The Royal Institution of Chartered Surveyors is the mark of property professionalism worldwide, promoting best practice, regulation and consumer protection for business and the community. It is the home of property related knowledge and is an impartial advisor to governments and global organisations. It is committed to the promotion of research in support of the efficient and effective operation of land and property markets worldwide.

Real Estate Issues

Series Managing Editors

Clare Eriksson   Head of Research, Royal Institution of Chartered Surveyors
John Henneberry   Department of Town & Regional Planning, University of Sheffield
K.W. Chau   Chair Professor, Department of Real Estate and Construction, The University of Hong Kong
Elaine Worzala   Director of the Carter Real Estate Center, College of Charleston, USA

Real Estate Issues is an international book series presenting the latest thinking into how real estate markets operate. The books have a strong theoretical basis – providing the underpinning for the development of new ideas.

The books are inclusive in nature, drawing both upon established techniques for real estate market analysis and on those from other academic disciplines as appropriate. The series embraces a comparative approach, allowing theory and practice to be put forward and tested for their applicability and relevance to the understanding of new situations. It does not seek to impose solutions, but rather provides a more effective means by which solutions can be found. It will not make any presumptions as to the importance of real estate markets but will uncover and present, through the clarity of the thinking, the real significance of the operation of real estate markets.

Further information on the *Real Estate Issues* series can be found at: http://eu.wiley.com/WileyCDA/Section/id-380013.html

Books in the series

Greenfields, Brownfields & Housing Development
Adams & Watkins
9780632063871

Planning, Public Policy & Property Markets
Adams, Watkins & White
9781405124300

Housing & Welfare in Southern Europe
Allen, Barlow, Léal, Maloutas & Padovani
9781405103077

*Markets & Institutions in Real Estate &
Construction*
Ball
9781405110990

*Building Cycles:
Growth & Instability*
Barras
9781405130011

*Neighbourhood Renewal & Housing Markets:
Community Engagement in the US and UK*
Beider
9781405134101

Mortgage Markets Worldwide
Ben-Shahar, Leung & Ong
9781405132107

*The Cost of Land Use Decisions:
Applying Transaction Cost Economics to
Planning & Development*
Buitelaar
9781405151238

*Urban Regeneration & Social Sustainability:
Best Practice from European Cities*
Colantonio & Dixon
9781405194198

Urban Regeneration in Europe
Couch, Fraser & Percy
9780632058419

*Urban Sprawl in Europe:
Landscapes, Land-Use Change & Policy*
Couch, Leontidou & Petschel-Held
9781405139175

Transforming Private Landlords
Crook & Kemp
9781405184151

Planning Gain
Crook, Henneberry & Whitehead
9781118219812

*Real Estate & the New Economy:
The Impact of Information and
Communications Technology*
Dixon, McAllister, Marston & Snow
9781405117784

Economics & Land Use Planning
Evans
9781405118613

Economics, Real Estate & the Supply of Land
Evans
9781405118620

*Management of Privatised Housing:
International Policies & Practice*
Gruis, Tsenkova & Nieboer
9781405181884

*Development & Developers:
Perspectives on Property*
Guy & Henneberry
9780632058426

*The Right to Buy: Analysis & Evaluation
of a Housing Policy*
Jones & Murie
9781405131971

Housing Markets & Planning Policy
Jones & Watkins
9781405175203

Office Markets & Public Policy
Colin Jones
9781405199766

*Challenges of the Housing Economy:
An International Perspective*
Jones, White & Dunse
9780470672334

*Mass Appraisal Methods:
An International Perspective for Property
Valuers*
Kauko & d'Amato
9781405180979

*Economics of the Mortgage Market:
Perspectives on Household Decision Making*
Leece
9781405114615

*Towers of Capital:
Office Markets & International Financial
Services*
Lizieri
9781405156721

Milestones in European Housing Finance
Lunde & Whitehead
9781118929452

*Making Housing More Affordable:
The Role of Intermediate Tenures*
Monk & Whitehead
9781405147149

Global Trends in Real Estate Finance
Newell & Sieracki
9781405151283

Housing Economics & Public Policy
O'Sullivan & Gibb
9780632064618

Dynamics of Housing in East Asia
Renaud et al
9780470672662

*International Real Estate:
An Institutional Approach*
Seabrooke, Kent & How
9781405103084

*Urban Design in the Real Estate Development
Process:
Policy Tools & Property Decisions*
Tiesdell & Adams
9781405192194

Real Estate Finance in the New Economy
Tiwari & White
9781405158718

*British Housebuilders:
History & Analysis*
Wellings
9781405149181

Milestones in European Housing Finance

Milestones in European Housing Finance

Edited by

Jens Lunde
Associate Professor
Department of Finance, Copenhagen Business School

Christine Whitehead
Emeritus Professor in Housing Economics
Department of Economics, London School of Economics

Registered Office
John Wiley & Sons, Ltd, The Atrium, Southern Gate, Chichester, West Sussex, PO19 8SQ,
United Kingdom.

Editorial Offices
9600 Garsington Road, Oxford, OX4 2DQ, United Kingdom.
The Atrium, Southern Gate, Chichester, West Sussex, PO19 8SQ, United Kingdom.

For details of our global editorial offices, for customer services and for information about
how to apply for permission to reuse the copyright material in this book please see our
website at www.wiley.com/wiley-blackwell.

Library of Congress Cataloging-in-Publication Data

Milestones in European housing finance / edited by Jens Lunde, Christine Whitehead.
     pages   cm
  Includes bibliographical references and index.
  ISBN 978-1-118-92945-2 (cloth)
1. Housing–Europe–Finance–History.   I. Lunde, Jens, editor.   II. Whitehead,
Christine M. E., editor.
  HD7332.A4M55 2016
  332.7′22–dc23
                                        2015026160

A catalogue record for this book is available from the British Library.

Set in 10/13pt Trump Mediaeval by SPi Global, Pondicherry, India
Printed and bound in Malaysia by Vivar Printing Sdn Bhd

1   2016

Contents

Notes on Contributors   xv
Foreword by David Miles, Professor of Financial Economics,
Imperial College, London   xxi
Acknowledgements   xxiii

**1 Introduction: Milestones in European Housing
    Finance since 1989**   **1**
   Jens Lunde and Christine Whitehead

   Why analyse developments in housing finance?   1
   Defining housing finance   3
   The countries   4
   Trends in mortgage systems   5
   Mortgage debt and house price increases – enabling each other?   7
   Conclusions   13
   References   14

2 European Housing Finance Models in 1989 and 2014   **15**
   Jens Lunde and Christine Whitehead

   Introduction   15
   Mortgage systems   16
   Funding the supply of mortgages   21
   Mortgage characteristics   25
   Overview   33
   References   35

**3 Australia's 25 Years with a Deregulated Housing
    Finance System: Looking Back and Looking Forward**   **37**
   Judith Yates and María Belén Yanotti

   The economic and institutional environment of the last 25 years   37
   Key milestones   39
   Impacts and implications of changes   43
   Emerging issues   48
   Conclusion   51
   Acknowledgements   51
   References   52

**4 Milestones in Housing Finance in Austria over
    the Last 25 Years**   **55**
   Alexis Mundt and Elisabeth Springler

   The economic and institutional environment of the last 25 years   55
   Finance milestones   57

Impacts and outcomes   66
Looking to the future   70
Acknowledgements   71
References   71

5   **Milestones in 25 Years of Housing Finance in Belgium**   **75**
    Sien Winters and Katleen Van den Broeck

    Introduction   75
    The Belgian housing finance system   76
    The economic and institutional environment of the last
    25 years in Belgium   76
    Milestones during the last 25 years of housing finance in Belgium   77
    Impacts   86
    Looking to the future   88
    Acknowledgements   89
    References   89

6   **Milestones in Housing Finance in the
    Czech Republic since 1990**   **93**
    Petr Sunega and Martin Lux

    Introduction   93
    Milestones in housing finance   95
    Impacts   102
    Future prospects   106
    Acknowledgements   106
    Notes   106
    References   107

7   **Milestones in Danish Housing Finance since 1990**   **109**
    Jens Lunde

    Introduction   109
    The economic environment of the last 25 years   110
    The Danish mortgage system   111
    Key milestones   113
    The impacts of these milestones over the last 25 years   117
    Parallel development in house prices and
    owner-occupiers' net debt   118
    The housing crisis, the national banking crisis and
    the Global Financial Crisis   121
    The aftermath   123
    The rescue operations   124
    Looking to the future   124
    Acknowledgements   125
    References   126

8   Milestones in Housing Finance in England   **127**
Kathleen Scanlon and Henryk Adamczuk

Introduction   127
The economic and institutional environment of the last 25 years   128
Milestones in private housing finance   128
Milestones in social and affordable housing finance   136
Impacts   138
Looking to the future   142
Note   143
References   144

9   Milestones in Housing Finance in Finland   **147**
Timo Tähtinen and Tommi Laanti

Introduction   147
Key milestones   148
Impacts and implications of changes   154
Looking to the future   161
References   162
Further reading   162

**10   Milestones of Housing Finance in France between 1988
and 2014: Is the French Credit System a Gallic Oddity?**   **165**
Christian Tutin and Bernard Vorms

Introduction: A quarter of a century later   165
Finance milestones   166
Specifics of French housing finance   171
Impacts   175
Looking to the future   179
Conclusions   180
References   181

**11   Milestones in the Development of the German
Housing Finance System in the Last 25 Years**   **183**
Stefan Kofner

The initial situation in 1989   183
Milestones at a glance   184
German reunification (1990): A friendly takeover
by the white knight?   184
The conversion of homeownership subsidisation from a tax to
a grant system (1996): Heading for a new balance of tenures?   186
Integration and deregulation of capital markets:
risks for the future?   187
Trying to run a housing system without subsidies   190

Measures to rescue the financial system since 2008   191
The dynamics of the German system of housing
finance since 1989   196
Notes   198
References   198

12 **Moving from an Authoritarian State System to an
    Authoritarian Market System: Housing Finance
    Milestones in Hungary between 1979 and 2014**   201
    József Hegedüs and Eszter Somogyi

From socialism to capitalism: the economic
and institutional environment   201
Finance milestones in the housing system   204
Impacts   214
The future of the housing finance system   216
References   217

13 **Housing Finance in Iceland: Milestones 1989–2014**   219
    Lúðvík Elíasson and Magnús Árni Skúlason

Introduction   219
The economic and institutional environment of the past 25 years 220
The bumpy ride of Icelandic housing finance   221
Impacts   232
Looking to the future   235
References   237

14 **Milestones in 25 Years of Housing Finance in Ireland**   239
    Padraic Kenna

Key milestones   239
Emerging issues   248
Conclusion   251
Acknowledgements   252
Notes   252
References   253

15 **Milestones in Housing Finance in the Netherlands, 1988–2013** 255
    Marja Elsinga, Hugo Priemus and Peter Boelhouwer

Introduction   255
Milestones over the three periods   256
Impacts   265
Reflection   270
Acknowledgements   271
References   271

16 **Housing Finance in Norway: The Last 25 Years**   **273**
   Rolf Barlindhaug

Introduction   273
The economic and institutional environment
of the last 25 years   274
Finance milestones   275
The financial crisis   281
Impacts of the housing finance milestones   283
Looking into the future   286
Conclusion   287
Acknowledgements   288
References   288

17 **Milestones of Housing Finance in Poland**   **291**
   Marta Widłak and Jacek Łaszek

Introduction   291
Housing finance milestones   292
Impact of housing finance milestones in Poland
in the last 25 years   301
Looking towards the future   307
References   308

18 **The Housing Finance System in Portugal since the 1980s**   **309**
   Romana Xerez and Jaime R. S. Fonseca

Introduction   309
Context: a legacy of family financing, the impact of
the 1974 revolution and the period to 1989   310
Milestones in the development of the Portuguese
housing market and housing finance since 1989   313
Impacts   319
Conclusions   321
Acknowledgements   323
References   323

19 **Evolution of the Housing Finance System in Russia**   **325**
   Maria Plotnikova, Andrey Tumanov and Evgeniya Zhelezova

Introduction   325
Brief review of basic features of the Soviet era housing system   326
The housing system during the transition to a market
economy (1990s)   328
Forming the basis for a housing mortgage financing
system (1997–2005)   329
Between the market and the state (2005–2013)   333

State programmes to stimulate housing demand and supply   333
The effect of the GFC   335
What lies ahead?   337
References   339

**20 Housing Finance in Slovenia: From a National Housing
Fund to a Bank-Driven System   341**
Andreja Cirman and Richard Sendi

The economic and institutional environment
of the last 25 years   341
Major policy changes   342
Impacts   353
Looking to the future   356
References   357

**21 Housing Finance in Spain: From the Liberalisation
of the Mortgage Market to Booms and Busts   359**
Irene Peña and Baralides Alberdi

The economic and institutional environment of
the last 25 years   359
Finance milestones   360
The impact of these milestones over the last 25 years   367
Looking to the future: financing into the future   372
References   374

22 Milestones in Swedish Housing Finance   375
Peter Englund

Background   375
Key milestones   378
Impacts   386
Looking to the future   389
References   390

**23 Housing Finance in Turkey over the Last 25 Years:
Good, Bad or Ugly?   393**
Yener Coşkun

Introduction   393
The Turkish housing finance system over the
last 25 years from a marketisation perspective   394
Finance milestones: The rise of marketisation and
changes in housing finance   400
Impacts of the transformation of the housing finance system 402
Future trends in housing finance markets   405

Gated communities and housing finance 405
Conclusions 408
Acknowledgements 409
References 410

24 **Milestones in EU Housing and Mortgage Markets** **413**
Jennifer Johnson, Lorenzo Isgrò and Sylvain Bouyon

Milestones in EU housing and mortgage markets 413
1990–2000 – Milestones: The Single European Market,
deregulation and consolidation and product innovation 413
2001–2008 – Milestones: EU focus on mortgage credit,
growth of covered bonds and adoption of the Capital
Requirements Directive (CRD) 418
2008–2014 – Milestones: Restoring financial stability,
consumer protection and unlocking long-term financing 421
Conclusion 428
References 430

25 **Following On From a Quarter of a Century of Mortgage Debt** **433**
Jens Lunde and Christine Whitehead

Introduction: 1989 and 2014 433
Trends in mortgage systems over the quarter century 436
The impact of the GFC 439
Conclusions: looking back and looking forward 443
References 446

Index 447

Notes on Contributors

Henryk Adamczuk is an Independent Researcher specialising in economic and financial aspects of housing markets. From 1988–2013 he was a senior lecturer at Birmingham City University. He participated in a major peer review study of housing in the European Union and has regularly presented at international housing conferences in Europe.

Baralides Alberdi is Director of the consultancy *Madrid Puerto Aéreo*. She is a specialist in housing finance and financial instruments and previously worked as head of the research department of the Mortgage Bank of Spain, the largest specialised mortgage institutions at that time.

Rolf Barlindhaug is a Senior Researcher at the Norwegian Institute for Urban and Regional Research. His research interests are housing finance, housing market analysis, supply-side studies, the relationship between municipalities and the housebuilding industry, housing policy instruments and residential mobility.

Peter Boelhouwer is Professor of Housing Systems at Delft University of Technology. He is chair of the OTB – Research for the Built Environment department and of the European Network for Housing Research (ENHR). His main research topics are comparative housing analyses, housing finance and economics and housing preferences.

Sylvain Bouyon is a Research Fellow at the Centre for European Policy Studies. He previously worked as an economist at the European Mortgage Federation and at the National Bank of Belgium.

Andreja Cirman is Associate Professor in the Faculty of Economics, University of Ljubljana. Her main fields of expertise are housing, real estate and sustainability, reflected in a variety of published articles, research works and consultancy projects in Slovenia and abroad.

Yener Coşkun is a Senior Specialist for the Capital Markets Board of Turkey and visiting lecturer at Izmir University of Economics and the University of Sarajevo. He has published three books and several journal and professional articles on housing finance, real estate, capital markets and history.

Lúðvík Elíasson is currently a Senior Economist in the Financial Stability department at the Central Bank of Iceland. Lately, he has been working for parliamentary commissions assessing the role of banks and housing finance during and after the 2008 financial crisis in Iceland.

Marja Elsinga is Professor of Housing Governance at TU Delft and Visiting Professor at Tongji University in Shanghai. She has 25 years of experience in housing research and publishes widely on topics including housing policy, social housing, housing affordability and housing equity release.

Peter Englund is Professor of Banking at the Stockholm School of Economics specialising in housing economics and finance. He was previously Professor of Economics at Uppsala University and Professor of Real Estate Finance at the University of Amsterdam.

Jaime R. S. Fonseca is an Assistant Professor at Lisbon University (ISCSP-UL), particularly interested in data analysis. His work has been published in international peer-reviewed journals such as *International Journal of Public Administration, Social Sciences Research* and the *Journal of Retailing and Consumer Services.*

József Hegedüs is a Sociologist and founding member of the Metropolitan Research Institute, established in 1989 in Budapest, Hungary. His research focuses on urban and housing issues after the transition in Eastern Europe. He is one of the editors *Social Housing in Transition Countries,* published in 2013.

Lorenzo Isgrò is an Economic Adviser at the European Mortgage Federation, where he coordinates the Statistics Committee and is responsible for the publication of *Hypostat,* a housing and mortgage statistics issue. Previously, he worked at the Dutch Central Bank and European Central Bank.

Jennifer Johnson is Head of Legal and Economic Affairs at the European Mortgage Federation, where she is responsible for the activities of the EMF's Legal, Economic and Valuation Committees. She has worked at the EMF for more than 12 years and publishes regularly particularly on regulatory issues.

Padraic Kenna lectures in housing and property law at National University of Ireland Galway and at the Centre for Housing Law, Rights and Policy. His research areas include legal and policy aspects of mortgages, property, housing and human rights.

Stefan Kofner is Professor of Housing Management at the University of Applied Sciences Zittau/Görlitz and director of the TRAWOS research institute. He has a background in economics and has participated in comparative research projects and publications about housing allowances, social housing, the private rented sector and housing finance.

Tommi Laanti is a Senior Analyst at the Department of Built Environment in the Ministry of the Environment (Finland). His field of work is government housing policy and housing finance subsidy systems.

Jacek Łaszek is a Housing Finance Economist. For more than 20 years he has conducted research studies, analysis and consultations concerning housing finance systems in Poland and other Central and Eastern European countries. He is Professor at the Warsaw School of Economics and a leading advisor at the National Bank of Poland.

Jens Lunde has been Associate Professor in the Department of Finance at Copenhagen Business School since 1984. He has previously taught in the Department of Economics at the University of Copenhagen and worked for the Danish Ministry of Housing and the Danish Building Research Institute. His main specialisms are in housing finance with a particular emphasis on the analysis of individual data.

Martin Lux, Sociologist and Economist, is Head of the Department of Socio-Economics of Housing at the Institute of Sociology, Academy of Sciences of the Czech Republic. He has led and consulted on several international and national housing research projects.

Alexis Mundt, Economist and Historian, works as a research associate at the IIBW – Institute for Real Estate, Construction and Housing in Vienna. His areas of research include housing economics, comparative social policy and evaluations of housing policy in Austria and Europe.

Irene Peña is Chief Economist of the Spanish Mortgage Association, a specialised professional association consisting of the financial institutions that have a major presence in the Spanish mortgage market. She is also a member of several working groups of the European Mortgage Federation and the European Covered Bond Council.

Maria Plotnikova is a Lecturer in Economics at Aberystwyth University. Her research interests are in regional and urban economics, comparative housing systems and housing privatisation, particularly in Russia.

Hugo Priemus is Emeritus Professor of System Innovation Spatial Development and was previously professor of housing at TU Delft. His research interests include housing policy, spatial planning, land policy and urban transport. He has regularly advised the Netherlands government on issues around housing policy and finance.

Kathleen Scanlon, Assistant Professorial Research Fellow at the London School of Economics, specialises in housing, urban affairs and governance. She writes about housing systems and financing of both private and social housing and has worked on projects for the Council of Europe Development Bank, the Inter-American Development Bank and the OECD.

Richard Sendi works as a Senior Researcher at the Urban Planning Institute of the Republic of Slovenia. He specialises in housing research and is the head of Housing Studies at the Institute. He is also the president of the Institute's Scientific Council.

Magnús Árni Skúlason is the Founder and Managing Director of Reykjavik Economics ehf. Prior to founding Reykjavík Economics he was Director of the Centre for Housing and Property Research at Bifröst University, where he was an Associate Professor in Economics until January 2007.

Eszter Somogyi is a Researcher at the Metropolitan Research Institute, Budapest. Her main fields of interest are urban sociology and housing policy. She focuses on housing affordability problems and the development of inclusive housing policy schemes for segregated areas.

Elisabeth Springler, Economist, is Study Programme Director at the University of Applied Sciences bfi-Vienna, Austria. Previously she was Assistant Professor at the Vienna University of Economics and Marshall Plan Chair at the University of New Orleans.

Petr Sunega is an Economist. His main research interests include tenure choice and labour oriented migration, housing finance and housing economics. He has published on these topics in books and journals including *European Sociological Review, Housing Studies* and *Urban Studies.*

Timo Tähtinen is a Senior Adviser at the Department of the Built Environment in the Ministry of the Environment in Finland. His field of work is housing and construction market analysis and he advises the Finnish government on a wide range of housing policy issues.

Andrey Tumanov has more than 10 years of experience researching housing finance issues and currently works as Market Analyst and Forecaster in the Market Analysis and Strategic Planning Department of the Agency for Housing Mortgage Lending, a Russian mortgage market development institution.

Christian Tutin is Professor of Economics at the University of Paris-Est Créteil (UPEC) and a member of Lab'Urba research laboratory. His research fields include housing economics and the history of economic thought. He is a leading specialist on housing policy in France and has edited a book on social housing in Europe with Claire Levy-Vroelant.

Katleen Van den Broeck is Senior Researcher in housing at HIVA Research Institute for Work and Society of KU Leuven in Belgium. She has a broad background of socio-economic research. At HIVA-KU Leuven she studied mainly housing access (discrimination) and quality issues and housing policy.

Bernard Vorms is the President of the *Conseil National de la Transaction et de la Gestion Immobilière* (The National Council of Property Transaction and Management). Previously, he was Director General of the *Agence Nationale pour L'information sur le lodgement* and President of the *Société de Gestion du fond de Garantie de L'accession Sociale.*

Christine Whitehead is Emeritus Professor of Housing Economics at the London School of Economics. She works mainly in the fields of housing economics, finance and policy. She has worked with a wide range of international agencies as well as regularly for the UK government and Parliament.

Marta Widłak is a Senior Economist at the National Bank of Poland. She conducts research and analysis on housing markets. Her study on the house price index construction was a pioneering work in Poland.

Sien Winters is Housing Research Manager at the HIVA Research Institute for Work and Society of KU Leuven in Belgium. Educated as an economist, she has studied and published on a wide range of housing policy issues in Flanders. She is one of the expert members of the Flemish Housing Council.

Romana Xerez is Assistant Professor of Housing Policies and Community, Neighbourhood Networks and Housing Policy at the School for Social and Political Sciences – University of Lisbon. Her research broadly focuses on the comparative housing regimes and welfare state reform after the 2008 crisis.

María Belén Yanotti is Associate Lecturer at the University of Tasmania (UTAS), Australia. She holds a PhD in Economics and Finance from UTAS. She works in household finance, with a particular focus on housing finance and mortgages.

Judith Yates is an Honorary Associate in the School of Economics at the University of Sydney. She has worked in the field of housing economics and finance for many years and has published widely in the fields of housing economics, finance and policy. She has served on numerous housing and finance advisory bodies, especially for the Australian government.

Evgeniya Zhelezova is Project Manager of International Relations in the Market Analysis and Strategic Planning Department of the Agency for Housing and Mortgage Lending. She is a qualified expert with almost 10 years of experience in housing finance.

Foreword

Twenty-five years ago European housing finance markets looked very different across countries – in some places they hardly existed. In many ways they now look rather more similar. Countries where there was limited availability of mortgage debt have seen the greatest financial liberalisation. Along the way there has been a very substantial rise in the stock of mortgage debt relative to GDP in most countries. We have also had a financial crash which has affected every country, though in very different ways. The effects of that financial crisis are still with us; they shall be felt for years to come. And in many countries – most obviously in Spain and Ireland – housing and housing finance was at the very heart of their economic crises. Even outside of the exceptional conditions that came after the financial crisis of 2007–2008, what happens in housing finance markets matters greatly for economies because the stock of housing is a large part of national and household wealth and its value and rate of change is dependent on the cost and availability of finance.

Understanding how housing finance has changed in Europe over the past quarter of a century and how it still differs across countries is therefore both interesting and important. This volume represents an invaluable aid to that understanding. Country experts have provided a detailed and consistent account of how systems of housing finance have evolved in each of 21 countries (20 of which are European; the 21st is Australia) as well as of how changes have impacted on national housing markets. It is based on the work done in the last 25 years by the ENHR (European Network on Housing Research) Working Group on Housing Finance; its appearance now is partly to celebrate their 25th anniversary.

The great strength of this book is that detailed and up to date information on housing finance systems is presented in a way which allows for informed comparisons between countries. This reflects the fact that a common set of questions was asked of those who wrote country chapters. The result is that we have here a rich stock of information on the same fundamental set of characteristics of housing finance markets. Given how diverse national systems have been, the experiences of different countries is of great value in uncovering some of the links between mortgage markets, housing market conditions and the wider economy.

Jens Lunde and Christine Whitehead have done a fine job in editing and assembling this volume. They also provide three overview chapters which draw out some of the lessons from the experience of this large group of countries. They look back over a quarter of a century which saw a great rise in the availability of mortgage finance. What emerges is that while housing finance markets have in some ways become more similar – because most countries where mortgage debt was negligible in 1989 have seen a great deal of financial liberalisation and so the availability of mortgages and the stock of housing debt is much higher – in other dimensions the differences are even greater. There is now a more diverse range of funding methods across countries than was the case 25 years ago. And the impact of the Global Financial Crisis that started in 2007 has been very different across countries – in many countries housing markets were hardly affected; in others the impact has been little short of devastating. This diversity of experience means that what happens next will not be uniform. It is far from clear that convergence in housing finance markets is coming, nor that such a thing would be desirable. The only way to judge those things is to pay attention to the differences in housing and mortgage markets that exist across countries and understand why they exist. That is one reason why a book like this which tracks the evolution of housing finance across countries and takes a detailed look at where we are now is immensely valuable.

David Miles
Professor of Financial Economics
Imperial College, London

Acknowledgements

The idea for this text was initiated at an ENHR international conference three years ago when we realised that our ENHR Housing Finance Working Group would be celebrating our 25th birthday as a full member in 2015. There was immediate enthusiasm for a project bringing together the experiences of different countries as housing finance markets developed across Europe over the lifetime of the group – although when we all agreed we doubt that any of us realised how large the task was going to be.

The editors would like to thank all 42 authors involved in producing this text for their commitment to the idea of the project to examine the milestones in European housing finance, the hard work necessary to bring all the material together and particularly for their continued enthusiasm. The book ended up including 25 chapters – one for each year! Everyone who agreed to contribute has actually done so (possibly a first in comparative housing research?) and all have then generously responded to the editors continuing requests – even when sometimes the timescale has been quite unreasonable. We are immensely grateful for what has been, throughout the last three years, a team effort.

We would also like to thank everyone who has taken part in the Housing Finance Working Group over the last 25 years. Many have been regularly involved in monitoring how housing finance markets have moved from the generally highly regulated (or non-existent) systems of the 1980s, to the late 2000s when housing finance was seen as a major cause of the Global Financial Crisis, and to now when well operating housing finance markets are seen as a core element in ensuring greater stability of both finance markets in general and the European economy. Without the continued involvement of working group members from an increasing number of countries the idea of documenting milestones could not have been realised. Our regular seminars with the European Mortgage Federation have also been particularly valuable. We would like to thank the Federation for their continued involvement and support.

The text could only be completed with the continued help of our publishers and particularly the support of Madeleine Metcalfe who has guided us through the complexity of bringing our 25 chapters together into a (hopefully) coherent whole.

Finally we offer our grateful thanks to Emma Sagor, our Administrative Assistant, who has, for the last six months, made it possible to bring the project to fruition. Without her involvement we would never have been able to meet our – extended – deadlines and it has been a joy working with her.

We very much hope that all those who have been involved will think the resultant text worth the effort. Thank you all again.

Jens Lunde and
Christine Whitehead

1

Introduction: Milestones in European Housing Finance since 1989

Jens Lunde[a] and Christine Whitehead[b]

[a] *Copenhagen Business School, Frederiksberg, Denmark*
[b] *London School of Economics, London, UK*

Why analyse developments in housing finance?

In 2008 many commentators blamed housing finance for the depth of the Global Financial Crisis (GFC). They also saw the dysfunctionality of that market as one of the core reasons why the crisis was not resolved relatively quickly but instead in many countries turned into recession and stagnation. At its simplest, the case against housing finance was that deregulation and expansion of housing finance markets had enabled consumers to become over-indebted; had allowed house prices to grow unsustainably; had introduced riskier mortgage instruments with low debt servicing requirements to help new buyers to afford these higher prices and existing owners to realise some of their housing wealth; had led to excess competition in the mortgage market with resultant mis-selling and poor treasury management; and, from the point of view of financial markets most importantly, had left financial institutions across the world over-exposed to risky mortgage and construction debt even in countries where finance systems remained quite heavily regulated.

Often the details behind this case for the prosecution against housing finance have been very much concentrated on United States experience (Reinhart and Rogoff 2009; Green and Wachter 2010). But there also appeared to be an important contagion story, especially with respect to institutional fragility and over-indebtedness not only in Europe but in markets across the globe. There were also many national and Europe-wide issues that helped destabilise both finance and housing markets. Indeed, growing problems of

Milestones in European Housing Finance, First Edition.
Edited by Jens Lunde and Christine Whitehead.
© 2016 John Wiley & Sons, Ltd. Published 2016 by John Wiley & Sons, Ltd.

affordability and over-exposure to risky debt finance saw many European housing markets turn down from 2006/7 before the decisive outbreak of the GFC in September 2008.

The actual story has clearly been far more complex. Prior to the crisis – and certainly before the turn of the century – housing finance systems and markets appeared to be working quite well, not only in support of owner-occupation but also for the development and ownership of rented housing. Financial markets in much of Europe had been deregulated and liberalised for more than two decades before the signs of crisis emerged. Indeed, housing was seen to be a particularly successful part of the deregulation and privatisation story – with lower interest rates, higher owner-occupation rates and greater choice for many households.

Experiences across Europe both in the long period of relative economic stability and growth before the crisis and of the impact of the crisis cannot be presented as a simple, coherent story. There were vast differences between countries with different housing histories, different regulatory frameworks and different market pressures. Even so, there were growing similarities within groups of countries that in the run up to the crisis saw higher indebtedness and higher house prices as linked and a matter of increasing concern (OECD 2006). Experience after the crisis was similar – with some fairly general trends within particular groupings but very different national experiences across Europe as a whole. Some indeed saw little more than a hiccup in the housing finance market itself (whatever the effect of the crisis on macro-economies and real housing investment) while others experienced major problems from which recovery has been very slow.

Looking at the longer term picture, the period extending from 1989 to 2014 is simply unique in housing and financial market cycles (except to the extent that in a number of countries change started a little earlier). House prices and mortgage debt started to move more closely in parallel and both showed unprecedentedly strong growth from the middle of the 1990s onward. Especially after the turn of the century, the rate of increase in house prices grew so far out of line with incomes that it was perceived of by commentators as a 'housing bubble' in many countries. These prices could not have been realised unless they were funded through easier and cheaper access to (mortgage) credit. Equally the large scale growth in outstanding loans could not have occurred had demand for larger loans not existed. Thus the expansion in housing credit is seen to have formed a commensurate 'credit bubble'.

The objective of this book is to take a longer term view of housing finance markets across Europe – examining the major changes that have taken place since the 1980s and how these have impacted on national markets, including at one end extreme highly developed systems that have been in place for decades and at the other newly emerging markets that are still in the early stages of development. It is also to ask whether there are clear patterns across these countries that can help explain developments and give some indication of what might happen over the next few years.

The initial impetus for the book came from the fact that the European Network of Housing Research (ENHR) working group on housing finance was set up in 1989, just at the time when deregulation had taken hold in many Western European countries and the borders with Eastern Europe were being broken down. The group started working together in that year to monitor changes and to examine the causes and consequences of these changes for housing finance and for housing markets and policy more generally (Turner and Whitehead 1993). The impetus for monitoring and analysis has been maintained over the years, involving more experts and more countries (Scanlon *et al.* 2008; 2011). The group was among those best qualified to conduct an overview of developments across Europe and comparable countries, looking at the similarities and complexities of housing finance and its relationship to housing markets at both national and European levels. The authors come from many different disciplines – not just finance and economics but also public administration, sociology and other social sciences. Most work in universities but also engage with governments, regulatory authorities and the industry. Some work directly with their national governments, although here they write in a personal capacity. As a result we have been able to bring together some 42 of the most knowledgeable specialists in the field to contribute to the text.

In the country chapters the authors clarify milestones in the development of national housing finance markets over the last quarter century, examine how finance has impacted on the operation of housing markets and identify the factors that have affected the benefits and risks faced by institutions, providers and consumers alike. Thus each country chapter has a similar structure but takes account of the specific attributes of the national market and particularly the role played by government and regulation. The authors trace the changes that they see as of particular importance over the 25 year period and identify stages in the development of the market. They then look at the outcomes of these changes and end by giving their views on possible future trends in national housing and housing finance markets.

The editors have, in addition to the introduction, contributed two chapters, one based on a questionnaire, the other on a careful reading of the material presented in the text and elsewhere in the literature to draw out common themes. Overall, therefore, the aim is to provide both a source document identifying what has happened and an evaluative document that looks at trends and outcomes from a comparative viewpoint.

Defining housing finance

The term 'housing finance' is often believed to apply simply to the operation of mortgage markets in the form of housing loans or mortgage loans that enable consumers – owner-occupiers and sometimes landlords – to borrow against the value of their housing asset. As such it allows those who wish to own their own home to spread required payments over the period of the loan, enabling them to afford to own that asset. Equally it enables landlords to lever in debt finance to allow them to purchase against the future rental stream.

However, housing finance is actually a much broader concept, including financing through the owners' own resources (i.e. their equity) and – where relevant – financing by subsidies. The initial equity (down payment) is often seen as ensuring that the purchaser has a stake in the value of the property, thus reducing the risks faced by the mortgagee. Over time as the mortgage is paid down, as is a common family life-cycle pattern and, especially if house prices rise, the owners' equity increases and becomes the predominant source of housing finance for the property.

Many European housing systems historically were dominated by governments in terms of both housing provision and subsidy to improve affordability. In these circumstances the sources of housing finance include public borrowing – normally on the sovereign debt market rather than specifically through housing institutions – taxation (both national and local) and subsidies in kind, notably in the form of public land. Over the last 25 years, government involvement in production and provision has fallen and been replaced by private sources of finance. The only offset especially in most North Western European countries has been in the growth of income related housing allowances.

Another complication is that debt financing may be used for other purposes than purchasing the housing asset – for housing purposes such as renovation, helping children to buy their own home or the purchase of white goods, but also for releasing equity to spend on other things, for instance acting as a pension, buying a car or going on holiday. Over the 25-year period many countries have come to allow equity withdrawal at the time of raising a new mortgage. Moreover, remortgaging has become important to many borrowers looking to take advantage of falling interest rates and new types of mortgage loans, creating potential to increase liquidity. These and other innovative mortgage instruments became an important source of business for the lenders in many countries.

Finally housing finance is provided not just to owners and investors but also to developers, helping them to fund the purchase of land and the process of construction up to the point when it moves into the asset ownership phase. In some European countries – especially those with high rates of investment – this became one of the most important factors affecting bank solvency at the time of the crisis.

The countries

The 21 countries examined in the book can be fairly readily categorised in traditional geographic and legal/institutional terms. The first 18 are fully located within Europe. We have in addition included two, Russia and Turkey, which are partially European (and have systems that look to the West) and one, Australia, which is Anglo-Saxon in legal/institutional terms but located on the other side of the globe. These help to exemplify how deregulation and liberalisation have been reflected in the globalisation of finance markets.

Secondly, within Europe there are five or six generally recognised groupings not specific to housing but based on governance, level of regulation and economic approach as well as geography, within which our sample might be identified. These include:

- Anglo–Saxon – perhaps the most market oriented countries in Europe, here represented by the UK, Ireland and outside Europe by Australia;
- Scandinavia – including Denmark, Finland, Iceland, Norway and Sweden linked geo-politically and in terms of their general approach to welfare. This group is often seen to incorporate the Netherlands and indeed France – and to a much lesser degree Belgium;
- Central European corporatist systems – exemplified here by Germany and Austria;
- Ex-communist countries, here including the Czech Republic, Hungary, Poland, Russia and Slovenia;
- Southern European countries – here Portugal, Spain and Turkey.

Because the issues around how housing finance has developed have been perceived as affected by underlying political objectives as well as legal, regulatory and particularly market pressures, commentators have tended also to categorise not only housing finance systems but also their impact on mortgage debt and house prices in a somewhat similar fashion (Girouard *et al.* 2007; Scanlon *et al.* 2011; Priemus and Whitehead 2014; Tutin and Vorms 2014). Once the details of individual country experiences are set out, it may well prove to be that groupings of this type do not apply consistently across different aspects of either housing finance market development or indeed in terms of outcomes. This is a core issue addressed in Chapter 2.

Trends in mortgage systems

Over the last 25 years across the world more countries introduced housing finance systems with mortgages secured against property. Other countries improved and expanded already existing housing finance systems. Financial institutions created new loan types, often with low initial payments and utilised a wide range of new approaches to increasing their lending in particular through capital markets and mortgage securitisation. In this context Green and Wachter, looking from a US perspective, presented the institutional changes in housing finance across the globe over the three decades before the crisis under the very expressive title: 'The Housing Finance Revolution' (Federal Reserve Bank of Kansas City 2007; Green and Wachter 2010).

As result of a wide range of initiatives, notably with respect to deregulation and liberalisation, housing finance systems became more efficient in their own terms and access to housing was increased. Some important reasons for the changes throughout these years have included: making entry into owner-occupation easier (although arguably house price increases have offset much of this benefit); reducing interest rates and improving lifetime affordability by access to debt; removing the 'dead hand' of government from housing; improving efficiency in housing finance and mortgage systems; and increasing competition through further liberalisation of institutional arrangements. In many countries these changes were seen as part of the deregulation of financial markets more generally; in others they were concentrated on housing finance. In all cases much of the efforts were directed towards developing structures to make mortgage loans more accessible by securing the loan against the value of the property; that is, using the house as collateral for the loan. Once this was possible, the borrower could get access to long term loans with lower interest rates, while the lender could receive a better credit quality in exchange. These changes enabled lower mortgage interest rates and market based terms and conditions, but they also occurred during a period where interest rates in most countries were deceasing often to unprecedented levels, in part because of declining general inflation. Importantly reducing interest rates became an important part of international monetary policy after the September 11th attack in 2001 and again after 2008 as a means of alleviating the GFC and the following recessions. In Europe this movement was further stimulated by the preparation for and creation of the Euro in January 1999.

These changes need to be seen against an economic backdrop. In particular the 25 year period has not been one of continued and consistent economic growth suddenly brought to a halt by the GFC. Nor has it been one of continuous house price increases, at least in real terms. In Europe and in many other countries across the globe there was a major property boom in the late 1980s that was suddenly and disastrously reversed at the end of the decade, resulting in major mortgage market problems – notably changing the tenure behaviour of younger households in more open-economy countries that were most affected – as well is in massive cutbacks in property investment of all types. In the 1990s, while in the main European housing markets were recovering and economies were entering a period of consistent growth that lasted until the mid-2000s, individual countries had their own crises – notably Finland and Portugal. From around 2006 downturns could be observed in many, although not all, national housing markets. The GFC did indeed initially hit almost everyone, although for varying lengths of time. The impact of the subsequent recession has affected growth rates and consumer spending across Europe but again to very different degrees – some have seen one downturn followed by an upturn; others have experienced two cycles; while still others have as yet hardly turned up. We can therefore reasonably argue that the 25 year period examined in this text has in many countries seen at least two economic cycles, with considerable uncertainty almost everywhere about what will happen in the next few years.

Mortgage debt and house price increases – enabling each other?

The expansion in mortgage debt

As we have already noted the period under discussion is unique in the long history of housing finance. A recent study by Jordá, Schularick and Taylor (2014) includes a long-run dataset covering disaggregated bank credit for 17 advanced economies since 1870. These countries, covering over 90 percent of advanced economy output, include 12 of the countries discussed in this book. Their data,

> …dramatically underscore the size of the credit boom prior to the global financial crisis of 2008. A substantial part of that boom occurred in a very short time span of little more than 10 years between the mid-1990s and 2008/9. For our 17 country sample, the average bank credit to GDP ratio rose from 79 percent of GDP in 1995 to 112 percent of GDP in 2007… (Jordá *et al.* 2014: 8).

The data also show how the composition of bank loan books changed. From 1870 until the mid-1980s the overall share of real estate loans remained around 40%,

> …whereupon we see the start of a global real estate lending boom for the past 30 years leading to a large jump in the ratio. As a result, the shares of mortgage and non-mortgage lending are now approximately the inverse of what they were at the beginning of the 20th century. (Jordá *et al.* 2014: 12).

Over the 25 year period, housing markets, house prices and not least housing finance became an increasingly important part of modern macro-economic analysis, especially with respect to business cycle dynamics and financial stability risks, as real estate lending booms were perceived to be followed by deeper recessions and slower recoveries. The rapid increase in household debt over the last four decades became a matter of international concern in the early 2000s and led to several large scale analyses notably from the Organisation for Economic Co-operation and Development (OECD), the

Bank of International Settlements and the International Monetary Fund (IMF), addressing the extent of the debt problem and its macro-economic implications (Bank of International Settlements 2006; IMF 2006; OECD 2006; Girouard *et al.* 2007). In 2012 the IMF used the OECD data on household debt to demonstrate that the more household debt increased before the outbreak of the GFC (and before earlier recessions), the stronger and the longer lasting were the negative effects on housing consumption, housing prices, private consumption, investments, GDP and unemployment (IMF 2012). The OECD also stressed that high debt levels make economies more vulnerable to financial instability (OECD 2013).

Finally therefore we look at the basic data on how mortgage debt and house prices have moved across the countries included in this text to provide a baseline for the analysis in later chapters. Table 1.1 (taken mainly from the annual *Hypostat* publication from the European Mortgage Federation) shows the ratio of residential mortgage debt (the majority of all consumer debt) to GDP for most of the countries included in this book. Mortgage debt includes mortgages secured against housing assets and in some cases also loans to households for residential and non-commercial purposes where personal guarantees are used, issued by private banks and lenders.

Table 1.1   Residential mortgage debt to GDP ratio, 1990–2013; selected years (%).

	1990	2000	2008	2010	2013
Australia	19	46	82	87	85
Austria			25.5	28.1	28.0
Belgium	20.3	27.7	39.6	45.4	49.5
Czech Republic			9.8	12.2	14.5
Denmark	70.1[1]	67.7	87.9	94.6	93.8
Finland			36.4	42.9	45.7
France	19.7	21.2	36.2	41.1	43.8
Germany	42.5	53.2	46.3	46.2	44.2
Hungary		1.4	21.2	25.6	18.9
Iceland[2]		88.4[3]	111.3	118.0	100.8
Ireland		31.0	82.6	65.2	57.8
Netherlands		68.2	99.6	107.8	104.9
Norway	49.4	39.1	50.5	66.8	64.1
Poland		2.1	14.2	19.0	20.7
Portugal		41.5	61.2	66.2	64.3
Russia			2.2	2.4	3.8
Slovenia		0.3	9.1	13.7	15.0
Spain	10.6	29.9	62.0	65.1	59.9
Sweden	47.3	44.6	61.9	83.5	80.9
Turkey			3.6	5.3	6.0
UK	54.5	55.8	70.1	83.2	80.6

[1] Figure from 1992.
[2] Household debt to GDP.
[3] Figure from 2003.
Sources: EMF (2014); for Australia data, RBA Table E02; for Iceland, Central Bank of Iceland.

Over the period of our analysis the Netherlands has generally had the highest residential mortgage debt to GDP ratio. These have been fostered by public guarantees, by maximum loan-to-value ratios (LTVs) as high as 120 percent (now lowered to 104 percent and planned to fall to 80 percent), unconstrained tax reliefs for mortgage interest (now increasingly limited especially for new buyers) and a shift from public to private financing particularly for social housing. Among those at the other extreme are Austria and Germany with much more limited growth in debt in relation to national income. Many other countries have seen increases in their debt-to-GDP ratios – at times by over 50 percent – with some of the strongest increases to be found among the countries that already had high debt ratios. Since the crisis the pattern has been more diverse with further rises in some countries and falls in others. These differences appear to be related as much to changes in GDP as to debt levels.

Some part of the rise in debt has 'natural' causes, although these are not generally enough to explain its rapid growth. Some countries eliminated or significantly constrained public housing finance systems so that debt financing was transferred to the private sector. Many countries supported owner-occupation based on increasingly available debt finance. In 1989 many Eastern European countries had no private commercial and mortgage banking sectors. They slowly started to put in place the legal and institutional arrangements necessary for the introduction of mortgage financing and once in place, usually experienced rapid growth rates in outstanding mortgage debt – although from very low levels.

Strong economic forces were also behind the growth in household and mortgage debt. The fact that interest rates continued to fall at least in money terms meant that the payments on loans were reduced significantly. Deregulation and liberalisation of finance systems in general and housing finance in particular over the last 25 years – and in the decade before for several countries – generally made it easier for those with lower incomes and wealth to enter the market and improved mortgage market efficiency. Rapid rises in house prices meant that more collateral was available against which to borrow. However, it also worsened housing affordability, which in turn meant people had to borrow more. Increasingly it also excluded people further down the market, at the same time as excluding those with limited resources.

Trends in house prices

A particular concern over the 25 year period has been the rapid rise in house prices across much of the globe, which has been mirrored in many European countries. These trends are seen to be related to growing incomes, easier access to credit, and especially after the turn of the century, to the inter-relationship between house price rises and the capacity to borrow.

Table 1.2   Average annual increases in real house prices, 1990–2014; selected periods (%).

	1990:1–1995:1	1995:1–2000:1	2000:1–2005:1	2005:1–2007:1	2007:1–2010:1	2010:1–2012:1	2012:1–2014:3
Australia	0.0	3.2	8.5	3.3	5.2	−3.8	4.7
Austria			−1.1	2.1	2.1	4.9	2.4
Belgium	2.5	3.4	5.1	8.2	2.0	0.6	0.3
Czech Republic						−3.1	0.2
Denmark	0.1	7.3	4.9	15.4	−7.2	−5.0	1.5
Finland	−9.7	6.3	3.0	5.7	0.5	0.2	−1.6
France	−1.6	1.3	9.3	9.0	−1.7	2.6	−2.3
Germany	2.1	−1.4	−2.8	−1.2	−0.2	4.1	3.6
Hungary					−4.6	−7.0	−2.8
Iceland				9.5	−8.8	1.9	3.0
Ireland	0.7	14.3	7.2	10.9	−9.4	−15.5	4.9
Netherlands	4.4	10.5	4.2	1.7	−0.9	−4.5	−5.1
Norway	−1.8	9.2	4.8	11.1	0.0	6.4	1.8
Portugal	0.0	1.9	−1.3	−0.8	1.0	−2.4	−3.2
Russia					34.4	4.1	−2.8
Slovenia					−2.5	−3.4	−6.1
Spain	−2.1	2.6	11.4	5.9	−4.6	−8.5	−4.9
Sweden	−6.6	5.2	6.5	9.4	3.0	−0.9	4.1
Turkey						2.3	6.6
UK	−5.4	6.8	10.7	4.4	−3.1	−2.5	4.7

Source: OECD House price statistics of 30th January 2015.

Table 1.2 shows the average annual rate of increase in real house price for especially relevant periods from 1990 to 2014 for all but one of the countries included in the text. Six countries only have data for some years in the OECD house price statistics used here while Poland is not included at all. In the years after 1995 and up to 2007 there are several examples of double-digit increases in real house prices, signalling overheated markets. After 2007 the picture is more blurred with several countries experiencing strong falls in real house prices, while a few countries experienced a weak upturn in real house prices. The change in real house prices that occurred during each country's period of increasing house prices and the following downturn after the peak year can be seen in Table 1.3 for the countries with house price indices for all the 25 years in the OECD statistics.

Bringing the two together

Figure 1.1 shows the trend in mortgage debt-to-GDP ratios for five of the countries with the highest ratios over the period. In the main it shows some declines in the early 1990s when countries were recovering from the sharp downswing in many economies from 1989 and the Scandinavian banking crisis (1988–1993) was unwinding. Thereafter, from around 1994, mortgage debt and therefore the ratio rose quite consistently and particularly rapidly after the turn of the century until the crisis. Thereafter trends in different

Table 1.3   National house price cycles (changes in real house prices since the first quarter of 1990*).

	Latest upturn period and peak quarter	Increase in real house prices through the upturn (percent)	Change in real house prices after the last peak quarter (percent)
Australia	1996:1–2010:2	129.6%	2.7%
Belgium	1990:1–2014:3	117.9%	[no price peak]
Denmark	1993:2–2007:1	175.8%	−25.1%
Finland	1993:2–2007:3	87.1%	−3.8%
France	1997:1–2007:4	116.6%	−7.2%
Germany	Peak 1995:1 Trough 2008:3	2008:3–2014:3 19.6%	−7.0%
Ireland	1987:2–2007:1	331.1%	−41.6%
Netherlands	1991:1–2008:4	177.0%	−24.3%
Norway	1993:1–2007:3	197.2%	16.3%
Portugal	1996:3–2001:2	15.9%	−18.8%
Spain	1996:3–2007:3	121.0%	−37.9%
Sweden	1993:3–2010:4	139.2%	5.8%
UK	1996:2–2007:4	169.6%	−6.8%

*Only countries with real house price indices for all 25 years.
Source: OECD House price statistics of 30th January 2015.

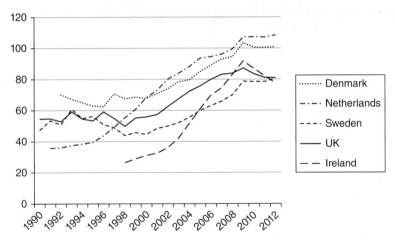

Figure 1.1   Residential mortgage debt to GDP ratio for five countries with among the highest ratios, 1990–2013 (%).
Source: EMF (2014).

countries went in different directions, reflecting variations in the depth of the crisis and the subsequent recession. Spain, perhaps to many people's surprise, is not part of this particularly high ratio group. However, it experienced the most rapidly growing ratio from a particularly low base in 1990.

It is worth remarking that in the residential mortgage debt-to-GDP ratio, the denominator – the Gross Domestic Product – is influenced not only by economic growth but also by developments in general prices. Therefore, an increase of similar size in both the debt to GDP ratio and in real house prices

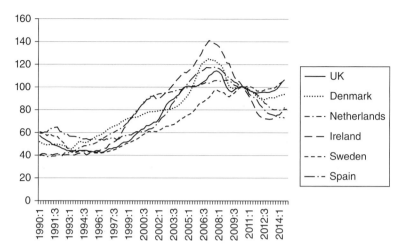

Figure 1.2   Developments in real house prices for the five countries plus Spain, 1990:1 to 2014:4 (2010 average = 100).
Source: OECD House price statistics of 30th January 2015.

means that nominal mortgage debt has increased more than nominal house prices. This has been the case throughout most of the long period of upturn.

Figure 1.2 shows the pattern of house price increases for the same countries together with Spain. It shows that in all six countries real house prices rose from the early 1990s, in all cases more than doubling – as seen in Table 1.3. Thereafter, Ireland experienced the greatest decline in real house prices, which were halved from the peak value in 2007:1 to the trough in 2013:1 when they started to rise again. Spain, Denmark and the Netherlands also experienced particularly strong downturns in real house prices after 2007.

Figure 1.3 on the other hand gives three examples of countries where house prices behaved in ways very different to those in countries with the highest debt ratios. Germany and Austria have experienced relatively little volatility, with prices in Germany actually declining for much of the period. In both countries, however, real house prices have risen quite significantly since the crisis. Belgium, like many of the other countries in our analysis, experienced continuing growth in real house prices until the mid-2000s with prices more than doubling but then, unlike the group in Figure 1.2, has since seen relative stability. All three countries have well-functioning housing finance systems and markets but also moderate residential mortgage debt-to-GDP ratios – although in Belgium the ratio has more than doubled since 1990 and has continued to rise since the crisis (Table 1.1).

Finally as is also seen in Table 1.1, mortgage debt (measured in terms of the debt-to-GDP ratio) has remained at similar levels in most countries after real house prices started to weaken. Debt levels have only been reduced in a few countries – with Ireland being the most remarkable example, followed by Iceland, Spain and Hungary, all of which have seen massive declines in new investment. This continued level of over-indebtedness is clearly a

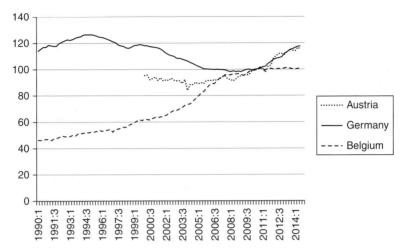

Figure 1.3 Developments in real house prices in Austria, Belgium and Germany, 1990:1 to 2014:4 (2010 average = 100).
Source: OECD House price statistics of 30th January 2015.

matter of concern especially in countries with large falls in nominal house prices and therefore significant issues around negative equity.

Conclusions

This introductory chapter has aimed to provide the rationale for the text, examining how housing finance systems have developed as deregulation and liberalisation have taken root in many European countries, others have started to develop these markets and still others have continued a more traditional path. It also points to some quite fundamental trends in mortgage debt and house prices that are part of the explanation for the financial crisis and points to reasons why many housing finance markets have not recovered – and indeed may not do so perhaps for decades.

The country chapters provide evidence that each national finance system has developed with specific national characteristics, even though the fundamentals of mortgage financing and markets are universal. The authors are able to look in detail at the changing role played by mortgage markets over the period and the varying reliance on other forms of finance. In some countries markets are still framed by central government policies; in others market pressures have dominated for three decades. At a general level it is clear that, in most countries, risks for both consumers and institutions have increased, although some types of risk are being modified by new regulations and other policy responses. Over the 25 years differences between housing finance systems across Europe have narrowed in some contexts but clear differences undoubtedly remain. These similarities and differences are characterised in the next chapter.

References

Bank of International Settlements (2006). *Housing Finance in a Global Financial Market*, CGFS Papers, no. 26, Basle: BIS.

EMF (2014). *Hypostat 2014. A Review of Europe's Mortgage and Housing Markets*. European Mortgage Federation, Brussels, November.

Federal Reserve Bank of Kansas City (2007). Housing, Housing Finance, and Monetary Policy. Symposium Proceedings. Federal Reserve Bank of Kansas City's Jackson Hole Symposium, 31 August–1 September 2007.

Girouard, N, Kennedy, M, and André, C (2007). *Has the rise in debt made households more vulnerable?* Economics Department Working Papers No. 535. OECD. Eco/Wkp(2006)63, January.

Green, R K And Wachter, S (2010) The housing finance revolution. In: *The Blackwell Companion to the Economics of Housing*, Smith, S and Searle, B (eds), Wiley-Blackwell, Oxford.

International Monetary Fund (IMF) (2012). Dealing with household debt. Chapter 3 In: *Growth Resuming. Dangers Remain. IMF World Economic Outlook*. April 2012.

International Monetary Fund (IMF) (2006). How do financial systems affect economic cycles? Chapter 4 In: *Financial Systems and Economic Cycles. IMF World Economic Outlook*. September 2006.

Jordá, Ò, Schularick, M and Taylor, AM (2014) *The Great Mortgaging: Housing Finance, Crises, and Business Cycles. National Bureau of Economic Research*. NBER Working Paper 20501.

OECD (2006). Has the rise in debt made households more vulnerable? *OECD Economic Outlook* 2006:2 no. 80. December, 135–158.

OECD (2013). Debt and macroeconomic stability. *OECD Economic Department Policy Notes* no. 16, January.

OECD (various years). *House price statistics* [Online], Available: www.oecd-ilibrary.org/economics/house-prices_2074384x-table17 (accessed 20 July, 2015).

Priemus, H, and Whitehead, C (2014). Interactions between the financial crisis and national housing markets. *Journal of Housing and the Built Environment* 29:2. 193–200.

Reinhart, C and Rogoff, KS (2009). *This Time Is Different: Eight Centuries of Financial Folly*. Princeton University Press, Princeton, New Jersey.

Scanlon, K, Lunde, J and Whitehead, C (2008). Mortgage product innovation in advanced economies: more choice, more risk *International Journal of Housing Policy* 8:2, 109–131.

Scanlon, K, Lunde, J and Whitehead, C (2011). Responding to the housing and financial crises: mortgage lending, mortgage products and government policies *International Journal of Housing Policy* 11:1, 23–49.

Turner, B and Whitehead, C (1993). *Housing Finance in the 1990s*. The National Swedish Institute for Building Research. Gävle and London. May.

Tutin, C and Vorms, B (2014). French Housing Markets after the subprime crisis: from exuberance to resilience, *Journal of Housing and the Built Environment* 29:2, 277–298.

2

European Housing Finance Models in 1989 and 2014

Jens Lunde[a] and Christine Whitehead[b]

[a] *Department of Finance, Copenhagen Business School, Frederiksberg, Denmark*
[b] *Department of Economics, London School of Economics, London, UK*

Introduction

The changes in housing finance markets and systems across Europe over the last 25 years – the subject of this book – can be examined in two ways: as a flow of changes that appeared over the timeline from 1989 to 2014, or as a comparison of the state of housing finance design, systems and market content in 1989 and the state of housing finance a quarter of a century later.

Developments in each country's housing finance system over the 25 years are presented by national authors for the 21 countries in the following chapters. This chapter compares the operation of housing finance systems around 1989 and then in 2014. Most of the chapter relies on the answers to a questionnaire sent by the editors to the authors of the national chapters. The questionnaire asked the respondents about how their mortgage system operated in 1989 or around that year and then again in 2014. In this way changes could be identified, while the dynamics of change are left to the individual chapters.

The questionnaire concentrated specifically on supply and demand in the mortgage market – that is, loans secured against residential property. It was in two parts. The first centred on the nature and importance of the mortgage

Milestones in European Housing Finance, First Edition.
Edited by Jens Lunde and Christine Whitehead.
© 2016 John Wiley & Sons, Ltd. Published 2016 by John Wiley & Sons, Ltd.

system employed at the starting date and at the present time. Authors were asked whether their mortgage market at each point in time was:

- Non-existent (so that owners had to use bank loans or raise family equity, otherwise they could not own);
- Highly regulated (limited to the most secure borrowers; used low loan-to-value ratios [LTVs]; only available from specialist providers and for short periods of time);
- One where some deregulation had been already been put in place before 1989 (usually after 1980 involving more lenders, more sources of funds and easier terms);
- Liberalised (with large number of lenders, competition among lenders, many instruments used and many sources of funds).

In the second part of the questionnaire the detailed characteristics of mortgage systems were identified. Here, the country authors were asked about the rules and norms for housing loans and lending around 1989 and again in 2014 and if these rules were simply usual business practice or legally based. The questions were grouped around:

- Credit assessments and the registration of the security behind the loans;
- The use of rules to limit the scale of mortgage loans (e.g. LTV, downpayment requirements, debt-to-income (DTI) ratios, loan terms);
- Access to foreign currency loans and to equity withdrawal;
- The funding methods used;
- The incidence of credit risk and how risk was shared (including the use of guarantees);
- Mortgage types available;
- How interest rates were set (fixed or variable as well as whether market or regulated); and
- Foreclosure processes.

In this chapter the answers and how they compare across countries are described and analysed. The editors, who are the authors of this chapter, are responsible for this analysis and for the opinions expressed.

Mortgage systems

The overall picture

Comparing the different national housing finance systems in 1989 and in 2014, we find large changes in many countries. Non-market financing through public budgets has nearly disappeared. Subsidisation of housing supply, especially social housing, from public budgets has been reduced. In many countries deregulation and liberalisation of the finance systems in general and housing in particular was already well underway but this process was intensified. Restricting loans for instance to new build housing units, renovation or modernisation have nearly disappeared. Other loan restrictions, directed at making lending more secure eased somewhat over the 25 years. Thus remortgaging and equity withdrawal have become widely accepted. Loans with longer terms and innovative new instruments have been introduced, often with the purpose of reducing borrowers' payments. Some of these changes were partly reversed after the outbreak of the Global Financial Crisis (GFC) so that 2014 may be more regulated than, say, 2008 but this is a matter for discussion in the individual chapters.

The answers to the questionnaires show that already in 1989 between a third and half of the countries included in this book had experienced some deregulation and liberalisation of mortgage markets, often starting around 1980 but sometimes earlier. In some countries, therefore, there were large numbers of national and international lenders working in a competitive environment and with an increasing number of instruments, a great deal more liquidity and easier terms. The majority of respondents found that liberalisation had made further progress and created considerable improvement over the 25 years. Only a few respondents – Iceland, Ireland and to some extent Belgium, together with the East European countries in 1989 and only Belgium and Ireland in 2014 – regarded their mortgage market as highly regulated.

Importantly, most East European countries established housing financial systems in the years after 1989. European Mortgage Federation (EMF) statistics show that Estonia, Latvia, Hungary, Slovakia and Poland had residential mortgage loan to GDP ratios above 20 percent by 2013 (EMF 2014). In several countries the process of liberalisation was, as remarked by the Spanish authors, also one of regulation in order to create a market.

Not surprisingly given easier access to credit across most of Europe, the answers to the questionnaire indicated that 'family equity' had declined in importance between 1989 and now. Family support across the generations has always been common and can be expected to continue to some degree, as lending to as well as renting out to children is quite normal in many societies; the reverse – children having older family members included in their household – is less common in industrialised societies especially in the context of ongoing urbanisation. Similarly, ordinary bank loans for housing purposes were more common around 1989 than now. Specialised mortgages, with funds raised by commercial or mortgage banks, operating with longer terms and based on the use of the borrowers' homes as collateral, have meant that the servicing costs are lower than for ordinary bank loans. The availability of such loans also increased access to owner-occupation but also to consumer debt.

The decline in equity financing

The use of equity as a source of housing finance for the initial purchase of the dwelling and thereafter over the lifetime of the mortgage was remarkably reduced between 1989 and 2014. To say this in another way, homeowners have generally become more leveraged over their housing careers. This might be regarded as a common milestone in European housing finance, and as a systemic change, resulting in significantly more risk for borrowers and lenders.

As is clear from Table 2.1, the effects of a number of changes have worked in this direction (although in some countries there have also been increases in outright ownership as owner-occupation becomes more normal among older households).

Housing finance models where first time homeowners could borrow at an interest rate below the market interest rate because they had already saved for a period of years beforehand, also at a reduced interest rate, were often part of regulated mortgage market systems. These models disappeared in nearly all countries by the end of the 1980s and the start of the 1990s as access to mortgage credit became easier. Only Austria, Germany and Hungary have some elements of this model left (through contract savings or *Bausparkasse*).

The homeowner's equity starts to be built up with the downpayment provided as part of an ordinary house purchase process. Respondents were therefore asked if there were rules with respect to the required downpayment for the first loan. In nearly all countries with mortgage systems in force in 1989, the usual business practice was to require a downpayment – generally varying between 10 to 20 percent. These rules were not part of national legislation.

As also shown in Table 2.1, downpayment requirements were slightly less common in 2014. In five countries, usual business practice no longer required downpayments. In the Netherlands, a guarantee system made it possible to borrow more than 100 percent of the purchase price. In France, the regulatory framework also enabled loans of more than 100 percent. Among the former central planned economies, only Russia required a downpayment – put in place when they established a market mortgage lending platform.

LTV regulations form an indirect requirement for downpayments, although many buyers, facing such requirements, might be able to find other borrowing channels (unsecured bank loans, family loans etc.). In the years after 2000, when mortgage credit rose strongly until around 2008, competition among banks and other suppliers in deregulated mortgage markets seems to have led to lower downpayment requirements. Thus, it has been claimed on many occasions that the housing market boom was fostered

Table 2.1 Some changes influencing the size of household equity.

Country	Downpayment for the first loan		Max term		Housing equity withdrawal available	
	1989	2014	1989	2014	1989	2014
Australia	Yes	At least 5%	25–30 years	30 years	No specific product for the purpose.	Yes
Austria	Yes	No	Yes	Usually 30 years (up to 40)	No	No
Belgium	Downpayment required	No	~20 years	30 years	No	No
Czech Republic	No	No	15 years	30 years	No	No specific mortgage loans for this purpose
Denmark	No downpayment required	5% of downpayment required from 1 Nov 2015	30 years	30 years	Mortgage equity withdrawal accepted Dec. 1992	Yes
England	Downpayment for first-time buyers normally over 10%	Probably around 20–25% and even with government support 5% but much lower in 2000s	20–25 years	No – but rarely over 25 years	Only implicitly on moving	Yes
France	Only for some banks	No	25 years (sometimes 30)	25	No	Yes (much less readily available than pre-2008)
Finland	20–30% (unless other collateral)	No	15 years	typically 30 years	No	No
Germany	Downpayment usually 20% of the assessed mortgage loan value as a minimum	Downpayment usually 20% of the assessed mortgage loan value as a minimum	No	No	Very rarely used in practice	Yes
Hungary	Yes	No	35 years	30 years	No	Possible, but not common
Iceland	Minimum equity contribution. Loosely enforced	Downpayment normally required	Lowered from 40 to 25 years in 1989	40 years	No	Yes

(continued overleaf)

Table 2.1 (*continued*)

Country	Downpayment for the first loan		Max term		Housing equity withdrawal available	
	1989	2014	1989	2014	1989	2014
Ireland	Yes	Yes	25 years	30 years	No	Yes
Netherlands	Yes, but this is a cyclical requirement.	Most first-time buyers have a mortgage guarantee that covers 104% LTV	25–30 is general practice	30 is general practice	Second mortgages are available	Yes
Norway	20% (unless other collateral)	15%	No	30 years	No	Yes, second mortgage widely available; a couple of institutions provide reverse mortgage
Poland		5% of downpayment		35 years	No	Yes. Home equity credit line secured on dwelling
Portugal	Yes	Yes	25 years – the general practice	No	Yes	Yes
Russia	No	45.9%	No	50 years	No	No
Slovenia	No	Only loans secured within Bausparkassen housing loan scheme	10 years	30 years	No	No
Spain	Yes	Yes	No	No	Yes	No
Sweden	Not in general	Not in general	Perhaps 50 or 60 years in practice	Perhaps 50 or 60 years in practice	At a penalty; i.e. cost is higher than the PDV of the interest gain	At a penalty; i.e. cost is higher than the PDV of the interest gain
Turkey			Relatively short terms	20 years; average 7.2 years		

by weak credit assessments, low downpayments and expectations that house price would continue to rise.

Falling inflation and interest rates over the 25 years, reaching their current extremely low levels after the GFC, have contributed significantly to a low equity/high leverage pattern among homeowners. In 1989 high nominal interest rates created front loading problems (in the US this was named the mortgage-tilt problem) as borrowers had difficulties in paying the high debt service requirements of the first years of the mortgage. Thereafter, high inflation led to a rapid reduction in the real value of both the debt repayments and the debt. These effects can be attributed to the 'inflation component' in nominal interest rates, which can be seen as the borrower's payment for the gradual reduction of the real value of the loan debt and as compensation to the investor as the real value of his/her saving declines over time.

In 2014, by contrast to 1989, first year debt service charges on nominal interest rate loans were extremely low – and in most countries lower than ever before. However, as a result there is only a very slow reduction in the real value of the debt. Thus homeowners' leverage ratios remain high and their equity remains low for many years after the initial purchase, unless house prices should start to increase more than consumer prices. If instead house prices fall, many more owners may become technically insolvent. In 2014 the ECB and other commentators have started to fear that such deflation might occur over the next few years resulting in an increase in the real value of the homeowners' and other property owners' debt burden.

As can also be seen from Table 2.1, homeowners' capacity to maintain high leverage ratios through their housing careers has also increased over the 25-year period. Loan terms have been lengthened significantly; interest-only mortgages have become available in several countries and remortgaging allows borrowing against home equity to become easier so that homeowners are enabled to make equity withdrawals, which by definition reduce equity financing. After the GFC and the housing market downturns countries tended to reverse their policies on access to interest-only loans and equity withdrawal (Scanlon *et al.* 2011). Maximum LTVs have also declined (Scanlon *et al.* forthcoming). These measures are discussed further in the individual country chapters.

Funding the supply of mortgages

The funding method is often seen as the determining variable that distinguishes and defines the different mortgage system models in use. In the literature these mortgage system models have been grouped into four major types: 'depository systems; directed credit (including provident funds, raised by payroll taxes and contractual savings schemes); specialised mortgage lending (through government-regulated or -owned banks or "covered bonds"...);

and more recently, secondary mortgage market systems through securitisation' (Green and Wachter 2007: 22).

This grouping already represented a change in mortgage system models. Through the 1980s and the 1990s ongoing reductions in interest rates lowered the market costs of funding for housing significantly and gradually eliminated the front loading problem. This rendered it possible to remove, or at least reduce, the serious burden on public expenditure that was associated with direct public sector funding and subsidies to housing finance. Falling interest rates also changed and indeed nearly eliminated the building society and Bausparkasse models, where savings were pooled to finance the purchase of homes. In these models intermediaries enabled households to finance the purchase of a house with loans at below market interest rates, if they had saved for some years before also at below market deposit interest rates. Such mortgage models were found in the UK, Germany, Austria, Spain and a few other countries. Some interest from Eastern European countries in these systems has disappeared or become much less important over the period.

A classification of mortgage systems currently in use suggests three types: (i) *deposit-financed mortgage systems*, where the bank/originator holds the loans on the balance sheet and uses deposits as the funding source; (ii) *securitised mortgage systems*, where mortgages are packaged into pools and where repackaging can be used to form different bond types, to be sold to investors and (iii) *covered bonds*, which are claims on the originator that are collateralised by pools of mortgages but where the underlying mortgages remain on the books of the originators (Campbell 2012: 17–19).

Table 2.2 clarifies what respondents identified as their most used funding methods around 1989. Funding with deposits through a banking model was the most common, either as the only funding method or in combination with the use of another method. However, among the model's disadvantages, deposits can be withdrawn on demand while mortgages cannot and 'deposit–financed lending usually involves an element of maturity transformation, particularly when mortgages are fixed rate. This exposes mortgage lenders to fundamental risk from changes in interest rates' (Campbell 2012: 17).

The second most usual funding method in 1989 was through covered bonds – again often in combination with other funding methods. Denmark used only covered bond to fund mortgage lending. Germany used *Pfandbriefe*, which formed a large part of the German market.

Even in 1989 some countries used several funding methods (see Table 2.2). Germany used not only Pfandbriefe but also deposits, unsecured bank bonds and even securitisation (on a small scale). Austria used 'deposits, inheritance, public subsidy loans for self-building of single-family houses by households, and public loans and covered bonds for multi-storey LPHA housing'. France used 'retail deposits and special saving schemes (*Epargne-logement*

Table 2.2   Funding methods used in 1989.

	Number of countries	Countries	Comments
No market lending	5	Czech Republic, Hungary, Poland, Russia, Slovenia	The mentioned deposits might be from ordinary banking activities and as basis for bank loans
Retail deposits only	10	Australia, Belgium, Czech R, Finland, Hungary, Ireland, Netherlands, Portugal, (Russia), Slovenia	France: Special saving schemes are seen as a subsidy arrangement
More than one funding method	9	Austria, UK, France, Germany, Iceland, Norway, Spain, Sweden, Turkey	
Retail deposits in combination with other funding methods	6	Austria, UK, France, Norway, Spain, Sweden	
Covered bonds only or in combination with other funding methods	7	Denmark, France, Germany, Sweden, Austria, Iceland, Spain	Denmark used only covered bonds with the same characteristics as the matching loans. In Germany Pfandbriefe formed a large part of the market

Note: the numbers add up to more than 21 countries, as some have been mentioned more than one time.

for home buyers and *Livret A* for social landlords)' but did not employ securitisation. The respondents' answer for the Netherlands was:

> Deposits through general banks were the most important source. Insurers and pension funds also had a market share. Covered bonds were used but only until 1980 by specialised mortgage banks. These banks became part of general banks after the crisis of the early 1980s. No securitisation.

What is clear is that no common 'European funding method' existed at that time – but that some systems had the potential for many different forms of funding, while others had only one model – or indeed no mortgage market at all.

Twenty-five years later, one of the most general and most important changes – 'milestones' – in housing finance has been that only a few countries now use deposits as the only funding source and a far more diverse range of funding methods is in place in most countries (see Table 2.3, which covers the same issues for 2014). Most fundamentally in all countries potential purchasers are able to borrow for house purchase under market conditions.

Table 2.3   Funding methods used in 2014.

	Number of countries	Countries	Comments
No market lending	0		All countries have access to borrowing at market conditions
Retail deposits only	2	Slovenia, Turkey	Only these two countries seem to rely solely on deposits as funding source
More than one funding method	18	Australia, Austria, Belgium, Czech R, UK, France, Finland, Germany, Hungary, Iceland, Ireland, Netherlands, Norway, Poland, Portugal, Russia, Spain, Sweden	
Retail deposits in combination with other funding methods	17	Australia, Austria, Belgium, Czech R, UK, France, Finland, Germany, Hungary, Iceland, Ireland, Norway, Poland, Portugal, Russia, Spain, Sweden	
Covered bonds only or in combination with other funding methods	18	Australia, Austria, Belgium, Czech R, Denmark, France, Finland, Germany, Hungary, Iceland, Ireland, Netherlands, Norway, Poland, Portugal, Russia, Spain, Sweden	Denmark used for the most part covered bonds, still with the same characteristics as the matching bonds. In Germany Pfandbriefe still formed a large part of the market

Note: the numbers add up to more than 21 countries, as some have been mentioned more than one time.

In particular, many commercial banks now use money market instruments as well as deposits to fund their mortgage lending. This use of money market instruments created some of the background behind the outbreak of the GFC in 2008.

The third big change in funding methods is that covered bonds are now used in 18 countries. Covered bonds are debt instruments secured by a cover pool of mortgage loans with the properties as collateral. Denmark still uses this mechanism almost exclusively as the means of financing mortgages. Germany equally uses Pfandbriefe. However, the importance of covered bonds differs a lot between countries. For example, the Polish respondent remarks: 'Only about 0.5 percent of mortgage funding is through covered bonds (approximately 99.5 percent of PLN lending is funded through retail deposits). So this is a rather negligible source of funding'. Even in Denmark, a small market in commercial bank housing loans has been created which relies on funding through deposits as well as covered bonds.

Both deposit funding and covered bond systems permit maturity transformation, which can create the risk of a 'mis-match' when combined with funds from wholesale money markets. 'However, in countries that have limited maturity transformation, covered bond systems have been impressively stable' (Campbell 2012: 19).

Covered bond legislation now exists in 26 out of 28 EU Member States, with Estonia and Malta as the exceptions, and in five other non-EU European countries, including Russia and Turkey. Through the market turmoil in and after 2008 the covered bond markets in general continued to function – although some banks needed state support and restructuring.

A rather different approach to using secondary markets has been the use of mortgage backed securities. Mortgage backed securities were increasingly used from the mid-1990s and became an important source of funding in the UK, Australia and Ireland with some issuance in most European countries during the early 2000s (Holmans *et al.* 2003). The market almost completely closed after the GFC because of problems experienced in the USA and was only just beginning to re-emerge in 2014.

Thus over the last 25 years funding has moved away from partly public or publicly subsidised frameworks and 'special circuit' models to banking models based on market priced deposits and also away from retail towards capital market funding, including both mortgage backed securities and covered bonds.

Mortgage characteristics

Mortgage models have been developed in each country within their own legislative and regulatory frameworks. As a result there are variations in loan characteristics and in how interest rates are set across countries, even though the same basic fundamentals need to be in place in any mortgage system. Over the 25-year period, as markets have become more embedded, the variance in mortgage characteristics has declined in part as a result of international competition and regulation.

Credit assessment

Even though the basis of most mortgages is that the property is provided as collateral, normal bank procedure within a market lending system has usually included a credit assessment when a borrower applies for a loan. Such credit assessments were legally required in four countries in 1989 but were usual business practice in some form in all countries – although the level of detail required varied greatly. An exception was Denmark, as mortgages were originated on the basis of the property value – called 'the value of the bricks' – until 1990, but large losses in the Danish mortgage banks in 1990 acted as an 'eye opener' and the regulation was improved to include an assessment of the borrower. Today, the basic credit assessment of loan applicants remains much the same as 25 years earlier and is now legally required in seven countries.

Property valuation and registration

As in 1989, it is normal procedure to assess the value of the property used as collateral for the mortgage loan. In some countries this information may also affect the interest rate charged to the borrower. In Finland, France and Germany, construction costs or the transaction price may be used instead of a valuation. A couple of East European countries in 1989 did not require a property value assessment or other market lending rules but since then they have established lending systems including property valuations. In 1989 the valuation process was generally based on business practice and was legally based in only five countries. Now there are 11 countries where it is legally based.

The public registration of ownership in some form of 'land register' was legally required in nearly all countries where there was a market lending system in 1989. Now almost all countries demand this public registration. Ireland was and is the only exception.

Similarly, the public registration of loans, secured against the property as collateral, was required in almost all countries with a market lending system both in 1989 and now. The exceptions were England and Ireland where other legally based systems apply.

Ownership and mortgage borrower registration rules are seen as important legal and often constitutional requirements in many countries in the same way as for other property rights, which is why they have generally been unchanged over the 25 years. The introduction of public registration of ownership rights and security for loans in the former central planned economies and in other countries initiating market lending systems sometimes required constitutional change.

Lending restrictions on access to a mortgage or housing loan

Earlier some housing financial systems were provided from public budgets or were subsidised directly or indirectly through the state or public entities. Then budget limits created natural barriers to the quantity of funding available. In some countries these were the only way to raise a loan for house purchase. In many nations in 1989 the use of special circuits of mortgage funding was in place. Where interest rates were below market interest rates there was a clear incentive to borrow – but allocations were often limited to those with secure incomes who could easily make the repayments. Equally there were queues or limits on the amount that could be borrowed sometimes based on past savings. In some instances these rules were adjusted and total lending regulated as part of the monetary and the finance policy.

Restrictions on borrowers' access to mortgage funding have traditionally only been a matter of usual business practice. The most widely used and best known restriction is an LTV rule, which applied in two thirds of the countries in our sample in 1989. Most countries allowed a maximum of around 80 percent but these were only legally binding in a couple of countries. France, Ireland, the Netherlands and four Eastern European countries did not use a LTV rule, even as part of business practice.

In 2014 all the countries included here used LTV rules. This might be seen as a milestone in European mortgage regulation and as in part reflective of the harmonisation process within the EU. The maximum allowed LTV increased in some countries but the questionnaire did not cover changes prior to the GFC that have since been reversed. In the Netherlands, Sweden and the UK LTVs certainly rose and have now fallen, as discussed in the individual chapters.

Another closely related and commonly used restriction on access to mortgages can be found in rules around the required downpayment when (first time) buying and borrowing (see Table 2.1).

Borrowers only had to fulfil specific rules with respect to a maximum of DTI ratio in Ireland, Norway, Portugal, Slovenia, Spain and Turkey in 1989. Of course in other countries the size of the debt and of the income is included in more general credit assessments so DTI rules may be unnecessary. Today DTI rules are in place in eleven countries but are not legally required except for in Hungary and Poland.

At least 11 countries used debt service-to-income ratios rules in the regulation of the mortgage market in 1989, although the regulation was only legally based in Iceland. The few examples of ratios mentioned are around 30 percent. By 2014 the respondents from 14 countries suggested that debt-service-to-income rules are usual business practice. However, the answers from all countries indicate that a cornerstone of all credit assessments is to verify that the borrowers will be able to pay their future debt service requirements.

Terms, currency employed and access to equity withdrawal

The generally available maximum term for a housing loan in each country was presented in Table 2.1. In 1989, these terms showed considerable variation between countries, ranging from 15 to 35 years. In countries with no market mortgage system available loan terms were usually much shorter. Only Sweden used longer terms, up to 50 or 60 years. The maximum terms were generally not a legal requirement. In most countries the most common length for mortgages was 20 or 25 years.

Now the maximum term has lengthened in half of the countries included here and is 30 years or higher in 14 countries. The maximum term is only legally based in two countries. The terms most usually available have also lengthened but they are still shorter than the maximum possible. In 1989 borrowers could generally only raise mortgages denominated in a foreign currency to finance owner-occupied homes in Australia, Germany and Slovenia (where it was possible but not common). This was usually because many worked in other countries or had incomes in another currency.

However, the capacity to raise housing loans denominated in another currency increased in several countries until the housing market turnarounds and the GFC in 2008. Borrowers and governments in a number of countries where foreign currency loans had become common then came to realise that there were serious downside risks involved in such loans. As a result these mortgages are now rarely offered or are even forbidden. Countries with recent 'bad experiences' with loans in foreign currencies include Iceland, Poland, Hungary and Slovenia.

To prohibit persons and households from equity withdrawal is impossible. A loan contract made on market conditions is a simple reallocation of the borrower's and, with the opposite sign, the creditor's consumption possibilities; no subsidies are involved. Moreover, there are obvious welfare gains to enabling lending to households as part of normal banking activities regulated within a national financial supervisory framework. In particular it helps to limit unregulated or even black market banking activities.

It was more usual to restrict such equity withdrawal through specialised lenders, especially when rates were held below market levels. Many restrictions were found across countries in 1989 and homeowners generally had high equity-to-housing value ratios after they had been owners for some years. Access to equity withdrawal by raising or extending a mortgage was highly restricted in nearly all the countries included here (Table 2.1). Spain and Portugal were exceptions but their legal access to housing equity withdrawal was not commonly used because of cultural and family traditions. In the Netherlands, owners had the capacity to raise a 'second mortgage'. However, equity can always be realised when the house is sold. Especially in inflationary periods, large housing equity withdrawals have been made at sale often funded by a larger mortgage (while providing a larger deposit) on the next home.

An important change during the last 25 years is that formal access to housing equity withdrawal was made possible in at least 14 of the countries in our sample. This structural change might also be seen as a regulatory milestone. However, there have been increasing calls for direct and indirect restrictions since the GFC, discussed in the individual chapters.

Credit risk and guarantees

The respondents to the questionnaire noted that the lender generally carries the credit risk associated with a loan contract. Therefore the lender has to include a risk premium when setting the interest rate. It is possible to separate the risk by issuing a guarantee for the payments and selling the risk to a guarantor through a financial intermediation process. Then the borrower pays a premium to the guarantor instead of paying a risk premium to the lender. This approach was used in some countries – in the Netherlands, Portugal and Slovenia around 1989. In others, notably Eastern European countries such as Hungary and Russia, public budgets took some of the risk. In Iceland, mortgage lending, and therefore risk carrying, was managed through a public fund until the end of 1989.

Little has changed between 1989 and 2014 in terms of the formal contracts. The lenders still carry the risk in 2014 – however, the use of insurance and guarantees has grown more widespread. Guarantees can be given from a public entity, an insurance company or a specialised guarantor. In 1989 guarantees for mortgages were mainly arranged by the public sector – some German states, Dutch municipalities and some Australian states. In Sweden the government offered guarantees to lenders who financed new (residential) construction. In Denmark mortgages were raised to finance social housing and guaranteed through the public sector.

The use of guarantees issued by specialised institutions seems to have been expanded slightly over the last 25 years. New guarantees have also been put in place in Australia for loans with LTVs above 80 percent and in the Belgian region of Flanders as insurance to guaranteed income. Some German states still offer loan guarantee schemes. In the Netherlands the National Mortgage Guarantee arrangement is used to ensure that high LTV rules can be maintained. The UK now has guarantees in place for some mortgages and for funds to support social housing investment. France and Russia also have some guarantee arrangements. The special Danish and Swedish arrangements remain unchanged.

Sometimes – but not included in the questionnaire – borrowers have access to insurance to ensure that they will be have adequate income to continue payments on their mortgages in the event of illness or unemployment. In France all lenders demand that borrowers insure against death and incapacity. In Ireland a life cover is required. However, where it is optional, insurance seems not to be popular. On the other hand, insurance protection with respect to the asset given as collateral is common. In particular fire insurance is a loan condition in several countries.

How mortgage interest rates are determined

Typically, a range of mortgage types has been offered in the mortgage market and more loan types were on offer in 2014 than in 1989. Here, we concentrate on identifying different interest rate setting rules.

The main issue is whether fixed, adjustable rate or variable interest rates are the norm in each country. In 1989, 11 countries answered that they had fixed interest rates or mostly fixed rates; six that they used variable rates or mostly variable rates. Only Finland used mostly adjustable rate mortgages.

The picture seems more varied in 2014 as more loan types are available than 25 years ago with even more in the period before the GFC (Scanlon *et al.* 2011). In 2014 only seven countries used mostly fixed interest rates; six used mainly variable interest rates; and four – Denmark, Hungary, Poland and Sweden – mostly used adjustable rate mortgages. Iceland used index linked mortgages, which carried fixed *real* interest rates. A couple of countries have shifted to mainly variable rates. But in almost all countries other options were available.

The length of the period over which a fixed interest rate is fixed as well as the rules for resetting variable interest rates remain very diverse. In 1989 the majority of those with fixed rate systems were for 5 years or less. In Germany, the most common fixed rate period was 10 years. In other countries rates were fixed for the full term of the mortgage. Even so, the general impression from the answers is that in 2014 the fixed interest periods have been shortened.

Another question asked for 1989 was: 'Is the interest rate determined: for each individual loan (like a bank loan); for all loans in a given category; or in relation to capital market conditions – for example, by a bond rate in 1989'.

This question showed important differences between housing finance systems in Europe. At one extreme, and the most used method, was the 'banking model', where interest rates are decided for each loan after negotiation between the bank and the borrower. This was the case in Australia, Austria, Finland, the Netherlands, Portugal, Slovenia, Spain, Turkey and the UK. Some answers suggested that lenders identified categories, based on information from the loan applicant about type of property, earlier savings, downpayment or LTV, loan term (or maturity) and so on. In some countries, Belgium, Czech Republic, France, Germany, Hungary and Iceland, borrowers belonging to well-defined categories had to be offered the same interest rates. In others both individual and group attributes helped determine the interest rate. However, 'credit quality' – that is, the borrower's credit worthiness – was not mentioned much.

At the other extreme example is the Danish mortgage system, where bonds are resold on the stock exchange, so interest rates move constantly reflecting market conditions. Thus Danish borrowers have to pay the same risk premium embedded into the interest rate for a given loan type and determined by the bond investors in the capital market. In addition the mortgage banks add a fee, which varies with the loan's LTV, type and main category of borrower.

In 2014 the banks had the power to determine the interest rate on each loan individually in only seven countries. Even then, the banks take into account certain 'rules' as well as capital market interest rates that they cannot influence. In addition, lenders include a margin that covers fees to the lender, which may be determined by competition or may be regulated.

The respondents were asked for 2014 whether the interest rate on an individual mortgage was determined directly by interest rates in the general capital market – for example, a LIBOR based interest rate and if so, how? In nearly all the countries, sometimes exclusively but usually as a possible choice, mortgages of this type are on offer based on some national reference interest rate index. Then the interest rate for the single loan is equal to this reference rate plus a margin (including a payment for credit risk) as determined by the individual lender.

Another question was whether the interest rate on an individual mortgage was influenced by special legal requirements? This was not usual. Caps and floors have been used in Spain and caps in Austria and Denmark but were not required by law. Hungary had restrictions on the interest rate adjustment for loans granted before 2011. In Belgium the 1993 mortgage law contained strict rules to protect the borrowers: no interest rate variation within one year with the maximum increase in interest rates limited to one percentage point after the first year and two percentage points after the second year where loans could be reset in the first three years. In Denmark a law introduced in 2013 restricts the annual increase in interest rates to five percentage points for loans with annual interest resetting.

The frequency of allowable interest rate changes is relevant for variable rate and adjustable rate mortgages. The variable interest rate can be changed when the lender decides in Australia, Iceland, Portugal, Turkey and the UK – and monthly in Norway and Poland. In other countries interest rates can be reset in accordance with rules specific to the mortgage instrument, usually an adjustable rate mortgage. Some of the answers also indicate that refinancing possibilities using the existing mortgage can be combined with the resetting procedure.

Two questions were asked about fixed interest rate mortgages in 2014, one about the period during which the loan was fixed; the other about the average actual fixed period. Table 2.4 summarises this information.

Foreclosures

A mortgage is a loan contract with the important feature that the borrower's property is used as collateral. This special attribute has the advantage for the lender that the property can be taken into possession after a default, that is, if the borrower does not deliver the promised payments. The owner-occupier thus loses the property but also the family home. From the point of view of the borrower, the use of the property as collateral reduces the interest rate on the loan. The extent of this deduction depends significantly on the costs and efficiency of the relevant foreclosure mechanism – especially as there are usually strict legal conditions.

The questionnaire included a number of questions around foreclosure in 1989 and in 2014. These covered how long the process took; whether any remaining debt was written off or whether there was full recourse for such debt; how often the procedures were used; and whether the rules were legally based.

Table 2.4   Fixed interest rate periods in 2014.

Country	The periods interest rates can be fixed for	The respondents' estimates of the average period
Australia	1–15 years	3 years
Austria	Short, medium and long	1–7 years
Belgium	The duration of loan up to 30 years or variable with initial fixed rate period: 1–3 years; 3–5 years, 5–10 years, more than 10 years (1 year minimum)	Wide range Average 17–18 years
Czech Republic	1, 3, 5, 10, 15, 20, 30 years.	5 years
Denmark	1–10 years for ARM mortgages. 30 years for FRM mortgages	No data. Also the length of this period varies over the cycle
UK	1–5 years.	1–2 years
France	No restrictions	Not known
Finland	Not answered	12 month EURIBOR is used in about 56% of the loans
Germany	Not answered	Not answered
Hungary	3, 5, 10 years	Mainly for state subsidised mortgage loans
Iceland	No restrictions. Commonly 3 years, 5 years or term of loan (typically 25 years or most commonly 40 years)	For non-indexed fixed-rate loan rates are fixed for either 3 or 5 years. The average in 2013 was 4.3 years based on new lending by banks and the HFF
Ireland	1, 2, 3, 4 and 5-year fixed rates are common. Longer terms available.	3 years
Netherlands	5 or 10 years most common, but up to 20 years with a higher rate	Between 5 and 10 years
Norway	The rate is fixed for the agreed period	62% of the loans in value terms have a period of 1–5 years, 22% less than 1 year
Poland	Not answered	Not answered
Portugal	No	No fixed
Russia	The rate is usually fixed for the whole period	The average period of mortgage is about 15 years
Slovenia	Up to 10 years	Between 5 and 10 years for combined rate loans. After this period the loan is variable rate based on EURIBOR + margin
Spain	Not used Other formulae based on initial fixed rate period are used. The most common initial fixed period is 3 years	Mortgage loans in Spain are mostly variable rate (normally can be reset every 6/12 months) Since 2008 'initial fixed period rate' loans have grown more popular The initial period in normally between 2–5 years; thereafter, it is usually variable
Sweden	Not answered	Not answered
Turkey	It can be fixed for whole loan period	Average period for the fixed interest rate is the most common length of term: 61–120 months

Note: The respondents' sources for the answers are not mentioned.

The characteristics of national foreclosure and bankruptcy systems are normally part of the legal fundamentals in a market based system. Even so they were poorly determined in many countries. Those respondents who answered said that it was legally based but many did not answer that specific question perhaps because it was obvious or perhaps because of lack of information.

Even in 1989 most Eastern European countries had some private ownership and some sort of foreclosure system. For instance, the Russian respondent wrote that, in 1989:

> As per the Russian Soviet Federative Socialist Republic's Civil Code, in-court foreclosure was allowed, however, with a provision on foreclosure of alternative assets permitted, that is, assets different from the collateral that would be sufficient to meet the collateral holder's claim.

However, clarifying these rules was often an important part of the development of well operating mortgage markets in Eastern and Southern Europe (Turner and Whitehead 1993).

Many respondents did not have the necessary information to answer the question about duration for 1989. In 2014 the average duration for foreclosure procedures was 2–3 years. The shortest durations, at a year or lower, were found in the Nordic countries. Iceland was the only country that noted that they have changed the laws on bankruptcy after the financial crisis – reducing the time taken from 7 to 2 years. They, like a number of other countries, notably Ireland and Spain, also developed legally based forbearance rules to address post crisis issues and allow borrowers to adjust their payments in relation to their income. In Hungary from 2011 a foreclosure quota system was applied to credit institutions.

There is a remarkable uniformity among the European countries on whether the remaining debt remains in place after foreclosure. In both 1989 and 2014 all had full recourse mortgages, that is, the uncovered debt after a foreclosure remains the responsibility of the borrower. In many cases, however, the best solution for both borrower and lender may be to make a voluntary agreement maybe including some write-down in the debt. Equally in some contexts personal bankruptcy, which normally involves a significant write down, may be a better solution for the borrower. This may be one reason why, rather against expectations, respondents generally said that foreclosure procedures were not often used, either in 1989 or in 2014.

Overview

The analysis in this chapter is restricted mainly to identifying the attributes of mortgage systems at around our starting date of 1989, their attributes in 2014 and the most important changes that have taken place between those two dates. It shows that housing finance markets now exist in all the countries included in this text and that these have mainly become more efficient, more accessible and cheaper both for lenders and consumers. As a result, in most countries debt finance has grown rapidly and the use of own equity has declined.

Overall legal systems associated with mortgage markets have become more transparent and have helped to ensure better operating markets. The choice of instruments has increased and the proportions of households able to purchase have become larger. Private funding mechanisms have also expanded – particularly through the use of wholesale and secondary markets. Public finance provision has been much reduced as have special circuits of housing finance.

The evidence presented here shows considerable convergence in how mortgage markets operate. Yet there remain many differences, reflecting different histories, development paths and cultures as well as different legal and regulatory systems. In all countries the objective is the same – to build finance markets that enable households to match their payments over their housing careers to their incomes and to widen the choice of property and tenure wherever possible.

With deregulation, liberalisation and market competition, risks faced by both lenders and borrowers have undoubtedly increased. This issue forms some part of the comparison presented here, together with discussion of instruments and regulation that can help mitigate consequent negative impacts. However, these issues are mainly best discussed once the evolution of debt finance in each country has been spelled out. We will therefore return to it in the final chapter.

One element that is clearly missing from the comparison is what has been happening in between the starting and ending dates, how changes have impacted on housing markets and particularly house prices, and in particular, what the effects of the GFC have been on mortgage systems and housing markets across Europe. These are matters for the individual country chapters. An initial review of the impact of the GFC on national housing finance markets, edited by Jens Lunde and Christine Whitehead and including contributions from all the country authors, was published in 2014 by the EMF (Lunde and Whitehead 2014).

Each country chapter follows a similar pattern starting from the ways that the national housing finance system has changed between 1989 and 2014; then identifying and explaining milestones for each country; examining the impact of changes in the finance market on housing systems; and looking to future developments. However – both because of differences between countries in how housing finance systems have operated and thus in what is regarded as important to understand developments over the last quarter century, and because of the different backgrounds and interests of the authors – each follows a somewhat different path. The result, we hope, is a rich tapestry that will help readers to understand where each country has come from, the strengths and weaknesses of national systems and possible ways forward.

References

Campbell, JY (2012). Mortgage market design. *Review of Finance* 17, 1–33.

EMF (2014). *Hypostat 2014. A Review of Europe's Mortgage and Housing Markets.* European Mortgage Federation. Brussels. November.

Green, RK and Wachter, S (2007). The housing finance revolution. In: *Housing, Housing Finance, and Monetary Policy.* Federal Reserve Bank of Kansas City, pp. 21–67.

Holmans, A, Karley, K and Whitehead, C (2003). The mortgage backed securities market in the UK: overview and prospects, *Housing Research Summary*, No 201, Office of the Deputy Prime Minister.

Lunde, J and Whitehead, C (2014). Milestones in housing finance across Europe. *Mortgage Info ENHR Special Edition*, August 2014, Brussels, EMF and ECBC.

Scanlon, K, Lunde, J and Whitehead, C (2011). Responding to the housing and financial crises: mortgage lending, mortgage products and government policies. *International Journal of Housing Policy* 11:1, 23–49, March.

Scanlon, K, Lunde, J and Whitehead, C (forthcoming) European housing systems after the crisis submitted to *International Journal of Housing Policy*.

Turner, B and Whitehead, C (1993) *Housing Finance in the 1990s.* The National Swedish Institute for Building Research. Gävle. May, pp. 311–330.

3

Australia's 25 Years with a Deregulated Housing Finance System: Looking Back and Looking Forward

Judith Yates[a] and María Belén Yanotti[b]
[a] School of Economics, University of Sydney, Sydney, Australia
[b] Tasmanian School of Business and Economics, University of Tasmania, Tasmania, Australia

The economic and institutional environment of the last 25 years

For the past 25 years, Australia's housing finance system has provided funds for households who own more than 95 percent of Australia's housing stock, as owner-occupiers and as private landlords. In the mid-1980s, at the start of the period under review, almost 90 percent of housing finance commitments went to owner-occupiers. The remainder went to investors. A review of its operation and of the factors that have affected the way it has functioned over the past generation provides an opportunity to consider its likely impacts over the next generation.

During the period under review, Australia's housing finance market was deregulated and transformed into a liberalised system. At the start of the period, mortgages for owner-occupation were provided by Australia's highly concentrated authorised deposit-taking institutions (ADIs) on a fully documented, full-recourse, variable-rate basis and fixed-rate mortgages represented less than a quarter of the owner-occupied mortgage market. Currently, variable-rate mortgages account for approximately 85 percent of all mortgages. Variable-rate mortgages dominate in countries where there is an incentive to pre-pay because mortgage interest payments are not deductible (as is the case

Milestones in European Housing Finance, First Edition.
Edited by Jens Lunde and Christine Whitehead.
© 2016 John Wiley & Sons, Ltd. Published 2016 by John Wiley & Sons, Ltd.

in Australia for owner-occupiers) (Ellis 2006). Investment loans were a relatively small component of housing finance and were likely to be assessed as shorter term, mortgaged small business loans. Lending standards were quite conservative, with a maximum debt service-to-income ratio of 30 percent and loan-to-value ratios (LTVs) of a maximum of 80 percent. After deregulation in the 1980s, competition increased with the introduction of new players in the market. A wider range of financial products were offered to both owner-occupiers and investors, measures of disposable income and property valuation methods were redefined, lending standards were relaxed and higher LTVs, backed by private loan mortgage insurance (LMI), were available. These trends were slowed by the post-2007 credit crunch. Today, 25 years later, the Australian mortgage market is still highly concentrated, with four major banks holding more than 80 percent of all mortgage debt held by ADIs (APRA 2013a: 7). Fully documented, full-recourse variable-rate loans still dominate but new finance commitments are now shared more or less equally between owner-occupiers and investors. No mortgage institution is government backed, and mortgage insurers have been privatised, although several regulatory authorities do supervise the market.

The changes in the housing finance system were consistent with the broad thrust of change that took place in Australia over the period. From the early 1980s, Australia experienced a series of microeconomic reforms that would transform its economy to a more market oriented, globalised economy. Financial markets were deregulated and entry was liberalised, tariffs were reduced, the dollar was floated, the labour market was made more flexible, income taxes were lowered as the base was broadened and the transition from discretionary monetary policy to a successful inflation-targeting regime was completed. In the early 1990s, however, Australia went into 'the recession we had to have', attributed to an asset price boom built on increased borrowing and to the 'relentless pressure' of high interest rates (with a cash rate that peaked at 18 percent in 1989). This experience highlighted the weaknesses of risk management within financial institutions. As a consequence, the 1990s saw the beginning of new arrangements for prudential supervision of these institutions.

The reforms of the 1980s and 1990s made a significant contribution to Australia's post 1990 financial and economic performance. Since 1990, Australia has experienced 22 years of consecutive economic growth, with an average growth in real GDP a full percentage point above the Organisation for Economic Co-operation and Development (OECD) average (OECD 2013a: 231). In the 5 years following the Global Financial Crisis (GFC), when the average OECD growth rate was negative, Australia's growth rate remained at 2 percent per year.

This growth has been driven by two booms: an internally generated credit boom that ended in the mid-2000s and an externally generated resources (iron ore and natural gas) boom, which is still to run its full course (Stevens 2013).

The credit boom was encouraged by tax and policy changes that, along with a low interest rate environment, encouraged investment in housing and demand for housing finance. Credit expansion was facilitated by deregulation of the financial system. It ended with the GFC as lenders' liquidity risk rose and the 'credit crunch' closed funding avenues for mortgage lenders. The commodity price and investment components of the resources boom, which began at the start of the 2000s, assisted in sustaining household confidence and taking Australia comfortably through the first decade of the 2000s. The strength of the anticipated third component of the resources boom, the export component, is likely to have a strong influence on whether this will continue. Garnaut (2013) provides an assessment of what he sees as the 'fateful' choices Australia will have to make during what he argues are its 'dog days' after more than two decades of extraordinary prosperity.

Both the credit and resources booms contributed to the increases in income inequality observed in Australia from the mid-1980s to the late 2000s. By the late 2000s, Australia's income inequality (as reflected in the Gini coefficient) had increased more than in most of the 34 OECD countries for which data are readily available (OECD 2013b: 67). Wealth inequality in Australia also increased (ABS 2013a: Table 3.1). These increases in inequality have had an impact on the way in which the mortgage market operates in Australia by contributing to the squeezing out of lower income, low wealth purchasers from the mortgage market.

This paper focuses on the reforms that laid the foundations for the economic and financial outcomes in Australia over the past 25 years, with a particular emphasis on the way in which these affected the demand for, and supply of, housing finance and its housing market. The next section outlines a number of key milestones that have affected Australia's housing and the housing finance systems. The section on impacts and implications of changes describes the changes that have arisen as a result of these reforms and provides a brief overview of some of their impacts. The section following that highlights emerging housing and finance issues that arise, in part, from increasing inequality. The final section concludes.

Key milestones

For the last 25 years, structural changes in Australia's housing and housing finance systems have been affected by a number of institutional and policy shifts that, with hindsight, caused substantial and on-going change. Such changes are defined here as key milestones. These key milestones can be categorised broadly as being related to deregulation and reform of the financial system, to fiscal policy changes reflected in several key transformations to the structure of Australia's income tax and transfer system, and to

Table 3.1   Key milestones.

Financial market changes	
1981–1985	Financial deregulation
1986	Secondary mortgage market established
mid-1990s	Development of the securitisation (particularly RMBS) market and emergence of new lenders (through use of securitisation)
1993–1996	Shift to independent monetary policy and inflation target (of 2–3%)
1995–1997	Privatisation of government owned financial institutions
1997–	Prudential regulation of financial institutions
Fiscal policy changes	
1985	Tax on real capital gains introduced (owner-occupied housing exempt)
1992	Tax advantaged (compulsory) Superannuation Guarantee Scheme introduced
1999	Capital gains tax changed to 50% discount on nominal gains
2001	Goods and services tax introduced
2012	Tax rulings changed to allow SMSFs to borrow on limited recourse basis
Housing policy change	
1990s	Commonwealth capital outlays cut; shifting to reliance on income support
2000s	First home buyer concessions
2008	Capital funding for public housing ceased
2008	National Rental Affordability Scheme (NRAS) introduced

housing policy responses to these changes. They are summarised in Table 3.1 and covered in more detail next.

The series of market developments covered in the introduction, such as the 1990–1992 financial crisis and the recent GFC, might also be considered as milestones because they resulted in structural changes in the housing finance system, highlighted potential failures in the system, prompted financial system inquiries and, hence, contributed to policy and regulatory changes.

Financial and regulatory reform

The key financial and regulatory reforms that transformed and globalised Australia's economic and financial system in the 1980s were the result of a major inquiry into its Financial System (AFSI 1981). Its recommendations led to the floating of the dollar, the relaxation of restrictions on foreign bank entry into Australia, the dismantling of exchange controls and the abolition of portfolio and interest controls on financial institutions. Subsequent to these changes, all existing government-owned financial institutions were privatised. One exception to this free-market trend was the establishment of state government-sponsored secondary mortgage market corporations in Australia in the mid-1980s.

Deregulation intensified competition in the financial sector in the late 1980s but prudential standards did not keep pace with market developments. High interest rates, poor lending practices and a severe recession contributed to the banking system experiencing significant losses in the early 1990s. The perceived failings of the existing regulatory structure led to the establishment of a second Financial System Inquiry to determine how regulation could be reformed to promote competition while preserving system safety and stability (for a historical perspective on the events following deregulation in the mid-1980s, see FSI 1997: Chapter 14). This set the basis for a tightening of regulatory oversight of risk-taking financial institutions and resulted in the formation of Australia's key regulatory agencies: the Australian Prudential Regulation Authority (APRA), which focuses on the stability of authorised deposit-taking institutions (ADIs); the Australian Securities and Investment Commission (ASIC), responsible for the regulation of financial products; and the Reserve Bank of Australia (RBA), which retains responsibility for monetary policy and systemic stability in the whole financial system.

A third inquiry into Australia's financial system was announced at the end of 2013 with the stated aim of 'determining how the financial system could be positioned to best meet Australia's evolving needs and support Australia's economic growth' (Treasury 2013). Whether this turns out to be a key milestone will only be able to be assessed with hindsight.

Fiscal policy change

The first of the key fiscal policy changes that can be regarded as a key milestone relates to Australia's taxation system. In 1985, a capital gains tax was introduced in response to a recommendation of a Review of the Australian Tax System (Australian Government 1985) that the income tax base be broadened. Owner-occupied homes were exempt from this tax. The capital gains tax applies to realised gains and losses and, until 1999, to real, rather than nominal, gains. In 1999, following the recommendations of a Review of Business Taxation, indexation provisions were removed but individuals receive a 50 percent discount on any capital gain realised on an asset held for at least twelve months. Owner-occupied housing remains exempt.

One anomaly that emerged with these changes was an asymmetric treatment of income and expense for investors. This has encouraged widespread use of so called 'negative gearing' by individual investors in residential rental property in anticipation of tax advantaged capital gains when property prices are expected to increase. Negative gearing occurs when mortgage interest payments used to finance an asset exceed the net income generated by that asset. In Australia, such loss can be deducted against income from any source. A similar incentive is likely to affect self-managed superannuation funds (SMSFs) as a result of a 2012 tax ruling that permits SMSFs to use limited recourse borrowing to finance property purchase. There is no mortgage interest tax deduction for owner-occupiers.

These incentives are reinforced by key policy changes in the mid-1980s affecting owner-occupied housing through the operation of Australia's means-tested age pension system. The family home is exempt from the assets test (introduced in 1985) and from the rules that apply to the value of investments held in the income test (introduced in 1994).

The introduction of a mandated and tax-advantaged Superannuation Guarantee Scheme in 1992 along with the continuation of tax concessions for voluntary contributions provide a further bias in the way in which Australia taxes income from savings and can be interpreted as an additional fiscal policy milestone. Details of the extent of the tax biases towards various forms of saving (including housing) can be found in the Henry review (AFTS 2009: 32–33). One impact of the introduction of compulsory saving is that an increasing share of household wealth is being invested in long term savings vehicles. As discussed later, these assets potentially could help fund housing in the future.

Housing policy change

Key milestones in housing policy in the past 25 years relate primarily to changes in the structure of tenure-based assistance. Throughout the period, housing policy had increasingly perverse effects. Indirect assistance through tax concessions increased, was poorly targeted and tended to add to demand rather than supply. Deposit assistance to first-time homebuyers (which was highly targeted and relatively ungenerous) was eliminated, direct Commonwealth involvement in public housing funding withdrawn, and rental assistance to private tenants rapidly expanded. The decline in explicit assistance for homeownership was reversed in 2000 when an untargeted First Home Owners Grant (FHOG) was introduced, ostensibly to compensate for the impost of the newly introduced goods and services tax (GST) (see Dungey *et al.* 2011 for an overview of first-time homebuyer schemes from 1990). However, it is argued that this simply brought forward purchase by those who would eventually have bought, and pushed up dwelling prices (e.g. Guest 2005). Its short term stimulatory impact was put to good use between 2008 and 2010 when a generous First Home Owners Boost (FHOB) made an effective contribution to sustaining demand in the post-GFC era.

With the exception of short-lived policies implemented from 2008, there has been little explicit support for rental housing and the supply of affordable private rental housing has declined. A significant housing stimulus package, introduced early in 2009 as part of the fiscal response to the GFC, provided a one-off boost to social housing. This reinforced a new National Rental Assistance Scheme (NRAS) introduced in 2008 with the aims of increasing the supply of affordable rental housing and encouraging large-scale institutional investment in rental housing. After a five year funding period under a Labor government, new funding for NRAS ceased with the election of a Coalition government in 2013.

The impacts of many of these key milestones contributed to Australia's resilience following the GFC. Explanations include its: responsive and timely policy actions; stable domestic institutional environment; resources boom; sound, resilient and well managed financial system; and effective regulatory and supervisory framework (see IMF 2012a and Davis 2013). These impacts and their implications are examined next.

Impacts and implications of changes

Impacts

The milestones described here contributed to the credit boom experienced in Australia for much of the period under consideration. The overall effect of financial and regulatory reforms was an increase in the supply of credit and a reduction in its cost. This resulted from increased competition arising from the entry of new lenders between 1985 and 1993 and, from 1996, the emergence of wholesale mortgage originators and mortgage brokers. Their participation was enhanced by technological advances and, in particular, by the growth of the residential mortgage backed securities (RMBS) market – which provided a relatively cheap funding source. The Australian securitisation market expanded rapidly between the mid-1990s and the recent financial crisis, reaching up to 7 percent of the total assets in the financial system by mid-2007. Non-bank lenders made use of this source of funds to introduce riskier low-documentation loans, interest-only loans and revolving credit lines.

Key milestones in fiscal and housing policy, together with increased competition in the mortgage market and the wider range of financial products available, provided an increasing incentive for households to make use of this cheaper and more readily available credit. As in most countries experiencing a credit boom from the mid-1990s to the mid-2000s, disinflation and the resultant downward shift in nominal interest rates increased household borrowing capacity (e.g. CGFS 2006). During this period, the ratio of debt-to-income for Australian households more than trebled. Besides tax incentives that encouraged demand, a number of additional factors encouraged a willingness to take on debt, including a one-off increase in borrowing capacity as a result of an increase in female workforce participation, a steady rise in household income over several decades and a reduction in the volatility of this income. Housing has been shown to be a superior good, with households being prepared to pay proportionally more on housing as income rises. Forced accumulation of illiquid long term savings in the form of superannuation provides a reason why households might be willing to take on debt in their pre-retirement years as accumulated superannuation holdings provide a means of paying off any debt remaining at retirement age.

As in a number of OECD countries, Australia's credit boom led to an increase in real house prices. Between 1980 and 1995, average annual real house price growth was just over 1 percent. Between 1995 and 2005, however, real house prices in Australia grew at more than 6 percent per year, with an average annual increase of almost 15 percent from 2001 to 2003. Since 2005 they have risen at an average of a little over 2 percent per year. One of the reasons why the credit boom had such a significant impact on dwelling prices in Australia is that, during the 2000s, Australia had an undersupply of dwellings (NHSC 2011). In part this arose because of its extremely inelastic supply response to rising dwelling prices (Caldera Sánchez and Johansson 2011). There is a host of reasons for a sluggish response but one is the difficulty that developers of multi-unit dwellings have in obtaining finance for construction despite urban development policies in Australia's major capital cities that encourage such dwellings.

The credit boom from the mid-1990s to the mid-2000s was fuelled primarily by demand from established households reflected in increased housing finance commitments to repeat-buyer owner-occupiers and to investors (see Figure 3.1). Established households have benefited most from the changes to the tax and transfer system described previously, can afford larger mortgages and have squeezed out first-time homebuyers, who are a relatively unimportant source of demand for housing finance in Australia, despite its growing population. During the 1990s, first homebuyers represented around 22 percent of new housing finance commitments. This fell to 19 percent during the 2000s despite the boosts given by various fiscal incentives to first homebuyers. By the early 2010s, it had fallen to below 15 percent.

From 1999, the share of new lending to investors rose from 30 percent to almost 50 percent in 2004, although a decreasing share of this lending has

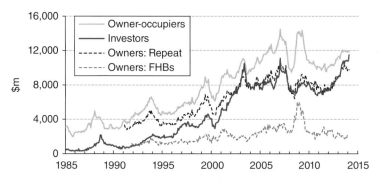

Figure 3.1   Housing finance commitments, Australia.
Source: ABS (2014), Cat. No. 5609.011, CPI adjusted ($2014); Cat. No.5609.09a for First Home Buyer data.

been for new construction. This growth was widely seen as a response to tax incentives that encouraged negative gearing, but a range of other innovations including home equity loans, split-purpose loans, deposit bonds and interest only loans also assisted. Much of this growth in investor demand was driven by anticipation of strong real capital gains in Australia's housing markets over a 20-year period.

For much of the duration of the credit boom, the household sector had become a net borrower rather than a net saver – with the result that banks had to look beyond deposits to fund their activities. From the mid-1980s until 2000, the household savings ratio declined dramatically from around 10 percent to close to 0 percent at the start of the 2000s, where it remained until the mid-2000s. However, with the onset of the GFC, the savings ratio rose dramatically. In the past few years it appears to have stabilised at its mid-1980s level of around 10 percent.

The end of the credit boom was, in part, engineered by a series of interest rate rises in which Australia's policy rate, the cash rate, was increased by three percentage points over a 6-year period from April 2002.

In stark contrast to the outcomes associated with the credit boom, the second boom that contributed to Australia's sustained real growth – the resources boom – has been associated with a rising savings ratio, reduced credit growth, and with debt consolidation facilitated by the reduction in interest rates that took place from 2008. In part, this reflects increased uncertainty associated with the events of the late 2000s and a lower appetite for risk. When interest rates fall, households with variable-rate loans are able to pre-pay their outstanding mortgage debt with no penalty simply by maintaining mortgage repayments at their previous level. Prepayments are facilitated by products such as home equity loans, redraw facilities and offset accounts. Between 2008 and 2013, households increased their prepayment mortgage buffer by a factor of three to 21 months of scheduled repayments (RBA 2013: 44).

One result of this slowdown in credit growth is that household debt-to-income ratios have stabilised since 2008 as seen in Figure 3.2. The rise in the ratio from the mid-1980s to mid-2000s can be regarded as a key summary of the housing finance impacts of the milestone changes outlined in this section.

The International Monetary Fund (IMF) has shown that larger run-ups in household debt tend to be associated with more severe and protracted housing busts and recessions. A stable household debt-to-asset ratio is seen as having the potential to mask a growing exposure to a sharp fall in asset prices which, in turn, can lead to household defaults, 'underwater' mortgages, foreclosures and 'fire' sales observed in a number of countries at the end of the 2000s (IMF 2012b: 89). A key question, therefore, is whether Australia's high debt to income ratio matters. The following subsection addresses this issue.

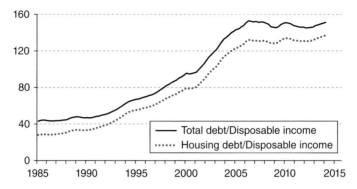

Figure 3.2   Australia's household debt ratios.
Source: RBA (2014), Table E2.

Implications of changes

Two opposing responses can be given to the question of whether Australia's high household debt-to-income ratio matters. These follow from the implications of the impact of the milestone changes made during the 1980s and 1990s. The first response, which might be called the official response, relates to economic and financial stability. The second relates to housing outcomes.

Economic and financial stability   The economic and financial stability response to whether Australia's high household debt-to-income ratio matters is a clear 'No'. The case for this response rests on a number of grounds.

- The trebling of the household debt-to-income ratio in the past 25 years is seen as a one-off shift to a 'new normal' equilibrium, following a structural response to deregulation and disinflation. The higher ratio is seen as sustainable because lower interest rates have reduced repayment burdens.
- Housing debt is held disproportionately by non-financially constrained households. Around 70 percent of mortgage debt is held by households in the top 40 percent of the income distribution, with sufficient equity buffers to withstand significant downturns in dwelling prices. One of the reasons why the GFC had less impact on dwelling prices in Australia than elsewhere was that the bulk of outstanding debt was held by non-vulnerable households.
- Less than 5 percent of households have both a high debt service ratio and low household income.
- Default rates in Australia are extremely low, and arrears rates have been well below 1 percent throughout the 2000s.

- When interest rates are below normal, lenders build in protection against interest rate risk by testing loan serviceability against 'normal' interest rates. This is seen as a distinguishing feature of lending for housing in Australia (APRA 2013b: 45).

Housing outcomes   While there was reasonable attention given to the impact of milestones on the housing finance system at the time of their introduction, their impact on the housing market was given little consideration. The second, opposing, response to the question of whether Australia's high household debt-to-income ratio matters arises from this. This response is a clear 'Yes'. Again, a number of reasons can be given for this. These relate primarily to the impact that the housing finance system has on housing outcomes.

- The rise in household debt is generally regarded as the primary facilitator of the unsustainable rise in real house prices that took place in Australia (as elsewhere) from the mid-1990s to mid-2000s. This growth in dwelling prices resulted in an increase in wealth for established households, and further enhanced their capacity to outbid first-time homebuyers with limited equity in the housing market.
- One outcome of this displacement has been a significant decline in home-ownership rates for younger households in the lower part of the income distribution. Figure 3.3 shows these declines.
- Declining age-specific home-ownership rates are resulting in an increasing share of households living in private rental housing. Lower income

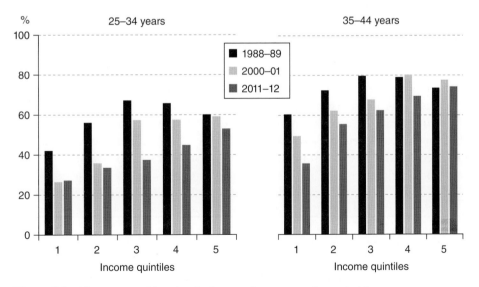

Figure 3.3 Homeownership rates by income for younger households.
Source: ABS (2005; 2008; 2013b); Surveys of Income and Housing, 2000–2001 and 2011–2012 and Household Expenditure Survey (1988–1989). Findings based on use of basic confidentialised unit record files.

households who have been squeezed out of homeownership increase the pressure on the lower end of the private rental market, leading to significant shortfalls in the supply of affordable rental dwellings for households in the bottom two income quintiles (NHSC 2012: 48).

Emerging issues

Two broad, inter-related issues emerge from the impacts and implications of the key milestones over the past 25 years. The first relates primarily to housing policy. The second relates to the implications this has for housing finance. Both are consequences of the shift to increasingly market oriented housing and housing finance systems. Both are likely to be affected by future trends in income and wealth inequality. These are summarised in Table 3.2 and covered in more detail next.

Housing policy

Housing policy issues relate directly to the key tenures that have been the hallmark of Australian housing provision. Despite considerable direct and indirect assistance, homeownership has become increasingly inaccessible for young households with low incomes and little accumulated wealth. Unless they have access to considerable equity, households in the bottom two quintiles of the income distribution have to meet their housing needs in the private rental sector. The question of whether, and in what form, government support should continue to be provided for homeownership, given that it is increasingly the domain of more affluent households, is a key emerging issue for the future.

A second, and even more pressing, issue is the question of how to increase the supply of affordable rental housing for households excluded from homeownership. An increase in the supply of multi-unit dwellings, more likely to be rented than the separate houses that dominate Australia's housing stock, has been restricted by finance constraints as developers requiring bank finance must achieve a significant level of pre-sales. This requirement has

Table 3.2 Emerging issues.

Housing policy	Housing finance
1. What form of government support for homeownership should there be?	1. How to limit share of housing finance to established households.
2. How to increase supply of affordable rental housing.	2. What is future role of superannuation funds in providing finance for housing?
3. How to finance affordable rental housing.	3. What finance instruments might be developed to fund affordable rental housing?

increased from around 50 to closer to 100 percent of debt since the GFC. While demand from both owner-occupiers and individual investors has been the source of finance from pre-sales, a decreasing share of this has come from investors over the past 25 years.

Whether current levels of individual investor demand will continue remains an unknown. Because investors are currently driven by tax advantages arising from capital gains, speculative tax-driven investor interest is likely to decrease with an anticipated slowdown in housing price growth to a more sustainable long run trend. This is also likely to affect the current emerging interest of self-managed superannuation funds in small-scale residential investment. Past experience also suggests that individual private investment in rental housing is unlikely to adequately serve the affordable end of the private rental market.

The final issue for housing policy, therefore, is how to provide a reliable source of private finance for affordable rental housing to sustain the embryonic affordable housing industry that began to emerge as a result of the policy initiatives implemented in 2008 and 2009. These initiatives were intended to develop more commercially sophisticated, larger community housing providers as a means of expanding the social housing system and to encourage institutional investment in social and affordable rental housing. The termination of the key initiative implemented to achieve these goals, the National Rental Affordability Scheme, and the lack of continuity in policy direction create a significant barrier to the willingness of institutional investors to become involved. Related to this housing policy issue is the need to clarify the role of government in articulating and achieving intended housing outcomes.

Housing finance

Emerging issues relating to housing finance are closely related to emerging housing policy issues. The first of these is how to limit the share of housing finance allocated to established households, and how to return the first-time homebuyer share at least to its historical norm. APRA (2013a: 22) sees credit risk as the principal source of risk for banks in Australia and suggests that prudent lending is critical. If banks tighten lending standards in response to new regulatory controls imposed under APRA's implementation of Basel III or to perceived increases in risk, borrowers able to access funds are more likely to be those with greater equity and with greater repayment capacities. In the main, they will be higher income and higher wealth owners upgrading or investors expanding their housing portfolios.

Macro-prudential regulation, introduced in a number of countries as a means of limiting the build-up of debt excesses, has included restricting the share of high LTV ratio lending (APRA 2013a: 27 but see also IMF 2013 for a full coverage of tools). This is not yet an issue in Australia, but any such constraint will further limit access to housing finance by first-time homebuyers. However, Australia implements sectoral capital requirements on residential mortgage loans by requiring higher risk weights on already high LTV loans. Since this paper was finalised (in mid-2014), continuing investor activity in key housing markets and the risk that this may exacerbate house price increases has led the Governor of the Reserve Bank of Australia to be more predisposed to the implementation of further prudential controls. However, he retains his scepticism about their likely effectiveness as a panacea (Stevens 2014; see also Ellis 2012). A key issue is how to limit speculative investor activity without harming access for marginal first homebuyers. While housing remains a tax-advantaged form of saving, unequal access to housing finance in order to accumulate housing assets will, in turn, reinforce existing wealth inequalities.

A second issue is the future role of the banks within the housing finance system. Currently, ADIs hold 50 percent of all financial assets in Australia but superannuation funds are showing by far the fastest growth (IMF 2012c: Box 4.3). The growth of this pool of long term savings raises the question of whether there might be a more appropriate way of using these funds to better match long term illiquid savings and investment – relative to the current dominant practice of bank housing finance that matches long term (albeit variable-rate) mortgages with short term deposits (Davis 2013: 44ff).

Davis (2013: 46) suggests that the consequences of a household portfolio allocation away from bank deposits into superannuation in the longer run means that banks must attract funds from sources other than household deposits or shrink in relative size. He argues this will require them to make greater use of new investments to create securities, which absorb the flow of super savings (see also Joye and Gans 2008).

This leads to a third housing finance issue: that of raising finance for what is intended to be a growing affordable housing rental sector. Currently, social housing providers in Australia have limited success in obtaining conventional bank finance and have more stringent conditions imposed on them than individual investors. They are required to have lower LTV ratios, are charged higher interest rates (more closely aligned to small business loans than to housing loans), and can only obtain relatively short term loans (for approximately 5 years), which exposes them to significant re-financing risks (KPMG 2010).

Institutional investors, identified as the most likely source of funds at scale, have indicated a considerable appetite for new forms of investment opportunities (beyond share markets and commercial property) that offer a secure form of longer term (10 years or more), low-risk investment, with return based primarily on cash flow. Such products would be attractive for superannuation funds wishing to match their pending liabilities as they transition from the accumulation to 'pension phase' (as their membership ages). However, achieving new forms of low-risk investment will require some form of credit enhancement (in the form of insurance, guarantees etc.) to overcome investor perceptions of risk, and to meet their yield requirements. With the loss of previous government owned financial inter-mediaries and insurance providers, new institutions will also need to be established to issue such securities.

Where the demand for housing finance from investors in rental housing is driven by expectations of capital gain, it is likely to be pro-cyclical (and, hence, potentially destabilising). Goodhardt has suggested there is a need for discussion on the types of innovation in housing finance that would encour-age counter-cyclical measures (reported in Crockett 2011: 40). New long term instruments, based on reliable cash flow rather than capital gains expectations, are more likely to achieve this goal and to result in better and more resilient housing outcomes than the system of housing finance that emerged in the 25 years following the mid-1980s wave of deregulation.

Conclusion

In conclusion, Australia experienced a number of reforms from the early-1980s to the mid-1990s that transformed it to a more market oriented econ-omy. These reforms had significant impacts on both its housing and housing finance systems. These impacts have generally been positive and were instru-mental in protecting Australia from the worst of the effects of the GFC of the late 2000s. However, they were less positive because of their perverse distributional outcomes. Fiscal changes provided increased incentives for households to invest in housing, both as owner-occupiers and as residential landlords. Financial market changes facilitated increases in demand, house-hold debt-to-income ratios and dwelling prices. Increases in income (and wealth) inequalities reduced the ability of economically disadvantaged house-holds to gain a foothold in the housing market and homeownership rates declined, particularly among lower income, younger households.

These outcomes suggest that, in the next 25 years, Australia will need to reassess the future of homeownership (and supporting policies) and to deter-mine how to increase the supply of affordable rental housing and how this should be financed. In doing so, it will need to decide what role government should play in a market oriented economy, which institutions are best placed to fund housing in the future and what instruments should be employed.

Acknowledgements

Earlier versions of this paper were presented at the EMF-ENHR Joint Seminar, 17–18 September 2013, Brussels and at the ENHR conference, 1–4 July 2014, Edinburgh. The authors would like to thank Mardi Dungey, Graeme Wells, Chris Stewart, participants at the seminar and conference and the editors, for helpful comments and suggestions.

References

Australian Bureau of Statistics (ABS) (2005) *Survey of Income and Housing 2000–01*, Confidentialised Unit Record File. Findings based on use of Basic CURF data.

Australian Bureau of Statistics (ABS) (2008) *Household Expenditure Survey 1988–89* (Second Edition), Confidentialised Unit Record Files. Findings based on use of Basic CURF data.

Australian Bureau of Statistics (ABS) (2013a) *Household wealth and wealth distribution 2011–12* [Online], Available: www.abs.gov.au (accessed 22 July, 2015).

Australian Bureau of Statistics (ABS) (2013b) *Survey of Income and Housing 2011–12*, Confidentialised Unit Record File. Findings based on use of Basic CURF data.

Australian Bureau of Statistics (ABS) (2014). *Housing Finance, Australia*, Cat. No. 5609.0, July 2014 [Online], Available: www.abs.gov.au (accessed 22 July, 2015).

Australian Financial System Inquiry (AFSI) (1981) *Campbell Report: Final Report* Australian Government Publishing Service, Canberra.

Australia's Future Tax System Review Panel (AFTS) (Henry Review) (2009), *Henry Review: Australia's future tax system: Report to the Treasurer, part 2, volumes 1 and 2* [Online], Available: www.taxreview.treasury.gov.au (accessed 22 July, 2015).

Australian Government (1985) *Reform of the Australian Tax System: Draft White Paper* Australian Government Publishing Service, Canberra.

Australian Prudential Regulatory Authority (APRA) (2013a) 'ADI industry risks', *Insight* 2013(2):4–39 [Online], Available: www.apra.gov.au/Insight/Pages/APRA-Insight-Issue-2-2013.aspx (accessed 29 July 2015).

Australian Prudential Regulatory Authority (APRA) (2013b) 'Loan serviceability standards in housing lending', *Insight* 2013(2): 40–54 [Online]. Available: www.apra.gov.au/Insight/Pages/APRA-Insight-Issue-2-2013.aspx (accessed 29 July 2015).

Caldera Sánchez, A and Johansson, Å (2011). *The Price Responsiveness of Housing Supply in OECD Countries, OECD Economics Department Working Papers, No. 837, OECD Publishing* [Online], Available: www.oecd-ilibrary.org/economics/the-price-responsiveness-of-housing-supply-in-oecd-countries_5kgk9qhrnn33-en (accessed 22 July, 2015).

Committee on the Global Financial System (CGFS) (2006) *Housing Finance in the Global Financial Market, CGFS Papers No. 26* [Online], Available: www.bis.org/publ/cgfs26.pdf (accessed 22 July, 2015).

Crockett, A (2011). *What Financial System for the Twenty-First Century?* Per Jacobsson Foundation [Online], Available: www.perjacobsson.org/lectures/062611.pdf (accessed 22 July, 2015).

Davis, K. (2013) *Funding Australia's Future: From where do we begin?* [Online], Available: www.fundingaustraliasfuture.com/fromwheredowebegin (accessed 22 July, 2015).

Dungey, M, Wells, G and Thompson, S (2011). First home buyers support schemes in Australia. *Australian Economic Review* 44(4): 468–479.

Ellis, L (2012) *Macroprudential Policy: A Suite of Tools or a State of Mind?. Speech to the Paul Woolley Centre for Capital Market Dysfunctionality Annual Conference, Sydney, 11 October 2012* [Online], Available: www.rba.gov.au/speeches/2012/sp-so-111012.html (accessed 22 July, 2015).

Ellis, L (2006). *Housing and Housing Finance: The View from Australia and Beyond, Reserve Bank of Australia Discussion Paper, 2006–12* [Online], Available: www.rba.gov.au (accessed 22 July, 2015).

Financial System Inquiry (FSI) (1997). *Wallis Report: Final Report* [Online], Available: http://fsi.treasury.gov.au/content/default.asp (accessed 22 July, 2015).

Garnaut, R (2013). *Dog Days: Australia after the Boom*. Black Inc., Collingwood, Victoria.

Guest, R (2005). A life cycle analysis of housing affordability options for first home owner-occupiers in Australia. *Economic Record* 81(254): 237–248.

IMF (2013). *Key aspects of macroprudential policy-background paper* [Online], Available: www.imf.org/external/np/pp/eng/2013/061013c.pdf (accessed 22 July, 2015).

IMF (2012a) *Australia: Financial System Stability Assessment, International Monetary Fund Country Report No.12/308, November* [Online], Available: www.imf.org/external/pubs/ft/scr/2012/cr12308.pdf (accessed 22 July, 2015).

IMF (2012b). *World Economic Outlook: Growth Resuming, Dangers Remain, April 2012* [Online], Available: www.imf.org/external/pubs/ft/weo/2012/01/ (accessed 22 July, 2015).

IMF (2012c). *Global Financial Stability Report, October* [Online], Available: www.imf.org/External/Pubs/FT/GFSR/2012/02/ (accessed 22 July, 2015).

Joye, C and Gans, J (2008). *'Aussie Mac: A Policy Proposal for Australia', The Selected Works of Joshua S Gans*[Online], Available: http://works.bepress.com/joshuagans/17 (accessed 22 July, 2015).

KPMG (2010) *Barriers to the creation of a long term affordable housing investment class* [Online], Available: www.kpmg.com/AU/en/IssuesAndInsights/ArticlesPublications/Documents/Barriers-to-the-creation-of-a-long-term-affordable-housing-investment-class-June-2010.pdf (accessed 22 July, 2015).

National Housing Supply Council (2012). *Housing Supply and Affordability – Key Indicators 2012*[Online], Available: www.nhsc.org.au/ (accessed 22 July, 2015).

National Housing Supply Council (2011). *State of Supply Report* [Online], Available: www.nhsc.org.au/ (accessed 22 July, 2015).

OECD (2013a). *OECD Economic Outlook*, Vol. 2013/1 [Online], Available: www.oecd-ilibrary.org/economics/oecd-economic-outlook-interim-report-september-2013_eco_outlook-v2013-sup1-en (accessed 22 July, 2015).

OECD (2013b). *OECD Factbook 2013: Economic, Environment and Social Statistics* [Online], Available: www.oecd-ilibrary.org/sites/factbook-2013-en/03/02/01/index.html?itemId=/content/chapter/factbook-2013-25-en (accessed 22 July, 2015).

Reserve Bank of Australia (RBA) (2013). *Financial Stability Review, March* [Online], Available: www.rba.gov.au/publications/fsr/2013/mar/pdf/0313.pdf (accessed 22 July, 2015).

Reserve Bank of Australia (RBA) (2014). *Household Finances – Selected Ratios, Table E2* [Online], Available: www.rba.gov.au. (accessed 22 July, 2015)

Stevens, G (2014). *Remarks to the Melbourne Economic Forum* [Online], Available: http://static.knowledgevision.com/account/brr/assets/attachment/RBA/RBA_Speech_QA_transcript_Glenn_Stevens_Governor_Thursday_25_September_2014.pdf (accessed 22 July, 2015).

Stevens, G (2013) *'Economic Policy after the Booms', address to The Anika Foundation Luncheon, Sydney – 30 July 2013* [Online], Available: www.rba.gov.au/speeches/2013/sp-gov-300713.html (accessed 22 July, 2015).

The Treasury (2013). *Financial System Inquiry – Draft Terms of Reference* [Online], Available: www.treasury.gov.au/ConsultationsandReviews/Consultations/2013/financial-system-inquiry-tor (accessed 22 July, 2015).

4

Milestones in Housing Finance in Austria over the Last 25 Years

Alexis Mundt[a] and Elisabeth Springler[b]

[a] IIBW-Institute for Real Estate, Construction and Housing, Vienna, Austria

[b] European Economy and Business Management, University of Applied Sciences BFI, Vienna, Austria

The economic and institutional environment of the last 25 years

Housing finance in Austria used to be dominated by own equity and subsidised public loans. From 1979, commercial banks slowly entered the market for mortgage financing, but throughout the 1980s around 96 percent of bank housing loans still received public subsidies, mostly in the form of interest or annuity subsidies (Url 2001: 85). Additionally, public low interest loans played a major part in housing finance. In 1990 an equivalent of around €34 billion in outstanding housing loans existed in Austria, of which 40 percent were public loans, 26 percent were loans by Contract Savings Banks and around 34 percent were (mostly) subsidised bank loans (Schmidinger 1992: 306; Table 4.1). New construction was largely dependent on own equity (48.5 percent equity ratio), especially with respect to single-family construction, which was largely in the form of self-build by households.

Looking at the situation in 2014, it is evident that there have been some changes, but compared to other OECD countries, these have been less incisive and many traditional Austrian housing finance features are still predominant: the importance of public (now regional) low interest housing loans; the engagement of Contract Savings Banks (and other special purpose housing banks, see next) and the predominance of own equity (savings,

Milestones in European Housing Finance, First Edition.
Edited by Jens Lunde and Christine Whitehead.
© 2016 John Wiley & Sons, Ltd. Published 2016 by John Wiley & Sons, Ltd.

Table 4.1   Volume and composition of outstanding housing loans, 1990 and 2013.

	1990	2013
Sum of outstanding housing loans in billion €	€38 bn	€111 bn
As share of GDP	28%	35%
Composition		
Banks and insurance companies loans	34%	63%
Contract Savings Banks loans	26%	15%
Public subsidised loans (regional subsidy schemes)	40%	22%

Source: OENB; Schmidinger (1992); Url (2001).

inheritance and self-building) in single-family housing construction. Market finance has, however, gained importance over recent last decades and the share of market finance without interest and annuity subsidies has increased considerably. When considering housing finance by commercial institutions (including loans from Housing Construction Banks and Contract Savings Banks) the value of outstanding mortgages was around €88 bn in 2013. Although that is an increase of 100 percent since 2003 it still only represents 28 percent as a share of GDP, which is low compared to many other western European economies (in Germany, the share is 45 percent while in The Netherlands it is 108 percent) (EMF 2013: 89). Foreign exchange loans (FX-loans) were particularly popular during the mid-2000s when interest and exchange rates were favourable. Since 2007 worsening conditions and surging repayment difficulties have led to a restructuring of FX-loans into Euro-denominated mortgages, and new FX-loans have been heavily curtailed by the Financial Market Authority. When considering the whole amount of outstanding housing loans in 2013 (see Table 4.1), its share of GDP is 35 percent compared to 28 percent in 1990. While commercial banks' share rose strongly, public loans and outstanding Contract Savings Banks loans lost importance over the years.

Throughout the period of investigation, there are some important features of the Austrian housing market that help determine the composition of housing finance. First, housing supply characteristics strongly influence the structure of housing finance in Austria and vice versa. Provincial low-interest loans or annuity grants in support of capital market loans are very important in the single-family housing sector and especially in the subsidised multi-apartment stock, which covers more than 60 percent of all high-rise construction. Additionally, there are three types of special purpose banks entrusted with the task to raise money for housing construction: the Mortgage Banks that issue covered mortgage bonds (*Pfandbriefe*), the Contract Savings Banks (*Bausparkassen*) and the Housing Construction Banks (*Wohnbaubanken*) (see next for more detail).

Second, the Austrian housing market is dominated by a very strong rental market segment, which is one of the largest in Europe. Renting is particularly popular in the capital city Vienna. An increasingly important role in the rental sector is played by Limited-Profit Housing Associations (LPHAs) that build and manage cost rent apartments mainly with the help of regional supply-side subsidies. The market for single-family houses, on the other hand, is strongly dominated by self-building by young households who also receive subsidies as well as relying on family capital contributions. Single-family house building by commercial builders for an anonymous market is very rare. Rather, households buy or inherit adequate building plots and commission builders for tailored projects or turn to the prefabricated housing industry. Internationally, these housing supply characteristics in Austria are quite unusual and explain the relative scarcity of market-oriented, commercial developers that dominate most English speaking countries (Ball 2012).

Third, looking at the tenure mix over recent decades, the owner-occupied housing stock did not increase in size. This in turn has kept household debt in relation to GDP low. Urban housing, which has been the main focus of building activity over recent decades, is dominated by high-rise construction in the form of mainly rental and increasingly owner-occupied apartments provided by LPHAs and institutional investors (Mundt 2013).

Summarising the trends over the last 25 years, it is clear that commercial housing finance gained importance in Austria but in a volatile fashion. Finance by special purpose housing banks acted as a buffer against these swings, for example by filling the financing gap during the Global Financial Crisis (GFC) when banks were reluctant to finance new production. Even the latest price boom was triggered more by the relocation of private household savings than by an increase in debt finance.

Finance milestones

To divide the last 25 years of Austrian housing finance in different phases, it is helpful to look at the development of real housing investment between 1989 and 2014. Housing finance in Austria is strongly linked to financing housing construction and new housing supply.

While single-family housing construction was very stable throughout the whole period, there was still a housing market cycle dominated by multi-storey housing construction (rental and owner-occupied apartments). The first phase between around 1990 and 1998 was a boom period, dominated by demand-led, multi-storey housing construction carried out by LPHAs and commercial providers, with a focus on subsidised loans. The second phase between 1998 and 2003 was characterised by decreasing real investment in housing and declining output numbers. At the same time subsidised regional loans decreased and private housing finance, heavily dependent on Swiss Franc (CHF) and Japanese Yen (JPY) denominated housing mortgages, gained importance. In 2004 housing construction picked up again, as did population growth and household formation. This phase is still continuing and was only slightly affected by the GFC. In fact, the Austrian housing sector was affected much less than many other European countries by the recent financial turmoil. Austria did not experience strong price increases or an extraordinary construction boom during the early 2000s. Austria rather followed a countercyclical trend of housing market development similar to Germany. Housing price dynamics and construction have been especially strong since 2009, unlike in most other EU countries (EMF 2013: section 2.3). Table 4.2 summarises important milestones in housing finance during these three phases. They will be discussed in more detail in the following sections.

Regional demand-led building boom 1990–1997

In the late 1980s Austria was characterised by comparatively high real mortgage interest rates. In 1988 these were around 8 percent, 2.5 percentage points higher than in Germany in the same year (Mooslechner 1990a: 93). The increase in mortgage interest rates for housing loans in the early 1990s further worsened market conditions for households obtaining mortgage loans (Schmidinger 2007: 419). However, interest rates decreased to approximately 6 percent in 1997 (OeNB). The downward trend was especially visible after Austria joined the European Union in 1995.

In the 1970s and 1980s, all forecasts predicted a stagnating or declining Austrian population, but in the 1990s quite the opposite happened. Large migration inflows (particularly following the Balkan wars) and changes in household formation led to a significant increase in demand for housing services. At the same time, smaller apartments were refurbished and combined, which reduced the housing stock. As demand for housing was strong, these developments called for a significant shift in the institutional settings to enable further housing production. The massive supply response was mainly carried out by LPHAs (see Box 4.1), which became major players on the Austrian housing market and were funded by regional low interest loans. Regional subsidies were strongly increased during this period (Lugger and Amann 2013). Additionally, the system of Contract Savings Banks was amended to provide an adequate legal framework for the operations of such banks. Housing Construction Banks were set up as new special purpose banks for attracting finance for subsidised housing projects.

Housing Construction Banks were introduced in 1993 with the main goals of countering the very high market interest rates on mortgage loans and providing long-term, fixed-interest loans to the housing sector, especially to providers of units for long-term rental (Schmidinger 2007).

Covered mortgage bonds provided by the Regional Mortgage Banks had before been the main method of refinancing for banks (see Box 4.2). Conceptually, those covered bonds were set up with maturities of up to 30 years, but due to interest rate developments their average maturity fell to

Table 4.2 Milestones in housing finance in Austria, 1980s to 2014.

	Institutional changes	Policy changes	Market changes
First phase: housing investment boom of the early 1990s			
End 1980s	Devolution of most housing agendas (especially subsidy schemes) to regions		Increase in interest rates
1980s–early 1990s		Regions develop their own bundle of housing policy measures, funding still from earmarked federal funds.	Liberalisation of the banking sector
1990		Access of commercial developers to housing subsidies in Vienna (competition)	
1993	Contract Savings Banks are restructured in new law (Bausparkassengesetz 1993).	Option to buy after 10 years standardised in LPHA new build if tenant contributions exceed €50/m²	LPHA rental apartments with option to buy continuously replace subsidised apartments for sale
1994	Housing Construction Banks take up issuing of Housing Construction Convertible Bonds (HCCB) and financing subsidised housing; refinancing by mortgage bonds is slowly replaced.		
1995	EU accession		EU accession leads to strong long-run decrease in interest rates
Second phase: housing production decline 1998–2003			
End 1990s	Municipalities continuously give up own construction and rely on LPHAs	Earmarking of federal housing policy funds is slowly lifted. 1st step: housing related infrastructure may be financed out of subsidy schemes.	FX-loans in JPY and CHF start to gain importance, together with repayment vehicles, in the form of interest-only loans.
2001		2nd step: Redemption of housing loans may be used for non-housing purposes	
Early 2000s	Federal Government reaches agreement to privatise own 60 000 social rental units. Process takes until 2004.	As a result, the share of public funds for housing finance decreases considerably, a trend that continues throughout 2000s.	FX-loans strongly gain importance.

(continued overleaf)

Table 4.2 (*continued*)

	Institutional changes	Policy changes	Market changes
Third period: stable increase in housing production 2004 onwards			
2005	Laws concerning mortgage bonds renewed; Contract Savings loans also opened for long-term care and education		
2008			New emissions of HCCB peak in 2008 raising funds for co-financing most subsidised projects.
2008/09		Abolition of earmarking of federal funds for housing policy expenses. Funding passes to regional discretion.	Restriction to FX-loans following repayment difficulties due to exchange rate development. Restructuring into € mortgages.
2010		Tax deductibility of HCCB purchase abolished	Consumer Credit Law 2010 in reaction to EU directive affects mortgages to households (stricter risk assessment, more transparency)
2012		Reduction in Contract Savings premium	

Box 4.1   Limited-profit housing associations (LPHAs)

LPHAs in Austria date back to the early twentieth century and have continuously gained importance since 1945. Their core function is to set up of a long-term social housing stock at below market rents directed at large parts of the population (Mundt and Amann 2010).

At the end of 2012, there were 192 active LPHAs in Austria, differing in their legal status and owner composition (Lugger and Amann 2013: 69). Cooperatives are owned jointly by their members while the limited-profit companies are owned by local or regional public bodies, religious institutions, trade unions, chambers, associations and parties. Apart from the ownership structures, there are only minor differences in legal status, since all LPHAs are regulated by the same law (the Limited-profit Housing Act of 1979), are embedded in the same supervisory structure and are represented by the same umbrella organisation (GBV). LPHAs have grown more significant and have increased their tenure share through high levels of construction output. The LPHA housing stock plays a crucial role in offering affordable housing choices to many households throughout their housing careers (Deutsch 2009).

The system employs a cost coverage principle. Cost rents are calculated at the estate level, and there is no rent-pooling at the LPHA level. A special mark-up for periodic renovation and maintenance works is considered. Today, LPHAs build frequently without subsidised loans but with market finance; cost rents apply nevertheless. Municipalities often approach LPHAs if they detect a lack of affordable housing in their area. Together they design projects and apply for subsidies from the regional government. Building plots are often supplied at low costs by the municipalities. Some regions have implemented tender procedures and competitions (e.g. Housing Developers Competitions in Vienna). Any profits made by the LPHA have to be reinvested either in the purchase of land or in refurbishment and new construction. Interest paid on own equity to the owners and shareholders is limited (for more detail, see Ludl 2007; Amann *et al.* 2009; Lawson *et al.* 2010; Mundt and Amann 2010).

---

between five and six years. So a new method of refinancing had to be implemented. Housing Construction Banks started to issue Housing Construction Convertible Bonds (HCCB) that are directed at private investors with a low risk profile. They were tax-privileged in two ways. Investment income tax exemptions amounted to higher after-tax returns of around 0.3–0.4 percentage points than comparable investments (Amann *et al.* 2005), contributing thus to the popularity of HCCB.

The effect of the tax exemption also accrues to the lender of Housing Construction Banks loans. Any funds raised through the sale of bonds have to be invested in high-volume new housing and refurbishment projects. Therefore, finance raised by HCCB is channelled into projects that the public believes deserve preferential treatment and have been chosen to receive subsidies through the various competitive selection processes organised by the regional governments. The system by which Housing Construction banks can raise money was thus deliberately designed as a

---

Box 4.2   Special purpose banks for housing finance in Austria

There are three important types of special purpose banks for housing finance in Austria. These are Regional Mortgage Banks, Contract Savings Banks and Housing Construction Banks. All of them have specific tasks appointed to them by several laws. Their main aim is to manage special purpose, closed circuits of finance for housing construction or housing purchases (Schmidinger 2007). Special purpose banks are closely monitored by public supervisory authorities. In many aspects they strongly differ from commercial banks, which are the main issuers of individual household mortgages.

Regional Mortgage Banks (Landes-Hypobanken)
Dating back to 1876, Mortgage Banks have the right to give out mortgage loans and refinance by covered mortgage bonds. While Mortgage Banks used to be in public ownership (by the nine regional governments), today they are universal banks and fully integrated with the commercial banking sector. Their focus is still on construction finance and municipal projects, but they also provide private and commercial loans. They operate in Austria and Central and Eastern European (CEE) countries. Covered mortgage bonds were slowly replaced by HCCB offered by the newly founded Housing Construction banks (see next), but they have regained popularity since 2009. Outstanding mortgage bonds amounted to €17 bn at the end of 2013, representing 19 percent of all outstanding mortgage loans.

Contract Savings Banks (Bausparkassen)
As in Germany, contract savings schemes have a long tradition in Austria. Since the 1950s there have been tax advantages for contract savings and loans. In 1973 the premium to contract savings was capped to counter regressive distributional effects. Contract savings are encouraged by state premiums and still enjoy considerable popularity. The finance raised has to be invested in housing, long-term care or education (Bauer 2009). Even the payback of these loans is earmarked for these tasks in order to create a long-term closed circuit of finance for housing construction. Outstanding loans at the end of 2013 were around €19 bn (€16.4 bn of which were housing loans).

Housing Construction Banks (Wohnbaubanken)
Beginning in 1994, the main task of Housing Construction Banks is to provide developers of affordable housing with medium to long-term low-interest loans (supply-side finance). Housing Construction Banks refinance themselves by issuing Housing Construction Convertible Bonds (HCCB) directed at private investors. HCCB are very popular due to their low risk profile and tax privileges. At the end of 2012, the volume of outstanding loans backed by HCCB was around €14 bn (i.e. around 17 percent of outstanding housing loans including regional loans). There are six Housing Construction Banks active in Austria today.

---

substitute to lesser-regulated private housing finance in order to secure long-term stability and an institutional setting to promote it.

In addition to the funds raised by HCCB, a new finance element was standardised in the LPHA housing system in 1993. If tenants contribute more than €50/m² (in 2014, more than €66.68/m²) to a new project, they were granted a right-to-buy (RTB) the apartment after 10 years. The contribution takes the form of a loan and is repaid (minus 1 percent depreciation per annum) if the tenant moves out. If the tenant chooses to buy the apartment after 10 years, the contribution is deducted from the sales price. Since the mid-1990s rental apartments with a RTB have mainly replaced subsidised apartments offered for direct sale, thus contributing to the consistently high rental market share.

The major institutional change in the late 1980s was the devolution of housing subsidy schemes from the federal level to the regions. In Austria there are nine provinces or regions, Vienna being one of them. Since the devolution of housing policy in two waves at the end of the 1980s, the regions have been responsible for designing their own housing subsidy schemes. Consequently, nine quite different housing subsidy schemes have evolved in the regions. Nevertheless, to a large extent, supply-side subsidies for new construction still dominate (Amann and Mundt 2013). This institutional shift also marked a change in the composition of housing finance. While during the 1980s around 64 percent of household debt was in the form of subsidised housing loans (Mooslechner 1990b: 161), by the end of the 1980s, the share of federally subsidised loans started to decrease quickly. During the early 2000s some regions sold their outstanding low-interest loans as packages to commercial banks, which further reduced the state share of outstanding housing loans, although favourable conditions for households stayed in place. Since 2008 the regions have received uncon-ditional transfers from the federal government and have financed housing subsidies out of their own budgets (see next).

1998–2003: Surge of foreign exchange mortgages

Landmark economic policy measures within the housing sectors reflect the aim of decreasing the direct role of the state (especially the nine regions) in housing subsidies. Earmarking taxes specifically for housing subsidies was removed gradually in the early 2000s. The redemption of former housing subsidy loans could be used for other regional policy areas other than housing. In turn, housing subsidies lost their predominance in real housing investment.

At the same time, market finance gained importance. Commercial banks continuously increased their role in housing finance by issuing individual mortgage loans. Even though there were no strict legal require-ments on commercial housing loans, low loan-to-value ratios (LTVs) of up to 80 percent and low debt-service to income ratios dominated the market. Variable interest rates were usually applied and maturities varied between 15 and 25 years.

While most mortgages were first denominated in the national currency (ATS) and then in Euros, this period of liberalisation of housing finance also saw an increase in FX-loans. In the late 1980s the proportion of FX-loans (mainly for non-housing investments) in Austria was already comparatively high, because companies used FX-loans to overcome exchange rate risks in international trade (Waschiczek 2002: 89). In the second half of the 1990s, the usage of this form of loan gained momentum starting in the most Western region of Austria, Vorarlberg, which borders Switzerland. Numerous Austrian citizens worked in Switzerland and aimed to hedge part of their exchange rate risks on their income by using mortgage loans denominated in CHF.

The model spread quickly and by 2002, 24 percent of all outstanding loans to Austrian households were FX-loans (Waschiczek 2002: 92). Especially after 1999, loans denominated in JPY became popular with Austrian households. The popularity of FX-loans stemmed from the much lower interest rates in Switzerland and Japan compared to the European Union. In 2003 average interest rates on new mortgage loans were 4.41 percent for Euro-denominated loans and only 1.18 percent for loans in JPY and 1.67 percent in CHF (OeNB). Exchange rate risks were insufficiently considered and FX-loans were strongly promoted by the banking sector and also the Austrian media, because first experiences in the regions of Tyrol and Vorarlberg of the early 1990s were very positive. Early FX-loans in Vorarlberg were rooted in the fact that households gained their income in CHF and wanted to avoid exchange rate risks, but the situation shifted when JPY became prominent and the more eastern regions of Austria joined the trend by embracing FX-loans. Households started to believe in 'auto-amortising' (Beer *et al.* 2008: 121) loans through exchange rate gains over time. FX-loans continued to gain ground with respect to new mortgages and reached a peak of 31.5 percent of all outstanding mortgages in 2008 (Schmidinger 2013).

Interest rates for FX-loans were mostly variable, at around 150 basis points over three months' LIBOR interest rates, and were mostly paid back via a repayment vehicle (e.g. life insurance plans, investment plans into stocks, shares and funds). The system was later criticised for not clarifying the risks to households appropriately.

Private finance gains ground in new housing boom since 2004

Unlike many other European economies Austria did not face a severe housing crisis in the aftermath of the GFC. The whole period from 2004 onwards is rather characterised by a new housing boom with private housing finance playing an increasingly important role in this development.

Important aspects of market change over this time period are the status of mortgage bonds and the reframing of the structure of FX-loans. The interest rate gap between loans denominated in Euros and in CHF diminished between 2004 and 2007, especially as fees for FX-loans were increased in 2004 (Thienel and Schuh 2007: 18). In addition, demand for FX-loans in JPY lessened due to the increasing awareness of exchange rate risks and many outstanding FX-loans were converted into Euro denominated loans. After its peak value in 2008 the share of FX-loans in all outstanding mortgages started to decline.

Private lending for housing construction and purchase increased throughout the period, as did household debt. The ratio of mortgage debt (only banks and special purpose banks, not regional loans) to GDP rose from 13.8 percent in 2002 to a peak of 27.9 percent in 2010 (EMF 2013). Total outstanding residential loans per capita (for the population over 18 years of age) almost tripled between 2001 (€4580) and 2012 (€12 261) (EMF 2013: 91). Furthermore, Austrian banks were heavily engaged in the extension of credit to the private sector in Central, Eastern and South Eastern Europe and the Baltic states, mainly by FX-loans. This activity was carried out more by their subsidiaries (indirect mortgage loans) than by Austrian banks themselves (direct mortgage loans). Between December 2005 and December 2009 their FX-loan portfolios more than doubled from €31 bn to almost €79 bn (Pann *et al.* 2010: 60). While some banks curbed lending in Central, Eastern and South Eastern Europe before the crisis, it was the intervention of central banks that avoided a prolonged liquidity squeeze and capital losses as a result of foreign currency positions. In fact, a very costly intervention by the Austrian state was required to prevent the bankruptcy of one Regional Mortgage Bank (*Hypo Alpe Adria*) that had accumulated excessive risks by financing real estate deals mainly in Southern and South Eastern Europe and had been protected by extensive guarantees by the region of Carinthia.

Despite the fact that Austrian households had not been directly negatively affected by a housing market crisis, international experience led to increased monitoring of household debt robustness in Austria. Changes were made in how banks were supervised as the high risks associated with repayment vehicles (which are in place for approximately 70 percent of FX-loans) became better understood. In 2007 stronger monitoring of the structure and volume of FX-loans was implemented within the banking supervision system. Additionally, the Austrian banking supervisory authority (FMA) changed the requirements by which households could obtain a FX-loan. New business is today only open to households with the lowest probability of default and income in matching currency. The conversion of outstanding FX-loans into Euro-denominated loans was strongly encouraged. Most remaining FX-loans operate as interest-only mortgages with repayment vehicles based on mixed funds or pension plans. Over the course of the GFC the performance of most repayment vehicles was far below their expected returns (Sellner 2011: 22). This leaves many households with a negative capital-loan gap at the present time today.

Uncertainty is also reflected in the volume of new loans given to households for housing purposes. Lending transactions to households decreased in Austria during the GFC. As the Austrian tenure structure is characterised by a strong rental market, this decrease in household mortgage financing was not reflected in a slump in housing production. On the contrary, data show a stable increase. Four important developments since 2008 can be summarised as follows:

First, refinancing conditions by commercial banks are today hardly able to adapt the maturity of bank loans to the 20–25 years that are standard for provincial subsidy loans. There is a high risk mark-up on bank loans with maturities of that length (Pilarz 2012). This explains the resurging importance of loans by Housing Construction Banks to provide long-term finance (see Box 4.2). Following strong growth rates between 2000 and 2007, the volume of outstanding HCCBs declined slightly between 2008 and 2012 because new issues were low and many tranches of HCCB from years with high levels of activity expired. Therefore, new projects could only be financed out of repaid building loans (approximately €600 mn per annum) (Schmidinger 2013). This changed in 2013 when yet again bond issues increased and raised some €1.3 bn.

Second, new construction is strongly financed by market loans at the moment, leading in part to a revival of covered mortgage bonds by the Regional Mortgage Banks. Covered mortgage bonds are similar to asset-backed securities but at all times remain on the issuer's consolidated balance sheet, that is, they continue as obligations of the issuer (Springler 2008). Their cover pools are dynamic. Cover pool assets are not included in insolvency proceedings and are therefore considered a very secure investment. The collateral is a pool of mortgage loans with low LTVs (below 60 percent).

Third, in 2012 the state subsidy to contract savings schemes was cut in half (now max. €18 per annum). This did not, however, affect the popularity of the instrument, which in the present framework offers high security. The contract savings scheme was never as costly to the state as it was for example in the Czech Republic since premiums were always heavily capped (Lux 2013).

Fourth, the level of mortgage debt has been stagnating since 2012 at around €110 bn (OeNB). Because of low interest rates many households are even using their saving accounts to pay back mortgage loans.

Impacts and outcomes

Despite the high exposure to FX-loans by Austrian households, the financial stability of housing finance overall seems to not be at risk. Empirical investigations (Beer and Wagner 2012; Fessler *et al.* 2012; Albacete and Lindner 2013) show that the major part of housing finance comes from the savings of individual households (Figure 4.1). While the risk assumed by households might increase because of the high share of FX-loans, the importance of

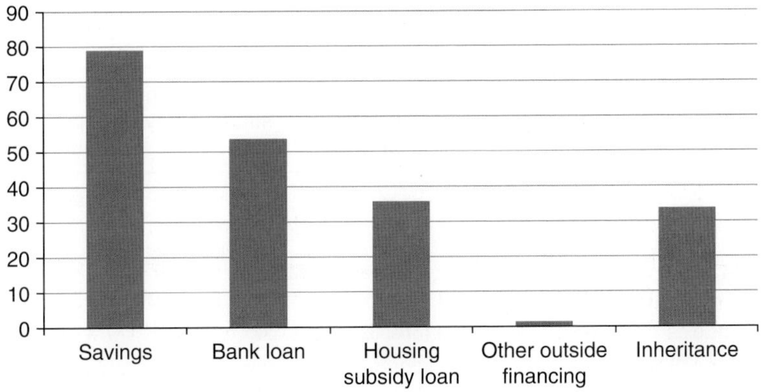

Figure 4.1 Major finance sources of households for housing purchase and self-building, 2012.
Source: Beer and Wagner (2012: 86).
Note: Based on survey data. Percentage of households using source (several sources are possible).

housing subsidy loans and the heavy reliance on inherited wealth point to the robustness of the system.

Housing finance in Austria is shaped by tailor-made financing components that were implemented and adjusted by political involvement and address housing segments and developers selectively. The importance of private housing finance was deliberately kept under control within the overall system. Table 4.3 summarises the financial sources used by various kinds of developers (or homeowners) and makes clear how the different elements work together. For one, the financing of LPHA affordable housing, which involves several tranches of finance with different levels of risk, has been described as an example of *structured finance* (Amann *et al.* 2009).

Why did the housing market in Austria survive the GFC better than other OECD countries? There are several influencing factors that can be identified:

- Mortgage debt exposure of households remains low. Since 2010, Austria's share of mortgage debt to GDP has stagnated at around 28 percent, which is low compared to many other western European economies (it is 45 percent in Germany and 108 percent in The Netherlands) (EMF 2013: 89). As mentioned previously, the low share of commercial mortgage finance for house purchases is the main reason for this. Out of the €164 billion in outstanding loans of the household sector, €110 bn are housing loans (OeNB 2Q 2013). Based on the Household Finance and Consumption Survey (2010), only around 18 percent of households have outstanding mortgage debt (Albacete and Lindner 2013: 60).

Table 4.3 Importance of housing finance elements according to housing segments and developers.

Finance element	LPHA (mostly rental with or without RTB)	Commercial developer (rental and for sale)	Self-building single-family	House or apartment purchase
Own equity	x	xx	xxx (also inheritance, e.g. building plot)	xxx
Tenants contribution (in exchange for RTB)	xxx	–	–	–
Regional subsidies (low interest loans)	xxx	x (possible in some regions)	xxx	x
Capital market loans (partly covered by mortgage bonds)	xx (especially loans covered by mortgage bonds)	xxx	xx	xx (between 1995 and 2008 strongly in CHF and JPY)
Housing Construction Banks loans (raised by HCCB)	xxx	x	–	–
Contract Savings Banks loans	x	–	xx	xx

Key: x = less important; xxx = very important.
Source: Author's presentation, see also: Czerny and Wagner (2003); Amann *et al.* (2005: 22); Beer and Wagner (2012); Schmidinger (2007; 2013); Schwebisch (2008); Mundt (2013).

- LTVs are traditionally low in Austria. The median initial LTV ratio rose from a range of 40–50 percent in the 1990s to around 60 percent in the past few years (Albacete and Lindner 2013: 65). As the size of the homeowner sector is also smaller than in most other countries, experience of financial distress concerning the repayment of mortgages in the light of the GFC remained limited. Nevertheless the debt burden of some income groups has increased in the past decades. Younger homeowners (age group 18–39) tend to have accumulated higher risk financing, with higher LTVs or FX-loans, but also simultaneously hold an above average share of guaranteed loans (Albacete and Wagner 2009: 80). The appreciation of the Swiss Franc has, however, led to considerable financial distress for some households. As a result FX-loans were restructured and curtailed.
- Contrary to many other OECD countries there was no drastic price boom before and price correction in the light of the GFC. Strong institutional interrelations led to comparatively smooth housing price increases and low housing costs throughout most of the last 25 years. Austria is one of the few European economies where overall housing costs (in both owner and rented markets) equate to only around 20 percent of total household income (Springler 2010). The large social rental housing share has contributed to this subdued price development. Even so, since 2008 prices have risen more rapidly, especially in the apartment sector, in Vienna and in most regional capitals (Mundt 2013). Demand is high because of population increases, household formation patterns and investment by private

households. Private households are increasingly relocating their savings into the purchase of real estate, which is considered a very safe asset. In the absence of price corrections in the aftermath of the GFC, which so strongly affected many OECD countries, Austrian households were not confronted with surging debt and negative equity. Also, relatively moderate increases in the unemployment rate combined with a low share of households with repayment mortgages have prevented a surge in repayment difficulties, which so strongly affected other countries. In this light, the high rental share in Austria and the dependence on own equity for single-family housing construction (or purchase) has contributed to the relative resilience of the housing finance system to external shocks.

- On a more general level, housing in Austria is treated as a 'consumption good' as opposed to an 'investment good'. For that reason continuity and stability of prices and production are a political priority. The latest price increases are seen as a matter of concern rather than as a welcome gain to real estate owners. This is a very different view from the one dominant in property-focused societies such as UK, US, Australia or Spain (Schwartz and Seabrooke 2009), where double-digit yearly house price increases before the GFC were sometimes overlooked by policy makers and sometimes greeted with enthusiasm. In Austria recent house price increases that affect the rental market quickly led to the call for higher volumes of social housing provision and the tightening of rent control. Declining rental housing affordability was a major concern in the national elections of fall 2013.
- Refinancing arrangements for housing finance are resilient because of special purpose banks and instruments such as the HCCB, covered mortgage bonds and the Contract Savings Banks. Securitisation of mortgages is not used in Austria. Even though legally possible, the costs involved with the placement of mortgage-backed securities by a financial institution on the capital market would only pay off if large volumes could be achieved (approximately €1.5 bn) (Schmidinger 2007: 404). The low LTVs of around 70 percent contribute to very good refinancing conditions for banks at the European Central Bank (Schmidinger 2013).
- Special purpose banks for housing finance and subsidy schemes from the regions function as a buffer against the volatile involvement of commercial banks in housing finance. The special purpose banks for housing finance have not been static, but have rather continuously adapted to the changing environment (e.g. Contract Savings Scheme).

Regarding the composition of tenure in Austria, there has only been one distinctive trend since 1981: while the rental market segment kept its relative size, the LPHA housing stock gained importance compared to the private rental and also municipal housing stock (Figure 4.2). Private rental apartments used to make up the major proportion of the rental market, but they have been overtaken by the social rental housing sector over the last

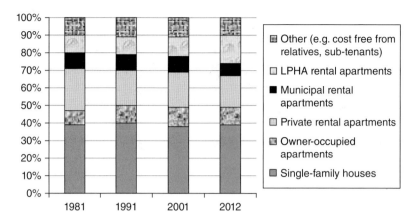

Figure 4.2 Housing tenure in Austria, 1981–2012.
Source: Authors' calculation according to Statistik Austria (2014); GBV (2014) and Janik (2013).

decades (as a result of the construction of cost rent social housing by LPHAs). This trend was encouraged by the availability of regional subsidies to LPHA housing construction and the strong demand for subsidised rental housing, which is not a residualised tenure in Austria, but popular with most income groups and young households (Matznetter 2002; Deutsch 2009; Lawson *et al.* 2010).

Looking to the future

An important objective in the future will be to maintain the strong institutional relationships between the social housing sector and the financial instruments provided by the market. The continuous withdrawal of state intervention and earmarked subsidies seems to be widening the gap between social housing demand and supply and eroding the existing system. As redemptions of housing subsidies now need not necessarily be reinvested in the housing sector, the capital available for future housing production is decreasing. In the current framework of public austerity most regions have reduced their subsidies to the housing sector (Amann and Mundt 2013). This further diminishes the ability of social housing policy effectively to address current needs. Consequently LPHAs rely more on commercial loans for their building activity, which leads to higher cost rents. In 2013, however, the downward trend in HCCB placements by housing construction banks was reversed, which generated additional finance for social housing projects. Additionally, the present boom in covered mortgage bonds might contribute to more housing finance becoming available in the future.

As for single-family housing construction and purchase, private bank mortgage loans have gained importance over the last decades, but to a comparatively moderate degree. The widespread current availability of low-interest mortgages has reduced the relative advantage of subsidised finance components such as Contract Savings loans and regional housing loans. The latter have also lost appeal due to tight requirements on building quality (energy efficiency and insulation). The availability of private finance seems to have contributed to the current price boom. In any case, own equity and savings increasingly play a smaller role, while mortgage debt is becoming more important. This development is strongly related to the low interest rate climate, which might be reversed in the future. As in the past, the other financing elements seem to be being retained deliberately in case of a change in the economic climate.

Even though the issuance of FX-loans to households is much more heavily restricted today, hidden risks in outstanding mortgages may emerge in the future. Since it will take until at least 2018 for the bulk of outstanding FX-loans to amortise, the eventual performance of the repayment vehicles that have been used in most cases is still uncertain. Preliminary analyses have shown that holders of FX-loans have higher risk buffers (total real estate wealth, household income and estimated potential rental income) than average mortgage holders (Beer *et al.* 2008: 129; Albacete *et al.* 2012; Albacete and Lindner 2013), but the true picture of repayment difficulties will only be revealed in the coming years.

Acknowledgements

The authors would like to thank Josef Schmidinger, Karin Wagner, Hannes Wohlmuth and Wolfgang Amann for their helpful comments and advice.

References

Albacete, N and Lindner, P (2013). Household vulnerability in Austria – A microeconomic analysis based on the Household Finance and Consumption Survey. *OeNB Financial Stability Report* 25, 57–73.

Albacete, N and Wagner, K (2009). Housing finance of Austrian households. *OeNB Monetary Policy and The Economy* Q3/09, 62–92.

Albacete, N, Fessler, P and Schürz, M (2012). Risk buffer profiles of foreign currency mortgage holders. *OeNB Financial Stability Report* 23, 58–71.

Amann, W, Ramaseder, S and Riss, O (2005). Effizienz des Systems der Wohnbaubanken in Österreich. Expertise im Auftrag der ARGE Wohnbaubanken, FGW, Vienna.

Amann, W, Lawson, J and Mundt, A (2009). Structured financing allows for affordable rental housing in Austria. *Housing Finance International* June 2009, 14–18.

Amann, W and Mundt, A (2013). Berichtsstandard Wohnbauförderung 2013. Study commissioned by the City of Vienna, IIBW, Vienna.

Ball, M (2012). Housebuilding and housing supply. In: *The Sage Handbook of Housing Studies*, Clapham, D, Clark, W and Gibb, K (eds), Sage, London, pp. 27–46.

Bauer, E (2009). Housing finance and housing providers in Austria: Performance in the light of the financial and economic crisis. In: *Financing Social Housing After the Economic Crisis*, CECODHAS(ed.), Cecodhas, Brussels, pp. 38–41.

Beer, C, Ongena, S and Peter, M (2008). Carry Trade auf Österreichisch: Was für Haushalte entscheiden sich am ehesten für Fremdwährungskredite? *OeNB Financial Stability Report* 16, 117–132.

Beer, C and Wagner, K (2012). Wohnkostenbelastung der österreichischen Haushalte: Ergebillionisse einer aktuellen Erhebung. *Geldpolitik and Wirtschaft* Q4/12, 82–95.

Czerny, M and Wagner, K (2003). Structural factors in the Austrian Housing and real estate market, *Focus on Austria, Vol. 3/2003*, Vienna.

Deutsch, E (2009). The Austrian social rented sector at the crossroads for housing choice. *European Journal of Housing Policy* 9:3, 285–311.

European Mortgage Federation (EMF) (2013). *Hypostat 2012. A Review of Europe's Mortgage and Housing Markets*. European Mortgage Federation.

Fessler, P, Mooslechner, P and Schürz, M (2012). Households Finance and Consumption Survey des Eurosystems 2010, Erste Ergebillionisse für Österreich, in: OeNB, Geldpolitik and Wirtschaft Q3/12, pp. 26–67.

GBV (2014). Jahreskompaktstatistik [Online] Available: www.gbv.at/Document/View/4477 (accessed 22 July, 2015).

Janik, W (2013). Wohnungsaufwand 2012. *Statistische Nachrichten* 6/2013, 478–491.

Lawson, J, Gilmour, T and Milligan, V (2010). International measures to channel investment towards affordable rental housing. *AHURI Research Paper. For the Government of Western Australia*, AHURI, Melbourne.

Ludl, H (2007). *Limited-profit Housing Associations in Austria* GBV, Vienna.

Lugger, K and Amann, W (2013). *Österreichisches Wohnhandbuch 2013* Studienverlag, Vienna.

Lux, M (2013). The Czech Republic: Locked between municipal and social housing. In: *Social Housing in Transition Countries. Routledge Studies in Health and Social Welfare No.10*, Hegedüs, J, Lux, M and Teller, N (eds), Routledge, London and New York, pp. 146–162.

Matznetter, W (2002). Social housing policy in a conservative welfare state: Austria as an example. *Urban Studies* 39, 265–282.

Mooslechner, P (1990a). Internationale Zinsentwicklung. In: *Zur Neugestaltung der Wohnungspolitik in Österreich*, Czerny, M (ed.), WIFO, Vienna, pp. 88–108.

Mooslechner, P (1990b). Makroökonomische Finanzierungsstruktur des Wohnbaus in Österreich. In: *Zur Neugestaltung der Wohnungspolitik in Österreich*, Czerny, M (ed.), WIFO, Vienna, pp. 142–169.

Mundt, A and Amann, W (2010). Indicators of an integrated rental market in Austria. *Housing Finance International* Winter 2010, 35–44.

Mundt, A (2013). Housing supply in Austria: Providers, motivation, competition. *Paper presented at the ENHR Conference 2013 in Tarragona, Spain*.

OeNB (Various years). OeNB Database on financial indicators [Online] Available: www.oenb.at/isaweb/dyna1.do?lang=ENandgo=initHierarchie (accessed 22 July, 2015).

Pann, J, Seliger, R and Übeleis, J (2010). Foreign currency lending in Central, Eastern and Southeastern Europe: The case of Austrian banks. *OeNB Financial Stability Report* 20, 60–80.

Pilarz, G (2012). Sozialer Wohnbau und Finanzmarktkrise. In: *Gemeinnützige Wohnungswirtschaft im Wandel. Grundlagen – Entwicklungen – Perspektiven* (eds. GBV/ÖMB/MVÖ), Fair Wohnen, Vienna, pp. 83–90.

Schmidinger, J (2007). Spezialkreditinstitute zur Wohnbaufinanzierung. In: *Österreichs Kreditwirtschaft. Von der Reichsmark über den Schilling zum Euro*, Frasl, E, Haiden, R and Taus, J (eds), NWV, Vienna and Graz, pp. 401–434.

Schmidinger, J (2013). Die Rolle von Wohnbaubanken und Bausparkassen bei der Wohnbaufinanzierung. *Written version of the presentation at OeNB Workshop on Housing Finance*, 2 October 2013, Vienna.

Schmidinger, J, Rießland, B and Negrin, E (1992). Überlegungen zur Neukonzeption der Wohnbauförderung und Wohnbaufinanzierung. *ÖBA (Österreichisches Bankarchiv)* 4, 303–312.

Schwartz, H and Seabrooke, L (eds) (2009). *The Politics of Housing Booms and Busts.* Basingstoke, Palgrave MacMillan.

Schwebisch, G (2008). Nachhaltige Immobilienfinanzierung im Spannungsfeld der Kapitalmarktvorschriften. In: *Die österreichische Wohnungsgemeinnützigkeit – Ein europäisches Erfolgsmodell*, Lugger, K and Holoubek, M (eds), Manz, Vienna pp. 269–280.

Sellner, C (2011). Fremdwährungsanteil bei Tilgungskrediten bei 86 percent – eine Analyse der Fremdwährungskreditstatistik. *OeNB Statistiken* Q1/11, 22–27.

Springler, E (2008). Wohnbaufinanzierung aus volkswirtschaftlicher Sicht. In: *Die österreichische Wohnungsgemeinnützigkeit – Ein europäisches Erfolgsmodell* (eds Lugger, K and Holoubek, M.), Manz, Vienna, pp. 281–292.

Springler, E (2010). Finanzkrise – finanzielle Belastung der Haushalte durch Wohnkosten. *Kurswechsel* 1/2010, 67–75.

Statistik Austria (2014). Census and microcensus data on main residences 1981, 1991, 2001 according to StatCube [Online] Available: http://statcube.at/superweb/login.do?guest=guest (accessed 16 October, 2014).

Thienel, P and Schuh, N (2007). Wachstum der Fremdwährungskredite geht zurück. Wesentliche Entwicklungen im inländischen Finanzwesen im dritten Quartal 2006. *OeNB Statistiken* Q1/07, 18–27.

Url, T (2001). Der Einfluss öffentlicher Fördermittel auf die Finanzierungskosten von Wohnbauinvestitionen. In: *Wohnungswirtschaft vor neuen Herausforderungen* (ed. Czerny, M.), WIFO, Vienna, pp. 79–118.

Waschiczek, W (2002). Fremdwährungskredite in Österreich – Effizienz – und Risikoüberlegungen. *OeNB Financial Stability Report* 4, 89–107.

5

Milestones in 25 Years of Housing Finance in Belgium

Sien Winters and Katleen Van den Broeck
HIVA – KU Leuven, Leuven, Belgium

Introduction

At first glance, the Belgian housing finance system appears to operate under market conditions. It has a large number of mortgage credit providers and the demand for mortgage credit is high. However, taking a closer look at what happened in this market over the past 25 years, it is clear that government policy has had a major impact on this market. It also helps to explain why the Belgian housing and mortgage credit markets evolved very differently from other European countries during and after the Global Financial Crisis (GFC).

In this chapter, after a short description of the Belgian housing finance system and an explanation of the economic and institutional environment, we describe the main trends and milestones in policy, housing markets and mortgage credit markets. These milestones are then linked together and analysed in order to explain the current situation in Belgium. Finally, the chapter concludes with a discussion of the main issues for the future of Belgian housing finance.

This contribution is mainly based on literature review. Apart from a large number of statistics provided by the Belgian Professional Union for Credit (UPC-BVK) – the trade association that deals with consumer credit and mortgage credit – and two recent Financial Stability Reviews from the National Bank of Belgium, developments in private housing finance in Belgium have not been documented in great detail. Therefore, some complementary interviews have been carried out to provide further context for the analysis.

The Belgian housing finance system

In principle, the provision of mortgage credit in Belgium is open to all potential providers. However, because of the complexity of Belgian legislation those in the market are mainly national mortgage credit providers. These are mainly banks that deal directly with borrowers. The Belgian mortgage credit market is fairly conservative in its product innovation. The characteristics of mortgage credit are still very traditional, with maturities typically between 20 and 30 years and interest rates fixed for the whole duration of the loan. Thanks to the prudent behaviour of banks and consumers, the risks for consumers are rather low and defaults remain limited. The potential risks for banks associated with mortgage credit are also considered to be relatively low. In the most recent years, however, a wide range of loan to-value ratios (LTVs) and debt-service-to-income ratios have become more available, which may increase risks in the future and cause the National Bank of Belgium to implement additional prudential measures.

Twenty-five years ago, around 1989, the Belgian housing finance system seemed even more cautious than it is today. The types of mortgage credit offered were limited and very conservative. Even in the absence of any strict regulation (there were no real mortgage credit laws before 1993), policy around credit institutions promoted this cautiousness. This resulted almost exclusively in fixed interest rates, loans with durations of no more than 20 years, and LTVs from around 75 percent to a maximum of 80 percent. To ensure prudential lending, a loan was only provided if the repayments were one third or less of the client's income. This rule has been quite stable over time (Damen *et al.* 2014).

Since 1989, three major types of transformation have occurred in the Belgian housing finance system: (i) changes in the regulatory framework; (ii) changes in the tax relief system that had effects on the mortgage credit markets; and (iii) experiments, with at first decreasing and then increasing caution. This will be explained in more detail in the section on housing milestones.

The economic and institutional environment of the last 25 years in Belgium

In the second half of the 1980s, Belgium was recovering from a long period of economic crisis. Employment and real income levels were increasing and confidence in the country's economic future was growing. Moreover, mortgage interest rates had dropped from 14.9 percent in 1982 to 8 percent in 1988. This resulted in increased house building and housing transactions (Buyst 1992). By the end of the 1980s and during the first years of the following decade, economic growth slowed down and interest rates started to increase again (Janssens and De Wael 2005). Meanwhile, government debt had been growing. In order to join the Euro zone and to comply with the Maastricht Treaty, strong and continued budgetary discipline was required.

In 1998, Belgium entered the European Monetary Union and in 2002 joined the Euro zone. The government succeeded in balancing its budget throughout the period 2000–2008. From mid-2008 onwards, the GFC hit Belgium and several Belgian banks faced severe problems. To rescue some of the largest banks, strong state interventions were necessary, which resulted in increased government debt.

From an institutional and political point of view, the reform of the Belgian state as a result of repeated governmental crises is one of the major developments of the last decades. The reform process started in 1970. From then on the powers and competences of the regions were gradually expanded. The reform of 1993 turned Belgium into a federal state consisting of 'communities' and 'regions'. In 1980, the three Belgian regions (Flanders, Wallonia and Brussels) obtained full power over almost all of their housing policies. However, control over two important policy instruments, housing taxation and rent regulation, remained with the federal government. Control over these two remaining instruments was transferred to the regions in mid-2014 (Winters 2013).

The three Belgian regions differ importantly in cultural and socio-economic background. Their housing markets, in turn, are also quite different, although the similarity in housing policy across the regions is remarkable (Vanneste *et al.* 2008). In all three regions homeownership is strongly encouraged, social housing is of rather limited importance and the private rental sector receives almost no public support (Winters and Heylen 2013).

Milestones during the last 25 years of housing finance in Belgium

The past 25 years of housing finance in Belgium have to be described in terms of gradual evolutions, rather than milestones. However, in line with the scope of this book, we will try to outline major events in Belgian housing finance. Table 5.1 provides an overview, and the following sections explain why these measures can be considered as milestones.

Table 5.1 Overview of milestones in Belgian housing finance.

1993	Mortgage credit law
2005	Introduction of *woonbonus* for homeowners
2009	Introduction of 'green loans' (abolished in 2010)
2015	Reduction of *woonbonus* in Flanders and in Wallonia

Policy change

Regulatory framework for private housing finance   The regulatory framework for private housing finance changed substantially over the last 25 years.
The first milestone is the mortgage credit law of 1993. Before 1993 no real
mortgage credit law existed, but rules stipulated in a Royal Decree (RD)
from 1936 (K.B. no. 225 from 7/1/1936) regarding the regulations of mortgage credit were applied. The RD was part of the financial recovery legislation put in place after the world economic crisis of the early 1930s and
placed strong emphasis on the protection of the borrower (Cousy 1992). Also
of importance is an RD from 1935 (K.B. no. 74 from 28/1/1935), which
focused on decreasing mortgage (and privileged claim) interest rates and
stipulated that loans had to be granted at a fixed interest rate of 5–6 percent.
In practice, however, interest rates increased to over 6 percent from 1964
onwards. Particularly in the late 1970s, as a result of the oil crisis and its
effect on long term interest rates, credit institutions could not maintain the
legally determined rates and there was consequently a large mismatch
between the stable interest rates they were obliged to offer on their asset
side and the volatile interest rates they had to pay on their liabilities side
(Cousy 1992). This difference was at its height in 1981 when the interest
rate on mortgage credit was 15 percent (Buyst 1992). Since variable interest
rates were not allowed by law, credit institutions offered loans with fixed
interest rates, which included a 5-year review clause. This clause stipulated
that at the end of each 5-year period the borrower could choose to either
repay the remainder of the loan or accept a new 5-year loan at the current
interest rate. Whenever this clause gave rise to severe upward adjustments
of interest rates, it received large amounts of media attention and strong
reactions from consumer organisations (Cousy 1992). However, most challenges to the clause were rejected by the courts. To protect consumers
against this practice and to allow the mortgage system to respond to changing market conditions (such as the movement towards deregulation in the
internal European market), the first real mortgage credit law was finally
designed in 1992 and came into effect in 1993.

After 1993, some aspects of mortgage credit became strongly regulated. For
example, interest rates were allowed to be variable but the law included limits on this variability and the allowed frequency of adjustment. A maximum
financial penalty was also set for early redemption by borrowers (National
Bank of Belgium 2012). Also as a result of the 1993 law, the duration of the
mortgage registration was extended from 15 to 30 years. Currently, there is
a debate over whether to increase the mortgage duration even further, from
30 to 40 years, in order to enable households to obtain credit into older age to
take account of increasing longevity (Beroepsvereniging van het Krediet 2014).

The Central Credit Register was established in 1985. This register is a
database hosted by the National Bank. At that time, it only had a negative

role listing all defaulters (de Corte and De Groote 2005). However, in order to prevent repayment problems and to protect consumers against excessive indebtedness), all consumer and mortgage credit loans were required to be listed from 2001 by the Central Credit Register law. For credit institutions it then became compulsory to check the credit status of their loan applicants in order to assess their solvency and ability to repay. If credit institutions do not check this list before they grant a loan, they face severe consequences if the debtor defaults.

In 2013 the National Bank of Belgium introduced additional prudential measures to protect against insolvency among credit institutions. These measures were approved by an RD, including a flat-rate five-percentage-point add-on to the risk weightings calculated by the banks in order to compute the minimum regulatory capital buffers required in the Basel II framework.

Housing taxation In 1989, Belgium had just finished an important tax reform, resulting in a decrease in the average marginal tax rate of personal income tax. In 1990, a number of increases in VAT rates followed the reform of income tax to compensate for decreasing tax revenues and to comply with European VAT regulations. New VAT reductions were also introduced at the same time and later extended. VAT rates for renovation activities were eased several times. Since 1996, the standard VAT rate has been 21 percent, with a reduction to 6 percent for all renovation activities on dwellings that are at least five years old.

Immovable property in Belgium is taxed in several ways, but there are also a variety of deductions. The tax base for income and property taxes is the 'cadastral value', a publicly assessed value for income from the property. The valuation of the housing stock was carried out in 1975 and, apart from a yearly indexation since 1991, the cadastral value has not been adjusted to account for market changes. As a result, on average the cadastral value is far below the real market value of most dwellings, and differences in cadastral values between dwellings reflect differences in market values only to a limited extent.

An important milestone in housing taxation, and as will be shown also for housing finance, was the reform of personal income tax in 2005. The principle of levying tax on income after the deduction of costs remained. However, imputed rents on dwellings inhabited by the owner and financed by a mortgage were no longer subject to income tax. Even so, all reimbursements and other costs (including interest payments, capital repayments and life insurance premiums) could still be deducted from taxable income up to a limit. Compared to the former system of income tax deductions, this so-called *woonbonus* meant that the average benefit per household increased greatly from around €2500 per household in 2004 to €4980 in 2005 (Damen *et al.* 2014; Goeyvaerts *et al.* 2014). Income from rental property was still taxed after debt interests were deducted, with additional deductions for capital repayments and life insurance premiums staying in place, albeit at less favourable levels than for owner-occupation.

In 2009, so called 'green loans' for energy saving investments were introduced as a crisis measure. The state paid 1.5 percent of the interest on these green loans and the remaining interest could be deducted from taxable income at a fixed rate of 30 percent. The measure was removed at the end of 2011.

Property taxes are levied by the lower levels of government. Imputed rents are also the tax basis for property taxes in Belgium. The regions set the basic rates and the provinces and municipalities levy a surcharge. The right to raise transaction taxes was transferred to the regions in 2002. In the years thereafter, all three regions reduced their rates and put exemptions in place, many of which favour individually owned dwellings. Notwithstanding these measures, transaction costs in Belgium remain very high compared to other Organisation for Economic Co-operation and Development (OECD) countries (OECD 2011).

Another fiscal measure with consequences for the housing market was the policy of fiscal amnesty introduced in 2004 with the aim of repatriating private savings from abroad. According to the banks, a large part of these savings were then spent on immovable property (Van Gompel 2013).

Regional housing policies   The regions have had control over social housing policy since the 1980s. Initially investment in social housing was negligible. Budgetary constraints, ongoing high expenses associated with past investments and slow implementation of the new regional competences constrained new investments. However, in 1991, as a reaction to the breakthrough of the extreme right in local elections, the Flemish government made social housing a political priority. In the following decades, investment in social housing in Flanders and the Walloon Region increased. In the Brussels-Capital Region, the bulk of financial investment in social housing was spent on renovation (Bernard 2008). Other regional policy instruments included subsidies for renovation and social ownership. Subsidies for new construction were introduced in Belgium in 1926 and had been an important policy instrument in the past but were gradually abolished. Today, the only subsidies for new construction are for energy saving investments. A common feature of housing policy in the three regions is that the private rental market receives the least support from the government. Furthermore, none of the three regions has a substantial system of housing allowances that aims to improve housing affordability for private tenants.

Of special interest for housing finance is the system of 'social mortgage credit'. Households with an income below a certain level can apply for mortgage credit with a reduced interest rate provided by (semi-)public institutions, financed through public and private means. The interest rate is dependent on income and household composition. In Flanders, each year around 4000 households are granted such a mortgage, mainly for the purchase of a dwelling. Another interesting Flemish policy instrument is the 'insurance guaranteed income', which was introduced in 2008 by which, if the borrower's income is reduced as a result of unemployment or invalidity, an insurance company contributes to the instalments for three years. The insurance fee is paid by the Flemish government.

Housing market change

Developments in the housing market during the last 25 years are more easily described in terms of gradual and continuous evolutions than in terms of specific milestones. The first key evolution is the growing share of owner-occupation, which rose from 60.8 percent in 1981 (Vanneste *et al.* 2008) to 68 percent in 2009 (Dol and Haffner 2010). The private rented sector declined gradually during the same period. Compared with other European countries, social housing in Belgium – which constitutes 7 percent of the total housing stock – is limited, and importantly, this proportion has not changed significantly in recent decades (Winters and Heylen 2013).

As in most European countries, dwelling prices have shown strong increases over the past 25 years (see Figure 5.1). After a decline in the early 1980s, a long period of recovery began in 1985. Nominal prices in 2012 were more than three times their level in 1992. The rate of increase accelerated particularly from 2005. When prices dropped in most European countries in 2007/8, house price growth in Belgium only slowed temporarily, with prices increasing again in 2009.

The number of transactions has been increasing over the past 25 years. The number of dwelling sales rose from 96 000 in 1990 to a peak of 127 000 in 2010 and 2011, with only a temporary decline during the years of the

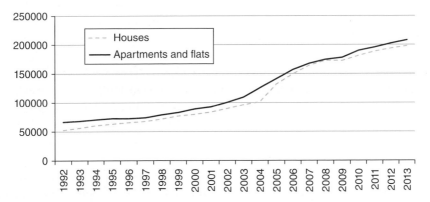

Figure 5.1 Average nominal prices of houses and apartments, Belgium, 1992–2012. *Source*: ADSEI (2014).

GFC. New construction on the other hand remained fairly stable with the number of new building permits issued oscillating between 40 000 and 60 000 per year. In contrast to what happened in a number of other countries, there was no boom in new residential building in Belgium during the period of strong price growth before 2008. Instead, Belgium saw only a slight upward trend during the five years before the crisis and a retreat to an average of 45 000 new building permits per year during the crisis. This corresponds with the building industry having a stable share of GDP during these years (Van Gompel 2013).

Changes in private housing finance

Expanding mortgage credit   As in many other countries, the overall debt ratio of households in Belgium increased significantly over the past 25 years from 20 percent of GDP in the 1980s to 57.8 percent in 2013. These levels, however, are still lower than the 65.5 percent average ratio in the Euro area (National Bank of Belgium 2014). This increase is to a large extent explained by an expanding mortgage credit market: the amount of new mortgage credit rose from €8.7 bn in 1996 to a record of €27.2 bn in 2011. Thereafter, only a weak decline to €25 bn in 2013 was recorded (UPC-BVK 2014).

The expansion is the result of an increase in the number of mortgage credit loans, the growth of the average loan size and a decline in the rate of amortisation of the outstanding stock (National Bank of Belgium 2012). Figure 5.2 shows the total amount of new mortgage credit and the number of new loans granted between 1996 and 2013 by the purpose of the loan. One key trend evident in this graph is the increase in the number of new loans for renovations in 2009 in reaction to the introduction of 'green loans', followed by a sharp drop in 2012 when this 'crisis measure' was abolished

The private housing finance system in Belgium is currently dominated by private banks. In 1989 the mortgage credit supply was nearly equally divided between the public and the private sector. The main suppliers were the public credit institutions (48.3 percent) and the savings banks (22.8 percent), followed by universal banks (14.4 percent) and insurance companies (13.6 percent). Public credit institutions were themselves financed mainly by private deposits (Pacolet 1989). Only a very small share of the mortgage credit supply came from mortgage companies (0.9 percent) (Buyst 1992). The dismantling of the last public credit institution (the Central Office for Mortgage Credit, established in 1936) started in 2000 and it was officially merged with a private savings bank in 2010.

Even though competition between the credit supply institutions increased, one in four (26 percent) purchasers of mortgage credit did not compare mortgage products (European Commission 2012). Most house buyers looking for a loan purchase their loan directly from the provider

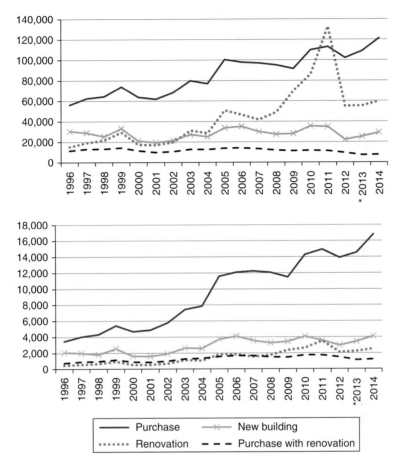

Figure 5.2 New mortgage credit according to the purpose of the loan: number of loans (top) and amount in million Euros (bottom), Belgium, 1996–2013.
Source: UPC-BVK (2014).
Note: From 2013, the number of mortgage providers in the statistics has extended, so there is a break with the figures before 2013.

(75 percent). The use of an intermediary or an advisor only started around 1995 and today, the use of intermediaries is still relatively low (22 percent) (European Commission 2012).

Around 1989, LTVs were usually around 75 percent or at most 80 percent. Between 1996 and 2006, the average amount of mortgage credit granted was linked to the average house price, resulting in a stable LTV of around 80 percent on average. However, when price increases accelerated in 2005, average mortgage credit did not follow and the average LTV dropped to below 65 percent in 2013. However, this average hides a wide distribution of LTVs. For households with limited personal funds, acquisition was only possible through mortgage loans with high LTVs. Around one-third of new sales volumes in 2013 had an LTV ratio of more than 90 percent. This sub-segment

Table 5.2 Breakdown of the outstanding mortgage loan stock according to indexed loan-to-value ratios (*).

LTV (%)	Share of stock (%)
≤80	71.5
80–90	10.6
90–100	10.3
100–110	2.8
≥110	1.7
NA	3.1

*Indexed LTVs are calculated as the ratio between the amount of the mortgage loan outstanding at reporting date (taking repayments of capital into account) and the assessed market value of the property.
Source: National Bank of Belgium (2014).

of high LTV loans has contributed to a large amount of outstanding loans with high LTVs, as Table 5.2 shows (National Bank of Belgium 2014).

Another recent trend in the Belgian mortgage credit market is the increasing maturity duration of mortgage loans. The share of loans with a maturity of more than 20 years increased from 33.5 percent of the stock by the end of 2007 to almost 44.6 percent four years later with an average of 23.5 years in 2013 in Flanders (for loans with a minimum duration of 15 years) (Goeyvaerts *et al.* 2014). Loans with a maturity greater than 20 years accounted for almost 50 percent of annual volumes since 2007 (National Bank of Belgium 2012). These increased maturities can be largely explained by the changes made to the tax regime in 2005, which provided an incentive for borrowers to extend the terms of their contracts (Damen *et al.* 2014).

Prudent mortgage behaviour   In 1989, banks usually assessed the solvency of potential borrowers using the rule that no more than one third of personal income should be spent on mortgage instalments. LTV was mostly kept below 80 percent. Furthermore, banks demanded deposit requirements. However, gradually, lending conditions were eased. In the last few years three-quarters of new loans have had debt-service-to-income ratios at origination of above 30 percent (National Bank of Belgium 2014). Since the financial crisis, banks have been stricter in adhering to their lending conditions, following recommendations from the National Bank.

The relative proportion of mortgages with fixed and variable interest rates has varied considerably from year to year in Belgium depending on the spread between the rates (Damen and Buyst 2013). Even so, the majority of mortgage credit involves fixed interest rates for the whole term of the contract, reflecting that borrowers in Belgium are rather risk-averse when taking out a mortgage (De Decker 2013). Before the 1990s, variable interest rates were officially prohibited but were of some importance during the following decade. Since 2005 fixed interest loans have regained importance. In 2012, loans with fixed mortgage rates for the whole term of the contract represented 56 percent of the total stock of mortgages (National Bank of Belgium 2012). Among new loans in 2013, 67.2 percent had fixed interest rates for the whole duration of the loan and for another 13.1 percent the interest rate was semi-fixed (fixed for a minimum of 10 years, then variable) (UPC-BVK 2014).

The prudent loan behaviour of lenders, which has also been imposed by law, results in a rather low proportion of arrears being registered by the Central Credit Register. The default rate rose slightly between 2007 and 2009, but dropped back to 1.6 percent in March 2012 (National Bank of Belgium 2012). Figures from the Eurosystem Household Finance and Consumption Survey (European Central Bank 2013) also illustrate that Belgian households are less financially fragile than households in the wider Euro area.

Risks and securities for banks Typically the repayment of debt is guaranteed by a mortgage, which is registered at quite a high cost (this requires the registration of the mortgage credit deed at the Registration Office and inscription of the mortgage guarantee in the Mortgage Register). It is also possible, however, to negotiate a guarantee on part of the loan through a cheaper mortgage mandate (where the loan provider is authorised to register the mortgage if he assumes the borrower is facing repayment problems). As the latter offers less security for the loan provider, it is more readily granted to borrowers with a reasonable level of personal resources (De Tijd 2012). At the end of 2011, 71 percent of mortgage credit was secured exclusively by a mortgage. The figures for mortgage credit secured by a mandate only (6 percent) or other type of guarantees (2 percent) are quite low (National Bank of Belgium 2012).

Most credit institutions demand an insurance to cover the outstanding balance. Banks that do not demand insurance can charge higher rates. Some credit institutions offer reductions in interest rates if the borrower agrees to buy the insurance to cover the outstanding balance from the same provider as the loan.

The domination of fixed interest rates and the limited variability of interest rates imposed by the mortgage credit law carry risks for the banks. When interest rates fall, banks cannot adjust the rates accordingly as (with fixed rates) borrowers are likely to refinance their loan, leaving the bank with a high funding cost. The banks include these risks in the commercial margins taken on mortgage credit.

Overall, the risks Belgian banks are carrying seem to be relatively low compared to other countries. The banks' calculations of risk weights (10 percent on average) are significantly lower than those applied by the standardised approach of the Basel II framework (35 percent). However, the National Bank of Belgium is warning that the internal risk models that banks use are calibrated on historical credit loss data, and therefore might be too low in less favourable market conditions. A sizeable group of borrowers in recent years may have extended mortgage maturities, loan sizes and/or debt service ratios in a way that could result in higher risks in the future (National Bank of Belgium 2014).

Funding   On the funding side, Belgium has seen large shifts from funding predominantly through retail deposits to increased funding via securitisations. In 2011 securitised mortgage credit constituted nearly half of the Belgian residential mortgage credit market (National Bank of Belgium 2012). The bulk of these securitisations took place after 2008 for liquidity purposes. Covered bonds and mortgage bonds have only been legally allowed since 2012 as a further attempt to meet the liquidity needs of credit institutions.

Impacts

In Figure 5.3, we present a framework that aims to explain the relationships between different aspects of housing finance in Belgium during the past 25 years. At the top of this framework is the mortgage market. This market has expanded considerably as the result of increasing prices for dwellings and land, increasing numbers of new loans and longer loan contract terms. These three factors are intertwined and are strongly influenced by both market conditions (dwelling prices, income, interest rates etc.) and policy (fiscal policy, mortgage credit law etc.).

It is clear that the expansion of the credit market over the past 25 years has mainly been the result of an expansion in transactions rather than new

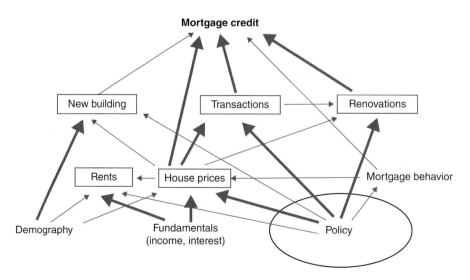

Figure 5.3   Framework for housing finance in Belgium during the past 25 years.

construction. Increasing prices, driven by growing household incomes and decreasing interest rates, fuelled this expansion. The general public believes that prices will continue to increase and therefore investing in residential property is a good opportunity for making capital gains. In this context, (Goeyvaerts *et al.* 2014) observe a growing number of second-time buyers. Additionally, younger generations in Belgium are more likely than their predecessors to opt to start by buying smaller dwellings with worse amenities, with the goal of selling them on and making a profit. In Flanders, the introduction of 'portability of transaction taxes' in 2002, by which duties paid on a first time home purchase can be offset against duties on a second property purchase, made these second-time purchases more attractive. Finally, fiscal policy seems to be a major factor in the increase in transactions. The amount of credit available expanded particularly after 2005, the year the new tax regime came into force. There is growing empirical evidence that the fiscal benefits from these tax reforms contributed significantly to the price increases (Van Reybrouck and Valenduc 2012; Goeyvaerts *et al.* 2014; Damen *et al.* 2014) and therefore indirectly stimulated the number of transactions and expanded the amount of credit. There was also a direct impact on mortgage credit in that the proportion of housing transactions financed with mortgages after 2005 was close to 100 percent, compared to 80 percent between 1995 and 2004 (National Bank of Belgium 2014), suggesting that some mortgage transactions were concluded solely for fiscal optimisation purposes.

Normally, increased prices stimulate new construction. In Belgium, however, the building industry has not responded to price increases as strongly as some other European countries. Price elasticity of supply is estimated to be very low in Belgium (Caldera Sanchez and Johansson 2011, Damen *et al.* 2014). This is partly because of legal obstacles (environmental planning and building regulations) to new construction and a shortage of new building plots, but also because of the rather static nature of the Belgian house building industry (Dol *et al.* 2010). In the past, private households in Belgium mainly viewed residential property as a stable and secure long term investment and house building was almost completely self-promoted, while the share of commercial development was rather low. Moreover, transactions were discouraged by high transaction costs. In such a market, supply does not respond as quickly and strongly as it does in a dynamic market. This helps to explains why a building boom was not seen in Belgium during the period of strong price increases. However, these trends do appear to be changing. Over the last two decades, the share of commercial developers has gradually increased and in 2012, new construction by private developers slightly outnumbered self-promoted building output (Dirickx 2013). Portability of transaction costs in Flanders (since 2002) and ongoing price increases also contributed to increased transactions.

There has been a strong increase in the number of loans for renovations in recent years, particularly between 2009 and 2012. This can be explained by the temporarily favourable tax treatment for energy saving investments ('green loans'). The abolition of this measure at the end of 2011 resulted in a sharp drop in the number of renovation loans in 2012. The *woonbonus* also probably helped to stimulate mortgage credit for purposes of renovations during this period (Goeyvaerts *et al.* 2014).

While fiscal policy seems to be a major factor behind the observed expansion of the mortgage market, the prudent behaviour of both mortgage lenders and consumers – reinforced by the restrictive mortgage credit law – inhibited even stronger expansion. This meant there was less room for product innovation than in many other European countries. Together with high transaction costs and a limited speculative building industry, this protected the Belgian housing market from even stronger price increases prior to the GFC and therefore probably also from a sharp drop in prices during and after the crisis. Other factors are also relevant, including the strong Belgian social security system, which kept purchasing power at a relatively high level throughout the crisis years (National Bank of Belgium 2012).

Looking to the future

Looking to the future, experts are interested in what will happen if/when the main driving forces behind the market change. Price development is particularly important in this context. If there are continuing and strong price increases in the future, the market will probably become more dynamic. If prices stabilise or decrease, the number of transactions will probably decrease, as will renovation investment. All of this will affect the volume of mortgage credit.

Changes in income and interest rates are the fundamentals that affect house prices. Both factors are dependent on global economic trends as well as national and local financial and social policy. The new governments that were formed at the regional and federal level in the summer and autumn 2014 agreed upon a strategy of austerity and announced a range of policies to promote public savings.

Of specific concern is the housing tax regime. From 2015 onwards, the regions are able to design their own tax policy for owner-occupied housing. Budgets for fiscal benefits were transferred accordingly, but only at 2014 levels. Budgetary costs, however, were expected to continue to rise. In a study in June 2014, Goeyvaerts *et al.* estimated that under current policies, the cost for the Flemish Region would rise from €1.3 bn in 2014 to €1.9 bn in 2020 and €3 bn in 2050. Goeyvaerts *et al.* have also pointed to the impact of the *woonbonus* on house prices and to its adverse effect on income distribution, confirming earlier expert assessments (Heylen 2013) and advice from the Flemish Housing Council on that topic (Vlaamse Woonraad 2012). The study concluded with a proposal for a very gradual reduction in tax benefits over a period of 25 years in order to avoid provoking shocks on the real estate market. In its coalition agreement of 24 July 2014, the Flemish government announced a cut in the *woonbonus* of one-third for new loan contracts from 1 January 2015. Furthermore, the deduction at the borrower's marginal tax rate was converted into a flat rate deduction of 40 percent. The Walloon government did not change the deductible amount, but like Flanders changed the rate to 40 percent fixed. Unlike both other regions, the Brussels region decided not to change the *woonbonus* tax benefit until at least 2017. In Flanders, the announced change caused a boom in transactions by the end of 2014. At this stage, it is not yet clear what the impact of these changes will be on prices and consequently on housing market activities and mortgage demand.

Although the risks related to mortgage credit are estimated to be low for the Belgian banks compared to other countries, the National Bank of Belgium considered it justifiable to implement some additional prudential measures aimed at strengthening the banks' resilience and reducing these risks. A first measure was the aforementioned flat-rate five-percentage-point add-on to the risk weightings calculated by the banks themselves. Other measures include assessment of the models used by banks to calculate the risks and requests for banks to carry out self-assessments and to develop action plans to redress identified weaknesses. These measures aim to prevent future imbalances in the residential property markets (National Bank of Belgium 2014). These measures could, however, also have a dampening effect on mortgage credit and, indirectly, on prices.

Acknowledgements

We owe special thanks to our contact persons from private banks and the National Bank of Belgium. We also want to thank Sven Damen for very useful literature advice and UPC-BVK for their comments on an earlier version of the chapter.

References

ADSEI (2014). Vastgoedprijzen [Online], Available: http://statbel.fgov.be/nl/statistieken/cijfers/economie/bouw_industrie/vastgoed/ (accessed 22 July, 2015).

Bernard, N (2008). Good and bad fortune of the plan for the construction of 5,000 (low- and middle-income) housing units in Brussels. *Journal of Housing and the Built Environment* 23, 231–239.

Beroepsvereniging van het Krediet (2014). *Jaarverslag 2013*. BVK, Brussels.

Buyst, E (1992). Het belang van het hypothecaire krediet in de Belgische economie. In: *Het hypothecaire krediet van de onafhankelijkheid van België tot de Europese Gemeenschap*, Belgische Vereniging voor het Onroerend Krediet (eds). BVOK, Brussels, pp. 165–178.

Caldera Sanchez, A and Johansson, A (2011). The price responsiveness of housing supply in OECD Countries. *OECD Economics Department Working Papers*, no. 837, OECD Publishing, Paris.

Cousy, HA (1992). Het juridische statuut van het hypothecaire krediet en de controle op de ondernemingen. In: *Het hypothecaire krediet van de onafhankelijkheid van België tot de Europese Gemeenschap* (eds Belgische Vereniging voor het Onroerend Krediet). BVOK, Brussels, pp. 133–164.

Damen, S and Buyst, E (2013). The myopic choice between fixed and adjustable rate mortgages in Flanders. *KU Leuven Center for Economic Studies Discussion Papers Series*, DPS13.15. Faculty of Economics and Business, Leuven, pp. 1–30.

Damen, S, Vastmans, F and Buyst, E (2014). The long-run relationship between house prices and income re-examined: the role of mortgage interest deduction and mortgage product innovation. *KU Leuven Center for Economic Studies Discussion Paper Series*, DPS14.09. Faculty of Economics and Business, Leuven, pp. 1–47.

de Corte, R and De Groote, B (2005). *Overzicht van het burgerlijk recht* (zesde editie). Kluwer, Mechelen.

De Decker, P (2013). *Eigen woning: geldmachine of pensioensparen?* Garant, Apeldoorn-Antwerpen.

De Tijd (2012). *Welke normen hanteren banken voor een woonlening?* 30 June 2012, p. 48. De Tijd, Brussels.

Dirickx, T (2013). *Uitdagingen voor wonen in Vlaanderen en de rol van de VMSW*. Woonforum 2013, 22 maart 2013 [Online] Available at: www.woonforum2013.be/Portals/40/documents/ ToonDirckx %20plenaire %20sessie.pdf (accessed 22 July, 2015).

Dol, K and Haffner, M (2010). *Housing Statistics in the European Union 2010*. Ministry of the Interior and Kingdom Relations, The Hague, The Netherlands.

Dol, K, van der Heyden, H and Oxley, M (2010). Crisis and policy interventions in Western European housing markets: do specific housing systems reduce the impact of the crisis? *Comparative housing research: approaches and policy challenges in a new international era*. Delft University of Technology, OTB Research Institute for Housing, Urban and Mobility Studies, Delft, The Netherlands, March pp. 24–25,

European Central Bank (2013). The Eurosystem Household Finance and Consumption Survey. Results from the First Wave. *Statistic Paper Series*, April 2013:2, 1–108.

European Commission (2012). Retail Financial Services. *Special Eurobarometer 373*, Wave EB76.1 – TNS Opinion and Social.

Goeyvaerts, G, Haffner, M, Heylen, K, Van den Broeck, K, Vastmans, F and Winters, S (2014). *Onderzoek naar de woonfiscaliteit in Vlaanderen*. CES – KU Leuven, Leuven.

Heylen, K (2013). The distributional impact of housing subsidies in Flanders. *International Journal of Housing Policy* 13:1, 45–65.

Janssens, P and De Wael, P (2005). *50 jaar Belgische vastgoedmarkt*. Roularta Books, Roeselare.

National Bank of Belgium (2012). Review of the Belgian residential loan market. In: *Financial Stability Review 2012*. National Bank of Belgium, Brussels, pp. 95–109.

National Bank of Belgium (2014). The Belgian mortgage credit market: recent developments and prudential measures. In: *Financial Stability Review 2014*. National Bank of Belgium, Brussels, pp. 113–122.

OECD (2011). Housing and the Economy: Policies for Renovation. *Economic Policy Reform 2011. Going for Growth*. OECD, Paris, pp. 1–24.

Pacolet, J (1989). *Marktstructuur en operationele efficiëntie in de Belgische financiële sector*. Doctoral Dissertation, Leuven: Faculteit der Economische en Toegepaste Economische Wetenschappen K.U. Leuven, publication number 205.

UPC-BVK (2014). *Statistieken. Hypothecair krediet: realisaties en aanvragen vanaf januari 2000 tot 2014 (S1)* [Online], Available: www.upc-bvk.be/nl/press/statistics (accessed 29 July 2015).

Van Gompel, J (2013). De Belgische vastgoed-en hypotheekmarkt. Ontwikkeling, waardering en toekomstvisie. *Bank-en Financiewezen* 2013:6, 439–457.

Vanneste, D, Thomas, I and Vanderstraeten, L (2008). The spatial structure(s) of the Belgian housing stock. *Journal of Housing and the Built Environment* 23, 193–198.

Van Reybrouck, G and Valenduc, C (2012). Chapter 3.4: Taxation of housing in Belgium: facts and reforms. In: *Property Taxation and Enhanced Tax Administration in Challenging Times*. Gayer, C and Mourre, G (eds). *Economic Papers 463*, October 2012, European Commission, Brussels.

Vlaamse Woonraad (2012). *Advies over de regionalisering van de woonbonus. Advies 2012/12.* Vlaamse Woonraad, Brussels.

Winters, S (2013). Belgian state reform as an opportunity to reorient Flemish housing policy. *International Journal of Housing Policy* 13:1, 90–99.

Winters, S and Heylen, K (2013). How housing outcomes vary between the Belgian regions. *Journal of Housing and the Built Environment* 29, 541–556.

6

Milestones in Housing Finance in the Czech Republic since 1990

Petr Sunega and Martin Lux

Department of Socioeconomics of Housing, Institute of Sociology, Academy of Sciences of the Czech Republic, Prague, Czech Republic

Introduction

The Czech Republic, like many other post-socialist countries, experienced growth in the share of owner-occupied housing after 1990. One of the necessary conditions for such growth was the creation of market-based financial instruments that facilitated the purchase and sale of dwellings on the housing market. The Czech housing finance system evolved gradually after 1993 and today can be classified as a deposit-based system, comprised of universal, mortgage and housing savings banks. Lenders use retail banking (deposits), housing savings and mortgage bonds to raise funds for mortgage (housing) loans. In contrast, securitisation in the form of mortgage-backed securities (MBS) never appeared in the Czech finance system. As of 2014 there are 14 universal banks in the Czech Republic that have a licence to issue mortgage loans and two specialised mortgage banks. Additionally, there are six housing savings banks that issue fixed interest rate housing loans.

The production of new housing before 1990 was centrally planned and financed especially by state subsidies either for *public housing construction, enterprise housing construction, cooperative housing construction* or *individual housing construction* (Lérová 1983). State subsidies for *public housing construction* supported the construction of state rental housing, and the resulting properties were managed by companies funded and operated by municipalities (national committees). This programme was fully funded

Milestones in European Housing Finance, First Edition.
Edited by Jens Lunde and Christine Whitehead.
© 2016 John Wiley & Sons, Ltd. Published 2016 by John Wiley & Sons, Ltd.

by the state budget. The *cooperative housing construction* programme, by contrast, was operated by building cooperatives and funded through the contributions of cooperative members, state subsidies and low-interest state bank loans (3 percent p.a., maturity up to 30 years). The *enterprise housing construction* programme was funded by public enterprises, state subsidies and state bank loans but was cancelled in 1981. Finally, *individual housing construction* (the construction of detached houses) was funded by home-owners, municipal subsidies (after 1967) and low-interest state bank loans (2.7 percent p.a., maturity up to 30 years). In sum, 56 percent of the total construction costs were funded by public budgets, 29 percent by inhabitants and 15 percent by state bank loans granted to inhabitants (Lérová 1983). While all *public housing construction* costs and the majority of *cooperative housing construction* costs (54 percent) were funded by the state budget, 69 percent of *individual housing construction* costs were funded by the home-owners themselves.

After 1990, the responsibility for securing housing transferred more from the state to individuals and their families. The policy of privatisation (Kemeny 1992) and the free-market ideology in the 1990s led to radical changes in tenure structure in favour of owner-occupied housing, though this institutional change has occurred far more slowly than in most other CEE countries. The change in tenure structure and abolition of the centrally planned system followed by the withdrawal of the state from financing new housing construction required the introduction of standard market-based housing finance instruments. The first such instrument was the housing savings scheme, introduced in 1993. Due to the generous state premium, the tax-exempt status of the interest from the housing savings scheme and the option to use the state premium for other than housing purpose, it became simultaneously very popular with households and burdensome for the state budget.

The concept of mortgage bonds first appeared in legislation in 1990 (Čechlovská 2005). However, due to the non-functional capital market, the first mortgage loans were not granted until 1995 when new and more thorough mortgage legislation was approved. The mortgage loan was defined as a purpose-built loan (i.e. a loan for dwelling purchase or for the construction of a dwelling) secured by real estate in the Czech Republic. The maximum loan-to-value ratio (LTV) for loans covered by mortgage bonds was set at 70 percent. Despite necessary legislation being approved in 1995, mortgage finance in the Czech Republic did not take off in practice until 2000 due to macroeconomic instability and high uncertainty following from the transformation of the Czech economy.

A 2004 amendment to the mortgage legislation eliminated the purpose-built requirement from the definition of the mortgage loan and this allowed banks to offer equity mortgages and mortgages on cooperative housing. Moreover, the amendment to the law eliminated the requirement that the property used as collateral for the mortgage loan had to be located within the Czech Republic; after the amendment, this property could be located in other EU countries. The liberalisation of mortgage provision accelerated the growth of the market, which peaked in 2008. The changes in housing finance were mirrored by changes in housing prices. Housing prices have peaked twice since 1998:[1] first in 2003, a year before the accession of the Czech Republic to the European Union, and second in 2008.

Between 1999 and 2008, the country maintained a high rate of GDP growth and a relatively low public budget deficit and public debt. This healthy macroeconomic performance was a consequence of several austerity measures applied by Czech governments during a mild economic crisis between 1997 and 1998. After 1999, the Czech Republic also enjoyed low rates of inflation and low inflation volatility. Low inflation and the traditionally high propensity among Czech households to save allowed Czech mortgage lenders to offer affordable interest on local currency (Czech koruna, CZK) mortgage loans. From 2005 to 2008, the average nominal rate for a 5–10-year fixed period loan in the local currency was around 5 percent per annum. Consequently, the outstanding mortgage balance as a share of total GDP grew sharply between 2001 and 2008 and has continued to grow until today. Between 1990 and 2013, the ratio increased from 0 to 22 percent.

The housing market was affected by the Global Financial Crisis (GFC) in the autumn of 2008. However, by 2009 it was already evident that the financial sector had returned to a healthy state and Czech banks remained profitable. No Czech bank was taken over or went bankrupt between 2008 and 2013. The default rate (for mortgage loan payments that are overdue by more than 90 days) increased from 1.6 percent in 2008 to 3.4 percent in 2012 and has remained stable since then. The decline in house prices was also relatively mild. Between the third quarter of 2008 and the second quarter of 2012, the nominal prices of flats (apartments) decreased by 20 percent, while the prices of detached homes dropped by only 3.7 percent and prices of plots actually appreciated; therefore, the aggregate residential price index decreased only by 9 percent between 2008 and 2012.

Milestones in housing finance

Taking into account trends in house prices, housing construction, macroeconomic performance, mortgage indebtedness, and the development and transformation of Czech economic institutions, we can divide the years between 1990 and 2013 into three periods that aid in the assessment of market-based housing finance in the Czech Republic:

1. A period of establishing new rules of the game (1990–2000);
2. A period of economic, housing and mortgage boom (2001–2008);
3. A period of decline and housing market crisis (2009–2013).

Period of establishing new rules of the game (1990–2000)

After the socialist system collapsed in 1990, new 'rules of the game' began to be introduced in all aspects of social and economic life. Despite the fact that housing was separate in many ways from main government reforms (Lux 2009), the changes in housing policy substantially transferred the responsibility for securing housing from the state to individual households and the provision of housing from the state to the market. These changes affected the size and type of housing produced, housing affordability (housing costs) and, most significantly, the structure of housing tenure.

In the Czech Republic, no right-to-buy legislation was passed in 1990s in contrast to most other post-socialist states. Consequently, the tenants in public rental housing did not receive the right to buy their dwellings under centrally set criteria. However, municipalities began to voluntarily privatise their housing. Flats were mostly sold to sitting tenants at a very low price, though conditions varied from one municipality to the next and the privatisation process was gradual, occurring slowly throughout the decades. According to the 2011 Census, rental housing formed 22 percent of total housing stock, of which 14 percent was privately owned and 8 percent was considered public housing. By comparison, in 1990 public housing represented 39 percent of housing stock. The marginalisation of public renting was therefore similar to that which occurred in the post-socialist states that applied right-to-buy policies, though the process in the Czech Republic was much slower. The homeownership rate increased from 57 percent in 1991 to 65 percent in 2011, which includes cooperative housing that has the *de facto* status of owner-occupied housing in the Czech Republic.

One of the first acts introduced after the change of political regime was a restitution of property expropriated by the communists between 1948 and 1989. According to the restitution legislation, the original owner or his/her heirs were the persons entitled to apply for return of property through restitution in kind. By 1993 most of the property transfers were completed. Approximately 7 percent of the national housing stock (and a much larger share in the centres of large cities) was returned to previous house owners. However, for a long time the Czech government maintained strong rent regulation, which applied to both municipal and private (restituted) running tenancies. Market rents could be charged only for newly signed rental contracts (after 1993) and regulated rents were kept very low, even under the management and maintenance cost level.

In 2006 the situation suddenly changed when Polish private landlord Hutten-Czapska won a case against the Polish state in a dispute before the European Court for Human Rights. The Court decided that the rent control breaches the rights of Polish private landlords and this decision opened the door for private landlords to require the public compensations. The Czech government prepared a plan to deregulate rents until 2010 (later prolonged to 2012 in big cities) to avoid payment of financial compensations to restituents. Recently, all rents, including existing and newly signed rental contracts in both the municipal and private rental sectors, have been liberalised. Beyond property restitution, the privatisation of former state enterprise-owned housing stock additionally contributed to the growth of private rental supply. Gradually, institutional investors began to enter the market. The share of private rental housing out of the total housing stock thus increased very quickly compared to the pace in more advanced countries, growing from almost 0 percent in 1990 to 7 percent in 1993 (as a result of property restitution), 12 percent in 2001 and 14 percent in 2011.

New market-based housing finance instruments were introduced throughout the 1990s. The first such instrument was the housing savings scheme (introduced in 1993). The housing savings scheme operates as a 'closed' system like in Germany or Austria (Bausparkasse), where loans are funded from the deposits of banks' clients. In other words, housing savings banks do not rely on any additional funding beyond the yields gained on the financial market from the investment of free financial resources in secure assets. The state supports the savings aspect of the scheme with a state premium – between 1993 and 2004, this was 25 percent of the sum of the annual deposit up to CZK 4500 (€175); this then decreased to 15 percent of the sum of annual deposit up to CZK 3000 (€117) after 2004 and further to 10 percent up to CZK 2000 (€78) after 2011. When a client does not wish to take a loan, the minimum savings period to be eligible for the state premium is six years (extended from five years in January 2004). When a client wants to take a loan from the scheme, the minimum savings period is two years. During the repayment phase the loan is paid back in annuity instalments and the interest rate is fixed for the whole maturity of the loan. There is a legal right to prepayment anytime during the maturity without any prepayment penalty. Funds acquired from the housing savings scheme are not bound to any particular use or purpose. The *Housing Attitudes 2001* survey (Lux *et al.* 2005) revealed that majority of people who used housing savings scheme were planning to use the funds for purposes other than housing.

In the Czech Republic the necessary legislation for the issuance of mortgage loans was passed in 1995. Mortgage financing did not spread as quickly as had been expected (Figure 6.1). This was mainly due to the macroeconomic situation, particularly the high rate of inflation and the high nominal interest rates on mortgage loans (in 1995 the nominal mortgage interest rates were around 11 percent). But there were also psychological reasons: people were wary of taking on a large debt for a long term (and unsure about their capacity to repay in the future) and there was still a feeling that living in debt was somehow immoral (Lux *et al.* 2005).

Since 1995, the state has provided interest subsidies for mortgage loans to tackle the 'tilt' problem that arose as a result of high inflation rates in 1990s. With high inflation, lenders charge high nominal interest rates.

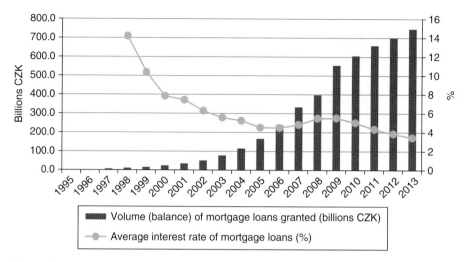

Figure 6.1   Total volume (balance) of mortgage loans granted and average interest rates on housing loans, 1995–2013.
Source: Czech National Bank (various years).

This creates an affordability barrier with annuity mortgages where initial payments are high. However, as time passes, loan repayments decline in real value through inflation, resulting in repayments constituting a declining share of a borrower's income. Thus, the high real values of payments at the beginning of a loan term prevent many households from qualifying for mortgages. At first these subsidies applied only to newly constructed housing, but later they were extended to support the purchase of older housing by young first-time buyers. The subsidy was directly linked to the development of interest rates in the economy. More precisely, the value of the interest subsidy was set for a given year according to the average nominal interest rate from newly granted mortgage loans to physical persons during the previous year. After interest rates fell below 7 percent in 2003, the subsidy was cancelled. Since 1998, borrowers have also been entitled to tax relief. They can deduct the sum of annually paid mortgage interest (up to CZK 300 000/€11 667) minus any state subsidies from their personal income tax base.

The Czech mortgage industry during the first period (1990–2000) only offered a limited number of products and the mortgage loan could be used until 2004 only for limited set of purposes related to the housing needs of the applicant. The interest rates of mortgage loans were fixed; mortgage loans with variable interest rates did not exist or were not used (Sunega and Lux 2007). The maximum loan maturity was 20 years, the maximum LTV ratio was 70 percent and the solvency criteria were applied more or less across the board to all applicants. The only mechanisms banks offered to make loans more accessible included the option to apply with a co-applicant, the supply of a broad range of interest rate fixings and various promotional activities including discounting the fee to set up a loan (Sunega and Lux 2007).

Period of booms (2001–2008)

The period between 2001 and 2008 could be described as a golden age for housing and mortgage markets in the Czech Republic; despite a short period of house price correction in 2004 when the housing bubble 'burst' after the country's accession to EU. This boom was accelerated by significant legal changes, most notably the deregulation of mortgage provision. After 2004, in conformity with changes in the legislation, mortgage loans were redefined to include every loan secured by real estate. The real estate used to secure the loan could be located in another EU member state or within the European economic area. Also after 2004, mortgage recipients were no longer required to use the loans for housing purposes and equity loans were introduced. The use of financial resources obtained from the issue of mortgage bonds was also broadened. The maximum LTV (70 percent) for mortgage loans financed by mortgage bonds remained but mortgage banks could use other sources (e.g. deposits or their own capital) to finance mortgage loans and thus were able to offer higher LTV loans.

In booming years, the maximum LTV rose to 100 percent, the maximum loan maturity to 30 years and mortgages with variable interest rates appeared – they were linked to financial market interest rates (usually the Prague Interbank Offered Rate – PRIBOR). Between 2005 and 2006 numerous innovative financial schemes appeared including equity mortgages, flexible mortgages, mortgages on cooperative housing, mortgage loans combined with housing savings or with life insurance ('interest-only') and mortgages without proof of solvency.

Flexible mortgages allow borrowers repeatedly to increase (up to 20 percent of the principal) or decrease (up to 50 percent of the annuity) the instalments on the mortgage loan, roll over the repayment of the loan for up to 12 months or interrupt the repayment of the loan for up to three months. The borrower can ask for increasing/decreasing instalments or to interrupt instalments only if he/she has properly paid instalments over the previous 12 months. Mortgage on cooperative housing allows borrowers to buy a cooperative flat (or share in a building cooperative, more precisely) without having other property as a guarantee for the mortgage loan. However, the co-op flat has to be transferred to private ownership within two years of the purchase; otherwise the loan has to be guaranteed by another piece of property owned by the borrower.

An 'interest only' mortgage is a mortgage loan combined usually with (capital) life insurance or a housing savings scheme. The borrower repays only the interest and the principal of the loan is repaid in a one-off payment funded by the life insurance or the housing savings scheme. The maximum

LTV of the loan can be up to 100 percent when combined with life insurance and up to 85 percent when combined with the housing savings scheme. The maturity of the loan is up to 30 years (life insurance) or up to 8 years (housing savings scheme). The interest rate is usually fixed for a 'fixing period' (in the case of life insurance) or fixed for the entire maturity of the loan (in the case of the housing saving scheme). Mortgage loans without proof of solvency were granted to borrowers without confirmation of income from employee(s) or tax returns verified by the tax authority of the borrower. However, the maximum LTV of the loan was limited to 50 percent and banks usually required the minimum collateral value of the property.

Figure 6.2 shows the share of various types of riskier mortgage products out of all mortgage loans provided between 2005–2009: mortgage loans with an LTV equal to or higher than 100 percent; mortgage loans with an LTV equal to or higher than 80 percent; loans granted without proof of solvency; combined (with other financial products, like life insurance or the housing savings scheme) and flexible mortgage loans; interest-only mortgage loans; and mortgage loans denominated in foreign currency. The data comes from the survey *Mortgage Credit in the CR 2010*, a one-off survey organised by the Socio-Economics of Housing Department at the Institute of Sociology, Academy of Sciences of the Czech Republic. The aim of the survey was to bridge the gap in officially provided statistics on the Czech mortgage market (there was no available data about LTV values, volumes and numbers of 'innovative' mortgage products granted etc.). The data should be therefore

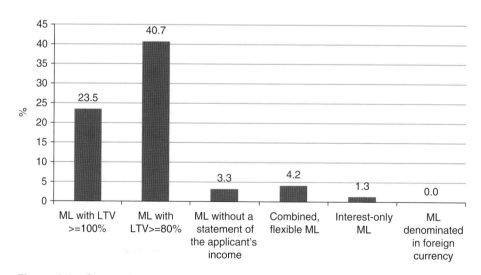

Figure 6.2 Share of mortgage loans (ML) by their specific criteria out of the total volume of ML provided to physical persons for housing, 2005–2009.
Source: Sunega and Lux (2011).
Note: The figures were calculated as weighted averages, where the weights were the volume of ML provided to physical persons for housing in individual years.

handled with caution, because it is impossible to verify their reliability. The provided LTV ratios are applied only when the loans are raised.

The volume of mortgage loans with an LTV equal to or higher than 100 percent on average makes up a relatively significant share (almost 1/4) of the total volume of mortgage loans provided in the observed period. However, the share of mortgage loans provided without requiring a statement of income from the applicant, the share of combined and flexible mortgage loans, and the share of interest-only mortgage loans all constituted relatively marginal shares of the entire volume of mortgage loans. The share of mortgage loans denominated in foreign currency, which was the main source of the problem in mortgage financing during GFC in some post-socialist countries (e.g. Hungary; see Hegedüs *et al.* 2011), was completely insignificant (0.06 percent of all mortgages granted in 2008). Owing to low inflation combined with low local currency deposit/loan rates, the Czech mortgage loan portfolio contained a high share of fixed-rate mortgages (43 percent of all mortgages granted in 2008).

Despite increasing mortgage debt, the total household debt in the Czech Republic was still considered to be relatively low because the total volume of deposits exceeded the total volume of loans: the ratio of volume of loans to volume of deposits reached 69 percent in 2012. However, prepayment penalties for fixed interest rate loans remained high, usually about 10 percent of the outstanding principal. These sanctions raised the cost of re-financing existing mortgage loans in the case of property sale, reduced competition and motivated clients to engage in riskier behaviour (clients were 'pressed' into fixed rates for the short term so as to avoid entirely forfeiting the option of mortgage loan prepayment).

A qualitative survey conducted in 2005 (Sunega and Lux 2007) revealed that Czech mortgage lenders were not experiencing a lack of resources or felt there was a need for additional financial arrangements. Short term money (i.e. deposits) was, in the opinion of mortgage loan providers, cheaper than emissions of mortgage bonds, and universal banks that provided retail banking were therefore in a favourable position compared to specialised mortgage banks.

Period of decline and housing market crisis (2009–2013)

After Lehman Brothers filed for bankruptcy protection in the US on 15 September, 2008, the ensuing uncertainty in the global financial markets and simultaneous credit crunch had an immediate effect on financial markets in Central and Eastern European countries (CEE). In the Czech Republic during late September and October 2008 there was a substantial drop in the activities of the interbank money market, an increase in the volatility of exchange rates with the Czech koruna depreciating continuously because of reduced investor confidence in the whole CEE region until the second quarter of 2009, and a slump in the stock market. The Czech National Bank reacted by lowering basic rates. For example, the rate for advances on collateral decreased cumulatively between August 2008 and December 2009 by 2.75 percentage points. However, these steps had only a limited effect on interbank money market rates and, consequently, on interest rates for mortgage loans. The monetary policy mechanism linking national bank rates to commercial rates was disrupted and as a result risk premiums increased substantially.

Instead, banks tightened their loan conditions. In practice this meant that the financing of new housing development through loans ceased and mortgage loans for households were tightened through reducing a maximum LTV or imposing a minimum income requirement on all new loan requests. The 'innovative' mortgage products of the boom period quickly disappeared from the market, although formally banks continued to offer these products to customers. Owing to liquidity constraints there was a real danger of a run on Czech banks. This spurred the Czech government to increase state guarantees for deposits from €25 000 to €50 000 in October 2008. In February 2010, the government doubled this state guarantee for deposits to €100 000.

The economic recession, which started during the final quarter of 2008, led to an annual decline in GDP of 4.5 percent in 2009. However, when compared to other CEE countries, the overall macroeconomic situation remained comparatively stable in the Czech Republic (see Table 6.1). In 2009 annual inflation dropped to 1 percent, registered unemployment increased to 9.2 percent, and although the state debt increased to 30 percent of GDP in 2009, total debt was at a level that allowed a temporary shock increase.

Despite the credit crunch, Czech banks remained profitable. No Czech bank was taken over or went bankrupt between 2008 and 2013. It should be noted in this respect that the Czech Republic is one of the few new EU member states whose banking sector is independent of external financing, despite the fact that almost all banks are owned by foreign capital. The main reason for this is the high ratio of deposits to loans resulting from the comparatively high propensity among Czech households to save. The acceptable increase in the default rate was partly due to the relatively conservative lending conditions applied by Czech mortgage lenders until 2004, but more likely stemmed from the large share of fixed rate mortgages and the marginal share of foreign currency mortgages.

Impacts

The ideology of privatisation championed by the new Czech governments in the 1990s changed the country from a nation of public tenants into nation of homeowners. The main driver of this structural change was the privatisation of public housing at 'giveaway' prices. The Czech Republic did not introduce a right-to-buy policy but municipalities gradually and voluntarily sold most of their housing stock to tenants. For tenants, this shift in many ways only a formal change (due to the fact that public renting under socialism

Table 6.1 Overall economic performance before and after the crisis.

Year	1999	2000	2001	2002	2003	2004	2005	2006	2007	2008	2009	2010	2011	2012	2013
GDP growth in constant prices	1.4	4.3	3.1	1.6	3.6	4.9	6.4	6.9	5.5	2.7	-4.8	2.3	2.0	-0.8	-0.7
Inflation rate (%)	2.1	3.9	4.7	1.8	0.1	2.8	1.9	2.5	2.8	6.3	1.0	1.5	1.9	3.3	1.4
Unemployment rate (%)	9.4	8.8	8.9	9.8	10.3	9.5	8.9	7.7	6.0	6.0	9.2	9.6	8.6	9.4	9.5
State debt as % of GDP	10.2	12.2	13.5	14.8	17.6	19.4	21.2	22.9	23.3	24.9	30.0	34.0	37.3	41.2	41.2

Source: Czech Statistical Office (various years).

resembled quasi-homeownership and the low rents paid by public tenants).
But the privatisation of public housing and the withdrawal of the state as a
direct provider of housing had a major effect on the nature of the housing
system, social norms, and people's expectations of the housing market. As
in other post-socialist states, rental housing has slowly developed a stigma
and is seen as transitory and residual housing; tenure neutrality in the Czech
Republic has been reduced and tenure structure has been skewed towards
homeownership.

However, thanks to the large-scale restitution of much of the housing
stock, the increasing interest of professional investors and rent deregulation,
private rental housing has become an important housing tenure in Czech
housing system. Unlike in most other post-socialist states, the housing
tenure structure thus remained more balanced and this fact, among others,
helps to explain the lack of a sub-prime mortgage market in the country.
Low-income households had an alternative to owner-occupied housing -
private renting supported by generous public housing benefit system.

Despite the increasing importance of owner-occupation in the housing
system, there were no market-based housing finance instruments in the
early 1990s that enabled market exchange. Due to high inflation and interest rates, commercial banking loans were inaccessible for the overwhelming
majority of households. Consequently, the government defined rules for
housing savings schemes, which were established in the Czech Republic as
early as in 1993. The highly subsidised savings schemes allowed newly
established special housing savings banks to offer housing loans with interest rates around 6 percent p.a. (while the interest on commercial loans
exceeded 15 percent p.a. in middle of 1990s).

However, due to high public subsidies, the housing savings scheme
became a very popular instrument for general household savings and the
payment of state premiums grew to be a substantial financial burden on the
state. By 2005, the state was contributing CZK 16 bn (€623 mn) to support
the housing savings schemes (Figure 6.3). In that time, public expenditures
on state premiums represented more than half of all state housing expenditure. Since 2006, these high levels of state support have been gradually
decreasing.

The loans from the housing savings scheme represented the only way in
which to obtain a loan with an affordable interest rate for purchasing a flat/
home during the period of high inflation at the beginning of the economic
transformation (until the end of the 1990s). However, after interest rates
began to decrease in the early 2000s and the number of traditional mortgages expanded, the housing savings scheme system that was fuelled by the
generous support of the state became ineffective.

The golden age of the Czech mortgage market that began in 2001, led to
increasing competitiveness and dramatic drop in mortgage lenders' margins.
The spread between the average cost of mortgage loans granted in 2004

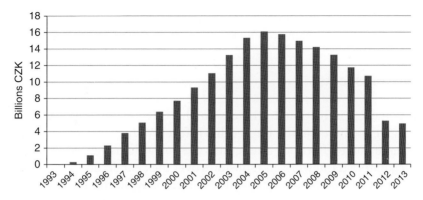

Figure 6.3 The volume of state support to the housing savings scheme, 1993–2013.
Source: Ministry of Finance (2008; 2014).

(i.e. the average mortgage interest rate) and (weighted) average costs of funding mortgage loans (i.e. rates on mortgage bonds, deposits, own capital) was low – between 1.07 and 1.35 percentage points.[2] The average gross margin, which was calculated as the difference between the average weighted[3] interest rate from mortgage loans granted by banks in 2000–2004 and the average annual gross yield of government five year bonds during the same period, was 1.44 percentage points, with the margin falling over time to a value below 1 percentage point in 2004 (Sunega and Lux 2007).

In 2008, housing and mortgage markets were affected by the GFC – however, its effect on both house prices and banks was relatively mild. The economic factors that helped the Czech mortgage market and banking system remain relatively healthy included: (i) a very short period of intensive mortgage boom before the crisis; (ii) sufficient financial resources from deposits and mortgage bonds (also thanks to the traditionally high propensity of Czech households to save); (iii) the rather low total indebtedness of Czech households; (iv) the positive structure of household debt; and (v) the fact that mortgage loans were denominated in local currencies and had mostly fixed interest rates (thus protecting borrowers from interest and exchange rate risks). One additional institutional factor was likely the more balanced housing tenure system in the Czech Republic that allowed low-income households (or households with unstable incomes) to stay in private rental housing and, consequently, kept the sub-prime mortgage segment relatively small (Hegedüs *et al.* 2011).

The Czech government's response to the economic crisis in the financial sector, beyond the previously mentioned higher state guarantees for deposits, was therefore limited. There were no mortgage rescue schemes, no special income supports for highly leveraged borrowers, no new regulations of the banking sector, and no moratorium on repossessions. The only government measures implemented were the postponement of rent deregulation in a number of the larger Czech cities and the introduction of state guarantees for loans to housing developers who built rental housing.

Future prospects

No dramatic institutional changes in the Czech mortgage and housing system are predicted in the foreseeable future. We may expect that the state will make some efforts to strengthen the social housing sector through a new regulatory framework and subsidies over the next decade. A combination of both private and public financial resources may be committed to exploring innovative social housing models, which may lead to the emergence of new, important housing finance segments in the future. On the other hand, no major changes to the institutional framework for private rental housing are expected as rent deregulation has already completed and a new Civil Code was introduced in 2014.

Even during the economic crisis, outstanding mortgage debt increased in the Czech Republic. A large part of this continued growth in the mortgage market was the result of old fixed mortgages being refinanced in recent years. As was the case previously, deposits and sales of mortgage (covered) bonds are providing sufficient resources to meet recovered loan activity and therefore we do not expect (at least not in next few years) that other forms of loan securitisation (MBS) will appear. New regulations will have to be in line with EU regulations but no specific national regulatory rules have been proposed. Ongoing discussions focus largely on how to improve the efficiency of the housing savings scheme, particularly whether further reductions in the state premium would be desirable and whether conditions should be placed on savings (including the state premium) to limit their use to not for housing purposes only.

Acknowledgements

This chapter has received financial support from the 'Centre of Excellence' project entitled 'The Dynamics of Change in Czech Society' which is funded by the Czech Science Foundation (Grant Agency of the Czech Republic, GACR, grant no. 14-36154G).

Notes

1   The Czech Statistical Office (CZSO) has issued a quarterly price index since 1998 (14 years) for flats, plots and detached homes. The data are derived from tax offices (non-random survey) based on declarations for a stamp duty. The data are transaction prices taken from contracts.

2   We used two methods to calculate the spread between the price of funds used by banks for financing mortgage loans and the average costs of mortgage loans (i.e. average interest rate). In the first case the costs of deposits were approximated by five year interest swaps – IRS (the spread was 1.07 percentage points in this case). In the second case we used as an approximation of (alternative) costs of deposits average yield to maturity of five year government bonds (the spread was 1.35 percentage points in this case).

3   The weights were the banks' shares in the total amount of residential loans granted to citizens up to 31 December 2004.

References

Čechlovská, Š (2005). Hypoteční bankovnictví v podmínkách české ekonomiky [Mortgage banking in the Czech economy]. *Aplikované právo [Applied Law]* 1, 87–111.

Czech National Bank (various years). ARAD data series system, Residents - loans to households (incl. NPISHs) – CZK+FC [Online], Available: www.cnb.cz/cnb/STAT.ARADY_PKG. VYSTUP?p_period=12andp_sort=1andp_des=50andp_sestuid=27368andp_uka=7andp_strid=AABBAFandp_od=199301andp_do=201502andp_lang=ENandp_format=0andp_decsep= (accessed 22 July, 2015).

Czech National Bank (various years). ARAD data series system, Bank interest rates on CZK-denominated loans by Czech households – new business (year averages) [Online], Available: www.cnb.cz/cnb/STAT.ARADY_PKG.VYSTUP?p_period=1andp_sort=1andp_des=50andp_sestuid=12864andp_uka=6andp_strid=AAABAAandp_od=200401andp_do=201502andp_lang=ENandp_format=0andp_decsep= (accessed 22 July, 2015).

Czech Statistical Office (various years). *Key macroeconomic indicators* [Online], Available: https://www.czso.cz/csu/czso/hmu_ts (accessed 22 July, 2015).

Hegedüs, J, Lux, M and Sunega, P (2011). Decline and depression: the impact of the global economic crisis on housing markets in two post-socialist states. *Journal of Housing and the Built Environment* 26, 315–333.

Kemeny, J (1992). *Housing and Social Theory*. London, New York: Routledge.

Lérová, I (1983). *Úloha bydlení v sociálně ekonomickém rozvoji. [The Role of Housing in Socio-Economic Development]*. SNTL, Praha.

Lux, M (2009). *Housing Policy and Housing Finance in the Czech Republic during Transition. An Example of Schism between the Still-Living Past and the Need of Reform*. Delft University Press, Amsterdam.

Lux, M, Sunega, P, Kostelecký, T, Čermák, D and Montag, J (2005). *Standardy bydlení 2004/2005: Financování bydlení a regenerace sídlišť. [Housing Standards 2004/2005: Housing finance and real estate housing refurbishment]*. Sociologický ústav AV ČR, Praha.

Ministry of Finance of the Czech Republic (Ministerstvo financí ČR) (2008). Základní ukazatele vývoje stavebního spoření v České republice [Basic indicators of the housing savings scheme development in the Czech Republic], [Online], Available: www.mfcr.cz/cs/soukromy-sektor/monitoring/vyvoj-stavebniho-sporeni/2008/zakladni-ukazatele-vyvoje-31–3-2008–1449 (accessed 22 July, 2015).

Ministry of Finance of the Czech Republic (Ministerstvo financí ČR) (2014). Základní ukazatele vývoje stavebního spoření v České republice k 31.12.2013 [Basic indicators of the housing savings scheme development in the Czech Republic at 31.21.2013], [Online], Available: www.mfcr.cz/cs/soukromy-sektor/monitoring/vyvoj-stavebniho-sporeni/2013/zakladni-ukazatele-vyvoje-stavebniho-spo-16984 (accessed 22 July, 2015).

Sunega, P and Lux, M (2007). Market-based housing finance efficiency in the Czech Republic. *International Journal of Housing Policy* 7, 241–273.

Sunega, P and Lux, M (2011). Systémová rizika na trhu bydlení v ČR, In: *Standardy bydlení 2010/2011: Sociální nerovnosti a tržní rizika v bydlení. [Housing Standards 2010/2011: Social Inequalities and Housing Market Risks].* Lux, M, Sunega, P, Mikeszová, M *et al.* (eds), pp. 99–108. Bernardyová Praha: Sociologický ústav AV ČR, v.v.i.

7

Milestones in Danish Housing Finance since 1990

Jens Lunde
Department of Finance, Copenhagen Business School, Frederiksberg, Denmark

Introduction

The quarter of a century that has passed since 1989 may well have been the most exciting and dynamic period ever seen in the Danish housing and mortgage markets. The period was framed by the banking and housing market crisis from the end of the 1980s up to 1993 and by three recent crises: the national housing, national banking and the Global Financial Crisis (GFC).

Before 1989, the Danish mortgage system went through a regulatory stop-go policy from 1970 to 1982. During that period the limitation on mortgage and bank loan availability reduced owner-occupiers' consumption possibilities. From 1982 onward, access to mortgage loans was gradually improved and the capital markets deregulated to reflect market conditions. This process was completed in 1992–1993.

Adjustable rate mortgages (ARMs) were introduced in 1996 and interest-only mortgages (IO) were introduced in 2003. The demand for both products was high because of their low payments, which made owner-occupied housing more affordable. In addition, lower interest rates affected housing prices and mortgage borrowing resulted in large increases in lending volumes.

The mature Danish housing and mortgage markets followed a strong cycle similar to that seen in many other countries. There was also an unprecedented upturn in housing and property markets, but the 'housing bubble' burst in 2006–2007, followed in 2006–2008 by the crises that had strong national as well as global roots. The downturns in the housing,

Milestones in European Housing Finance, First Edition.
Edited by Jens Lunde and Christine Whitehead.
© 2016 John Wiley & Sons, Ltd. Published 2016 by John Wiley & Sons, Ltd.

property and mortgage markets turned into a recession and seriously affected the macro economy, such that in 2014, GDP (in 2010 prices) was still below its 2008 level.

Denmark uses an efficient and internationally highly respected mortgage system. The reverse side of this efficiency is that the household debt is among the highest in Europe.

The economic environment of the last 25 years

By the end of the 1980s, the balance in the Danish economy was more or less restored. The double-digit rates of inflation at the start of the 1980s were lowered to 2.6 percent by 1990. The interest rate for 30-year annuity mortgage bonds reached an all-time high of 21.3 percent in September 1982 but was down to 10.8 percent at the start of 1990. The policy of solving internal imbalances by depreciation of the exchange rate had successfully been replaced by stable exchange rates, linked to the Euro.

Since 1982, the Danish central bank has – with governmental agreement – ensured that the exchange rate for the Danish Krone should 'shadow' the Deutsche Mark and, since 1999, the Euro. This policy remains in place with the central bank stating in March 2015 (after the financial turmoil around the Danish Krone) that maintaining a stable exchange rate was the primary and single target in fixing the interest rate policy. Other targets, such as for example, stabilising the internal Danish economic cycles, are not included (Danmarks Nationalbank 2015).

Tenure structure

The housing stock at the start of 2011 was 2 745 000 dwellings. Of these, 49.2 percent were owner-occupied, 7.3 percent private cooperative housing, 14.1 percent private rental housing and 18.9 percent social housing; 1.6 percent was owned by a public organisation and – possibly because of bad registration of household movement – 6.4 percent had no defined owner in the register.

Taxation

The taxation rules for owners of residential properties are that all pay land taxes, while the income and capital gains taxation rules in the four tenures differ significantly: from 'tax free' to near full taxation.

Social housing associations and private cooperative housing organisations are 'tax free' as they are exempt from income tax and capital gains taxation. Owner-occupiers are taxed through a property value tax of 1 percent of the publicly assessed property value. But because of the 'tax freeze', the property value tax is normally calculated on the 2001 publicly assessed property value plus 5 percent. For most borrowers interest expenditures are deductible at a tax rate of 29.6 percent. Owner-occupiers are exempt from capital gains taxation.

Owners of private residential rental properties face nearly the 'full' income tax scheme. Their annual net rent surplus is taxed with generally similar rates above 50 percent, whatever personal or company taxation rules are followed. And their capital gains are taxed at realisation at the same rates but can be 'rolled over' to another property. For long term pension savings invested in properties both the net rent surplus and the capital gains are taxed annually at 15.3 percent.

The Danish mortgage system

The Danish mortgage system is efficient, based on capital market interest rates and is technically 'cheap' from a borrower perspective.

An owner-occupied house or flat can be financed with a mortgage up to 80 percent of the property value. At the time of purchase, commercial banks often financed the rest of the purchase price, at least until 2015 when new regulations were put in place that required a downpayment of 5 percent. Mortgage loans are mostly provided by specialised mortgage banks, but commercial banks obtained the capacity to use covered bonds to finance housing loans in 2008.

The same basic model is used when issuing mortgage loans to all property types. The maximum loan-to-value ratio (LTV) is tied to the type of property: 80 percent for residential properties, 70 percent for agriculture, 60 percent for commercial properties and summer homes and 40 percent for plots.

The mortgage bank must ensure that the loan applicant can service the new mortgage loan and is able to service the debt on a 30 years fixed interest rate mortgage (FRM) with instalments: a rather soft condition given the currently low long term interest rates. The mortgage bank must also assess the property value before a mortgage is offered. The mortgage bank carries the credit risk on the loan.

The Danish mortgage system has existed since 1797. A mortgage loan is funded by a sale of mortgage bonds with exactly the same market value as the loan, issued in a specific bond pool. The bonds in the package have the same characteristics and thus a one-to-one correspondence to the issued loans. This forms the 'principle-of-balance' between the loans and the bonds. Thus Danish mortgage bonds differ from the general type of covered bonds as 'in the European model a dynamic portfolio of mortgage loans back the bonds' (Lea 2010: 20). In this pass-through model the borrower pays the debt services to the mortgage bank that withholds the fees and passes the rest through to the bondholders.

By matching bonds and loans, the interest rate risk is, in principle, removed from the mortgage bank's balance sheet. Originally the system contained a 'corner-solution' in that all loans/bonds carried fixed coupon interest rates over the whole loan term. From 1996 onwards, ARM loans were issued using the same funding model, but the incident arising in 2008 uncovered a serious systemic risk simply not recognised from the start.

Danish mortgage banks offer several loan types. Demand is highest for ARM loans. Both ARM and fixed interest mortgages (FRM loans) can be combined with an interest-only facility, which is also in high demand. These IO-loans contain an interest-only period of 10 years before the debt is repaid over the remaining part of the term – for example, during the last 20 years for a 30-year loan.

Mortgage bonds are sold on the stock exchange (OMX). Mortgage bonds are, in principle, continuously priced over the day on the capital market and are thereby fully transparent. The interest rate spread between short-term mortgages and state bonds is normally around 0.2 percentage points for comparable paper.

Fees to cover the mortgage bank's administration costs and risk at lending are added to the borrower's interest rate. These fees are usually less than 1 percent, depending on the actual LTV and the type of loan. The credit risk is estimated as the average risk for borrowers with the same degree of leverage and for the loan type, and not for the specific borrower. The mortgage model therefore follows a consistency principle, where mortgage borrowers face the same interest rate for identical mortgage products. This principle can be traced back to the historical roots of mortgage banks as cooperative organisations of borrowers, who had common interest to pool safe loans (with collateral) into portfolios to obtain as low interest rates as possible. This means of setting mortgage interest rates differs from commercial banks' administratively determined variable interest rates, which include elements of individual risk premiums.

On the stock exchange the interest rates for mortgage bonds with identical characteristics but issued by different mortgage banks are always nearly identical. Fees differ very little between the mortgage banks. Despite there being few lenders, the mortgage market is transparent and competitive.

FRM loans can be prepaid at par (100) on the settlement days (usually four) each year. The imbedded call option is paid by the borrower through a higher market interest rate. Alternatively matching FRM bonds can be bought in the market and delivered to the mortgage bank as required, when the market interest rate is above the printed bond interest rate. When the interest rate falls, the FRM borrower may exercise the option to prepay at par, financing the exercise by a new FRM at the lower interest rate level and thus capture the benefits of reduced debt servicing. ARM loans can be repaid on the date set for refinancing the bonds or by buying the short-term bonds at the market price, normally not far away from par.

The borrower only has to pay a market determined service fee to make a prepayment, as both the mortgage banks and commercial banks have a business interest in enabling the activity. The Danish model has never contained any penalty payments at prepayment. The mortgage bank adds the transaction costs to the debt. There has been huge prepayment activity over a long span of years with falling interest rates. Of course the extent of prepayment activity has varied but it has accelerated again through 2014 and the beginning of 2015, as interest rates for 30 year annuity bonds continued to fall.

The Danish mortgage system has a strong reputation internationally for being liquid, efficient, cheap and stable as well as for creating affordability and an easy and cheap prepayment option. The funding method employed and the 'balance principle' make the system efficient and transparent and the loans are 'cheap'. In this context, Bob Pannell of the UK Council of Mortgage Lenders gave a highly positive evaluation of the Danish mortgage system through the title of his article: 'Denmark: Probably the Best Housing Finance System in the World?' (2003). Michael Lea in a paper for the Harvard Centre looked at alternatives to the US mortgage systems and found that 'the Danish system offers the prospect of a real improvement in the US system' (Lea 2010: 25). Lea praises the balance principle, which removes the interest rate risk from the lender as well as the access to prepayment through buying bonds on the market, which 'allows automatic deleveraging as rates rise and reduces the probability of negative equity' (Lea 2010: 17). Recently, John Campbell argued that the USA has much to learn 'from the Danish implementation of the European Covered Bonds system' (Campbell 2012: 1).

Key milestones

Institutional and regulatory changes of the mortgage system

Table 7.1 summarises key milestones in the regulation of the Danish mortgage market and banks system throughout the study period. Access to mortgages became tightly regulated from 1970 onwards, almost to the same extent as a central planned economy. During the deregulation of the mortgage market and banks through the 1980s, ridiculous barriers facing owner-occupiers' and firms' access to mortgage funding were removed. However, mortgage loan conditions remained a part of the economic policy.

In 1992–1993 the deregulation process was completed. The ability to a raise mortgage, together with the capacity to make equity withdrawal up to a LTV of 80 percent, without regard to the use of the loan proceeds as in the years before, became available. The full use of annuity loans was re-introduced and the maximum term for loans was 30 years.

Traditionally, Danish mortgage loans carried fixed interest rates, while nearly all other countries had some element of variable rates. In 1996 nearly

Table 7.1 Milestones in regulation.

Year	Regulatory changes
1987	Tax reform – reduction of the tax rate for deducting interest expenditures.
1989	Institutional reform of the mortgage system and banks' conditions to implement EU directives.
1992 (May)	Refinancing of mortgage loans for owner-occupation with a 30-year term. Possible to raise a new mortgage loan by 100% of expenditures on renovation and improvement of owner-occupied dwellings, up to the 80% LTV.
1992 (December)	Access for owner-occupiers to raise 30-year mortgage loans for equity withdrawal without a specific loan purpose.
1993 (May)	Reintroduction of annuity loans for owner-occupied dwellings.
1993 (June)	Reintroduction of so-called cash loans. Right to carry the original tax exemption on old high interest cash loans through to a new loan as deductible interest expenditures.
1994*	Tax reform: Reduction of the tax rate for deducting interest expenditures and reduction of the imputed rent from 2.5 to 2.0% on the taxation of owner-occupiers.
1996	Adjustable rate mortgage (ARM) legally accepted and introduced by a mortgage bank.
1999	The maximum term was increased from 35½ to 50½ years for index linked mortgage loans for social housing (IS loans).
1999*	Tax reform: The 'Whitsun package': Reduction of the tax rate for deducting interest expenditures. Imputed rent taxation of owner-occupiers was transformed to a property value tax.
2002*	Tax freeze on property value tax. Annual land tax for a property must not increase by more than 7%.
2003	Interest-only mortgages introduced with a 10-year interest-only period.
2007	Covered bond law, including the European Union's Capital Requirement Directive, brought into national legislation.
2008	Systemic risk in refinancing ARM loans with short term bonds identified. Reduced through government intervention and market operations. 'Bank Packages' and other rescue operations to secure the effective functioning of the bond market.
2014	The maturity of 1- and 2-year mortgage bonds automatically prolonged for 1 year, if the interest rate is 5 percentage points or more above the interest rate at the previous auction.

*The parliamentary decision was made earlier but the reform was introduced in this year.

200 years of tradition was broken when a mortgage bank started to offer ARM mortgages: the borrower obtained a contract for a 30-year loan with interest rate resetting after 1, 2, 3, 4, 5... or 10 years, financed by the sale of matching bonds at annual auctions. After 2000 many borrowers refinanced to ARMs, and the fraction accelerated further around 2008. In January 2015, ARMs accounted for 65 percent of owner-occupier mortgages, 74 percent for private landlords, 88 percent for agriculture and 90 percent for industry, offices and shops. The financial engineering activity continued with the introduction of 'guarantee-loans': an ARM mortgage with an interest rate cap to limit the possible increase in the interest rate. Seven percent of outstanding mortgages were guarantee loans in January 2015.

In October 2003 it became possible to issue interest-only mortgages (IOs) where the borrower only pays interest up to 10 years and then repays the debt over the next 20 years (for a 30-year loan). After 5 years IOs had a market share of 50 percent, fast penetration for a new brand. In January 2015, IOs accounted for 51 percent of outstanding mortgage debt.

The European Union's Capital Requirement Directive including a new covered bond definition was implemented in Danish legislation in 2007 and was effective from 2008. The most important change was that the mortgage bank was required to perform regular validations of the borrowers' LTV, and not just at the time of issuance of their mortgages as earlier. Borrowers with existing mortgages are not required to put up more collateral if their LTV rose above the 80 percent as a result of falling house prices. However, the mortgage banks had to add extra collateral to comply with the requirement. Reflecting this, the 2007 legislation introduced junior covered bonds with more limited security than the issued covered bonds but a better security than for any other capital element. At the same time commercial banks were allowed to issue covered bonds to finance properties (Gyntelberg *et al.* 2012).

Tax policy changes

The clear imbalance in the taxation treatment of the four tenures around 1990 has remained in place up to 2015. Tax conditions for owner-occupiers were changed through a series of 'tax reforms' from 1987 on. These reduced the personal tax rates for wage earners at which net interest expenditures were deducted and slightly reduced the taxation of imputed rents on owner-occupied properties.

Under the first wider tax reform of 1987, interest income and expenditure, including the imputed rent of 2.5 percent of the assessed property value for owner-occupiers, were taxed at 50 percent but only for wage earners. The impact of the reduction in the interest payment after tax depended on the owner's marginal tax rate but was generally around 10 percentage points. As a result the taxation of capital and labour income was separated. The self-employed could deduct interest expenditures from their income before tax. In 1994, the interest tax rate was reduced to 44 percent and the taxable imputed rent was lowered from 2.5 to 2 percent.

The 'Whitsun' package in 1999 contained the largest reduction in the tax rate for deducting net capital expenditures against taxable income to 33 percent (in the 'average' municipality), a reduction of 14 percentage points. Imputed rent taxation was transformed into a 'property value tax' – of similar size – at 1 percent of the public assessed property value. A further change was put in place in 2010, when the tax rate for deducting interest expenditure up to 50 000 DKK (100 000 DKK for spouses) was reduced by 1 percentage annually until 2019.

In 2001 the government declared a 'tax freeze' on the property value tax, which was generally to be calculated on the publicly assessed property value in 2001 plus 5 percent. The average efficient property tax rate was estimated for 2013 to be around 0.6 percent of the actual market value of owner-occupied dwellings (Møller and Parum 2013).

The 2001 tax freeze also included land taxes: the annual land tax for a property was to increase by a maximum of 7 percent. Even so, land taxes will continue to increase over the coming years and will be particularly high in the capital area.

The market milestone: falling interest rates

The interest rates on 30-year mortgage bonds peaked in the summer of 1982 rising above 21 percent. Over the following decades interest rates fell fairly consistently (see Figure 7.1). This was possibly the most important driver behind the unprecedented upturn in house and property prices from 1993 to 2007 and the associated credit expansion.

The European Central Bank (ECB) increased the monetary policy interest rates from 2005. This had a significant influence on Danish rates. However,

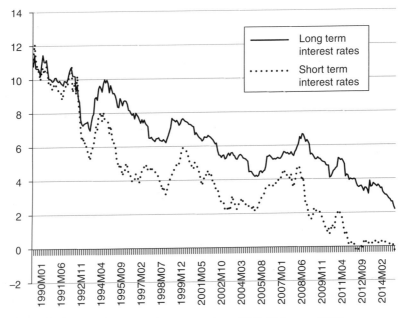

Figure 7.1   Development in Danish interest rates, 1990–February 2015.
Notes: Interest rate, callable mortgage bonds, 30 years maturity (annuity), percent p.a. After December (2012): average long term mortgage interest rates.
Interest rate, central government bonds, 2 years (bullet issues), percent p.a. After December (2012): average short term mortgage interest rates (resulting in a 0.2 percent increase in rates shown).
Source: For 1990-2012M11: Statistic Denmark; For 2012M12-2015M2: Association of Danish Mortgage Banks.

during the GFC the rates were reduced again. Since then low interest rates have been among the policy measures used by the ECB and the Danish central bank.

Indeed, even negative interest rates were observed in 2012 for the two-year state bond. The data change after December 2012 in Figure 7.1, from a two-year state bond to short term mortgage rates, elevated the short term with about 0.2 percent.

After the appreciation of the Swiss Franc in January 2015, the Danish central bank used the interest rate weapon to neutralise market speculation in an appreciation of the Danish Krone. As a result short-term mortgage interest rates also became negative at the start of 2015.

The interest rates for 30 years mortgage bonds include a payment for the embedded call option in the bonds, as the loans can be prepaid at price 100. Long term interest rates have fallen significantly over 25 years and reached an all-time low at the start of 2015. At their lowest during a few days at the start of 2015, 30-year FRM financed with 1½ percent bonds were offered. At 12 o'clock on March 10, 2015, the internal rate of returns on the 30-year 2 percent annuity Nykredit bond was 2.15 percent and 2.19 for the IO bond with the same characteristics. At the same time, the 10-year state bond (without a call option at price 100) carried an internal rate of return at 0.25 percent.

The impacts of these milestones over the last 25 years

House price development

The decline in interest rates reduced debt service expenditures for owner-occupiers when buying, made it possible for households to service a higher debt and enabled them to buy a more expensive flat or house. At the time that the mortgage is granted the banks' credit assessment considers the payments in light of the regulatory rule that the loan applicant must be able to service a 30-year FRM loan with installments. Therefore, when interest rates fall, the system creates an 'automatic' increase in possible purchase prices and thereby the borrowers' raise larger loans.

In 1992, the housing market was in a poor state. Real house prices had dropped by more than one-third; around 25 percent of owner-occupiers were technically insolvent; and annually more than 10 000 owner-occupiers were in foreclosure. However, after the positive result of the referendum on the Edinburgh treaty in 1993, interest rates started to fall. House prices reached a trough in the second quarter of 1993 and turned around.

From that trough, Danish real house prices started a long and nearly unbroken ride upwards and the rate of increase even accelerated after 2003 to a peak in the first quarter of 2007 (see Chapter 1, Table 1.1 and Figure 1.2). From trough to peak the total increase in real house prices was 177 percent – in the OECD area Denmark was only outpaced by Ireland, the Netherlands and Norway (Lunde 2009).

Denmark also experienced a 'building boom', as prices of existing houses rose above building costs. Housing investment was 6.8 percent of GDP in 2006, double the 3.3 percent in 1993. Building and modernisation of one-family houses was especially active.

After the 2007 peak, prices of houses, flats and other properties fell significantly. Real house prices declined by 29 percent between the peak and the second quarter of 2012 and have only improved 5 percent up to early 2015. The fall was nearly as much as in the two previous housing crises from 1979 to 1982 and from 1986 to 1993. The fall in real house price since the peak compared with that in the Netherlands and was only exceeded in Ireland and Spain.

Parallel development in house prices and owner-occupiers' net debt

Structurally, Danish owner-occupiers are highly levered as seen by the stable, and high, LTV ratios for established owner-occupiers. This reflects the fact that Danish house price development was mirrored by a similar strong and unprecedented increase in housing debt. As a result, owner-occupiers' net debt and housing wealth have moved in parallel.

This is confirmed at the micro level for the single owner-occupier families. Tax statistics are used to identify the family's net debt (mortgage and bank loans minus financial assets) and compare this to the family's housing wealth as measured by the publicly assessed property value. Owner-occupier families, excluding the self-employed, can be divided into deciles in relation to the size of their net liability-to-housing wealth. The data presented in this section and later, show the value for the family exactly on the mentioned decile (Lunde 2012b).

The LTV ratios (net debt-to-housing wealth ratios) for the median established owner-occupier in different age groups are shown in Figure 7.2. These stable ratios show that the families' housing wealth and net debt have moved in parallel for 'younger' owner-occupiers below 40 years of age. However, owners above 40 years of age have increasing LTV ratios meaning they have become more indebted. This can be explained partly by low inflation and interest rates, which maintain the real value of the debt services that have been almost unchanged over the years. It can also be partly explained by the fact that, for borrowers with IOs, the debt remains unchanged for the first 10 years.

Around 20–25 percent of owner-occupiers have been technically insolvent over the last 25 years – with liabilities greater than asset values. An exception

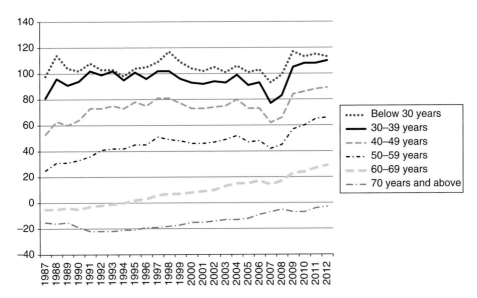

Figure 7.2 Net liabilities-to-housing wealth for the median owner-occupiers (excluding the self-employed) in different age groups, 1987–2012.
Source: Danish tax statistics.

is found around the house price peak in 2007. The LTV level for median owners below 40 years of age has been above 100 percent since 2009 and in some earlier years, around half of younger owner-occupiers were 'under water'. The underlying data show that around 40 percent of the owners between 40 and 49 years of age, more than 20 percent of the owners between 50 and 59 years and more than 10 percent between 60 and 69 years of age were technically insolvent (Lunde 2012b).

The high level of technical insolvency is a 'natural' consequence of the Danish tradition of first-time buying with nearly no downpayment. By definition they started 'under water'. If house prices start to fall, they are 'locked in' and cannot move up the housing ladder as they would otherwise choose to do.

The frequency of technical insolvency has been rather stable over the whole period but as house prices fell between 1986 and 1993 a high number of owner-occupiers suffered foreclosure. When the housing prices turned around in 2007 only slightly more owners fell into arrears or ended in foreclosure – particularly because interest rates were highly reduced after 2008 and many owner-occupiers were able to refinance with ARMs.

Owner-occupiers' net liabilities-to-income ratios

Owner-occupiers' debt has increased much more than their incomes since 1994. For the 'median owner' the net liability-to-income (before tax) increased 121 percent to 2012. The upturn in the net liability-to-income

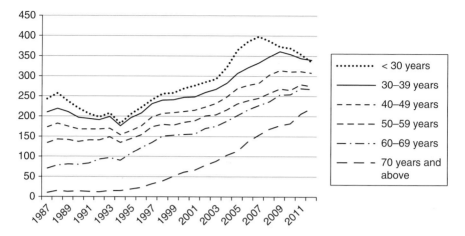

Figure 7.3 Net liabilities-to-gross income ratios for owner-occupiers (excluding the self-employed) for the 20 percent with highest ratios, by age, 1987–2012.
Source: Danish tax statistics.

ratio lasted until 2011, when the underlying deleveraging started to influence the ratio.

The net liabilities-to-gross income ratios for owner-occupiers in the eighth decile in the different age groups are shown in Figure 7.3. Thus in these decile values, 20 percent of owners have an even higher ratio than shown by the decile line. In these groups, a deleveraging process started in 2008 for owners below 30 years of age and in 2010 for all below 60 years of age. Only owners above that age have not deleveraged yet but their debt ratios are anyway somewhat lower. At the macro level, Danish families' household debt-to-disposable income peaked in 2009 (Lunde 2012a).

Owner-occupiers below 40 years of age also experienced a fall in their net liabilities-to-income ratios from 1988 to 1994, while the 'older' owners have experienced a nearly uniform increase in their debt, compared to income, since 1987.

Development in owner-occupiers' net interest expenditures-to-gross income ratios

The combined effect of the increase in owner-occupiers' indebtedness and the fall in interest rates is seen through the development in their net interest expenditures-to-gross income ratios. The ratios are highest in the younger age groups, as is to be expected from a life-cycle perspective, but their ratios have also been falling over the 25 years. For owner-occupiers over 60 years of age, net interest expenditures-to-gross income ratios have slightly increased. The age dependent differences in debt service burden have thereby been narrowed.

The tightening of the interest rates in 2005–2006 is observed in Figure 7.4 for the owners in the eighth decile, where the 20 percent with

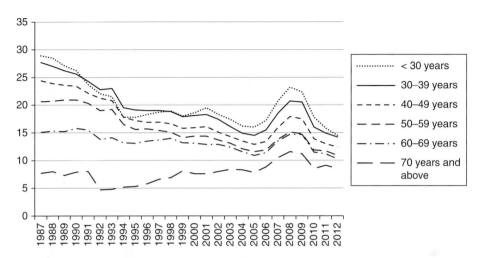

Figure 7.4 Net interest expenditure-to-gross income ratios for owner-occupiers (excluding the self-employed) for the 20 percent with highest ratios, by age, 1987–2012.
Source: Danish tax statistics.

the highest interest payment burden are found. Their ratios increased sharply and form a 'peak' as shown. This contributed seriously to the drop in house prices that followed. The rise in interest payments was reversed with the large-scale rapid reductions in interest rates after the outbreak of the GFC in 2008.

Interest rates and owner-occupiers' net interest expenditures have reduced further since 2012 and, therefore, the owner-occupiers' interest payments must have also been further reduced. But high interest rate risks remain.

The housing crisis, the national banking crisis and the Global Financial Crisis

The long period of expansion in house prices and activity seen since 1993 was not sustained. House prices could not continue to increase more than consumer prices in the long run. And only few 'soft landings' in housing markets have been seen internationally. The relatively modest increase in interest rates from the summer 2005 became the Danish bubble/bust factor. And in the summer 2005 the number of houses and flats sold peaked and started to fall abruptly. Building activity also fell steeply from the peak in private house building starts a year later. At the same time market prices for houses and flats in the capital region peaked as well. Finally, house prices at the national level peaked in the first quarter of 2007.

Denmark experienced a triple crisis in 2007–2008: a housing crisis starting in 2007, a banking crisis in 2008 and shortly after that the outbreak of the GFC. All three crises appeared independently of one another but clearly each single crisis intensified the consequences of the others. In 2011 the Euro-crisis added to the problems. Denmark was already in recession and in 2014 real GDP was still 3.3 percent below its 2007 level. The housing crisis became the epicentre for the recession in the Danish economy and appeared before the next on the crisis time line: the Danish banking crisis. 'Often, however, banking problems arise not from the liability side but from a protracted deterioration in asset quality, be it from a collapse in real estate prices...' (Reinhart & Rogoff 2009: 9).

The first forced buy-out of a small bank happened in January 2008 but it had not been unusual for small banks to be bought out or merged. However, over the summer of 2008 a larger provincial bank also failed. Behind the Danish banking crisis was the fact that banks had financed strong lending growth from 2000 onwards by issuing short-term bonds and borrowing from foreign credit institutions and funded less by deposits: a risky funding mix, especially at the beginning of the outbreak of the GFC (Abildgren and Thomsen 2011). A similar approach to funding partly created the implosion of the US financial system in 2007–2008 (Reinhart & Rogoff 2009).

Another important feature was the large part of their lending with collateral behind the loans. This is normally attractive to banks and consumers, as collateral makes the loans more secure and the borrower is enabled to pay a lower interest rate. 'But unlike other loans, the cash flow to repay a property loan is not independent of collateral, with changes in vacancy rates or rental values being immediately reflected in the resale value of the building' (Davis 1995: 297). A large part of the commercial banks' losses and write downs were on loans to building firms or loans with residential and commercial properties as collaterals.

Between 2008 and 2013 the Danish FSA stopped activity in 19 commercial banks because they could not provide the required capital base. Of these, 13 banks were transferred into the 'bad bank' construction called 'Financial Stability'. In total, 62 banks became more or less 'voluntarily', merged or stopped operating for other reasons. No mortgage banks stopped.

Thus the banking crisis became to some extent a crisis of the markets for commercial and rental residential properties. The banks however took only minor losses on owner-occupier loans. The number of foreclosures was much lower than during earlier housing crises. This time, owner-occupier borrowers were able to service their debts, which have kept the numbers of foreclosures low. An important explanation for this, besides the low interest rates, was that ARMs increased as a proportion of owner-occupiers' loans from 46 percent in March 2008 to 68 percent in August 2012.

The GFC started with the collapse of the subprime market in the USA in 2007. Liquidity dried up in the markets, whose participants lost confidence in each other, and the crisis then deepened as a result of the bankruptcy of Lehman Brothers in September 2008.

All financial markets, including those in Denmark, were affected. In September–October 2008 the Danish mortgage market was particularly exposed, but the balance principle did ensure that the mortgage bonds issued had the same financial characteristics as the loans in the pool. The Danish mortgage bond market continued to work in the autumn of 2008, while other paper and capital markets ceased to function.

The interest rates on both short- and long-term bonds increased considerably up to the second quarter of 2008 (see Figure 7.1) and the spread to swap rates widened. In early December, Danish mortgage banks had to execute the annual ARM-refinancing of 1-year bullet bonds, and then 'spreads widened but the refinancing was done at a rate of 5.25 percent in a period when the majority of covered bond markets in Europe were effectively closed for new issuance' (Gyntelberg *et al.* 2012: 56–58). Therefore, Campbell could conclude: 'The Danish system proved relatively stable even during the global financial crisis' (2012: 28).

The aftermath

Since 2008, households' nominal debt has remained nearly stable, although the mix has changed with slightly more mortgages and fewer bank loans being raised. From 2009 on, the household debt-to-GDP ratio fell reflecting the deleveraging process. As seen previously, deleveraging had already started among the most indebted owner-occupiers. In an analysis of owner-occupier families' LTVs and consumption prior to and after the financial crisis it was found that 'families that were highly leveraged prior to the financial crisis reduced consumption during the crisis more than comparable families with less pre-crisis leverage' (Andersen *et al.* 2014: 23). This deleveraging effect has contributed considerably to the fall in private consumption and to the economic stagnation observed at least until 2015.

The many technically insolvent owners were simply 'locked in', as the commercial and mortgage banks will normally not allow a family to move unless they repay the loans. For young families their way up the housing ladder was broken or – at best – delayed. So the numbers of sales fell and the housing market dried up.

House price changes after the crises have been rather uneven across the country. After a strong turn around, prices of both flats and houses in the capital have started to increase but are not yet up to the level before the housing crisis. At the other end of the market, usually related to the degree of urbanisation and thereby often in small villages, houses are unsaleable, the inhabitants cannot move and many have to find 'an arrangement' with their bank. Moreover, often they cannot raise a mortgage as no one can fulfil the mortgage banks lending criteria that the house can be sold at a similar price in the near future, as the market is not really functioning.

The rescue operations

The Danish central bank lowered government interest rates in 2008. As the primary and single target for the Danish monetary policy is to maintain a stable exchange rate against the Euro, the Danish economy is indirectly influenced by the ECB's interest rate and quantitative easing policy.

The Danish government and parliament established five 'bank packages' in the period October 2008 to October 2010 (Abildgren and Thomsen 2011). Of particular relevance to housing finance was an agreement for the pension sector from October 2008, which prevented a 'fire sale' of mortgage bonds from the pension funds. No rescue operation schemes for borrowers have been introduced or even proposed.

The possibility of activating the mentioned systemic risk associated with ARM loans' refinancing is very small – but if it were to happen, the consequences would pose an enormous systemic threat. To reduce the systemic risk associated with ARM that can occur at refinancing, the mortgage banks initially split the auctions for short-term mortgage bonds into several auctions over the year instead of a single one in December.

A new law was passed in 2013 to reduce this systemic risk and to spread the risk of sudden interest rate increases or of turmoil on foreign exchange markets. The maturity of one- and two-year bonds is automatically prolonged for one year with 5 percentage points added to the interest rate, if without this adjustment the interest rate at the auction would be 5 percentage points or more above the interest rate at the previous auction.

New 'soft' regulatory changes have been put in place after the crises. The Danish FSA introduced a 'supervisory diamond for mortgage-credit institutions' (Danish FSA 2014). 'Systemic important' financial institutions have been defined and all mortgage banks included because of the importance of a secure mortgage system. The mortgage banks have increased fees and tried to differentiate the fees in relation to expected risk on the different loan types; most for ARM and IO loans.

Looking to the future

The Danish mortgage model with capital market determined interest rates has maintained its high international reputation as an efficient, sophisticated and cheap mortgage system. On the other hand, over two decades, Denmark has had the highest household debt-to-disposable income ratio among OECD members and the second highest residential mortgage-to-GDP ratio in the EMF statistics. After the 'repair' of the systemic risks embodied in the refinancing of one- and two-year bonds, the model for the Danish mortgage system has been relatively little affected by the crisis.

Low payment ARM loans still cover around two-thirds of outstanding mortgages. This has created a large upside interest risk for owner-occupiers, farmers and other mortgage borrowers in the current low-interest environment. At some point the ECB's interest rates will be 'normalised'. The interest-only period for the first IO loans expired in 2013 and many borrowers will try to refinance to a new IO loan in the years to come. To make this possible, they must fulfil the LTV requirement. Otherwise their debt services are doubled – at best – and for borrowers with ARMs the increase will be much higher. Most deferred amortisation periods will come to an end during 2019–2023 (Dam *et al.* 2014: 57).

The high levels of Danish household debt were criticised by OECD, IMF and BIS at the start of 2012. Afterwards, the central bank and the Ministry of Business and Growth analysed the position of all households with mortgage loans. The central bank found that: 'Given the current economic outlook, the extent of the indebted families cannot, however, be assumed to pose a threat to the household sector or the financial sector' (Andersen *et al.* 2012: 3). The Ministry undertook a stress test and found that an interest rate increase to five percentage points would increase the fraction of households with a debt service ratio-to-disposable income above 50 percent from 4.8 percent to 12.1 percent. The Ministry did not find the result alarming. (Erhvervs- og Vækstministeriet 2013). Neither of the two analyses includes how the house prices and the housing market would react.

On this basis it has to be maintained here that Danish owner-occupiers' are exposed to any large and especially fast interest rate increase. Together with the high debt-to-housing wealth and high debt-to-gross income levels observed, this indicates high risk and acts as a threat to financial stability over the coming years. New changes in taxation and in regulation may well be introduced. The central bank clearly wants to avoid a new 'housing bubble' arising from the current low interest rate regime and repeated its proposals in the recent economic survey for: (i) a reduction in the maximum LTV ratio for deferred amortisation loans (IOs), (ii) a reversal of the freeze on the property value tax to restore the link between property value tax and house prices and so help stabilise house prices, (iii) a reduction in the tax value of interest expenditure deductibility and (iv) changed conditions on the market for private and social rental housing (without mentioning the type of changes) (Dam *et al.* 2014). However, financial engineering could easily be used to create similar products, if access to mortgage loan products such as ARMs and IOs is reduced or even stopped.

Acknowledgements

The data for this chapter were made available by 'Lovmodelsekretariatet' of the Danish Ministry of Business and Growth. I am grateful for these data as well as for the important personal support, willingness and enthusiasm I have had from Nicolai S. Møller and Martin Ulrik Jensen, who have provided me with the basic statistics.

References

Abildgren, K and Thomsen, J (2011). A tale of two Danish banking crises. *Monetary Review 1st Quarter 2011*, Part 1, 121–141.

Andersen, AL, Christensen, AM, Nielsen, NF, Koob, SA, Oksbjerg, M and Kaarup, R (2012). The wealth and debt of Danish families. *Monetary Review 2nd Quarter 2012*, Part 2, 1–40.

Andersen, AL, Duus, C and Jensen, TL (2014). *Household debt and consumption during the financial crisis: Evidence from Danish micro data.* Danmarks Nationalbank Working Papers 2014: 89.

Association of Danish Mortgage Banks (various years). Realkreditrådets statistikker [Online]. Available: www.realkreditraadet.dk/Statistikker.aspx (accessed 22 July, 2015).

Campbell, JY (2012). Mortgage market design. *Review of Finance* 17, 1–33.

Dam, NA, Hvolbøl, TS and Rasmussen, MH (2014). A multi-speed housing market. *Danmarks Nationalbank, Monetary Review, 3rd Quarter 2014*, pp. 43–63.

The Danish FSA (2014). *Supervisory diamond for mortgage-credit institutions.* 11 September.

Danmarks Nationalbank (2015). *Monetary Review. 1st Quarter.*

Davis, EP (1995). *Debt Financial Fragility and Systemic Risk. Revised and Expanded Edition.* Clarendon Press, Oxford.

Erhvervs- og Vækstministeriet (2013). Gældsudgifter i husholdninger med realkreditlån. *Vækstpolitisk Tema, Nr. 2.*

Gyntelberg, J, Kjeldsen, K, Nielsen, MB and Persson, M (2012). *The 2008 Financial Crisis and the Danish Mortgage Market.* In: *Global Housing Markets. Crises, Policies, and Institutions,* Bardhan, A, Edelstein, RH, Kroll, CA (eds). Kolb Series in Finance, Miami, Florida, pp. 53–68.

Lea, M (2010). *Alternative Forms of Mortgage Finance: What Can We Learn From Other Countries?* Paper prepared for Harvard Joint Center for Housing Studies National Symposium. Harvard Business School. February 18, 2010 (revised April 14, 2010).

Lunde, J (2009). Boligcyklen i dyster fase: Boligprisernes vej ned ad en rutsjebane. *Finans/Invest.* 7:Oktober, 5–14.

Lunde, J (2012a). Husholdningsgælden – et dansk bidrag til gældskrisen? *Finans/Invest.* 6:September, 18–26.

Lunde, J (2012b). En analyse af de danske familiers gældsætning og finansielle sårbarhed. *Finans/Invest.* 7:November, 18–27.

Møller, M and Parum, C (2013). Den omstridte ejendomsværdiskat. *Finans/Invest,* 6/13:September, 6–13.

Pannell, B (2003). Denmark: Probably the best housing finance system in the world? *CML Housing Finance, Winter.*

Reinhart, C and Rogoff, KS (2009). *This Time Is Different: Eight Centuries of Financial Folly.* Princeton University Press: Princeton, New Jersey.

Statistic Denmark (various years). *Data for research* [Online] Available: www.dst.dk/en/TilSalg/Forskningsservice (accessed 22 July 2015).

8

Milestones in Housing Finance in England

Kathleen Scanlon[a] and Henryk Adamczuk[b]

[a] London School of Economics, London, UK
[b] Birmingham City University, Birmingham, UK

Introduction

In 1989, English housing finance providers were starting to take advantage of the freedoms afforded by financial deregulation in the 1970s and 1980s. The special circuit of housing finance based on retail deposits through building societies had already been dismantled and building societies were starting to demutualise and become banks. Securitisation had an increasing role in the mid-1980s. A range of mortgage types had been available since the early 1970s. Almost all mortgages were on variable rates. Interest rates and inflation were high – mortgage customers were paying up to 15 percent on new loans – but real house prices had just started a decline that would last 6 years.

By 2015, the landscape looked very different. An increasing proportion of owner-occupiers had no mortgage; building societies' dominance of the mortgage market had evaporated; most mortgage products had interest rates fixed in the short term and consumers increasingly used the internet and brokers to shop for mortgages. Mortgage tax relief had disappeared in 2000 and interest-only mortgages had all but disappeared. Since the Global Financial Crisis (GFC), wholesale funding markets have remained very limited, except when supported by the government. Tighter regulation has reinforced lenders' caution in the wake of the GFC, making access to mortgage finance more difficult for all but the lowest-risk borrowers – despite historically low interest rates.

Milestones in European Housing Finance, First Edition.
Edited by Jens Lunde and Christine Whitehead.
© 2016 John Wiley & Sons, Ltd. Published 2016 by John Wiley & Sons, Ltd.

The economic and institutional environment of the last 25 years

The 1980s saw deregulation of mortgage lending (and of financial services generally), but regulatory oversight grew increasingly stringent after 2000 and the GFC gave it added impetus. Lenders' behaviour towards consumers, formerly governed by an industry code of practice, was in 2004 brought formally into the regulatory ambit and since 2014 has been even more tightly constrained.

At the start of our quarter century, interest rates in England began to fall as inflation declined rapidly. From a high of nearly 15 percent in October 1989, the Bank of England reference rate fell to 6 percent in 1996. It then rose slightly and fell again; the figure (now called the Bank Rate) has not exceeded 6 percent since 2000. Remarkably, for 5 years since March 2009, the rate has been unchanged at 0.5 percent. Mortgage interest rates followed a similar trajectory; a borrower could expect to pay about 15 percent on a new loan in 1989, while today mortgages are available with initial rates below 1.5 percent – or even below 1 percent.

These declining interest rates did not enable a concomitant rise in owner-occupation: although the owner-occupation rate rose in the first half of the period, it has now fallen to almost exactly the same level as in 1989 (64 percent). Importantly, access to mortgage finance has grown more difficult in recent years, especially for first-time buyers.

Milestones in private housing finance

Table 8.1 presents our milestones in housing finance in chronological order. Each serves as a trigger for wider discussion about developments in a particular aspect of the mortgage landscape, and for that reason may appear

Table 8.1   Milestones in housing finance in England, 1988–2015.

Phase	Year	Milestone
Deregulation and expansion	1988	1. End of dual mortgage tax relief for unrelated couples
	1988	2. 1988 Housing Act introduces private finance for social housing
	1989	3. First building society becomes a bank
	1996	4. Introduction of 'Buy-to-Let' mortgages
	1999	5. Regulator addresses endowment mortgage mis-selling
	2000	6. Mortgage tax relief ended
Crisis	2008	7. Nationalisation of Northern Rock
Post-crisis and recovery	2010	8. Coalition government cuts capital investment for social housing and introduces the affordable rents regime
	2012	9. Funding for Lending scheme introduced
	2013	10. Help to Buy and guarantees introduced
	2014	11. The Mortgage Market Review comes into effect

in a slightly different order in the text. In particular, milestones 2 and 7, which relate to finance for social rather than private housing, are discussed in the next section.

Taxation

As early as 1974 the government started taking steps towards abolishing mortgage tax relief by limiting the amount on which it could be claimed, first at £25 000 and then from 1983 at £30 000 (Whitehead *et al.* 2005). However, interest payments were deductible at individuals' marginal rate of tax, and unmarried couples and individuals buying homes together could *each* receive mortgage relief.

Milestone 1 (1988): End of dual mortgage tax relief for unrelated couples   Our first milestone, in March 1988, was the announcement that the dual deductibility for unmarried couples would be withdrawn. There was a 5-month grace period between the announcement and the change in the regulation, which triggered a rush to beat the deadline and a massive incentive for unrelated individuals and couples to buy together. At the same time, it was announced that the basis of local property tax would change, breaking the link with property values and effectively reducing tax payments on higher-value homes. The combined effect of these two policy changes contributed to a surge in transactions and house prices. UK house prices, which had been rising more rapidly than inflation for most of the previous two decades, reached their peak in 1989, then fell in real terms for 6 years.

At the beginning of our period, tax relief was equivalent to about 19 percent of gross mortgage interest paid (Holmans and Whitehead 1998), but continued to be progressively whittled away. Higher-rate relief was abolished in 1991 and the rate of subsidy separated from the tax rate in 1994. By 2000 the relief had been entirely abolished for owner-occupiers (Milestone 6). It is still available for buy-to-let investors as they pay tax on net rents.

Industry structure and retail environment

In the 1970s, the mortgage market was dominated by building societies that had roots in the eighteenth century. These mutually owned institutions, often locally based, were limited to taking retail deposits and lending on housing. They were regulated separately from the banking system, which gave them certain tax advantages over banks and contributed to their domination of the market (they accounted for up to 96 percent of mortgages loans in the 1970s).

Successive pieces of legislation in the 1980s, culminating in the Building Societies Act 1986, allowed building societies to raise some funds on the wholesale market, provide more mainstream banking services and convert into banks on balloting their members (depositors and borrowers). Members tended to vote yes in light of the generous windfalls on offer; the average Halifax member, for example, received shares worth more than £2400 in the new bank. This gave building societies a route out of what many had increasingly perceived as a dead end.

Milestone 3 (1989): First building society becomes a bank   Our next milestone, in 1989, was Abbey National's transformation from building society to bank. Most other major lenders followed from 1995 onwards.

By 1997 the market share of banks (including these former building societies) exceeded that of building societies. But the institutional landscape was not vastly changed – the major players in the 1990s mortgage market were actually the same institutions as in the 1980s. Truly radical changes did come later as a result of the financial crisis (see next). Some societies chose not to convert: in 2013, five of the top 20 mortgage lenders by balances outstanding were building societies, including the third-largest (CML Table MM10).

Online transactions have become more important in the mortgage market, particularly in the initial shopping-around phase. Twenty-five years ago the home buyer would have sat at a desk in a building society or bank branch to discuss options with a salesperson – and probably paid no transaction fee. By 2014, many dealt not directly with mortgage lenders but rather with brokers – and paid high arrangement charges. The shift was for two reasons: first, the number of physical branches of banks and building societies fell dramatically in the last 25 years (Britain was considered to be very 'overbanked' in the 1970s) and indeed a number of lenders now have no physical retail outlets at all. Second, it became increasingly difficult for the average consumer independently to consider all the options, because the number of mortgage products offered has increased enormously – one product-comparison website listed 1794 mortgage products for home buyers, and 1634 for remortgages, in November 2014 (www.moneysupermarket.com).

The widespread use of information technology might have been expected to reduce the costs to the consumer of mortgage transactions, but instead they have risen. Lenders have increasingly competed for customers on the basis of 'headline' mortgage rates, and have therefore changed their pricing structures. Many loans now carry extra charges – on average around £1000. These fees generally do not vary by loan size, so are regressive in that they disproportionately affect borrowers taking out small mortgages. In addition, the typical new loan offers a low fixed or tracker interest rate for only a few years, after which the rate rises; borrowers who want to continue to pay low interest rates must remortgage and pay another set of fees.

Mortgage products

Until the mid-1990s, residential mortgages were aimed at owner-occupiers; specific financial products for would-be landlords became available with our next milestone.

Milestone 4 (1996): Introduction of 'buy-to-let' mortgages In 1996 a group of lenders introduced dedicated mortgages to fund the acquisition of rental property. Since the early nineteenth century the UK's private rented sector had been in long-term decline as households aspired to owner-occupation and rent controls depressed landlords' returns. The Housing Act of 1988 deregulated the private rental market, increasing the attractiveness of rented property as an investment, but prospective landlords still generally had to fund acquisitions by commercial loans or remortgaging their own homes.

In 1996 the Association of Residential Letting Agents (ARLA), in collaboration with a small group of mortgage lenders, announced a new type of loan to target this market: the buy-to-let mortgage. Buy-to-let lenders based mortgages not on the borrower's salary income but on the prospective rental income from the investment property. The following year, a change in the law made it easier for landlords to regain possession of their properties from tenants, further increasing the attractions of rented property as an investment.

Buy-to-let has now entered the language as a generic term, and the introduction of dedicated mortgages has been credited with turning rented property into a normal investment class for private individuals – in effect creating an entire new industry. In the first half of 1999 there were 58 800 outstanding buy-to-let mortgages (less than 1 percent of the market); by mid-2014, there were nearly 1.6 million, accounting for more than 14 percent of all loans. New buy-to-let lending fell sharply during the GFC but has since recovered to some degree.

The buy-to-let mortgage was the most important new product during the period, but not the only one – the UK market has long been one of the world's most innovative (Scanlon *et al.* 2008). The primary goal of many of these innovations was to reduce initial repayments. As Miles (2004) observes, many borrowers choose a loan on this basis but have a limited understanding of other product characteristics.

The early 2000s also saw strong growth in the proportion of interest-only loans. Such mortgages had long been a feature of the UK market in the form of endowment mortgages; what was new was the de-linking from specified repayment vehicles in the wake of the endowment 'scandal' (see next). By 2007, some 24 percent of new mortgages were interest-only loans with no specified repayment vehicle – but by 2013, in the wake of new regulations tightening access to mortgages (see next), only 4 percent of new loans for owner-occupiers were on an interest-only basis (CML Table ML6). This product type was still common for buy-to-let borrowers, for whom it remains tax-efficient.

Regulation

The typical mortgage customer 25 years ago would have been offered a choice between an endowment and an annuity mortgage, and the majority chose the endowment option. These were two-part products: first, an interest-only loan with a term of 25 years; second, a linked insurance policy or 'endowment', into which the borrower paid a set amount every month. This policy was operated not by the mortgage lender but by an outside fund manager, and invested mainly in stocks and shares. The idea was that when the loan matured the value of the insurance policy would permit the borrower to repay all or part of the principal with possibly a sum left over.

Milestone 5 (1999): Regulator addresses endowment mis-selling
Endowment mortgages were generally available from the early 1970s but became increasingly popular in the 1980s, peaking at 83 percent of new mortgages in 1989 before declining to a low of 12 percent in 2002 (CML ML6). The changing economic circumstances of the mid to late 1990s exposed the risks inherent in the model: the forecast rates of growth for the investments underlying the endowment turned out to be too high, and many borrowers found their maturing endowment policies did not cover the proportion of the mortgage principal they expected. There was a public and political outcry, and the lenders were accused of 'mis-selling'.

From 1999 providers were required to update borrowers regularly about the performance of their endowment policies, and specifically about the likelihood that they would not repay their mortgages. This was novel, as 'under the conditions of endowment policies, a policyholder is not legally entitled to know whether the investment is on track to repay the debt' (Financial Ombudsman Service 2001, quoted in Severn 2008). If a borrower could prove that the provider or adviser had not informed them of the risks inherent in endowment mortgages – or had not properly established their attitude to risk – they were entitled to compensation from the lender to put them in the position they would have been in had they instead taken out a repayment mortgage.

In all, around two million customers submitted complaints to their endowment providers, of whom a substantial number were successful. This led mortgage lenders to split the sale of investment policies from the sale of mortgages; interest-only loans were still available but mortgage lenders no longer required borrowers to have investment plans in place for repayment of the principal. This opened the door for consumers to take out interest-only loans *without* any particular plan for repaying the principal. This option was increasingly taken up from 2005, and by 2008 such loans accounted for a third of new mortgages and remortgages – clearly a highly risky position that only came to an end with the GFC.

Endowment policies were not the only products subject to mis-selling. Mortgage payment protection policies that insured against sickness, unemployment and other losses in income became popular in the mid-1990s encouraged, although not subsidised, by government in response to the 1989 crisis (Ford 2000). Take-up was quite high but by 2008 there were clear concerns about their attributes and the Financial Services Authority again stepped in.

While the 1980s and 1990s were a period of deregulation, by the early 2000s the pendulum had begun to swing back. In 2004 the mortgage industry's voluntary code was supplanted by an official rulebook, and in 2005 the Financial Services Authority (FSA) instituted the Mortgage Market Review (MMR), a wide-ranging examination of the mortgage lending practices of UK banks; this was given new impetus by the financial crisis (see next).

The financial crisis[1]

One of the remarkable stories of the first years of the twenty-first century was the rise of Northern Rock, which more than tripled its assets over a few years to become the country's fifth-largest mortgage lender. It began life as a building society but moved away from its roots to seek funding in the wholesale markets, and by June 2007 only 23 percent of its liabilities were retail deposits. The rest were securitised notes, funds from wholesale money markets and covered bonds – much of it borrowed on a short-term basis (Northern Rock 2008).

In 2007 rising defaults on US subprime mortgage loans caused problems in the market for US residential mortgage backed securities (RMBS). These spread rapidly to other countries as it emerged that many non-US institutions also held such assets. In mid-2007 Northern Rock found it could no longer re-finance its short-term debt. This was not a reflection of the quality of its loan book, which was relatively good, but rather the result of the near-collapse of the interbank lending market.

Milestone 6 (2008): The nationalisation of Northern Rock   On learning of Northern Rock's problems, the Bank of England arranged for a liquidity facility. News of this leaked, triggering a panic by depositors, who queued in their thousands at the bank's limited number of branches to withdraw their savings. In response the government guaranteed all deposits in Northern Rock, but was forced to nationalise the company in early 2008 in what was to be the first of a series of government rescues.

Mid-2007 represented the high point of the UK housing market. Transactions and then house prices fell dramatically after that. Lehman

Brothers declared bankruptcy in September 2008, marking the beginning of a financial crisis that affected institutions across the globe. The UK industry was badly affected and underwent massive upheavals in 2008 and 2009 with a wave of mergers (many officially encouraged or forced) and government take-overs (Whitehead and Scanlon 2012). Only Barclays and HSBC, of the top 10 lenders in 2006, were relatively unaffected. Some of the others were eventually absorbed by other firms. The government is still the majority shareholder in Royal Bank of Scotland and retains a substantial holding in Lloyds.

The centralised lenders that relied so heavily on securitisation and wholesale funds were particularly affected by the crisis, and many stopped new lending for a period of months or years. Mainstream lenders with access to retail funds turned to these, including in particular the repayment of existing mortgages, to maintain activity. Gross lending did not decline dramatically, since more than a million households still had to refinance short-term discounted fixed-rate mortgages (Croft 2007), but net lending collapsed almost completely.

Milestone 10 (2013): Introduction of 'Help to Buy' and other guarantees

Lending remained depressed for years after the crisis. In its 2013 Budget, the coalition government addressed the growing political issue of lack of access to mortgage finance. It introduced in England the 'Help to Buy' programme, which consisted of two schemes: first, a government equity loan of up to 20 percent of the value of a new home from April 2013 (now extended to 2020); second, a mortgage guarantee for purchasers with small deposits (at least 5 percent) from January 2014. The price ceiling for both components was set at £600 000, which covered the vast majority of housing transactions in the UK – in 2010, only about 6 percent of mortgage transactions were for properties worth more than £500 000 (DCLG Live Table 532). The equity loan was available only for new homes, but the mortgage guarantee could be used to purchase existing properties. There was no income limit for eligibility and purchasers did not have to be first-time buyers, but could not own other homes.

Critics questioned the wisdom of the government backing high LTV loans, particularly while at the same time the regulator was arguing, in the context of the Mortgage Market Review, that high LTVs were a strong indicator of risk. Economists were also concerned that the scheme might increase house prices rather than incentivise new supply.

Milestone 11 (2014): The Mortgage Market Review (MMR) comes into effect

The idea of the MMR was to 'ensure continued access to the mortgage market for the vast majority of customers who can afford it, while addressing the tail of poor mortgage lending seen in the past' (FSA 2012: p. 6). The new regime is paternalistic, substituting regulations for consumer decisions about what product would best suit them (except for the very wealthy, who are explicitly excluded). In April 2014, the date of our next milestone, the new rules took effect. They limit lenders' ability to offer some less conventional products. So-called self-certification mortgages (where the borrower does not have to provide proof of income), which made up almost half of new loans between 2007 and the first quarter of 2010 were effectively banned (Edmonds 2014: 5). Lenders can still offer interest-only loans but must ensure that borrowers could afford repayments on a standard annuity mortgage or have a credible strategy for repaying the principal. In assessing affordability of loan repayments, lenders now must take into account borrowers' other household expenditure as well as the possibility of future interest-rate rises.

Lenders had already adopted much more conservative lending policies in the wake of the GFC: loan-to-income and loan-to-value criteria were tightened significantly (100 percent LTV loans, once common, had disappeared completely by 2009). But more stringent affordability assessments led consumers to complain about intrusive questions, and the interest-rate stress tests mean some borrowers qualify for smaller mortgages than before – or do not qualify at all. The FSA estimated that the numbers affected would be small, but the trade body for mortgage lenders predicted a major impact. The system has been in place for less than a year, so it is too early for considered assessment, but worries that MMR rules may stifle growth in the market have not been alleviated.

Funding

Historically, UK mortgage lending was funded by retail deposits, but the deregulation of the sector in the 1980s opened the way for other funding models, including securitisation. The foundations for securitisation of mortgages in the UK were laid in 1986 with the passage of the Financial Services Act and the Building Societies Act. The process is as follows: a mortgage originator sells residential mortgages to a special-purpose vehicle, which then issues debt to investors. This debt is redeemed by the cash flow from the underlying mortgage pool in the form of RMBS. The concept was an American import first put into practice by subsidiaries of US banks, although procedures had to be tailored to the UK legal and tax system.

During the 1980s and 1990s specialised mortgage lenders dominated the securitisation market, but in the late 1990s more traditional lenders – in particular Abbey National and Northern Rock – became active (Holmans *et al.* 2003). Securitisation grew rapidly when first introduced in 1987 but then fell sharply because of changes in the UK housing market and decreases in the margins between mortgage rates and LIBOR (Pryke and Whitehead 1994). From the mid-1990s, though, the market again grew strongly, and 'between 2000 and 2007, the total amount outstanding of UK RMBSs and covered bonds rose from £13 billion to £257 billion, with growth in the amount outstanding in 2006 alone amounting to £78 billion' (Crosby 2008b: 12).

US investors became the main overseas purchasers of UK RMBS; they bought 31 percent of those issued between 2005 and 2007, compared to 34 percent for UK investors (Crosby 2008b). This opening-up of UK mortgage funding to an international market was initially welcomed, but it left the UK industry vulnerable to contagion when the US subprime market collapsed. Faced with essentially closed markets, specialist non-bank lenders almost stopped making new mortgage loans; of 10–12 specialist lenders in 2007, only about three were still accepting new business in late 2008 (Crosby 2008a).

Milestone 9 (2012): Funding for Lending Scheme (FLS) introduced In 2012, concerned by the continued weakness of lending to households and businesses, including mortgage lending, the UK Treasury and the Bank of England announced the Funding for Lending Scheme (FLS). Banks and building societies were allowed to borrow Treasury bills at below-market rates for extended periods and then they could raise cash by employing them as collateral for borrowing or substituting them for their own reserves. The goal was to reduce the cost of funds and increase lending to the 'real economy'. To incentivise new lending, the scheme was structured so institutions that increased lending paid lower interest rates. Each eligible lender could borrow up to 5 percent of their outstanding loan portfolio, plus the amount of net new lending over an 18-month period.

Bank calculations suggested that at the time of introduction, the cost of funds under FLS was about 100 basis points below market (Churm *et al.* 2012). However, they recognised that there was no certain link between loan rates and the cost of funding. Other concerns were (i) that the scheme crowded out normal borrowing and a return to normalisation through vanilla securitisation and the use of covered bonds; (ii) that indebtedness to the Bank of England had to be unwound, leaving the market short of funds in the medium term.

Milestones in social and affordable housing finance

This section discusses how developments in the financing of social and affordable housing over the last quarter-century have framed the social sector of today.

In 1989 local authorities were still the dominant providers of social housing in the UK with 23 percent of the total stock, down from 33 percent in 1980. Housing associations were just emerging as social providers with 3 percent of the stock. Right to buy, introduced by the Conservative government of

1979, was the main source of this decline together with capital spending reductions (Pawson and Mullins 2010). Borrowing by local authorities counted as public sector borrowing and was subject to Treasury cash limits, whereas housing associations fell outside the public borrowing and accounting regime. These changes meant almost all new social-housing development would be done by associations.

Milestone 2 (1988): The Housing Act introduces private finance for social housing   The Housing Act 1988 changed the basis on which new social housing was financed. The average 85 percent up-front government grant was replaced with lower rates of grant topped up by borrowing on the private finance market. Associations were regulated by the Housing Corporation (now the Homes and Communities Agency) but there were no government guarantees as existed, for instance, in The Netherlands.

The 1988 Act also gave housing associations powers to set their own rents to cover costs up to market levels. This was underpinned by the continued availability of housing benefit for tenants on low incomes, which was available to both social and private landlords. Local authorities were also permitted to transfer their stock to newly-created regulated provider landlords if residents voted in favour, in a process known as Large-Scale Voluntary Transfers (LSVTs), although the earliest transfers pre-date this Act.

Through building new homes and transfer from local authorities, the housing association sector grew from 3 to 11 percent of the English housing stock over the period 1988–2013. The sector is very diverse, ranging from specialist agencies to generalist groups with development and management arms. There are about 1500 active associations. Of these, 339 large organisations own or manage at least 1000 social homes and account for more than 95 percent of the sector's 2.6 million units (HCA 2014).

Traditional providers grew through development and acquisition, financed partly by social housing grant and partly by private finance. The debt profiles of Large Scale Voluntary Transfer (LSVT) providers are different: they were debt financed when created, then re-financed in accordance with their business plans.

Housing associations have been active in developing new tenure models, both to meet housing needs and to provide income for their social activities. With shared ownership, for example, purchasers buy a proportion of the equity in a property, pay rent to the association on the remainder and may staircase up to 100 percent ownership. Later shared equity models were introduced that depend upon a government-supported equity loan. Associations are now becoming active in the private rented sector as well as building for sale, as government grant continues to be reduced.

Housing associations have had few difficulties in raising private finance. Interest rates, initially some 2 percent above LIBOR, fell to as little as

30 basis points above, very similar to the rates achieved in The Netherlands with government guarantees (Whitehead 1999). The financial crisis had a short-term impact on their borrowing capacity as banks restructured their portfolios and tried to increase interest rates on new borrowing. However, associations have increasingly raised funds through the bond market – where interest rates remain very low – often obtaining up to AAA ratings from the major agencies. By 2013, £73.5 bn of private finance had been raised, half through the capital market in the form of bonds (HCA 2014).

Milestone 8 (2010): Coalition cuts back capital grants and introduces the 'affordable rent' regime Social landlords traditionally offered secure tenancies at rents well below market levels. Affordable rent tenancies were a new model introduced in 2010. These tenancies had shorter, fixed terms, with rents higher than social rents – up to a maximum of 80 percent of market rent. These were supported by much lower grants – around £20 000 per unit as compared to around £50 000 per new-build social dwelling in 2008–2011. Associations meet the gap through borrowing, using reserves and cross-subsidising from outright sales and equity sales. In essence, the affordable rent model replaces capital subsidy for social housing with revenue subsidy through housing benefit, which is paid to some two-thirds of housing association tenants.

Linked to the new regime was a further policy change, which falls under Milestone 10: the Affordable Housing Guarantee Scheme. This scheme, introduced in 2012, guarantees borrowing to provide affordable rented housing and lowers the costs of that borrowing. A similar scheme was introduced to support private rented sector development.

In 2014 the Homes and Communities Agency, which regulates the sector, was very positive about the outlook. The gross book value of housing association properties increased by £9.1 billion to £118.6 bn, while capital grants had increased by £641 mn (1.5 percent) to £43.8 bn. But long-term loans had increased by much more (£4.4 bn, or 8 percent, to £47.9 bn) and as new development attracts less grant, housing associations that intend to develop must generate greater surpluses from existing operations (HCA 2014).

Impacts

The private financing of the housing association sector is generally considered to be a success story. There have been no bankruptcies, though lapses of management have been identified and weak associations have been encouraged to merge by the regulator. The largest 250 associations own over two million homes, a greater concentration than under the local authority housing models before 1980. The difference is that most large associations hold stock across regions and sometimes across the whole country.

Although housing associations have responded to the new affordable rent model in the current funding cycle, there are questions as to whether it will erode their capacity to maintain output levels as grants are cut further. The main concern must be that over 50 percent of housing association income comes from housing benefit and the current government is trying to limit that bill.

Developments in the financing of private housing have been more complex and less tied to government policy. The mortgage system sits at the nexus between the wider financial services industry, the housing market and the economy as a whole. Changes in the mortgage landscape therefore often reflect developments well outside the narrowly drawn borders of the industry itself. Mortgage lending is also cyclical. Thus at the beginning of our period, in 1989, interest rates were high, but so was mortgage borrowing. Now demand is far lower and credit heavily constrained, even though interest rates are very low.

This cyclicality is evident in the development in mortgage transactions since 1989 (Figure 8.1). The amount of new loans was flat during the house-price decline of the early 1990s, then rose to a peak in 2007 before dropping dramatically in 2008 and 2009. The immediate cause was the GFC, which reduced house prices (and expectations about house prices), slashed lenders' appetite for risk, and led regulators to adopt a much more paternalistic and prescriptive approach to mortgage lending.

We are now six years on from the worst of the crisis and house prices have recovered in much (though not all) of England – and in London and the

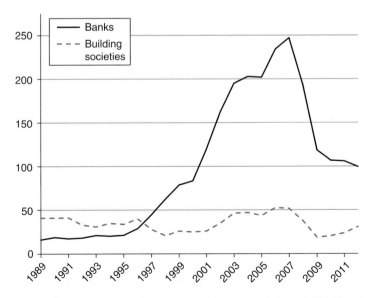

Figure 8.1 New mortgage advances by type of lender, 1989–2012 (£ billions).
Source: CML Tables MM4 and MM8.

South East – have exceeded earlier peaks. The economy is returning to health and the population is growing faster than in most European countries. Interest rates are at historic lows and the expectation is that they will not increase for at least a year. There is no lack of appetite for house purchase; the vast majority of households aspire to own their own homes. Yet, new mortgage lending remains far below pre-crisis levels (Figure 8.1 and Figure 8.2).

The reason is prudence (or fear, depending on your point of view). Lenders and regulators alike feared a repetition of the lax lending practices that contributed to the financial crisis. The new MMR rules eliminate many of the mortgage types that first-time buyers relied on: pure interest-only, high-LTV and self-certification loans. The rule also mandated a much more stringent assessment of loan affordability – one that excludes many potential buyers. These rules were arguably redundant, at least initially, as lenders themselves had already become dramatically more conservative in their underwriting practices.

Housing and pensions are the two largest financial assets of most households. The rule changes under the MMR reduce consumer choice; the explicitly paternalistic rationale was that borrowers did not understand the risks and could not be trusted to make the best decisions. At the same time, however, dramatic changes in pension regulations, which took effect in April 2015, give consumers much *more* control over the use of their pension funds. Many will no longer be required to buy an annuity and can even withdraw the entire balance as a cash lump sum. This is being heralded as a brave and common-sense reform even though research indicates that consumers understand even less about pensions than they do about mortgages (Franklin and Creighton 2015).

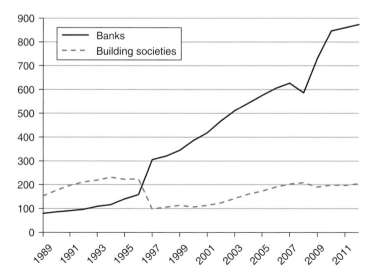

Figure 8.2 Mortgage balances outstanding by type of lender, 1989–2012 (£ billions).
Source: CML Tables MM4 and MM8.

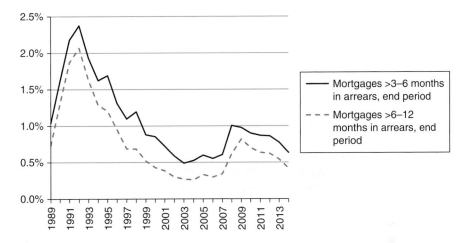

Figure 8.3   Arrears, 1989–2013.
Source: CML Table AP1.
*Mortgages between 3 and 6 months in arrears 1989–1993 input by author.

It should be noted that this caution was *not* triggered by a sharp increase in possessions, which despite expectations, did not rise much in the most recent financial crisis. In the housing market downturn that marked the beginning of this period (1989–1996), interest rates were high and possessions spiked (Figure 8.3). But in recent years interest rates remained low, which meant that those who kept their jobs could generally afford to pay their mortgages. The low possession rate also reflected widespread lender forbearance.

Figure 8.4 shows that the proportion of households with mortgages fell across all age groups in the last decade, but most markedly for younger cohorts – the proportion of 25–34-year-olds with mortgages dropped by more than 20 percentage points, from 56 to 34 percent. The size of the down payment now required to enter the housing market in many parts of England is prohibitive for many young people. The average age of a first-time buyer in England has risen to 30 and 32 in London (Halifax 2015). A high proportion of those who buy do so with parental help.

The English mortgage system is one of the world's most developed. In the early 1990s, a report by Diamond and Lee for Fannie Mae suggested that the UK system was the best developed praising it for its responsiveness to demand and robustness in the face of housing market volatility (Diamond and Lea 1992). A report by consultants Mercer Oliver Wyman (2003) rated it against several benchmarks, including 'product completeness' (the range of mortgage products offered), finding that UK lenders offered a wider range of products than in most other countries.

Some features of the English product offer seem resistant to change. Despite Miles' finding in 2004 that many households would on reasonable

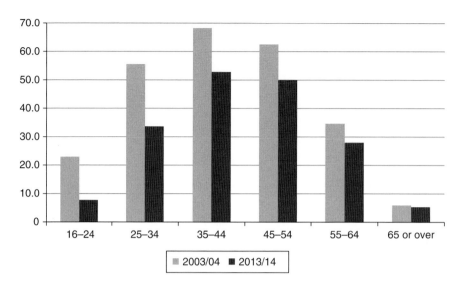

Figure 8.4 Households with mortgages as percent of all households by age group, 2003/04 and 2013/14.
Source: English Housing Survey (2013/14).

assumptions be better off with long-term fixed-rate mortgages (Miles 2004), there is still little appetite for these products, common in countries such as the USA and Denmark. While there has been some increase in uptake of fixed-rate loans, the fixes are short (1–5 years). UK borrowers have yet to be convinced by the merits of the long-term fix, especially because short-term rates are so low and past evidence shows they have often been better value if higher risk. For those who manage to assemble a down payment, the ongoing cost of owner-occupation can be much lower than rents in the private rented sector.

The mortgage-lending industry is now more concentrated than it was in 1989, and no longer dominated by building societies (although many of the leading lenders were once building societies). The government still has major holdings in large lenders that were bailed out during the financial crisis, including 23.9 percent of Lloyds Banking Group, the UK's largest mortgage lender in 2015. This is already changing as the government sells its share holdings, and in any case the lending behaviour of these firms does not appear to differ markedly from competitors.

Looking to the future

The owner-occupation rate in England has been falling since 2003 and is likely to continue to do so (Figure 8.5). Tightened mortgage availability is one of the drivers, though far from the only factor.

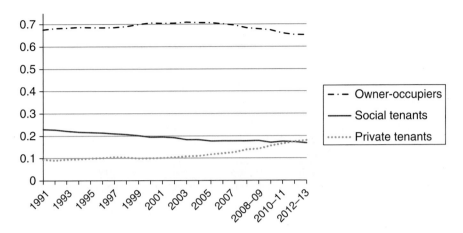

Figure 8.5 Housing tenure in England, 1980–2013/14.
Source: English Housing Survey (2013/14).

Interestingly, there has been a marked change in the composition of owner-occupiers. Two years ago, the number of outright owners exceeded those buying with a mortgage for the first time. Again, mortgage availability is not the only – or even the main – factor at play: this also shows the increase in the cohort of (usually older) owner-occupiers who have paid off their mortgages.

A continued fall in owner-occupation has implications that go beyond the housing market. Owner-occupied homes, together with pensions, are the major stores of wealth for most English households. It has long been the expectation that older people can draw on this wealth to cover the costs of care in old age, and to supplement their pensions. To the extent that tighter conditions on mortgage finance constrain access to owner-occupation and indeed to remortgages, this will have widespread effects on the economies of individual households as they age, as well as on government finances.

Lastly, it is inevitable that interest rates will eventually begin to rise. When they do, borrowers with long-term fixed rate mortgages may (finally) look prescient. Even a small increase will be large in percentage terms, since rates are so low. Nevertheless, most recent borrowers should be able to cope with a rate rise because of the precautionary stance forced on lenders by the MMR. The bigger effect will be on house prices, as higher interest rates feed through to monthly payments. Consumers will be able to borrow less, putting downward pressure on house prices. In overall economic terms this would be a good thing.

Note

1   This section draws on Whitehead and Scanlon (2012), which offers a fuller exploration of the events of the GFC as they affected the English mortgage market.

References

Churm, R, Leake, J, Radia, A and Srinivasan, S (2012). The Funding for Lending Scheme, *Bank of England Quarterly Bulletin.*

Council of Mortgage Lenders (CML) (various years). Online Statistical Tables [Online] Available at: www.cml.org.uk (accessed July 2015).

Croft, J (2007). Time bomb for 1 million mortgagors, *Financial Times* 2 June 2007.

Crosby, J (2008a). *Mortgage Finance: Interim Analysis.* HM Treasury, London.

Crosby, J (2008b). *Mortgage Finance: Final Report and Recommendations.* HM Treasury, London.

Department of Communities and Local Government (DCLG) (various years). Live Statistical Tables. [Online] Available: www.gov.uk/government/statistical-data-sets/live-tables-on-housing-market-and-house-prices (accessed July 2015).

Diamond, D and Lea, M (1992). The decline of special circuits in developed country housing finance, *Housing Policy Debate* 3(3): 747–777.

Edmonds, T. (2014). Mortgage Market Review. House of Commons Library Standard Note SN/BT/5808 [Online] Available at: www.parliament.uk/briefing-papers/sn05808.pdf (accessed 24 July, 2015).

English Housing Survey (2013/14). Online Datasets [Online] Available at: http://data.gov.uk/dataset/english_housing_survey (accessed 24 July, 2015).

Financial Ombudsman Service (2001). *Annual Review 2000/2001.*

Financial Services Authority (FSA) (2012). Mortgage Market Review: Feedback on CP11/31 and final rules. Policy Statement 12/16 [Online] Available at: www.fsa.gov.uk/static/pubs/policy/ps12-16.pdf (accessed 29 July 2015).

Ford, J (2000). MPPI take-up and retention – the current evidence, *Housing Finance* 45, Council of Mortgage Lenders: London.

Franklin, B and Creighton, H (2015). Making the system fit for purpose: How consumer appetite for secure retirement income could be supported by the pension reforms. International Longevity Centre, UK [Online] Available at: www.ilcuk.org.uk/images/uploads/publication-pdfs/Pensions_Reform_Report_Web_(final).pdf (accessed 24 July, 2015).

Halifax (2015). Number of first-time buyers in 2014 at highest since 2007. [Online] Available at: www.lloydsbankinggroup.com/globalassets/150106-ftb-annual-review-final.pdf (accessed 24 July, 2015).

Holmans, A and Whitehead, C (1998). *Housing Subsidies and Tax Reliefs for British Households,* Council of Mortgage Lenders, London.

Holmans, A, Karley, K and Whitehead, C (2003). *The mortgage backed securities market in the UK: overview and prospects.* Housing Research Summary, No 201, Office of the Deputy Prime Minister, 2003.

Homes and Communities Agency (HCA) (2014). *Global Accounts of Housing Providers* [Online] Available at: www.gov.uk/government/uploads/system/uploads/attachment_data/file/370753/global_accounts_2013_full.pdf (accessed 24 July, 2015).

Mercer Oliver Wyman (2003). *Study on the Financial Integration of European Mortgage Markets.* EMF, Brussels.

Miles, D (2004). *The Miles Review: The UK Mortgage Market: Taking a longer-term view. Final report and recommendations.* HM Treasury, London.

Northern Rock (2008). *Annual report and Accounts 2007* [Online] Available at: www.n-ram.co.uk/~/media/Files/N/NRAM-PLC/documents/corporate-reports/2007-annual-report.pdf (accessed 29 July 2015).

Pawson, H and Mullins, D (2010). *After Council Housing: Britain's New Landlords.* Palgrave MacMillan.

Pryke, M and Whitehead, C (1994). An overview of mortgage-backed securitisation in the UK. *Housing Studies* 9:1, 75–101.

Scanlon, K, Lunde, J and Whitehead, C (2008). Mortgage product innovation in advanced econo-mies: more choice, more risk, *International Journal of Housing Policy* 2008: 2.

Severn, D (2008). *The Financial Ombudsman Service and mortgage endowment complaints* London: FOS [Online] Available at: www.financial-ombudsman.org.uk/assets/pdf/DavidSevernReport.pdf (accessed 24 July 2015).

Whitehead, CME (1999). The provision of finance for social housing: The UK experience. *Urban Studies* 36: 657–672.

Whitehead, C, Gibb, K and Stephens, M (2005). *Evaluation of English Housing Policy 1975–2000 Theme 2: Finance and Affordability*. HMSO, London.

Whitehead, C and Scanlon, K (2012). Europe's selective housing bubble: The UK. In: *Global Housing Markets: Crises, Institutions and Policies*, Bardhan, A, Edelstein, R and Kroll, C (eds), John Wiley & Sons, Inc., Hoboken, NJ.

9

Milestones in Housing Finance in Finland

Timo Tähtinen and Tommi Laanti
Ministry of the Environment, Department of the Built Environment, Finland

Introduction

In Finland in the mid-1980s universal banks were the main mortgage lenders although the government also had an important role as a lender. Finland's financial markets were tightly regulated. The supply of finance for households was limited. The mortgages available had short maturities, about 5–8 years, and a typical loan-to-value ratio (LTV) was between 50 and 80 percent. On the other hand, mortgage interest payments were deductible from high marginal tax rates, and there was a high inflation environment. Consequently, there was a large amount of unsatisfied credit demand. In the mid-1980s about 63 percent of Finns were owner-occupiers.

Today housing finance is readily available. Mortgages are almost entirely provided by universal banks, of which the two largest OP-Pohjola Group and Nordea Bank together have a market share of almost 70 percent. The mortgage maturity is typically 20–25 years and the LTV is typically 70 percent, although loans up to 100 percent are possible. The government, which used to grant housing loans itself, offers partial state guarantees for household mortgages. The proportion of Finns who are owner-occupiers, at 65 percent, is little higher than in the 1980s.

The changes began in the mid-1980s with the liberalisation of the financial markets. The immediate consequence was a credit boom, which led to rapid economic growth and to an economic and housing market bubble. The boom soon turned into an economic downturn in the early 1990s, which hit

Milestones in European Housing Finance, First Edition.
Edited by Jens Lunde and Christine Whitehead.
© 2016 John Wiley & Sons, Ltd. Published 2016 by John Wiley & Sons, Ltd.

Finland exceptionally hard and led to the collapse of asset values and to record high unemployment levels. During the recession of the early 1990s Finland joined the European Exchange Rate Mechanism (ERM), made a major tax reform and liberalised the rental market. The development of housing finance continued; a state guarantee system for mortgages was introduced in 1996, and Finland joined the Economic and Monetary Union (EMU) in 1998, placing further downward pressure on general interest rates. The abolition of stamp duty on mortgages in 1998 opened the way for increased competition among banks for mortgage customers and led to longer maturities and lower margins. Finland enjoyed strong economic growth from 1995 until the financial crisis of 2008. This steadily increased the demand for owner-occupied housing. The financial crisis of 2008 and the subsequent increase in banking supervision have turned the clock back. Banks have become more conservative in their lending policies and have both increased their interest rate margins and now look more carefully at individual borrowers.

Key milestones

Over the last 30 years, housing and housing finance have been shaped by a number of institutional and policy changes. These changes, or milestones, can be categorised as being related to deregulation and reform of the housing finance market, to housing and fiscal policy and to the economic environment (Table 9.1).

Deregulation, boom and collapse: 1985–1995

Until the middle of the 1980s both banks' deposit rates and lending rates were linked to the Bank of Finland's base rate, which itself was very low in real terms. The Bank of Finland controlled the banks' liquidity with quotas and penalty rates on marginal funding. The banks applied credit rationing to their customers. Homebuyers needed to save up to 20–50 percent of the price of the dwelling in a bank's saving account before getting a mortgage. The maturity of the loans was only 5–8 years.

The regulation on banks' lending rates and mortgage pricing was abolished in 1986 and foreign capital movements were liberalised. A year later the Bank of Finland ceased to give guidelines for, for example, pre-saving requirements, further enhancing mortgage market competition. In January 1988 mortgage interest rates were allowed to be linked to market interest rates, whereas they had previously been tied to the central bank's base rate (Booth *et al.* 1994). This led to HELIBOR-rates (Helsinki EURIBOR) becoming the most popular interest rates to which to tie mortgage interest rates.

Table 9.1 Milestones.

	Housing finance market	Housing and fiscal policy	Economic environment
Years 1985–1989	Abolition of interest rate controls and shift to free pricing of mortgages (1986) Bank of Finland ceased to give guidelines on e.g. pre-saving (1987) Mortgages could be linked to market interest rates (earlier to Bank of Finland's base rate) (1988)		Economic boom (1988–1990)
Years 1990–95	Legislation for household debt settlement was introduced (1993)	Rents on new contracts were freed from rent control (1992) Tax reform: mortgage interest payments were no longer directly deductible from income, and covered only 25% of the interest payments (1993) Old rent contracts were freed from rent control (1995)	Recession (1990–1993), which led to 18% unemployment (in 1994), collapse of housing production and house price crash
Years 1996–2007	The legislation for covered bonds was changed (1999, 2003, 2010) Maturities on mortgages began to lengthen (around 2000)	A partial state guarantee was introduced for mortgages (1996) Stamp duty was removed from mortgages (1998) Non-profit legislation was introduced for social housing (1999)	There was strong economic growth during the whole period, led by the mobile phone industry (Nokia). The Finnish currency joined the ERM system (1996) and the Euro in 1999. House prices began to increase in 1996 and continued to do so almost continuously until 2008.
Year 2008–	The banks' funding became more difficult; lending was reduced and loan margins were increased. Financial supervisory authority issued guidelines to lower the risks of mortgage finance (2010) Legislation on binding LTV ratios comes into force (2015)	A rise in free market rental housing investments (from around 2008) The existing first-time buyer subsidy system (ASP) was improved (2009) Phasing out of the mortgage tax relief system began (2012) The transfer tax for house purchases was increased and the tax base widened (2013)	Financial market crisis hit Finland in the autumn of 2008. Interest rates went up and economic growth became heavily negative in 2009 and again in 2012 and 2013. The demand for owner-occupied housing slowed down and demand for rental housing increased.

These changes increased the availability of housing finance significantly; even 100 percent loans became possible. Loan maturities also lengthened, but only somewhat, to 10–12 years. The change benefited the banks, which could not only increase their lending but also lower their funding costs and risks as the mortgages became tied to market based interest rates. The banks, however, put too much weight on increasing their mortgage business and far too little on the risks of doing so.

The changes also benefited the borrowers, as loan maturities grew longer and in particular it became possible to take larger mortgages with lower saving requirements or without any pre-savings at all. As a result the housing market became 'crazy', and in 1988 there were almost 60 000 first-time purchases, which is three to six times the average amount. The stock of housing loans increased in 1988 by 24 percent and in 1989 by 16 percent. These were very significant figures given the short loan maturities and large amortisations on existing loans. Jännäri and Koskenkylä (1995) discuss the reasons for the boom (existence of unsatisfied credit demand, growth strategies of the banks, lack of control and supervision, lack of political will etc.) and argue that similar experiences after deregulation took place in other countries, most notably other Nordic countries at the same time.

An economic boom followed the deregulation in 1988–1989 with very high employment levels, rising consumption and falling savings ratios. Residential construction was booming and house prices skyrocketed. The boom turned into a bust in 1991. Finland's GDP growth was negative from 1991 to 1993 declining by 12 percent over that period. Unemployment increased from 3.2 percent in 1990 to 16.4 percent in 1994. At the same time Finland faced a bank crisis and a real estate market crash, with house prices dropping by nearly 50 percent.

After the crash, the banks changed their lending policies and became more conservative; personal sureties were no longer accepted and LTVs dropped to between 60 and 80 percent of value. Obviously, this further weakened the housing market. Forced sales increased significantly and remained at a high level until 1996. In many cases households still had debt left after the sale. Personal sureties given to guarantee other persons' mortgages also caused large problems during the recession as the guarantor was made to pay in the case of the borrower's default. Where there were debt payment difficulties, legislation in 1993 made it possible to agree a debt settlement. It also made it possible to retain one's own home if the indebtedness solely arose from the mortgage and the settlement was financially viable. Debt settlements were used most actively between 1994 and 1997. The state also paid interest subsidies to households with serious mortgage payment difficulties. Both measures helped to save homes.

The deregulation of the rental market in the first half of 1990s helped to revive the free rental market, which had suffered from rent controls since 1967. Deregulation took place during the recession and its effect was an immediate increase in the availability of free market rental dwellings. From 1990 to 2000 the number of free market rental dwellings grew by more than 100 000 units, while the number of owner-occupied dwellings stayed roughly the same in the aftermath of the recession. The proportion of free market rental dwellings in the total stock increased from 11 to 15 percent over the decade. In addition, counter cyclical support measures were given during the recession to state supported social housing production, which led to an increase in the supply of social rental housing.

The fact that interest payments were income tax deductible at high marginal tax rates was an important factor affecting mortgage demand in the 1980s right up to the housing boom at the end of the decade, because it led to negative real after-tax interest rates for the whole of the period. During the recession, the tax system was reformed extensively and from 1993 onwards only 25 percent of mortgage interest payments were deductible. The percentage was set at 30 percent for first-time buyers as an additional subsidy. Importantly, they were deducted from the tax payable, which lowered the impact of the subsidy considerably, especially for high-income earners. Saarimaa (2010) found that high-income groups (who had very high marginal tax rates) responded by reducing their mortgage borrowing. The general principles remain in place but the percentages have changed slightly in line with the tax rate for capital income taxation. Landlords can also deduct the interest payments from their capital income. Only housing related loans are tax deductible.

Strong economic growth and improving mortgage availability: 1996–2007

Economic growth slowly picked up in the mid-1990s. After the recession, growth was fast and remained so until 2008. Real GNP grew a staggering 72 percent in the years 1994–2007 while the unemployment rate dropped from 16.4 percent to 6.4 percent. The key to economic growth in this period was the success of Nokia (a mobile phone company) and the electronics industry around it. Rapid economic growth and rising incomes played a major role in increasing owner-occupied housing demand.

The weakness of the Finnish currency was reflected in high interest rates during the early 1990s. Finland joined the European Community in 1995 and the EU movement towards a common currency provided Finland with a way to restore the creditworthiness of its currency and lower these high interest rates. The Finnish mark was added into the ERM in 1996 and Finland joined the Euro in 1999. Much of the low interest rate environment ever since can be credited to the existence of the ERM and later the EMU and the Euro.

The demand for owner-occupied housing stayed low for many years because of high unemployment but also because the banks had turned to more conservative lending practises. In 1996 a partial state guarantee was introduced for mortgages, with the aim of substituting this for personal sureties (which had resulted in individual bankruptcies among guarantors) and improving the functioning of the housing market. There is a one-time guarantee fee, which was originally 1.5 percent of the guaranteed amount and has later been increased to 2.5 percent. The guarantee covers a maximum of 20 percent of the loan (the most risky part). There is also a maximum value of the guarantee. The guarantee was popular from the beginning. Based on a survey of home purchases in 2001, the state guarantee was used in 29 percent of purchases and in the case of first-time buyers the share was as high as 54 percent (Johnson and Tarkoma 2004). Although commercial alternatives were gradually developed, the state guarantee has remained important and in 2012 there were still state guarantees on mortgages worth some €12 bn (15 percent of all mortgages). So far, the guarantee losses have been very small in comparison to collected fees, but have been slowly increasing in recent years.

One small fiscal policy change stands out in this period as having a large impact on housing finance. Because Finnish mortgages are over-whelmingly tied to short-term interest rates, their amortisation is typically very flexible and the mortgage can be paid off in full at almost any time. When in 1998 stamp duty was removed from mortgage agreements, it removed a major transaction cost associated with changing the mortgage lender. This opened the way for increased competition in housing finance. It became typical to shop around when taking a new or larger mortgage but also while servicing an existing mortgage. At the same time banks began to collect service payments on services that used to be offered for free and new saving instruments were introduced. As a result, banks could further lower their margins, as they had created other sources of income. Consequently, banks began actively to attract customers with mortgage offers as having a large customer base increased in importance. Partly for this reason, house purchase numbers picked up by some 30 percent in the early years of the century and were at their highest in the years between 2005 and 2008.

Legislation regarding the ownership of social housing by non-profit organisations was introduced in 1999. The legislation defined the scope of social housing and set limits on the profits that could be made and how they could be used. The aim was to ensure funds were used in the social housing sector and to improve the viability of social housing providers. This legislation, together with the rise of business-oriented rental housing provision has gradually led to a major change in the ownership of rental housing. The largest non-profit operators have gradually turned more and more towards the free rental market sector, because their owners are increasingly looking for returns on their investments and the legislation limited their profits and actions within social housing. The social sector is now mainly based on municipally owned operators. Social housing used to be financed by state loans through the Housing Fund of Finland. During the recession in the 1990s, the state moved towards providing state guarantees to enable market financing to be employed more heavily. Since 2007 social housing has been financed solely by financial institutions with the state providing a guarantee for the loan. The Housing Fund of Finland acts as the guarantor of the loan and may also pay interest subsidies and in some cases grants for the borrower.

The financial market crisis and a weak economy: 2008–present

Interest rate levels started to increase in 2006, but the economy, especially in terms of construction, remained strong until 2008. Demand for owner-occupied housing gradually declined, but it was only in the early autumn of 2008 that this lack of demand started to lead to new housing projects being put on hold. Banks began to have problems in funding because of the global financial market crisis and general interest rate levels jumped upwards. The economic slowdown led to a decline in GDP of 8.3 percent in 2009.

In the housing sector, counter cyclical measures were directed at rental housing production during the years 2009–2011. This led to new operators entering the market. The high returns on free rental market investments have also had an impact and new housing funds have been set up in order to invest in rental housing production. The slow-down in owner-occupied housing production also forced building companies to look for new customers and the rental housing funds have benefited from this.

There was an immediate rebound in economic growth in 2010 and 2011. The owner-occupied housing market, after an initial price drop in the winter of 2008–2009, also recovered rapidly contrary to the experience in many other European countries (Marrez and Pontuch 2013). Economic recovery and record low mortgage interest rates (about 2 percent for new loans since 2010) revived the owner-occupied housing market and house pricess continued to climb towards new records, which were reached in 2013. The number of sales, however, did not recover, but remained some 15 percent below the years before the financial crises. Because the economy remains weak and has been further affected by the Crimean crises in 2014, nominal house prices turned slightly downwards in 2014.

The financial crisis also led to changes in how banks and the mortgage market operate. The worldwide concern over excessive debt led to discussions about new rules, and this has had an impact on Finland. Funding for mortgages had been based on general bank funding, that is, customer deposits, short-term loans and bonds. Customer deposits had been by far the most important source of funding. This has now changed as a result of the growth in covered bonds.

The legislation for covered bonds was improved in 1999, 2003 and especially in 2010 in order to expand the banks' longer term funding opportunities. In 2004 there were practically no covered bonds issued, but since then the market has been gradually increasing. The banks have set up subsidiaries, which use covered (residential) bonds as a funding method. The legislation of 2010 broadened and deepened the market and the stock of covered bonds has more than doubled since to 26 million in the 2013, about 30 percent of mortgage lending. At the same time short term funding has been declining. This way the banks are preparing for new rules that require the maturity of the funding to better match the maturity of lending.

The Financial Supervisory Authority has in recent years been concerned about consumer protection as well as the risks faced by banks. One area of concern has been the lending practises of the banks with regard to mortgages. The authority issued guidelines in 2010 with regard to lending practises. These included that banks should not in general use higher than 90 percent LTVs and should make scenario calculations on debt servicing based on 6 percent interest rates. In 2011 the financial supervisory authority found in its survey that 44 percent of first-time buyer mortgages had a LTV higher than 100 percent (Palmroos and Nokkala 2011). High LTVs were found also in some cases where the borrower had poor ability to pay. Interest rate margins were also not correlated with the credit risk of the borrower. Consequently, there was room for improvement in risk management.

Mortgage tax relief began to be phased out gradually in 2012, so that by 2018 only 50 percent of interest payments will be taken into account when making the deduction. At the same time mortgage tax relief has lost its importance because of the low interest rate level.

There has been a subsidy system for the first-time buyers since 1982. It is based on pre-savings, on which the banks pay an above market interest rate, and an interest subsidised mortgage. The system was very popular in the 1990s, and at its height (in 1992) accounted for 15 percent of all new mortgages. The system was updated in 2009 and has been very popular since with 4000 new loans being granted in 2013.

Impacts and implications of changes

The milestones described here contributed to a sea change in Finnish housing finance from 1985 to 2014. Besides economic growth, deregulation of financial markets, Finland's participation in the process towards setting up the Euro, improvements in the competitive environment of the lenders and the beneficial development of the interest rate level have been key to this development.

As a result the terms on which housing finance is available have improved quite dramatically. Consequently, households have been able to take on more debt to finance their home acquisitions. However, it is difficult to assess the quantitative benefits of this development. There are definitely some clear drawbacks in terms of risks and the worsened situation of first-time buyers because of higher house prices in today's housing market. The share of owner-occupiers has increased only slightly during the time period, but this can also be explained by ongoing urbanisation, as there is typically a higher share of rental housing in larger cities than elsewhere.

There have been many changes since 1985, but the mortgage loan product itself has not experienced any major changes, apart from maturities becoming longer. First, universal banks are the only lenders in the market, whereas the government used to have a role as a lender in the 1980s and in beginning of the 1990s. Second, Finnish mortgages have been and are variable rate mortgages. Fixed rate mortgages have had a very limited role in Finnish housing finance. Their share has normally been well below 10 percent of all housing loans, and the latest information from 2013 reveals that only 1.6 percent of the housing loans were made at fixed interest rates. The origin of this approach lies in the fact that EURIBOR rates replaced the central banks' base rate as the main market interest rates to which mortgage interest rates were tied at the end of the 1980s. The almost continuous decrease in interest rates since 1992 has made short-term interest rates a superior choice throughout this period. Third, although mortgages can have amortisation free periods of up to a couple of years, they are all basically repayment mortgages. Bullet loans exist, but they have short maturities and are used for interim financing.

Impacts

In the mid-1980s housing finance was scarce, fulfilling the pre-saving requirement was a challenging task, interest rate margins were high and loan maturities were short. In 2014 all these elements of housing finance have significantly improved from the perspective of the borrower.

The decline in interest rates and inflation that the EMU area has experienced over the last 20 years is quite remarkable in itself. Interest rate margins have declined since the deregulation of the financial markets (Figure 9.1). In 1990 the average interest rate margin was about 2.5 percentage points. The margin began to decline in the end of 1990s and declined gradually until around 2008, when the average margin was about 0.5 percentage points. The financial crisis of 2008 changed this, and average loan margins have risen to around 1.5 percent since the beginning of the crisis as the banks adjust to the new regulatory environment. On the other hand the decrease in interest rates on new mortgages in this period is quite remarkable.

Longer maturities have also reduced monthly payments. In the mid-1980s maturities were well below 10 years. They began to lengthen only gradually after the deregulation of the financial markets (Kosonen 1992a). As late as 1999 the average maturity of a mortgage was only 11 years and a typical new mortgage had a maturity of 15 years. Only 3 percent of mortgages had a maturity longer than 15 years. At this time Finland was well behind the European norm, and even more behind its Nordic neighbours (ECB 2003).

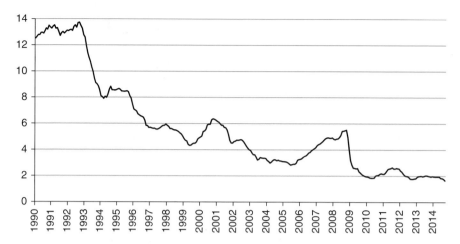

Figure 9.1   Interest rate on new mortgages in percent.
Source: ECB Statistics.

However, the banks started to change their behaviour, using mortgages as a vehicle to attract customers and to offer longer maturities. In 2008 the average maturity of new loans was 18.8 years, but the maturity of a typical new mortgage was 25 years, and 10 percent of the loans had maturities of 30 years. Since 2008 mortgage maturities have become shorter. In the spring of 2014 the average maturity was 16.9 years and the most typical new mortgage had a maturity of 20 years. Furthermore, only about 2 percent of new mortgages have maturities over 25 years.

The pre-saving requirement in the mid-1980s was between 20 and 50 percent. When the financial markets were deregulated, 100 percent LTV loans became available almost immediately. The recession of the early 1990s resulted in more conservative lending policies, but during the last 10 years or so, 100 percent mortgages have again become possible, and as was described in the previous section, quite common for first-time buyers. Consequently, in addition of mortgages becoming cheaper, they have also become readily available without years of pre-saving.

Implications of changes

All the changes described here – cheaper loans, longer maturities and the relaxation of pre-saving requirements – have increased the number of households who are able to borrow. Obviously, the changes have also increased the size of a mortgage a given household can take (Figure 9.2). From 2002 to 2013 the number of households with housing debt increased by 32 percent and the average size of a mortgage grew 4.5-fold, although there was practically no change in the share of owner-occupiers.

The total amount of household housing debt has increased in a similar way (Figure 9.3). In 1985 there was about €10 bn of housing debt, which

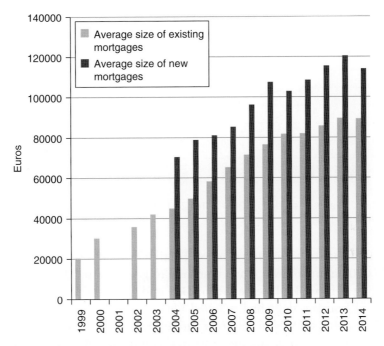

Figure 9.2 Average size of existing and new mortgages in Euros.
Source: Federation of Finnish Financial Services.

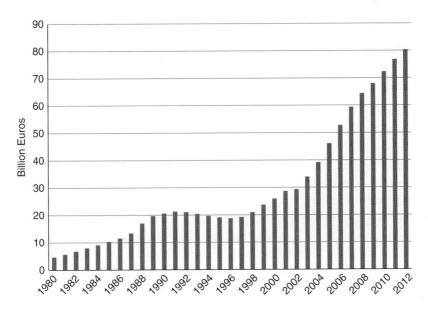

Figure 9.3 Households mortgage stock in billion Euros.
Source: Statistics Finland.

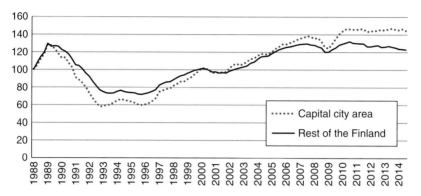

Figure 9.4   Real house prices, 1988–2014 (2000 = 100).
Source: Statistics Finland.

doubled during the following 5 years. Total debt then remained at the same level of €20 bn until 1998, when it started to grow again. The fastest growth in housing debt took place between 2000 and 2010 and by the end of 2012 household housing debt had reached €80 bn. By international standards, Finnish housing debt is not among the highest; in 2012 housing debt was 44 percent of the GDP while the Euro area average was 47 percent. However, the increase has been rapid and significant.

House prices were very volatile in the late 1980s and early 1990s. Since 1995 there has been little volatility, but almost a steady increase. House prices have increased faster than incomes and faster than rents (measured by price/earnings). There are a number of reasons for this steady increase. First, household incomes have increased steadily since the recession. With rising incomes, households have been investing more in housing. Second, the increase in the average mortgage size and in total housing debt has an inter-active relationship with house prices. Additionally, better mortgage terms and lower interest rates have made it possible to pay more for housing. House prices have increased as a result, requiring more borrowing (Figure 9.4). Consequently, there has been a mutually reinforcing process between these two trends. Oikarinen (2009b: 137) found that there is a stable co-integration relationship in the Helsinki Metropolitan area between real housing prices, real income and loan-to-GDP ratio, which would mean that the loan-to-GDP ratio would capture the changes in the long run relation-ship between house prices and income that we would expect from credit market liberalisation (in the period 1975–2006). Third, the rapid increase in house prices after the 1990s depression made owner-occupied housing look like a sure bet, which has further fuelled demand.

Housing standards and quality of housing have unquestionably improved a great deal in this period. For example, sewage, hot water and central heat-ing have become almost universal. Technology and materials have improved as well, but this likely explains only a small part of the increase in house prices. One improvement, however, is obvious: housing space per person has increased since 1990 from 31 m² per person to 40 m² per person, an improvement of 29 percent, which by itself is quite remarkable

Access to owner-occupancy seems to have improved between 1995 and 2005, as the number of first-time buyers increased steadily. The share of first-time buyers in total purchases increased from only 16 percent in 1995 to 24 percent in 2005. According to statistics owner-occupied housing has become more common among younger households (under 40 years old) since the 1990s, whereas there are fewer owner-occupiers among the middle aged (45–54 years old). Since the financial crisis, however, there has been a significant drop in the number of first-time buyers (Figure 9.5).

The share of owner-occupiers was 63 percent in 1980. Over the next 10 years, helped by deregulation of the financial market, the share increased rapidly to 71 percent. A decade later in 2000, the share had dropped back to 63 percent as many householders lost their jobs and homes during the recession. Thereafter, the strong economy up to 2008 and improvements in housing finance reversed the figures, and by 2013 the share of owner-occupation had risen to 65 percent. But lately this increase has ceased. André and Garcia (2012) looked at the price-to-rent and price-to-income ratios for Finland and found that both of have risen rather steadily since the recession in the 1990s, but whereas the price-to-income ratio was about in line with the long term average, the price-to-rent ratio in 2010 was about 40 percent above the long term average. This coincides well with the recent downward development in first-time buying, explained by the high house prices in relation to rents. As a result of all these ups and downs there has not been much change in the proportion of owner-occupiers over the whole period since 1980.

Figure 9.5 Number and share of first-time buyers. (2009–2011 no data on first-time buyers is available.)
Source: Statistics Finland.

On the negative side, the increase in household debt in itself increases the financial risks faced by households. Given that the average loan is now 4.5 times larger than in 1999, households could potentially face considerably more severe problems should household members lose their jobs or fall ill. The risks of debt are further increased by the preference of Finns for short term interest rates. The Euro zone has lowered the variance of interest rates making that risk smaller. The continuation of the low interest rate environment is, however, shaping households' beliefs and contributing to more risky behaviour. This behaviour could become costly should there be sudden or large upward changes in interest rates.

These two risks are somewhat mitigated by the fact that nowadays about every third loan is protected against large interest rate increases by interest rate caps and about every third borrower has personal insurance in case of unemployment or illness. So far the credit losses from mortgages, with the exception of the recession in 1990s, have been low in Finland and have remained so. After the financial crisis credit losses from mortgages in 2009 and 2010 were only 0.02 percentage points of the mortgage loan stock annually.

To summarise, there seem to be clear benefits from the development of housing finance in terms of better access to homeownership. It is also obvious that mortgage lending today is no longer about having good personal connections to bank managers but is based on quantifiable attributes of the borrower. This makes the market more efficient. Housing standards are also higher. The drawbacks of the development are also obvious. House prices have increased considerably putting particular pressure on first-time buyers. Households' debt holdings have multiplied in a very short time period, increasing the risks for the households and the housing market. The debt burden has also increased in the sense that households used to pay back their mortgages within 10 years or so, whereas it now takes about 20 years. The problem has been that the supply of housing has not adequately increased to address increases in demand. The price elasticity of housing supply has been estimated to be in the range of 0.15–0.66, which shows a positive, but not a very strong reaction (Mäki-Fränti *et al.* 2011). Therefore, one cannot escape the conclusion that much of the benefits from improvements in housing finance have resulted in higher prices (and more debt), and a golden opportunity to improve housing and housing affordability has been lost to some extent. Marrez and Pontuch (2013) conclude that the Finnish housing market,

> ...has merely been responsive to structural changes in underlying supply and demand factors. And further, the decreasing affordability and rising price-to-rental ratios have mostly been driven by changes in financing costs, demographic developments, as well as by limitations to land supply and moderate construction activity.

Looking to the future

Weak economic growth has been key to housing market development during the last few years and has led to slightly falling nominal house prices in 2014. Rising unemployment and the lack of new jobs are currently affecting the demand for owner-occupation. It seems likely that differences in house price development across regions, which have been small, will become larger in the future. There are fears even today that, in more remote regions and in smaller municipalities, home sales will become increasingly difficult and dwellings will be left empty. Lately, this has generated some political discussion.

The banks have addressed the lower demand for owner-occupied housing by lowering the mortgage interest rate margins in order to compete for customers. At the same time the variance in margins has widened depending on the creditworthiness of the borrower, which is an indication of improvements in the banks' credit evaluation processes.

The concern about the use of high LTVs has led to a legislative process being put in place to introduce binding LTV limits. The limits will be set initially at 95 percent for first-time buyers and at 90 percent for existing owners (the banks will not be able to give a higher mortgage but other loans will be available). The financial supervisory authority will be given the further power to decrease the LTV limit by 10 percentage points during housing market booms in order to lower the risks to households and the banks. The system is set to come into force in June 2016.

Academic researchers have also raised a discussion around the tax-preferred status of owner-occupancy (Saarimaa 2009). The argument is that the tax benefits (mortgage tax relief, tax free sales after two years of occupancy and lack of imputed rent income taxation) given to owner-occupancy make owner-occupation financially a superior choice in comparison to renting. Yet there is very little evidence that there are relative benefits to owner-occupation in general (via spill-over effects to the neighbourhood etc.). Further, there might be some general detrimental effects from owner-occupancy (like less willingness to move to take up a job and more risks in terms of less diversified household asset portfolios). The discussion is concentrated on how to make the tenures more neutral. The ongoing gradual reduction in mortgage tax relief is one step towards this goal. Also working against owner-occupancy is the fact that further decreases in interest rates are virtually impossible. With the gradual lowering of mortgage tax relief and interest rates already on the rise there will be increases in the cost of borrowing.

It therefore seems likely that the demand in the housing market has shifted and is shifting towards renting. Ongoing urbanisation and increased immigration to Finland will put pressure on the rental market, as the share of rental housing in larger cities is about 50 percent. In addition, as André and Garcia (2012) found, the price-to-rent ratio is currently 40 percent above its long-term average, which suggests that choosing owner-occupancy over renting is historically expensive at the moment. Attention is therefore likely to turn more towards rental sector both in the development of housing policy and of housing finance.

References

André, C and Garcia, C (2012). *Housing Price and Investment Dynamics in Finland*, OECD Economics Department Working Paper No. 962.

Booth, G, Glascock, J, Martikainen, T and Rothovius, T (1994). The financing of residential real estate in Finland: An overview. *Journal of Housing Research* 5:2, 205–227.

ECB (2003). *Structural factors in the EU housing markets*. European Central Bank.

ECB (various years). European Central Bank Statistics [Online] Available: www.ecb.europa.eu/ stats/html/index.en.html (accessed 24 July, 2015).

Federation of Finnish Financial Services (various years). Statistics [Online] Available: www.fkl. fi/en/material/statistics/Pages/default.aspx (accessed 24 July, 2015).

Johnson, M and Tarkoma, J (2004). *Osakeasunnon ostajat ja valtiontakaus: tilastollinen selvitys vuonna 2001 osakeasunnon ostaneista, ympäristöministeriö.*

Jännäri, K and Koskenkylä, H (1995). Suomen pankkikriisin syiden tarkastelua, *Kansantaloudellinen aikakauskirja* 91:vsk-1/1995.

Kosonen, K (1992a). Asuntopolitiikka ja asuntorahoitus Suomessa ja Länsi-Euroopassa – Vertaileva tarkastelu, *TTT Katsaus* 3:86, 1992.

Marrez, H and Pontuch, P (2013). Finland's high house prices and household debt: a source of concern? *ECFIN Country Focus.*

Mäki-Fränti, P, Lahtinen, M, Pakarinen, S and Esala, L (2011). Alueellisten asuntomarkkinoiden kehitys vuoteen 2013. *PTT työpapereita* 131, 29 p.

Oikarinen, E (2009b). Household borrowing and metropolitan housing price dynamics – Empirical evidence from Helsinki. *Journal of Housing Economics*, 18:2, June 2009.

Palmroos, P and Nokkala, J (2011). *Otantatutkimus henkilöasiakkaiden asuntoluotosta*, Financial Supervisory Authority.

Saarimaa, T (2010). Tax incentives and demand for mortgage debt: Evidence from the Finnish 1993 Tax Reform, *International Journal of Housing Policy* 10:1, 19–40.

Saarimaa, T (2009). Tutkimuksia omistusasumisesta, verotuksesta ja portfolion valinnasta, *Kansantaloudellinen aikakauskirja* 3, 371–375.

Statistics Finland (various years). Statistics [Online] Available: www.stat.fi/til/index_en.html (accessed 24 July, 2015).

Further reading

Finanssialan keskusliitto (2014). *Asuntolainamarkkinat Suomessa 2014*, www.fkl.fi/ materiaalipankki/esitysaineistot/ppt/Asuntolainamarkkinat_Suomessa.ppt.

Kajanoja, L (2012). *Asuntojen hinnat, kotitalouksien velka ja makrotalouden vakaus Suomessa*, BoF Online February 2012.

Kivistö, J (2012). *Suomen asuntohintakehitys ja siihen vaikuttavat tekijät*, BoF Online 4.2012

Koskela, E, and Viren, M (1991). *Inflation, Capital Markets, and Household Saving in Nordic Countries*, University of Helsinki.

Kosonen, K (1992b). *Housing finance in Finland: Institutional features and recent developments*. ENHR Meeting Hague, 12 April 1992.

Nykredit markets (2013). *Nordic Covered Bonds – Finland, A Handbook*

OECD (2014). *Economic Surveys Finland.*

Oikarinen, E (2009a). Interaction between housing prices and household borrowing: The Finnish case, *Journal of Banking & Finance* 33.

Schauman, H (2012). *Asuntomarkkinat ja kotitalouksien velka – pohjoismainen vertailu,* BoF Online May 2012.

Säylä Markku (2012). *Uusi elämäntapa velkaannuttaa ja vaurastuttaa,* Hyvinvointikatsaus April 2012, Tilastokeskus.

Tilastokeskus (2013). *Velkaantumistilasto.*

Tuomainen, P (2013). Suomalainen asuntorahoitus vuosina 1999–2011, Itä-Suomen yliopisto.

10

Milestones of Housing Finance in France between 1988 and 2014: Is the French Credit System a Gallic Oddity?

Christian Tutin[a] and Bernard Vorms[b]

[a] UPEC (Université de Paris Est Créteil) and Lab'urba, Paris, France
[b] Conseil national de la Transaction et de la Gestion immobilières (CNTGI), Paris, France

Introduction: A quarter of a century later

In 1990, most of the distinctive characteristics of the French system of housing finance were already in place. The mortgage loans market was 'incomplete' and has remained so. But the structure of the banking sector has changed since then, with the reinforcement of big universal banks and the near disappearance of specialised circuits, which was the joint product of the real estate crisis of the 1990s, disintermediation and deliberate state policies. In the second half of the 1990s, the upsurge in house prices was fuelled by lower interest rates and longer loan maturities, but without endangering the banking system.

After the crisis, the French finance system has proven to be robust enough to resist the destabilising effects coming from the US and the peripheries of the Euro zone, even better than other strongly regulated systems such as in Germany. There was no clear evidence of a credit crunch for homebuyers.

The post-crisis recovery of the market was succeeded by stabilisation in 2012. Thereafter, house prices have declined slowly, the volume of new construction has returned to the low level of 2009 – although still higher than the lowest levels of the 1990s – while transactions on existing homes remain below their record levels of 2007 and 2011.

Milestones in European Housing Finance, First Edition.
Edited by Jens Lunde and Christine Whitehead.
© 2016 John Wiley & Sons, Ltd. Published 2016 by John Wiley & Sons, Ltd.

Finance milestones

At the end of the 1980s, the housing finance system reflected both the financial reforms of the mid-1980s and the reform of public aids, which were profoundly reshaped in 1977 (Lefebvre *et al.* 1991). Economically, the latter was aimed at reducing the role of the specialised financial institutions in housing finance and replacing the direct form of building subsidy (bricks and mortar) with support geared towards providing financial assistance to households in the housing market (personal allowances). The new system remained in place until 1995.

Personal allowances were supposed to be cheaper because they would decrease as real and nominal income increased with inflation and growth. Politically, the aim was to foster homeownership, but without giving up the construction of social rented housing. The objective of giving financial support simultaneously for homeownership, the social rental sector and, since 1986, private renting has been and remains a constant of French policy. It has never been called into question by any change of government, even if some experts from the ministry of finance wished to reduce the role of the public rental sector and refocus it progressively towards people in the lowest income brackets.

The period 1978–1984 was the only time when a large increase in the proportion of homeownership was achieved, with the symbolic threshold of 50 percent homeownership being surpassed in 1984.

In the 1980s, the most dramatic changes in housing finance were the result of globalisation, decreasing inflation and interest rates after 1982 (Figure 10.1). The dramatic fall in nominal long run interest rates was one of the main triggers for the upturn in the housing market, which resulted in a boom in prices up to 1991. This took place while deregulation and finance disintermediation (the fact that large companies gained direct access to the financial market) had sharpened the interest of universal banks in individual customers and private developers. Thus, universal banks were able to gain the market share of the specialised mortgage lenders.

But once deflation declined (after 1985) the very high level of interest rates (both nominal, around 10 percent – and real, about 6 percent) meant that support for homeownership became less and less effective. Ultimately, the system put in place in 1977 was jeopardised by low inflation and the slowdown in economic growth and household incomes, rather than by new trends in housing finance.

Low income homebuyers who had taken public subsidised mortgages (so called PAP loans – *Prêts d'Accession à la Propriété*, mainly distributed by the Crédit Foncier) with fixed rates but progressive instalments could not meet their monthly payments. To help them, the government encouraged people to refinance outstanding mortgages. At the same time, a law introduced in 1989 enhanced consumer and borrower protection allowing a judge

Table 10.1 Milestones – Housing finance in France.

Date	Macro context and housing markets	Housing policy	Finance
1988	Economic growth over 3% Nominal interest rates below 10% Inflation under 6%	1989: Re-regulation of private rents on existing contracts (new contacts free)	1984–1985: Financial reforms 1985: Creation of the CRH (Caisse de refinancement hypothécaire) 1989: Neiertz Act
1991 1993	Downturn of the housing market Economic recession For the first time since 1945, inflation rate lower than in Germany	Enlargement of personal allowance (APL)	Creation of the FGAS (Fonds de Garantie de l'Accession Sociale) Fall of the Crédit Lyonnais, rescued by the state jointly with the Crédit Agricole
1995		End of the public subsidised mortgages (PAP), replaced by zero interest loans (PTZ) Most generous fiscal incentives for buy-to-let investors End of interest deductibility for homebuyers	Second bailout of the Crédit Lyonnais (CDR = Bad bank)
1997–2002	Interest rates under 5%. Strong economic recovery. Real estate boom	2000: SRU Act (Solidarity and Urban Renewal), implementing social mix requisites	New loans for social rental (PLUS) Urban planning reform
2004–2006		ENL Act (National Compromise for Housing)	2005: PTZ extended to existing homes 2006: Introduction of reverse mortgages and equity withdrawal (under very strict conditions)
2007	Subprime crisis Fiscal package (tax cuts)	Interest on housing loans again deductible MOLE Act (Mobilisation for Housing and Against Exclusion)	BILLIONP closes two investment funds in the US (starting point of the financial crisis in France)
2009	Economic recession Downturn of the housing market	2009: Stimulus package	Fall of Dexia bank
2010 2011 2012	Fast recovery of the market Interest rates below 3.5%	Austerity budget. Fiscal incentive for buy-to-let investors suppressed Fiscal incentive for buy-to-let investors reintroduced Market interest deductibility suppressed	PTZ reduced
2013	New historical low of interest rates on housing loans Sharp drop in housing starts		
2014	Economic stagnation New historical low for mortgage interest rate (2.95%)	ALUR Act (Housing Affordability and Renewed Urban Planning), including private rents regulation (on new contracts) and the creation of the GUL: Universal Guarantee of Rents	PTZ enlarged

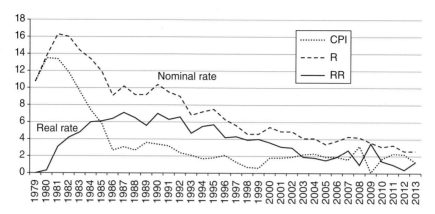

Figure 10.1   Consumption price index and interest rates (nominal and real) France 1979–2013.
Abbreviations:
CPI: Consumer Price Index (percentage annual change).
R: Long run nominal interest rate (treasury bonds 10-year).
RR: Real interest rate.
Source: INSEE *Comptes de la nation*.

to lower the interest rate of an outstanding loan for over-indebted households. At the beginning of the 1990s, public interest in homeownership reached a historic low. The number of PAP loans oscillated around 160 000 per year from 1978–1982, but declined to 55 000 in 1990 and 30 000 in 1992 and 1993 (Lefebvre *et al.* 1991). Finally, in 1995 the zero interest loan (PTZ – *Prêts à taux zéro*), distributed by all banks and directed at low and middle-income first-time buyers of new houses replaced the PAP subsidised mortgage loan system. Initially designed for new houses and existing ones with a large share (54 percent plus) of improvement works as the PAP was, the PTZ was extended to existing homes with no improvement work required in 2005.

Meanwhile, the real estate boom of the second half of the 1980s was followed by a crisis beginning in 1991–1992 and lasting until mid-1997. The banking system was put under strain, mainly through developers' insolvency, which resulted in a profound restructuring of financial circuits but not in any dramatic change in lending practices.

Towards mainstream lending

Specialised mortgage lenders were seriously hit by the downturn of the market from 1992 to 1997 after having been weakened by the refinancing of outstanding mortgages by mortgagors in the second half of the 1980s. All have now disappeared as independent financial entities. They were restructured, not through bankruptcy but through mergers or (re)purchase by big banks. The Crédit Foncier de France lost an essential part of its activity with the end of PAP in 1995, and had to be absorbed by the Caisses d'Epargne in 1999, which in turn merged in 2009 with the Banques Populaires to form a new banking group, BPCE (Banques Populaires Caisses d'Epargne). The La Hénin bank merged in 2000 with the Comptoir des Entrepreneurs in a new entity called Entenial, which then merged in 2005 with the Crédit Foncier de France, which itself was already in the hands of the Caisses d'Epargne.

A special mention must be made of the failure of the Crédit Lyonnais in 1993. This was the most dramatic bank failure in France since the 1930s. The bank, which was the first European banking network at that time, avoided formal bankruptcy only because the state opened a 'bad bank', the Consortium de Réalisation (CDR), to deal with its toxic assets and thanks to its integration into the Crédit Agricole banking group, the biggest retail bank in France. It is only in 2013 that the CDR completed its activity. The last episode was the planned closure of the Crédit Immobilier de France (CIF).

In the 2000s, there were only two surviving 'special circuits' by which housing could be financed. The first one is for social housing, through long run loans provided by the *Caisse des Dépôts* (CDC, the last remaining public financial institution) for social landlords, who are their own developers. The CDC uses market loans through the Livret A, a special tax exempted saving instrument, which is the most popular saving product in France. The loans granted to social landlords by the *Caisse* represent more than 70 percent of the *habitations à loyers modérés* (HLM) construction costs, which allow them to be free of any market finance (Levy-Vroelant *et al.* 2014). The other 'special circuit' works through the Epargne Logement (housing savings plan), a dedicated saving scheme that benefits from preferential tax concessions, set up in 1965 (CEL – *Compte Epargne Logement*) and 1970 (PEL – *Plan Epargne Logement*). The PEL is for longer duration deposits (10 years) and gives more advantages to the savers. In both cases, the advantage depends upon the actual level of market interest rates. Their role is to make homeownership more affordable through subsidised lending (under market subsidised rates) and to accumulate funds, which can be used by households as downpayments, but mostly by the banks as a funding source. The current very low interest rates means that the utility of *Epargne Logement* is limited for households, but its major role is as a funding source for banks, given that the part of the money collected through this scheme that must be used for residential loans still represented 35 percent of total mortgage funding in 2007. This proportion dropped to 26 percent in 2012.

The recent rise of covered bonds

The banks have substantial internal resources through deposits, capital market funding (bond issues) and regulated saving schemes, like the *Epargne Logement* mentioned previously. Deposits still represent half of the banks' resources.

In general, although the proportion of the funds raised from the market has increased, the use of specific financial products is still very limited. The main change is the rise of covered bonds since 2007. The bonds, which played a negligible role in the 1990s rising to 10 percent in 2007, are thought to now represent nearly 25 percent of the total of outstanding loans (€874 bn in 2012), of which 6 percent are issued by the public entity CRH (*Caisse de Refinancement de l'Habitat*). While several countries allow ordinary credit institutions to issue covered bonds subject to the segregation of the cover pool in their balance sheet, France requires the set-up of an *ad hoc* company – the *SCF* – totally distinct from the other companies of the group to which it belongs and exclusively dedicated to the issuance of covered bonds, named *obligations foncières*, and the management of the assets backing these issues (the 'cover pool'). Three main covered bond-issuing structures exist in France today: *sociétés de crédit foncier, sociétés de financement de l'habitat* and the CRH. The CRH is a credit institution created in 1985 by the French government with an explicit state guarantee as a central agency in order to issue bonds designed for refinancing residential mortgage home loans granted by the French banking system. The duration of those bonds is between 5 and 10 years. The spread with the EURIBOR of 6 months is very low.

Securitisation plays a minor role. Repeated initiatives from the Crédit Foncier – the last one in 2014 – remain very limited. As a result residential mortgage backed securities (MBS) account for only 2 per cent of total lending.

In France, the development of housing finance investment products was associated with none of the abuses that, elsewhere, allowed the lender to transfer the debt and to become disinterested in the final repayment of the loan. Nor did equity withdrawal develop. *Hypothèque rechargeable*, a kind of equity withdrawal, became legal in 2007 but was practically impossible and was ruled illegal again in 2013.

Fiscal incentives and tax rebates

After personal allowances, which represent the main form of public aid to housing (€16.4 bn in 2011, almost entirely devoted to tenants), the second largest contribution from the state to housing (€12.5 bn) is through tax rebates and exemptions, which are mainly in favour of buy-to-let investors and social landlords. Most of those fiscal benefits involve aids to 'producers' (buy-to-let investors and social landlords), in place of former 'bricks and mortar' aids, which are now very limited.

Fiscal incentives for buy-to-let investors were introduced for individual buyers to offset the flight specifically from housing by institutional investors (they were still investing in commercial centres and offices). This was partly the consequence of the financial reforms of 1985–1986, and partly an effect of stringent monetary policies, along with non-neutral fiscal policies.

These meant that the yield on residential assets became less and less favourable while financial assets became both more profitable and more liquid. Against a commitment to let for a certain number of years (generally nine years) and conditional on the observance of rent and income ceilings, the investor is allowed to deduct part of his investment from his income tax. The first fiscal incentive for buy-to-let investors was introduced in 1986 by Paul Quilès, a socialist Minister of Housing, and the most advantageous one was put in place in 1995 by André Périssol. The last one, introduced by Cécile Duflot, imposed lower rent and income ceilings than the previous ones. Thanks to those incentives, the stock of private rental units was stabilised, despite the withdrawal of institutional investors from rental housing. Their involvement now represents less than 5 percent of the rented housing stock. In the pre-crisis years, some 60000 to 70000 housing units (mainly small apartments) were being developed for individual buy-to-let investors.

The social rental sector also benefits from tax rebates through property tax exemptions (for 15 years) and VAT (5 percent reduced rate for new social units). Such fiscal aids are now more important than direct aids to investment.

As regards mortgagors, interest costs had long been deductible. But it was considered ineffective as a boost to homeownership and thus was abandoned in 1995. Reintroduced in 2007 by Nicolas Sarkozy, it was suppressed again in 2011 because of its budgetary cost.

Specifics of French housing finance

Universal banks lending to financially stable households

A small number of universal banks have thus become the main distributors of residential loans. Apart from this, the traditional characteristics of the French credit system remained unchanged so that, despite the continuous rise in housing debt, the financial fragility of banks and households did not increase.

The same pattern of credit supply is used for homeowners and for buy-to-let mortgagors, even if the rate of default is slightly higher for investors. A key element in risk control is related to the organisation of the credit sector, both in terms of the way loans are financed and secured (securitisation, covered bonds, deposits etc.) and the fact that the lenders manage the loan until full amortisation. The bank usually keeps the loan in its books without securitising it. The credit provider is not able to avoid the consequences if the borrower defaults on payment; or, at the very least, the risk must be identifiable and traceable. The banks carefully evaluate the risk of the transaction. More than 85 percent of new housing loans are made by universal banks. For the banks mortgage loans are, above all, a way of attracting new customers and promoting loyalty among existing ones. In particular they require borrowers to place their income payments into the bank via direct debit.

While lenders in most countries take into account the value of the property as collateral (to the point where the term mortgage implies both a guarantee and a secured loan) along with the income of the borrower, the French, with very few exceptions, focus their attention solely on the credit-worthiness of the borrower. This is why the lender almost never asks for an asset valuation, even though it is going to provide the finance: the value of the security is assumed to equal the amount of the transaction or the construction cost. On the other hand, banks tend to exclude potential borrowers who are not in stable employment or cannot insure against death or disability (Vorms 1998). Data based credit assessments do not exist.

No break in the link between the originator and the mortgagor

The various stages of the mortgage process are mainly handled by the lender. The proportion of loans brokered by agents and other go-betweens has increased over the last few years but remains below 20 percent of residential loans. Banks never delegate the responsibility to grant the loan to these intermediaries. The institution that approves the loan manages it until it is fully amortised and usually holds it on its balance sheet throughout that period.

Arrears and defaults therefore have a direct effect on their financial results, except those arising from loans to the lower income first-time homebuyers, who are guaranteed by the *Fonds de Garantie de l'Accession Sociale* (SGFGAS, installed 1993). So, the lender maintains the link with the borrower until the loan is fully amortised.

The 'caution': an alternative to the mortgage deed for low risk mortgagors

Most housing loans are not properly mortgages. The guarantee consists of a so-called caution (bond insurance), which is an unconditional guarantee given by a specialised financial entity (lending institution or insurance company, in some cases health insurance *Mutuelles*). This guarantee is the undertaking pledged by a third party, the 'caution' in return for a fee to pay the borrower's debt in case of default by the borrower. It simply has to be shown that the borrower has defaulted for the guarantee to come into force, which at the first request must be paid by the guarantor. Moreover, if the credit institution wishes, most caution companies take charge of the debt recovery process in the case of default. The benefit of this guarantee over the mortgage is evident to the lender: it ensures the return of its funds within a short period and at the same time removes the management of contentious issues. The paperwork for obtaining a guarantee is less than for a mortgage and does not involve a notary. The decision to accept or reject an applicant is, in general, very quick. In the case of late payments, the guarantor who has paid the debt takes on all the rights that the creditor had against the debtor. If an amicable solution is not found, the guarantor can put in place a 'judicial mortgage' and use all available methods of enforcement. The caution companies also differ in their status: some are credit institutions, while others are insurance companies. It is a very profitable activity that feeds into net banking profits as most mutual guarantee companies belong to banks. The companies only give their guarantee on less risky mortgages, so the losses are very limited while the cost of the guarantee is determined to ensure it is less than that of a mortgage deed. There is public registration of the loan secured against the property for loans with a mortgage deed but not for those with a caution, and above all the caution company pays the bank a generous commission for the brokering and the processing of the mortgage applications. This specifically French system of surety reduces risk to the bank and as a result nearly 60 percent of all loans are not registered as a mortgage deed.

The caution system was not affected by the Global Financial Crisis (GFC). More generally the losses of the French banks after the GFC were only linked to their investment in American MBS. No losses occurred with French borrowers, except with respect to a very small share of buy-to-let loans. Even so, this system is currently jeopardised by the Basel authorities. The main caution company, Crédit Logement, has been converted in an insurance company, which is more expensive in terms of capital requirements.

A superficial examination could suggest that the French caution is similar to private mortgage insurance in America or mortgage indemnity insurance in the UK. These are arranged to cover the part of the loan that exceeds a given loan-to-value ratio (LTV). These types of insurance are designed to allow access to credit for borrowers with little downpayment. These insurance policies are different from the caution in three essential respects. First, in legal terms, these insurances are complementary to the mortgage that is still required in all cases, whereas the caution is an alternative to a mortgage deed. Second, the caution guarantees all of the debt. Third, in terms of function, mortgage protection insurance is required when the percentage of the LTV is higher than a certain percentage, 70 or 80 percent; on the contrary the caution insures those cases with the least risk, especially those with a low LTV.

A guarantee fund dedicated to low income homebuyers

At the other end of the risk spectrum, mortgages for low income homebuyers are guaranteed by a public guarantee fund for social homeownership, the *Fonds de Garantie de l'Accession Sociale* (FGAS), whose mission is to make sure that low income first-time buyers can access homeownership.

In 1995, when the state was preparing to remove dedicated financing schemes, it wanted a reassurance that low income first-time homeowners would not be excluded by an overly selective credit policy being applied by some banks and wanted to ensure the ability to obtain an offer of credit on conditions similar to households with higher incomes. It is for this reason that the FGAS was established. It guarantees the risk for the lenders without taking the responsibility to manage their risk. It also helps lower the mortgage rates offered to modest borrowers in two ways: on the one hand, by compensating part of the costs of default and on the other, by inducing an economy of equity capital thanks to the guarantee given by the government were the fund to be depleted. Thus it keeps down the lenders' costs, allowing them to offer almost the same interest rate to low-income and affluent borrowers. The guarantee pays in case of borrower default to compensate for all losses defined in terms of a decrease in the actuarial rate of return expected by the credit institution granting the loan, taking into account ancillary expenses incurred in relation to the debtor. Finally, it is a guarantee of last resort, which, in principle, is used only when all other guarantees or sureties have been used. The fund requires that the loans it guarantees are secured by a mortgage guarantee. At its inception, the fund was financed equally by contributions from credit institutions and the government. In 2005, the very low level of claims since the establishment of the fund led the government to recover money that had been accumulated in the scheme. The scheme remained the same, but the fund was replaced with a direct guarantee given by public authorities.

Ancillary guarantees and consumer protection

If credit institutions bear the consequences of losses associated with the loans they grant, certain practices allow them to protect themselves from the consequences of what one might call 'the risks of life' (death, unemployment etc.). No lenders will issue a mortgage without an ancillary Death and Disability Insurance. France has very strong and effective regulation in relation to the provision of consumer information and protection, particularly as regards the borrower. This approach is reinforced by the strict attitude that judges and the legal framework have taken in relation to lending to individuals. This should be seen as a reflection of the emphasis that French society places on responsible lending, and indeed an attitude of mistrust with respect to the role of credit (Vorms 2012).

The law on usury forbids a lender from deviating by more than one third of the average rate of interest charged for loans of a similar nature, which, in times of low interest rates, represents a very narrow margin, for example, 1.33 percent when rates are 4 percent against 3.33 percent when they rise to 10 percent. Equity withdrawal is not practised. While amortised loans at fixed rates for the whole term account for the vast majority of the loans made (more than 97 percent in 2014), the law also imposes a ceiling on the compensation that can be required for early repayment of a fixed loan of 3 percent of the outstanding debt or 6 months' interest. In the case of job mobility or death, no prepayment penalty can be demanded.

Finally, in all the French *départements*, the Ministry of Housing manages, in partnership with local authorities, housing professionals and associations, *ADIL/agences départementales d'information sur le logement*, housing counselling agencies whose job is to offer free, impartial advice to the public on all housing issues. Those considering buying a house can explore their individual purchase and financing plans with an independent specialist who has links with banks and other professionals. It is important to note that these advisors have absolutely no intermediary or brokerage role.

As a result of this highly regulated system, the default rate is very low and foreclosures are mere exceptions. This is not wholly a good thing: many considered before the financial crisis of 2007 that the downside of this satisfactory situation was the overly restrictive nature of the credit supply (Taffin and Vorms 2007) and its impact on consumer choice. After the crisis, these critics have been forgotten.

Impacts

Impact on tenures

Regarding the structure of tenures, there was no dramatic jump in the last three decades (Table 10.2). Since the 1970s, the proportion of homeowners has been slowly but steadily increasing, from 46 percent of households in 1970 to 52 percent in 1984 and 58 percent now. Taking account of population growth this implies more than five million more homeowners since 1984, and nearly 10 million since 1963. Thirty-two percent of homeowners

Table 10.2 Housing tenures in France (millions of housing units, and percentage of the total stock).

	1970	1984	1990	1995	2000	2008	2012
Homeownership	7.35 (43.6%)	10.7 (51.9%)	12.1 (55%)	12.8 (54.9%)	13.8 (55.7%)	16 (57.8%)	16.4 (58%)
Private rental	7.39 (43.9)	6.6 (32%)	6 (27.3%)	6 (25.8%)	6.25 (25.2%)	6.6 (23.75%)	6.7 (23.5%)
Social housing[a]	2.1 (12.5%)	3.3 (16.1%)	3.9 (17.7%)	4.5 (19.3%)	4.7 (19.1%)	5.1 (18.4%)	5.3 (18.5%)
Housing stock (main dwellings)	16.8	20.6	22	23.3	24.8	27.7	28.5

[a] Enlarged definition (INSEE), including SEM (Sociétés d'économie mixte) and other non-HLM public housing.
Source: INSEE *Comptes du logement* (2012).

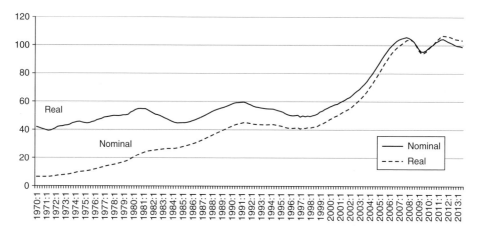

Figure 10.2 House Price Quarterly Index.
Based 2010 = 100
Source: OECD (various years).

still have a formal mortgage deed. Their number decreased slightly after the subprime crisis (4.95 million households in 2012, as compared to 5.5 million in 1990 and 5.25 in 2000) (INSEE, *Comptes du logement*, various years).

Forty-two percent of households are tenants, 44 percent of which are in social housing and 56 percent in the private rental sector. Thanks to continuous buy-to-let fiscal incentives, the private rental stock has been maintained, despite the fact that, since the beginning of the 1980s, institutional investors have moved out of the residential market. Thus, French households have a real choice and are not urged to become homeowners. Buy-to-let investment is one of the favourite investments of French households.

In the pre-crisis decade, the easier credit conditions made the progression to homeownership possible but at the same time they were a powerful trigger of house prices. As shown in Figure 10.2, the upsurge of house prices is unprecedented and has not been stopped by the crisis. The number of first-time buyers did not decline during the housing boom, thanks to increased urban sprawl, which was the only way of maintaining access to cheap homeownership for modest households, while it became a subject of growing concern for urban planners.

Impact on markets

In the second half of the 1990s, steadily declining interest rates and the return of sustained growth caused an upturn of the housing market, with a strong acceleration in price rises after 2003 (the reasons for which are still unclear), even after allowing for longer loan maturities as an additional and powerful driver (Tutin 2013; Tutin and Vorms 2014, and Figure 10.2).

As shown in Figure 10.3, house price rises were clearly sustained by credit, but the residential mortgage debt to GDP ratio remains very low in comparison with other European countries even if it has increased steadily

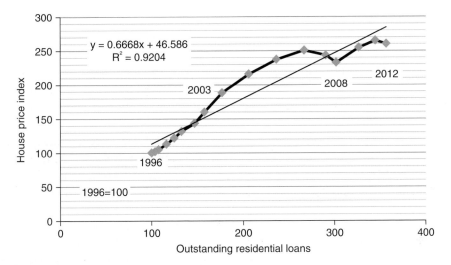

Figure 10.3   House price index and residential debt.
Based 1996 = 100
Source: EMF *Hypostat*.

over recent years, from 20 percent in 1997 to 43 percent in 2012 (and 65 percent of disposable income). This ratio has increased since 2007, as a result of a 34 percent increase in total outstanding residential loans (from €652 to €874 bn in 2012). The amount of residential debt per capita grew from €4200 to €13 500 between 1996 and 2012 (+357 percent).

Current estimates (e.g. Friggit 2011; Antipa and Lecat 2013) maintain that, once credit conditions (low rates, longer durations and high LTV ratios – up to 100 percent) plus income and demographic trends are taken into account, 15 percent to 30 percent of the 2012 price level remains unexplained. Moreover, the price-to-income ratio is still at least 60 percent over its long run value.

How can this over-valuation be explained? Given the post-crisis resilience of the housing market, it is not clear that there was even a bubble. In Tutin and Vorms (2014), we suggested that a self-sustained disequilibrium dynamic was at work, arising from changes in location patterns and residential behaviour. This resulted in continuous pressure on central cities and best valued areas in general, where the demand does not rest on income and borrowing capacity but rather on prior asset holdings. In other words, a majority of buyers are already homeowners; their bidding capacity is not adversely affected by price rises, so effective demand can be sustained. Whatever the reason, it is clear from Figure 10.3 that, at least between 2003 and 2008, price increases have exceeded what was funded by the rise in housing debt.

Impact of the crisis

In the years 1992–1997, the banking system was seriously and negatively affected by the decline in house prices, which contributed to the global recession of 1993–1994. During the real estate crisis of the 1990s, private developers were severely damaged, including the biggest, Christian Pellerin, which failed. Banking credit to private developers and real estate agents was a matter of concern. This was not the case after 2007. The financial crisis of 2007–2008 resulted in a sharp drop in the number of transactions and construction projects, but mortgagors were not seriously affected, and house prices soon returned to their pre-crisis level after a short break in 2008 and 2009.

A very small number of banks (namely the BILLIONP, Natixis – a subsidiary of the *Caisses d'Epargne* – and the Belgian-French Dexia bank) were seriously threatened, but only because of their risky investments in US MBS.

The rates of default and possessions hardly increased, and despite the refinancing difficulties the banks faced, there was no credit crunch for would-be homeowners except more stringent requirements for bridging loans. Moreover, the stimulus package introduced in 2009 involved support for the construction of social rented housing, tax incentives for investment in the private rental sector and very generous subsidies to encourage the construction or purchase of homeownership for low-income households. This element of new construction was mainly single family houses in less expensive areas, where the incentives have had an effective trigger effect and where construction could begin less than one year after the loan was made available, whereas it takes at least two years before the construction begins for a block of flats and three years for social housing blocks.

The financial crisis did not result in significant changes in the housing finance system, but has rather postponed attempts to change what was considered an overly constrained credit supply, namely by introducing some 'English speaking countries' practices'. Before the crisis, the public authorities' (entirely legitimate) objective was to open up access to credit for atypical borrowers (Taffin and Vorms 2007). For obvious reasons, these prospects were forgotten after 2007. The French mortgage loans market thus remains 'incomplete'. The only novelty introduced to satisfy foreign lenders was the creation of 'positive' borrowers' files, which were finally dismissed by the Supreme Court (*Conseil Constitutionnel*).

A record number of 326 000 PTZ were granted in 2011, among which 190 000 were dedicated to transactions in existing homes (and only a quarter of to low income households), which partly explains the recovery of prices after 2010. Existing homes have been excluded since 2011 and government subsidies for PTZ were drastically reduced in 2012, so that the number of PTZs fell to less than 80 000 in 2014. In order to boost the housing market, PTZs will now again be available for refurbished existing homes. At the same time, the social rented sector – whose position was seriously questioned in the pre-crisis years but became an important component of the stimulus package in 2009 – was reinforced. For example, in 2009 the state urged social landlords to buy 30 000 housing units from private developers. And the number of loans to social landlords was increased, so that – given the decline in private building – the proportion of social units out of the total of newly built houses, now approaching 30 percent, has not been as high since the beginning of the 1970s. Attitudes to the social sector have thus improved and the ways it is financed, which were supposed to be obsolete, appear secure.

Looking to the future

Housing analysts are now faced with the same questions raised in 2007 when the financial crisis was just beginning: what will happen to prices and volumes in the coming years? Are we going to observe a gentle decline in values and quantities (exchanged and produced), or a dramatic fall? For the moment, the average reduction in house prices has been very limited, but can now be observed in all regions and cities, including Paris *intramuros* (where prices were nonetheless 20 percent above their 2007 level at the end of 2013). Further, a growing differentiation can be observed in 2014 between tight markets, like Lyon or Paris, and some medium size cities, like Perpignan or St Etienne, where related to economic depression the drop in prices is much more pronounced, with a yearly decline of 5–10 percent. Finally, the volume of new construction, with 350 000 housing starts in 2014, fell back to its low 2009 level, although this is higher than the depressed average of the 1990s (around 300 000).

The high level of public debt, which was amplified by the crisis, will tighten the financial constraints on public spending on housing. The amount of zero interest loans has already decreased from €2.6 bn in 2011 to €0.82 bn in 2012, 2013 and 2014.

Despite the fact that public subsidy remains at a high level (around €42 bn in 2012, representing 2 percent of GDP), when it comes to fostering homeownership, these aids have become rather ineffective (i.e. not sufficient to maintain affordability) in tight markets where land prices are at the highest. For example, the PTZ is of no use in tight markets (the so-called zone 1). As regards personal allowances, they are effective for tenants in the low income brackets and for mortgagors in difficulties, but no longer work to improve affordability among new homebuyers.

In the more expensive markets, where excess demand goes hand in hand with low elasticity of supply, prior ownership of assets is more important than income when buying a dwelling. For instance, in less expensive markets, a first-time buyer can borrow 100 percent of the price of a dwelling whereas in Paris, the downpayment represents a large share of the price. Thus the more expensive markets are the least sensitive to mortgage rates, and prices in those tight markets are more driven by asset values than by income. This creates growing obstacles for new entrants to the market – especially for young people. As prices rise, access to property depends less on income and more and more on either personal or family assets.

Conclusions

For French housing finance, the main result of both the financial reforms of the 1980s and the crisis of the 1990s was the near disappearance of specialised operators in housing finance. But there was no major change in lending practices, or in the way the banks obtained their funds. Housing policies have been remarkably consistent from the late 1980s until now, mainly directed towards personal allowances rather than bricks and mortar, and have been increasingly based upon fiscal incentives for all tenure types. Finally, given the strong resilience manifested by housing markets (in terms of prices *and* to a lesser extent in terms of volumes), the housing finance system has not been affected by the GFC.

On the whole, the evolution of the housing loans market did not increase the fragility of the banking system. The transformation of the housing finance system has reinforced the role and market power of universal banks, but does not threaten their robustness. Although French public debt is significant, household debt remains very sustainable.

The GFC endangered neither mortgagors nor the capacity of banks to issue residential loans. It seems as if it has rather reinforced the particular features of the French housing finance, whose robustness accounted a lot for the strong resilience of housing markets since 2008. The peculiar system of long run loans for social landlords has even made it possible for France to be almost the only country in Europe (with Denmark) currently able to build more social housing after the crisis than before. However, surprisingly, the French banks are currently under huge pressure from the Basel authorities urging them to be closer to the English speaking countries standards: replace fixed rate mortgages by variable rates, weaken the caution scheme and develop securitisation in place of the current funding mix. Even if the aim of these transformations is to secure the finance system, it is through the transfer of risk from lenders to borrowers and investors, which seems paradoxical since this was the very cause of the subprime crisis. And this crisis proved that once over-indebtedness of mortgagors becomes systemic, no firewall can protect the lenders from its consequences and if it occurs, this evolution will not take place in the short term.

Regarding market functioning, as was the case in the 1980s, the changes after the mid-1990s were mainly the result of the sharp drop in interest rates rather than institutional change.

More generally, the credit system and housing policies operate as buffers against external shocks and cyclical up- and downturns, so that volatility is reduced and institutional changes are slower and less violent than in many other countries. But the deterioration of the macro-economic context probably means that the long lasting resilience of French housing markets has come to an end.

References

Antipa, P and Lecat, R (2013). 'Bulle immobilière' et politique d'octroi de crédits: enseignement d'un modèle structurel du marché français de l'immobilier résidentiel. *Débats et politiques – Revue de l'OFCE* 128, 163–188.

EMF (2014). *Hypostat 2013*. EMF, Brussels.

Friggit, J (2011). Quelles perspectives pour le prix des logements après son envolée? *Regards croisés sur l'économie* 9, 14–32. La Découverte, Paris.

INSEE (various years). *Comptes du logement*, [Online], Available: www.insee.fr.

Lefebvre, B, Mouillart, M and Occhipinti, S (1991). *Politique du Logement – 50 Ans pour un Échec*. L'Harmattan, Paris.

Levy-Vroelant, C, Schaefer, J-P and Tutin, C (2014). Social housing in France. In: *Social Housing in Europe*, Scanlon, K, Whitehead, C and Fernández Arrigoitia, M (eds). John Wiley & Sons, Ltd, Chichester, pp. 123–142.

Taffin, C and Vorms, B (2007). *Elargir l'accès au crédit au logement des emprunteurs atypiques* [Online], Available: www.anil.org/publications-et-etudes/etudes-et-eclairages/2007/elargir-lacces-au-credit-au-logement-des-emprunteurs-atypiques/ (accessed 5 August 2015).

Tutin, C (ed.) (2013). Ainsi vont les prix … In: *Etudes Foncières*, 165:Sept–Oct.. ADEF, Paris, pp. 35–62.

Tutin, C and Vorms, B (2014). French housing markets after the subprime crisis: from exuberance to resilience. *Journal of Housing and the Built Environment* 29, 277–298.

Vorms, B (1998). *L'accession à la propriété et la maîtrise des risques*, Plan Urbanisme, Paris: Construction Architecture, p. 95.

Vorms, B (2012). The effectiveness of the French credit system faced with the challenge of budgetary restrictions. *Housing Finance International* Summer, 20–24.

11

Milestones in the Development of the German Housing Finance System in the Last 25 Years

Stefan Kofner
TRAWOS-Institute, Zittau, Germany

The initial situation in 1989

The German housing finance system in 1989 can be described as traditional. The instruments used were aligned and tested; they ensured a stable development of the system and provided a high degree of resilience. In itself, the system did not and does not generate threatening macro-economic risks.

Within the primary mortgage markets there was no experimenting and few compromises were made on the requirements for capital adequacy and personal creditworthiness. The large market penetration of the building society sector (*Bausparkassen*) and a developed rental sector ensured that there was little demand for risky mortgage loans. On the funding side, tradition also ruled. The system was bank dominated and used traditional funding instruments almost exclusively, such as mortgage bonds and deposits. Almost all mortgages remained on the balance sheets of their originators. Finally, the structure of the supply side of primary mortgage lending was well-balanced and stable, with large market shares held by regionally rooted public and cooperative banks and an important and strictly regulated mortgage bank sector.

These structures only allowed for limited innovation, competition and high-risk lending policies. The banks that were able to take bigger risks were large niche players like state banks (*Landesbanken*) and mixed mortgage banks, which profited from public guarantees or regulatory loopholes.

Milestones in European Housing Finance, First Edition.
Edited by Jens Lunde and Christine Whitehead.
© 2016 John Wiley & Sons, Ltd. Published 2016 by John Wiley & Sons, Ltd.

In East Germany the initial situation of the housing market in 1990 was similar to the situation in many Central and Eastern European (CEE) countries. Residential investment, both in terms of total volume and spatial distribution, was centrally planned in the GDR (Sydow et al. 2005: 319). The corresponding credit funds were provided by the central budget. New residential development was also heavily subsidised, since the rents were far below cost (Topfstedt 1999: 441). For the most part, however, there was very little investment in preserving the stock of old buildings.

Milestones at a glance

It is not easy to identify milestones in the development of the German system of real estate finance over the last 25 years. Milestones are government actions that have shaped the system in the long run. The focus is thus on the *ex post* identification of crucial decisions and the discussion of the consequences of alternative courses of action. In this sense, the concept of milestones is closely linked to that of path dependence. Milestones are key events that have set the system on specific development paths.

In the case of Germany, the first major event was reunification almost 25 years ago. At that time, fundamental decisions about the economic transformation of the East German system of housing provision had to be made. Interestingly, different paths have been chosen for different policy areas here in many fields as elsewhere in post-socialist countries.

The most fundamental and enduring political decision in the last 25 years was the introduction of the Euro, which was announced in 1992 and fully introduced in 1999. The convergence criteria agreed upon at the Maastricht Summit and other factors initiated a long-term process of convergence, although with undesirable side effects.

Germany, of course, could not escape from the Global Financial Crisis (GFC). Decisive intervention of the government was required to rescue the banking system. However, the German economy and the German labour and housing markets have become surprisingly robust during the crisis.

The events in Table 11.1 have been identified as key milestones in the long-term development of housing markets and housing finance in Germany.

German reunification (1990): A friendly takeover by the white knight?

Since the German reunification, the East German housing market has undergone a fundamental transformation. This is true for multiple elements of the system, such as ownership structures, tenancy laws, the organisation of housing finance and housing investment, the funding environment and not least, the demographic framework of the housing market.

Table 11.1   Key milestones.

1 Oct 1990	**German reunification**
1 Jan 1996	**Conversion of home ownership subsidisation from a tax to a grant system**
1999–2005	**Integration and deregulation of capital markets**
1 Jan 1999	Euro introduction
19 July 2005	Elimination of guarantors' liability for savings banks and Landesbanken
19 July 2005	Abolition of the specialist bank principle for mortgage banks
2006–2008	**A housing system without subsidies**
1 Jan 2006	Abolition of declining balance depreciation scheme for new residential developments
1 Jan 2006	Abolition of the homeownership grant
2008–2014	**Measures to rescue the financial system**
5 Oct 2008	German government's patronage declaration of German bank deposits
7 Oct 2008	EU finance minister's rescue package
13 Oct 2008	Guarantee declaration of the functionality of the Pfandbrief Market
17 Oct 2008	Creation of the Special Fund for Financial Market Stabilisation (SoFFin)
2008 et seq.	Bail-out of several banks considered systemically relevant
July 2009	ECB covered bond purchase programme 1 (CBPP1)
8 Dec 2009	Extension of the eligibility period for the cyclical short-time working allowance

After the reunification, German housing policy was faced with the task of releasing the central government from its central position in housing provision and decentralising and privatising investment and financing decisions. In addition, it was thought that rents should reflect market rents in the housing market at least in the long run.

As compared to other post-socialist transition countries a very specific development path was followed in East Germany. First of all, German housing policy was reluctant to promote tenant privatisation. Secondly, new construction of rental housing and the modernisation of the existing housing stock were subsidised heavily for a number of years via special tax depreciation schemes. And finally, the regulatory framework was gradually approximated to the West German model. The heavy subsidies of the reconstruction years created the conditions for a relatively smooth transition.

Demographic development in East Germany also contributed to the relaxation of the market. The region continued to experience a very sharp drop in births. Also, full freedom of movement resulted in massive net emigration to the West. Largely as a result of these migration patterns a housing shortage developed in many cities of the West in the 1990s. Despite the sharp decline in population in the East, the number of households did not initially drop because of the consistently decreasing size of the average household. However, in the 1990s, a huge excess supply of dwellings arose. In response, incentives for housing demolitions were created and were especially attractive for public housing companies. The demolition rates achieved in recent years have taken some pressure off the market in the East.

In many ways, the specifics of the transformation approach of the East German housing market in the 1990s reflected the West German experience in the post-war decades. In addition, the housing policy of the GDR had restricted the formation of individual homeownership. To be sure, it made a difference that the 'acceding territory' did not have its own central government after 1990, which could have limited its openness to 'foreign' models and experiences. In short, for various reasons many other CEE transition countries that experienced mass privatisation of the state-owned housing stock took a fundamentally different path of transformation than East Germany from the very beginning.

The conversion of homeownership subsidisation from a tax to a grant system (1996): Heading for a new balance of tenures?

Since its introduction in 1996 until its abolition in 2006, the centrepiece of the homeownership subsidy system in Germany was the *Eigenheimzulage*, or first-homebuyer allowance. It replaced the previous model in which tax subsidies were offered for homeownership via a manipulated investment good model. The old funding model allowed the deduction of depreciation and interest on mortgage debt from income tax; the imputed rental value was set deliberately too low, however. Criticism of the tax incentive model centered particularly around its regressive distributional effect. This was also seen as a disadvantage for the relatively income-poor East German households. In contrast, the allowances scheme newly introduced in 1996 was independent of the tax situation of subsidised households.

With the Eigenheimzulage, a tangible incentive for homeownership for broad sections of the population had been created. A family with two children initially received up to DM 8000 in grants over a period of 8 years for a newly built home, a total of 64 000 DM (for further details, see Stephan 1996). However, despite the fact that the scheme privileged new construction, it did not in the end have a large effect on the number of residential completions. Although completions of one- and two-family buildings increased by over 25 percent between 1996 and 1999, completion rates fell consistently for 10 years after the turn of the millennium.

Integration and deregulation of capital markets: risks for the future?

German capital markets have widened and deepened as a result of the introduction of the Euro and they have become even more integrated into the global financial markets. Special features on the regulatory side like the privileges of the public banking sector and the special position of the mortgage banks were eliminated. In hindsight, one tends to weigh the risks of those tentative deregulations higher.

The introduction of the Euro (1999)

After the Treaty of Maastricht was signed in February 1992 the faith that financial markets had in the future for a monetary union solidified only gradually. The Euro was introduced as an accounting currency on 1 January 1999 and the capital markets immediately switched to the new currency. Independent of the issuer (public or private), new publicly traded securities have been issued only in Euros since then. The German federal government also made sure that its outstanding tradable debt securities were switched to the Euro in 1999 in order to prevent a market split between Deutschemark (DM) and Euro-denominated listed capital market securities.

In the bond market, the Euro was a success story right from the start. Thus, the volume of European corporate bonds has multiplied since the creation of the European Monetary Union. Although the German capital market has benefited from the broader investor base, this effect is likely to have been weakest in Germany because the DM bond market in terms of volume, liquidity, and the participation of international investors was already in the lead in Europe.

The German *Pfandbrief* (the German type of covered bond) market has shown significant growth since the introduction of the Euro. Perhaps more importantly than this, the market for public Pfandbriefe benefited from the growing involvement of international investors. The volume of outstanding German mortgage Pfandbriefe, on the other hand, only grew between 1995 and 2003. Thereafter, it has consistently declined.

In contrast to many other Euro zone countries the introduction of the Euro did not have a significant impact on the development of mortgage rates in Germany (EMF 2003: 8). Since 1994, there has been a decline in interest rates. According to the EMF, between 1994 and 1998 German mortgage rates dropped from 8.8 to 5.3 percent. However, this may be attributed more to the sustained decline in inflation in the early 1990s than to the introduction of the Euro. It does not seem plausible that the impending introduction of the Euro would have had a significant rate cutting effect in a traditionally hard currency, low interest rate country like Germany. The German bond market did not play the role of 'safe haven' either before or after the introduction of the Euro. This role was only assumed during the Euro crisis. Between 1999 and 2006, however, capital flows were clearly directed to the European periphery and not to the centre.

Thus, the German housing market showed no visible reaction to the introduction of the Euro. Despite declining mortgage rates after the turn of the millennium, the housing market remained weak. Housing completions fell ever further and transactions and house prices remained stagnant at best. No positive effect was observed as a result of a relaxation of mortgage credit standards.

The German housing market actually started to revive during the GFC. No signs of a mortgage credit crunch were observed in Germany. The increasing demand may be attributed to the extremely low mortgage rates (as a result of the extraordinary monetary policy of the European Central Bank) and the widespread perception of the German residential real estate as a crisis-proof investment by domestic and foreign investors.

Elimination of guarantors' liability for savings banks and Landesbanken (2005)

Until 2005, German public savings banks and Landesbanken (principal banks of the states that function as the central savings banks in their territories and are intended to drive regional economic development) profited from public guarantees, which gave them a competitive advantage in funding costs. The European Commission regarded these advantages as unfair and took action before the European Court. After a transition period (18 July 2001–18 July 2005), the institutional liability and the state guarantees had to be abolished. However, old liabilities and new liabilities incurred during the transition period still were given by the guarantees (Fischer *et al.* 2012: 18).

The abolition of the guarantee liability has had a significant impact on the lending business of savings banks/Landesbanken: the funding costs for new debt have risen and the credit terms of savings banks and private banks have been aligned. The public banks were forced to introduce a more risk-sensitive pricing of credit. Additionally a fundamental discussion has emerged about the legal form of savings banks to improve flexibility of obtaining equity capital and to facilitate mergers (conversion into private legal forms etc.).

At the level of the Landesbanken, there is a direct connection between the abolition of the guarantees and their inglorious role in the financial crisis. In advance of the 2005 deadline, most Landesbanken issued bonds beyond measure simply because they could do so under the warranty umbrella at still more favourable terms (Fischer *et al.* 2012). They did not know, however, what to do with this massive inflow of means. Thus the temptation grew to engage in risky credit portfolio business practices, such as the purchase of asset-backed securities.

Abolition of the specialist bank principle for mortgage banks (2005): An incorrect signal?

Until 2005 mortgage banks were the most important specialised banking group in Germany. Different from universal banks these special banks were limited in their business activity to mortgage and public lending. Their loans served as a collateral pool for the Pfandbriefe. Only high-quality loans (60% loan-to-value [LTV], first-rank, conservative valuation) registered into the 'cover register' and regularly examined by the 'cover pool monitor' were eligible as Pfandbrief collateral. In order to further minimise risk the duration of the Pfandbrief bonds almost matches that of the corresponding loans.

Apart from the specialised banks some mixed mortgage banks (for historical context, see Bellinger 2005: 48) and public credit institutions including the Landesbanken also had the right to issue Pfandbriefe although they were universal banks. The public issuers profited from public guarantees and hence top ratings and favourable refinancing conditions (Hagen and Kullig 2004: 1135).

Thus, the specialist bank principle had already been largely undermined when the Pfandbrief issuance monopoly of the privileged institutions was finally removed through the Pfandbrief Act, which came into force on 19 July 2005 (Volk 2006: 146). It was replaced by a licence system: the issuance right has been limited to licensed (universal) banks since then. Well-proven instruments from the existing mortgage bank legislation (e.g. the extra-low mortgage lending limit, regular cover pool examinations, the coverage principle and the preferential right of the Pfandbrief creditors in case of an issuer insolvency) were also taken over.

The Pfandbrief as a funding source is now open to every bank that fulfils the minimum requirements. The permission presupposes that the bank operates the Pfandbrief business regularly and lastingly and has suitable rules and instruments for the management of the associated risks. Furthermore the bank must have an appropriate organisational structure, qualified staff and resources for granting cover loans and issuing Pfandbriefe. In stipulating these conditions, legislators were seeking to ensure that the licensed banks conduct their Pfandbrief businesses seriously and lastingly. 'Opportunistic business strategies of a short-term nature' (Hagen 2008: 8) were clearly discouraged.

The Pfandbrief is still a major funding source of mortgage credit in Germany although with decreasing importance for housing finance. In retrospect, the abolition of the specialist bank principle may have been a wrong signal, but it was no major cause of the financial crisis. As a preventive measure, only a tightening and narrowing of the scope of the specialist bank regulation would have been promising.

Trying to run a housing system without subsidies

With the abolition of the homeownership grant in 2006, the era of home-ownership subsidies available for broad strata of the population ended in Germany. Interestingly, the declining balance depreciation for new private rental accommodation was abolished at the same time. Thus, the neutrality of housing policy against the two tenures was preserved by and large. With these decisive cuts in the subsidy system, the German government without doubt entered new ground in housing policy. The role of housing as a merit good was fundamentally put into question.

Abolition of the declining balance depreciation scheme for new residential developments (2006)

The German private rented sector is regarded as a stabilising force and a means of making housing consumption more affordable. It is characterised by security of tenure and second-generation rent controls. The housing policy of the post-war era not only subsidised social housing, but also ensured sufficient incentives for the private sector (Earley 2004: 28). New residential development was promoted from the beginning by various tax privileges (Kofner 2003: 328):

- capital gains tax exemption for rental properties held privately for a longer time period;
- a declining balance depreciation allowance until 2005 (after which it has become linear);
- the ability to set losses from letting against other income (negative gearing) to ensure the effectiveness of the depreciation allowance.

In Germany, the depreciation rules were changed repeatedly over time, but included an element of subsidisation (tax depreciation running ahead of economic depreciation) most of the time between 1949 and 2005. Before the cancellation of the scheme in 2006, 40 percent of the initial value (purchase price or production costs of the building without the value of the land) could be written off in the first 10 years. The depreciation schemes applicable in earlier years were even more favourable for investors for the most part. The resulting tax deferral effect created an important investment incentive. Private landlords with a high marginal income tax rate in particular profited from the declining balance depreciation. The policy also indirectly sought to relax housing markets and keep rents low.

However, since 2006 only linear depreciation has been allowed; the annual depreciation for residential buildings is 2.0 percent for all residential buildings completed after 31 December 1924. These rates apply regardless of whether the building is held as a business or personal asset. In very old buildings, or buildings in a bad state of construction, the remaining lifetime is to be reduced accordingly. It is likely that fiscal consolidation was an important motive for this change of legislation.

The housing market was not unaffected. Low completion numbers in the years after 2005 may be partly explained by the imbalance between the red tape still in force and the abolished tax compensation for private residential development. The financing system was affected by the change in the depreciation rules in terms of a decline in demand for mortgages for privately financed multi-family housing.

Abolition of the homeownership grant (2006):
Did we give it up too early?

The homeownership grant (*Eigenheimzulage*) was abolished on 1 January 2006. The elimination only applied to new cases, however. The ones already receiving the grant, continued to do so until the end of the eligibility period.

Nowadays owner-occupied homes are treated as consumption goods for tax purposes. Thus no deduction of interest is possible. The most important instrument promoting homeownership is the subsidisation as a pension scheme (the so-called 'Riester pension'). Depending on rate of return assumptions, homeownership can have a tax advantage here as compared with financial investments.

For the financial sector, the abolition of the homeownership grant was not good news. As a consequence the affordability of homeownership worsened considerably. The Eigenheimzulage had an equity capital-replacing character from the perspective of the lender. However, banks have not tried to compensate for this by lowering their creditworthiness criteria. A certain relaxation of the situation has been achieved only by the steadily declining capital market and mortgage rates.

Measures to rescue the financial system since 2008

It was a surprise to many that the German banking system was so exposed to the contagion risks of the financial crisis. The extent of the problems endangered the stability of the whole system. To this day, however, this is difficult for many people to recognise because they did not experience exaggerations and debt excesses in the domestic retail markets. Only determined action of the federal government and the international institutions, however, has allowed the country to cope with the situation.

The German government's patronage declaration of
German bank deposits

In October 2008, there were indications in Germany of bank runs for the first time since the 1930s. After dramatic negotiations on the last weekend of September 2008, the federal government together with private banks announced a rescue package for the ailing mortgage bank Hypo Real Estate with a value of about €35 bn. However, the private banks withdrew their warranties on 4 October because they concluded that the capital needs of the Hypo Real Estate were substantially higher than initially assumed.

According to the former Chancellor's Office Minister's promise the respective federal government's declaration was a:

> ...response to information provided by the Bundesbank, that there is a conspicuous behaviour of bank customers. People withdrew cash in large amounts from counters and ATMs. That was all below the threshold of systemically dangerous, but above the threshold of non-compliance.

The guarantee of savings was apparently introduced as a reaction to well-founded concerns that the matter could grow into a bank run if a new rescue package for Hypo Real Estate could not be presented in time (de Maizière and Braun 2013).

On the 5 October 2008, the Chancellor announced,

> ...the federal government says on this day that we will not allow the failure of a single financial institution to bring about an imbalance of the whole system. Therefore we are working hard to ensure the Hypo Real Estate... We tell the savers and depositors that their deposits are safe. This is also what the federal government stands for.[1]

Finance Minister Peer Steinbrück also assured depositors that they had nothing to fear as a result of the Hypo Real Estate crisis. The statements were obviously improvised and left inquiring journalists with many questions as to their scope and true meaning. Furthermore, no sources of financing were named. The statements were not legally binding and therefore they provided no reliable guarantee for German citizens. However, the federal government has said it will uphold its political commitment and take appropriate action if and when it becomes necessary (German Bundestag plenary proceedings 16/182). Be that as it may, the declarations served their purpose, and the banks have not been stormed. The government has additionally confirmed the continuing validity of the warranty given in 2008.

EU Finance Ministry's rescue package

The EU Finance Ministry's rescue package, which included the commitment to bail out any bank constituting a systemic risk in the banking market and common principles for the re-capitalisation of ailing institutions (F.A.Z., 8 October 2008, Nr. 235, 11), was another milestone to re-establish trust in the stability of the financial system.

Given the interconnectedness of the financial systems of individual European countries this Memorandum was of great importance for the stability of the German banking system. A purely national shield against the contagion risks from the collapse of a non-German European bank would have been short-sighted.

In reality, too many systemically important banks had to be bailed out by the governments of Germany and other European countries. It turned out that the nationally organised systems of regulation and banking supervision in Europe were very deficient. The European financial system was further undermined by the existence of shadow banks and conduits in Ireland and other financial markets. Their risks would eventually impact on the parent companies in Germany and elsewhere. The banking systems of individual countries such as Ireland and Spain were exposed to such risk that the national governments were overwhelmed with their stabilisation and had to take the help of the European institutions.

Guarantee declaration of the functionality of the Pfandbrief market

Another milestone was the German government's declaration in the Explanatory Memorandum of the Financial Markets Stabilisation Act (*Finanzmarktstabilisierungsgesetz*) from 13 October 2008:

> The special statutory provisions in Germany mean that Pfandbriefe are already safe – throughout the more than 200-year long history of the product there has never been a default of a German Pfandbrief. The German government will ensure that this continues to be the case in the future as well. As far as the functionality of the Pfandbrief market requires it the federal government will take further legal measures to ensure the safety of the Pfandbrief in the short term.[2]

This institutional letter of comfort went beyond the general guarantees for the German banks. Also it was absolutely costless for the Pfandbrief market and it was interpreted as covering all Pfandbriefe including existing issuances.

The president of the association of German mortgage banks commented on 27 November 2008:

> ... the Federal Government made clear that the Pfandbriefe are safe and therefore not in need of any public guarantees. There is nothing more to say than that. Public guarantees could permanently damage the Pfandbrief market. Suspicions could easily gain ground that there was a quality defect in the Pfandbriefe which had made public support necessary.

Creation of the Special Fund for Financial Market Stabilisation (SoFFin)

The Financial Market Stabilisation Fund (SoFFin) is a temporary special fund that was established on 17 October 2008 in an emergency procedure. The fund has a volume of €480 bn (€80 bn for the purchase of troubled assets and the recapitalisation of financial institutions and another €400 bn for guarantees of debt and liabilities of beneficiary companies). Beneficiary institutions must pay a 'competitive yield' or 'reasonable return' to the fund in return (Schrooten 2011: 356). Since 2011, the fund is no longer actively stabilising markets, but manages and monitors stabilisation means already granted.

The biggest customers of the SoFFin were the Hypo Real Estate, Commerzbank, IKB Deutsche Industriebank, and three Landesbanken. Up to 28 February 2013 the SoFFin was able to reduce its liquidity guarantees, which had peaked in 2010 at €168 bn, to €3.7 bn, and capital assistance, which peaked at €29.4 bn in 2010, to €18.8 bn. Greater commitments still existed at Commerzbank, Hypo Real Estate and Portigon (formerly WestLB) (FMSA 2014).

The creation of a national rescue facility for faltering banks was a milestone in stabilising the German financial system. The SoFFin has saved several systemically important banks from collapse, including at least two institutions that played a strategic role in real estate financing.

Bail-out of Hypo Real Estate, IKB Deutsche Industriebank, SachsenLB, BayernLB, WestLB, Commerzbank, HSH Nordbank, Aareal Bank and others

The German banks got into trouble because of their foreign wholesale lending activities. At home high standards were applied to the creditworthiness of private borrowers, particularly in the granting of housing loans. High LTVs and innovative types of loans, such as interest-only mortgages (IOMs) or foreign currency loans, remained the exception.

The German banking system was especially vulnerable because of its exposure to the risks in the US mortgage market (Kofner 2008: 49–53). Some banks maintained huge conduits that were focused on investment in the US subprime market (i.e. in residential mortgage-backed securities and collateralised debt obligation, their valuation was almost exclusively dependent on the development of subprime mortgages in the US). The conduits were equipped with virtually zero equity capital and did not appear on the balance sheets of their initiators. These quasi-banks have operated on a large scale outside of banking regulation and banking supervision and they have pursued such transactions that were not allowed to their parent companies.

The key problem for conduits was on the liabilities side of their balance sheets, where they had refinanced their mostly long-term assets only for the short-term. In case of a problem with the rollover of short-term funding, the parent companies had given very generous credit lines to the conduits. Banks engaged would have gone bankrupt if the governments had not intervened with guarantees, capital injections and arranged mergers motivated by concerns about the stability of the banking system.

The largest single rescue operation was the bail-out of the Hypo Real Estate bank in early October 2008 (Kofner 2008: 122–124). The bank's focus was on commercial real estate and public finance. Hypo Real Estate faltered not least because its Irish subsidiary Depfa could no longer refinance its large public sector loan book at the interbank market.

An insolvency of Hypo Real Estate would have been particularly harmful to the Pfandbrief market, which is widely regarded as a cornerstone of the German financial system. Fear was in the air that in case of the insolvency of a major issuer, the Pfandbrief would not be available as a source of refinancing of the banking system any longer, possibly indefinitely (Ruhkamp 2008). The consequences for the availability of real estate loans and the real estate market would certainly have been fatal. The rescue of this bank with total assets of €400 bn was thus justified by the magnitude of the possible contagion effects.

ECB Covered bond purchase programmes

In 2009 the ECB launched 'one of its most innovative non-standard measures', the first Covered Bond Purchase Programme (CBPP1). Under this initiative the Eurosystem purchased €60 bn worth of investment-grade covered bonds between July 2009 and July 2010 (see González-Páramo 2011 for the ECB's objectives). The CBPP1 programme stimulated a reactivation of covered bonds being issued in the primary market (Beirne *et al.* 2011).

When covered bond markets came under significant pressure again due to the intensification of the sovereign debt crisis, the ECB decided to launch CBPP2 in October 2011 and purchased covered bonds in the amount of €16.5 bn between November 2011 and October 2012.

The Eurosystem decided to target covered bonds because of the particular importance that this asset class has for the financing of banks and the real economy in the Euro area. However, it is unlikely that the programs were launched as a response to the situation at the German Pfandbrief market. Since early 2009 there were increasing signs that the Pfandbrief market was about to pick up noticeably (Kofner 2009). The temporary liquidity problems in the Pfandbrief market cannot be equated with the complete breakdown of the markets for credit securitisation in the course of the financial crisis. Compared with other mortgage funding instruments the Pfandbrief fared reasonably well and was able to maintain access to liquidity by and large. The development of the swap spreads of German Pfandbriefe as compared to other types of European covered bonds or to senior unsecured bank debt substantiates this point (Hofer and Kofner 2010).

Extension of the reference period for the cyclical short-time working allowance to 18 months

The German economy as a whole was affected by the global recession, but during the crisis the German Federal Government managed to maintain the confidence of financial markets and to support economic stabilisation through exceptional measures. During the crisis, the German economy performed relatively well, and in 2010 and 2011, the growth rate was twice the average of the EU27.

The development of the labour market is of utmost importance for the safety of outstanding mortgage loans. Germany was able to significantly reduce its unemployment rate in the midst of the GFC. Unemployment rates fell significantly (from 7.5 percent in 2008 to 5.5 percent in 2012) and the economic position of private households generally remained stable. The average unemployment rate in Germany is now about half that in the Euro zone and the EU 27.

It was crucial for this favourable development that in 2009, when German real GDP shrank by more than 5 percent, no mass layoffs took place in large companies. This was made possible by the extension of short-time allowances for underemployed people (*Kurzarbeitergeld*) and the widespread use of working-time accounts in large companies (Schnitzler *et al.* 2012). The eligibility period for the short-time allowance was extended from 6 to 24 months in early 2009. In addition, employers were also relieved from part of their social security contributions.

The employment effect of the policy was tremendous. Since the beginning of 2009, working hours have been logged for more than two million workers and in some industries almost one in three employees was affected.

The dynamics of the German system of housing finance since 1989

The German housing market is characterised by some special features. First of all there is a very low rate of homeownership and the rental sector is very important. Small private landlords play the most important role in the private rented sector. They operate under a focused low-cost subsidy system. The financial institutions (not so much regulation, but traditional lending habits) are clearly on the conservative side. Risky mortgages are not granted for either apartments or for homes. In particular, the high level of credit quality is guaranteed by the mortgage lending value calculation, the high standard of personal creditworthiness required from borrowers, the low level of house price to income (HPI) and LTVs and the low incidence of Adjustable Rate Mortgages (ARM), Interest Only Mortgages (IOM) and other 'innovative' mortgage products (Kofner 2008: 90–94). The refinancing of residential mortgages is bank-dominated, meaning the loans remain on the balance sheets of their originators for the most part. Traditional funding instruments such as deposits, bonds and mortgage bonds dominate. In contrast, securitisation and short-term loans from other banks play only a minor role. These structures have a favourable influence on loan quality.

The proliferation of Bauspar savings contracts helps to further dampen the demand for risky loans.

In 1989 the supply side structure of the German housing market was not significantly different to today. Furthermore, the tenancy laws from the late 1980s do not differ significantly from the laws in force today. Lately, however, a slight tightening of regulation has been observed. More strikingly, the subsidy system is entirely different than it was 25 years ago. Both homeownership and the construction of private rented blocks have been intensively promoted by the tax system throughout this period until the year 2005.

On the financing and refinancing side innovations have tried but failed to be taken up on a large scale. Serious regulatory changes hit public sector banks (abolition of public guarantees) and mortgage banks (abolition of the specialist bank principle). The structure of the suppliers of primary mortgage credit has changed: the retail market share of the mortgage banks has decreased, whilst the savings banks and the cooperative banks (i.e. the small and regionally rooted banks) were able to expand their market position. These structural changes may even have reduced the appetite for lending risk or an extension of the product range. On the other hand, the two largest mortgage banks have failed dramatically with their internationalisation strategies.

Thus, the German system of housing finance has undergone no fundamental change in the last 25 years, although of course the subsidy/tax relief system has changed. Nevertheless, four once-in-a-century events changed the financing conditions and the structure of the supply side: the German reunification, the introduction of the Euro without a political union, the sub-prime mortgage crisis and the subsequent Euro zone sovereign debt crisis. All events except for the Euro introduction had a shock-like character. They were not virtually unpredictable, but the political institutions were not prepared and were forced to improvise.

The first important challenge was German reunification. The banking system in East Germany had to be reorganised, the modernisation of the housing stock had to be supported with incentives, and solutions had to be found for the problems of housing sector debt from the socialist period and the low homeownership rate in the East. The last 25 years have seen a lot of progress on these issues, but there are still shortcomings: for example, in many places, there is an excess supply of housing, modernisations are often not profitable given the low rents and by far not all historic buildings have been saved.

The introduction of the Euro had no severe impact on Germany. In particular, no strong interest rate reduction effect occurred as it had in Spain or Italy. The financial crisis on the other hand has hit the German banking system relatively hard. The worst effects resulted primarily from indirect exposure to the US mortgage market. Particularly affected were some state banks (Landesbanken), but private mortgage lenders also suffered.

Large sums of government money kept a number of 'systemically important' banks afloat. In hindsight it appears that the experiment of internationalisation and modernisation of the banking system failed due to inexperience. Some public and mortgage banks as well as their regulators and supervisors particularly suffered from this lack of experience. The European Banking Union now offers the opportunity of a more neutral and professional approach to banking supervision.

Faced with the Euro zone debt crisis, the German economy was well prepared after years of political reforms, wage restraint and relative budget discipline. Helpful of course was the fact that there had been no housing bubble in Germany. Consequently, the emphasis of post crisis policy was on the supply side of the (wholesale) finance market while in most other countries there was more concern about consumers and mortgage products.

Notes

1   A. Merkel quoted from www.spiegel.de/wirtschaft/merkel-und-steinbrueck-im-wortlaut-die-spareinlagen-sind-sicher-a-582305.html. Translated by the author. No responsibility is taken for the correctness of citation and translation.
2   Translated by the author. No responsibility is taken for the correctness of citation and translation.

References

Beirne, J, Dalitz, L, Ejsing, J, Grothe, M, Manganelli, S, Monar, F *et al.* (2011). The impact of the Eurosystem's covered bond purchase program on the primary and secondary markets, *European Central Bank Occasional Paper Series* No. 122, January.

Bellinger, D (2005). Einige Betrachtungen zur Geschichte der deutschen Hypothekenbanken, *Immobilien & Finanzierung* 56:2, 48–51.

Earley, F (2004). What explains the differences in homeownership rates in Europe? *Housing Finance International* September 2004, 25–30.

EMF (European Mortgage Federation) (2003). Hypostat 1992–2002, Brussels.

Fischer, M, Hainz, C, Rocholl, J and Steffen, S (2012). Wie wirkt sich der Wegfall staatlicher Garantien auf die Risikoübernahme von Banken aus? *ifo Schnelldienst* 18:2012, 65. *Jahrgang*, 17–21.

Federal Agency for Financial Market Stabilisation (FMSA) (2014) Instruments of SoFFin [Online] Available: www.fmsa.de/de/fmsa/soffin/instrumente/massnahmen- www.fmsa.de/en/fmsa/soffin/ (accessed 29 July 2015).

González-Páramo, J (2011). Member of the Executive Board of the ECB (2011). The ECB and the sovereign debt crisis. Speech at the XXIV Moneda y Crédito Symposium, Madrid, 4 November.

Hagen, L (2008). The legal framework for issuing Pfandbriefe. In: *The Pfandbrief 2008/2009: Facts and Figures*, vdp Verband Deutscher Pfandbriefbanken, pp. 6–15.

Hagen, L and Kullig, S (2004). Pfandbrief bleibt Pfandbrief? *Kreditwesen*, 57:29, 1135–1137.

Hofer, T and Kofner, S (2010). The German residential mortgage market before, during and after the financial crisis: business as usual? Paper prepared for the *European Network of Housing Research International Housing Conference*, Istanbul, Turkey, 4–7 July 2010.

Kofner, S (2003). Die Formation der deutschen Wohnungspolitik nach dem Zweiten Weltkrieg – Teil III. In: *Deutsche Wohnungswirtschaft*, 55. Jg., Heft 12, S. 322–334.

Kofner, S (2008). *Die Hypotheken- und Finanzmarktkrise*, Fritz Knapp Verlag.

Kofner, S (2009). The German Pfandbrief system facing the financial crisis. Paper prepared For *the European Network of Housing Research International Housing Conference, Prague, Czech Republic*, 28 June–1 July 2009.

de Maizière, T and Braun, S (2013). *Damit der Staat den Menschen dient. Über Macht und Regieren*, Siedler-Verlag.

Ruhkamp, S (2008). Der Offenbarungseid. *F.A.Z.* v. 30.9.2008:229, S. 13.

Schnitzler, L, Seiwert, M and Schumacher, H (2012). Wie die Krise ihren Schrecken verliert: So trotzen BMW & Co. mit Flexibilisierung der Flaute. *Wirtschaftswoche* v. 27.11.2012.

Schrooten, M (2011). Bankenrettungsfonds: Chancen und Risiken. *Wirtschaftsdienst* 91:5, 356–358.

Stephan, R (1996). Die Neuregelung der Wohneigentumsförderung. In: *Der Betrieb*, Heft 5, pp. 240–248.

Sydow, M, Kofner, S and Sander, C (2005). Wohnungsmarkt, Wohnungspolitik und Wohnungswirtschaft in den neuen Bundesländern. In: *Grundlagen der Wohnungs- und Immobilienwirtschaft*, Kühne-Büning (ed.), 4th edn, Fritz Knapp Verlag, pp. 319–343.

Topfstedt, T (1999). Wohnen und Städtebau in der DDR. In: *Geschichte des Wohnens, Vol. 5, 1945 bis heute: Aufbau – Neubau – Umbau*, Flagge, I. (ed.), Deutsche Verlags-Anstalt Stuttgart, pp. 419–562.

Volk, B (2006). Germany. In: *Covered bonds beyond Pfandbriefe*, Golin, J (ed.). Euromoney Books, pp. 134–159.

12

Moving from an Authoritarian State System to an Authoritarian Market System: Housing Finance Milestones in Hungary between 1979 and 2014

József Hegedüs and Eszter Somogyi
Metropolitan Research Institute, Budapest, Hungary

From socialism to capitalism: the economic and institutional environment

In the last three decades, Hungary has undergone a radical social, economic and political transition. Despite being a small country without significant natural resources, Hungary has always been strongly connected to the global economy. The housing finance system in Hungary moved from a state controlled authoritarian system in the 1980s to a fully developed liberalised system in the 1990s. This was followed by a lending surge in the early 2000s that lasted until 2008 when the full impact of the Global Financial Crisis (GFC) reached Hungary. The GFC left the housing finance system in a state of confusion and regulatory measures were quickly introduced, some of which were considered 'unorthodox'.

Looking over the past 30–35 years, it is possible to distinguish four main stages in the development of the housing finance system and the housing market in Hungary, each characterised by a different economic and institutional environment. These can be categorised as:

- 1979–1990 Moving towards an authoritarian market society under socialism.

Milestones in European Housing Finance, First Edition.
Edited by Jens Lunde and Christine Whitehead.
© 2016 John Wiley & Sons, Ltd. Published 2016 by John Wiley & Sons, Ltd.

- 1991–2000 Transition to a market society: initial recession and recovery.
- 2001–2008 Dynamic growth and irresponsible fiscal policy: state and market failures.
- 2009–present Crisis management: from 'orthodox' to an 'unorthodox' approach.

The first stage lies technically outside the remit of this book, which starts in the late 1980s. However, because of the very radical changes that took place both before and after that date it seems appropriate in the Hungarian context to start with the decade before the fall of the Berlin Wall. Without understanding the pre-transition housing finance system, especially the house-price bubble, economic recession and housing loan crises prior to transition, it would be difficult to explain the main trends in the 1990s. The economic hardships faced by Eastern European socialist societies in the 1980s were rooted in the inefficiency of state socialism. However, the process of their economic decline was exacerbated by the oil price crisis of 1973. Hungary came very close to state bankruptcy in the early 1980s and, as a last resort (with the implicit consent of the Soviet Union), joined the IMF in 1982, gaining access to the financial resources of the international capital market. The government introduced several measures to support the decentralisation of the state sector (e.g. local councils and state companies gained more independence, the second economy was partially acknowledged, foreign investments were intensified and a two-tier bank system was introduced). By the end of the 1980s foreign debt and debt service had increased, increasing the budget deficit as part of an aggravated fiscal crisis. Concurrently, economic productivity was stagnating, forcing the political elite to eventually accept the inevitability of a regime change as the Soviet Union dissolved.

From 1990 to 2000, Hungary moved from a state controlled planned economy toward a liberal market economy through relevant economic strategies such as price liberalisation, privatisation of state-owned enterprises and the consolidation and privatisation of banks. As a result of the transitional recession GDP fell by 15 percent in the first part of the 1990s. After introducing a strict austerity programme in 1996 (the so-called Bokros programme) the economy started to recover and by the end of the decade the GDP gradually returned to its pre-transition level. The informal economy remained vast, estimated to account for 25–33 percent of the GDP between 1990 and 1997 (Lackó 2000). Poverty also became an important problem as social and regional inequalities continued to grow, albeit at a slower pace than during the previous decade.

Beginning in 2000, economic policy became more optimistic and shifted its focus from austerity to a demand-oriented model (in which housing finance played an important role). Global economic prosperity and the money market boom only fuelled irresponsible government policies. In 2004

Hungary joined the European Union, further fostering the belief in economic growth. A major element of the development during this period was the intensive growth of the residential mortgage market, initially supported by huge state subsidies (until 2004) and later through foreign resources, especially mortgage loans denominated in foreign currency with low variable interest rates and high risk factors for the borrowing households.

Foreign Direct Investments continued to flow into Hungary, which, thanks to the increase in EU Structural Funds, contributed to growth in the economy. Household consumption funded by loans continued to increase until September 2008, while industrial production, employment and exports fell. The irresponsible fiscal and monetary policy left Hungary with a fragile and vulnerable economy, weakened even further by the detrimental effects of the GFC in 2008.

Between 2008 and 2010, the government followed traditional crisis management policies by taking an IMF loan of $25 bn, introducing austerity measures such as government expenditure cuts (affecting housing subsidies, pensions, salaries in the public sector and more) and levying special taxes on banks and energy service companies. The government successfully decreased the budget deficit from 9.2 percent of the GDP in 2006 to 3.3 percent in 2010 and kept inflation under control at 4.2 percent in 2009 (as opposed to 6.1 percent in 2008). Nevertheless, the Hungarian economy grew by only 1 percent in 2007 and contracted by 6.3 percent in 2009.

After 2010, the new conservative government (which was elected in 2010 and re-elected in 2014 with a two-thirds majority) introduced an unorthodox economic (and political) regime, which deployed populist measures to move toward an authoritarian political system. As a method of crisis management, this policy tried to avoid the economically necessary direct austerity measures and instead utilised economic reserves (like the private pension funds) and imposed special taxes on foreign owned companies (banks, energy companies and commercial companies). At the same time, it froze utility prices (a subsidy to all activities), introduced a regressive flat rate income tax and cut social expenditures. These developments were considered by some observers as a step toward building up 'crony capitalism'. However, long term recovery necessitates austerity measures, either by cutting expenditures (decreasing salaries etc.), by imposing taxes, or by allowing inflation (through devaluation of the national currency) to decrease living standards and increase productivity through lower wages. The government did not have a master plan to restructure the economy and the measures taken appeared more like a series of *ad hoc*, trial-and-error decisions. These political changes had an impact on housing finance in two main ways: they placed the blame on banks for the crisis and they eliminated the foreign exchange (FX) loan portfolio, which set a political constraint on devaluation.

Consequently, the new government's very different approach was dubbed an unorthodox policy in the media. Thanks to its strong political support, the government was able to expand its powers so that when its fiscal plan to increase the deficit was rejected by the EU, the government started a 'freedom fight' against foreign-owned banks and international companies.

Finance milestones in the housing system

Although there have always been time-lags between major policy decisions and the ensuing change in the institutional legislation and market processes, the development of the housing finance system has remained closely connected to larger political and economic periods in Hungary (See Figure 12.1).

1980–1989: Introducing market elements in the housing system under budgetary pressure

Hungary represented one of the most liberal models of the centrally planned economy, which could partly be explained by the political consolidation of the Kádár administration (the first secretary of the communist party from 1956 to 1988) following the 1956 Revolution. The introduction of the 'new economic mechanism' in 1968 illustrated the desire for a more decentralised and more efficient economic system, which was vastly curtailed by the collapse of the Prague Spring in 1968. The housing system had a dual 'market' structure. In the *state sector*, there were different, directly controlled allocation channels (typically affecting not only the council housing stock, but the privately owned urban prefabricated housing stock as well) where income and need factors helped determine who obtained that housing. In the *private sector*, household income and informal social networks played determining roles. Both sectors worked within the limits of the central planning system, which regulated the supply of building material, accessibility of labour for private construction, the construction industry and access to finance. Moreover, the amount of property owned by individual families was also controlled: one family was legally allowed to own only one primary housing unit and one secondary unit.

The housing finance system in the socialist housing model was based on the centrally controlled state-owned bank (National Saving Banks – referred as 'OTP' in this article, based on its Hungarian acronym), appropriations from the state budget and, as a supplement, contributions from state-owned companies. The typical loan product (35-year, low fixed interest rate loans at around 1.5–3 percent) can also be considered as involving subsidy. There was no proper underwriting procedure in place; instead, eligible households assigned by the state housing agencies (councils, large state-owned enterprises, OTP and housing cooperatives) as potential buyers had automatic rights to the subsidy and the loan. In 1973, for example, 35 percent of the

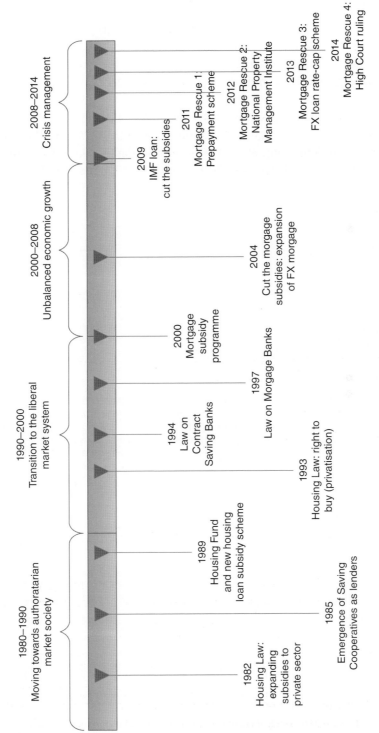

Figure 12.1 Main milestones in the development of the housing finance system.

total investment in the state controlled sector was financed through loans, 53 percent through budget subsidies and 12 percent from households' savings, while in the private sector the respective contributions were 24 percent, 1 percent and 75 percent respectively (Hegedüs and Tosics 1996: 249). An official salary requirement provided a safeguard against the risk of non-payment or default and, thanks to wage security and full employment policies, lending did not present any significant risk to OTP.

As the macroeconomic conditions of Hungary worsened at the turn of 1980, housing policy became more open to the market in the hope that increasing the incentives for private actors to invest in housing could ease the budgetary burden while maintaining the volume of the output (See Figures 12.2 and 12.3). Financial disadvantages faced by the private sector

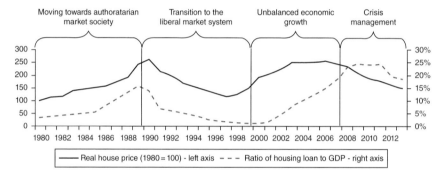

Figure 12.2   House price and loan to GDP ratio in Hungary, 1980–2013.
Sources: House price data from 1980 to 1998 are expert estimates based on OTP price data, surveys and other sources; from 1998, FHB (2014).
Data on new construction are from Central Statistical Office (various years).
Data on the housing loan portfolio between 1980 and 1985 are from OTP (1986).
Housing loan portfolio data between 1986 and 2014 is from Hungarian National Bank Statistics (various years).

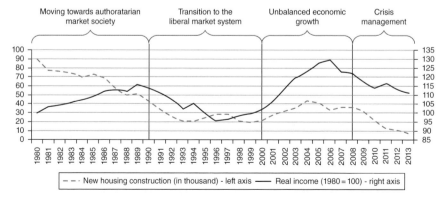

Figure 12.3   Housing construction and real income in Hungary 1980–2013.
Source: Central Statistical Office (various years).

Table 12.1 Tenure structure, 1970–2011.

	1970	1980	1990	2001	2011
Owner Occupied	66.5%	71.5%	72.3%	90.0%	88.0%
Municipal housing	33.3%	28.3%	19.0%	3.7%	2.7%
Corporate housing	–	–	3.7%	1.0%	1.0%
Private rental and other	0.3%	0.2%	5.0%	5.3%	8.3%
Total	100.0%	100.0%	100.0%	100.0%	100.0%

Source: Central Statistical Office (various years).

were diminished by making private single-family house building (self-help construction) eligible for construction subsidies, increasing the upper ceiling of the OTP loan, permitting the use of an employers' credit and even offering local council housing grants. As a result, the proportion of owner-occupation increased (Table 12.1). Other measures to promote private investment involved increasing the supply of available land (Hegedüs 1992). From 1985 small savings cooperatives had the right to issue housing loans, which in principle introduced competition within the sector. Despite this, OTP retained its monopoly position in the housing finance system (it controlled 85 percent of the loan portfolio in 1989).

In spite of the policy changes, housing output decreased in the late 1980s (Figure 12.3). Market house prices increased by 150 percent between 1980 and 1989 (Figure 12.2) and OTP had difficulty selling new subsidised apartments in multi-unit buildings in some cities because of their high cost and a shift in preferences (as well as the subsidisation of single family home construction).

The other – and more important – signs of the crisis were the increase in interest rates and the technical bankruptcy of the OTP. The outstanding housing loan portfolio increased rapidly in the 1980s, from 3 percent to 14 percent of the GDP between 1980 and 1989. The portfolio of long maturity and fixed low rate loans (1–3 percent) in the books of OTP and other saving cooperatives led to a huge increase in budgetary outlay as the nominal interest rate increased.

1989–1999: Transition to a market-based housing finance system

The housing finance system technically went bankrupt in 1988. Housing subsidy reached 3.3 percent of GDP in 1989 (World Bank 1991), which was unmanageable. Consequently, the housing finance system – or more precisely the housing finance subsidy scheme – was changed in 1989. The interest rate for housing loans was increased from 3 percent to 18.8 percent (still not market rate; the rate of inflation was 17 percent in the same year) and adjustable-rate mortgages were introduced as a standard loan product where the interest rate was subject to negotiation between OTP, the Central Bank (MNB) and the Ministry of Finance.

To decrease the budget burden, the new government in 1990 levied a 'special tax' on persons who borrowed in the 1980s. It offered two options to the borrowers: (i) either half of the loan would be discharged and the remaining part would be paid back at market rate or (ii) the total outstanding loan would henceforth carry a fixed 15 percent interest rate. By 1997, 83 percent of the loans had been paid back using the first option, amounting to 6 percent of the average GDP between 1989 and 1996. Even with this reduced burden, subsidies related to these old loans represented a huge share of the housing budget (49 percent and 29 percent of the housing subsidies in 1992 and 1994 respectively) (Hegedüs and Tosics 1996: 88).

The other major change in the housing sector was the drastic 'give-away' privatisation programme, which had started at the end of the 1980s but gained real momentum with the Housing Law of 1993, which gave sitting tenants the Right to Buy (or to purchase their rental home at a discount). From 1990 until 2001, the municipally owned public rental stock decreased by 74 percent, from 721 000 to 189 000. Sitting tenants typically paid 10–15 percent of the market price. This resulted in grave consequences for social housing policy after the transition, but it also meant an immediate relief for the budget, partly in the form of revenue from the sold housing stock and partly from the redemption of state subsidy from the rehabilitation of municipal stock.

In the second half of the 1990s two new housing finance institutions were set up: contract savings banks and mortgage banks. State subsidised contract savings became very popular and by 2000, 8 percent of the households had contract savings accounts. These were far more a savings product than a housing loan. The popularity of the contract savings schemes was partly because loan conditions became far less favourable with the introduction of the new interest rate subsidy system.

The housing subsidy system was very volatile in the 1990s. Changes to the subsidy system to compensate for the introduction of VAT on housing investment in 1994 had a temporary effect on housing output (see Figure 12.3). Interestingly, this was the result of a regulatory mistake. The construction subsidy for families with three or more children was increased by so much that it covered the *total* cost of the construction in less developed regions. Small entrepreneurs entered the market and took advantage of this subsidy scheme, which had a very controversial social impact. The government's housing policy papers adopted the recommendations of the World Bank and other international agencies; they laid down the principles for separating the subsidy system from housing finance and for targeting subsidies to households in need.

The housing mortgage market and housing output shrank during periods of high inflation, despite attempts to introduce deferred payment mortgages (DPM) and other housing construction subsidies. The proportion of GDP going to housing decreased from 13 percent to 2 percent and new construction dropped from 50 000 to 20 000 between 1989 and 1999. The typical loan product was a variable rate loan in HUF (Hungarian Forint) with a small interest rate subsidy and limited size tax exemption for mortgage repayment (Hegedüs and Várhegyi 2000). At the end of the 1990s, the positive macroeconomic changes had an effect on households' behaviour; house prices increased by 150 percent in the three years before mortgage expansion started in 2000.

2000–2008: Emergence of the mortgage market

The period between 2000 and 2008 was characterised by the emergence and rapid expansion of mortgage lending in Hungary. By 2000 the overall economic performance of the country had improved considerably; the GDP grew by 4 percent in 2000 and the fiscal deficit had decreased to 2.9 percent. Furthermore, the unemployment rate fell to around 5–7 percent and after a long period of decline house prices increased by 150 percent in real terms between 1998 and 2000. Residential real estate prices decreased by 40% in real terms between 1990 and 1998. This context paved the way for new policy measures and also had a positive effect on housing demand. The government started to introduce a more intensive housing policy focused on the stimulation of housing construction, which was considered to be a main driver of economic growth. The most significant element of this policy was the *support for housing mortgage* introduced in 2000 to make mortgages more affordable (Hegedüs and Somogyi 2005). An additional element in the subsidy programme was the Personal Income Tax (PIT) mortgage payment allowance. Although this had existed since 1994, use of the allowance was increased substantially during the early 2000s.

Originally the level of interest rate subsidies was modest and eligibility criteria were restricted. Political pressure claiming that only the upper-middle class was supported by the subsidy scheme and strong lobby activity backed by the construction industry and later by banks resulted in increased subsidisation levels and extended eligibility between 2000 and mid-2003. The interest rate of subsidised loans fell to around 4–6 percent by 2002, while market interest rates of housing loans remained at around 14 percent. Moreover, in 2002 the government increased the subsidy for contract savings and the housing construction grant, which was introduced in 1971 to help families with children to enter the homeownership market by contributing to their downpayment.

As a consequence of these heavily subsidised mortgage loans, the loan portfolio rapidly increased from a level of HUF 190 bn in 1999 to HUF 1500 bn by 2003 (8 percent of the GDP in 2003). The net value of the mortgage subsidy was 50–70 percent of the loan (taking into account the two interest rate subsidies and the PIT allowance), the same level as in the late 1980s (Hegedüs and Várhegyi 2000: 1637). It became clear that the level of subsidisation was not sustainable. Furthermore, the social equity effect of the mortgage programme was strongly regressive, with the upper 20 percent of households by income distribution receiving 60 percent of the total subsidy and the upper 40 percent of households receiving 80 percent (Hegedüs and Somogyi 2005: 199–202).

After a long political discussion the government substantially decreased subsidies for the newly issued mortgage loans at the end of 2003. PIT exemptions for mortgage repayment were phased out gradually and were eventually abolished in 2007.

The cut in subsidies did not stop the expansion of the market as new foreign exchange (FX) mortgage loans were introduced, which seemed more affordable than the HUF loans with reduced subsidy. The growth in the stock of outstanding FX housing mortgage and home equity loans is shown in Table 12.2. Annual new lending in foreign currency went from almost zero in 2004 to 90 percent of the mortgage portfolio in 2007. The interest rate of Swiss franc (CHF) loans was around 6 percent, while the market interest rate for HUF loans was above 10 percent. As Hungary was an EU member and most banks operating in the country were in European ownership, concerns about financing were dismissed. Valkovszky (2000), an analyst of the Hungarian National Bank, argued that the growth of housing credit will increase the vulnerability of the Hungarian economy, even if households borrow in HUF instead of FX, as the source of the loans has to be financed from foreign markets due to the low level of savings in the economy. Until 2008, it was considered very improbable that the value of the HUF would decrease so much that the financial advantages of the FX loan would be lost. Even in early 2008, there were plans to introduce an incentive

Table 12.2   The stock of outstanding mortgage backed housing loans and equity loans, 2000–2013.

	HUF housing mortgage loans	FX housing mortgage loan	FX home equity loan	Total	(in billion HUF)	HUF/CHF	HUF/EUR
2000	98%	2%	0%	100%	190.8	173.9	264.9
2001	98%	2%	0%	100%	327.2	166.2	246.3
2002	98%	2%	0%	100%	794.6	162.4	235.9
2003	99%	1%	0%	100%	1531.9	168.3	262.2
2004	84%	7%	9%	100%	2140.2	159.3	245.9
2005	67%	19%	14%	100%	2731.6	162.3	252.7
2006	51%	28%	21%	100%	3544.5	157.0	254.3
2007	38%	35%	28%	100%	4548.4	152.4	253.4
2008	26%	41%	33%	100%	6156.3	177.8	264.8
2009	24%	42%	33%	100%	6303.9	182.3	270.8
2010	21%	42%	37%	100%	6681.6	222.7	278.8
2011	22%	39%	38%	100%	6677.4	255.9	311.1
2012	27%	34%	39%	100%	5579.7	241.1	291.3
2013	28%	34%	39%	100%	5370.9	242.1	296.9

Source: Hungarian National Bank (various years).

to convert HUF subsidised loans to FX loans in order to decrease the fiscal pressure on the government (Hegedüs 2010).

Another important change in the mortgage lending system began in 2004 when the volume of equity loans surpassed housing loans. The equity loans also had low interest rates, but the related underwriting procedures were much looser as they were backed by one or more real estate units. The loosened underwriting conditions (e.g. no proper income checking) and irresponsible lending practices were a result of both the competition among banks and the poor performance of the Bank Supervision Authority. This meant that competition among banks developed in the field of risk taking rather than in price reduction.

2008–2014: Crisis management

The consequences of the financial crisis on the housing sector in Hungary were very much like those experienced elsewhere (Scanlon *et al.* 2012). Annual new housing construction decreased from an annual output of 36 200 units to 7300 units between 2008 and 2013; real house prices were more than 30 percent lower in late 2013 than in early 2008; housing transactions decreased by 40 percent in the same period and the share of non-performing loans increased from 5 percent to 20 percent between 2008 and 2014.

The initial response by the interim government (2009–2010) to the crisis focused on managing the fiscal deficit, which was one of the conditions of the IMF loan (see Figure 12.1). An important element of the fiscal adjustment programme was the drastic cut of housing subsidies; two mortgage interest subsidies and the housing construction grant were abolished.

The government introduced an 'orthodox' policy to manage the housing finance crisis. It launched gradual, step-by-step rescue programmes targeted at households who faced hardships in paying the mortgage (e.g. because of unemployment, health issues) and negotiated with banks and construction companies. Such measures introduced included options to restructure mortgage loans including an optional temporary decrease of monthly payments and a mortgage-to-rent scheme that offered preferential loans to local authorities to buy repossessed homes and let the original owner remain as a tenant in the property. However, these programmes were approached cautiously for fear of possible uncontrolled fiscal effects; consequently, they had no effect on the stock of nonperforming loans.

Another important measure was the introduction of a moratorium on foreclosures up to 1 September 2009, which was later extended until 1 July 2012. The moratorium was meant to provide protection for defaulting borrowers until a more complex rescue programme could be launched. However, the two year moratorium posed a risk to the stability of the financial system because the expectation that defaulting households could rely on help from the government increased the share of nonperforming loans

(HNB 2010). The moratorium has remained an issue of public debate: radical civil groups have demanded that the moratorium remain, but in 2011 the government made a compromise, phasing out the foreclosure moratorium through a yearly quota. The quota applied to properties worth below HUF 30 million with a rate of 3 percent in 2012; these standards gradually rose to 5 percent by 2014 (that is that a maximum 3 percent and 5 percent of properties with non-performing loans can be foreclosed). The actual number of foreclosures, however, reached only 75–85 percent of the quota due to the weak housing market and the banks choosing other solutions rather than foreclosing. Nevertheless, right after the last election, in May 2014, the new parliament introduced a moratorium again for an undefined period, until a final solution for the defaulted FX mortgage borrowers is agreed upon.

The government housing policy was focused on the problem of the FX loan portfolio. In 2011, the government launched the so-called Home Protection Programme, which introduced three main measures to 'rescue' the FX borrowers (early FX loan repayment scheme, FX loan rate cap scheme and rent-to-own scheme). No other housing policy targets were given attention by the government housing programme. One possible explanation is that FX borrowers represented a political threat in the case of the devaluation, which seemed a possible strategy for economic recovery. Nevertheless, there was no initial 'master plan' and the different measures were introduced in an *ad hoc* way, frequently modified by fine-tuning political and administrative interventions.

The *early FX loan repayment scheme* was the first important measure introduced, which ran from September 2011 until the end of February 2012. It allowed borrowers to repay their FX mortgages in full at only HUF 180 to the Swiss franc when the franc was trading at HUF 235–250. As a result, almost a quarter (23.3 percent) of mortgage loans were repaid, amounting to HUF 984 bn at the discounted exchange rate (PSZAF 2012). Just under a third of the early repayments were covered by new loans and 70 percent of the repayments were financed through households' savings. According to analyses, 15 percent of the repaid sum was connected to the informal economy. The gross loss of the programme was close to HUF 400 bn (0.5 percent of GDP), which was shared between the banks and the government at a ratio of 70 percent to 30 percent. As a consequence of the programmes, wealthier families could afford to pay off their FX loans resulting in the banks losing their best customers; the share of the nonperforming loans increased from 6 percent to 19 percent.

The *FX loan rate cap scheme* was introduced in 2012. It put an exchange rate cap on repayments and opened a special account for the exchange rate differential. Due to the number of low applicants, the eligibility criteria were eased several times to make it more accessible and attractive for borrowers. Once qualified, interest components above the exchange rate limit were paid by the bank and the government (at a ratio of 1:2); borrowers had to repay only the principal part, including the interest on the latter. The preferential rate period will last until June 2017 at the latest, but there has been uncertainty surrounding the accumulated debt on the special account at the end of the programme. Despite the government's active encouragement to enter this programme, it never gained much popularity: between 2011 and 2013 around 40 percent of eligible households chose this option (178 thousands 178 000 borrowers in total). The somewhat contradictory government communication led borrowers to expect more advantageous programmes in the future.

A *rent-to-own scheme* was introduced in 2012, managed by the newly established National Asset Management Company (NAMC). NAMC can buy a limited number of delinquent loans and offer a renting option to the former debtor. By mid-2014, NAMC had purchased almost all of the 25 000 units that they had planned to buy. The NAMC will pay the banks 35–55 percent of the value given in the original mortgage contract. The scheme targets the most vulnerable of borrowers who have children. Despite its good intention, this programme cannot solve the deep insolvency of most impoverished families. A significant problem of the scheme is that a substantial proportion of the families targeted by the scheme cannot even afford the low rent set by the law due to pre-existing debt (e.g. for public utility fees). The scheme does not provide a private insolvency solution to the former debtor. While the programme may be the largest social housing programme since 1989, problems surrounding the financing and maintenance of the sector remain unsolved.

Reacting to the existing social problems created by the mortgage crisis, spontaneous civil, self-organised movements have emerged to help the victims of the FX mortgage loans. These movements have been responsible for organising demonstrations, protesting against banks and the government and launching court procedures against banks, typically with the support of the extreme right-wing political parties. The government from time to time attempted to integrate them into public administration, but they remained quite independent. By 2013, the various court cases launched by the movements were brought to the Hungarian Supreme Court (Curia), which ruled in favour of the banks. The politicians (the prime minister among them) criticised the Curia, claiming it was biased towards the banks. On 16 June 2014, the Curia's ruling was modified: firstly, the court concluded that the practice of 'rate spreads' (using different rates for buying and selling currencies) was unfair and that the banks should have to use the Hungarian National Bank central rate; secondly, the Curia declared that the unilateral modification of the loan contract (e.g. interest rate) by the banks was unfair and the monthly instalment should be recalculated compensating the borrowers; thirdly, the Curia declared that the exchange rate risk should be borne exclusively by the borrower. The final measure of the rescue programme was the introduction of a governmental mandate for FX mortgage borrowers to convert their FX loans to HUF based loans at a current market based FX – HUF exchange rate (1 CHF = 256.47 HUF, 1 Euro = 308.97 HUF). The future initial interest rate of the converted FX mortgage loans is also regulated and cannot be changed for three years.

The radical wing of the civil movement was not pleased with the decision as they wanted to nullify the original contract, placing the cost of the exchange rate risk on the banks. The government (and the ruling party) exploited the disappointment of borrowers and anti-bank sentiment and even encouraged the popular blaming of banks

Impacts

The development of the housing finance system in the last decades faced several crises. Nevertheless, housing conditions have improved faster than in comparable countries in the region. One element of the housing financial crisis was the over-investment in housing both in the 1980s and 2000s, which was not justified by the economic fundamentals.

Beginning in 2000, the housing finance market started to develop with the help of a contradictory mortgage subsidy system. In 2004 the mortgage subsidy programme was severely cut, but the development of the mortgage market did not stop as low cost and high risk FX loans replaced the subsidised HUF loans. The potential risks (HUF exchange risk and interest rate risk) were underestimated by all stakeholders. The government controlled institutions (Financial Supervisory Authority, Hungarian National Bank) and pro-government politicians were content with the development contributing to the economic growth. The opposition who argued that the cut in subsidies in 2004 would hold back the potential growth of the market did not demand control over the expanding FX loan portfolio. Households who did not understand the risks of FX equity loans were eager to secure them, while the banks followed a logic of moral hazard and introduced less careful underwriting procedures under the assumption that the government would step in if the macroeconomic conditions worsened. Nevertheless the rapid growth of mortgage lending resulted in the construction of 340 000 units, which was a 40 percent more than in the 1990s.

While the mortgage portfolio increased rapidly, competition did not result in a decrease in interest rates (the spread remained very high for HUF loans), which hints at collusive behaviour. By the time the GFC hit the country, the economy had already been weakened by fiscal irresponsibility (a large deficit and increasing debt) and macro-economic failure (low growth). The housing finance system was extremely un-regulated and the banks had extreme power to set the cost of the loans, change the interest rates, regulate the exchange rates and more, powers that were not visible at the time of the growth but became evident during the crises and became the source of popular conflicts.

After 2009, the management of the crisis largely followed international trends, which meant the introduction of macroeconomic austerity programmes, changes to the regulatory environment of the banks and improvements in consumer protection (these are summarised in Table 12.3). In the meantime, the banks gradually changed their behaviour, accepted a common code of conduct and introduced refinancing schemes to help borrowers facing hardship in paying their instalments. Nevertheless, they still depended on government intervention to help borrowers in financial

Table 12.3   Impact of the main measures after the GFC in Hungary.

Programme name	Measures	Impact on		
		Borrowers	**Banks**	**Government**
Early FX loan repayment scheme	Possibility to repay FX loan at a discounted rate.	The programme had a huge regressive effect socially.	Most of the costs were borne by the banks (HUF 300 billion) and their portfolio worsened.	Government gave tax exemption for banks up to 30% of the cost (less tax revenue).
FX loan cap scheme	Introduced a cap on the exchange rate and deferred the capital payment.	The borrowers had no confidence in the programme as the future cost was not clear.	This programme was quite acceptable for the banks, their losses were manageable.	Government's attempts to persuade borrowers to join the programme result in continuously changing conditions.
Rent-to-own schemes – National Asset Management Company	The state buys a certain part of defaulted loans and property and use the latter as public housing.	The eligible foreclosed borrower can stay in the property as a tenant paying very low rent.	It allows banks to sell their worst portfolios to the government.	Most of the cost was paid by the state.
Regulation of banks to compensate borrowers	Compensation of the borrowers for banks' 'rate spread' practice and unilateral modification of the interest rates.	The payment burden of the borrowers will decrease.	Banks must pay an estimated cost of HUF 900–1000 bn.	Government hopes that reducing borrowers' burden will boost demand in the household sector without bank insolvency.
Law on compulsory conversion of FX loans to HUF loans and maximised interest rate	With very few exception borrowers are obliged to convert their FX loans to HUF loans on current market exchange rate.	Borrowers are forced to close their position at the current market exchange rate.	The conversion on market exchange rate is favourable for the banks but their loss can be increased because of the maximised interest rates.	National Bank makes profit on the conversion of FX to HUF.

difficulties. This 'organic' development, which in reality could not improve the situation of the defaulting borrowers on a large scale, was stopped by the second Orban government in 2010. The government radically changed its policy toward the banking sector and introduced a series of political measures (called the 'FX loan rescue programme') to re-allocate the cost of the mortgage crisis among stakeholders. Orban's unorthodox policies have been directed against the banks and an approach which has proven popular in the political rhetoric.

The mortgage rescue programme in Hungary, interestingly, benefitted rich households first (thanks to the prepayment scheme) at the cost of the banks and the majority of the costs of the other programmes were placed on the bank sector as well. There are only estimates about the final cost of the mortgage rescue programmes: the cost of the early prepayment programme was HUF 300 bn; corrections made on the bases of the Curia decision are estimated to amount to an additional HUF 900–1000 bn for the banking sector above the extra tax introduced in 2011. The cost of the interest rate cap is estimated to have resulted in a yearly loss of HUF 100 bn for the sector. The financial advantages on the FX borrowers' side includes an estimated decrease in monthly payments of around 25–30 percent and a projected decrease in outstanding debt of around 16 percent. The government's contribution is the partial forgiveness of the state tax on banks. These rescue programmes seem to display a larger trend of the economy and society moving again toward a centralised and authoritarian market economy.

The future of the housing finance system

The mortgage crisis and the postponed, long-lasting rescue programmes created a great uncertainty in the market. After 2008, there was a steep decline in mortgage finance, new construction decreased to a 100 year minimum and the rate of housing transactions fell to a third of what it had been thus far in the 2000s. A main policy of the Hungarian National Bank was to reduce the base rate to stimulate economic growth and, consequently, the interest rate of the mortgage loans substantially decreased to a level of 5–9 percent by 2014. Although the trend of decreasing housing transactions, housing constructions and mortgage lending seemed to stop in 2014, forecasts are still cautious about the rate of future increase.

According to the government's plans, a bill is currently being negotiated on the conversion of FX loans, though it remains unclear what exchange rate will be forced on the banks by the parliament. Additionally, the prime minister has expressed his preference of increased Hungarian ownership in the banking sector. The logic of this unorthodox economic policy dictates a scenario where most banks that are active in the mortgage market will be closely regulated by the government, in a very similar way to how they were regulated before 1990. The typical loan product, the total amount of the loan issued, the underwriting rules and more will be determined by the government and the Hungarian National Bank. The extra tax on banks, the central regulation of loan products and the provisional manner of converting the FX loan portfolio into HUF-based loans indicate the government's intention to recreate a state controlled system. We cannot predict how 'successful' the government will be in clearing up the market and achieving this aim.

There is no clear sign that the economy is recovering. One scenario is that the government will have to devalue the Hungarian currency in order to make the Hungarian economy competitive in the global market. If this is the case, then any plan to reinstate a fully controlled authoritarian economy will have to be sacrificed and there may be a chance for a return to a more mainstream economic policy with the normalisation of the economic system (that is, a withdrawal of the extreme state control over the economy). Even under this scenario, Hungary's future housing finance system is likely to be a more conservative and highly regulated one. Several new regulative elements have already appeared in the system. These are partly consistent with the European/international efforts towards a more prudent lending system. Foreign banks probably will play a more limited role, although they are still committed to staying in the Hungarian market, and FX loans will become marginal.

As a consequence of the recent developments, cash-based transactions have become more common in the housing market (as they were in the 1990s), at least for a while. The government and the banks must rebuild trust in the financial institutions as it was lost in the process of the mortgage rescue programme. One possibility is that after experiencing the negative effects of the high risks associated with homeownership, households will prefer to shift toward a rental solution. However, this shift will not be possible without a major change to the subsidy system, the tax treatment of housing and the legal regulation of the different tenures.

References

Central Statistical Office (various years). Construction Statistics [Online] Available: http://ksh.hu.

FHB (2014) FHB House Price Index. www.fhbindex.com/FHB-Index/FHB-House-Price-Index (accessed 29 July 2015).

Hegedüs, J (1992). Self help housing in Hungary. In: *Beyond Self-Help Housing*, Matey, K (ed.), pp. 217–231. Profil Verlag, München.

Hegedüs, J (2010). Towards a new housing system in transitional countries: The case of Hungary. In: *Housing Market Challenges in Europe and the United States*, Arestis, P, Mooslechner, P and Wagner, K (eds). Palgrave MacMillan, New York, pp. 178–202.

Hegedüs, J and Somogyi, E (2005). Evaluation of the hungarian mortgage program 2000–2004. In: *Housing Finance: New and Old Models in Central Europe, Russia and Kazakhstan*, Hegedüs, J and Struyk, RJ (eds). LGI Books, Open Society Institute, pp. 177–208.

Hegedüs, J and Tosics, I (1996). Hungary. In: *Housing Policy in Europe*, Balchin, P (ed.), Routledge, London and New York.

Hegedüs, J and Várhegyi, É (2000). The crisis in housing financing in the 1990s in Hungary. *Urban Studies* 37:9, 1610–1641.

Hungarian National Bank (HNB) (2010). *Report on Financial Stability.* Hungarian National Bank. 2010 December.

Hungarian National Bank (various years). *Market Information Statistics* [Online] Available: http://mnb.hu.

Lackó, M (2000). Hidden Economy: an Unknown Quantity? Comparative analysis of hidden economies in transition countries, *The Economics of Transition* 8:1, 2000.

OTP (1986). *Országos Takarékpénztár jelentése a lakásépítési, -hitelezési, és –értékesítési tevékenységről a 6. Ötéves terv időszakában (1980–1985), OTP, 1986, Budapest,* Report on Housing Construction, Housing Loan and Real Estate Activity of OTP in the 6th five-year plan period (1980–1985), OTP 1986, Budapest.

PSZAF (2012). *Éves jelentés, 2012 (Annual Report, 2012 of Bank Supervision Authority)* Pénzügyi Szervezetek Állami Felügyelete.

Scanlon, K, Lunde, J and Whitehead, C (2012). *Post-crisis Mortgage and Housing Markets in Europe: A Comparative Review.* London, Copenhagen.

Valkovszky, S (2000). Hungarian Housing Market. *Working paper,* Hungarian National Bank.

World Bank (1991). World Development Report World Development Report 1991: The Challenge of Development.

13

Housing Finance in Iceland: Milestones 1989–2014

Lúðvík Elíasson[a] and Magnús Árni Skúlason[b]
[a]Central Bank of Iceland, Reykjavík, Iceland
[b]Reykjavik Economics, Reykjavík, Iceland

Introduction

Housing finance in Iceland is available from banks, pension funds and the government owned mortgage lender, the Housing Financing Fund (HFF). The most common term for a new mortgage is 40 years, although shorter loans are also available (Central Bank of Iceland 2014). A variety of mortgage types has emerged over the past 5 years with choices of indexed loans (where amounts evolve according to the consumer price index), real or nominal interest rates, which are variable or fixed for a period of years or even the whole term of the loan, and annuities with a ceiling on paid interest and negative amortisation. Interest rates are generally determined by mortgage type by each lender. The most prolific lenders during the past few years have been the banks that have increasingly turned to covered bonds to finance their mortgage portfolios. The HFF, which only offers inflation-linked fixed rate mortgages, has accumulated significant losses in recent years due to increased risk-taking about 10 years ago, and is uncompetitive. The housing finance system is currently under revision and the government is considering a limited role for the HFF, shifting its focus to peripheral markets.

Twenty-five years ago the housing financing system was heavily revised. Financing of mortgage lending at the National Housing Authority (NHA, the HFF's predecessor) was switched entirely over to mortgage backed securities in late 1989, matching the mortgages in average duration and

Milestones in European Housing Finance, First Edition.
Edited by Jens Lunde and Christine Whitehead.
© 2016 John Wiley & Sons, Ltd. Published 2016 by John Wiley & Sons, Ltd.

interest rates. The NHA maintained its share as the main mortgage lender for new homes, but emphasis on financing general transactions in the housing market was increased. Lending terms were restricted with maximum loan length shortened to 25 years and interest rates effectively raised to eliminate the subsidy inherent in the earlier system where mortgage rates were fixed regardless of the terms on the NHA's funding.

The NHA (and subsequently the HFF) retained its virtual monopoly in the mortgage market until 2004. Its lending had grown steadily, increasing its emphasis on financing regular market transactions while diminishing its role as a social institution. In 2004 the HFF restructured its financing and eased its lending terms. During that year the private banks entered the mortgage market on competitive terms, rapidly gaining market share.

The economic and institutional environment of the past 25 years

Iceland has been suffering rampant inflation for decades. Increased emphasis on price stability appeared to have brought inflation down to single digits by the late 1990s (Snævarr 1993; Andersen and Guðmundsson 1998). As inflation targeting was implemented in March 2001 the *króna*, however, fell significantly causing a spike in inflation in early 2002. The situation was soon calmed and inflation remained under control again until 2008.

Traditionally, Iceland has been a two-pillar economy with foreign revenues coming from fisheries and energy intensive industries, and lately the export base has been diversified with tourism in particular playing an important role. The exchange rate was determined by law, until the formation of a foreign exchange market in 1993 (Central Bank of Iceland 2001). Deregulation of capital movements was completed in 1990–1995 (Kristinsson 2002). Between May 1993 and March 2001, the exchange rate was kept within a narrow band around a target based on a currency basket. The band was widened twice and eventually the exchange rate floated freely, from March 2001, until capital controls were put in place in November 2008.

In 1994 the European Economic Area (EEA) was formed as Iceland, Norway and Liechtenstein gained access to the European Community's internal market, entering into a free trade agreement based on free movements in goods and services, persons and capital. Privatisation of financial institutions and other government firms during 1992–2007 generated revenues amounting to 12.6 percent of GDP (in 2008 prices). Following privatisation, and operating within the EEA, the Icelandic banks grew rapidly by multiplying their lending in Iceland as well as in other countries (Hreinsson *et al.* 2010).

Tradition of owner-occupied housing

Social housing as well as other private housing has predominantly been owner-occupied since the beginning of a social-housing programme in the 1930s (Stefánsson *et al.* 2013). The ratio of owner-occupied homes to rental housing topped at 89 percent in 1990. Real interest rates became positive in the late 1980s and in the 1990s the capital account was opened. Feasible alternatives to housing for storing values emerged. In addition housing allowance for renters was introduced in 1995. The focus of housing financing policy on ownership, however, remained. Around 80 percent of homes were owner-occupied between 1995 and 2007 but the ratio has fallen since then, as housing financing once more became difficult to access following the bank failures in 2008.

The bumpy ride of Icelandic housing finance

Short overview of housing financing from 1989 to 2014

Over the past 25 years housing policy in Iceland became synonymous with housing finance. The system has evolved from focussing on financing new buildings to financing general market transactions. It also moved away from assisting mainly those with low income and little assets to assisting everyone. The government owned and guaranteed HFF increasingly took on risk in order to allow borrowers access to larger mortgages at lower interest rates (Stefánsson *et al.* 2013). A timeline of how these changes evolved is shown in Table 13.1.

The three large Icelandic banks entered the mortgage market in 2004. This happened after the banks were privatised, the funding of mortgages was moved to the market and following a pre-announced market advance by the HFF. Fierce competition for customers between the three large banks, some savings banks and the HFF resulted in excessive risk taking, increased access to credit, higher house prices and elevated household debt. As a result, households in general became more vulnerable to economic and financial shocks while risk was building up in the economy. Although defaults increased after the large banks failed in 2008 the recent governments have been focussing on reducing households' payment burden. Several measures have been introduced and the emphasis has been on postponing the full effects of unsustainable household debt by shifting the cost to taxpayers.

Since 1980, Icelandic mortgages have, as a rule, been indexed to the price level (Box 13.1). It is only since 2011 that non-indexed mortgages have gained any ground, and some foreign exchange (FX) linked mortgages were issued during 2003 to 2008. The main mortgage lender throughout most of the period was the NHA/HFF. Pension funds also lent to members and the

Table 13.1 Timeline showing milestones in housing finance in Iceland during the past 25 years.

		National Housing Agency / Housing Financing Fund		Banks		Pension funds
	Government policy	Financing	Lending	Financing	Lending	Lending
Early 1980s Increased access to loans, emphasis shifts towards market transactions rather than new building, government supports funding		Government contribution, bond sales to pension fund			Top up loans, indexed, high real rates, 5 to 10 year term	Mostly indexed loans, various terms, generally strict conditions
1986		Increased emphasis on bond sales to pension funds, government contribution	Indexed annuities, maximum term 16 to 31 year Maximum loan amounts increased. Loan term extended to 40 years			
1988	Tax system simplified. Interest rate support.					
1989 Market financing of mortgages	Market table bonds	Housing bonds	Maximum loan period cut to 25 years			
1995	Rent support					
1995			Loans lengthened to 40 years			

Theme	Year	Government / Housing fund	Lending	Banking / Market
Social functions of the government housing fund weaned out	1999	Housing Financing Fund. Workers building fund (social housing program) retired. HFF bonds.	Introduction of additional loans. Additional loans program retired	
Private sector provision in competition with government fund	2004	New bonds	Prepayments	First lien loans on comparable terms with the HFF
	2004		Further easing of lending. 90% LTV	
	2006			FX loans
	2007			HFF finances bank mortgages. Covered bond
Debt restructuring	2008	Banks taken over by the financial supervisor		New banks formed. Loans transferred at a discount
Rekindling competition under capital controls	2009		Prepayments	
	2010			FX loans illegal. Non-indexed loans
	2011	HFF refinanced	Government support	
	2013	HFF refinanced, again	Government support	

Box 13.1   Indexed mortgages

A part of the interest on debt is intended to cover the anticipated cost due to inflation, which causes the value of the currency to deteriorate. If the agreed upon interest rate is based on expectations of higher inflation than materialises then the value of the repayments will be greater than anticipated. Thus the lender benefits at the borrower's expense. If inflation turns out to be greater than expected, the borrower gains while the lender receives less valuable repayments than intended. Unanticipated inflation transfers values randomly between borrowers and lenders in this manner. This inflation risk is greater the longer the period until repayment, and the greater uncertainty is about future inflation. If inflation is high and unstable then long term lending may become costly, bearing high interest rates reflecting this risk. Variable interest rates are a partial cure, but fluctuations in the amounts paid can be extreme with an increased risk of defaults. Indexing the payments to the price level yields a repayment schedule in constant prices, that is, in real terms, thus eliminating the inflation risk. Indexed mortgages have been common in countries with a history of high and variable inflation, such as Israel, Mexico, Chile and Iceland (Elíasson 2014).

When the NHA was set up in the mid-1950s its lending was partly indexed. In 1979 new legislation allowing for full indexation of debts and assets was enacted. For a quarter of a century, between 1980 and 2005, effectively all mortgages were fully indexed (Jónsson 1999; Stefánsson *et al.* 2013).

Although there have been variations in different attributes of Icelandic mortgages, the typical Icelandic mortgage over the past 25 years has been a fixed rate indexed annuity. The repayments are thus fixed in real terms and are calculated according to the formula:

$$A_t = (r/n)\left[1 - 1/(1 + r/n)\right]^{-nT} X(P_t/P_0)$$

where A_t is the period t payment (fixed in real terms), r is the (fixed) real interest rate, n is the number of payments per year, T is the length of the loan in years, X is the initial loan amount, P_i is the value of the price index used for indexation in period i. The formula is therefore identical to the one used for annuities except that the real interest rate is used rather than the nominal rate, and the payment is scaled by the deviation of the period's price index from its effective value when the loan was issued.

---

commercial banks often made top-up loans on higher liens. Over the past 10 years the banks increased their presence in the mortgage market and added significantly to the variety of mortgage types available.

During the period from 1989 to 2014 three milestones in housing financing can be identified. The first occurred when financing of the NHA was switched to marketable bonds matching the mortgage-terms. The second was when the HFF as established in 1999 and the focus shifted further towards financing market transactions and away from social objectives. The third milestone was in 2004 when the private banks entered the market.

Starting point: the '1986 system'

In 1986 the NHA changed the funding of its mortgages and eased the lending terms considerably. The maximum loan amount was doubled for builders and increased six-fold for buyers of used houses. The loan amount was adjusted every 3 months in line with changes in the building cost index and was based on the share of the borrower's pension fund invested in financing the NHA. The real interest rates were kept unchanged from the previous years at 3.5 percent, while the term of the loans was lengthened to 40 years.

The mortgages carried 3.5 percent real rates but bonds sold to the pension funds to finance the mortgages had higher rates leaving the NHA with a negative carry of 2.5 to 5.5 percent and between 5 and 8 percent in the social housing programme. The NHA depended therefore on equity infusions from the government to balance the budget. This system was unsustainable and within a few years the programme was restructured, again!

First milestone: housing bonds

In 1989 the NHA restructured its financing and started issuing marketable bonds. The emphasis was on matching the maturity profile and interest rate burden of payments to the terms on the loans made to homebuyers. The mortgages were inflation-linked annuities with 25 years' repayment period, with an option of 40 years as of 1996. The housing bonds which funded the mortgages were also inflation-linked and had either 25- or 40-year maturity matching the loans. The financing bonds, however, were bullets, while mortgages typically had quarterly payments. In order to channel mortgage payments to the bond holders, housing bonds were regularly drawn by a lottery and paid in full. A call option for the bonds, in order to meet prepayments of mortgages, was introduced through additional lottery draws or buybacks in the market. New issues were regularly introduced to better reflect the maturity of loans and their interest rates. This led to a plethora of housing bond series and the total amount issued in each was limited.

Housing support through the tax system Various tax deductions, including interest on housing debt up to a fixed amount, were ceased as the income tax system was simplified in 1988. A means tested interest rate rebate was introduced instead, available only to those building or buying a home for the first time. As housing bond issuance started in 1989, mortgage interest rates increased and the housing subsidy was replaced by a partial interest rate benefits, serviced through the tax system. This system is still in place. The right to the interest rate benefits is linked to income levels and net assets, thus preserving a hint of a social housing system. Since 1995, income related housing allowances have been available to those paying rent and extra housing allowance to low-income families in the larger municipalities.

Second milestone: the Housing Financing Fund

When the HFF was formed in 1999 it took over the functions of the NHA. Before the introduction of market financing the Government Building Fund was used to finance regular loans by the NHA and the Workers' Building Fund financed low-income and other social housing. These funds were re-capitalised by the government and merged with the HFF.

Changes were made to the social housing programme when the HFF was formed. Previously loans on favourable terms had been available for the purchase of owner-occupied social housing, to those who qualified, by falling below certain maximum income and asset levels. Instead additional loans by the HFF with the cooperation of municipalities were introduced. Additional loans carried a marginally higher interest rate than regular loans and were used to top up loans to as much as 90 percent of the value of the housing unit. The maximum asset and income levels were raised such that significantly more applicants qualified for additional loans than those who previously had the option of borrowing through the social housing lending programme. Applications for additional loans were processed by housing committees in each municipality. The amount lent through the additional loans programme consistently exceeded plans and they were significantly more prone to collecting arrears than regular loans (Félagsmálaráðuneytið 2004).

The HFF continued to grow and consolidate its position as the virtual mortgage monopoly in Iceland during the first years of the century. In 2003, its lending rose above 7 percent of GDP for the first time (Figure 13.1) where it stayed for 3 years. Originally the government's housing fund solely

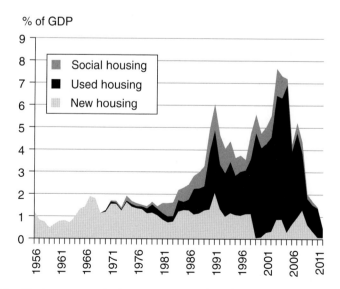

Figure 13.1 Mortgages made by government housing agencies (NHA and HFF).
Source: Stefánsson *et al.* (2013).

financed the purchase of new housing but after the mid-1980s, the emphasis shifted to financing market transactions.

Financing of rental housing The NHA started lending to municipalities, which had been building rental apartments as early as 1965. In 1988 the NHA began lending to building societies, both for social and other private housing (Hagfræðistofnun 2011). Between 1999 and 2012, about 20 percent of HFF's lending was to builders of rental housing, building societies, building contractors and developers. A significant number of these loans have generated losses at the HFF due to the lack of a regulatory structure (Stefánsson *et al.* 2013).

Mortgage restructuring at the HFF in 2004 A committee for reorganisation of the HFF's bond issues was formed in 2001. Its mandate was to suggest changes to the bonds that the fund issued, which would simplify it and support interest formation in the markets. The committee submitted its report in October 2003.

The changes to the HFF's funding which were implemented in July 2004 were largely based on the committee's suggestions. The HFF started issuing one type of bond, HFF bonds, which were inflation linked annuities with biannual payments. From then on, loans have been paid out in cash rather than by the marketable housing bonds. Three HFF bond series were issued, maturing in 2024, 2034 and 2044. Later in the year, a third series, maturing in 2014, was also offered.

By simplifying the bond issues the HFF hoped to attract foreign investors. Increased demand would then push down domestic interest rates, thus lowering the cost of houses for Icelandic homebuyers. Attempting to lower interest rates further still, the HFF decided to make the new bonds non-callable. Still borrowers were, against the suggestions made by the committee, allowed to prepay their mortgages without a penalty. This significantly increased the credit risk borne by the HFF. Particularly as interest rates were expected to drop, which in fact was one of the goals the HFF sought by changing its bond issues.

In December 2004 the HFF's maximum loan amounts and loan to value ratios (LTVs) were raised. This change had been in preparations since before the parliamentary elections in 2003 when the Progressive Party's promise of increased access to mortgages at the HFF, and in particular 90 percent LTV, became the main election issue and in fact one of the cornerstones of the government's policy statement.

Real interest rates on the HFF's mortgages had been fixed at 5.1 percent since 1994 until they were dropped to 4.8 percent following changes to the fund's bond issuance in July 2004 and further to 4.15 percent by the end of that year. The maximum loan amount had been raised from ISK 8 mn to ISK 9.2 mn in December 2003 and it was increased twice in 2004. Following further increases in 2005 and 2006 the maximum loan amount reached ISK 18 million, roughly doubling in size over 3 years.

In December 2004 the HFF act was changed allowing the HFF to increase the LTV on all new loans to 90 percent. Such high debt ratios were previously exclusively for borrowers meeting the fund's low-income and asset criteria.

Credit checks for HFF mortgages had been carried out by the commercial banks. In August 2004 the banks moved aggressively into the mortgage market. Rather than continuing to rely on their services the HFF shifted its credit checks to its webpage, counting on mortgage borrowers to perform them themselves (Stefánsson *et al.* 2013), which may have, in combination with higher LTVs and loan amounts, contributed to the deterioration in asset quality at the HFF.

Third milestone: the banks enter full force

The changes made to the HFF's funding in 2004 seriously hampered its ability to handle competition, limiting its options to manage risk in case of prepayments of mortgages.

This was done despite repeated warnings by various government agencies and others that the banks would soon begin advancing into the mortgage market (Institute of Economic Studies 2003; Central Bank of Iceland 2004b; Stefánsson *et al.* 2013). A few weeks after the HFF changed its funding, precisely that happened.

The International Monetary Fund (IMF) welcomed this change in the mortgage market, pointing out that this would allow the banks to 'strengthen their balance sheets by increasing the proportion of mortgage loans' (IMF 2004). The IMF, however, stressed that the financial supervisor would 'need to closely monitor the evolution of banks' balance sheets as they continue their expansion into the mortgage market.' Otherwise duration mismatches and foreign currency risk exposure could undermine their profitability. The IMF emphasised that policymakers should 'focus future reforms to the HFF on enhancing its ability to fulfil social objectives rather than increasing its ability to compete with banks' (IMF 2004).

Privatisation of the banking sector was completed in early 2003 (Box 13.2, based on Skúlason, 2012). The formerly government owned banks had good credit ratings and they seized the opportunity given by the low interest rates and ample supply of funds in international markets to grow their balance sheets to 10 times Iceland's GDP. They increasingly lent in foreign currency to Icelandic companies, particularly those in export sectors that had foreign currency revenues providing a natural hedge against FX-risk. The banks also financed the advance of many Icelandic companies in foreign countries as well as establishing their own branches and subsidiaries abroad.

The banks' main role in the mortgage market had for decades been providing additional lending at higher liens at high interest rates (often 9–10 percent real rates) and with shorter repayment periods (often 5–10 years). By shifting their emphasis to first lien mortgage lending in 2004 the banks

Box 13.2   Timeline: From a controlled economy to free market economy and back again

- 1994 – Iceland joins the European Economic Area in an agreement between the European Free Trade Association and the European Union.
  - Four Freedoms of Goods, Capital, Services and People.
  - Gave Icelandic companies and financial institutions access to European Capital Markets.
- 1998 – First step in privatisation of the state-owned banks when they were listed on the Icelandic Stock Exchange.
- 2001 – Age of Easy Money Starts as a consequence of the Internet bubble and 9/11.
- 2002 – Full privatisation of the two government owned banks.
  - Landsbanki (19 October 2002). Samson buys 45.8 percent of the bank's shares for ISK 12.3 bn.
  - Bunadarbankinn (17 November 2002) (Agricultural Bank of Iceland). The so-called S-group buys 45.8 percent of the bank's shares for ISK 11.9 bn.
  - Privatisation completed in 2003.
- 2003 – Spring: The Government of Iceland announces gradual increases in loan-to-value (LTV) to 90 percent and an increase in the maximum mortgage amount over a period of few years. The highest mortgage was ISK 9.7 mn at that point in time and 65 percent LTV (70 percent for first-time buyers).
  - 2004 – July 1: Change in the funding of the governmental owned Housing Financing Fund (HFF). Real interest rates were lowered from 5.1 percent to 4.8 percent on new mortgages. Interest rate exposure of the public becomes history, due to the introduction of cash-only loans instead of bonds.
  - 2004 – August 23: The newly privatised banks enter the mortgage market full force with higher maximum loan of ISK 25 mn and 80 percent LTV. Real interest rates fell to 4.4 percent. It was foreseen that the public would refinance more expensive loans, for example, lucrative overdraft loans of the banks, with new and cheaper mortgages. Hyper-competition in the mortgage market.
  - 2004 – November 8: Islandsbanki offers 100 percent LTV. General LTV is 90 percent.
  - 2004 – November 22: Real interest rates lowered generally to 4.15 percent.
  - The market is additionally fuelled at the same time with generous interest rate benefits from the government to homeowners.
  - This was in effect a deregulation of the housing mortgage markets, which resulted in higher house prices in the Reykjavik Capital Region, driven by strong economic growth and demographic change because of immigration.
- 2007 – Peak in the housing market.
- 2008 – October: Collapse of the Icelandic banking system.
  - 29 September, 2008, Glitnir Bank collapses and is put into a receivership by the Financial Supervisory Authority.
  - 8 October, 2008, the Financial Supervisory Authority puts Landsbankinn into a receivership.
  - 8 October, 2008, Great Britain evokes anti-terrorist legislation on Iceland, that is, freezes the assets of Landsbanki and the Icelandic Authorities and its institutions.

- 9 October, 2008, the Financial Supervisory Authority puts Kaupthing Bank into a receivership.
- 24 October, 2008, IMF and Iceland outline $2.1 bn loan plan.
- November 28, 2008, draconian capital controls put in place.
- 2010 – April 12: Report of the Special Investigation Commission on the 2008 banking sector crash.
- Banks re-enter the market.
- 2010 – December: Real housing prices hit the bottom. Down by 36 percent in real terms from its peak in October 2007.
- 2013 – July 2: Report of the Special Investigation Commission on the HFF.

improved the quality of their loan portfolios by increasing lending secured by assets. Mortgage lending was also favoured by the risk weights of bank capital used in Basel regulations facilitating faster lending growth. In addition, some Icelandic bank managers assumed that interest rates would continue to fall, making mortgages with fixed real rates above 4 percent for 40 years a good business opportunity (Stefánsson *et al.* 2013).

In early 2003 the investment bank Kaupþing merged with the newly privatised Búnaðarbanki to form the largest bank in Iceland. The bank wanted to increase its share in the local retail market and in August 2004 Kaupþing offered 40 year indexed mortgages with real rates below the rate offered at the HFF. Kaupþing also allowed refinancing of existing mortgages, effectively introducing households to a new low-cost method for equity withdrawal. The other large banks responded immediately by offering comparable mortgages in order to prevent Kaupþing from attracting their customers.

The HFF immediately suffered massive prepayments (Figure 13.2). It lowered its interest rates to match the competition from the banks and in December 2004 it was allowed to raise the LTV to 90 percent. The banks were generally offering 80 percent LTV without restrictions on the amount, but various restrictions applied to loans up to 90 percent LTV or in some cases 100 percent, often limiting the loan amount to 25 mn krónur (Stefánsson *et al.* 2013).

The HFF flooded with cash from prepayments and rather than buying its own bonds in the market it looked for ways to earn interest on its cash balance. A buy-back of HFF bonds would have realised losses from the risk taken by the fund when it changed its funding in 2004. Between 2004 and 2005 the HFF purchased mortgage portfolios from the banks, thereby financing its competitors, to the tune of ISK 95 bn or 10 percent of GDP at the time (Stefánsson *et al.* 2013). This enabled the banks to increase their mortgage lending further still, adding to the HFF's prepayment risk. In addition, mortgages issued by the banks were partially financed through issuance of mortgage backed securities, which totalled about ISK 175 bn during 2006–2008. Legislation on covered bonds was passed in the parliament in 2008.

FX lending   Mortgages in foreign currency baskets had been offered since late December 2003. This practice first became popular after the Icelandic *króna* depreciated by 22 percent in the first half of 2006. An increasing

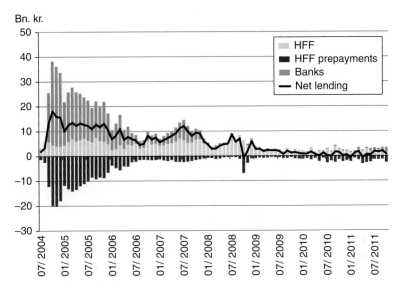

Bn. kr.

Figure 13.2   Monthly mortgage lending by banks and the HFF, prepayments at the HFF and total lending by banks and HFF net of prepayments at the HFF (net lending), 2004–2011.
Source: Stefánsson *et al.* (2013).

number of households demanded FX-linked mortgages, which were popularised by discussion in the media and by some members of academia. In 2007 the banks were experiencing rising borrowing rates in international markets. The banks boosted their foreign currency assets, for example by offering FX-linked mortgages domestically, meeting the households' appetite for currency risk. This kept the currency risk off the banks' balance sheets, but increased their counter part risk as domestic borrowers were increasingly short in foreign currencies.

FX-linked borrowing by households was virtually non-existent until 2003. In January 2004 4.5 percent of households' debt was FX-linked, 13 percent at the end of 2007 and 23 percent only 3 months later (Central Bank of Iceland 2008). This resulted in another burst in demand in the housing market as well as rekindling the rate of prepayments at the HFF.

Financial crisis: bank failures   At the height of the global financial crisis in the fall of 2008 Iceland's three large banks failed and their estates are still undergoing winding-up process. New banks were established by transferring many domestic assets (including mortgages) and domestic deposits to new companies. Transactions in the housing market came to a halt in late 2008 and housing investment stalled. The new banks have started to issue covered bonds to partially finance their mortgage lending.

Latest trend: introduction of non-indexed mortgages   No FX-linked mortgages have been issued since 2008 and FX-linked mortgages were ruled illegal by the Supreme Court in June 2010. New mortgages issued during the past 3 years have either been indexed or non-indexed. Nominal interest rates have been unusually low since the introduction of capital controls in late 2008. This explains the increased demand for non-indexed loans. During the first half of 2013 about 58 percent of new mortgage lending was indexed and 42 percent non-indexed (Central Bank of Iceland 2013). Although interest rates on non-indexed mortgages are relatively favourable at the moment, they are usually either floating or, at the minimum, reset every 3–5 years. In some cases the interest on index-linked mortgages is also reset every 5 years.

Impacts

The development of real house prices

During the 8-year period of economic stagnation from 1988 to 1995 real house prices barely moved (Figure 13.3). As the economy recovered from the slump, real prices started to rise. The transfer of the social housing programme into the general mortgage programme with additional loans up

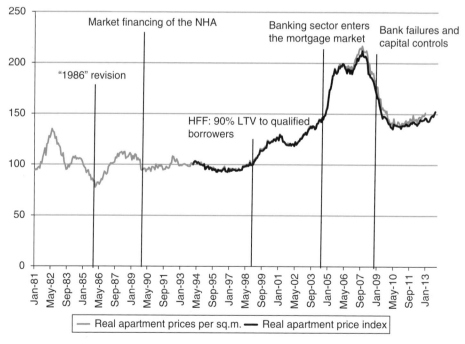

Figure 13.3   Real prices of apartments, 1981–2013 (January 1994 = 100).
Sources: Registers Iceland, Statistics Iceland, author's calculations. The figure shows two real house price series. The house price index for apartments in the capital region adjusted for changes in inflation (starting in 1994) and the cash price per square metre in apartment buildings in the capital region adjusted for inflation (starting in 1981).

to 90 percent in 1999, and the relaxation of constraints on receiving such additional aid, played its part in increasing demand for housing. By June 2003, real house prices exceeded the previous peak reached more than 20 years before and have stayed above that level ever since. The upward trend in real house prices during the twentieth century was sustained by urbanisation and a resulting rise in land values.

The price increases in early 2003 could be justified as a realignment of house prices from a state of suppression and the 2003 levels of real house prices were sustainable according to a 2003 study (Institute of Economic Studies 2003). In a 2004 report on the economic effects of then proposed changes to the HFF's lending the Central Bank of Iceland emphasised that the expansionary effects would be exaggerated due to their timing as credit constraints were relaxed at the height of the business cycle. The immediate effects would be increased indebtedness of households, increased spending on consumer goods, an inflation spurt and higher interest rates. In the long run the financial system would weaken as LTVs would be higher. Increased household debt could lead to a lower consumption path in the long run as debt-service increased (Central Bank of Iceland 2004a). Elíasson and Pétursson (2009) predicted a 25 percent rise in house prices a year after the HFF relaxed its credit terms and a similar rise in housing investment for the 2 years after, but these effects would then gradually die out.

In 2004 international investors searching for yield increasingly shipped their funds to Iceland. The newly privatised Icelandic banks tapped international bond markets and in 2005 foreign banks, sovereigns and private companies started issuing Euro bonds in the Icelandic currency. The HFF fund changed its issues to better suit international investors. At the same time the privately owned commercial banks expanded their portfolios of domestic assets by increasing their mortgage lending. In addition the HFF went ahead with its market advance, raising LTVs and loan amounts even more aggressively than originally intended (Stefánsson *et al.* 2013). House prices in Iceland started to rise rapidly and by the end of 2005 they had doubled in real terms from 7 years earlier. A second wave of heightened demand came in 2007 when banks increasingly offered FX-linked mortgages. Real apartment prices in the capital region reached an all-time high in October 2007. After the onslaught of the financial crisis and the failure of Iceland's three largest banks a year later, real house prices plummeted. By December 2010 they had lost 36 percent in real terms since the peak in 38 months. The exchange rate was supported by wide spread capital controls, which were put in to effect in November 2008, isolating domestic financial markets and real house prices have trended upwards since 2010 due to lack of investment opportunities within Iceland.

Households' debt Indebtedness of the household sector was rising during the final years of the twentieth century (Figure 13.4). Total household debt

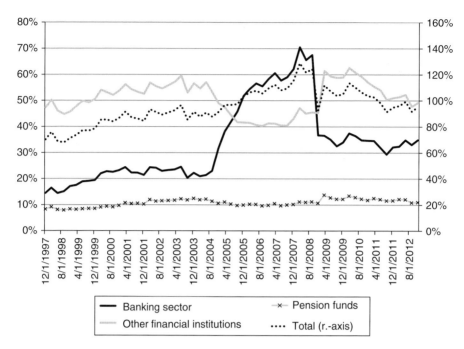

Figure 13.4 Debt of the household sector to the banking sector, other financial institutions (mostly the HFF), and to pension funds, as a percentage of GDP, 1997–2012. *Source*: Stefánsson *et al.* (2013).

increased from about 70 percent of GDP in 1997 to 100 percent in 2005. It continued to rise, reaching almost 130 percent of GDP in the first quarter of 2008, but has since then declined, largely due to the illegality of FX-linked loans that were written down, and is hovering around the 100 percent level.

Figure 13.4 also shows that the banking sector increased its lending to households from roughly 20 percent of GDP in the years prior to 2005 to about 70 percent in 2008. The credit-boom supported consumer spending and fuelled the expanding current account deficit. While total household debt increased significantly there was also considerable transition of debt from other financial institutions (the HFF) to the banking sector. The significant drop in debt to the banking sector in 2008 is a result of the failure of the banking sector. Although a large share of the banks' domestic assets were transferred to the new banks it was done at a discount and some of the debt remained with the failed banks.

Post-crash debt relief   The sharp fall of the Icelandic *króna*, which depreciated by 36 percent in the space of three months in the autumn of 2008, fuelled inflation. The economy went into a recession with GDP dropping by 12.8 percent between Q3 2007 and Q2 2010. Unemployment rose to previously unheard of levels, peaking at 9 percent in the second quarter of 2009.

Real (and in some cases nominal) wages fell. Real debt either increased (in the case of FX-linked loans) or stayed unchanged (in the case of inflation-linked loans). The purchasing power of disposable income fell significantly. Mortgage arrears increased while property values fell. In terms of purchasing power, household income fell to 2003 levels.

Over the past 5 years, various debt restructuring programmes were enacted either by individual banks or by the government. This included amendments to the bankruptcy laws, debt forgiveness on mortgages exceeding 110 percent of estimated property value and the introduction of household receivership. The most determined risk seekers who had opted for FX linked mortgages were rewarded as an expanded supreme court ruled, by a narrow margin, that these loans had in fact been illegal and they were written down to their original amount in *krónur*, adjusted for payments. A later ruling found that the original foreign currency interest rate still applied to these contracts. The Supreme Court thus distanced the determination of interest rates from the currency, rewarding those who took on higher risk. Discontent spread among more prudent mortgage borrowers who had opted for indexed debt in *krónur*, which demanded a corresponding write-down on their outstanding debt. According to a report by Central Bank staff 27.5 percent of households were categorised in financial distress in autumn 2009 and 37 percent of households had negative equity in their homes, compared to 6 percent 4 years earlier (Ólafsson and Vignisdóttir 2012). Plans for further government financed write-downs of mortgage debt, particularly aimed at those who are not in dire need for it, were introduced by the government late in 2013.

Looking to the future

Currently the Icelandic banks and pension funds appear more than able to meet the demand for housing finance at market determined interest rates. A wide variety of mortgages is available at the banks with choices of fixed or floating interest, indexation, annuities or fixed instalments.

The government is dealing with the dire situation of the HFF. Accumulated losses at the HFF, mostly due to the increased risk taken on as the fund swapped its funding in 2004 and insufficient risk management of the ensuing prepayments, amounted to ISK 100 bn at the end of 2012 and future losses were estimated in the ISK 32 bn to ISK 170 bn range in the Parliamentary report of the Special Investigation Commission on the HFF (Stefánsson *et al.* 2013). At 2012 prices these losses amount to between 8 percent and 16 percent of GDP. The eventual level of losses will depend on the rate of interest, which is currently low due to the capital controls.

The HFF has not issued new bonds since January 2012. It has repeatedly received equity injections from the government amounting to ISK 51 bn over

2011–2014, or close to 3 percent of GDP. Losses are expected to continue to accumulate and prepayments continue to exceed new lending at the fund.

Since 2010, the Ministry of Welfare has been analysing and developing housing policies for the future. Rather than focussing on restructuring of housing policy and accepting that there does not appears to be need for a government run mortgage bank to finance normal housing transactions, the HFF appears, according to a 2011 report from the Ministry, to be expected to play a significant role in housing financing (Velferðarráðuneytið 2011). Additional reports on housing policy were published by the Ministry in 2012 focussing on specific details of housing policy rather than on the framework or the role of the government in housing financing. One of the issues discussed in the reports from the Ministry of Welfare is the introduction of housing subsidies, intended not to discriminate between tenure choices (Velferðarráðuneytið 2012).

In April 2013. a working group at the Ministry of Welfare issued a report on the outlook and future role of the HFF (Velferðarráðuneytið 2013). It suggested that the role of the HFF would be restricted to general mortgage lending with strict LTV caps and lending to municipalities and non-profit building societies that provide rental housing at low rates. In addition the HFF would have the role of supplying housing finance in general or in specific areas in the case of market failure.

Similar ideas were put forth in a report contracted by the Ministry in 2014. It further recommended the HFF be closed down and the structure of the mortgage market would be adapted to something closer to the Danish model, leaving out, however, many amendments made there over the past 15 years which have eased access to lending and lowered payment burden excessively.

It is not necessary for the government to compete in a market sufficiently addressed by private firms. Although withdrawing the HFF from the market for general mortgages, where it is not playing any role beyond what the private sector is already doing, does not, however, solve the problem.

Excessive risk taking by banks, in particular in supplying mortgages, should also be addressed by imposing banking regulations, which are counter-cyclical with respect to housing market swings. The Icelandic experience is in agreement with recent experiences from other countries and emphasises the need for a framework for handling the risk of household debt running wild when access to mortgages is relaxed during upswings in the market.

The Central Bank has mentioned in its publications the possibilities of introducing counter-cyclical policy tools in the mortgage market to hinder over-accumulation of household debt during housing market booms as a part of a macro-prudential policy tool-box (Central Bank of Iceland 2010). One possibility is linking financial institutions' capital adequacy requirements to maximum LTVs. Another possibility is implementing dynamic provisioning by linking loan-loss contributions to credit growth. Yet another method considered is linking the weights used to calculate capital ratios according to Basel rules to macro-economic conditions. Special treatment of foreign currency mortgages is also under consideration, for instance, lower limits on LTVs for foreign currency loans (Central Bank of Iceland 2012).

Housing financing in Iceland repeatedly undergoes restructuring. The main theme of increasing government involvement in general housing financing appears, however, to be under real scrutiny for the first time in decades. Reinventing housing financing, searching for successful models in neighbouring countries, is, however, difficult. Even the most robust housing financing models have strayed from their roots lately and may be faltering, having succumbed to extended low-interest rate environments and aggressive financial innovations.

References

Andersen, PS and Guðmundsson, M (1998). Inflation and disinflation in Iceland. *Working paper* 1. Central Bank of Iceland, Reykjavík.

Central Bank of Iceland (2001). The Icelandic foreign exchange market. *Monetary Bulletin* 2001/3. Central Bank of Iceland, Reykjavík.

Central Bank of Iceland (2004a). *Efnahagsleg áhrif breytinga á fyrirkomulagi lánsfjármögnunar íbúðarhúsnæðis.* Central Bank of Iceland, Reykjavík.

Central Bank of Iceland (2004b). *Umsögn um frumvarp til laga um húsnæðismál.* Alþingi, Reykjavík.

Central Bank of Iceland (2008). *Financial Stability 2008.* Central Bank of Iceland, Reykjavík.

Central Bank of Iceland (2010). *Monetary policy in Iceland after capital controls: Report from the Central Bank of Iceland to the Minister of Economic Affairs.* Report no. 4, December 2010. Central Bank of Iceland, Reykjavík.

Central Bank of Iceland (2012). *Prudential rules following capital controls: Report of the Central Bank of Iceland to the Minister of Economic Affairs.* Special publication no. 6, August 2012. Central Bank of Iceland, Reykjavík.

Central Bank of Iceland (2013). *Financial Stability* 2013/2. Central Bank of Iceland, Reykjavík.

Central Bank of Iceland (2014). *Financial Stability* 2014/1. Central Bank of Iceland, Reykjavík.

Elíasson, L (2014). Indexation 101 *Economic Affairs* 6. Central Bank of Iceland, Reykjavík.

Elíasson, L and Pétursson, TG (2009). The residential housing market in Iceland: Analysing the effects of mortgage market restructuring *Housing Studies* 24:1, 25–45.

Félagsmálaráðuneytið (2004). *Skýrsla nefndar um mat á framkvæmd viðbótarlána.*

Hagfræðistofnun (2011). *Þróun á húsnæðismarkaði og samanburður við önnur lönd.*

Hreinsson, P, Benediktsdóttir, S, and Gunnarsson, T (eds) (2010). *Aðdragandi og orsakir falls íslensku bankanna 2008 og tengdir atburðir.* Rannsóknarnefnd Alþingis, Reykjavík.

Institute of Economic Studies (2003). Áhrif rýmri veðheimilda Íbúðalánasjóðs á húsnæðisverð og hagstjórn *Report no. C03:06.* Institute of Economic Studies, Reykjavík.

International Monetary Fund (IMF) (2004). *Staff Visit Concluding Statement,* October 25, 2004.

Jónsson, BB (1999). Financial indexation and interest rate policy in Iceland. *Working paper* 5. Central Bank of Iceland, Reykjavík.

Kristinsson, HS (2002). The Icelandic bond market. *Monetary Bulletin* 2002/1, 36–45. Central Bank of Iceland, Reykjavík.

Ólafsson, TT and Vignisdóttir, KÁ (2012). Households' position in the financial crisis in Iceland. *Working paper* 59. Central Bank of Iceland, Reykjavík.

Skúlason, MÁ (2012). Housing debt crisis in light of a major banking crisis in Iceland: Restructuring of household debt in Iceland – an example for other indebted countries? *EMF Hypostat 2011*, 21–24. European Mortgage Federation.

Snævarr, S (1993). *Haglýsing Íslands*. Heimskringla, Reykjavík.

Stefánsson, SH, Flygenring, KÞ and Heiðarsson, JÞ (eds.) (2013). *Skýrsla rannsóknarnefndar Alþingis um Íbúðalánasjóð o.fl*. Rannsóknarnefnd Alþingis um Íbúðalánasjóð o.fl., Reykjavík.

Velferðarráðuneytið (2011). *Húsnæðisstefna – skýrsla samráðshóps um húsnæðisstefnu*. Velferðarráðuneytið, Reykjavík.

Velferðarráðuneytið (2012). *Skýrsla vinnuhóps um húsnæðisbætur*. Velferðarráðuneytið, Reykjavík.

Velferðarráðuneytið (2013). *Skýrsla starfshóps um framtíðarhorfur og framtíðarhlutverk Íbúðalánasjóðs*. Velferðarráðuneytið, Reykjavík.

14

Milestones in 25 Years of Housing Finance in Ireland

Padraic Kenna

Centre for Housing Law, Rights and Policy, National University of Ireland, Galway, Ireland

Key milestones

Over the past quarter century, Ireland experienced the most dramatic and pervasive economic and institutional changes in its history. These may be defined in three phases, comprised of a number of key milestones, beginning with the slow emergence of the economy and society from underdevelopment up to the mid-1990s (see Table 14.1). This was followed by a rapid and tumultuous growth in housing finance and development, which, after 2007, led to the most rapid decline in house prices and state finances in the world.

Slow growth until the mid-1990s

The private finance system for owner-occupied housing – both for developers and mortgagors – was already in place by the end of the 1980s, with a deregulated market but supported by significant government intervention.

In Ireland, after Independence, a political and ideological fascination with property as the basis of Irish democracy had led to major state intervention and support to owner-occupiers (through grants and subsidised loans). By 1965, the people of Ireland lived 'in what might be regarded as the world's most heavily subsidised houses built under the *aegis* of a most complex set of State economic supports' (Pfretzschner 1963: 125). Social housing, too, was promoted for the labouring classes (and latterly those outside the labour market), but often to promote economic growth or sectoral interests (Kenna 2011).

Milestones in European Housing Finance, First Edition.
Edited by Jens Lunde and Christine Whitehead.
© 2016 John Wiley & Sons, Ltd. Published 2016 by John Wiley & Sons, Ltd.

Table 14.1   Key milestones.

1. Slow growth to mid-1990s	
1980s onwards	Growing economy, Foreign Direct Investment (FDI), Single European Act 1986
1989–1994	Financial deregulation and Building Society demutualisation
2. Rapid growth – mid 1990s to 2007	
1997–2007	Economic boom linked to FDI and the Euro, leading to increased population and new household formation
1997–2007	Gross National Product increases by almost 300%
1998–2007	House price bubble and massive growth in mortgage lending
1999	Ireland joined the Euro zone
2001 and 2007	Asset Covered Securities Acts creating framework for covered bonds and securitisation
2002	Euro into circulation accompanied by low ECB interest rates
2004	Enlargement of the European Union
2004–2008	Major expansion in bank borrowing from abroad
2004	Redefinition of 'affordability' of mortgages
3. Crash of 2007 and after	
2008	Collapse of banking system and State guarantee of all bank liabilities
2008	Recession as construction and related industries collapsed
2008–2013	Rise in mortgage arrears
2009	Legislation incorporating consumer law into mortgage law for 'housing loans' and first Code of Conduct on Mortgage Arrears (CCMA)
2009	Establishment of National Asset Management Agency (NAMA)
2010	Intervention of the 'Troika' and €67.5 bn. conditionally made available to the State through the EFSF, EFSM, IMF and other country bilateral loans. Nationalisation of most lenders and all building societies.
2010	Central Bank Reform Act establishes the Central Bank of Ireland as the single unitary body responsible for both central banking and financial regulation
2012	Finance Act – ending all mortgage tax reliefs by 2017
2013	Mortgage Arrears Resolution Targets for mortgage lenders
2014	ECB Single Supervisory Mechanism regulates main mortgage lenders in Ireland

More recent State promotion of private housing finance can be traced to the White Paper of 1964, which was proposed to 'be the Government's policy to ensure conditions favourable to private investment in housing' (Government of Ireland 1964: 47). Further deregulation of housing finance, which also involved demutualisation and mergers among building societies, occurred in the 1980s. Accompanied by a contraction (including a massive tenant purchase scheme) and residualisation of social housing from the 1980s, the ingredients were present for a house price boom and major demand for mortgage lending, once household formation began to increase.

Economic policy changed its focus in the 1960s to try to stem the tide of emigration and to generate employment by inviting foreign corporations to establish operations in Ireland. From the early 1980s, Ireland's economy had begun to develop significantly, with the establishment of global pharmaceutical, electronics and other high-skill manufacturing corporations. This was accompanied by a growing Europeanisation of the economy. Ireland had signed the Single European Act 1986 leading to a single market by 1992. These policies led to a population increase from 3.5 million to 4.5 million between

1986 and 2011 (29.6 percent). Numbers of households also increased from 964 882 to 1 649 408 (71 percent) in that period, while housing units rose from 976 304 to a total of 1 994 845 (80 percent increase excluding vacant units).

Rapid growth from the late 1990s to 2007

Ireland joined the single European currency (Euro zone) in 1999 (with the Euro coming into circulation from January 2002), attracting major foreign investment as the only English speaking Euro zone country. Unemployment dropped from 16 percent in 1994 to 4 percent in 2001. Of course, increasing housing need and demand corresponded with the growth of urbanisation and industrialisation. A new low interest rate environment, coupled with rising employment and income levels, led to increasing demand for housing. Low levels of private or social rented stock steered new households towards owner-occupation and increased demand for mortgage credit. Figure 14.1 illustrates this pattern, showing the widening gap between newly developed social and private (owner-occupier) housing from the late 1980s and the absolute predominance of access to new housing through owner-occupation in the 'boom years' 2000–2007. This trend corresponds with trends in the number of loans issued, the rise in house prices and the values of mortgage loans as shown in Figure 14.2, later.

By the late 1990s this economic development alongside population and household growth was leading to dramatic increases in house prices, which were becoming unaffordable for average income households. The Government commissioned the iconic Bacon Reports from the late 1990s, which proposed a range of measures to increase the supply of new homes, such as increasing the supply of land for housing development and speeding

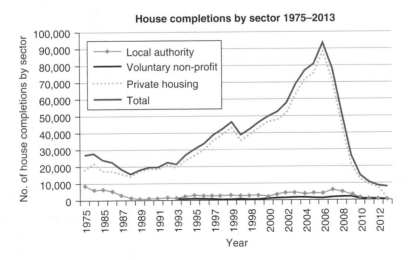

Figure 14.1   House completions by tenure 1975–2013.
Source: Central Statistics Office (various years).

up the planning process (Bacon and Associates 1998; 1999; 2003; Bacon and MacCabe 2000). However, the *laissez-faire* state housing policy continued, with planning and zoning becoming the key instruments for state involvement in the housing system alongside traditional maintenance of the property systems through the state land registration system and legal and state safeguarding of the contract, property exchange and mortgaging system. This situation resulted in many political scandals and public inquiries, as the availability of development finance led to rocketing land values and political pressures for rezoning and planning permissions (Mahon 2012).

After 2000, house prices continued to rise, and construction activity was also boosted by various property related tax-relief schemes (Goodbody 2005). Together with historically low interest rates and the huge increase in lending (including for buy-to-let properties, holiday homes and equity withdrawal), political and fiscal measures encouraged the excesses in the construction sector that were to characterise the years between 2002 and 2007 (Donovan and Murphy 2013). Increased availability of mortgage finance and more relaxed lending criteria created an Irish property bubble, which also encompassed commercial property development and other lending (McCarthy and McQuinn 2013).

Growth and complexity of mortgage lending   The growth and complexity of Irish mortgage lending between 2002 and 2007 was historically unique. Following the liberalisation measures (Everett and Kelly 2004), the Irish mortgage market experienced: significantly increased levels of mortgage lending; higher loan to value ratios (LTVs); growth in the types of variable, fixed rate, interest only and tracker mortgages; longer mortgage terms; and changes in funding sources of mortgage lenders (Doyle 2009). Figure 14.2 illustrates the pattern of growth in value of Irish residential mortgage lending. The growth from 1988 to 1995 was relatively modest compared to the explosion of mortgage lending, which occurred between 2002 and 2007. The total number of

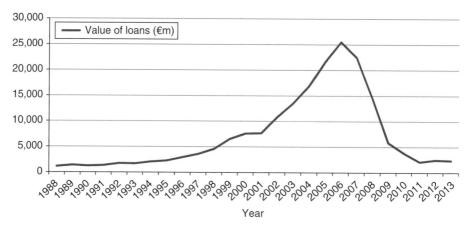

Figure 14.2   Total value of new mortgages issued, 1988–2013 (€ million).
Source: McCarthy and McQuinn (2013), p. 18.

mortgages issued also rose from 31,000 in 1990 to 111,000 in 2007, before dropping to 13,615 in 2013. The average amount of individual mortgage loans issued increased €40,140 in 1990 to €229,300 in 2006 and then down to €17,400 in 2013. The total value of outstanding loans for house purchase according in Ireland rose from €43.8 bn at the end of 2002 to €123.7 bn at the end of 2007, and then declined to €78.3 bn by end 2013 (Central Bank of Ireland 2015).

One of the features of the Irish property bubble years (2002–2007) was the growth of buy-to-let investment borrowings. Indeed, at the end of 2013 there were 145 530 residential mortgage accounts for buy-to-let properties with a value of €29.7 bn, accounting for 22 percent of all outstanding residential mortgage loans. Some 39 250 (27 percent) of these accounts were in arrears, with 21.1 percent in arrears of more than 90 days. The balance outstanding on arrears of more than 90 days was €8.7 bn, equivalent to 29.2 percent of the total outstanding balance on all these buy-to let mortgages.

A recent study showed that while interest-only mortgages account for a relatively small proportion of the market, these have higher levels of arrears than standard principal-and-interest mortgages (Kelly *et al.* 2014). Such mortgages were mainly issued to buy-to-let investors on tracker mortgages, in the period 2005–2008, at high LTVs. As a substantial number are due to revert to higher principal-and-interest repayments in the next few years, this could pose difficulties for borrowers in making repayments.

Another development was the introduction of 100 percent LTV mortgages, which grew from 6 percent of new loans in 2004 to 26 percent in 2006. Some 10 percent of new residential mortgages issued in 2007 were for the purpose of mortgage equity withdrawal (Doyle 2009: 84).

In the boom years (2002–2007) of Irish housing finance a range of products were developed. Table 14.2 shows the diversity of mortgage products available in the period 1997–2009 in Ireland.

Between 2004 and 2008 the majority of residential mortgages issued by Irish banks were tracker mortgages. While these loans are now very affordable and well performing there is a risk that when European Central Bank (ECB) rates increase, some of the borrowers who purchased homes at the highest prices of the bubble may be under pressure.

Table 14.2 Extent of types of Irish mortgage products.

	1997	2006	2009
Fixed rate mortgage products:	93	71	82
- 1–3 years	60	41	56
- 3–5 years	24	18	21
- Fixed greater than 5 years	9	12	5
Variable rate mortgage products	44	78	45
- Standard variable-rate mortgages	34	19	43
- Tracker mortgages		57	2
- Other (including current saver account, discount and 3-in-1 mortgages)	10	2	–

Source: Doyle (2009: 81).

Following the Asset Covered Securities Act 2001 (and 2007), which provided a framework for covered bonds and securitisation of mortgages, Irish mortgage lenders managed part of the additional risk of increased lending through securitisation. This led to some €25 bn in outstanding covered bonds, backed by mortgages in 2012, and total outstanding residential mortgage-backed securities of €51.2 bn in 2012 (Linn *et al.* 2014: 61; EMF *Hypostat* 2013).

As shown in Figure 14.3, large-scale borrowing by Irish credit institutions from outside Ireland (including mortgage lenders with headquarters outside Ireland) grew from just 10 percent of GDP in 2002 to some 60 percent (€110 bn) by early 2008, before declining dramatically. It has been suggested that this over-lending, financed by foreign borrowing by Irish banks, was a key element in the banking crisis (Honohan 2010: 20).

Affordability   Average variable mortgage interest rates in Ireland declined gradually from a peak of 16.25 percent in 1982 to 7.5 percent in 1994, 3.81 percent in 2003 to 3.25 percent in 2012 (CSO and *Hypostat* 2013). In this context, the question of affordability of housing mortgages began to be redefined after 2000, when low Euro zone interest rates became prevalent. While traditional models of lending based on multiples of annual incomes had been firmly established, these metrics were no longer seen as appropriate in a climate of low interest rates, rising equity values and increased availability of mortgage finance. Indeed, this changing definition of affordability towards ability to service the mortgage debt allowed for mortgages based on higher multiples of earnings to be advanced. In many cases lenders included unverified income (Duffy 2004). The situation was exacerbated by the arrival

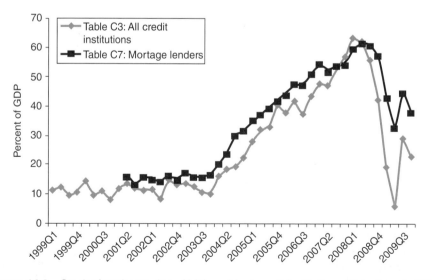

Figure 14.3   Stock of net borrowing of Irish resident credit institutions from abroad, 1999 Q1 to 2009 Q4.
Source: Honohan (2010: 33).

of lenders from the UK and elsewhere offering over 100 percent LTV and interest only loans, creating competition among all lenders for the pool of new borrowers.

Figure 14.4 shows nominal new house prices nationally (although there were higher increases in Dublin), with over 500 percent increases between 1988 and 2007. By mid-2007 the average second-hand house price had increased to almost 12 times the average industrial wage in Dublin.

It is clear that the increasing average mortgage amounts between 1995 and 2007 reflected, or perhaps influenced, the increase in house prices. There was an increasing excess of mortgage lending on each unit purchased. This led to reckless consideration of the underlying financial value of the housing being mortgaged and, indeed, to the ability of borrowers to repay in the event of a recession. The unsuitability of the mortgage products offered to each borrower can now be questioned, but the exuberance of the period led to poor consideration of such matters at the time. As the former Minister for Finance at the time of the banking collapse stated '[T]he biggest impropriety in the banking sector was the degree and pattern of reckless lending' (*Dáil Éireann* [Parliament] Debate, Vol. 720 No. 2, 28 October 2010).

The 2007 crash and after

Ireland stands out, both for its expansion of housing finance, the large growth and collapse of house prices and the impact of housing finance on its economy and society. The result of this explosion of credit is that household debt in Ireland (which includes mortgage and personal debt) remained elevated at over 180 percent of disposable income at the beginning of 2014 (Central Bank 2014). The Central Bank has pointed out that 'the household sector remains highly indebted and vulnerable to economic shocks, falls in income and increases in interest rates' (Central Bank 2014: 10).

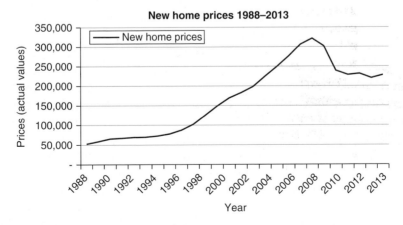

Figure 14.4   New home prices (national, including apartments), 1988–2013 (€).
Source: Central Statistics Office (various years).

Since the Global Financial Crisis (GFC) in 2007/2008, there has been a collapse, not just of house prices which have declined by an average of 50 percent (more is some areas), but of all the main lending institutions in the state. Following the state guarantee of these banks' liabilities, there has also been a collapse in the state's finances and indeed a general recession with high levels of unemployment. Banking debt has become sovereign debt, and in 2010, the Irish Government agreed to the Programme of Financial Support and Memorandum of Understanding with the European Union (EU) and the International Monetary Fund (IMF). This required that the banking system be restructured and recapitalised, and €67.5 bn was conditionally made available through the European Financial Stability Facility (EFSF), the European Financial Stabilisation Mechanism (EFSM) and the International Monetary Fund (IMF), with bilateral loans from the UK, Sweden and Denmark. Ireland exited this arrangement in December 2013, but the level of government debt remains high.

A consequence of the financial crisis is that today, almost all of the Irish banking sector has been nationalised, with the state owning 99.8 percent of Allied Irish Banks and Educational Building Society, 100 percent of the former Anglo-Irish Bank and Irish Nationwide Building Society (which has now been almost fully liquidated), 99.5 percent of Permanent TSB and 15 percent of the Bank of Ireland. In a rather unedifying end to the building society tradition in Ireland, the last two remaining societies (down from 11 in 1984) – Educational Building Society (with over 400 000 members) and Irish Nationwide Building Society – were merged with banks in 2011 by legislation, having engaged in excessive lending for property development and commercial property investment (Credit Institutions (Financial Support) Act 2008).

At the end of 2014, there were 764 567 mortgages on principal private dwellings (many properties have more than one mortgage) with a value of €107.4 bn. Some 136 564 (18 percent) were in arrears, with 96 474 (13 percent) in arrears over 90 days. Some 60 422 (7.9 percent of total) were in arrears over 360 days and of these some 33 589 (4.4 percent) were in arrears over 720 days. The Government *Housing Policy Statement* (2011) outlined a commitment to prevent households losing their homes as a result of mortgage related arrears. *The Programme for Government (2011–2016)* set out a range of measures to help households struggling to meet mortgage commitments from becoming homeless. The Central Bank of Ireland (which regulates mortgage lenders) set targets in March 2013 for lenders to arrange 'proposed' solutions for mortgages in arrears, with 45 percent of arrears cases to be resolved by the end of 2014 (Central Bank of Ireland 2013). 'Forbearance' arrangements have been developed for a third of the 15.5 percent of mortgagors in arrears. However, the number of initiated possession proceedings for mortgage arrears has escalated from 838 in 2012 to 3846 in 2013 and to approximately 12 000 in 2014, although the numbers of properties taken into possession remains around 4–700 per annum.

Sub-prime loans or residential mortgages issued by non-bank lenders accounted for 2 percent of all residential mortgage accounts outstanding at the end of December 2013 (2.5 percent in value terms). These sub-prime lenders were regarded as 'retail credit firms' and only became subject to regulation by the Central Bank from 1 February 2008. There were some 17 789 such loans on primary dwellings in March 2014, amounting to €3316 bn, with arrears of €1880 bn, or 57 percent of their loan book. Significantly, these are not subject to the Central Bank Mortgage Arrears Resolution Targets (MART) of 2013, although the consumer protection codes do apply. During 2012, sub-prime or non-bank lenders accounted for 24 percent of total properties repossessed following court orders, and 15 percent in 2013. One third of the 20 000 state low cost-home ownership loans (LCHO) were in arrears over 90 days.

While bank home mortgage lending by two main Irish banks grew by over 100 percent between 2002 and 2008, some of this was to UK borrowers. However, this flow of credit was dwarfed by development and property lending, which saw increases of 300–400 percent in the period. Indeed, the collapse of development and property lending with unsustainable and non-performing loans led initially to the collapse of the main banks and then to the establishment of the National Asset Management Agency (NAMA) in 2009. NAMA was involved in the acquisition and transfer of over €71 bn in loan assets involving 850 debtors and more than 11 000 individual loans collateralised by 16 000 individual properties. Approximately two-thirds of the assets backing those loans are located in Ireland, with most of the remainder located in the UK, in smaller concentrations in the US and throughout continental Europe. In exchange for these loans NAMA issued Government-guaranteed securities to the five participating financial institutions. However, a significant proportion of these loans is related to commercial property development (including residential sites), rather than direct housing mortgages.

Housing finance has had a major impact on tax and state finances. One significant legacy of the construction and housing lending boom was the collapse of tax income from that sector, with devastating consequences for state finances. Public expenditure had become reliant on property and development-related tax revenues, which by 2006 made up 18 percent of total fiscal income. This collapsed to 2.6 percent of total tax revenues by 2010, and the resulting crisis in the state finances led to the IMF/ECB bailout programme in 2010. The Irish State expends approximately €1.3 bn per annum on the support of rented housing (Department of Public Expenditure and Reform 2012: 1). In addition, the State provides significant tax benefits to home owners and investors, including the cost of providing mortgage interest relief, which in 2011 was €1.1 bn. (NESC 2014a: 2). Under the Social Welfare Acts the state provides financial support to those who cannot afford mortgage or rent payments through the Mortgage Interest Supplement and Rent

Supplement, which totalled €55 mn and €423 mn, respectively, in 2012. The Finance Act 2012 provided that all schemes which facilitate tax relief on mortgage interest payments will end in 2017.

One of the consequences of the housing related financial crisis was an examination of the failure of banking regulation. A number of expert reports on the causes of the financial crisis in Ireland highlighted regulatory weaknesses and the inadequacy of 'principles based' regulation (Honohan 2010; Reglin and Watson 2010; Commission of Investigation into the Banking Sector in Ireland 2011). The prudence and conduct of business regulation had apparently been strengthened by the Central Bank and Financial Services Authority of Ireland Act 2003, but this proved ineffective. The Central Bank and Financial Services Authority of Ireland Act 2004 established the Financial Services Ombudsman. However, the division of responsibilities between the Governor of the Central Bank of Ireland and the regulatory agencies established under the Act 'was novel and contained the hazard of ambiguous lines of responsibility especially in the event of a systemic crisis' (Honohan 2010: 36). The Central Bank Reform Act 2010 established the Central Bank as the single unitary body responsible for both central banking and financial regulation, reformed the regulatory structure for financial services with a new statutory fitness and probity regime for directors and certain executives of banks, and amended other legislation to strengthen regulation. From November 2014, the European Central Bank (under the Single Supervisory Mechanism) will now directly supervise the largest Irish banks.[1] A Parliamentary Committee of Inquiry into the banking crisis commenced in December 2014.

Emerging issues

In the wake of the financial and housing crisis many emerging issues are challenging existing housing policy norms (Norris and Coates 2014). Ireland's rate of homeownership peaked at 80 percent in 1991 and has now declined to around 70 percent. The most recent Census (2011) showed that of the total of 1 649 408 units in the State, some 566 776 units (or 34.4 percent) were owner-occupied without a mortgage/loan; 583 148 units (or 35.4 percent) were owner-occupied with a mortgage/loan. Within the rented sector there were 305 377 units, or 18.5 percent of tenure, while social housing tenure comprised some 156 000 units or 9.5 percent of tenures (CSO Census 2011). Since the census this pattern may well still be changing quite rapidly.

Morgenroth suggest that in the period to 2021 some 180,000 new households will require housing, mainly in the Dublin region (Morgenroth 2014: 14). Although in the past accessing owner-occupied housing has been the preferred choice for most emerging households, private renting is becoming more accepted, with regulation of tenancies and a regulatory authority now in place (Duffy *et al.* 2014). In any case, restrictions on mortgage lending arising from Mortgage Credit Directive[2] and other influences will inevitably lead to a greater demand for rented housing. As a result of these pressures the private rented sector is expected to provide for over 25 percent of households by 2020 (PRTB 2014).

The consequences of the housing finance and market crash have sparked an emerging debate on the future pattern of housing tenure in Ireland. Clearly, this will vary across social groups and will depend upon levels of new household formation, immigration patterns, average incomes, expectations of and actual house price increases, access to mortgage credit and the availability of tenure options (NESC 2014b). House prices are now rising again and the expectation of house price inflation is likely stimulate owner-occupation as an investment. Indeed, in 2013 Irish house prices were still 3.7 times higher than in 1994 in nominal terms and 2.5 times higher in real terms. Therefore, the attraction of renting may be short-lived (NESC 2014b: 47). Today, the question of mortgage eligibility is being defined again in terms of multiples of annual income. The Central Bank of Ireland has now proposed measures to restrict new lending for principal dwelling houses (PDH) to 80 percent LTV, and to 3.5 times gross annual incomes in an effort to ensure that borrowers and lenders can withstand potential economic or property market shocks in the future without financial distress (Central Bank of Ireland 2014).

One key issue is tenure choice, and this requires the creation of an affordable, secure and sustainable rental sector to provide a balance to the dominance of owner-occupation with mortgage as the principal route into housing.

Currently, the private rented sector is dominated by individual private landlords, with 65 percent of landlords owning one property, and a further 17 percent having two properties. Rents are not regulated and security of tenure is relatively weak. A recent report (NESC 2014b) which examined the opportunities and barriers for the development of this sector suggests that while private renting has some advantages – low-entry costs, no investment risk and flexibility – the disadvantages can often outweigh those benefits. Private renting offers less security of tenure than renting from a local authority, and future rents are determined by market prices, which also creates uncertainty for tenants. Recent rent rises have far outpaced rises in incomes and wages. However, the report also suggests that Ireland should seek to emulate European States, which have made private renting more affordable and attractive, while also providing tenants with security of tenure and more predictable rents. The Private Residential Tenancies Board (PRTB) suggests that the arrival of Real Estate Investment Trusts (REITS), introduced in the Finance Act 2013, is a significant step towards professionalising the private rented sector (PRTB 2014). The PRTB also suggests that the tax regime for investing in residential investment property is less favourable than for commercial property, and subsidies, taxation and regulation are key factors.

However, affordability problems in the private rented sector continue to drive increasing numbers of households on to social housing lists, although the concept of social housing itself is being redefined to include those in private rented housing on long-term rent supports. A recent report (NESC 2014a) which examined future demand, supply and funding options for social housing in Ireland reiterated the view that the developer-led private housing production system, where access is determined by availability of mortgage finance, would exclude up to a third of new households who are on low incomes or have special housing needs. The central problem (which was left unresolved in the NESC Report) was that if private developers (and financiers) do not take the lead in the production of new housing, who can?

Blending of mortgage law with consumer law

Mortgage law has traditionally been regarded as part of property or land law, and in Ireland much of this dates from pre-Independence. However, as part of the updating and consolidation of land law (in preparation for electronic conveyancing), the Land and Conveyancing Law Reform Act 2009 (LCLRA) introduced a new concept of a 'housing loan' into the law of mortgages. This differentiates mortgages on principal primary residences from all other mortgages. A 'housing loan' (as defined in S. (1) of the Consumer Credit Act 1995, as amended) broadly means a loan to a consumer to acquire or renovate a dwelling, whether a principal private residence or not). A 'consumer' is defined as a natural (as opposed to a legal) person acting outside the person's business. Once the mortgage is regarded as a 'housing loan', then lenders must obtain a possession order to recover possession in the Circuit Court rather than the High Court (a process which is less expensive and more localised). The LCLRA also enables a court to adjourn possession proceedings for two months where the borrower in arrears is likely to repay the mortgage and arrears, or to instruct a Personal Insolvency Practitioner to make a Personal Insolvency Arrangement proposal to creditors.

The Code of Conduct on Mortgage Arrears (CCMA) was originally introduced in 2009 and revised in 2010, 2011 and 2013. This involves a structured framework, setting out lender obligations in cases of mortgage arrears, which could include restructuring, voluntary sale, or mortgage-to-rent. The lender must operate a *Mortgage Arrears Resolution Process* when dealing with arrears and pre-arrears cases. However, in *Irish Life and Permanent v Dunne*[3] the Supreme Court confined the legal effect of the CCMA to one issue – the obligation on a lender not to bring legal proceedings within the short moratorium period provided in the CCMA.

Conclusion

Ireland experienced a massive economic boom from the late 1990s to 2007, followed by a collapse of its financial system in 2008. Gross National Product (GNP) at current prices had risen from €40 bn in 1994 to €164 bn in 2007, with a corresponding increase in capital formation in housing. In many ways, the housing boom can be understood as forming part of the economic boom itself, but with widespread negative and unforeseen consequences. However, the crash was confined to specific sectors of the economy – although the largest impact of the following recession was on areas which were linked with construction and housing related industries.

Ireland's period of unprecedented economic growth abruptly came to an end amid the fallout of the GFC. However, domestic factors including the irrational exuberance of mortgage lending created a crisis in all bank credit ratings and interbank trust. The state guaranteed all banking liabilities in 2008, and then provided major resources to ensure liquidity and recapitalisation of Irish banks. In 2010, the state agreed a financial package with the so-called 'Troika'– the EFSF, EFSM, IMF – as lenders of last resort and other country bilateral loans as part of a financing package amounting to €85 bn to cover these costs and shortfalls in fiscal income to maintain state services. The result was a General Government Debt of €203 bn at the end of 2013 – representing 124 percent of GDP – and is expected to decline to 107 percent of GDP by end 2018 (National Treasury Management Agency 2014: 14). This burden of debt adopted by the state continues to limit government options for public expenditure on housing. Interest expenditure on general government debt is expected to stabilise at 14 percent of government revenues in 2016. Membership of the EU Stability and Growth Pact requires Ireland to reduce its government national debt to GDP ratio, and this implies on-going fiscal and spending adjustments. Legislation enacted in 2009 created a new category in Irish mortgage law of 'housing loans' and integrates consumer protection into these 'housing loan' mortgages. The courts have incorporated this legislation into mortgage case law and the subsequent regulation of the balance of power between individual borrowers and corporate lenders is creating a unique and innovative set of precedents in Europe. In March 2013 the Central Bank set 'performance targets' for the major mortgage lenders to resolve mortgage arrears cases, and rising repossessions proceedings are creating public concern.

However, possessions and evictions in Ireland have been low compared to other states experiencing mortgage lending crises. Indeed, Government policy has been sympathetic to distressed borrowers, but promises a different form of regulatory approach. The *Programme for Government 2011–2016* states that:

> … more protection is needed for homeowners with distressed mortgages… We will ensure that the Central Bank and Financial Regulator supervise credit institutions' mortgage lending practices comprehensively and intensively. Where credit institutions fail to adequately control mortgage lending risks, the Central Bank will impose loan-to-value ceilings on mortgages, caps on loan-to-income multiples, limits on the term of new mortgages, and more rigorous procedures for verifying borrowers' incomes… (Department of Taoiseach 2011).

Irish mortgage lenders have been recovering from the economic downturn, previous lending policies and a reliance on global finance and over the next 2–3 years, the impact of the Banking Union will become apparent. This will affect the mortgage finance market especially alongside the introduction of the Basel III regulations and the EU Mortgage Credit Directive (2014), which aims to create an EU wide mortgage market with a high level of consumer protection. Stricter lending criteria, which consider the suitability of mortgage products for consumers and the underlying and long term housing values, will significantly impact on the nature of Irish housing. As a consequence, it is anticipated that, as in many European countries, mortgage lending will be more restricted than in the past, resulting in increasing reliance on the rental sector.

Acknowledgements

I am grateful to Patricia Coonan, Anne McGrath, Donna Shiel and Padraic Ward for their assistance.

Notes

1 See *Article 127(6) of the Treaty on the Functioning of the European Union and Council Regulation (EC) No 1023/2013* (the 'SSM Regulation').
2 Directive 2014/17/EC of the European Parliament and of the Council of 4 February 2014 on credit agreements relating to residential immovable property and amending Directives 2008/48/EC and 2013/36/EU and Regulation (EU) No 1093/2010.
3 Courts are not empowered to inquire into the fairness or failure to agree an alternative payment arrangement of any proposed 'solution' proposed by lenders.

References

Bacon, P and Associates (1998). *An Economic Assessment of Recent House Price Developments.* The Stationery Office, Dublin.

Bacon, P and Associates (1999). *The Housing Market: An Economic Review and Assessment.* The Stationery Office, Dublin.

Bacon, P and Associates (2003). *Medium Term Projections of the Supply and Demand for Apartments in Dublin City Centre.* Peter Bacon and Associates, Economic Consultants, Wexford.

Bacon, P and MacCabe, F (2000). *The Housing Market in Ireland: An Economic Evaluation of Trends and Prospects.* The Stationery Office, Dublin.

Central Bank of Ireland (2015). Table A.5.1 Loans to Irish Households – Purpose and Maturity [Online] Available: http://www.centralbank.ie/polstats/stats/cmab/pages/money%20and%20banking.aspx.

Central Bank of Ireland (2014). Consultation paper CP87, Central Bank of Ireland, Dublin.

Central Bank of Ireland (2013). Mortgage Arrears Resolution Targets 13 March 2013, [Online] Available: www.centralbank.ie/press-area/press-releases/documents/approach%20to%20mortage%20arrears%20resolution%20-.pdf (accessed 29 July 2015).

Central Statistics Office (CSO). (2011) *Census 2011.* CSO, Cork.

Central Statistics Office (various years). Statistics [Online] Available: www.cso.ie/en/index.html.

Commission of Investigation into the Banking Sector in Ireland (2011). *Misjudging Risk: Causes of the Systemic Banking Crisis in Ireland.* The Stationery Office, Dublin (The Nyberg Report).

Department of Public Expenditure and Reform (2012). *Social Housing Supports, Comprehensive Review of Expenditure.* DPER, Dublin.

Department of the Taoiseach (2011). Programme for Government 2011–2016, Government of Ireland, Dublin [Online] Available: www.taoiseach.gov.ie/eng/Work_Of_The_Department/Programme_for_Government/Programme_for_Government_2011–2016.pdf (accessed 29 July 2015).

Donovan, D and Murphy, AE (2013). *The Fall of the Celtic Tiger.* Oxford University Press, Oxford.

Doyle, N (2009). Housing finance development in Ireland. *Central Bank Quarterly Bulletin,* 75–88.

Duffy, D (2004). A note on measuring the affordability of homeownership, *ESRI Quarterly Economic Bulletin*, Summer, 71–78.

Duffy, D, Byrne, D and FitzGerald, J (2014). Alternative scenarios for new household formation in Ireland, *Quarterly Economic Commentary*, Spring 2014 ESRI, Dublin.

European Mortgage Federation (EMF) (2013). *Hypostat 2013, A Review of Europe's Mortgage and Housing Markets.* EMF, Dublin.

Everett, M and Kelly, J (2004). Financial liberalisation and economic growth in Ireland. *Quarterly Bulletin*, Autumn, Central Bank of Ireland, Dublin.

Goodbody Economic Consultants (2005). *Review of Area-Based Tax Incentive Renewal Schemes, Final Report*, Department of Finance, Dublin.

Government of Ireland (1964). White Paper, *Housing, Progress and Prospects.* The Stationery Office, Dublin.

Honohan, P (2010). *The Irish Banking Crisis: Regulatory and Financial Stability Policy 2003–2008 – A Report to the Minister for Finance by the Governor of the Central Bank.* Central Bank, Dublin.

Kelly, J, Kennedy, G and McIndoe-Calder, T (2014). Interest-only mortgages in Ireland. *Central Bank of Ireland Economic Letter Series*, 2014: 5.

Kenna, P (2011). *Housing Law, Rights and Policy.* Clarus Press, Dublin.

Linn, A, Kelly, A and Bailey, S (2014). Irish residential mortgage-backed securities – preliminary analysis of loan-level data, Central Bank of Ireland. *Quarterly Bulletin* 04/October 14.

Mahon, AP (2012). *The Final Report of the Tribunal of Inquiry into Certain Planning Matters and Payments*. The Stationery Office, Dublin.

McCarthy, Y and McQuinn, K (2013). Credit conditions in a boom and bust property market. *Central Bank of Ireland Research Technical Paper, No 8/RT/13.*

Morgenroth, E (2014). *Projected Population Change and Housing Demand: A County Level Analysis, ESRI Research Note*. ESRI, Dublin.

National Economic and Social Council (NESC) (2014a). *Social Housing at the Crossroads: Possibilities for Investment, Provision and Cost Rental*. NESC, Dublin.

National Economic and Social Council (2014b). *Homeownership and rental What Road is Ireland on?* (No. 138) NESC, Dublin.

National Treasury Management Agency (2014). *Annual Report and Accounts for year ended 31 December 2013*. NTMA, Dublin.

Norris, M and Coates, D (2014). How housing killed the Celtic tiger: anatomy and consequences of Ireland's boom and bust, *Journal of Housing and the Built Environment* 29:2, 299–315.

Pfretzschner, P (1965). *The Dynamics of Irish Housing*. IPA, Dublin.

Private Residential Tenancies Board (PRTB)/Housing Agency (2014). *Future of the Private Rented Sector*. PRTB, Dublin.

Regling, K and Watson, M (2010). *A Preliminary Report into the Sources of Ireland's Banking Crisis*. The Stationery Office, Dublin.

15

Milestones in Housing Finance in the Netherlands, 1988–2013

Marja Elsinga, Hugo Priemus and Peter Boelhouwer
OTB Research for the Built Environment, Faculty of Architecture and the Built Environment, Delft University of Technology, Delft, the Netherlands

Introduction

In this overview we consider the period since 1988, when the ENHR Working Group on Housing Finance was set up. Among the changes in housing finance, we selected the most strategic changes as milestones. We consider a milestone as something that caused a substantial change in housing finance, at least with hindsight. We not only distinguish milestones in the past that proved to be milestones; we also identify *candidate milestones* that we think have the potential to make a substantial change in the next decade. The chapter focuses on national housing policy since the government is central to the Dutch housing finance market and the housing system as a whole.

In this paper we distinguish three periods to describe the Dutch housing finance system. The first period (1988–2000) started in 1988 when a Parliamentary Inquiry on Building Subsidies took place and marked an end to the era in which subsidies for housing were self-evident. In 1989 the Housing Policy Memorandum of Secretary of State Heerma (1989) was published. With hindsight, we can conclude that this was the beginning of two decades of privatisation and deregulation including a number of important policy changes such as the Grossing Act, the end of general supply subsidies in social housing, the start of the National Guarantee Fund for owner-occupied housing, deregulation of financial markets and the development of new financial mortgage products.

Milestones in European Housing Finance, First Edition.
Edited by Jens Lunde and Christine Whitehead.
© 2016 John Wiley & Sons, Ltd. Published 2016 by John Wiley & Sons, Ltd.

This period was followed by a period (2000–2008) of confusion and fundamental debate about the Dutch housing finance system and its key features, such as mortgage interest income tax deduction and the role of social housing associations. These discussions were on the political agenda, but did not result in any substantial policy change in this period. However, the state aid letter from the European Commission in 2005 started a discussion on the social rental sector that would lead on to fundamental changes.

The third period (2008–present) started with the global financial crisis (GFC). In the Netherlands this resulted in an economic recession and stagnation in the housing market. This provided the impetus for the government to realise substantial changes in the owner-occupied market: reregulation of the mortgage market, adjustments in mortgage interest tax relief and the introduction of a landlord levy for regulated rented housing. Many changes in the finance system have taken place that are adversely affecting the current housing market and are considered candidate milestones.

The remainder of this contribution will describe milestones during these three periods in the next section, deal with the impacts in the following section and finally present some reflections in the final section.

Milestones over the three periods

1988–2000: privatisation and deregulation

The Heerma Memorandum   In the 1980s the general policy of supporting homeownership and reducing public rental housing, followed by the Thatcher Government in Britain, can be regarded as a trendsetter in many European countries (Boelhouwer and Priemus 1990). In line with this approach in 1989 the Heerma Memorandum on Housing Policy (Heerma 1989) marked a strong realignment of Dutch housing policy. General points of departure were: reductions in housing subsidies, encouragement for homeownership, hiving off government tasks and deregulation (Boelhouwer and Priemus 1990). This change in housing policy was the political reaction to the Parliamentary Inquiry on Housing Subsidies (Parlementaire Enquêtecommissie Bouwsubsidies 1988).

The Heerma Memorandum brought substantial change to the organisation of social rental housing, giving them more independence and incentivising entrepreneurship among the housing associations. To reduce future expenditures on supply subsidies Heerma (1989), encouraged by the Maastricht Treaty to reduce government deficits, proposed a number of measures: the abolition of long-term subsidy obligations for social rental housing, shorter subsidy durations for new cases, future subsidies that were less related to interest costs and the sale of social rented dwellings and high annual rent increases to compensate for this. The last was related to the aim of encouraging homeownership. For the owner-occupied sector the political message was on the one hand a reduction of supply subsidies and on the other a continuation, even a gradual increase, in fiscal support for home-ownership. The most remarkable aspect of the Heerma Memorandum was that it was not only an announcement but that it has been implemented almost completely. This policy document was the beginning of a long period of deregulation and privatisation: a typical milestone.

The mortgage market   The mortgage market was liberalised in the period 1988–2000. Covered bonds had only been used by special mortgage banks until 1980. These banks became part of the general banking system in the 1980s. Also many lenders entered the Dutch mortgage market; all the big consumer banks, several insurance companies and some international banks were active. Not only could the client make a choice between many mortgage suppliers, but there was also a variety of mortgage products available at that time. These mortgage products were steered by fiscal legislation (see section on new mortgage products that follows). Since the end of the 1980s, it became more and more common to keep the downpayments as low as possible or even to buy interest only mortgages. As a result monthly payments were reduced significantly, which were partly capitalised into higher house prices financed through higher mortgage loans. This led to much higher risk profiles and house price inflation. During the period between 1997 and 2001, there were double digit house price increases every year. The main reduction in risk was due to interest on most mortgages being fixed for a period of either 5 or 10 years. Via the Bureau of Credit Registration (BKR), buyers were also checked with respect to other debts. It was possible to buy a first house without any deposit.

New mortgage products: maximising tax benefit   Mortgage interest relief was introduced for homeowners in the Netherlands by the Pierson Cabinet in 1893, even before the Housing Act was enacted (1901). A deduction-based system was introduced in 1971 whereby owner-occupiers were taxed on the 'imputed rent', expressed as a percentage of the estimated value of the occupied dwelling (Van der Schaar 1987; 1991). However, the imputed rent tax did not fully counterbalance the mortgage interest tax relief. Later, as more people became homeowners, the gap between the imputed rent and the market rent of the home became even wider. So since the 1970s mortgage tax relief was no longer a neutral fiscal policy, but became more and more a tax subsidy supporting the growth of homeownership.

As in many other countries, the Dutch mortgage market was deregulated in the 1980s and 1990s (Priemus *et al.* 1994). The deregulation of mortgage markets made room for product innovation. In the Netherlands this resulted in the development of new mortgage products with lower monthly expenditures and allowing borrowers to gain the maximum benefit from the fiscal policy (Van der Schaar 1987). In 1985 the savings mortgage was introduced in the form of an interest only mortgage loan linked with a savings account. This enabled the borrower to benefit from maximum mortgage interest deduction for the whole period of the loan – usually 30 years. After 30 years the product guarantees that the savings will be enough to pay off the mortgage in full. Later on the investment mortgage was added. This product is similar to the savings mortgage; the only difference is that the savings account is replaced by an investment account which implies that there is no guarantee that the money in this account is enough to pay off the mortgage after 30 years. Remarkably, these products were accepted by the fiscal authority for mortgage interest deduction. These products were overtaken in terms of market share between 1988 and 2000 by the interest-only mortgage. This product enables maximum mortgage interest deduction for 30 years, without any wealth accumulation. Another important change in mortgage provision was the introduction of two-earner mortgage criteria in 1993. Until then, only the first income in a household was taken into account by the lender. The combination of fiscal policy, the availability of the mortgage guarantee and the new mortgage products substantially improved accessibility to homeownership. The policy focus was on improving access; there was little concern or discussion about the increased risks for these buyers. With hindsight we call the acceptance of new mortgage products such as the savings mortgage by the Dutch fiscal authority a milestone: the start of a period in which mortgage interest deduction maximisation was an increasingly accepted strategy for households.

Guarantee fund for owner-occupied housing   In 1956, the Netherlands introduced a government-backed municipal guarantee system to improve the accessibility and affordability of home-ownership. Each municipality developed its own guarantee system. In the early 1990s three shortcoming of this system needed to be addressed: the regulations had to be standardised, the efficiency of the fund had to be improved and a strong capital reserve position had to be built up. This led to the establishment of the Homeownership Guarantee Fund in November 1993 (Waarborgfonds Eigen Woningen, or WEW, in the Netherlands). The WEW is a private, non-profit organisation that is supported via counter-guarantees by central and local governments. The WEW became operational in 1995. It took over all the existing municipal guarantees and almost all municipalities discontinued their own systems. The WEW lending regulations are the same throughout the country and the rates and conditions are subject to annual approval by the Dutch Housing Ministry and the

Association of Netherlands Municipalities (Elsinga and Dol 2003; Priemus *et al.* 2007). The main purpose of the WEW is to lower the home-ownership threshold, particularly for households in low- and middle-income groups and to be a safety net in case of negative equity. The WEW guarantee covers 100 percent of the amount borrowed. This enables first-time buyers in particular to get a mortgage and buy a house without their own equity. To qualify for the guarantee the borrower must meet the criteria with respect to debt servicing – there is a maximum debt-to-service ratio that guarantees 'safe lending'. Moreover, the borrower has to pay an upfront fee of 1 percent of the mortgage loan. The fee is supposed to be for recovering cost.

Social Housing Guarantee Fund (WSW) and the Central Housing Fund (CFV)

In 1983, the Social Housing Guarantee Fund (*Waarborgfonds Sociale Woningbouw*: WSW) was set up as a private institute to enable the coverage of the financing needs of housing associations. At first, only guarantees for housing improvement were provided. In 1988 it became possible to obtain guarantees for financing the construction of new dwellings. The WSW provides the participating associations with access to the private capital market at the lowest costs. Since then, the WSW has granted guarantees to lenders for loans for new construction, housing improvement, acquisition of dwellings, and nursing and retirement homes. The WSW has a triple security structure. The primary security is formed by the financial resilience both of the association itself and the entire sector through the participation of the Central Housing Fund (see next). Before the WSW approves an application from a housing association, it tests the creditworthiness of the applicant. The secondary security consists of the capital assets of the WSW, which are created by a single capital contribution from the State and the fees the associations pay to obtain guarantees. The tertiary security is formed from the ultimate responsibility of the State and the local authorities that share this task equally (Van der Schaar 1991). The attractive interest rates on loans secured by the WSW demonstrate the great confidence that lenders have in the fund, which until recently had an AAA rating. This confidence is largely an outcome of the ultimate security provided by central and local governments (Priemus 1995).

Besides the private WSW, the Dutch social housing sector also has a public institute: the Central Housing Fund (*Centraal Fonds Volkshuisvesting*: CFV). This fund has two important tasks: financial supervision (since 1998) and financial support for weak housing associations (since 1988). Associations in a poor financial position can appeal to the CFV for assistance. The CFV is a mutual fund established by and for housing associations. To this end, each association contributes annually to the fund.

2000–2008: confusion

Mortgage interest deduction and mortgage products   Since 1971 mortgage interest relief has supported homeownership, pushing up house prices. It became a politically sensitive topic that became manifest with the reform of the Dutch income tax policy. In 2001 a substantial change in the tax system took place. A box structure for income tax was introduced, with box 1 including income from employment, box 2 including business income and box 3 including income from wealth. This resulted in the main in a more coherent and consistent income tax policy. However, in theory, owner-occupied dwellings as an investment good should be in box 3, but for political reasons they were put in box 1. The explanation for this is that if the owner-occupied dwelling were in box 3, this would mean the end of a specific mortgage interest tax deduction. This was considered politically too delicate. Thus for political reasons a substantial inconsistency was introduced with respect to owner-occupied dwellings. There were two changes introduced with respect to the deductibility of mortgage interest; the period of deduction was changed from unlimited to 30 years (Haffner 2002) and mortgage interest deduction could only apply to one dwelling per household. This tax reform, a potential milestone, did not change the principles behind the mortgage interest deduction. Much more important was the impact of the relaxation of mortgage provision conditions: LTV for new mortgages increased to 125 and LTI standards became more flexible. Moreover, it was in this period that interest-only mortgages became popular as a way of making homeownership more accessible. House prices increased substantially in this period and therefore affordability was under pressure.

Social housing under discussion   At the turn of the century the social rental sector had considerable surplus equity, which increased from 11 percent in 2001 to 16 percent of the total balance sheet in 2005. This surplus was at least one of the reasons why the sector became the subject of political discussion, the key issue being whether the housing associations, with large amounts of capital, are active enough to justify their special financial position. Many questions were raised about the future of the social rental sector (see WRR 2004; Conijn 2005; Commissie De Boer 2005; SER 2005; VROM-raad 2005; 2007; Commissie Schilder 2006; Stuurgroep Meijerink 2008). This led to the introduction of corporation tax for housing associations in 2008. However, all these thoroughly written reports did not result in either a clear government vision or in policy changes.

In this period another discussion started that only later had an impact. This was the discussion about state aid and the possibly anti-competitive position between housing associations and commercial investors arising from the guarantees provided from the social housing guarantee fund (Elsinga *et al.* 2008; Gruis and Priemus 2008).

In response to the European Commission's concerns the Dutch government took several measures to adjust the system, the main ones being:

1. Defining an explicit maximum rent limit for social rental housing (for which state aid is allowed);
2. Allocating at least 90 percent of social rental dwellings to a target group limited by a maximum income;
3. Restricting state aid (in the shape of indirect state guarantees for housing associations' loans guaranteed by the Social Housing Guarantee Fund (WSW).

This new policy was designed in 2007/2008, published in 2009 and implemented in 2011 (Gruis and Elsinga 2014).

2008-Present: effects of the GFC

The financial crisis   In 2008 the Netherlands was hit by the GFC (Global Financial Crisis), which had a dramatic impact on Dutch international banks, in particular ABN-AMRO, ING and SNS Reaal, which were supported heavily by the National Government. the Netherlands' economy underwent a triple dip with economic decline in 2009, 2012 and 2013. The financial-economic crisis hit the Dutch housing market severely, partly as a result of the very large size and international orientation of the Dutch banking sector.

Since 2008 house prices have declined, the number of housing transactions went down dramatically and the construction of owner-occupied housing plummeted. The credit crunch has made lenders more wary of granting mortgages. As a result, access to mortgage loans and thus homeownership became much more difficult. The financial crisis forced the government to reconsider their policies on homeownership. This resulted in some reregulation of the mortgage market and gradual changes in mortgage interest tax relief. These measures seriously harmed the housing market in the short run. We identify these as candidate milestones since they may be the start of a period of higher risk awareness. The future will learn whether these measures are temporary or the start of a structural change in housing finance.

Reregulation of the mortgage market   After the effects of the crisis became clear in the Netherlands, the Dutch government introduced several policies to stimulate the housing market (Van der Heijden *et al.* 2011). These measures, however, provided only some relief in the period 2008–2010.

In March 2011 the Ministry of Finance, the AFM (Financial Market Authority) and the banks and insurers signed an agreement to curtail 'peak mortgages' (mortgages that exceed the value of the property). This agreement has led to a new code of conduct for mortgage financing (GHF), which came into force in August 2011 (Nederlandse Vereniging van Banken 2011). This new GHF was the base for a range of austerity measures in mortgage lending practices. For instance, the maximum loan-to-value ratio (LTV) for mortgage loans decreased from 120 to 106 and then to 104 percent (and will decrease to 100 percent in 2018 and maybe to 80 percent in the longer run), and restrictions have been imposed on co-financing expenditures for upkeep and renovation. In addition, it became far more difficult for lenders to provide tailor-made solutions (e.g. higher LTVs or loan-to-income ratios, LTIs) by means of so-called 'explain mortgages' (loans that deviate from the 2006 code of conduct). The implication is that the volume of explain mortgages plunged from roughly 25–30 percent in 2012 to less than 5 percent in 2013. Finally, for households without someone in permanent employment it became much harder to get a mortgage.

There are three reasons for these rigorous interventions in the Dutch mortgage market (Boelhouwer 2013). The size of the debt is perhaps the most important. The Dutch national mortgage debt has more than doubled since 1999, from €298 bn to €665 bn in 2013 (Figure 15.3). This makes the Netherlands the front-runner in Europe. The total size of the Dutch residential mortgage debt as a percentage of GDP is one-third larger than the UK's and more than twice as big as Germany's (EMF 2012). The exceptional international position occupied by the Netherlands has not escaped the notice of international institutions such as the International Monetary Fund (IMF), the Organisation for Economic Co-operation and Development (OECD) and credit rating agencies. They see the Dutch mortgage debt as a financial risk and recommend again and again that it be reduced. The Dutch Ministry of Finance in particular is afraid that the high debt level will prompt the rating agencies to lower the country's credit rating. the Netherlands has lost its triple-A rating and is now rated as AA+ by Standard and Poors, although it still has a triple-A rating from Fitch and Moody. The consequence of this is that the Netherlands will have to pay more to finance its sovereign debt. Lowering the credit rating by one class can be expected to lead to an estimated increase in annual financing costs of between €4 bn and €5 bn.

A second reason to consider strong intervention by international institutions is that in their opinion the high national mortgage debt puts individual households, banks and the government (through revenues foregone from mortgage interest deductibility) at too much risk. Given the sharply increased impact of mortgage interest deductibility on government finances and its open-ended nature, the decision to intervene is understandable. On the other hand, for quite a while the Netherlands has had the lowest level of mortgage payment arrears and the fewest number of repossessions in Europe (Neuteboom 2008; Van Hoek and Koning 2012). Furthermore, as Neuteboom

(2008) has demonstrated, when corrected for the national context, the Dutch are certainly no more risk-prone in the mortgage market than other European countries. The British are the exception to this general attitude with a higher propensity to take risk.

The third reason to reduce the level of mortgage indebtedness is the rule that has been imposed on banks since Basel III and the plans to form a European Banking Union. Banks were required to increase the amount of their own financial reserves (i.e. to recapitalise). All Dutch banks passed the European stress test in 2014. The savings ratio for Dutch households is very high by international standards. However, those savings are held by the pension funds and are thus unavailable to the banks as collateral for their mortgage portfolios. Before the credit crisis, this was not an insurmountable problem. The Dutch banks could borrow on favourable terms on the international capital market and could sell their bundled mortgages on the same international capital market by means of securitization. Because of the financial crisis this option had recently almost entirely disappeared, while the interest on the equity investment needed for their recapitalisation had increased sharply. Since mid-2012, incidentally, Dutch banks have again been trading mortgages through securitisation programmes. The consequence of this specifically Dutch funding or deposit problem is that since 2008 the mortgage interest rate has been roughly 1.5 percent higher than in neighbouring countries. Before 2008, these interest rates were virtually identical. And these high Dutch mortgage interest rates have reduced the borrowing capacity of households.

Revision of mortgage interest deduction   Another remarkable change is the gradual adjustment in fiscal policy. For many decades the policy and its burden on the national budget appeared a politically delicate topic, preventing discussion that could have resulted in substantial changes. In January 2013, however, the Dutch government introduced restrictions on mortgage interest tax relief so that it is no longer available for interest-only mortgages for first-time buyers. New homebuyers therefore can only obtain mortgage tax relief on of annuity or linear mortgages (both of which have 30 year repayment periods). For a medium priced house in the Netherlands, this will lead to an increase in the cost of a mortgage of approximately €40000. This is considered a substantial change. Existing mortgage borrowers also face a minor change: a reduction of 0.5 percent point interest each year for the next 28 years for households in the highest tax bracket, so that after 28 years the tax deduction for higher-income groups will have fallen from 52 to 38 percent. For the national government this is an income-neutral scheme: higher-income households will receive compensation in the form of a reduction in income tax affecting housing and mortgage markets rates (VVD-PvdA 2012). These changes provide a substantial benefit, particularly for first-time buyers. Announcing such reductions in mortgage tax relief was considered political suicide in the past decades, but recently the changes were passed in parliament without too many problems. Such changes can probably be explained by the growing national awareness among Dutch voters and politicians that current fiscal policy is not sustainable.

A landlord levy for the social rental sector   Since the mid-1990s, political support for the social rental sector has deteriorated year after year. This led to the start of an official Parliamentary Inquiry on Housing Associations in 2013.

There are a number of reasons for this deterioration in support. The first reason is repeated criticism that the hybrid social rental sector is inefficient by definition, since it lacks discipline from either the market and or government (Conijn 2005; Buiter *et al.* 2006; Koning en Leuvesteijn 2010; SER-CSED 2010; Commissie Hoekstra 2012). A second reason, providing empirical evidence for the first, is the very generous collective employment agreement available for housing association employees and the fact that, since 2008, no less than 110 housing association directors have received incomes exceeding the so-called 'Balkenende standard' (i.e. earning more than the prime minister). A third reason is around problems of integrity associated with irresponsible investments in about 30 housing associations, which have received a great deal of public attention. The loss of €2 bn in 2012 through trading in derivatives by Vestia, the largest housing association in the Netherlands, resulted in more negative publicity. As a result all other housing associations had to pay an extra fee to the Central Fund, raising the potential risk of moral hazard of the guarantee system of WSW and CFV (De Jong 2013).

So far this has not led to any change in government supervision, but it did result in a landlord levy. The landlord levy requires housing associations to pay a levy to the national government. This levy pushes housing associations to sell dwellings, to increase rents towards market levels and to reduce investment and maintenance. In other words, it is a measure apparently aimed at reducing the social rental sector and solving the government's financial problems. This is a substantial change as compared to the past when government supported social landlords financially to provide adequate housing for affordable rents.

Overview

Table 15.1 provides an overview of milestones and *candidate milestones* and demonstrates that major changes outside the Dutch housing market – such as the need of the government to cut budgets because of the Maastricht treaty, the competition rules of the European Commission, the GFC and Basel III – resulted in changes in Dutch housing finance policy.

Table 15.1 Milestones and *potential milestones* in three periods.

	Major institutional changes	Policy changes

1988–2000	• Thatcher as trendsetter in EU
	• Maastricht Treaty
	• Deregulation of mortgage markets worldwide
		• Heerma Memorandum
		  • Grossing Act
		  • Key role social sector funds
		  • Guarantee Fund Homeowners
		• New mortgage products accepted by fiscal authority

2000–2008	• State aid letter European Commission	• New allocation rules for social housing (2009)
2008–now	• Global Financial Crisis • Basel III	• Reregulation of Dutch mortgage market; tighter conditions for mortgage provision • Revision of mortgage interest deduction • Landlord levy

Impacts

The housing finance market

The previous sections discussed milestones in policies relevant for the housing finance market. This market consists of a mortgage market for homeowners and a market for loans for housing associations. The major providers in the mortgage market are the Rabobank, de ABN, ING, SNS and AEGON currently covering 77 percent of the mortgage market (Table 15.2), which is around €650 bn. The main providers of loans for housing associations are BNG and the Waterschapsbank, both public banks. The total amount of loans to housing associations is around €78 bn, while their own equity is €32 bn (CFV 2013).

Whereas not so much changed in terms of who provides mortgages, the products they provide have changed substantially over the years as shown in Figure 15.1 as a result of innovations in the mortgage market that were approved by the tax authority. The linear mortgage and the annuity mortgage, which were dominant in the late 1980s, declined in the 1990s and the start of the financial crisis, but are now re-emerging due to the adjustment of the income tax policy. Innovation in the mortgage market led to new products, and the savings mortgage and the life insurance mortgage became more and more important during the 1990s. Later on, the investment mortgage was added. All products maximise mortgage interest relief by maximising interest payments and building equity to pay off the mortgage at the end of the term in different ways. In the late 1990s a new type of mortgage became popular: the interest only mortgage. Figure 15.1 demonstrates the enormous popularity of this product. In the 2000s there has been a substantial increase in the number of 'other mortgages' mostly involving combination mortgages: an interest only mortgage in combination with another mortgage type. These are expected to become less popular with the introduction of the new conditions for mortgage interest relief from 2013 (Elsinga and Dol 2003).

Table 15.2 Market shares in the Dutch mortgage market.

	2004	2010
Rabobank	25.7%	30.2%
ING	21.7%	20.2%
ABN AMRO	14.3%	20.0%
SNS	11.2%	6.7%
Fortis	8.4%	With ABN AMRO
AEGON	1.3%	5.6%
BNP Paribas*	0.5%	7.7%
Other	16.8%	9.6%
Market share largest four	72.9%	77.1%

*Has withdrawn from the Dutch market.
Source: Netherlands Competition Authority (NCA) (2011: 20).

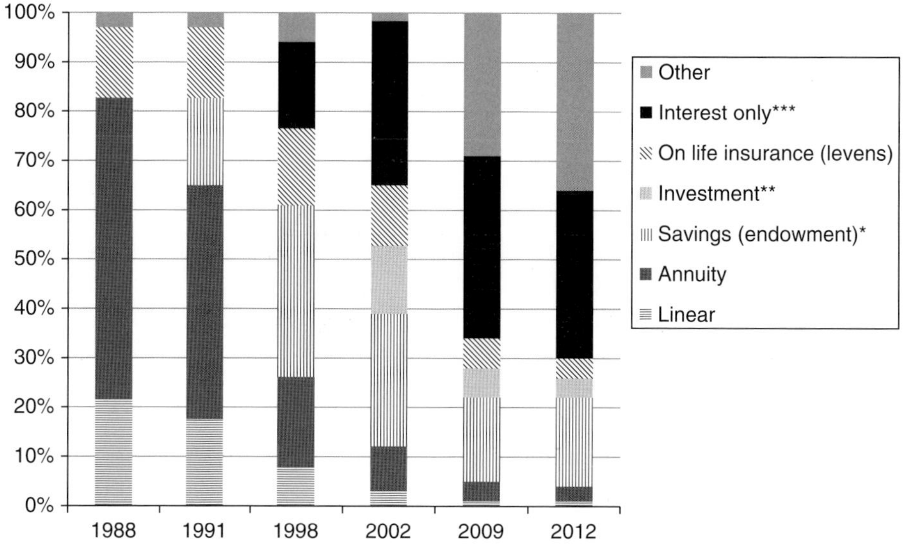

Figure 15.1 Types of outstanding mortgages by homeowners, 1988–2012.
*Did not exist until end of 1980s
**Introduced in second half of 1990s
***100% interest only mortgages from late 1990s
****Growth mortgage = based on future income growth, mostly abandoned after 1980s housing market crisis
Source: WoON-survey (2012), Ministry of the Interior.

The impacts of the identified milestones

The impact of the Heerma Memorandum was enormous. It was introduced at the beginning of an era in which housing subsidies changed from self-evident to non-existent. They introduced a period in which privatisation and deregulation were key to the policy discourse and were accepted widely. However, the peculiarity of the Netherlands was that privatisation and deregulation were applied mainly to the rental market. No more direct subsidies were provided and social housing changed from a sector for all into a sector more and more targeted at low income groups. Subsidies were no longer provided to the commercial rental sector and as a result this sector has continued to decline over the last decades. However, financial support was still provided to homeowners in the form of mortgage interest tax relief for products that maximised that relief and a government backed mortgage guarantee for homeowners. The overall impact of this period of privatisation and deregulation was to boost the owner-occupied market (Figure 15.2), an enormous increase in house prices (Figure 15.3) and a substantial growth in mortgage debt (Figure 15.4). The effect of privatisation was also to increase the importance of hybrid organisations such as housing associations and the National Mortgage Guarantee Fund. Hybrid organisations were meant to combine the best of public interest and market forces.

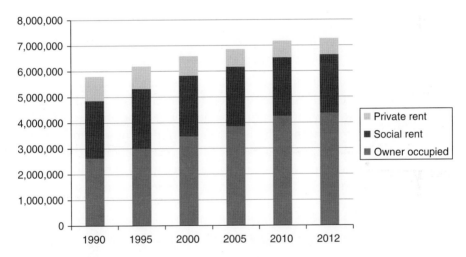

Figure 15.2 Tenure in Dutch housing stock, 1990–2012.
Source: Statistics Netherlands.

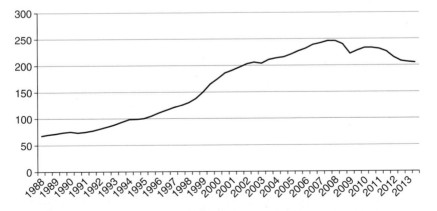

Figure 15.3 Nominal house prices, the Netherlands, 1990–2013 Q2.
Source: NVM (Dutch organisation for real estate agents).

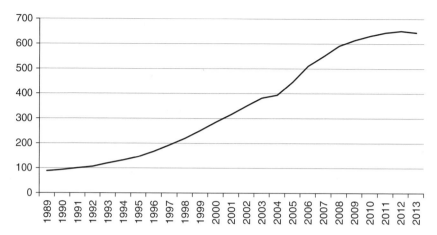

Figure 15.4   Mortgage debt in the Netherlands, 1988–2013.
Source: Dutch National Bank.

Attitudes to this boost for homeownership and hybrid organisations started to change shortly after 2000. The burst of the 'Dotcom'/Internet bubble harmed belief in continued economic growth. The enormous burden of mortgage tax relief on the government budget became a matter of debate as did the role and position of housing associations. These were criticised more and more as inefficient organisations that harmed competition because both market and democratic pressures were lacking. All this coincided with a letter from the European Commission criticising the Dutch social rental sector for the imbalance it created in the Dutch housing market and the negative impacts on the level playing field with commercial investors. In other words, key features of the Dutch housing system were topics of fundamental debate. However, the debate did not result in any immediate substantial policy changes.

Finally, this fundamental debate about the system was fuelled by the effects of the GFC which in the Netherlands resulted in the nationalisation of ABN in 2008 as well as state support for ING and SNS Reaal. This crisis in the housing market can be considered a milestone in housing finance, housing policy and the housing market in the Netherlands. Because the Dutch economy was in trouble, the government gave priority to supporting the recovery in financial markets, including the mortgage market and improving the government budget. This led to some reregulation of the mortgage market and adjustments to income tax policy. These measures had a negative impact on the owner-occupied housing market. This helps to explain why, contrary to owner-occupied markets in other European countries, the Dutch owner-occupied market is still suffering seriously from house price decrease (Figure 15.3), a low level of transactions (Figure 15.5) and low production levels (Figure 15.6) (Scanlon and Elsinga 2014). Moreover, claims to the Guarantee Fund for Owner Occupation increased from around

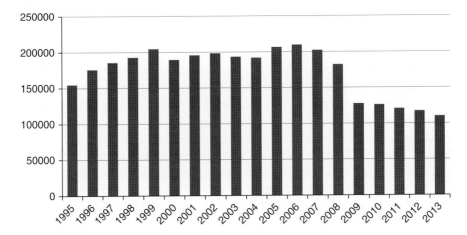

Figure 15.5 Transactions in housing in the Netherlands, 1989–2013.
Source: Statistics Netherlands.

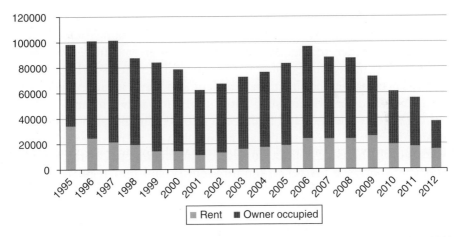

Figure 15.6 Housing production (completed) by tenure in the Netherlands, 1995–2012.
Source: Statistics Netherlands.

1000 in 2007 to more than 4000 in 2013. The average amount claimed increased in the same time to €39 000 (WEW 2014). In 2014 the owner-occupied housing market seemed to reach the bottom.

It was not only the production of owner-occupied dwellings that fell; the production of social housing also decreased considerably after the introduction of the landlord levy. In the meantime the level playing field discussion about the rental market resulted in a compromise with the European Commission and concrete changes in the allocation rules for Dutch social rental housing. From 2011, social rental housing became targeted mainly at lower income groups. Gradually, the Dutch social rental sector is changing from a sector for all into a sector helping the lower income groups.

Reflection

For the Netherlands, the period of deregulation and privatisation meant an enormous boom in house prices and mortgage debts. Moreover, it led to a more market oriented approach in the social rental sector: with housing association becoming financially independent and given the opportunity to undertake commercial activities. This period was followed by a period of confusion and debate which led only to further debate and no policy changes. Then in 2008 the Netherlands and the Dutch housing market were hit by the GFC, which resulted in a number of policy changes but no clear strategy for reforming the housing market.

Currently, the owner-occupied market is still struggling as compared to other housing markets in Europe. The social housing sector remains a topic of debate and criticism without any clear perspective about the future. The private rental market is identified by the government as a solution and a tenure to be stimulated. However, investment in this sector is limited and government financial support is not on the cards. At the same time housing affordability is becoming a high priority political issue. For first-time buyers, housing expenditure is increasing because of the obligation to repay mortgages in order to qualify for mortgage interest relief. For tenants, expenditure is increasing because of the substantial rent rises that landlords regard as necessary to be able to pay the landlord levy. Housing expenditure-to-income ratios are increasing particularly for new entrants into the housing market (Haffner and Boumeester 2013). The developments in the housing market in the last 25 years have led to an increasing gap between insiders in the housing market, to a large extent protected by the very slow decline in mortgage tax relief, tenure security and rent regulation, while new entrants face high housing costs and less protection.

The imposition of limits on mortgage interest tax deductions is probably a first step to reducing the tax support of homeownership more generally. A question is whether the reregulation of the mortgage market is to be seen only as a short term answer to the crisis or as a structural system change. It is clear that the mortgage market has to adjust to the modified tax regime, which probably brings with it a substantial reduction in demand for interest only mortgages and more or less for mortgage debt overall. Thirty-one percent of the housing system is waiting for what will happen after the results of the Parliamentary Inquiry on Housing Associations. It has become clear that the social rental sector is no longer a sector for all income groups and that the influence of local governments and tenants on the strategic policy of housing associations will increase in the near future (Parlementaire Enquete Commissie Woningcorporaties 2014).

Considering the developments over the last 25 years, the conclusion is that major institutional changes outside the housing market have impacted enormously on the Dutch housing finance system. This may explain why these fundamental adjustments are not underpinned by a clear and broadly supported strategic view about the future of the Dutch housing finance system.

Acknowledgements

With thanks to Kees Dol for the statistics.

References

Boelhouwer, PJ (2013). How financial markets and institutions disrupt the Dutch housing market, 2013, *Paper: ENHR Tarragona International Conference, Overcoming the crisis: integrating the urban environment*, 19–22 June, Tarragona, Book of abstracts, p. 39.

Boelhouwer, P and Priemus, H (1990). Dutch housing policy realigned. *the Netherlands Journal of Housing and Environmental Research* 5:1, 105–119.

Buiter, W, van Dalen, H, van Eijffinger, S, Koedijk, K, Teulings, C and van Witteloostuijn, A (2006). Over goede intenties en harde wetten van de woningmarkt (REA-advies)[About good intentions and the housing market]. *Tijdschrift voor Politieke Ekonomie* 27:6, 20–24.

CFV (Central Fund for Housing) (2013). *Sectorbeeld*. Baarn: Central Fund for Housing.

Commissie De Boer (2005). *Lokaal wat kan, centraal wat moet: nieuw bestel voor Woningcorporaties* [Local if possible and central what is necessary: a new arrangement for housing associations]. Advice for Aedes vereniging van woningcorporaties and Ministerie voor Volkshuisvesting, Ruimtelijke Ordening en Milieu.

Commissie Hoekstra (2012). *Eindrapportage Commissie Kaderstelling en Toezicht Woningcorporaties* [Final report on framework and supervision of social rental housing]. The Hague.

Commissie Schilder (2006). *Advies toezicht op woningcorporaties.* [Advice for supervision on housing associations]. De Nederlandsche Bank DNB, Amsterdam.

Conijn, J (2005). *Naar een duidelijke taakafbakening en heldere sturing* [Towards clear division of responsibilities and clear steering], RIGO, Amsterdam.

De Jong, R de (2013). *De balans verstoord* [The balance disturbed], Aedes, Den Haag.

DNB (Dutch National Bank), *Statistics DNB*, Den Haag: Dutch National Bank.

Elsinga, M and Dol, C. (2003). *De geschiedenis van de Nationale Hypotheekgarantie* [The History of the Dutch Government Mortgage Guarantee], WEW, Zoetermeer.

Elsinga, M, Haffner, M. and van der Heijden, H (2008). Threats for the Dutch unitary model. *European Journal of Housing Policy* 8:1, 21–37.

EMF (2012). *Hypostat.* Brussels: European Mortgage Federation.

Gruis, VH and Priemus, H (2008). European Competition Policy and National Housing Policy: International implications of the Dutch Case, *Housing Studies* 23:3, 485–505.

Gruis, V and Elsinga, M (2014). Tensions between social housing and EU-regulation, *EStaL (European State Aid Law Quarterly)* 13:3, 463–469.

Haffner, MEA (2002). Dutch Personal Income Tax Reform 2001: an exceptional position for owner-occupied housing. *Housing Studies* 17:3, 521–534.

Haffner, MEA and Boumeester, HJFM (2013). The affordability of housing in the Netherlands: an increasing income gap between owning and renting? *Housing Studies* 25:6, 799–820.

Heerma, E (1989). *Nota Volkshuisvesting in de Jaren Negentig: van bouwen tot wonen* [Housing in the Nineties Memorandum: from building to living], Sdu Uitgevers, Den Haag.

Koning, P and van Leuvensteijn, M (2010). *De woningcorporatie uit de verdwijndriehoek.* [The housing association out of the Bermuda Triangle]. Centraal Planbureau (CPB), Den Haag.

Ministry of the Interior (2012). *WoON-survey 2012*, Den Haag: Ministry of the Interior.

Nederlandse Vereniging van Banken NVB (2011). *Gedragscode Hypothecaire Financiering* (GHF) [Code of conduct for mortgage loans], NVB, Den Haag.

Netherlands Competition Authority (NCA) (2011). *Sectorstudie Hypotheekmarkt* [Sector study Mortgage market, Den Haag: NMA.

NVM (Dutch organization for real estate agents) (n.d.). *Wonen en Marktcijfers* [Housing statistics], Nieuwegein: NVM.

Neuteboom, P (2008). *On the Rationality of Borrowers' Behaviour. Comparing Risk Attitudes of Homeowners.* DUP Science, Sustainable Urban Areas 21, IOS Press, Amsterdam.

Parlementaire Enquêtecommissie Bouwsubsidies (1988). *Rapport Parlementaire Enquête Bouwsubsidies* [Report: Parliamentary Inquiry into Property Subsidies], Staatsuitgeverij, Den Haag.

Priemus, H (1995). How to abolish social housing? The Dutch case. *International Journal of Urban and Regional Research* 19:1, 145–155.

Priemus, H, Elsinga, M and Cao, L (2007). Public mortgage guarantee: Risks for the *Tax Payer? Housing Finance International* 21:4, 16–23.

Priemus, H, Kleinman, M, Maclennan, D and Turner, B (1994). Maastricht Treaty: Consequences for national housing policies, *Housing Studies* 9:2, 163–182.

Scanlon, K and Elsinga, M (2014). Policy changes affecting housing and mortgage markets: how governments in the UK and the Netherlands. *Journal of Housing and the Built Environment* 29:2, 335–360.

SER (2005). *Ondernemerschap voor de publieke zaak* [Entrepreneurship for public aims]. SER, Den Haag.

SER-CSED (2010). *Naar een integrale hervorming van de woningmarkt* [Towards an integral reform of the housing market]. SER-CSED, Den Haag.

Statistics Netherlands (CBS) (various years). *Statistics for housing.* Den Haag: Statistics Netherlands.

Stuurgroep Meijerink (2008). *Nieuw arrangement: overheid – woningcorporaties* [New arrangement: government – housing associations]. (Advies stuurgroep Meijerink, in opdracht van Aedes en de minister van WWI).

Van der Heijden, HMH, Dol, CP and Oxley, MJ (2011). Western European housing systems and the impact of the international financial crisis. *Journal of Housing and the Built Environment* 26:3, 295–313.

Van der Schaar, J (1987). *Groei en bloei van het Nederlandse volkshuisvestingsbeleid* [Growth and florishing of Dutch Housing Policy]. Delftse Universitaire Pers, Delft.

Van der Schaar, J (1991). *Volkshuisvesting: een zaak van beleid* [Housing: a policy matter]. Het Spectrum, Utrecht.

Van Hoek, T and Koning, M (2012). *Situatie op de Nederlandse hypotheekmarkt* [Situation at the Dutch mortgage market]. EIB, Amsterdam.

VROM-raad (2005). *Voorbij of vooruit: woningcorporaties aan zet.* [Over or forward: it is the housing associations' turn]. VROM-raad, Den Haag.

VROM-raad (2007). *Tijd voor keuzes. Perspectief op een woningmarkt in balans.* [Time for choices: perspective of a housing market in balance]. VROM-raad, Den Haag.

VVD-PvdA (2012). *Bruggen bouwen; regeerakkoord VVD (Conservative Party) and PvdA (Social Democratic Party).* The Hague.

Waarborgfonds Eigen Woningen (WEW) (2014). *Annual report*, Zoetermeer: WEW.

Waarborgfonds Sociale Woningbouw (WSW). (Social House-building Guarantee Fund) (WSW) (2011) *Annual report.* WSW, Huizen.

WRR (2004). *Bewijzen van goede dienstverlening* [Proof of good service], WRR, Den Haag.

16

Housing Finance in Norway: The Last 25 Years

Rolf Barlindhaug
*Norwegian Institute for Urban and Regional Research (NIBR),
Department for Housing and Environmental Planning Research,
Oslo, Norway*

Introduction

Over the last 25 years, lending conditions for homebuyers in Norway have been influenced by numerous factors, including: the banking crisis of the late 1980s; monetary policy which responded to various macro-economic challenges; the increasing role of financial supervision; changing international conditions; the reduced role of state banks in housing finance and a housing policy that changed its focus to target vulnerable groups.

Major changes in the supply of finance were driven by the merger and concentration of Norwegian financial companies and by the entrance of foreign actors into the domestic market. Private banks provided 90 percent of household mortgages when covered bonds were introduced in 2007. After that point, the share of credit companies increased and reached 47 percent at the end of 2011.

Lending conditions today are more flexible than they were in the beginning of the period, reflecting a change away from a focus on individual savings behaviour and customer loyalty, to competition among lenders with a stronger focus on collateral. In credit assessment terms banks today use a residual model. A household dependent amount for subsistence expenses is deducted from disposable income. To qualify, one has to be able to repay the loan and to cope if the interest rate were to increase by 5 percentage points. In addition, a deposit of 15 percent of the purchase price is required. If it is a

Milestones in European Housing Finance, First Edition.
Edited by Jens Lunde and Christine Whitehead.
© 2016 John Wiley & Sons, Ltd. Published 2016 by John Wiley & Sons, Ltd.

collateral loan, loan-to-value (LTV) rates can be up to 100 percent. Variable interest rates are preferred, but fixed interest rates or combination loans where part of the loan has a fixed interest rate are also offered.

After World War II, homeownership became the preferred tenure in Norway fuelled by a tradition of self-employed small farmers and a negative view of being dependent on contractual relationships. Consequently individual ownership dominated, but collective ownership through housing cooperatives was also common (Annaniassen 2006). Today, nearly 80 percent of households in Norway are individual homeowners, co-owners in condominiums or co-owners in a housing cooperative. This is largely similar to the proportion at the beginning of the 1990s. Homeownership is favourably taxed and general housing policy seeks to stimulate homeownership for most of the population. For most private households, a house is their dominant asset and a mortgage their dominant liability.

The economic and institutional environment of the last 25 years

The macro-economic development

A growth in consumption and investment from 1984 – financed by an increased take-up of debt, an expansive fiscal policy, a drop in oil prices in 1986 and strong income growth – led to a powerful cost shock for Norwegian companies and large imbalances in the Norwegian economy, followed by a devaluation of the Norwegian Krone (NOK) and high interest rates for several years. Together with a gradual reduction in marginal tax rates on capital incomes, this implied an increase in real interest rates after tax, leading to a decline in house prices from 1988. The decline in the growth of wages and costs from 1989 laid, however, the basis for low inflation and a decline in nominal interest rates from 1992.

The state economy and state finances grew stronger after 1993 as a result of significant growth in oil revenues (Steigum 2010). The bank crisis was handled well: a market-based financial and credit system had been established and tax reform had been implemented. House prices more than doubled over the next 10 years.

The state's pension fund (oil fund) was established in 2001. A political decision implied that a maximum of 4 percent of the fund could be used annually to balance the annual government budgets. In the same year, the Stoltenberg Government instructed Norges Bank to adapt monetary policy so that inflation would remain steady at 2.5 percent. In the case of a possible recession, the state then had the muscle to intervene and the ability to lower the key policy rate. A recovery in demand for Norwegian export products and a sharp improvement in terms of trade laid the foundation for the boom that followed.

The business cycle turned in the beginning of 2008, and in the wake of the financial crisis the situation worsened sharply. The unemployment rate increased, but compared with most other countries, the reduction in production and employment in the Norwegian economy was modest. High growth in demand for the products and services from the petroleum sector in 2008 and 2009 helped to curb macro-economic decline. From the second half of 2008, Norges Bank gradually reduced the key policy rate to 1.25 percent. High debt and a low share of fixed interest loans quickly led to an increase in the disposable income of Norwegian households. Fiscal policy was significantly adjusted and the government presented a fiscal stimulus package of NOK 20 bn to mitigate the negative impact of the financial crisis in the Norwegian economy. Together with government support measures for the financial sector, this helped to stabilise the economy. Lower interest rates quickly resulted in an improvement in the housing market and eventually increased demand from households. Gradually, activity in the economy picked up again.

Finance milestones

Introduction

In this section, we look more closely at how the financial market and housing finance have evolved over the last 25 years in Norway. Table 16.1 shows the major milestones related to housing finance in three periods and will be described in more detail in the following sections.

From regulation to competition and a banking crisis

Between 1983 and 1988, the majority of direct regulations on the credit market were removed. Under a strict regulatory regime banks were able to hand-pick the best and most secure customers (Meld. St. 21: 2010–2011). The deregulation led to strong competition among credit institutions resulting in great pressure to acquire new customers. Deregulation led to a strong credit expansion, and over the course of a four year period in the latter half of the 1980s, lending volume was doubled. Loans from mortgage companies and finance companies in particular exhibited large growth.

As a result of the fall in domestic demand and consumption in 1987, banks and finance companies experienced heavy losses on loans and guarantees, and the following year the first banks lost their equity. The losses on loans increased from 0.5 percent of total assets in 1987 to 4.5 and 1.9 percent, respectively, in commercial banks and saving banks in 1991 when the losses were at their highest. The banking crisis showed that banks did not make adequate credit assessments in a deregulated market.

Table 16.1   Important milestones influencing housing finance in Norway.

Milestone	1980–1989	1990–1999	2000–2013
Institutional	Deregulation, competition and concentration	Introduction of the state's Bank Guarantee fund (1991) and the Bank Investment fund (1991) Norway becomes a member of the European Economic Area	Stronger capital requirements introduced for financial institutions Introduction of the Norwegian Banks' Guarantee Fund (2004) and the Norwegian State Finance Fund (2009)
Regulatory	Deregulation of the housing market	The key policy rate based on fixed exchange rates	The key policy rate based on inflation target (2001)
Mortgage funding	Mostly deposit Banks could issue bonds (1987)	Mostly deposit	Covered bonds introduced in 2007
Mortgage finance	LTV-rate: max 80% Loan 1.5–2.5 times income	From late 1990s: High proportion of 100% LTV rates	Home equity line of credit in 2006 From 2011: LTV-rate: max 85% Residual model with subsistence expenses used in credit assessment
Taxation	Gradual reduction in marginal tax rate on capital incomes	Taxation system changed in 1992	Tax on imputed rent removed
Housing policy	Subsidies concentrated on the finance of new built dwellings	Subsidy on loans for new construction removed A more targeted individual housing policy introduced	

The new regime established additional requirements for risk assessment, assessment of solvency and internal control of the loans that were given. The changes in the financial markets in the 1980s led to the introduction of rules that would apply to all financial institutions to ensure fair competition conditions for both national and foreign enterprises. The banks were capitalised through their own guarantee funds, but they also were supported from the state's bank guarantee fund, which was created in 1991. Because the crisis had made investors cautious about investing in Norwegian banks, the state established a Bank Investment Fund in the fall of 1991.

The structure of the finance institutions

At the beginning of the 1990s, the formal mortgage suppliers included saving banks, commercial banks, insurance companies, mortgage companies, finance companies, pension funds and state banks. Credit companies issued bonds, while banks mainly obtained their funds through deposits from the retail market.

In 1990, there were 142 saving banks in Norway, a reduction from 493 in the 1970s (Meld. St. 21: 2010–2011). The commercial banks, which held lower loan volumes than the saving banks, included 23 companies, the same number as in the 1980s, but a reduction from 40 in 1970. Only 14 of the commercial banks offered loans to private households in 1990. Two of these were foreign owned.

Further consolidation followed. Several banks merged and other banks were put under public administration. In the fall of 1991 the state took over 100 percent of the shares in two commercial banks (Fokus and Kredittkassen) after the share capital was lost. The shareholders of a third bank (DnB) accepted a write-down of the shares. After supplying DnB with new share capital, the state held 100 percent of the shares for a short period of time, while today the government's stake is around one-third. Today the role of the state's Bank Investment Fund is limited to holding shares in DnB Holding ASA. By the end of 2010, there were 114 saving banks and 31 commercial banks in the Norwegian market; the number of commercial banks increased between 2005 and 2010, while the number of savings banks declined somewhat.

In accordance with the balance principle, loans provided by credit companies had an interest rate lock-in period, while banks primarily operated with variable interest rates. From 1987, banks were allowed to issue bonds to improve the match between the maturity and interest terms on their assets and liabilities. From that point on around 20 percent of the banks' funding was made through the issuance of bonds.

In 1992 Norway accepted the EEA Agreement, and it was put into force in 1994. This influenced the development of the financial market in the years that followed. As a result of the work of the Cook commission the 12 EU-countries agreed that the banks should have a capital-asset ratio of 8 percent, with assets weighted according to risk. This requirement proved valuable for Norway after 1993. Capital adequacy requirements create a buffer in the form of primary capital to account for the risk that businesses bring with them. It provides protection for depositors and creditors. One argument for introducing capital-asset ratios as requirements is that banks are covered by a state guarantee and household deposits are secured by the state, up to a certain limit.

The changing role of the Housing Bank

The Housing Bank, established in 1946, financed a significant portion of newly-built dwellings. Since loans from the Housing Bank were subsidised, it was given an annual quota for these loans. By the mid-1990s, the state bank committee was concerned that the Housing Bank's significant role could have adverse effects for the rest of the credit market (NOU 1995: 11). The Housing Bank at that time was a significant player in one of the least risky parts of the credit market (first-priority loans for housing), while the rest of the Norwegian banks traditionally held relatively risky loan portfolios. The state bank committee was concerned that in the early 1990s there was a considerable over capacity in the Norwegian credit market. The Housing Bank's loan business could not be justified on the basis of general competition in the credit market (NOU 2002: 2). The committee recommended maintaining the Housing Bank in a number of riskier areas to achieve a different distribution of credit as compared to what private banks might choose. One such area was the provision credit to disadvantaged borrowers.

The government agreed with the committee's conclusions that the main purpose of the state banks should be to provide credit to socially disadvantaged borrowers who could not obtain financing in the rest of the credit market. The state banks should also take important distributional goals into account, inter alia, in the field of housing finance.

After 1996, market-based principles were applied when determining the interest rate on loans from the Housing Bank and on loans given through the local authorities. These are based on interest rates on government securities (Treasury bills) with a remaining maturity from 0 to 3 months, plus an interest margin of 1 percent. All loans are subject to a variable rate or a fixed interest rate with a 5-year lock-in period. The state no longer granted interest rate subsidies to new loans from the Housing Bank. The share of loans provided for new construction which were financed by the Housing Bank declined significantly; in the first half of the 1990s, 79 percent of loans given for new construction were from the Housing Bank, whereas between 1996 and 2013, the Housing Bank financed only 33 percent of new housing.

When the subsidised loans for new construction were removed, more emphasis was put on individual investment cash grants. Thus, as a result of the findings of the state bank committee in 1995, housing policy was changed from being universal to highly selective.

The main Norwegian housing policy instruments – the start-up loan and the individual investment cash grant – are designed to promote homeownership. Applications for start-up loans can be lodged with the local authority as a form of full or supplementary financing to facilitate entry into the housing market. Start-up loans are primarily intended for first-time buyers who are unable to access the private mortgage market. In the case of repossession, any loss is shared between the local authority (25 percent) and the Housing Bank. The interest rate is not adjusted to compensate for the higher level of risk that is incurred. Nearly half of applicants are turned down, mostly because they are unable to afford the annual housing expenses.

Investment cash grants may be provided along with start-up loans to first-time buyers. The objective is to help particularly disadvantaged households to own a home. The grants are available to households with permanently low incomes who would not otherwise qualify for a start-up loan. These one-time grants constitute about 20 percent of the purchase price. A tenure-neutral housing allowance scheme for households with low incomes and high housing expenses is an additional supplement to the finance instruments.

A scheme called 'home savings for the young' is directed at young people up to age of 33. The maximum savings amount was recently increased from NOK 150000 to NOK 200000. Customers get a tax credit of 20 percent of an annual maximum savings amount of NOK 25000 until the ceiling is reached.

Risk, increased LTV ratios and the introduction of covered bonds

At the end of the 1990s when house price inflation was high, reports showed that 25 percent of new loans had an LTV of more than 80 percent and a significant percentage of these loans were given without any collateral or guarantees (The Norwegian Financial Supervisory Authority 2000). Over the next few years, the proportion of loans that had an LTV of more than 80 percent increased to 32 percent (The Norwegian Financial Supervisory Authority 2003a). Half of these loans were given without additional security.

Banks were being exposed to different types of risk. A strong increase in house prices, followed by a large build-up of debt, increased credit risk. By having a substantial stock portfolio, banks were also exposed to market risk. Strong growth in lending combined with weak growth in bank deposits increased the liquidity risk. A slightly lower loan growth in 2002, combined with increased deposit growth in the wake of the fall in the stock market, stabilised the situation to some degree. As the main problem was an unstably high proportion of short-term funding, the answer to the problem was better capitalised banks.

Those who had entered into fixed-rate deals in the late 1980s were bound by high interest rates, while the interest rate in the 1990s dropped sharply for those who had variable interest rates. These experiences contributed to the low demand for fixed rate deals in the mid-1990s when only 1 percent of new loans were fixed interest mortgages. This share, however, increased to 13 percent by the end of the 1990s when both inflation and interest rates had fallen. Fixed interest rate mortgages are given for a period of 1, 3, 5 or 10 years, with the right to renew the loan. A premium has to be paid to the lender when wishing to terminate the contract during the binding period because of falling interest rates.

Until 2002 there was a strong market concentration in the finance sector. Even so, this was less in Norway than in the other Nordic countries. Norway also experienced a rise of so-called mixed financial companies and increased foreign influence through acquisitions and the establishment of foreign affiliates. Competition led to the interest margin falling sharply in the period 1993–2002 (The Norwegian Financial Supervisory Authority 2003b).

At the same time capital adequacy increased for most banks, but some still had low capital adequacy and it was recommended that they reduce their lending volume or improve their core capital coverage. The Norwegian Banks' Guarantee Fund was established under a legislative amendment in 2004, as an amalgamation of the Commercial Banks' Guarantee Fund and the Savings Banks' Guarantee Fund.

In 2007, legislation opened up for covered bonds in Norway. Covered bonds were issued, secured in a loan portfolio consisting of public loans, mortgages secured in residential property or other real estate. These bonds have priority over other debts and are often called housing bonds because they are made up of mortgage portfolios. The mortgages in such a portfolio will, according to the rules, consist of loans with LTVs up to 75 percent. The security of the loans, in relation to the market value, must at all times exceed the value of the bonds. If not, further security has to be raised, for example, in the form of government bonds. The system involves lower risk mark-ups and should provide lower mortgage interest rates than the use of unsecured bonds. The scheme has resulted in lower funding costs and lower liquidity risk for the banks. Covered bonds have since been one of the banks' main funding sources. Only companies that are licensed as a mortgage company with that stipulated purpose can issue these bonds in Norway (The Norwegian Financial Supervisory Authority 2014). Covered bonds are issued by 23 companies, most of them wholly-owned by Norwegian banks.

Transfers of well-secured loan portfolios to wholly-owned mortgage companies have led to some concern about the mother banks' weakened loan portfolios. This has also raised questions about restrictions in the opportunities to transfer such well-secured loans and whether the equity requirement of banks should be further increased. But the Norwegian covered bond system is designed so that the credit risk remains in the banking system. Credit institutions may have a significant credit risk in that the remaining term on the mortgages is on average 10 years, while the funding through covered bonds has maturities of 3 and 5 years.

Credit institutions may be exposed to foreign exchange risk when issuing in foreign currency and interest risk when issuing bonds with fixed interest rates in a situation where most of the mortgage loans are provided with variable interest rates. Credit institutions may enter into derivative deals to secure themselves against these risk factors (The Norwegian Financial Supervisory Authority 2012). Covered bonds have given Norwegian banks a greater opportunity than in the past to retrieve capital in international markets, since the demand from Europe for secured bonds has been high.

One purpose of introducing covered bonds in Norway was to improve competition among lenders, while another was to provide a broader selection of financial instruments. Two additional goals – the lowering of interest rates on mortgages and increasing the share of fixed interest loans – have not been achieved.

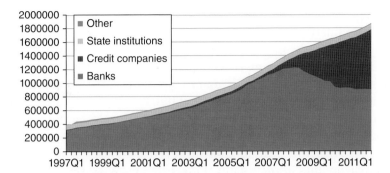

Figure 16.1 Loan secured in housing given to households, after institution, in million NOK. *Source*: Statistic Norway.

Nyhus (1991) offers an overview of mortgage lending. In 1990, banks had a market share of 51 percent, while the state banks had a 23 percent market share and the credit companies and insurance companies held 13 percent each. From 1985 to 1990 the credit companies doubled their market share against a reduction for state banks.

As can be seen in Figure 16.1, the banks' share of household mortgages had already risen to 80 percent by 1997. All volume increase from 1997 to 2007 came from bank lending. After introducing covered bonds in 2007 credit companies increased and reached a share of 47 percent at the end of 2011.

The financial crisis

Norway was less affected by the financial crisis compared to other countries. According to the NOU (2011: 1) this was probably because of a combination of luck, skill and caution. The failure of international financial markets nevertheless led to acute funding challenges for Norwegian banks and comprehensive changes to regulatory measures were implemented. For the Norwegian banks the financial crisis first and foremost was a liquidity crisis and not a solvency crisis, with the biggest test being their ability to withstand losses. Thanks to high equity and earnings, the Norwegian banks had a good starting point from which to hold up against any losses.

Norwegian authorities conducted a series of measures to improve the banks' access to liquidity, both to help to maintain their lending activities and to prevent solvent banks from having payment problems. Among other measures, Norges Bank injected large amounts of liquidity into the banking system, the maturity of liquidity was extended, and collateral requirements for loans were temporarily eased. In October 2008, the government established an arrangement in which banks could obtain government securities in exchange for covered bonds. Banks that participated in the arrangement could obtain finance through the sale of the government securities directly or by borrowing in the market using the government securities as collateral. In addition the Government Finance Fund was created in 2009 to put the Norwegian banks in a better position to maintain normal lending activities by providing solvent banks with core capital.

Credit companies again played an important role because the banks moved their housing loans to their own specialised credit institutions in conjunction with the introduction of covered bonds. A high demand for secured instruments in the financial markets in the last few years may also have helped to increase the proportion of covered bond funding. The increase in covered bond funding occurred at the expense of other types of bonds (e.g. senior bonds).

Compared with the Norwegian banking crisis of the 1990s, the effects of the Global Financial Crisis (GFC) have been mild. Also, while the banking crisis in the 1990s had a domestic origin, resulting from excessive debt accumulation by households and firms and subsequent solvency problems in the banks, this financial crisis originated from outside.

It appears that economic recessions last longer when the decline has its roots in financial imbalances (Meld. St. 12: 2012–2013). This was the case in several countries in the late 1980s and early 1990s, as well as in the United States and many European countries in 2008. In the years before the recent GFC, house prices in many countries had risen to levels that in hindsight turned out to be unsustainable. House prices in Norway did fall in the second half of 2008. After stabilising in 2009, however, house prices began to increase again quite markedly. This increase was in strong contrast to the trend in many other OECD countries and is related to the Norwegian economy, which has coped fairly well throughout the GFC.

This financial crisis did not reveal significant inadequacies in the financial market regulations in Norway (NOU 2011: 1). In certain key areas, Norwegian regulations were somewhat stricter than in many other countries and stricter than what have been the minimum requirements in the EU. This situation contributed to the Norwegian financial institutions being better capitalised at the outbreak of the crisis.

The large reduction in risk weights for mortgages under the Basel II regulations meant that it was relatively more favourable for the Nordic banks to provide mortgage loans than business loans. Lower risk weights however gave less need for capital in the banks. The excess equity could be paid back to the owners or be used for loan growth. The financial crisis led to increased concerns about the banks' liquidity risk and, in 2010, the Basel Committee issued recommendations on the first harmonised international quantitative liquidity requirements (Basel III). These recommendations were updated in 2013 and came into Norwegian law through the EEA Agreement.

Impacts of the housing finance milestones

The banking crises in 1988–1993

In the 1980s both the housing and credit markets in Norway were deregulated. Price regulations in the housing market was mostly abolished in the early 1980s and completely abolished at the end the decade. The repeal of price regulation on dwellings in housing cooperatives was of particular importance, especially in the major cities. On a national basis, dwellings in housing cooperatives amounted to approximately 15 percent of the housing stock. In the cities the proportion was larger. The residents of these dwellings had strongly increased their equity and reached a good starting point from which to climb further in the housing market more broadly, not only within the housing cooperative sector.

Before the deregulations a household first had to save and establish a long customer relationship with a bank before it could borrow a maximum of 80 percent of the purchase price. In the wake of the credit market's deregulation, the competition between institutions led to aggressive marketing and an intensified battle for loan customers including poor credit assessments (NOU 1992: 30). The valuations of properties were often based on the value of similar properties that had been recently traded. In the late 1980s the main rule was that a loan should constitute three times a household's income. After the deregulations, mortgages were primarily given based on downpayment possibilities (Barlindhaug 1996).

The high house price inflation provided the basis for a lending increase within the rules that already applied to collateral. Lack of credit valuation and high LTVs led to a huge potential for loss when house prices began to fall, the unemployment rate increased, the tax system was reorganised and people's income expectations were lowered. Households prioritised paying interests and instalments on their mortgages and reduced other consumption. In the end, the banks' losses on housing loans were modest. Their losses on loans to shopping centres and commercial buildings were much greater.

In the beginning of the 1990s the relationship between the size of the loan and income determined the maximum loan amount. In the beginning of the 1990s the rule was that loans should be 1.5–2.5 times income. When judging repayment ability, banks increased the actual interest level by 2–3 percent points. Without any collateral, the LTV had to be 80 percent or lower, often less for mortgage and insurance companies. Some banks gave LTV rates around 100 percent if payment ability was high.

It was common to distinguish between first and second priority loans, where the first priority loan amounted to max 60 percent of the purchase price. Those who bought a new house with a first priority loan from the Housing Bank were usually in need of another loan as well, a so called 'top loan'. The household then had to deal with two credit institutions instead of one. The total management costs of securing loans from the credit institutions were thus larger than if one bank had given the entire loan (NOU 2002: 2).

During the crisis at the beginning of the 1990s Norges Bank had a system for setting interest rates and for trying to keep the foreign exchange rate constant. As a result, despite high rates of unemployment and falling house prices, interest rate levels were high. This was especially serious for home-owners hit by unemployment as housing expenses were high at the same time that house prices were falling. This situation increased the probability that households would default on their mortgages. The proportion of mort-gage loans that went into default in the household market increased to a peak of around 6 percent in 1992 (The Norwegian Financial Supervisory Authority 2013). This rate fell to around 1 percent by the end of the 1990s and has since remained stable, both during and after the financial crisis.

The problems households faced at the beginning of the 1990s were addressed partly by government measures – such as start-up loans, mecha-nisms for refinancing expensive top loans and a debt settlement law for households facing major difficulties – and partly by a range of individual solutions negotiated directly between the credit institutions and clients, including interest rate reductions and debt write-downs.

House prices increased in the period to follow, undoing the price decline observed between 1988 and 1992. For those who had the opportunity to increase housing consumption when moving, something most people do when they change residence, it was an advantage to move when house prices were still low. But a number of households with negative equity as a result of the price slump could not finance a new property and were locked into their existing property. At the bottom, in 1992, the number of transactions in the owner-occupied market amounted to 1.7 percent of the number of households in Norway. In the period 1993–1999, this proportion increased to an average of 2.6, while after 2005 the share has been at around 3.7 percent.

The period of growth from 1993–2007

House prices rose consistently after 1993 but still remained below construc-tion costs. With credit readily available, it appeared inevitable that prices would continue to rise. The risk for lenders of not getting back the loan by any default and foreclosure was therefore seen as small.

The state bank committee's report in 1995 initiated a major discussion about the role of the Housing Bank in financing the construction of new housing. The subsidised loans from the Housing Bank made it difficult for the private credit institutions to provide well-secured mortgage loans, which in turn decreased their willingness to take risks on other customers. During the early 1990s crisis the Housing Bank financed almost all new construc-tion and kept up building activity. This intervention was therefore positive for the construction industry and employment in general. On the other hand the high supply of new homes encouraged the fall in house prices and made the situation worse for households facing serious payment problems. This policy revealed a contradiction between the importance of maintaining steady activity in the residential construction sector and the risks that such an intervention would reinforce and extend the decline in house prices.

The driving forces behind the rise in house prices in Norway are fairly similar to those seen in other countries. Income growth has been high for many years, with rising employment and strong growth in real wages. Housing demand has been supported by low interest rates, population growth, general optimism among households and banks and easy access to credit. The supply of credit must also be seen in the context of strong competition among banks over market shares in the mortgage market. The rise in house prices was followed by a sharp increase in household debt burden, as measured by gross debt as a share of disposable income, from the turn of the millennium up to the cyclical peak at the end of 2007. In 2000 average household debt amounted to 1.2 times disposable income and increased to just under twice the disposable income in 2007. In subsequent years, the debt burden remained fairly stable, but has risen again in recent years to exactly twice disposable income in 2013. This level is high, both historically and compared with other countries. In Figure 16.2, nominal house prices and debt per household are indexed. Since 2001 debt per household has increased faster than nominal house prices.

The financial crisis and its aftermath: the period 2007–2013

Beginning in 2010 The Norwegian Financial Supervisory Authority required a deposit of 10 percent, later increased to 15 percent. The intention was to curb the strong housing demand and thus reduce house price inflation in the market for existing dwellings. Another intention was to avoid a situation where homebuyers could face negative equity after a possible fall in house prices, which in turn could decrease demand for other goods and services.

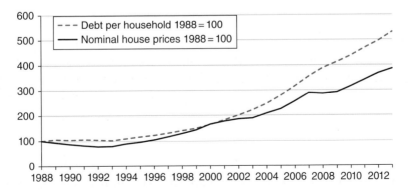

Figure 16.2 Nominal house prices and debt per household (Index 1988 = 100).
Source: Statistic Norway and NIBR.

Mortgages today are mainly given with variable interest rates on market conditions. The normal repayment period on the mortgage is 20 years after the annuity principle, but there is a lot of flexibility. The largest banks provide up to a 30-year repayment period. Interest rates increase with the size of the LTV ratio. Two out of five young homebuyers now get help from parents with residential finance. Parents can help in four different ways, either by being partly responsible for the loans, by using their own property as collateral, by giving cash advances on inheritance as a lump sum or by taking out loans on their property and giving the amount as a gift.

Johannessen *et al.* (2013) show that the ownership rates among young people have decreased slightly since 2007, but compared to other European countries, the rate is still very high. Of all young people between 20 and 35 years of age, 52 percent were homeowners in 2012, compared to 55 percent in 2007.

The new conservative government wants to soften the requirements set by the Norwegian Financial Supervisory Authority, but has not yet formally changed the guidelines, only emphasised practice. Banks now use more discretion and are considering individual customers in terms of future wages, liquidity and solvency. They can give loans with LTV rates higher than 85 percent, but can no longer go to 100 percent. At the same time regulations for the use of the start-up loan have been tightened. Only those on permanently low incomes but who have the ability to repay the mortgage can now apply for a start-up loan.

How monetary policy is designed has implications for the property owners' risk exposure. One source of risk is fluctuation in interest rates. The current housing price level and high debt burden can create significant liquidity pressure for households with small margins. How banks account for interest rate increases in their lending policy, therefore, has an effect on the household's financial resilience (Aarland and Astrup 2013). Norges Bank now determines the key policy rate in order to achieve an inflation target of 2.5 percent. This monetary policy regime affects the risk exposure to property owners in general. The economy-wide inflation rate is determined by the level of activity and the employment level. For Norges Bank to reach the inflation target, the bank must, therefore, as a simple generalisation, set the key policy rate high when employment levels are high and vice versa. For homeowners, this means that unemployment and interest rates are negatively correlated. Variable interest rates can be seen as a kind of liquidity insurance against unemployment, which one does not get at fixed rates.

Looking into the future

In 2010 the governor of Norges Bank expressed the view that the Norwegian housing finance system is undeveloped and immature. Variable interest rates comprise a large element of the system and fixed-rate loans are not very customer-friendly because it is expensive to buy oneself out of contracts with fixed interest rates. Norway does not have a secondary market over which it could spread the risk (Nettavisen 2010).

Norway may face significant challenges in the future. For a small, open economy changes in the international economic environment are of particular importance. The financial crisis and measures to counteract it have resulted in major financial and economic costs for the government. The cost and the distribution of these measures raises the question of what role the financial sector should have in the future, what activities within the economy as a whole are served by engaging in the sector and who should bear the costs of problems in the sector (NOU 2011: 1).

The State Bank Commission (NOU 1995: 11) felt it was important that a broad set of measures should be employed to ensure that the financial sector in Norway is robust and appropriate. Taxes or fees should supplement regulation and supervision in a useful manner. The sector should also be more transparent about the activities and risk-taking of financial institutions, including the banks' own calculation of capital requirements.

The maturity of the banks' funding has increased and makes the banks more robust against the risk of short-term failure of the funding. Nevertheless, several Norwegian banks are some distance off from meeting the soon-to-be-introduced international requirements for liquidity, even after changes in the definition have made the requirement easier to reach. The banks also do not meet the expected future requirements for long term stable funding. In 2013 the Norwegian Government instructed the banks to employ stricter capital requirements than their foreign competitors were imposing. At the same time Norway wished that the operations of the banks would be subject to the same solvency requirements that applied in the country where the business is run (i.e. the host country's regulations).

Homeownership is strongly tax favoured in Norway, although it is unlikely to have played any significant role in the current financial crisis. The Commission's view is that the current tax bias for housing investment clearly has undesirable aspects, including that households are probably more vulnerable to fluctuations in house prices. The Commission therefore recommended that the taxation of housing should be brought more in line with the taxation of other assets.

Conclusion

Deregulation of the housing and credit markets in the 1980s laid the foundation for aggressive marketing and an intensified battle for loan customers. The banking crisis, experienced between 1988 and 1993 and resulting in falling house prices, revealed that the banks were making poor credit assessments in the deregulated market. This led to stricter lending guidelines.

After 1993, growth in the Norwegian oil economy alongside high income growth and low unemployment led to continuous house price inflation and a strong increase in average household debt. The business cycle turned in the beginning of 2008. Norges Bank gradually reduced the key policy rate and fiscal policy was used to support the economy. Strong monetary and fiscal stimuli alongside a range of government support measures to the financial sector contributed to stabilising the situation.

Since the financial crisis, a deposit of 15 percent is now required to secure a loan as an attempt to curb the strong demand for housing and thus reduce house price inflation and debt growth. In addition, Norwegian banks were instructed to impose stricter capital requirements than their foreign competitors. In this context it is important to remember that middle-aged groups have strongly contributed to the debt growth and that increased lending also must be seen in relation to the volume of new construction.

Low interest rates and favourable taxation of homeownership still increase house prices and lending. Some households will have payment problems if interest rates rise, but the worst scenario will be if an interest rate increase leads to reduced demand for other goods and services followed by high unemployment.

Acknowledgements

This work is supported by the Housing Bank with NOK 75 000.

References

Aarland, K and Astrup, KC (2013). *Økonomisk risiko og boligeie.* NIBR-rapport 2013: 16.

Annaniassen, E (2006). *En skandinavisk boligmodell? Historien om et sosialdemokratisk eierland og et sosialdemokratisk leieboerland.* Temahefte 1/06. NOVA.

Barlindhaug, R (1996). Boliger belånes til pipa. *Samfunnsspeilet* nr. 4/96. SSB.

Johannessen, K, Astrup, KC and Medby, P (2013). *Unges etablering på boligmarkedet – er stigen trukket opp?* NIBR-rapport 2013: 16.

Meld. St. 12 (2012–2013). *Perspektivmeldingen.*

Meld. St. 21 (2010–2011). *Finansmarkedsmeldinga.*

Nettavisen (2010). *Gjedrem hudfletter norsk boligfinansiering,* [online], Available: http://stocklink.no/mobile/Article.aspx?id=63418 (accessed 29 July 2015).

NOU (1992). *Bankkrisen.* Finans og tolldepartementet. p. 30.

NOU (1995). *Statsbankutvalget. Statsbankene under endrede rammevilkår.* Finans- og tolldepartementet.

NOU (2002). *Boligmarkedene og boligpolitikken.* Kommunal og regionaldepartementet.

NOU (2011). *Bedre rustet mot finanskriser. Finanskriseutvalgets utredning.* Finansdepartementet.

Nyhus, EK (1991). *Tilbydere på det private utlånsmarkedet – en oversikt.* Arbeidsnotat nr. 12/1991 SNF.

Statistics Norway (various years). Banking and Financial Markets Statistics [Online] Available: www.ssb.no/en/bank-og-finansmarked.

Steigum, E (2010). *Norsk økonomi etter 1980 – fra krise til suksess*. Working Paper Series 4/10 CME/BI, Juni 2010.

The Norwegian Financial Supervisory Authority (2000). *Boliglånsundersøkelsen 2000*.

The Norwegian Financial Supervisory Authority (2003a). *Boliglånsundersøkelsen 2003*.

The Norwegian Financial Supervisory Authority (2003b). *Tilstanden i finansmarkedet 2002*.

The Norwegian Financial Supervisory Authority (2012). *Letter to the Ministry of Finance*. 3 October 2012.

The Norwegian Financial Supervisory Authority (2013). *Finansielle utviklingstrekk*. November 2013.

The Norwegian Financial Supervisory Authority (2014). *Finansielt utsyn 2014*.

17

Milestones of Housing Finance in Poland

Marta Widłak and Jacek Łaszek
National Bank of Poland, Warszawa, Poland

Introduction

In 1989 there was no private housing finance system in Poland. During the first 10 years following the dissolution of the Soviet Union, very little housing was financed through private funds from the banking sector because of high interest rates. Instead the official government financing programme was a semi-market saving scheme that was strongly subsidised by the state. This financing scheme was established during the socialist era (in the 1980s), but was gradually phased out during the 1990s. Other forms of public finance for the housing sector during the former regime included communal housing and state enterprise housing. These were cancelled step-by-step during the first stage of political transformation. A new programme of non-profit social rented housing focused on medium and lower income groups was introduced in 1995 and continued until 2008. This programme, however, was very costly and inefficient, so its impact on meeting housing needs was low.

Poland's accession into the EU in 2004 led to an inflow of foreign capital and accelerated the growth of the Polish economy. Easy access to foreign finance along with stable rates of inflation and growing household incomes resulted in strong demand for housing. The period between 2005 and 2008 was one of unprecedented growth in mortgage loans (mainly Swiss Franc [CHF] denominated loans that were granted through universal banks). This buoyant market situation was slowed by the Global Financial Crisis (GFC). Since then, mortgage market regulation has strengthened. The availability of mortgages has decreased significantly because of the crisis and because the availability of CHF denominated loans has been curtailed. At the same time, the state has continued the policy of gradually withdrawing its role in financing housing.

Milestones in European Housing Finance, First Edition.
Edited by Jens Lunde and Christine Whitehead.
© 2016 John Wiley & Sons, Ltd. Published 2016 by John Wiley & Sons, Ltd.

The end of 1989 was a truly historic breakthrough for Poland as this was the year in which its political, economic and social transformation began. The 25-year period of transformation of the housing sector and its financing that followed was dominated by a change of state policy that made home-ownership more popular, albeit with a fairly random policy of subsidisation. The withdrawal of the state's role in housing finance was accompanied by the development of private financing through mortgages. At the same time, attempts to develop a system of social rented housing largely failed. The excessively restrictive law protecting the rights of tenants was not changed and prevented the creation of a rented housing sector throughout this period. The policy emphasis on owner-occupation and the absence of a rental market means that households have virtually no tenure choice in Poland.

Housing finance milestones

Taking into consideration the changes in housing policy, construction of new housing units, trends in prices of housing units and changes in basic housing finance schemes, one can divide the last 25 years into three periods:

1. The beginning of the creation of a housing market and a regime change from publicly-financed housing to a private savings and mortgage credit finance scheme (1990–2001).
2. Economic, housing and mortgage market boom (2002–2008).
3. Economic, housing and mortgage market slowdown as a result of the GFC (2009–2013).

Taking a closer look at the identified periods, we can enumerate certain milestones from within housing policy, housing finance and changes in market dynamics. These main events determined the path of housing finance in Poland during the period of economic transformation and are described in Table 17.1.

First stage – housing market creation

This stage (1990–2001) can be briefly characterised by the following trends:

- A gradual change in the common understanding of the role of the state in housing finance;
- Deregulation of the housing sector as a result of the wider economic transformation rather than purposeful, strategic long term housing policy;
- Introduction of new schemes for public subsidies for housing (for new construction of both cooperative and owner-occupied housing);

Table 17.1 Milestones in Polish housing finance, 1989–2013.

No.	Date	Milestone
1	1989/1990	Regime change. The collapse of the communist system and the transition from a centrally planned economy to a free market economy. The beginning of the restructuring of the finance mechanisms for cooperative housing, both existing and new.
2	1991	The start of assistance from the World Bank, European Bank for Reconstruction and Development and USAID, focused mainly on developing a programme for transitioning from a socialist housing sector to a market system.
3	1991–1997	The adoption of certain legal acts concerning (among other topics): • tax subsidies for private housing construction (1991) • residential tenancies and housing allowances (1994) • condominium law (1994) • land (1997) • the new programme for nonprofit social housing – TBS (1995).
4	1997/1998	The Act on Mortgage Covered Bonds and Mortgage Banks. An increase in the share of banks providing first mortgages not subsidized by the state. An increase in the number of developers and a distinct growth in bank loans for financing developer projects.
5	2001	Significant reduction in the construction subsidy through the liquidation of the greater part of the tax relief of 1991. Imposition of VAT on developer construction. The significant reduction in the programme of housing allowances and the tightening of the law protecting tenants blocked the possibility of creating a rental housing market.
6	2001/2002	A significant decrease in inflation to below 10% and growing demand for mortgages.
7	2004–2005	EU accession and foreign capital inflow. Beginning of mortgage, price and housing construction boom.
8	2006	The beginning of the regulation of universal banks granting loans for the purchase of housing – Recommendation S. The final removal of income tax relief; the introduction of a new government subsidy programme, the so-called RnS (Rodzina na Swoim).
9	2008/2009	The end of the mortgage, price and construction boom and housing market stabilisation as a result of the GFC; the end of CHF denominated mortgage loans.
10	2011–2013	The development of prudential regulations connected with housing finance provided by universal banks (amendments to Recommendation S, Recommendation T, Recommendation J).
11	2012–2013	Legal act on the protection of home buyers rights, (the so-called Developer Law); Further cuts to the public subsidy for private housing (the so-called MdM scheme that replaces RnS).

- Creation of a legal and economic environment enabling the establishment and development of a mortgage market;
- State withdrawal from financing of housing construction and thus a breakdown in housing investment.

Programmes of reform of the housing sector   The moment that market transformation began, fundamental disparities in the Polish housing economy emerged: while a low share of public expenditure was being devoted to the maintenance of housing stock and a low share of private resources were used to finance the housing stock, a relatively high level of subsidies and high share of public resources was devoted to financing housing construction. During the period of transformation there was no credible programme of reform introduced for the housing sector. After 1991 Poland benefitted from the support of international institutions. The core schemes helping to build a housing market were formulated by the World Bank, the European Bank for Reconstruction and Development and the United States Agency for International Development (USAID) (Łaszek 2004a). The long term programmes launched by these institutions supported the development of a housing market by laying the foundations for developers and commercial banks to finance housing construction.

In the period discussed here, certain legal acts were changed or established. These concerned: the role of the state in housing construction and its financing processes; a reduction in subsidies for housing construction; changes to ownership rights in association with privatisation; and housing allowances. Next, we briefly summarise the most important legal changes that established the new institutional framework.

Public financing   In the early 1990s, the existing public subsidies for loans for housing cooperatives were replaced by a new scheme of public subsidies and allowances. Income tax deduction was possible for most housing construction expenditures: the purchase of land; personal contributions to the housing cooperative; extensions to buildings for residential purposes; housing renovation or modernisation; construction of multifamily buildings for rent and the purchase of land for rental housing construction. *Ad valorem* taxes and mortgage credit subsidies were not introduced at a large scale. The current property tax is a low, nearly lump sum tax paid for each square metre.

Questions of what was to be done with land owned by the state were solved only in 1997. The new law, among others, defined the responsibilities of municipalities in relation to the purchase, supply of utilities and transfer of land for housing purposes, especially for multifamily investments.

Privatisation of the housing stock   The next important step was privatisation of the existing stock. The so-called Condominium Law (1994) was implemented to protect ownership rights and to enable the privatisation of buildings owned by municipalities or state enterprises. It laid the foundation for construction by developers, which had previously been carried out through cooperatives because of the lack of a suitable legal framework.

Privatisation of the housing stock was the programme with the strongest impact on consumers, who were given assets of enormous value. This created the basis of a housing market in the largest cities of Poland but it was also an accidental transfer of wealth of high value. The housing stock was often sold to the existing residents for symbolic sums (public and company stock was sold for about 10 percent of estimated construction costs). Privatisation concerned mainly public and company-owned housing stock, and to a certain degree cooperative housing, where the so-called cooperative tenants' rights (similar to rental rights) were transformed into cooperative-ownership rights (similar to homeownership rights). To a limited extent (less than 10 percent), cooperative apartments were also converted to full private ownership. Privatisation concerned only the urban housing stock, as housing in rural areas was already in private ownership.

Rental and social housing   The Act concerning the regulation of rents and protection of tenants in communal, municipal and private housing was also changed. It empowered municipalities to establish rent levels, allowing rent increases that had been necessary for a long time. It introduced the possibility of eviction for non-payment of rent without an obligation to provide substitute premises. The Act also established a new housing allowance scheme, which was the first attempt towards subsidies that targeted low-income households. The obligation to provide housing allowances for members of housing cooperatives and owners of single-family housing, however, fell on municipalities, which was not an appropriate way to rationalise the public housing policy (Merrill *et al.* 1998).

Further changes made in 2001 introduced heavy restrictions on private residential rental agreements and maintained excessive protection for tenants. Following these changes, it became practically impossible for the owner to terminate a tenant's contract and rents were frozen at very low levels. Moreover, allowances introduced in the mid-1990s were also restricted. This was an attempt to reconcile the rights of tenants of old apartments who had held their tenancy under communism with tenants entering since the transition and to avoid accusations of unequal treatment of citizens. In reality, these changes have halted any development of a rental housing market over the last 25 years and boosted the popularity of owner-occupied housing financed through the banking sector.

Some additional attempts were also made to satisfy the housing needs of middle and low-income groups. The institutional and regulatory rules for a contractual savings system and non-profit social rented housing scheme (so-called TBS) were introduced in 1995. Public funds to support these programmes were channelled into the National Housing Fund (Chiquier 2006). The contractual saving system functioned until 2001 when tax relief was abolished.

Private financing   At the same time, following the German model, some attempts were made to establish mortgage covered bonds as a tool for refinancing housing loans. The covered bond and mortgage banks, however, were heavily regulated by a new law. Consequently, despite later law amendments, mortgage banking and the mortgage bond market are rather dormant in Poland.

From about 1997 there was a significant increase in financing housing through bank loans supported by retail deposits. The first commercial (i.e. non-subsidised) mortgages were granted in Poland at the beginning of the 1990s, when the creation of the banking sector started. This took place alongside the launch of a World Bank programme (the creation of a mortgage fund) and the creation of the Polish–American Mortgage Bank. These institutions introduced simplified procedures for credit assessment and granting mortgages based on the experience of developed countries, mainly the US (*Fannie Mae*). The first instruments introduced were housing loans denominated in US dollars and double-indexed. The loan service was indexed to the wage index while the remaining equity was indexed to 13-week government bonds. Problematically, the data on wages was half-year lagged, which, in a situation of high inflation, caused payment shocks. Later, the bank Powszechna Kasa Oszczędności Bank Polski (PKO BP) changed the remaining equity index to the 12-month average deposit rate (from the five biggest banks) plus a fixed margin. The bank also introduced an additional product, which was similar to a Deferred Interest Mortgage (DIM) although the payment rate was adjusted in discrete steps according to the ratio of payment to outstanding loan. Full DIM loans, which were quite popular in Hungary, were never fully accepted in Poland, even though they guaranteed a predictable cash-flow and could be refinanced with covered bonds. Both of these products and the standards for granting loans were copied by the remaining banks, which also mainly adopted double indexed loans. These instruments remained dominant throughout the first stage of housing finance development until about 1999.

Until 1994 the mortgage market was dominated by two main players – PKO BP and the Polish-American Mortgage Bank (PAM) – as well as several banks clustered around the mortgage fund created by the World Bank programme, of which the largest was Powszechny Bank Gospodarczy (PBG) from Łódź. The mortgage fund programme was spread between these two groups. At the turn of 1997/1998 almost all of the existing universal banks were competing on the mortgage market (Merrill 2000; Łaszek 2004a). The largest universal bank in terms of assets, PKO BP, retained its dominant position on the mortgage market until about 2001 and even after 24 years it is still a major player in the sector with a market share estimated at about 30 percent in 2013.

Despite the increased involvement of banks in housing finance, the loans they granted were relatively small. This was a consequence of low household incomes, high interest rates and prudent policies by the banks, which translated into low credit ratings, which meant that the loans made were of significantly lower value than that of the collateral. The typical value of loans granted between 1997 and 2000 by PKO BP was between 30 000–40 000 Polish Zloty (PLN) and by Bank Polska Kasa Opieki Spółka Akcyjna (PKO SA) it was PLN 60 000–70 000. For comparison, the average monthly gross salary in the enterprise sector was PLN 1157 in 1997 and PLN 2057 in 2000.

The basic types of residential mortgage loans that developed during these early years in Poland included loans for financing newly-built apartments, loans for existing apartments, and loans for renovations and modernisation. This remains the case today.

At first the majority of the banks based their interest rates on the so-called base rates of the bank, which usually included the costs of obtaining funds, risk premiums and profit. Under pressure of competition in the second half of the 1990s they began to move towards independent indexes based mainly on the Warsaw Interbank Offer Rate (WIBOR). While bank margins reached 7–9 percentage points above the contractual index between 1996 and 1999, they fell to a level of 3.5–4.5 percent in 1999.

Housing construction The gradual development of the mortgage market and the increased role of private housing finance, along with new laws and regulations concerning real estate management, created a good climate for the development of housing construction in Poland. Around 1997 many new private firms emerged, developing mainly multifamily buildings intended for sale or private rental. The share of these investments grew gradually in relation to other types of construction, mainly cooperative housing. The role of cooperative housing construction gradually declined as 'old loans' (granted to a large extent in the 1980s and highly subsidised by the state) slowly expired. However, throughout this first period, developer projects still faced quite unequal competition from the housing cooperatives, which continued to benefit from subsidised loans and were in possession of large tracts of land (a legacy of the former housing economy).

The formation of the private housing investment market in Poland largely occurred between 1997 and 2001. In 2000 the building tax relief was withdrawn and VAT was imposed on construction carried out by developers. This was also the moment when the supply of new housing began to exceed demand. Anticipation of the removal of tax relief and the introduction of VAT caused a sudden increase in demand for housing units completed by December 2001. After this date demand for new construction declined and as a result many developers went bankrupt. Consequently, there was a fall in the number of completed projects, building permits, newly-started housing units and total construction. The market would not begin to recover until 4 years later.

Second stage – the boom

This stage (2002–2008) can be characterised mainly by the following milestones:

- The development of the mortgage market and progressive growth of PLN and CHF denominated mortgage lending, primarily through universal banks.
- A further reduction in public subsidies for housing (in particular the change from more advantageous tax relief to the limited Rodzina na Swoim [RnS] programme, financing some parts of mortgage interest for a short period).
- The beginning of mortgage lending regulation by banking supervision (mainly with respect to foreign currency [FX] loans).
- Reduction and termination of the TBS programme, alongside the introduction of some efforts to reverse the tenant protection act.

For Poland, 2001 was a seminal year characterised by regulation changes, a breakdown in housing construction, major improvements in overall economic conditions and a substantial drop in inflation. The second stage, beginning around 2002 and finishing at the end of 2008 (when the GFC started), could be called the mortgage credit boom period. At first, together with the drop in inflation, mortgage loans in PLN became more popular and available. This helped housing investment to recover slowly. However, the true breakthrough was EU accession, when banks got access to FX loan financing. In part, because of a lack of previous experience in FX lending and a lack of established lending standards in this field, CHF denominated mortgage loans became dominant on the market. They were the lowest priced product eagerly granted by banks, which were fiercely competing to gain more clients. The mortgage boom started in the middle of 2005 and lasted for about 3 years. In this period FX loans dominated the market (Figure 17.1). Banks' margins on mortgage loans, which in 2002 were between 2.0 and 2.5 percent, fell between 2007 and 2008 to 1.5 percent (and have now returned to the current level of 2.0–2.5 percent).

The mortgage lending and house price boom were also fuelled by the fast growth of GDP and incomes and the growing need for housing driven by rises in the number of marriages, birth rates and the proportion of the population of working age. Additionally, there was substantial migration from rural areas to the cities. Until 2006, households could to some extent still take advantage of the remaining tax allowance when buying or building new housing units. In 2006 the remaining part of the previous tax allowance was totally withdrawn and replaced by a new programme subsidising housing purchases – the so-called Rodzina na Swoim (RnS). The new subsidy had a quite limited effect on public expenditure. The state paid some part of mortgage interest but only for the first eight years of the mortgage. Unfortunately, to some extent this subsidy was distributed to banks and developers, who offset it in house prices and interest rates for mortgage credit.

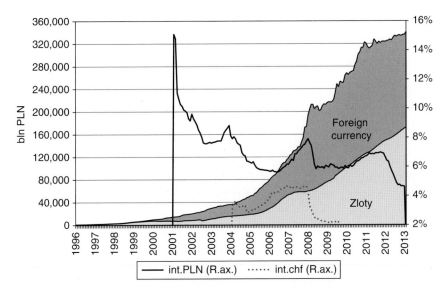

Figure 17.1 Mortgage loans and average mortgage interest rates.
Source: NBP.

The first regulation of banking mortgage products issued by the banking supervision authority (Recommendation S) was not introduced until the middle of 2006. This regulation was rather liberal and did not restrain banks from granting very risky CHF denominated (and, since 2008, Euro denominated) mortgage loans.

The TBS programme was gradually reduced during this second period, and after 2010 funding for new TBS projects was stopped completely. There were attempts to stimulate financing for the private rented sector through legal regulations designed to circumvent the excessive tenant protection law. However, the new regulations were easy to challenge and did not really reduce the risk to the investor. The sector involving individually rented housing remained informal and no professional rental housing stock was created. A vibrant rental market, however, is needed to increase the responsiveness and dynamism of housing markets and to enhance the soundness of mortgage markets (Chiquier 2006).

Third stage – the slowdown

This stage (2009–2013) can be characterised in brief by the following milestones:

- Further regulation of mortgage lending by banking supervision (tougher mortgage standards) and some deregulation of the mortgage covered bonds market;
- Further reductions in public subsidies (cancellation of VAT tax relief for building materials and a switch from the remaining interest subsidy [RnS] to a lower up front subsidy called MdM);

- A slight decline followed by stabilisation in house prices, combined with a growing supply of new housing;
- Steady revival in the overall economic situation.

The stabilisation of the housing market, the moderate slowdown in demand for housing, and above all restricted access to bank loans – the only significant source of housing finance in Poland – began in 2009 after the outbreak of the GFC. However, neither Polish debtors nor the banking sector have been heavily affected by the GFC.

In the third quarter of 2008 the Zloty began rapidly to lose its value, resulting in some problems with the portfolio of loans denominated in foreign currency and restrictions imposed on new loans. Primarily, these problems concerned the refinancing of FX loan portfolios and exchange rate shocks. The National Bank of Poland was ready to provide extra liquidity for the banking sector, but in the end banks did not use it. Since the banks had to finance the growing value of FX denominated loan portfolios, a deposit war began, leading to an increase in the interest rate on loans in PLN. Investment in apartments and mortgage portfolios began to show losses. Consequently, the supply of unsold, new housing units in the six largest cities increased from approximately 12 000 at the beginning of 2006 to over 30 000 in 2008 and over 38 000 by Q3 of 2010. The impact of the GFC on borrowers was also limited. The impact of the weakening PLN on the denominated credit instalments was, to a large extent, compensated for by the fall in interest rate (most of the CHF denominated loans were variable interest rates linked to the London Interbank Offered Rate: LIBOR).

Nevertheless, the GFC forced the banking supervision body further to tighten regulations relating to mortgage products and the banks' exposure to credit risk connected with the housing market (new Recommendations S, T and J). This mainly concerned universal banks, since mortgage banks were regulated conservatively by the act which created them. In particular, FX denominated loans were restricted and then practically blocked by the regulations connected with capital requirements, established rules on credit-worthiness and the introduction, for the first time, of rules for LTV and DTI (80 and 50 percent thresholds of the latest were shifted to coming years due to the downturn in the economy). Obligations to monitor the housing market and make use of professional databases for valuation and assessment of market risk were also introduced.

A further change in the government housing subsidy programme from RnS to MdM in 2013 had a disruptive influence on the market. This change restricted state assistance in housing finance even further, and is now the last existing form of subsidy for private housing in Poland.

The Polish housing system has been characterised by a specific dichotomy. Despite the lack of a formal rental housing sector, tenants have been protected much more than homeowners, while house purchasers have borne the full risk of the development process. Only after the end of the housing boom and the experience of the economic crisis did legislators manage to pass a law to protect buyers of developer-built housing. The so-called developer law introduced in 2012 resolves at least formally the issue of protecting buyers through the introduction of, among other things, an escrow account and bank supervision of the investment process.

Impact of housing finance milestones in Poland in the last 25 years

The main impacts of these housing finance milestones can be briefly summarised as follows:

1. A housing market has emerged, based on private ownership of housing, mortgages and individual preferences. There has been a gradual change from perceiving housing as a social good and an element of employment policy to a tangible private asset and an element of lifestyle.
2. These milestones have led to changes in the basic characteristics of the housing sector – in terms of the move to market prices for both housing costs and prices, the volume of housing construction and investment, the ownership structure, the way that building firms operate and the system of housing finance.
3. The massive transfer of former public housing wealth to the population laid the foundations for the housing market and influenced the consumer and social behaviour of population.
4. Mortgage finance has become almost the only way to acquire a home. Public support has been reduced for all income groups (even for those on the lowest incomes), and consequently affordability has become a problem for newly forming households. Additionally, there is a lack of reasonable and long term housing policy which includes programmes for social and rental housing.
5. The rapid privatisation of the housing stock and the diminishing role of public housing finance has thus resulted in the rapidly growing popularity of owner-occupied housing and, in turn, a neglect of rental and social housing.

Impacts on the outputs and structure of housing construction

The transformation of the production sphere had a positive impact on the sector in the long term, eliminating ineffective, large state enterprises and expensive but poor quality production based on prefabricated technology. However, in the early period of Poland's economic transformation, there was a collapse in housing production. Amongst different demand factors the most important were a sudden fall in public housing finance and the lack of availability of loans from banks, which could not be compensated for by cash expenditure from the population. Nevertheless, in the longer term, adaptations occurred within the housing market and the wider economy, and consequently the level of construction began to grow.

The transformations that occurred during the 1990s significantly changed the size and investment structure of housing construction in Poland (Figure 17.2). The share of the private sector grew (to 89 percent in 2013) while the share of housing cooperatives fell (to 5 percent) and company and communal housing also fell considerably (to 6 percent). There were also significant changes in the spatial distribution of housing construction. Today, new housing construction is concentrated in the largest urban areas with the highest development and income potential. In 1991 25 percent of new apartments were built in major urban areas (provincial capitals); in 2000 the share was 50 percent and in 2012 it stood at 58 percent. However, little has changed in the structure of individual housing (single family) construction and its financing. This is concentrated in rural areas and smaller towns, where it was and is by far the dominant form (in 2013 it constituted 55 percent of all housing construction). During the socialist period, this segment was already primarily financed by private owners without the participation of the state. While this has not changed, since the 2000s the share of bank lending to finance construction in the single family home sector has grown consistently. Nevertheless, bank lending remains the main form of finance for multi-family housing construction (especially in the largest cities in Poland). Cooperative housing construction, which was very highly subsidised by the state, reached its climax in the years 1990/1992, and ultimately died in the

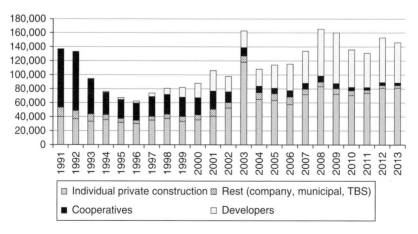

Figure 17.2 The size and structure of housing construction in Poland.
Source: Central Statistical Office.
Note: The change in individual housing construction in 2003 is purely statistical and results from some legal changes.

years 1995/1996. After this period the only remaining cooperatives operated on a commercial basis and competed on the market with developers. Their market share continues to decline, while the share of construction produced by private development companies grew from a few percent in the middle of the 1990s to over 45 percent in 2001 and 89 percent in 2013.

A specific kind of developer emerged in the Polish market in the 1990s (Łaszek 2004b). These developers realise investments with the funds (pre-payments) of future homeowners, supplemented sometimes with loans. Investments realised by this method often proved to be extremely risky for the clients, as well as very profitable for the developers. It was not until the 2012 Act that regulations were introduced protecting the interests of developers' clients.

The structure of the development sector changed for good with accession to the EU and the credit boom in the years 2005–2008. In part as a result of the inflow of foreign capital, strong developer firms emerged and dominated the markets in the largest cities. The credit boom strengthened these firms as their high profits enabled them to raise additional capital. The credit boom also resulted in the emergence of significant land banks and forced the creation of procedures to speed up the preparation of land for investment. Therefore, the earlier barrier limiting access to building land was reduced.

Mortgage, price and construction boom

As a result of the mortgage boom (2005–2008) and income and demographic growth, the demand for housing flourished, causing unprecedented growth in house prices and construction (see Figures 17.2 and 17.3). Very fast growth in demand meant that housing investment projects were offered for sale at very early stages of development thus carrying a high risk. This also means that the actual rise in real prices, especially in early stage of the boom, was even higher than that measured statistically. In stable market conditions, such projects are usually characterised by higher premiums for the risk and lower prices, but this was not the Polish case. High demand also caused an increase in the price expectations of building firms and producers of building materials; consequently, inflation occurred in the construction and building materials market. The increasingly high prices of apartments and their growing supply resulted in an increase in unsold housing stock on the market.

The GFC halted the growth of imbalances in the housing market in Poland. The effect of the economic downturn was a fall in the prices of housing, which remain low in nominal terms and only slightly higher in real terms (Figure 17.3). This took place despite significant reductions of foreign capital inflow on the credit markets. Despite the economic downturn, the financial situation of Polish developers was satisfactory. Also banks did not experience as much turmoil as in other countries and continued to guarantee access to mortgages in PLN. FX denominated lending was, on the other hand,

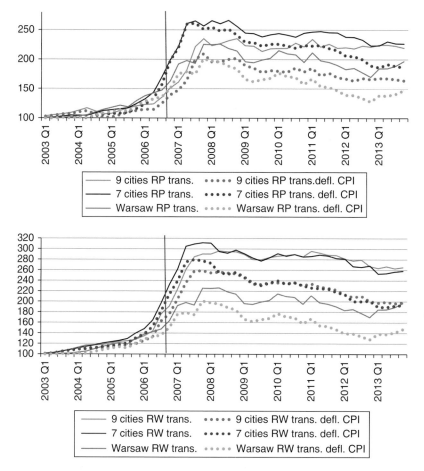

Figure 17.3   House price dynamics in Poland – new construction (upper part) and existing stock (lower part).

Source: NBP (2014).

Note: The vertical line divides data into asking price data (to 2006 Q3) and transaction price data. Groups of 9 and 7 cities relates to the biggest Polish cities being provincial capitals.

Abbreviations: 'Trans.' means these are transactions not asking prices; 'Defl. CPI' means that the nominal prices have been deflated with the CPI.

curtailed, mainly due to the lack of funding, the weakening of PLN and a fear of deepening systemic risk. Regulations on mortgage lending, including of FX denominated loans, have only been tightened since 2011.

Mortgage banking system development

Beginning in 1990, the state withdrew relatively quickly from financing construction, leaving it to private savings and mortgages funded by deposits in the banking system. However, the risk associated with the construction sector together with prohibitively high interest rates arising from very high inflation resulted in virtually no interest in providing this form of finance through the banking system. Until about 1997, the only housing construction financed by the banks involved the old, expiring, cooperative investment loans granted by PKO and subsidised by the state. By the end of the 1990s, despite growth in the mortgage market, the primary source of funding for housing projects remained the personal resources of the population. Financing by cash was the main way of funding the much smaller construction volume produced during the first half of the decade. Mortgages played a supportive role and were paid to the developer as cash installments. Because of the lack of mortgage collateral they were often granted on terms that were unfavourable to the client, but justifiable by the risk. During the 2000s, as interest rates fell and prices remained relatively low for the borrower, FX denominated mortgages became more widespread and larger loans began to appear, particularly in the major cities.

The share of bank loans in housing finance increased between 2000 and 2002 from 17 percent to almost 30 percent, and in subsequent years loans have become the basis for financing housing construction. The decisive year was 2004 when Poland joined the EU and thus gained access to international financial markets. The credit and price boom between 2005 and 2008 was largely funded by the supply of CHF denominated mortgages (see Figures 17.1). Today, between 50 and 60 percent of funding for housing construction comes from bank loans, with the rest funded by the personal funds of the population.

Choice of a mortgage banking model

In the last decade, changes in mortgage banking were related mainly to changes in market trends, products and regulation. In this area, one of the main issues has been the choice of the model of financing (either by universal or mortgage banks).

In practice, the Polish mortgage banking system was created and developed on the basis of universal banks. Specialised mortgage banking, so far, has not developed beyond the experimental stage.

One problem mortgage banks faced was the restrictive credit conditions imposed on them by the law (concerning the quality of mortgage covered bonds) in combination with a complete lack of prudential regulations related to mortgage lending and housing loans until 2006 granted by universal banks. This asymmetry, despite the subsequent amendment to the law, practically removed any 'business sense' argument for creating mortgage banks.

The second problem was the cost of funds. The benchmark for specialist mortgage institutions used has been treasury bonds that were more expensive than the cost of deposits available for universal banks. This very quickly condemned mortgage banks to foreign denominated loans supplied from foreign parent banks or commercial loans. As a result, mortgage banks in

Poland were created as specialised institutions around large universal banks or as part of large corporate groups, and therefore had to compete with other universal banks that belonged to those same groups.

The main weakness connected with the creation of mortgage banks in Poland was the lack of a clear vision of how the sector would function in the long term. Despite carrying a systemic risk, FX denominated loans apparently solved the problem of housing affordability – they replaced good housing policy and were, especially in the initial period, very profitable for the banks. The initial lack of adequate mortgage regulation as well as their relatively late introduction has not resulted in significant losses for banks thus far (currently the percentage of non-performing loans does not exceed 4 percent). However, the potential risk associated with these portfolios, as the experience in other countries has shown, is significant.

Public financing

Throughout the 1990s public funds for housing were allocated mainly for existing cooperative commitments (about 60–65 percent of the state budget allocated for the needs of housing) and direct or indirect support for households that already had an apartment (about 20 percent). In the first half of the decade they mainly financed construction of cooperative housing under the old obligations, and in the second half of the decade they were associated with subsidising existing homes. Between 1999 and 2000, the share of budget funds allocated to housing finance rose slightly, because of the larger-scale construction of social housing through the TBS programme.

The estimated subsidies for cooperative housing construction (through price subsidies to companies, free transfer of land and inflation) amounted to about 50 percent of total investment funds. Credit for cooperatives financed 40 percent of construction and, thus, it can be estimated that the actual share of finance for new housing that came from private individuals in the 1980s did not exceed 10 percent. In the first half of the 1990s that proportion jumped to 80 percent while both credit and subsidies were negligible. After 2010, the share paid by households themselves can be estimated at around 50 percent, with the rest from debt finance. This shows the dramatic scale of fluctuations in housing finance.

The state budget has indirectly stimulated housing investment and renovation through tax relief on personal income. The scale of this was significant; at the end of the 1990s income tax deductions for investments amounted to about PLN 7 bn annually and the actual sum of tax relief (i.e. the reduction in government revenue) was approximately PLN 2 bn, which was equivalent to more than 50 percent of the total budgetary resources allocated to this sector. Beginning in 2001, the state gradually started to withdraw these allowances. Through the RnS programme (2006), the state funded a portion of mortgage interest, but this was replaced by the recently introduced MdM programme (2013), by which the state gives a smaller grant subsidy (5–10 percent of the value of the loan).

Looking towards the future

It seems that in the coming years the system of private financing of owner-occupied housing construction via the banking sector will be maintained The recent government subsidy programme introduced in January 2014 (MdM) is in fact the next step in phasing out state financial support for the sector. In the coming years, because of the need to reduce public spending, one can expect a further reduction in subsidy. The current housing situation in Poland (around 356 housing units for every 1000 inhabitants) lags far behind the developed countries in the Euro zone, although it is consistent with the level of GDP. As Poland's GDP per capita catches up with other EU countries, housing demand should grow. The factors pulling in the opposite direction include the projected decline in population and expected out-migration to other EU countries. The importance of privately funded owner-occupied housing (which today constitutes about 97 percent of new construction) and the absence of public programmes to provide financial and regulatory support for social housing and the rental market (in various forms) results in low efficiency in the entire housing system. This in turn carries serious consequences for the whole economy.

The mortgage portfolios of universal banks have become significant, and the risks associated with these portfolios – in particular with respect to that part denominated in foreign currencies – are substantial. The quality of the portfolios denominated in PLN is relatively low. Under these conditions, stricter credit requirements – imposed by the regulator to help ensure a better liquidity balance – can change profitability and be a factor in renewed interest in mortgage banks. Furthermore, it seems that the planned easing of the regulations for specialist mortgage banks will probably wake up this practically dormant mortgage segment to some extent. However, any expansion of mortgage banks will probably result in more loans and securitised receivables associated with the most expensive housing and commercial real estate.

Finally, there has been growing criticism of Polish housing policy concerning the lack of available rental and social housing especially in the context of a surplus of developer housing on the market. This has led in 2014 to the launch of a programme involving the purchase of developer housing for rental purposes. However, preliminary estimates show that this programme is focused on the same income group as the MdM subsidy. Consequently its introduction in the current environment of strong budget pressures may well result in a waste of public money. Thus, the rental market and the lowest income groups remain excluded from adequate housing without any systemic solutions concerning their housing conditions in sight.

References

Central Statistical Office (CSO) (various years). [Online], Available: http://stat.gov.pl/obszary-tematyczne/przemysl-budownictwo-srodki-trwale/budownictwo/budownictwo-mieszkaniowe-tablice-przegladowe-od-1991-r-,6,3.html (accessed 29 July 2015).

Chiquier, L (2006). Poland – Housing finance policy note, *World Bank Working Papers*, No 37143 [Online] Available: http://documents.worldbank.org/curated/en/2006/03/7034239/poland-housing-finance-policy-note (accessed 29 July 2015).

Łaszek, J (2004a). *Sektor nieruchomości mieszkaniowych w Polsce. Stan i perspektywy rozwoju*, Monografie i opracowania, Nr 525, Szkoła Główna Handlowa w Warszawie, Warsaw.

Łaszek, J (2004b). Bariery rozwoju rynku nieruchomości mieszkaniowych w Polsce, *Materiały i studia nr 184*, NBP, Warsaw.

Merrill, S, Lawrence, R, Garnett, H, Urbańska, W, Kozłowski, E, Łaszek, J (1998). *Local Government Rent Policy and Best Practice in Poland: The Need for Rent Reform and an Improved Housing Allowance Program*. The Urban Institute, Washington [Online] Available: http://pdf.usaid.gov/pdf_docs/Pnacj143.pdf (accessed 29 July 2015).

Merrill, S (2000). *A decade of building housing finance in Poland. Challenges at the outset of the new century*. The Urban Institute, Washington [Online] Available: http://pdf.usaid.gov/pdf_docs/Pnacj152.pdf (accessed 29 July 2015).

NBP (2014). *Informacja o cenach mieszkań i sytuacji na rynku nieruchomości mieszkaniowych i komercyjnych w Polsce; Quarter report*, NBP, Warszawa [Online] Available: www.nbp.pl/publikacje/rynek_nieruchomosci/ceny_mieszkan_09_2014.pdf (accessed 3 August 2015).

18

The Housing Finance System in Portugal since the 1980s

Romana Xerez and Jaime R. S. Fonseca
School of Social and Political Sciences/University of Lisbon,
Centre for Public Administration and Public Policies, Lisbon, Portugal

Introduction

Portugal has been experiencing financial problems since the 2007–2008 Global Financial Crisis (GFC) and has had to follow a strict austerity programme overseen by the Troika (European Union [EU], European Central Bank [ECB] and the International Monetary Fund [IMF]). The economy has contracted sharply, with house prices falling and unemployment rising. This has affected all sectors, especially the construction industry (Banco de Portugal 2013). The sector has fallen into debt, with almost 40 percent of credit formally in default. The economic situation has also adversely affected households. In 2011 the household budget survey (INE 2012) showed that housing expenses (including water, electricity, gas, condominium insurance, cleaning, minor repairs, rent and mortgage repayments) accounted for 29.1 percent of overall household spending. The housing cost overburden, when the ratio of annual expenditure on housing compared to disposable income is higher than 40 percent of total income, was 10.4 percent in 2010 and 11.7 percent in 2011.

Housing is financed in three major ways in Portugal: through public funds in the case of social housing, through family financing and through bank loans. The Portuguese housing finance system has supported high rates of construction, which in turn has driven strong growth in the housing market in recent decades. Because of this, however, supply has outstripped demand. In 2011, the number of dwellings in Portugal exceeded the number

Milestones in European Housing Finance, First Edition.
Edited by Jens Lunde and Christine Whitehead.
© 2016 John Wiley & Sons, Ltd. Published 2016 by John Wiley & Sons, Ltd.

of households by 45 percent (INE 2011). About 32 percent of dwellings were second or vacant homes, representing an increase of 2.7 percent between 2001 and 2011. Almost half the vacant homes were for sale and had been built after 1990. Some of these vacant homes are inherited properties, but a significant number are the result of growing rates of second homeownership, especially in areas near the beach such as the Algarve. Over 50 percent of owner-occupiers had monthly mortgage repayments of between €250 and €500 (INE 2011).

Today, the credit market is more regulated and it is much more difficult to access housing credit. Loan-to-value ratios (LTVs) are lower and loan maturities are longer (40–50 years) (European Central Bank 2009). Portugal has seen an increase in the proportion of people renting (INE 1991; 2001; 2011) and increasing numbers of people defaulting on mortgages, sometimes resulting in foreclosure and eviction. However, according to the Bank of Portugal there has been no real estate bubble in Portugal. To explain these realities we need to look at how Portugal's housing finance system developed into what it looks like today.

Housing has always played an important role in Portugal, but the Portuguese housing market and housing finance system have undergone considerable changes as a result of various economic and social impacts. The building boom that began in the 1980s was in response to the previous period, lasting many decades, of housing need and shortages. Several factors combined to encourage this increase in output, including cultural values related to housing, a legacy of family financing, public policies, Portugal's accession to the European Union, privatisation, liberalisation and expansion of the housing finance market and the role of housing in the welfare state (Xerez and Fonseca 2013). Interestingly, while the situation in Portugal between 1989 and 2009 was characterised by expanding homeownership and housing credit, deregulation and access to large sources of funds and loans with high LTVs and 20-year maturities, this contrasts sharply with the present position.

This chapter begins by discussing some of the main social, economic and political factors underpinning the housing finance system in Portugal during the boom period. It then analyses the housing market and discusses three milestones and their implications, before closing with a few concluding remarks.

Context: a legacy of family financing, the impact of the 1974 revolution and the period to 1989

In Portugal, as in the other Southern European countries, family has played an important role in both the financing and the provision of housing through self-promotion (Allen *et al.* 2004; Fahey and Norris 2011; Minas *et al.* 2013).

In Portugal before the GFC, it was common for families to provide financial support for down payments on property, to contribute financially towards monthly outgoings (be they related to housing or services like education) and to assist in the repayment of housing loans. After the crisis, these roles of family support have changed because of increasing unemployment and reductions to pensions. Portuguese mortgage loans are frequently secured by collateral and/or personal guarantors, usually family members, which reduce the risks of financial instability. More than 90 percent of borrowers are covered by collateral guarantees and about 10 percent by personal guarantors (Banco de Portugal 2013). Since the crisis, the extent of family support has changed due to increasing unemployment and reductions to pensions. Nevertheless, the role of family in Portuguese housing finance is very significant and more in-depth research is needed to fully understand how changes to this tradition of family support may impact housing markets and the housing finance system.

In addition to the large role traditionally played by families, the Portuguese housing market has been very significantly influenced by the events of the 1974 revolution (Perista and Baptista 2007). Although this research largely focuses on trends and milestones from 1989 onwards, the revolution greatly contributed to the development of a unique housing finance system in Portugal and therefore must be discussed to establish the political and socio-logical context for what happened after the late 1980s.

Housing was a significant social problem after the 1974 revolution. In the mid-1970s, about six million Portuguese were living in poor condi-tions. Moreover, half a million people had emigrated from the former Portuguese colonies in Africa and needed homes. Because there was an insufficient supply of dwellings, many people were forced to live in sublet unsuitable properties, which were particularly poor in the metropolitan areas. During this period, the state began to show a willingness to imple-ment a positive housing policy. In the mid-1970s and 1980s the political response to the housing shortage was to encourage homeownership, which influenced the economic and institutional environment of the housing market and its regulation. The right to a home became a constitutional right in 1976, and the Ministry of Housing became primarily responsible for ensuring that it was achieved.

The post-revolution period was characterised by macro-economic insta-bility. This led to two agreements with the IMF between 1978–1979 and 1983–1985, which implemented credit limits to prevent excessive monetary expansion. Banks were nationalised after the revolution in 1975, but they were reprivatised between 1985 and 1989. Liberalisation of the banking system occurred in the late 1980s, later than in most EU countries: the first Portuguese private bank emerged in 1986; the stock market was set up and the majority of lending rates were liberalised except for housing credit in 1988; and the full liberalisation of deposit rates and capital movements occurred in 1992 (Antão *et al.* 2009). The market share of state-owned banks decreased from 74 percent in 1990 to 24 percent in 1996. Portugal's financial integration with Europe allowed interest rates to converge towards lower and less volatile levels. This process increased competition among banks and marked a new phase in Portugal's economic development (Banco de Portugal 2009).

Some important innovative policies and programmes were introduced during the post revolution period that further influenced the economic and financial context. Towards the end of the 1970s, governments sought to revive the housing and construction sector in order to create jobs and address housing needs. The Bank of Portugal introduced special conditions for funding the sector, and public policies promoted homeownership. Loans were intended particularly to assist low-income families in exercising their right to housing. Housing cooperatives, created in the late 1970s, were also designed to ensure the population had access to homes. Legislation created a financial system that incentivised the purchase and construction of new dwellings through lower interest rates supported by the state, the Bank of Portugal and banks. Although this system contributed to the development of the construction sector and increased the number of home loans, these measures could not address the difficulties faced by the lowest-income families. Consequently, these groups became the target of social housing policies from the late 1970s.

Economic and financial problems and a painful IMF intervention at the end of the decade, which had a particularly negative impact on housing costs and rising interest rates, led to an almost unbearable financial burden for many households. New support measures were created and new legislation was introduced to regulate lending and create financial incentives for the purchase, construction, improvement and expansion of housing. New social housing legislation was passed in 1983. This policy was designed to provide low-income families who were unable to purchase a home with an allowance to enable them to rent one. A mass social housing construction programme was introduced. Even so, social housing represented only about 3 percent of the total amount of the housing stock.

Governments introduced housing savings accounts to help develop the housing market and overcome the crisis. In the 1980s, the different governments in collaboration with the Bank of Portugal and other banks introduced further credit measures in support of homeownership.

The mortgage system and market at the end of the 1980s underwent significant deregulation as part of the wider liberalisation and Europeanisation of the Portuguese economy. The repayment period for most mortgage loans was about 20 years. Now the mortgage system has changed enormously becoming far more regulated, with repayment periods expanded to as high as 50 years.

Another important issue has been taxation. The main tax on landlords in Portugal is the Municipal Property Tax (IMI), based on property valuations. Urban property tax rates range between 0.3 and 0.5 percent. Municipalities determine the applicable rate, which can vary by about 30 percent. This tax was increased after 2012 as a result of Troika influence. In 2008, while the transactions costs of purchasing a dwelling including taxation in the EU14 countries accounted for on average 5.3 percent of the property price (and 11.4 percent in neighbouring Spain), in Portugal it was much lower (2.5 percent) (European Mortgage Federation 2010).

The 1980s state welfare crisis and more liberal public policies gave rise to decentralisation, in which social housing was transferred to local munici-palities (Ferreira 1987; Plano Estratégico de Habitação 2007; Guerra 2011). After joining the European community in 1986, access to European funds had an immense impact on the finance and expansion of social housing in Portugal. Toward the end of the 1980s, social housing tenants were given the option to buy their homes. Although this enabled families with few financial resources to be homeowners, the debt repayment terms (three times the minimum wage) were only compatible with long maturity and high LTV (100 percent) loans. In effect, these policy changes led to social housing being seen in a policy sense as a temporary or transitional solution.

In all, the 1980s were a period of financial liberalisation, economic expan-sion and development of the construction sector to boost employment. Entry into the European community boosted the economy and consumer confidence. As a result of the high inflation rates, privatisation and growth in the housing market experienced during the 1980s, Portugal entered the next decade with an optimistic outlook on its social and economic future. With this context established, the next section explores three periods of key milestones in the last 25 years of housing finance.

Milestones in the development of the Portuguese housing market and housing finance since 1989

Table 18.1 details the three main milestone periods in the development of Portuguese housing finance and the key events in each period.

Figure 18.1 charts the relationship between house prices and the key milestone periods identified in this chapter: in the first milestone period, there was a sharp increase in house prices during the building boom; there is a more moderate increase during the second milestone period leading towards the GFC; and after the crisis, we see prices begin to decline. Figure 18.1 also compares Portuguese house price trends with Spain, Germany and the Netherlands. It suggests that the Portuguese economic cycle has followed a different pattern to some of its European comparators.

Table 18.1   Timeline of housing finance and regulation milestones.

First milestone 1989–2002 Homeownership	Second milestone 2002–2007 Financial innovation	Third milestone 2008 onwards Crisis and regulation
External Factors		
IMF Intervention	2002 Introduction of the Euro	2008 Lehman Brothers filed for bankruptcy
1986 Accession to the European Union 1993 Single Market 1999 Announcement of Euro		2008 Global Financial Crisis
Legislative and Policy Changes		
Right to housing	Financial innovation products	Regularisation of defaults and PERSI
Article 65, Portuguese Constitution	Credit institutions must give customers information on interest rates and other loan costs	Action Plan for the Risk of Non-compliance – PARI (2012)
Housing savings accounts (1986–1989) Right to buy (1988) Subsidised loans (1998–2002) Covered bonds (1990–1998) Securitisation (1999–2002)		Responsible lending (2014–2016)

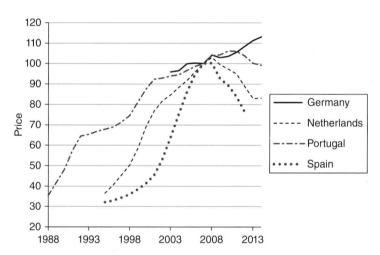

Figure 18.1   House prices in Portugal, Spain, Germany and the Netherlands (2007 = 100).
Source: European Central Bank.
Key: RPP.H.GR.N.TF.00.2.00.

First milestone: Homeownership and credit liberalisation between 1989 and 2002

Financial liberalisation began in the 1980s when the banking system was opened to the private sector. What followed was the modernisation of the financial system, the emergence of new financial institutions and products, the liberalisation of interest rates, the abolition of credit constraints and the liberalisation of capital movements in late 1992. Privatisation increased capital market liquidity, which allowed the credit market and, in particular, the mortgage market to develop for both investors and families (Banco de Portugal 2004).

The first housing finance milestone, which began in 1989 and ended in 2002, was a period of increasing homeownership and credit liberalisation (see Table 18.1). Homeownership incentives, private house building, household savings, housing savings accounts, interest subsidies and covered bonds were key features of this milestone period.

Homeownership incentives and easy access to credit expanded borrowing during this time. According to the Banco de Portugal (2013) between 1980 and 1992 the ratio between the value of mortgage loans and housing owned by households increased from 4 to 8 percent. From 1993 onwards, this ratio grew much more rapidly to about 39 percent in 2004. The large numbers of households able to move from the rented sector to homeownership helped to push up house prices (Figure 18.1) and associated with this increase, mortgage debt grew over the next few decades.

House building in Portugal has increased by over 20 percent in each decade since the 1970s, but growth rates have slowed over time; building increased by 27 percent in the 1970s, 22 percent in the 1980s, and 21 percent in the 1990s (INE 2013). The decline of renting in Portugal was facilitated by this increased output, the decline in mortgage rates (from 17 percent in 1984 to 1.7 percent in the early 2000s) and the fact that rent legislation became outdated (INE 2013).

Until recently rents were kept very low, a legacy from the legislation of the mid-1960s. This rent freeze made the rental market highly unattractive to landlords (Perista and Baptista 2007); consequently, the private rental market now only represents about 18 percent of housing in Portugal (INE 2011).

The 1990s witnessed economic expansion, a housing market boom, credit liberalisation, subsidised mortgages from raised income taxes, an increase in housing construction permits (Figure 18.2), more second homes and changes in tenancy trends. Significantly, many more Portuguese people became homeowners with the help of a loan or a mortgage (Figure 18.3).

In the 1990s the Portuguese economy became more integrated with Europe and more globalised. The creation of a single market in 1993 and the outcomes of the introduction of the Euro in 1999 had decisive effects on housing in Portugal. Being part of the single market led to financial liberalisation, especially with respect to home loan interest rates.

The mid-1990s witnessed growth in private consumption as a result of expansion in employment, income and consequently consumer confidence. Household wealth increased as a result of developments in the capital markets and rises in real estate prices. At the same time, interest rates were low, which increased the number of housing loans and subsequently household debt. The flourishing housing market in the 1990s was based in addition on social and economic factors such as increased immigration and an increase

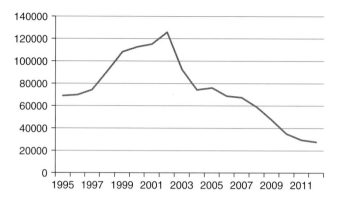

Figure 18.2   Housing construction permits.
Source: INE (2013).

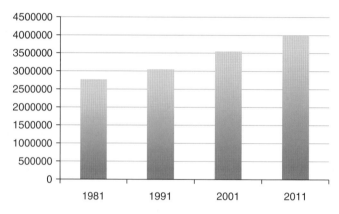

Figure 18.3   Homeowners with loans or mortgages.
Source: INE (1991; 2001; 2011).

in the number of people in their twenties and thirties, the liberalisation of mortgages and the introduction of new financial instruments that extended and subsidised credit.

The borrowing capabilities of Portuguese families changed profoundly over this period as financial assets grew faster than disposable income. In 1995, Portugal had one of the lowest housing-debt-to-GDP ratios, while it currently has one of the highest. In the second half of the 1990s, a large number of families had access to the debt market. Lower nominal interest rates, improved bank credit facilities, the increasing values of real estate and the vast supply of homes were some of the reasons for the high demand for housing and consequent household borrowing.

From 1999 to 2002 debt continued to grow faster than disposable income (Banco de Portugal 2008). Housing construction continued to benefit from lower interest rates and improvements in the financial circumstances of Portuguese households. The use of bank loans to buy homes was already high and increased further. Subsidised loans and sharp declines in interest rates contributed to the growth in mortgages.

The 1990s were also a period of financial innovation. Covered bonds for housing mortgages and construction first appeared in Portugal in 1990. The legislation at this time allowed Portuguese banks to issue covered bonds. The legislation was later changed in 1995, and then again in 2006, to allow the extension of eligible credits and provide for a financial instrument based on underlying mortgage loans, guaranteed by central governments, regional authorities or local authorities in an EU member state. This gave rise to a new kind of credit institution – specialist mortgage lenders.

Market determined interest rates and increasing bank competition led to the need for a more transparent market and the publication of comparable information between institutions, allowing customers to compare loan rates. In 1994, the banks were required to inform customers about the costs of real estate loans, including the annual percentage rate (APR).

Securitisation operations appeared in Portuguese financial institutions in 1997, despite the lack of regulation. The legal framework for securitisation transactions was introduced in 1997 and amended in 2002.

Second milestone

After 2002, following the introduction of the Euro and the rules of the Stability and Growth Pact, which introduced control of public finances to ensure that the country's inflation and interest rates would drop, the Portuguese economy stagnated. The housing market also changed in the early 2000s. The construction sector slowed down in 2001 (Figure 18.2) and new subsidised mortgage loans were ended in 2002. The macro-economic situation began to worsen significantly. New rules from the Bank of Portugal issued in 2003 signalled a move toward tighter regulation and following this all banks were required to provide additional information when granting loans (Banco de Portugal 2003). The rules laid out the details that were to be included in the standardised information sheet, including the cost of opening and keeping an account and payments required during the life of the loan. According to the Banco de Portugal (2004) the number of new mortgage contracts decreased. Subsidised credit ended in 2002, which led to a significant increase in household indebtedness. This slowed two decades of a building boom in Portugal; however, banks responded to these trends by introducing creative credit products. This marked the second key milestone period in the Portuguese housing finance over the last 25 years: the 5 years between 2002 and 2007, which can be characterised as the pre-crisis period. Portugal experienced a deteriorating housing market during this period and increased difficulty in accessing loans due to economic problems.

The innovative products introduced in the early 2000s made it possible to convert short term liabilities into liabilities based on medium/long term collateral and typically a mortgage. There was a grace period in the early years of the loan and the possibility of deferred payments for a significant portion of the loan and other means of reducing payments in the early years of a mortgage. Banco de Portugal (2004) made successive reductions in interest rates. This more competitive environment in the mortgage market resulted in easier access to financing for those households that met the criteria. LTVs increased between the early 2000s and 2006, and the maturity of loans expanded to 30 years or more in order to respond to the signals of the decreasing housing market. Spreads were lowered and the banks were less stringent when approving home loans. Despite some reduction in sales and construction, house prices and borrowing increased in this period, consistent with the evidence from most developed countries where housing finance practices have encouraged homeownership by reducing monthly debt servicing costs in the early years of the loan. Long term, this can result in higher repayments for the borrowers and a fragile housing finance system (Scanlon *et al.* 2008).

The low interest rates and favourable contractual terms offered by banks continued to encourage home purchases and mortgage debt. These conditions have led to continuing financial stress because of Portuguese families' debt servicing costs compared to disposable income. Portugal has one of the highest household debt rates in the Euro zone (Banco de Portugal 2005). Overall, household indebtedness during this second period was very high, especially as a result of housing purchases and mortgage lending. The number of mortgage contracts increased by nearly 4 percent in 2004 alone.

In late 2005, there was a slowdown in mortgage lending and a rise in defaults on bank loans, followed by a rise in interest rates in 2006. Economic growth slowed during this period, and while unemployment began to rise, consumer confidence fell. Nevertheless, banks slightly relaxed their home loan conditions and there continued to be demand for mortgages.

The 2005–2009 Strategic Housing Plan pointed towards greater government involvement in the housing system, introducing strategic proposals for the design, implementation, monitoring and evaluation of housing, urban renewal and renting policies. They also introduced Door 65 in 2007, a special programme designed to boost the public and private rental market by reversing depopulation in city centres.

Finally, European legislation on responsible lending was implemented in Portugal in 2006. It laid out a comprehensive set of rules of conduct and requirements to be fulfilled by credit institutions.

Third milestone

Since 2009, Portugal has experienced a situation of economic recession, characterised by continued growth in public debt, austerity policies, the nationalisation of failed banks, external interventions (bailouts) and difficulties in controlling the deficit (Leite 2010; Lourtie 2011; Aguiar-Conraria *et al.* 2012; OECD 2014). Since the crisis annual GDP growth has averaged about 0.5 percent, in comparison to rates of more than 3 percent recorded after 1976.

As a consequence of the crisis, the Portuguese authorities took an even more regulated attitude towards credit institutions and bank customers. Additionally, they sought to reduce household debt levels with new legislation concerning the monitoring of public and private institutions.

The Action Plan for the Risk of Non-Compliance (PARI) was set up in 2012 to monitor loan agreements, detect default risks and implement rapid measures to prevent default. A Default Regulation Scheme (PERSI) was also implemented, together with the Banco de Portugal (2012) Instruction 44/2012, which detailed rules for reporting information on debtors in very difficult monetary circumstances who needed to renegotiate their mortgage contracts. Credit institutions must now assess the financial capacity of the consumer in trouble and where feasible, submit appropriate proposals to regularise the consumer's financial situation in line with their goals and needs. These measures are intended to finish by the end of 2015. However, while defaults remain very low, PARI does not seem to have been effective in directly preventing mortgage defaults, which have increased in the last two years and will grow further in forthcoming years.

The Troika has played an important role in the Portuguese housing system during this third key period. In particular it imposed legislative measures to encourage people to pursue rental rather than owner-occupation in order to try to develop the rental market in Portugal and reduce household debt (Troika 2011).

Impacts

The increase in household spending in the late 1990s was a result of a wave of optimism arising from a favourable business cycle and predictions of good prospects for future earnings after Portugal joined the Economic and Monetary Union in 1993. Positive developments in the Portuguese labour market, based on favourable job prospects, were associated with a better financial situation for many households. The macro-economic situation contributed to high levels of consumer confidence. This and a reduction in interest rates led to strong growth in consumption, especially home purchases financed by loans (Banco de Portugal 2013). The slowdown in the economy after 1999 and the rise in interest rates in 2000, combined with excessive household indebtedness, had a negative impact on the construction sector in 2001. Nevertheless, demand for housing loans remained quite high until around 2005.

Even before the GFC, mortgage loans from banks to households had begun to decrease as a result of the rising interest rates and the high levels of indebtedness among Portuguese families. The decline in consumer confidence may, however, have been the main factor responsible for this decrease in building permits and demand for home loans. In 2007 as a result of the international economic slowdown and rising interest rates, demand for housing loans decreased. The first decline in the mortgage market in Portugal occurred in the second half of 2007 and the first quarter of 2008 (Banco de Portugal 2008).

The default indicators in 2009 were very high and were associated with a sudden drop in economic activity in late 2008. Home loans, however, showed relatively low default levels, about 2.5 percent less than in consumer credit and 6 percent less than unsecured loans for other purposes. The relatively low figure for default on mortgage loans according to the Banco de Portugal occurs because of the comparatively small proportion of mortgage borrowers who have few financial resources (2013). Portugal, therefore, was unlike many countries where lending to families with limited resources was more prevalent, such as the US. Debt maturities in Portugal are some of the highest in Europe, in some cases up to 40 or 50 years.

The credit market bank survey suggests that banks made significant changes to mortgage policies before the start of the financial crisis (Banco de Portugal 2014). These changes included introducing stricter criteria for granting loans but placed fewer restrictions on products that adapted debt service to customers' financial capacities. As a result there was an increase in the number of requests to extend mortgage repayment times and to renegotiate older loan agreements. A time series analysis shows that longer mortgage periods are associated with greater competition and activity in the housing and mortgage markets.

There was a progressive increase in LTV from the early 2000s until the GFC. There was a reduction in margins at the same time. These data suggest an increase in competition between banks. After 2007, a rise in unemployment and the household tax burden, a decrease in household purchasing power, falling housing prices and a riskier mortgage market, made mortgage banks increase restrictions and reduce LTV. At the end of 2012, about half of the portfolio of loans to households for housing had LTVs below 70 percent, 35 percent had higher LTVs at 80 percent and 16 percent had LTVs above 90 percent (Banco de Portugal 2013).

One of the mortgage attributes that has changed substantially is loan maturity, which has increased significantly. There has been a trend towards longer repayment periods for mortgage contracts over the last decade. According to the bank lending survey, in 2007, more than 65 percent of loans had maturities of over 30 years (Banco de Portugal 2014). Approximately 36 percent of loan agreements were for 40–50 years, among the highest in the Euro zone (European Central Bank 2009). It should be noted, however, that Portugal also had the largest number of younger customers.

Portuguese mortgage loans have a low probability of default and a high recovery rate (Banco de Portugal 2008). This is because these loans relate to the households' own home and real assets are used as collateral. Additionally, there is a stigma associated with defaulting on mortgages, which might partly explain the relatively low number of non-performing loans in Portugal. Furthermore, Portugal did not experience excessive increases in real estate prices (Figure 18.1) unlike other countries, such as Spain.

Mortgage loans account for about 80 percent of debt in Portugal (*Official Journal of The European Union* 2014). Most mortgage loans are for housing and banks usually perceive this type of credit as low risk because of the safe-guard of private guarantees and the fact that there seems to be no real estate bubble in Portugal (Banco de Portugal and INE 2012; Costa and Farinha 2012; Banco de Portugal 2014).

From 2008 onwards, there was a decrease in mortgage loan activity as banks were more restrictive in granting credit and spreads increased, particularly for riskier borrowers. Guarantee requirements were also made stricter and transaction costs were higher.

The number of mortgage loans entering default remained low after the 2008 crisis. This is almost certainly because the percentage of low-income households with access to the mortgage market in Portugal remains very low (Farinha 2007). Furthermore, mortgage loans decreased from 2006, particularly after the GFC. There are now significant signs of improvement in the housing market. The confidence indicator with respect to construction and public works increased in July 2014 to its highest level since November 2010 (INE 2014a). This rise was due to an increase in orders and a decrease in unemployment. Expectations for housing purchase and construction have also improved. Rising housing prices and a significant pickup in buyer interest in Portugal are signs of growth in the housing market. According to the house price index (INE 2014b) there was a 4 percent increase in home prices in the first quarter of 2014, the largest gain in the last four years. Real estate transactions grew by 16.7 percent in early 2014.

Conclusions

Evidence suggests that there have been three distinct periods, which can in a sense be called milestones, of the development of Portugal's housing finance system, housing market and regulation over the last 25 years. These milestone periods must be set in the context created by government intervention in the post-revolution period in the late 1970s and 1980s in response to housing needs and shortages affecting about 60 percent of the population. Another legacy of this post-revolution period has been the right to a home, which has led to homeownership being seen as central to more than two decades of policy. Government policy promoting homeownership, the optimistic economic outlook and rapid increases in household income were the main reasons for the expansion of the housing market in Portugal. Between the mid-1970s and the 1990s, housing became a cornerstone of the welfare state. Portugal, because of its unique legislative context, its long building boom and the comparable absence of a housing bubble, offers an interesting case for research and international comparison.

As economic and housing market conditions changed for the worse appropriate policy and regulation responses from both Portuguese and international institutions have become necessary, not just with respect to managing the mortgage market but at a more general level.

First, the crisis gave rise to new social risks associated with rising housing costs, foreclosures, evictions, repossessions and possible homelessness. These factors disproportionately affect more vulnerable groups and can have deep macro-economic and financial consequences. Changes to social housing and housing allowance policy in Portugal are therefore necessary to address these emerging risks.

Second, as the number of people renting rises – and the number of homeowners declines – legislation is needed to protect people from volatile markets and economic instability.

Third, there need to be improvements to the way risk is managed in the finance and housing market in the post-crisis context. These may include the introduction of a more extensive credit information system, the strengthening of existing legal rights, improvements to publicly available loan information, and an increase in the quality of financial instruments.

This chapter's findings suggest that the development of the housing finance system in Portugal over the last three decades is closely associated with social, economic, political and cultural factors. These include the relative importance of individual homeownership over renting, the role of family support in housing finance, various pieces of legislation concerning the design of loans and the promotion of private housing, public policies which promote the purchase of homes and the virtual absence of a rental market in Portugal because of both rent controls and favourable mortgage conditions.

The results of this research suggest a need for further studies to assess the importance of family financing in funding housing in Portugal. Additionally, the recent increase in the maturity of loans to 40 or 50 years – some of the longest maturities offered in Europe – may be hiding the longer term costs of high indebtedness in Portugal, which could have effects on the national, European and international markets. Portuguese policy makers should thus devote significant attention to housing and housing finance when crafting future public policies.

Acknowledgements

The authors are grateful to the editors, Christine Whitehead and Jens Lunde, for their invaluable, helpful comments over the course of this research and on previous versions of this paper. They would also like to thank Pedro Rodrigues, Maria Olinda Garcia and Luísa Farinha for their insightful comments and suggestions. All opinions expressed herein are, however, the sole responsibility of the authors.

References

Aguiar-Conraria, L, Alexandre, F and Pinho, M (2012). O euro e o crescimento da economia portuguesa: uma análise contrafactual. *Análise Social* 47(203): 298–321.

Antão, P, Boucinha, M, Farinha, L, Lacerda, A, Leal, AC and Ribeiro, N (2009). Financial integration, financial structures and the decisions of households and firms. In *The Portuguese Economy in the Context of Economic, Financial and Monetary Integration*. Lisboa, Banco de Portugal, pp. 415–539.

Allen, J, Barlow, J, Leal, J, Maloutas, T and Padovani, L (2004). *Housing and Welfare in Southern Europe*. Blackwell, Oxford.

Banco de Portugal (2003). *Instrução 27/2003*. Sistema de Instruções do Banco de Portugal Banco de Portugal, Lisboa.

Banco de Portugal (2004). *Relatório Anual*. Banco de Portugal, Lisboa.

Banco de Portugal (2005). *Relatório Anual*. Banco de Portugal, Lisboa.

Banco de Portugal (2008). *Relatório Anual*. Banco de Portugal, Lisboa.

Banco de Portugal (2009). *A Economia Portuguesa no Contexto da Integração Económica, Financeira e Monetária* Banco de Portugal, Lisboa.

Banco de Portugal (2012). *Instruction no. 44/2012*. Banco de Portugal, Lisboa.

Banco de Portugal (2013). *Relatório de Estabilidade Financeira and Maio 2013*. Banco de Portugal, Lisboa.

Banco de Portugal (2014). *Bank Lending Survey |Results for Portugal |July 2014*. [Online]. Available: www.bportugal.pt/en-US/EstudosEconomicos/Publicacoes/IBMC/Publications/Results_jul_e.pdf (accessed 3 August 2015).

Banco de Portugal and INE (2012). *Inquérito à situação financeira das famílias 2010* [Online], Available: www.bportugal.pt/pt-PT/EstudosEconomicos/Publicacoes/ISFFamilias/Publicacoes/isff_2010_p.pdf (accessed 3 August 2015).

Costa, S and Farinha, L (2012). Households' indebtedness: a microeconomic analysis based on the results of the households' financial. In: *Financial Stability Report*. Banco de Portugal, Lisboa.

European Central Bank (2009). *Housing Finance in the Euro Area*. Occasional Paper Series no 101. European Central Bank, Brussels.

European Mortgage Federation (2010). *Study on the Cost of Housing in Europe*, European Mortgage Federation, Brussels.

Fahey, T and Norris, M (2011). Housing in the welfare state: rethinking the conceptual foundations of comparative housing policy analysis. *International Journal of Housing Policy* 11(4): 406–452.

Farinha, L (2007). O endividamento das famílias portuguesas: evidencia recente com base nos resultados do IPEF 2006–2007. In *Relatório de Estabilidade Financeira*, 2007. Banco de Portugal, Lisboa.

Ferreira, AF (1987). *Por uma Nova Política de Habitação* Edições Afrontamento, Porto.

Guerra, I (2011). As políticas de habitação em Portugal: à procura de novos caminhos. *Cidades, Comunidades e Territórios* 22: 41–68.

INE (1991). *Censos 1991*. Instituto Nacional de Estatística, Lisboa.

INE (2001). *Censos 2001*. Instituto Nacional de Estatística, Lisboa.

INE (2011). *Censos 2011*. Instituto Nacional de Estatística, Lisboa.

INE (2012). *Inquérito às Despesas das Famílias 2010–2011*. Instituto Nacional de Estatística, Lisboa.

INE (2013). *Estatísticas da Construção e Habitação 2012*. Instituto Nacional de Estatística, Lisboa.

INE (2014a). *Business and Consumer Survey*. Instituto Nacional de Estatística, Lisboa.

INE (2014b). *Housing Prices Index: Press Release*. Instituto Nacional de Estatística, Lisboa.

Leite, AN (2010). A internacionalização da economia portuguesa. *Relações Internacionais* 28: 119–132.

Lourtie, P (2011). Portugal no contexto da crise do euro. *Relações Internacionais* 32: 61–105.

Minas, C, Mavrikiou, PM and Jacobson, D (2013). Homeownership, family and the gift effect: the case of Cyprus. *Journal of Housing and the Built Environment* 28: 11–15.

OECD (2014). *'Better Policies' series Portugal reforming the state to promote growth*. OECD, Brussels.

Official Journal of The European Union (2014). *Directive 2014/17/Eu of the European Parliament and of the Council on Credit Agreements for Consumers Relating to Residential Immovable Property*. European Commission, Brussels.

Perista, P and Baptista, I (2007). Portugal: the sense of home. In: *Home Ownership: Beyond Asset and Security*, Elsinga, Decker, P, Teller, N and Toussaint, J (eds). IOS Press, Amsterdam, pp. 201–224.

Plano Estratégico de Habitação (2007). *Contributos para o Plano Estratégico da Habitação 2008–2013* [Online] Available: http://habitacao.cm-lisboa.pt/documentos/1234211200Q4s TG0sq1Kb68JW7.pdf (accessed 3 August 2015).

Scanlon, K, Lunde, J and Whitehead, C (2008). Mortgage product innovation in advanced economies: more choice, more risk. *International Journal of Housing Policy* 8(2): 109–131.

Troika (2011). *Memorando de Entendimento sobre as Condicionalidades de Política Económica* [Online] Available: www.portugal.gov.pt/media/371369/mou_20110517.pdf (accessed 29 July 2015).

Xerez, R and Fonseca, JRS (2013). A comparative analysis of housing systems in the southern European countries and Germany: how the Portuguese case matters? Paper presented at the workshop *The Housing Markets of Southern Europe in Face of the Crisis*. 1–5 December, Goerlitz.

19

Evolution of the Housing Finance System in Russia

Maria Plotnikova[a], Andrey Tumanov[b] and
Evgeniya Zhelezova[b]

[a] *Aberystwyth University, Penglais, Aberystwyth, Ceredigian, Wales, UK*
[b] *Agency for Housing Mortgage Lending, Moscow, Russia*

Introduction

Before and after the change to a market economy in the early 1990s, the housing finance policy objective has remained the same: facilitating housing provision for the population. In the Soviet Union, this objective was achieved through increasing the housing supply by building state-owned housing, which would then be distributed to households free of charge. Housing loans were available only to households who became part of a limited number of cooperatives to supplement the savings they used to finance construction of multi-family buildings. The equivalent of buying a dwelling on a secondary market was exchanging dwellings with other households. Increasing new supply aimed to alleviate the housing shortage that was pervasive in the Soviet Union and carried on into the post-reform period. This housing shortage was experienced particularly in cities.

After the change to a market economy the means of achieving the objective of housing provision have changed from building housing to enabling households to buy housing on the housing market. The housing market had to be created through privatisation of existing housing. The market was thin with a limited number of transactions that only wealthier strata of the population could afford: hence the need for mortgage finance. Housing finance policy came to incorporate the development of mortgage finance institutions and a legal foundation. The mortgage industry is the smallest

Milestones in European Housing Finance, First Edition.
Edited by Jens Lunde and Christine Whitehead.
© 2016 John Wiley & Sons, Ltd. Published 2016 by John Wiley & Sons, Ltd.

among transition countries but has been growing rapidly. It is dominated by state banks but the majority of households still do not earn enough to qualify to take out a mortgage. Another important dimension of housing finance policy after the change to a market economy has been the subsidisation of housing demand through various subsidy schemes for poorer households and special categories of households, such as young families. This dimension of housing finance policy is path-dependent on the Soviet system of housing distribution where, to this day, households on waiting lists receive free housing from the state.

Brief review of basic features of the Soviet era housing system

The salient features of the socialist housing model were the dominance of public ownership of housing, strong socialist tenancy rights, subsidised housing provision and limited cost recovery from tenants, a state monopoly in construction and housing maintenance and the absence of property rights and land markets.

Throughout the Soviet period, housing was owned, financed and built by the state. In the Soviet Union the share of housing under state control was much higher than in other countries: 78 percent in the former Soviet Union versus 56 percent in Poland, 34 percent in Czechoslovakia (1988), 33 percent in Romania and Slovenia and 25 percent in Hungary. Because of the state monopoly resources were used inefficiently as construction enterprises did not have to compete on the market and were always financed by the state. Since the objective was to build more to satisfy the excess demand for housing, the emphasis was on the quantity of housing produced at the expense of housing quality. State-owned housing was allocated to households on the basis of need defined by average living space per household member. The low rent that residents had to pay contributed to the distortion, so the quality of housing was low and the shortage of living space manifested in long waiting times in the housing 'queue'. Strong tenancy rights (tenants could not be evicted except for safety reasons) signified quasi-ownership of the dwelling with the right to reside passed on to descendants of the original occupants. The possibility of moving to another dwelling could only be realised through exchange. This often involved long chains of exchange and illegal side payments.

State-ownership was primarily an urban feature. In rural areas and small towns individual family houses were privately built and owned. Individual home building could be part-financed by loans from state banks. Another form of state ownership that was common during this period was enterprise housing. A large proportion of housing was built and owned by enterprises to house their employees. Enterprise-housing was common in industrial towns.

To help solve the problem of the housing shortage from the 1960s the government started to allow housing cooperatives in which households contributed a portion of construction cost. The overall share of cooperative housing has been 8–10 percent. Only households living in over-crowded conditions (not exceeding 5–7 m per person) were allowed to participate in cooperatives, which meant that cooperative housing existed primarily in large cities. Cooperative housing was financed through savings and loans from state banks provided that private savings amounted to 40 percent of the loan. The interest rate for individual house building was 2 percent, while housing construction cooperatives were charged 0.5 percent. Both were below the 3 percent annual bank deposit rates. The fact that the lending rate was lower than the deposit rate illustrates how cross-subsidisation between industry sectors was prevalent in the Soviet economy.

The following sections review the major milestones in the transformation of Russia's housing and housing finance system over the last 25 years. The key periods discussed include the transition to a market economy (1990s), the formation of a housing mortgage finance system (1997–2005) and a subsequent phase characterised by limited access to cheap, long-term finance and low construction volumes (2005–2013). The major milestones within these periods are summarised in Table 19.1.

Table 19.1 Milestones.

Year	Regulation	Policy	Market Behaviour
1991–1993		Housing Privatisation	Mass-scale privatisation of housing by sitting tenants
1993–1998	Laws enabling the development of mortgage financing adopted	The state Agency for Housing Mortgage Lending (AHML) established	Increase in private construction
1997–1998 financial crisis		Government support curtailed due to budgetary squeeze	Lull in construction, decline in house prices and bank lending
2004–2007	Housing Code adopted in 2004	Securitisation of mortgages National Housing Project launched in 2005	Housing and mortgage market growing
2008–2009 financial crisis		Anti-crisis measures in housing and mortgage market; ARHML established	Decline in mortgage and housing markets followed by recovery
2014–2015 Recession		'Social' Mortgage	Decline in mortgage lending followed by recovery

The housing system during the transition to a market economy (1990s)

In the 1990s, the key objective of the state was to put in place an institutional and legal basis for the housing sector to function in the free market economy. The objective of housing reforms was to rectify the distortions that came about as a result of reliance on the socialist housing model (Hegedus and Tosics 1996). Basic laws governing both the relations in the housing and financial spheres–that is, the respective chapters of the Civil Code and the Banks and Bank Activity Law–were enacted in this period. The Law 'On the foundations of the federal housing policy' that came into force on 24 December 1992 enabled the institutional reforms in the housing system to take shape in the coming years.

In this early period of transition to a market economy, the government's endeavours were primarily aimed at creating conditions for market mechanism to work in the housing sector. The most important of these reforms was housing privatisation, which started in 1991. It enabled tenants to acquire their unit (initially at little cost and, since 1992, for free) simply by applying for the transfer of ownership. The original terminal date for privatisation was scheduled to be 1 January 2007; however, it was extended more than once (1 March 2010 and 1 March 2013) and is now set at 1 March 2015.

Economic relations that existed under the planned economy, including housing finance, unravelled and gave way to market coordination. Privatisation of the construction industry was necessary to reduce the inefficiency of large, highly vertically integrated construction companies. The construction industry was privatised quickly because of its high expected profitability. New construction firms were also established but total construction volume still declined in the 1990s: in 1990: 61.7 million m^2 were commissioned, in 1995, 41 million m^2 and in 2000, 30.3 million m^2 (Figure 19.1). At the same time, as a result of the liberalisation of home-ownership rights, private owner-building was growing rapidly: in 1991 5.4 million m^2 of such housing was commissioned, in 1996, 10.0 million m^2 and by 2000, 12.6 million m^2.

The government's support to enable households to buy or build houses was extremely limited because of the lack of financial resources. It mainly involved support for individual owner-building. As part of the federal programme 'Own House', adopted in 1996, the state contributed to the introduction of new technologies and the development of modern designs for single family homes. It also provided grants for building detached houses for households who needed amounts up to 70 percent of the construction cost and developed financial mechanisms for raising funds from banks.

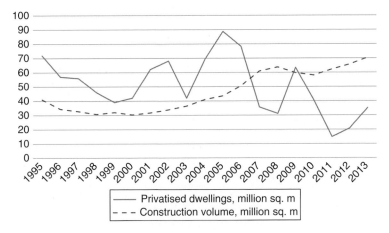

Figure 19.1 Housing construction and housing privatisation dynamics, 1995–2014.
Source: State Statistical Service, authors' calculation.

Forming the basis for a housing mortgage financing system (1997–2005)

As a result of the housing reform conducted during the 1990s, the housing construction sector was privatised, and housing privatisation was underway peaking in 1992–1994. However, housing transactions were few and it became ever more evident that to achieve the functioning housing market that was required, the ability to buy housing had to be enabled. This was to be achieved through developing the mortgage industry and through subsidising households in need of better living conditions who could not get a mortgage on market terms. The Law on Mortgages (1998) was aimed at facilitating the development of a mortgage industry and subsidies to purchase housing began to be allocated to qualified households.

The subsidy worked through allocating housing certificates (vouchers) to qualified households for the purchase or construction of housing. The difference between the value of the housing certificates and the price or construction cost of the dwelling was to be paid by the household from savings or through borrowing. Such subsidy amounts ranged from 5 to 70 percent of the construction cost or the purchase price of the dwelling. The value of the certificate was determined by how much the household earned above the minimum wage and how long the household had spent on the waiting list for social housing. It was also based on regional house prices, household composition and the living space area calculated using the household-size based norm: 33 m² for 1 person, 42 m² for 2 persons and 18 m² per person if a household included three or more members. For certain categories of people (military servicemen, rescue workers, survivors of Chernobyl and other catastrophes) who are subsidised out of the federal budget, the subsidy amount might reach 100 percent. The State Statistical Agency reported in 2003 that as a result of households taking advantage of these programmes the amount of private and privatised housing increased (Institute for Urban Economics 2004). The amount of privatised housing increased because in order to buy a new dwelling, many households had to sell the old dwelling to pay for the difference between the price and the amount of housing voucher money. Selling the old dwelling was possible only when the household owned the dwelling.

Housing construction finance

During this period housing construction was mainly financed by households, who purchased dwellings in multi-family buildings in the early stages of construction. Lower prices at the beginning of construction (up to 30–40 percent off the retail price of the finished dwelling) increased housing affordability (and thus demand for housing) and made investments very attractive (returns on investment could reach 50–70 percent per year when selling the completed dwelling within 1–2 years). Such schemes were therefore very popular and attractive despite the high risks of developer failure to meet obligations on time. The situation of postponed construction occurred frequently during the economic crisis of 1998, when developers could no longer finance the completion of one project by selling future apartments in another.

An unpredictable rise in construction material prices led to bankruptcy among developers and a growth in so-called defrauded homebuyers. Households that invested in construction were also exposed to the risk of being sold the same apartment as someone else because of fraud or non-transparent and unregulated relations between the developer and its contractors. It was common practice for a developer to provide apartments under construction to a contractor in exchange for materials and/or services. Households buying an apartment from a contractor were exposed to the risk that the contract between developer and contractor might be terminated leading to the cancellation of the contract between household and contractor. Inflation was in double digits in the 1990s and even if the invested funds were returned when the contract fell through, inflation had eroded the value of their initial investment making it less likely that they would be able to afford another housing purchase. To address these issues, in 2005 the federal law on shared participation in construction was adopted. This law provides protection to households and regulates relations between households and developers. In particular, the state system of registration of shared participation contracts was established; to avoid multiple sales of the same apartment developers were obliged to attract household investment only within the framework of this law. However, during the 2000s developers tried to avoid compliance with this law and continued to try to transfer risks to investor-households.

Financing housing maintenance and major renovation of multi-family housing

The problem of dilapidated housing stock originates in the distortions embedded in the socialist housing system whereby the state was severely resource constrained and did not provide adequate maintenance, focusing on doing only the necessary repairs. The ratios of income to combined rent and utility payment were low in the socialist countries – ranging from a high of 12 percent in Bulgaria to the lows of 2.7 percent in Czechoslovakia and 2.5 percent in the Soviet Union. No capital cost recovery was included in the rent, contributing to the problem of deferring maintenance into the future and creating a backlog in renovation. The under-financing of long-term maintenance was exacerbated after the transition to the market system.

The backlog of maintenance carried over from the past has been prohibitive to finance for residents, especially those on low-incomes. Multi-family housing management largely remains in the hands of municipalities. Private management companies are not common except in new buildings with wealthier residents. The main reason behind the lack of progress in the management of multi-family urban housing has been the uncertainty over financing long-term maintenance (Plotnikova 2009). Management companies have been reluctant to take on the management of buildings needing major renovation (or buildings with low income households) in fear of having to finance unanticipated expenses. In 2012 the Housing Code was amended to incorporate provisions to ensure residents' contribution to maintenance of their buildings. These long-awaited legal provisions also specify the uses of accumulated funds.

Mortgage finance

The development of mortgage finance required that a legal foundation and a set of laws such as the Law on Mortgages (1998) were adopted. Another milestone was setting up the state Agency for Housing Mortgage Lending (AHML) in 1997. The agency received statutory funding in 1998, which has subsequently been increased. AHML's objective is to facilitate the banks in issuing mortgage loans. The agency refinances mortgage loans by buying them from banks and issuing mortgage-backed securities (MBS) to attract funds to finance mortgage lending. It provides mortgage insurance, guarantees mortgage backed bonds of issuing banks and facilitates common standards among mortgage issuers seeking AHML's guarantees for their mortgage-backed bonds. AHML was tasked with creating these mortgage market institutions where there were none. These took time to develop, particularly as AHML's functioning was interrupted by the financial crisis of 1997–1998.

The 1998 financial crisis, characterised by portfolio investment flight from developing countries' fledgling financial markets, affected the Russian economy and significantly slowed the implementation of state housing policy. It started as a currency crisis when the Ruble was attacked by speculators but quickly evolved into a public debt and fiscal crisis. The government announced a moratorium on servicing its foreign debt. There were runs on the banks and many lost their foreign currency savings as the Ruble depreciated. Banks stopped lending so that construction ground to a halt and activity on the housing market slowed down significantly.

In 2000, in order to stimulate the mortgage market in the aftermath of the crisis, new policy targets for housing mortgage development were set out in the Housing Mortgage Development Concept in 2000 and subsequently revised in 2005. In 2004, banks were allowed to use foreclosure procedures on mortgaged property to recover the balance on mortgage loans when the borrower failed to comply with the mortgage agreement. AHML started refinancing mortgage loans in 2002.

The Law on Mortgage Securities (2003) provided the possibility of banks issuing covered bonds in parallel with the state-agency AHML issuing MBS. Khmelnitskaya (2014) suggests that there was competition (exemplified by lobbying in Parliament to pass enabling legislation) between the AHML government-owned agency model based on the American Fannie Mae and the 'European' decentralised model based on banks trading covered bonds backed by mortgages. But the state-mortgage agency model took hold and the bank-based model did not. Mortgage-backed bonds have been issued by banks but there was little demand from investors for these bonds because of their high risk. Later AHML extended its reach to guaranteeing mortgage-based bonds issued by lending banks hence reducing their risk and increasing the MBS market. The 2004 Law also allowed for building societies to be established. Such savings schemes were established to allow prospective borrowers to invest in them. The building societies could not have survived without having been subsidised by the state because the savings were eroded by inflation and housing price appreciation.

Despite these efforts the need for mortgage instruments is underscored by the fact that Soviet style housing exchange still takes place mostly in the low quality segment. Real estate agencies have been acting as stores of information on available properties. They serve as the intermediary or clearing house in the transactions where (in many cases) apartments are exchanged with a side payment to compensate for the difference in market value. The chain of exchange in some instances may be long and coordination is required for households to move in and out of the dwellings. These transactions are possible in the absence of commercial bank loans since fewer liquid assets are needed for such transactions.

To support the developing housing and mortgage market and increase the affordability of housing, the government introduced several housing-related deductions from taxable personal income. Households can deduct the costs of construction or purchase of an individual house (including the costs of land) up to 2 million Rubles and interest payments on the mortgage. If the dwelling is sold after it has been owned for more than 3 years the owner does not pay income tax (13 percent) on the sale. If the dwelling has been owned for less than 3 years the taxable income is reduced by the amount of the purchase price or 1 million Rubles (the average price of a 50 m² apartment was about 1.5 million Rubles at the end of 2004).

Between the market and the state (2005–2013)

Housing privatisation resulted in high home-ownership rates but the volume of transactions in the housing market was low, a characteristic of a 'thin' market. New owners were 'poor owners' who could not sell because few had the ability to buy. Housing affordability efforts were concentrating on the demand-side, and it was evident that the low effective demand could be increased through the development of the mortgage industry. But interest rates on mortgage loans remained very high because the lenders had little access to cheap long-term finance. On the housing supply-side low construction volumes were not sufficient to satisfy the modest effective housing demand and housing prices were increasing.

State programmes to stimulate housing demand and supply

In order to increase housing affordability the Package of Federal Laws to Develop the Affordable Housing Market was adopted at the end of 2004. It included the new Housing Codex, which spells out the state's obligation to provide housing only for low-income households. This underscored the attempt to get away from the legacy of the Soviet housing model where housing was viewed as a right and the state was providing housing to households living in sub-standard or overcrowded conditions.

Earlier housing policy efforts aimed at the supply-side had an enabling function; that is, they provided a legal and institutional framework for the functioning of the housing market and the mortgage industry, while the actual money was spent on subsidising demand.

In 2005 the Federal Government stepped up its involvement in the housing market by unveiling a comprehensive programme aimed at providing the population with 'quality affordable housing': the so-called National Priority Project in the Area of Housing (other National Projects are in provision of affordable health, support of education and promotion of agriculture). The National Housing Project reached beyond earlier efforts to stimulate demand and incorporated supply-side measures aimed at reducing construction costs at the pre-construction stage. These included financing municipal provision and maintenance of infrastructure, such as connecting building lots to utility mains and zoning.

The National Housing Project also included measures reflecting the government's commitment to subsidising housing demand. One spending priority area has been to subsidise the deposit for young, first-time buyer families. Another is to subsidise house purchase for certain categories of households, such as military servicemen, or those who worked in harsh or risky conditions (e.g. above the Arctic Circle). The National Housing Project, an ongoing programme still in place, exemplifies the housing system that has retained a strong legacy of subsidised housing coupled with the application of market reforms aimed at owner-occupation.

Household incomes continued to grow up to 2008 as the economy was expanding because world oil prices were on the rise. While construction volumes increased, these were not enough to offset the growth in effective housing demand facilitated by government-sponsored programmes. Housing became less affordable in 2006 and prices peaked in 2007 and 2008, the least affordable years during the measured time period. From 2009 housing became more affordable and continued to become more affordable through to 2014.

Development of mortgage backed securities

In the mid-2000s the economy was expanding and the mortgage market was growing rapidly. Even though it was starting from a low base, the amount of mortgage origination increased 367 percent between 2005 and 2006 and 112 percent the year after. The increase in market size was accompanied by the lowering of the mortgage interest rate from 14.9 percent at the end of 2005 to 12.6 percent at the end of 2007. Mortgage downpayments also declined. In the first few years of mortgage issuance foreign currency loans were common because the interest rates on foreign currency loans were lower than on national currency loans. Thus borrowers ignored exchange rate risk even though the experience of the 1997–1998 financial crisis and Ruble depreciation were in the recent past. The proportion of foreign currency mortgage loans in 2005 was 44 percent. While the amount of foreign currency mortgages increased in subsequent years with a peak in 2007 of over 118 billion Rubles (€3.3 bn), the percent share steadily declined reaching 21.3 percent in 2007 and 6.2 percent in 2009. At the same time more risky mortgage products began to be offered, such as mortgages in non-major foreign currencies.

The first MBS issue took place in 2006–2007. The issue was oversubscribed by domestic and foreign investors. AHML played an instrumental role in early securities issues. The other major issuer was the state-owned VTB Bank.

The Global Financial Crisis (GFC) had a negative impact on the Russian MBS market. All investors left the market except for the AHML. Thereafter, however, the dynamic growth in the mortgage market in 2011–2013 and the implementation of AHML and Vnesheconombank programmes to purchase MBS from mortgage-lending banks increased the interest of commercial banks in securitisation mechanisms. In 2013 Residential Mortgage Backed Security (RMBS) issuance volumes reached 140 billion Rubles and senior tranche ratings were the same as or even higher than sovereign (country) ratings. However, the RMBS market is yet to develop to its full potential: in 2013 the ratio of RMBS issued to originating mortgages was only just over 10 percent.

The effect of the GFC

The GFC caught up with the Russian financial system in 2008 with the banks experiencing serious liquidity shortages. Mortgage Lending volume declined four-fold between 2008 and 2009 while the number of mortgage transactions declined less than three-fold, implying that the average size of a mortgage loan was declining. Average mortgage interest rates increased from 12.9 percent to 14.3 percent (Figure 19.2) and the average mortgage term was reduced from 18 to 16.5 years between 2008 and 2009. As the economy contracted, the delinquency rate on all personal loans, including mortgage loans, increased. The volume of delinquent mortgage loans continued to increase up to 2011 (Kosareva and Tumanov 2011).

The decline in mortgage issuance and of consumer loans that are used to finance housing purchase contributed to the decline in transactions in the

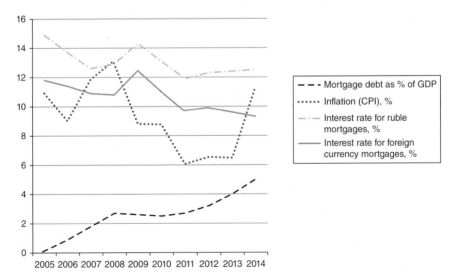

Figure 19.2   Mortgage debt, mortgage interest rates and inflation, 2005–2014.
Source: State Statistical Service, AHML calculations.

housing market. In 2009, the number of transactions in the housing market declined by 13.3 percent year-on-year. Housing prices also went down in nominal terms (by 3.7 percent between 2008 and 2009). Construction volumes declined by about 15 percent between 2007 and 2010.

The main idea behind the anti-crisis housing measures was to prevent the contraction of the housing construction and mortgage lending markets. The government together with state agencies such as the Agency for Housing Mortgage Lending, the Russian Housing Development Foundation, the Fund for the Promotion of the Housing and Utility Sector Reform and state-owned banks implemented the anti-crisis policy measures relating to housing finance. Measures included:

- AHML was recapitalised to the extent of 60 billion Rubles. These additional funds were to be used to refinance and reschedule mortgage loans for borrowers who could no longer afford to continue paying their mortgages as a result of the crisis;
- To assist households in trouble and mitigate the effects of the financial crisis, AHML founded the Agency for Restructuring of Housing Mortgage Loans – ARHML (a subsidiary of AHML). ARHML was tasked with rescheduling mortgage loans for borrowers who either became unemployed or whose earnings were reduced as a result of the crisis. Those eligible for support were granted a stabilisation loan to cover up to twelve monthly payments, any arrears (except for penalties) and insurance payments. For those for whom the basic loan support was not enough because of crisis-induced income loss there was a provision to allow their payments to be rescheduled. Additional support included AHML buying borrowers' mortgages and pledges from the lending banks to avoid foreclosure of their homes. ARHML support was later channelled into assisting insolvent borrowers from vulnerable categories such as borrowers from company towns who in the absence of support to pay their mortgage would stand to lose their only housing.
- In a measure that targeted a large segment of potential mortgage-holders, from 2009 the government allowed the 'maternal subsidy' (a one-off inflation-indexed sum paid by the state to mothers at the birth of their second or other subsequent child that could be put towards healthcare, education or improvement of housing conditions, but not earlier than 3 years after the birth of the child) for households with two or more children, to be spent on the improvement of housing conditions including repayment of mortgage loans immediately after childbirth/adoption.
- In addition to the measures to help borrowers suffering from the effects of financial crisis, the government strengthened its efforts to stimulate the market that had slowed down during the crisis.
- So that the government could continue to meet its social obligation to provide free or subsidised housing to certain categories of households, the

municipalities were enabled to purchase apartments at construction stage to make it possible for construction projects to be completed.

- The banks received financial support from the government totalling 250 million Rubles to maintain a maximum 11 percent mortgage interest rate for the purchase of newly built housing. The maximum loan-to-value (LTV) ratio on mortgage loans eligible for securitisation was increased from 70 to 80 percent in order to make mortgages more affordable to offset falling effective demand during the financial crisis.
- In addition to demand-side measures, the government used supply-side instruments to improve infrastructure and so facilitate the construction of housing that was affordable to middle-income households. The government also set up the Housing Development Foundation tasked with providing infrastructure on federally owned land and auctioning it to construction companies. This was intended to reduce overall construction costs and thus make housing more affordable.

The housing and mortgage sectors started to recover in 2010. At the end of 2010 ARHML had completed its task of assisting debtor households and its mission and name were changed. Mortgage lending surpassed pre-crisis levels and continued to increase. Arrears of over 90 days declined to 2.5 percent, down from 7.3 percent at the height of the crisis.

By 2012 mortgage debt had grown to 3.2 percent of GDP (Figure 19.2), which is still well below the figure for Eastern European countries where the ratio of mortgages to GDP varied from 6.6 percent in Romania to 32.6 percent in Croatia for the same year.

What lies ahead?

Lending volumes have been growing primarily as a result of the expansion of unsecured consumer lending. Steps taken by the Bank of Russia to improve the resilience of Russian financial system post-crisis served as the main driver behind the mortgage lending market growth from mid-2013. Responding to the high level of accumulated risk, the regulator introduced a set of measures tightening banking regulations for unsecured lending and revised minimum reserves rates, capital requirements and risk ratios for unsecured consumer loans. As a result, banks began adjusting retail lending strategies to refocus on a broader share of less risky secured lending. This development indicates that mortgage lending has the potential to act as a growth driver for the national economy and not merely for the banking sector.

From a long-term perspective, mortgage finance has a high growth potential in Russia as the share of mortgage debt in GDP is low in comparison to other countries. This potential is reinforced by the continuing need of the population for affordable housing. Facilitating mortgage lending can play a vital role in helping to boost consumer demand so long as improving housing conditions continues to be one of the most essential needs for Russian households. Mortgage lending can also boost growth in the construction sector and related industries through multiplier effects.

On a cautionary note, experience in other countries shows that the over-financialisation of housing aimed at fuelling the economy can make both the financial sector and the economy more susceptible to financial crisis. And over-reliance on mortgage finance renders the original intent, that of making housing more affordable, unachievable for regular citizens suffering from the crisis.

One important challenge for mortgage finance will be its resilience to macroeconomic shocks. The Russian economy has been subjected to many of these: as world oil prices stopped increasing in 2013 and declined in 2014, Russia's GDP growth slowed down to just over 1 percent in 2013 and came to a halt in 2014. Economic sanctions imposed against and by Russia in 2014, reduced or re-oriented trade and the decline in foreign direct investment affected different sectors in varying ways in what currently looks likely to generate stagnation of overall GDP. It was always difficult for Russian banks to secure long-term financing. The sanctions imposed on banks cut their access to long-term financing from international sources. Banks increased mortgage interest rates and decreased LTVs. Many banks stopped mortgage lending altogether, especially after the Central Bank raised the refinancing interest rate to 17 percent in November 2014.

The government has now taken steps to prevent the implosion of the mortgage system by subsidising banks to offer a so-called 'social mortgage' interest rate of 12 percent, while the Central Bank lowered the refinancing rate to 12.5 percent by May 2015. The subsidy is not meant to be long-term as the Central Bank is expected to lower the refinancing rate as the economy recovers, thus decreasing the size of the subsidy. However, the subsidised interest rate applies to new construction, only leaving secondary mortgage lending at market interest rates. Other variants of the social mortgage approach involve a government subsidy towards a reduced price for the dwelling or to allow the price per square metre to be fixed at a 'social' level that the household could afford with the help of a mortgage. The social mortgage is to be implemented in 2015 and AHML is tasked with overseeing its implementation by local governments. As with previous housing subsidy schemes, only certain household categories are eligible for a social mortgage. These include: households living in dwellings where space per person is below 18 m^2 or those living in dilapidated housing or buildings that are due for demolition; young families with one or more child where parents are aged under 35; families receiving maternity capital and families with three or more children; veterans of military actions; members of the military building (mortgage-saving) societies; and state and municipal executives and employees of large monopsony-enterprises in towns where the monopsonist is the principal employer. The role of the social mortgage as part of housing finance policy intervention underscores that to make sense of the housing finance system in Russia it is important to understand the interaction between market forces and the legacy of the socialist housing model, resulting in policies that are path-dependent on the latter.

While the banks have curtailed their lending, alternative lending schemes have emerged including developers selling apartments to customers in stages, for example requiring four quarterly payments. However, only a small portion of households would have access to finance to afford to pay for the property in the course of 1 year. With the overall decline in housing and consumer loans direct financing by households at the construction stage is likely to become even more prevalent. This underscores the overarching need to develop housing construction finance mechanisms that get away from the practice of end-users financing construction by paying for their dwelling before it is built.

Another challenge for the banking system is to develop its ability to satisfy the growing demand for financing to support residential development used entirely for the rental sector, as well as financing of infrastructure projects to enable such residential development.

Overall, the evidence of the last 25 years shows that the massive shift from state owned to private housing and to a lesser extent from state finance to market provided finance has taken time and resources in the form of housing demand subsidies. The legacy of state intervention makes it difficult to develop a true market particularly one accessible to lower-income homeowners.

However, there have been real advances in setting up the institutional basis for the mortgage system to evolve, for example the establishment of AHML and legal provisions for the secondary mortgage market. The development of mortgage finance will depend on the structure and evolution of the banking industry.

Into the longer term, housing remains a popular target for investment for Russian households, which will ensure growth of the mortgage industry in the future.

References

Hegedus, J and Tosics, I (1996). Disintegration of the East-European housing model. In: *Housing Privatization in Eastern Europe*, Clapham, D, Hegedus, J, Kintrea, K and Tosics I (eds). Greenwood Press.

Khmelnitskaya, M (2014). Russian Housing Finance Policy: State-led institutional evolution. *Post-Communist Economies* 26:2, 149–175.

Kosareva, N and Tumanov, A (2011). Housing market in Russia: Lessons of the mortgage crisis. In: *Global Housing Markets: Crises, Policies, and Institutions*, Bardhan, A, Edelstein, R and Kroll, C (eds). John Wiley & Sons, Inc., Hoboken, NJ.

Plotnikova, M (2009). Managing privatised housing: The case of Russia. In: *Managing Privatized Housing: International Perspectives*, Nieboer, N, Gruis, V and Tsenkova, S (eds). Wiley-Blackwell, Chichester, UK.

Institute for Urban Economics (2004). *Evaluation of the Scale and Dynamics of Changes in Effective Housing Demand and Housing Production in Russia*, Report prepared for OJSC Foreign Trade Bank in 2004.

State Statistical Service (various years). Federal State Statistical Service [Online] Available: www.gks.ru/wps/wcm/connect/rosstat_main/rosstat/en/main/ (accessed 29 July 2015).

20

Housing Finance in Slovenia: From a National Housing Fund to a Bank-Driven System

Andreja Cirman[a] and Richard Sendi[b]

[a] *University of Ljubljana, Faculty of Economics, Ljubljana, Slovenia*
[b] *Urban Planning Institute of the Republic of Slovenia, Ljubljana, Slovenia*

The economic and institutional environment of the last 25 years

The last 25 years have been turbulent for the Slovenian housing finance system. Previously a communist country, Slovenia constituted one of the six republics of the Socialist Federal Republic of Yugoslavia, which was created in the aftermath of World War II. In 1991, Slovenia – separated from the Federation – declared independence and abandoned the communist political doctrine, replacing it with a market economy. The shift from a planned to a market economy presented tremendous challenges that involved major transformations in the political, social and economic spheres including, of course, housing finance. As was the case in other Central and Eastern European countries, political doctrine obliged the state to provide housing for all citizens during the period of communist rule. This obligation was abruptly terminated upon the adoption of the market system. Instead of state provision, an enabling principle was adopted as the basic approach by which measures aimed at achieving the country's new housing policies were to be implemented. The state would, henceforth, provide assistance through various forms of benefits but only to those groups of the population that were not capable, financially or otherwise, of solving their housing needs.

Milestones in European Housing Finance, First Edition.
Edited by Jens Lunde and Christine Whitehead.
© 2016 John Wiley & Sons, Ltd. Published 2016 by John Wiley & Sons, Ltd.

The new housing policy specified two categories of tenure for which (indirect) state funding could be provided: social housing and not-for-profit housing (the category *social housing* was later abolished, leaving only the *not-for-profit* classification in use).

It is possible to identify several milestones in housing finance in Slovenia during the last 25 years. Among these, the most important ones are: the introduction of a market economy and the adoption of the 1991 Housing Act; the creation of the National Housing Fund; the offer of long-term housing loans; the introduction of mortgage lending; the introduction of a national housing savings scheme and the introduction of a subsidy scheme for first-time homebuyers (see Table 20.2, later).

The events of the last 25 years have significantly affected the system of housing finance in Slovenia and, consequently, the country's housing situation. After the initial drastic fall in public sector production throughout the 1990s, the level of new construction gradually picked up and increased consistently from 2000, peaking in 2008 when almost 10 000 new dwellings were completed. Until 2007 the Slovenian economy enjoyed a favourable economic environment and high growth rates in production, employment and investment. However, in 2008 the major macro-economic trends reversed and the country entered a recession as a consequence of the Global Financial Crisis (GFC) that began in 2008. Average annual house prices started to decline slowly. Partly due to much more cautious demand because of the grim macro-economic outlook, but mostly due to the banks being overburdened with non-performing loans, new housing construction sharply decreased after 2009, as did the number of housing starts.

Major policy changes

The 25 years since 1989 can be divided into four distinct periods in terms of the characteristics of housing finance as illustrated in Table 20.1.

The pre-market economy period

Prior to the introduction of the market economy, Slovenia implemented a fairly effective housing construction policy, which was financed from a variety of sources, the most important among these being contributions by

Table 20.1   Development of housing finance in Slovenia.

Pre-market economy period	The period dominated by the National Housing Fund	Bank-driven system	Bank crisis period
(before 1991)	(1991–2001) 199(19919991999)	(2001–2008)	(2008–)

state-owned companies, employees, the Social Security Fund and banks. Before its abolition, this system provided a stable source of financing that enabled the then state-owned construction companies to realise various mass housing projects, thus ensuring a steady supply of new dwellings in multi-family residential neighbourhoods. State funded housing provision was primarily meant for the social rental sector, albeit a small proportion of it could be sold on the market by construction companies, the purchase predominantly financed by loans often provided by employers. With a fixed nominal rate and high inflation, these loans often resulted in a negative real interest rate.

The abolition of the pre-market housing finance system meant that construction companies were suddenly deprived of a steady source of financing. As a result, some went into liquidation while others were privatised and broken down into smaller, specialised units (Sendi 1999). The immediate consequence was, inevitably, a sharp decline in the level of state financed housing construction.

Notwithstanding the declared objective (ideological utopianism) to provide housing for all citizens, the state was never able to achieve this goal. On the contrary, family housing (mostly self-built) constituted 67 percent of the total housing stock at the time of the introduction of the market economy. The main sources of financing were favourable company loans, personal savings and commercial loans (Lavrač and Verlič-Christensen 1996). It is important to note that a very large majority of self-built homes were constructed on land already owned by the future homeowner or their relatives, which meant that no costs were incurred in purchasing the land (Kos 1984).

The introduction of a market economy was an event that brought with it major political and socio-economic transformations. As such, the early 1990s were marked by the adoption and implementation of numerous new laws intended to facilitate the necessary adjustments to the new political system. In the housing sector, the introduction of a market economy meant the execution of extensive housing policy reforms. These reforms were implemented through the New Housing Act that was adopted towards the end of 1991 (see Table 20.2).

In addition to abolishing the system of financing new housing construction, the new housing law introduced several other housing policy reforms with immediate as well as long-lasting impacts on housing finance and provision. These included: the abolition of the stocking of house building land by municipalities, the privatisation of the public housing stock, restitution of previously nationalised property and the creation of the National Housing Fund as the principal governmental institution (parastatal body) responsible for implementing national housing policies.

Abolition of municipal building land stocks   The efficient implementation of housing construction programmes during the pre-market economy

Table 20.2   Major milestones in housing finance in Slovenia.

Year	Event
1991	• Introduction of a market economy • Adoption of New Housing Act • Abolition of the system of financing new housing construction • Abolition of municipal land stocking practices • Privatisation of public housing stock • Restitution of previously nationalised property • Creation of National Housing Fund
1992	• Provision of favourable interest long-term housing loans
1997	• Introduction of mortgage lending
1999	• Introduction of the National Housing Savings Scheme
2001	• Transformation of the National Housing Fund into a real estate fund
2006	• Introduction of a subsidy scheme for young family first-time homebuyers

period was also guaranteed by an elaborate mechanism for securing house-building land. This was essentially a land planning system that enabled municipalities to operate what used to be known as *Municipal Building Land Banks*. Through this system, municipalities could secure land, service it with the necessary communal infrastructure and keep it ready for housing construction and other community purposes. The acquisition and holding of such land stocks was abolished by the 1991 Housing Act.

Privatisation of public housing stock   The 1991 Housing Act also provided for the privatisation of public housing dwellings which, at the time, were owned by local authorities, state-owned companies and various government institutions. This measure offered the possibility of purchase by sitting tenants of the housing unit they were occupying at a considerably reduced price and under very favourable payment terms (Stanovnik 1994; Sendi 1995; Mandič 1999; Cirman 2006; Sendi 2009). The proceeds from privatisation were distributed in the following way: 10 percent to the Restitution Fund, 20 percent to the National Housing Fund and 70 percent to previous owners of the social housing stock (firms and municipalities). At the end of the privatisation process, some 66 000 social housing units were sold and with these sales the rental tenure was reduced from 31 percent in 1991 to 11 percent in 1993 (Hribar 1994; Žnidaršič and Hribar 1995). By 2011, the rental sector had been further reduced to 9 percent (7 percent social and 2 percent private rental tenure).

Restitution of previously nationalised property   Restitution refers to the return of property that had been nationalised (forcefully taken over by the state from private owners) after World War II to its rightful owners. At the time of the introduction of the market economy, there were about 13 000 nationalised dwellings. According to the data provided by the ministry responsible for housing, over two-thirds of these properties have so far been returned. Like privatisation, the restitution of nationalised dwellings resulted in the reduction of the public rented stock, which also contributed the massive decline in the rental tenure stated above.

While privatisation and the restitution of dwellings negatively impacted on the size of the rented sector, the restitution of land had a serious impact on the availability of house-building land. The reestablishment of property rights on land resulted in a scarcity of land for housing construction, leading to sharp increases in land prices.

The creation of the National Housing Fund   Another major reform measure introduced by the 1991 Housing Act was the creation of the National Housing Fund (NHF). Created as the main governmental institution responsible for implementing national housing policy (set out in the National Housing Programme), its major tasks were (and continue to be) to finance the implementation of the National Housing Programme, facilitate new housing construction and promote renewal and maintenance of the existing housing stock. The NHF was, indeed the dominant housing finance institution in Slovenia throughout the 1990s.

Period of domination of the NHF

The initial activity of the NHF was to support the construction, renovation and maintenance of housing by offering long-term housing loans on favourable terms to households and to non-profit housing organisations. With almost €60 mn of outstanding loans by the end of the nineties, the NHF had grown into the biggest housing finance institution in the country.

According to the Housing Act, the NHF was entitled to receive 20 percent of the revenue from the sale of the previous social rental stock and in two decades after the privatisation, it has received €208 mn from this source for its operations. The state was also legally obliged to support the NHF financially and there were periodical transfers of funds from the central government budget to the fund between 1995 and 1999. Since these funds were not sufficient to enable it to carry out all of its activities, the management of the NHF decided to raise additional funds by issuing debentures.

With its lending activity in the 1990s the NHF contributed to the demand as well as supply side of the housing market. On the demand side it used the funds to disburse low interest rate loans to households. In 1995, the interest rate in real terms for those loans was 3 percent, in comparison with the average banking real interest rate of 12.8 percent. A typical loan in Slovenia in the 1990s was an index-linked loan. The last tenders were carried out in 2001 and 2002, with a real interest rate of 1.75 percent to 2.25 percent and a maturity of 10–20 years. The amount received depended on the size of the household and income. Special groups, such as young households and disabled people were treated preferentially. The criteria for loan distribution were set by the NHF.

Similar to banking practices, the loans could be secured a lien on the property, guarantors or an insurance company. They were granted by public tenders that were usually heavily oversubscribed. Therefore, a proportional reduction of requested amounts was necessary. The use of loan proceeds was limited to housing, but no limitations were placed on size or price. However, each tender was limited to a certain use for the loan proceeds, for example renovation, construction and purchase. By 2002 the NHF had carried out 20 tenders for low interest rate loans to households amounting to almost €300 mn. In 2001 commercial and savings banks and the NHF shared the market by a ratio of approximately 2:1.

The NHF also tried to stimulate the supply of non-profit rental housing. After privatisation the Slovenian housing market suffered a severe shortage of affordable rental housing. However, because of the institutional arrangements for non-profit rental housing provision with low rents, which included heavy regulation, the poor capital base and difficulties in accessing building land, the demand for the NHF's loans by non-profit housing associations remained relatively low.

The housing situation – with decreasing affordability due to rising housing prices – called for changes in the housing policy at the end of the 1990s. The challenges for the NHF were how to ensure further access to affordable loans and how to stimulate supply while ensuring affordable housing. In order to achieve this, two new instruments were introduced: the National Housing Savings Scheme (NHSS) in 1999 and withdrawal by the NHF from direct lending to households in 2001. This shift in its strategy enabled it to start investing directly in the provision of housing.

The NHSS was introduced as a tool for encouraging long-term savings, at the same time aiming to increase the supply of affordable, long-term housing loans. The Scheme was modelled on the Austrian Bausparkassen system. It consisted of 5- and 10-year savings contracts with a selected commercial bank. The interest rate for the 5-year contract was TOM + 1.65 percent and TOM + 3 percent for the second type of contract (TOM being an interest rate used as a proxy for inflation, set by the Bank of Slovenia on the basis of average inflation in the past three months). Every 12 months the government granted a premium of 8.33 percent of annual savings for the 5-year contract and 10.42 percent for the 10-year contracts. After the period of contractual saving, the savers participating in this scheme could secure a favourable housing loan. The banks were obliged to provide savers with a loan, which had to be at least double the sum and double the maturity they had managed to save. With the 10-year contract, the saver could obtain a 20-year loan with a pre-fixed interest rate of TOM + 3.8 percent. The 5-year contract gave the saver the right to a 10-year loan at an annual interest rate of TOM + 2.45 percent. For NHSS loans, banks were not allowed to charge additional costs for granting the loan or for its administration. The loan proceeds had to be spent on housing while the proceeds from savings were not limited to housing. The first saving contracts within the NHSS were released in 1999. Because of the limited amount of subsidy, the number of available contracts was restricted and after issuing almost 22 800 contracts in a week, the scheme was 'sold out'. By the end of 2003, 82 644 contracts had been concluded, the majority for a period of 5 years.

The NHSS was introduced in order to force the banks to provide a more competitive supply of housing finance (Housing Fund of the Republic of Slovenia 2005). At the time there was actually no real system of mortgage finance in Slovenia, since only a small proportion of housing loans was secured by mortgages. High real interest rates of around 6 percent in 1999 enabled banks to charge relatively high interest margins. The transactions costs amounted to 3–5 percent of the loan amount. For funding these housing loans, which typically had maturities between 10 and 20 years, Slovenian lenders primarily used saving deposits with maturities of up to 1 year with relatively high interest rates (Butler *et al.* 2002). By the end of 2004 the total amount of accumulated savings and premiums from the NHSS amounted to 3.9 percent of aggregate bank savings and 38.9 percent of long-term deposits with commercial banks in Slovenian Tolars (SIT) or foreign currencies (the NHSS reports in 2004 and 2005 do not provide data regarding the accumulated interest on savings).

A survey among the NHSS participants who took up the initial 22 800 contracts indicated a very high potential demand for loans (almost €264 mn); however, by the end of 2004 only €41.9 mn was actually borrowed (Bank of Slovenia 2005). There are at least two reasons for this relatively low demand. On the one hand, by 2004 the housing loans offered by the banking sector were competitive enough to keep reducing the number of savers exercising the right for the NHSS loans. This was the result of macro-economic stabilisation policies, the intention of entering the European Monetary Union by 2007, increased competitiveness of the banking sector and, above all, decreasing interest rate trends on worldwide financial markets. On the other hand, for an average participant, the total amount accumulated through 5-year saving in NHSS together with the potential loan amounted to an equivalent of only 16 m² of an apartment in Ljubljana and was therefore seen as insufficient to purchase an average-priced dwelling. Some savings were probably diverted to consumer spending, which recorded a relatively high rate of growth in 2004.

The Scheme definitely had an important impact on the banking sector. In the first few years the funds from the NHSS presented a relatively favourable source of finance for commercial banks. However, in 2002 deposit interest rates in the Slovenian economy started to decrease and by mid-2003 fell below the rates offered by the NHSS, thus reducing the attractiveness of the scheme's deposits as source of funding for the banks (Ribnikar *et al.* 2005).

Because of the very restrictive conditions the NHSS set for the banks (they, not the saver, were obliged to repay the premiums to the government if the saver did not opt to take out a housing loan within 1 year after the saving period ended) and the very inflexible terms of the scheme relative to the dynamics in financial markets, the banks no longer responded to the call to participate in the programme in 2004 and 2005. Consequently, although the government amended the scheme in 2006 the instrument gradually faded out of the market.

Towards the end of 2006, the NHF introduced a new financing instrument known as the 'Subsidy for young family first-time home seekers'. As the criterion for eligibility, the *young family* was defined as a 'household of one or both parents with one or more children, adoptees or stepchildren, provided that at least one of the children is not yet of school age during the year of submission of the application for the subsidy'. Initially, the subsidy amounted to €160 per member of the family but was increased to €300 in 2007. A young family was eligible for the subsidy for a maximum period of 8 years. This type of subsidy was primarily provided as financial support for the purchase or construction of a new dwelling, or for the reconstruction or conversion of an existing building for residential purposes. Beyond this type of subsidy, there was also a subsidy scheme intended for young families residing in private rented housing. In addition to the conditions described previously, eligibility criteria in this case also included the requirement that at least one of the parents had successfully completed education and was not older than 28 years (or 30 years in the case of having completed doctoral studies) in the year when the call for applications was announced. The rent subsidy was available for a maximum of 2 years. This clearly shows that the subsidy scheme, as a finance instrument, was primarily intended to promote homeownership and not renting. However, this subsidy was abolished in 2012 as part of the austerity measures adopted to deal with the consequences of the financial crisis that occurred in 2007.

Bank driven period

In the past, as well as at the present, there have been no banking institutions in Slovenia that have specialised solely in housing finance, though most banks offer housing loans as one of their financial products. Mortgage loans – or house-purchase loans secured by the dwellings themselves – were introduced in Slovenia only in 1997. Prior to that, housing loans were secured exclusively by guarantors (up to four creditworthy people had to stand surety to repay the loan in the case of the debtor's default) or insured by the insurance companies (with these insurance policies the banks transferred all the recovery procedures and associated risks to the insurance companies). The government did not offer any specific subsidies for housing loans disbursed by commercial banks. Unfortunately, there are no data available on the volume of housing loans outstanding in the 1990s (only total outstanding long-term loans to households). Outstanding long-term loans to households increased from 5.5 percent of GDP in 1995 to 8.7 percent of GDP in 1999 (authors' calculations based on SI-STAT data portal and Bank of Slovenia *Monthly Bulletin* 2004). However, there was a tax relief on loan repayment with a credit up to 3 percent of taxable income, which was reduced in 2005 to 2 percent for principal repayment and an additional 2 percent for interest and then completely abolished in 2006.

High real interest rates and high inflation meant that housing loans in Slovenia in the 1990s were limited to 5- to 10-year annuity loans (Housing and Mortgage Loans in Slovenia, 2002). Even in 2003, 23 percent of new housing loans had a maturity of under 10 years and only 4 percent were over 20 years. However, the trend was positive. By 2007, only 17 percent of new housing loans had a maturity of under 10 years and already almost 40 percent were over 20 years (Bank of Slovenia 2009).

From 2003, Slovenia also faced a trend of significant cuts in bank interest rates as a result of nominal convergence of domestic interest rates with the country's entry into the EU. The banking sector was faced with intensified competition and was struggling for higher market shares in loans. A lower interest rate was the most important factor behind the steep rise in lending activity by the banks. In 1999, the annual growth rate reached above 20 percent, but thereafter, strongly decreased and remained below 10 percent until 2003. The total household lending growth rate accelerated again in 2004. There were several factors for the growth in household lending (Bank of Slovenia 2005): strengthened economic growth; the low level of interest rates that encouraged consumer spending; the low household borrowing rate in recent years and a consequent rise in creditworthiness among the public; and the flexibility, lower cost and simplicity of banks' consumer and housing loan offers. Housing loans made a significant contribution to the rise in household lending. Year-on-year growth was constantly above that for total household lending (Figure 20.1).

Part of this growth in housing loans was due to the possibility of taking out foreign currency loans. Throughout the period between May 2002 – when households were first able to borrow foreign currency from banks – and the middle of 2004, the proportion of household lending in foreign currency was negligible. After Slovenia joined the ERM II (a mechanism which ensures that exchange rate fluctuations between the Euro and other EU currencies do not disrupt economic stability within the single market) in 2004, the net flow of household loans denominated in foreign currency grew very rapidly and the majority of these were housing loans. In 2006 only 32 percent of outstanding housing loans were in domestic currency; 47 percent were in Euros or Euro-indexed loans and 21 percent in Swiss Francs (CHF) (or indexed to CHF). The high proportion of foreign currency borrowing was due to EURIBOR-tied interest rates being more favourable

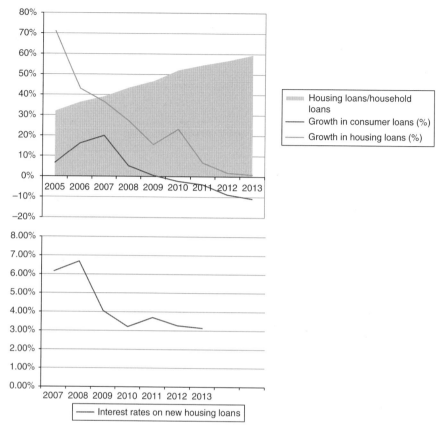

Figure 20.1   Growth in housing loans (left) and of interest rates on new housing loans.
Source: Authors on the basis of data published by the Bank of Slovenia in various *Monthly Bulletins*.
Note: Includes loans in which the agreed interest rate is variable or fixed for up to 1 year.

than domestic currency-indexed loans and to diminishing currency risk as a result of Slovenia's entry into the European Monetary Union in 2007. In 2007 the proportion of housing loans in Swiss francs climbed to 29 percent increasing the proportion of households that are exposed to foreign currency risk (Bank of Slovenia 2008). In 2007, 78 percent of such loans with variable interest rate.

In the early 2000s, mortgage secured loans played a smaller role in housing finance than they did in more developed financial systems. One obstacle to the development of mortgage lending in Slovenia was that a relatively large proportion of real estate ware not registered with the land register. Given the inefficiency with respect to the foreclosure of mortgages (the process could take years), a feature of housing lending in Slovenia was the widespread use of loan insurance by insurance companies. In 2004, 35 percent of new housing loans were insured by insurance companies and 32 percent were secured by a mortgage. In 2007 the proportion of loans insured by insurance companies decreased to 11 percent and the proportion of mortgage loans increased to 70 percent. Mortgages have in general longer terms (up to thirty years), a lower interest rate and a higher loan principal. Typical payment to income ratio was 33 percent, although in the case of higher incomes and housing loans with a pledge on real estate, this can also reach up to 60 percent. The average loan-to-value ratio (LTV) for outstanding loans in 2007 was 60 percent.

In 2006 the government adopted legislation permitting the banks to issue mortgage backed securities. However, no securitisation of residential mortgages has taken place. Before the financial and economic crisis banks fuelled their high lending activity with funds acquired abroad. The situation changed with the outbreak of the GFC and, in the following years, the banks were forced to repay a large part of their debts to the international wholesale markets. Restrictions on the funding side have also resulted in a reduction in lending to the non-banking sectors.

Bank crisis period

Slovenia, a Euro zone member country since January 2007, was hugely affected by the GFC that broke out in 2008 in the USA and started seriously to impact on the Slovenian economy towards the end of 2009. The International Monetary Fund (IMF) has reported that Slovenia's real GDP experienced one of the largest falls in the Euro area, a decline of about 10 percent from peak to trough (IMF 2012). While the economy showed signs of a slight recovery in 2010, this positive trend was interrupted in the second half of 2011 by the continued escalation of the Euro area crisis. After 2 years of decline Slovenian GDP is expected to grow by 2 percent in 2014 with steady increases forecasted for 2015 and 2016 (Institute for Macroeconomic Analysis and Development 2014).

The construction sector has been the worst affected and, according to the IMF report, will continue to decline. The credit crunch left the majority of construction companies without the funding required to continue their building activity. The ensuing decline of liquidity in the real estate market resulted in a growth of arrears among construction companies, eventually leading to the bankruptcy of major firms. According to data provided by the Agency of the Republic of Slovenia for Public Legal Records and Related Services, in 2012 bankruptcies were most common in the construction and the financial intermediation sectors (Figure 20.2).

This situation notwithstanding, the 2012 IMF report still found the balance sheet of the household sector to be relatively strong:

> In 2010, household assets excluding real estate (113 percent of GDP) exceeded total household liabilities (35 percent of GDP) by a large margin, and were relatively liquid, with slightly over 50 percent in cash or bank deposits. Household liabilities are mostly consumer and mortgage loans

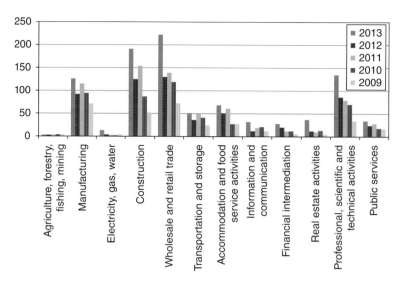

Figure 20.2　Number of bankruptcy proceedings initiated against firms by sector.
Source: Authors on the basis of data provided by the Agency of the Republic of Slovenia for Public Legal Records and Related Services (2014).

from banks with an average maturity exceeding 15 years, and the average loan-to-value ratio for housing loans is around 60 percent. The debt-to-disposable income ratio stood at 53 percent in 2010 (compared to close to 100 percent in the Euro area) (IMF 2012: 10).

In spite of the apparently positive situation, there is, arguably, one crucial issue of future concern. The implementation of austerity measures, job losses and stagnation or decline in wage levels are all already significantly impacting on the growth of disposable income. The adverse economic situation, which has been reflected in a decline in purchasing power, is gradually reducing household consumption and household saving. According to the Bank of Slovenia, household disposable income declined for the first time in 2012, by 1.7 percent. This has contributed to weakening consumer confidence, a growing uncertainty about income prospects and to greater caution in the spending behaviours of households. Consequently households have reduced their liabilities to all sectors. The Bank of Slovenia reports that the value of outstanding consumer loans declined by 8.8 percent in 2012 while the stock of housing loans has been stagnating since the second half of 2012.

The second issue of concern is the real estate price risk. The IMF reports that residential and commercial real estate prices increased by 40–50 percent from 2005 to 2008. After the emergence of the GFC, prices slowly started to fall in 2009 and it is estimated that there had been a general decline in real estate prices of around 10 percent by 2012. Currently, the potential for economic growth in the medium term that would eventually also have a positive impact on housing finance opportunities remains low. According to the Development Report 2013 published by the Institute for Macroeconomic Analyses and Development (IMAD), the continued deleveraging of banks and enterprises and the need for further fiscal consolidation, alongside limited sources of financing for the state and private sector, will remain the main factors that may continue to hinder a faster recovery of the Slovenian economy.

Impacts

The policy shifts introduced after the adoption of a market economy have had a variety of impacts on the country's housing finance system, its general housing situation and, especially, its current tenure structure. First, the abolition of the previous system of housing finance, which had contributed to the maintenance of a relatively stable housing supply, inevitably resulted in a sharp decline in the level of new public sector housing construction throughout the first decade following the introduction of housing reforms (Figure 20.3).

It is, however, worth noting that the level of new housing construction in the private sector continued at comparable levels even after the introduction of housing reforms. The explanation for the stability of housing production in the private sector is that such housing has always been predominantly constructed at the initiative of individual families without significant state support (Sendi 1999).

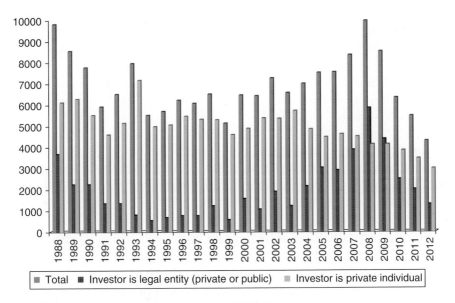

Figure 20.3 Dwellings completed by year, 1988–2012.
Source: Statistical Office of the Republic of Slovenia (2014).

The decline in the level of new construction in the public sector consequently resulted in a growth in unmet demand for housing. At the same time, housing demand was also stimulated by macro-economic stabilisation, coupled with decreasing inflation and interest rates, a growing number of households, loan disbursements by the National Housing Fund, increased competition and improved access to funding in the banking sector. This resulted in a strong increase in housing prices. Prices in the capital city Ljubljana (denominated in Euros) grew on average by 4–7 percent a year in the 1996–2004 period, although this growth slowed after the introduction of the NHSS in 1999. House prices, however, started to fall in 2009 as a result of the GFC.

Before the outbreak of the financial crisis house prices had grown continuously in Slovenia for almost two decades. As a result of the deregulation of the banking sector and the benefits enjoyed by the country after joining the Exchange Rate Mechanism (ERMII) and the Economic and Monetary Union (EMU), the availability of housing finance increased so that developers as well as households had better access to loans for the development, construction or acquisition of housing. The inflation stabilised, loan maturities increased and interest rates followed the trends in the Euro area.

Eventually, the banks successfully took over the role of the provider of housing finance from the NHF and channelled increasing amounts of funds into the housing market. The stable macro-economic environment and the entrance of a large 'second baby-boom generation' to the housing market led to strong pressures on the demand side of the market. However, as a consequence of the limited availability of building land, lengthy development procedures and high risks involved in these procedures, the supply side of the market was very rigid and could only react to the signals on the demand side with huge delays. Consequently housing prices increased, with the highest growth in the capital city and in tourist destinations. This happened despite the fact that the NHF intervened on the supply side of the housing market by contributing almost 5 percent of total new construction between 2002–2007 and almost 12 percent in the central Slovenian region (the area of highest demand) and was selling its dwellings at below market prices. Regardless of the benefits of better access to housing finance, Slovenian households continued to face decreased housing affordability throughout the period 2001–2007 as a result of constantly growing housing prices.

Stimulated by increases in real estate prices and strong demand, investors reacted with numerous new real estate projects that heavily benefited from the high liquidity and cheap financing offered by the banks. However, because of complex administrative and planning procedures, the majority of this increased output entered the market late in the period 2006–2009 (see Figure 20.3). This resulted in a large amount of unsold real estate property, the bankruptcy of numerous developers and construction companies, a huge amount of real estate-linked non-performing loans within the banking sector and an almost complete halt in housing construction. In 2012 the proportion of non-performing loans in the whole banking system stood at 14.6 percent. However, households remained relatively low-risk (with only 3.8 percent of their classified claims more than 90 days in arrears), partly as a result of their low level of indebtedness (Bank of Slovenia 2013). Since 2008, however, falling housing prices have contributed to increased housing affordability, but only few households are in a position to benefit from this improvement because of the prevailing uncertain economic situation.

While, on the one hand, the financial crisis led to a gradual fall in housing prices, it also had a very serious impact on housing construction activity. The credit crunch that led to the collapse of some of the major construction companies resulted in a sharp decline in the number of housing starts, which fell from almost 11 000 starts in 2007 to just over 3000 in 2012 (Figure 20.4).

Another major impact of the policy changes implemented during the last 25 years has been the further growth of home ownership while the rented sector has gradually dwindled to minimal levels. According to the 2011 census data, home ownership accounted for 92 percent of the total dwelling stock, an increase of 25 percent on the level of home ownership in 1991. The privatisation of the public housing stock, the restitution of previously nationalised property, the loan practices of the NHF, the operation of the NHSS and the implementation of the housing subsidy scheme are all measures which favoured home ownership and contributed considerably to the constant growth of that tenure.

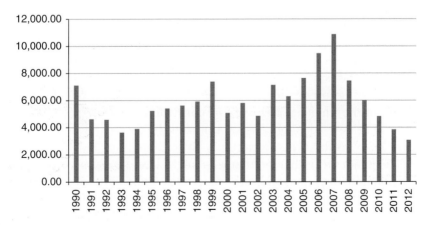

Figure 20.4 Housing starts by year, 1990–2012.
Source: SI-STAT data, Statistical office of the Republic of Slovenia.

Looking to the future

The financial crisis revealed many unsustainable business models within Slovenia's banking sector as well as in the housing development and construction sectors. A huge amount of the housing stock, leveraged with an abundance of cheap funds before the crisis, was left unsold on the market leaving the banks struggling with massive amounts of non-performing loans.

The supply side of the housing market is today faced not only with a low demand for newly built dwellings but also low profits and high risk. Practically all large construction companies that are capable of managing larger construction projects have become bankrupt and the banks have almost completely stopped financing new real estate investments. Although the demand for social housing has soared with rising unemployment, fiscal austerity measures have, to a large extent, prevented the municipal housing funds from responding. Consequently, the housing construction industry is facing an all-time low level of activity. From its peak in 2008, when nearly 10 000 new dwellings were completed, the level of new housing construction fell to a mere 4307 in 2012. A similar downturn can be seen in the number of building permits issued for new construction, which decreased from a peak of 9414 permits in 2007 to only 2700 in 2012 (SI-STAT data, Statistical Office of the Republic of Slovenia).

Generally, it may be argued that the introduction of a market economy and its accompanying policy changes have been the most important factors in the evolution of housing finance in Slovenia over the last 25 years. As a major element in the shift to a market economy system, Slovenia's housing policy has predominantly supported the demand side of the housing market, mostly orientated towards the promotion of home ownership. The non-profit rental segment of the market has suffered from inadequate institutional and financial arrangements and offers a safety net only to a very small proportion of the population. Government policies have reduced the rental sector, especially the public rental sector, to an almost negligible size. Introducing new housing policies with specific housing finance mechanisms for increasing the supply of rented housing must be one of the principle objectives of the new National Housing Programme that is currently in preparation.

Another important challenge for future housing finance concerns the current effect of the financial crisis on the construction industry. The decrease in the level of new housing construction and the drastic fall in the number of starts may result in a substantially lower supply of housing in future years. The major worry here is that this might later be a source of potential pressure on housing prices when the macro-economic situation stabilises. It is hoped that this problem will be effectively dealt with after the successful implementation, by the government, of the measures intended to revive and restore an efficient banking system.

References

Bank of Slovenia (2004). *Monthly Bulletin, December 2004*. Ljubljana.

Bank of Slovenia (2005). *Financial Stability Report*. Ljubljana.

Bank of Slovenia (2008). *Financial Stability Report*. Ljubljana.

Bank of Slovenia (2009). *Financial Stability Report*. Ljubljana.

Bank of Slovenia (2013). *Financial Stability Report*. Ljubljana.

Butler, SB Merstallinger, P, and Duebel, A (2002). *Policy Report: Legal Aspects of the Slovenian Mortgage Banking System*. Ministry of Finance, Ljubljana.

Cirman, A (2006). Housing tenure preferences in the post-privatisation period: The case of Slovenia. *Housing Studies* 21:1, 113–134.

Housing Fund of the Republic of Slovenia (2005). *Report on the National Housing Savings Scheme 2 2004*. Ljubljana *(in Slovene)*.

Hribar, B (1994). *Research Results: Household Consumption Survey 1991 and 1992 (in Slovene)*. Statistical Office of the Republic of Slovenia, Ljubljana.

Institute for Macroeconomic Analysis and Development (2014). *Spring forecast of Slovenia's main macroeconomic aggregates*. Ljubljana.

International Monetary Fund (2012). *Republic of Slovenia: Financial system stability assessment*. IMF Country Report No. 12/325, December 2012.

Kos, D (1984). *Predstavitev rezultatov javnomnenjskih raziskav o rezidencialnih aspiracijah* (Results of a public opinion poll on residential aspirations). Urban Planning Institute of the Republic of Slovenia, Ljubljana.

Lavrač, I and Verlič-Christensen, B (1996). Slovenia. In: *Housing Policy in Europe*. Balchin, P (ed.). Routledge, London, pp. 307–313.

Mandič, S (1999). Stanovanje, kakovost življenja in spremembe v zadnjem desetletju. Housing, quality of living and changes in the last decade. In: *Družboslovne spremembe na Slovenskem: ob 40-letnici ustanovitve Inštituta za sociologijo Univerze v Ljubljani.*, Boh, K (ed.). Družboslovne razprave, 15:30/31, pp. 186–208.

Ribnikar, I, Cirman, A, Čok, M, Groznik, P and Košak, M (2005). *Financing Purchase or Construction of Owner-Occupied Dwellings in Slovenia (in Slovene)*. Faculty of Economics, Ljubljana.

Sendi, R (1995). Housing reform and housing conflict: The privatisation and denationalisation of public housing in the Republic of Slovenia in practice. *International Journal of Urban and Regional Research* 19:3, 435–446.

Sendi, R (1999). Housing construction in the transition period: Slovenia's non-starter situation. *Housing Studies*, 14:6, 803–819.

Sendi, R (2009). Management of privatised housing: Slovenia. In: *Management of Privatised Housing: Internal Policies and Practice*, Gruis, V, Tsenkova, S and Nieboer, N (eds), Wiley-Blackwell, Oxford, pp. 229–255.

Stanovnik, T (1994). The sale of the social housing stock in Slovenia: what happened and why. *Urban Studies* 31:9, 1559–1570.

Statistical Office of the Republic of Slovenia – SI-STAT data portal (n.d.). [Online] Available: www.stat.si/statweb (accessed 29 July 2015).

Žnidaršič, E and Hribar, N (1995). *Research Results: Household Consumption Survey 1993 (in Slovene)*. Statistical Office of the Republic of Slovenia, Ljubljana.

21

Housing Finance in Spain: From the Liberalisation of the Mortgage Market to Booms and Busts

Irene Peña[a] and Baralides Alberdi[b]
[a] *Spanish Mortgage Association, Madrid, Spain*
[b] *Madrid Puerto Aéreo, Madrid, Spain*

The economic and institutional environment of the last 25 years

Over the last 25 years, housing finance in Spain experienced a huge transformation which allowed the creation of one of the largest home ownership markets in Europe. In the late 1980s a new-born mortgage market began to emerge in a context of economic growth and increased political stability after Spain joined the European Union in 1986. The mortgage market developed its main features over the following years and new legislation was approved to support this progress.

Between 1986 and 1992 the market was in a process of liberalisation with more lenders entering the market, more sources of funds available and easier terms for borrowers. Credit assessment, collateral appraisal and a greater harmonisation with European norms were already in place. However, loan-to-value ratios (LTVs) were still low and interest rates were mostly fixed to term, at highs of around 17 percent. The main funding tools were retail deposits and mortgage bonds. From 1992 to 1996 the Spanish economy entered into a recession that affected the mortgage market prompting an increase in arrears and a drop in gross mortgage lending.

After the recession, the Spanish economy entered a period of strong growth and high liquidity. Access to capital markets at very low spreads and

Milestones in European Housing Finance, First Edition.
Edited by Jens Lunde and Christine Whitehead.
© 2016 John Wiley & Sons, Ltd. Published 2016 by John Wiley & Sons, Ltd.

the outstanding levels of competition between financial institutions encouraged a drop in mortgage interest rates, improving the affordability of housing. Housing demand increased exponentially, boosting the residential market but placing upward pressure on house prices.

The onset in 2008 of the Global Financial Crisis (GFC) forced the housing sector to a standstill, both in terms of supply and demand, which had already been softening since 2006. The liquidity constraints and the adjustments in the real estate market were quickly passed on to the wider economy triggering a contraction in GDP and a fast increase in unemployment levels. Unbalanced real estate developments contributed to financial sector distress, forcing institutions to face severe restructuring and recapitalisation processes in order to restore confidence in the financial system and the flows of credit. Today, some signs of reactivation of the market have been observed in light of a sounder and fully liberalised financial sector.

Finance milestones

Table 21.1 summarises the key milestones in the development of Spain's housing market finance system.

The birth and rise of the mortgage market: 1981–2007

The starting point of the housing market finance system in Spain was the approval of 'the mortgage law' in 1981. Until then, mortgage activity was limited to savings banks, deposit institutions of a social nature that were linked to the public sector and were legally restricted to operate in their respective domestic region. Savings banks' sources of funding were exclusively short-term deposits. The only institution with authority for issuing covered bonds (*cedulas hipotecarias*) was the Mortgage Bank, a state owned bank focused on granting loans for social housing. This meant that there was no competition in the market and that the growth of credit was limited to the evolution of deposits. Tight lending standards characterised this period, with low LTVs and high fixed interest rates.

The objective of the 1981 mortgage law was to widen the market by allowing all financial institutions to grant mortgage loans and to issue the securities necessary to fund them. The security within the granting and contractual process was also increased and a detailed regulation of the valuation companies was put in place. This new legal framework and its subsequent legal developments helped to increase competition among financial institutions and to reduce the operational costs and length of the process. By the late 1980s, total outstanding residential mortgage debt-to-GDP almost doubled from 15 percent in 1983 to 25 percent in 1992. Furthermore, as a consequence of the incorporation of the European regulation on financial

Table 21.1 Milestones timeline.

Year	Financial Regulation	Policy change	Market change
1981	Mortgage Market Law.	Deregulates mortgage market.	Increases lending competition and availability of credit.
1992	Law on real estate investment and mortgage funds.	Creates indirect tools for investing in real estate market and mortgage securitisation.	Changes not enough to open and develop the rental market. Good results for mortgage securitisation.
1994	Law on subrogation and modification of mortgage loans.	Fosters competition among credit institutions.	Decreasing long term interest rates and conversion from fix to variable.
1994	Law on urban leasing.	Reduces tenant's rights.	More freedom for landlords although feeble impact.
1998	On securitisation.	Securitisation of other categories of assets besides mortgage loans.	Dramatic increase in mortgage securities issues.
2007	Reform of 1981 mortgage market law.	Grants liquidity, reduces interest rates risks, and introduces more flexibility to the mortgage market.	Difficult to assess due to the burst of the GFC.
2009	Creation of FORB.	Merger and concentration processes and solutions for credit institutions not viable.	Dramatic reduction in number of financial institutions, mainly Savings Banks.
2009	Rental market.	Introduces new investment figure the SOCIMIs (Spanish REITs).	SOCIMIs not attractive to market (i.e. taxation).
2012	Financial Assistance Program (MOU).	Recapitalisation of financial institutions and segregation of troubled assets (SAREB).	Soundness of financial sector.
2012	Rental market.	SOCIMIs' tax harmonisation with REITs.	SOCIMIs taking off.
2013	Law to protect mortgagee, debt restructuring, and social rents.	Amends some aspects of enforcement procedures.	Reduction in the number of foreclosures and evictions procedures already in 2013.

institutions into national law, the operational geographic limitations of the savings banks ended and from 1988 onwards, the savings banks had freedom to open branch offices throughout the Spanish territory.

In parallel to the bullish evolution of the home ownership market, rented housing had been diminishing in Spain since the 1960s as policy

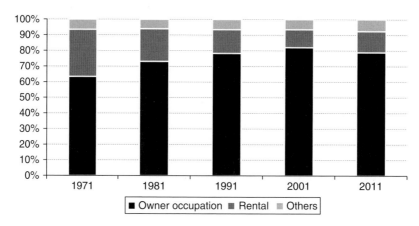

Figure 21.1   Distribution of main dwellings by housing tenure (percentage of dwellings).
Source: INE Census (2014).

became more oriented towards stimulating economic activity than towards social goals (Figure 21.1). Social housing was increasingly provided via the owner-occupied sector instead of developing a social rented housing sector (Alberdi 2014). In the mid-1980s there was an attempt to reverse this trend by liberalising the rental sector. This was only focused on new leases and had little success. In 1992, Real Estate Investment Funds were created as indirect investment vehicles in order to increase capital flows to foster the rental sector. However, the restrictive regulation of these instruments limited their success as well. In a further attempt, a new law on Urban Leasing was passed in 1994, which established free agreement between parties for the amount of the rent and the duration of the lease and eased eviction procedures. This law did not represent a sufficient liberalisation and rental housing remained residual.

In the 1990s, housing finance developed in a highly competitive environment. During that period and in a context of decreasing interest rates, credit institutions went into what has been known as a 'mortgage credit war'. It was initially led by Santander bank in 1992, the first institution that increased its client portfolio through the reduction in mortgage interest rates for clients coming from other financial institutions. This competitive strategy was soon followed by the rest of the financial institutions. This allowed all mortgages, both new and outstanding, to benefit from the reduction of interest rates. This phenomenon was mainly feasible thanks to the creation in 1994 of the capacity to subrogate a mortgage loan. The mechanism of subrogation allows either a change of debtor (changing the debtor but keeping the mortgage in the same bank) or a change of creditor (moving the mortgage from one bank to another) with the aim of modifying either the interest rate from fixed to variable and/or the level or the loan period with low or no cost for the borrower.

This mechanism also allowed lenders to rapidly increase their clients' portfolios by introducing finance opportunities earlier in the funding process. Financial institutions went from only funding the purchase of housing to funding real estate developers and, by the end of the period (2006–2007), to financing the purchase of land. By lending to real estate developers financial institutions reached a wider customer base as households buying new homes were given new incentives (through loan conditions and taxes) to take their loans from the developer. However, this action dramatically increased the exposure of financial institutions to real estate risks, especially when they started to grant money for purchasing land.

In this new mortgage market, the client became the focus of financial institutions and the mortgage loan was understood as a powerful tool of cross selling. It is worth noting that in the mid-1990s long-term variable interest rate loans – mostly linked to Madrid Interbank Offered Rate (MIBOR rate) – started to be commercialised in order to allow the client to benefit from decreasing long-term interest rates that fell from 17 percent in 1989/1990 to 9 percent in 1996. According to the Bank of Spain, at the end of 1997, 86 percent of the outstanding balances of mortgage loans on housing were already variable interest loans; by the end of 2002 this had risen to 98 percent (Alvarez and Gómez 2003).

The unprecedented growth of mortgage lending recorded over this period was possible thanks to the parallel development of collateralised debt instruments. In 1992 mortgage securitisation funds were created. The objective of the introduction of the mortgage securitisation funds was to improve liquidity by making it easier to mobilise residential mortgage loans, reducing final costs. Later on, in 1998, the government created 'Asset Securitisation Funds', or ABS, in order to facilitate the securitisation of other categories of assets. The assets of this kind of fund are securitised rights for credit, whereas the liabilities correspond to the bonds issued. Finally, in 2002 public sector covered bonds were introduced to the market along with Mortgage Transfer Certificates.

Another important component of housing policy in Spain over the last 25 years has been the development of a system for designating land for development. Although successive land laws were approved in 1990, 1998 and 2007 by the central government, standards have to be approved by regional governments and the responsibility for applying these standards falls entirely with the town hall. Most regional governments also passed their own land laws. The 1990 law maintained elements of the previous system where different kinds of land were designated for development which sometimes meant that land was not brought forward by owners. Each individual town hall determined criteria when drawing up their general plans that identified the medium-term availability of building land and, therefore, placed upward pressure on its price (Alberdi and Levenfeld 1996). The reform of 1998 was intended to liberalise the system and reduce house prices by increasing the amount of available land. However, in spite of the spirit of this reform, land prices notably increased during this period as a result of speculation and of artificial scarcity caused by the planning system. Essentially, land was one of the main reasons for the rise in house prices. Land taxation (i.e. licenses, transfers) represented more than 50 percent of town halls' income during the boom years. The 2007 Land Law was aimed at stopping expropriations and reducing the price of urban land, but was not tested due to the onset of the GFC that completely froze the land market.

Finally, taxation during the period also favoured homebuyers, contributing to the idea that Spaniards had an increasing appetite for property. Fiscal deductions that applied to first purchased residences started in 1977 (Galapero 1999) and were maintained until 2010. They were restored at the end of 2011 only to be eliminated again at the beginning of 2013. On the other hand fiscal incentives for the rented sector were very limited.

The crisis period and the renaissance of the mortgage market: 2007–present

The outstanding growth of residential activity supported by a vigorous mortgage market ended abruptly in 2008 when the GFC hit and credit dried up. Spanish lenders faced different episodes of funding constraints resulting from the turmoil in the European wholesale funding market. The high levels of exposure to the real estate sector, the uncertainty regarding the value of mortgage collaterals and the increase in arrears (especially in commercial lending to real estate developers) generated a problem of confidence in the soundness of the financial sector. In view of these problems, the government and the Bank of Spain started taking measures in 2009. The first was the creation of the Fund for the Orderly Bank Restructuring (FORB) (see Box 21.1) to manage the restructuring of credit institutions and resolution processes. One of the first actions of the FORB was to consolidate the savings bank sector in order to restore confidence in the system. FORB granted financial support to merger processes when requested to do so by the entities concerned. The reform of savings banks followed and in 2010 rules were set up to allow savings banks to issue top-quality capital, facilitate access to capital markets and also to make management and governing bodies more professional and subject to greater market discipline.

In spite of these reforms the huge weight of real estate loans remained on the banks' balance sheets, which continued to put at risk the viability of a substantial part of the Spanish banking system. This forced the government to ask for assistance of up to €100 bn from the Euro group in June 2012 to support Spain's injured banking sector. This assistance was established by a Memorandum of Understanding (MoU) and was conditional on specific policy measures being introduced in regards to the financial

Box 21.1   Restructuring of the banking sector: the FORB and the SAREB

When the GFC began in 2008, it was predicted to have a limited impact on Spanish banks as they did not include Special Investment Vehicles or toxic assets, but rather utilised a traditional retail banking model. On the funding side banks had no long-dated maturities for mortgage bonds (around 10 years) and did not have short-term liquidity problems. Provisioning rules were straightforward and transparent. But the financial crisis still impacted Spanish banks that had built up weaknesses during economic boom periods, including sharp growth in credit – mainly in the construction and real estate sectors – that progressively raised their doubtful assets and their provisions. These imbalances were more acute for most of the savings banks that had exceeded their capacity, expanded outside their geographical area and employed a singular stakeholder model that complicated their capacity to issue equity.

Since 2009 a range of measures have been taken to increase the resilience of the sector in response to the GFC. This included addressing the uncertainty of the funding market, increasing provisioning and transparency, promoting mergers between savings banks and creating the FORB as a backstop if funds were not obtained in the market. To address the uncertainty of the funding market, guarantees for banks issuances of new debt and the acquisition of high quality assets were granted. However, the restrictions of liquidity, together with higher capital requirements and provisions, limited the supply of credit and increased its price. At the same time its demand had also been affected by the uncertainty of the setting.

In the summer of 2010 wholesale markets reopened for Spanish banks, but economic weaknesses persisted and the pressure of Irish debt generated contagion effects. Potential access to wholesale markets was once again made harder. In November 2010 the Bank of Spain required banks to publish full details of their lending to the construction and real estate sector, their volume of wholesale funding and their liquidity situation. In February 2011 savings banks were asked to increase their capital requirements to 8 percent – or to 10 percent if funding on wholesale markets was in excess of 20 percent and if at least 20 percent of their share capital had not been placed with third parties.

Between 2010 and 2013, the situation of Spanish banks remained difficult, with net interest margins under pressure, rather flat business volumes, and the need to continue making loan loss provisions to write down assets. Additionally, there was no lending yet to real estate companies or to households. Between 2011 and 2012 the sovereign crisis also affected the banks, and even the public guarantee proved harmful to them with the sovereign ceiling causing issuing problems. Risk premiums against Germany increased dramatically in the first term of 2013 and remained high for the whole year reaching a maximum of 630 basis points in July. This decreased, however, to below 200 at the beginning of 2014. Banks took refuge in the ECB using mortgage bonds in exchange. Between 2012 and 2013 the ECB announced they would be buying public debt in the secondary markets and making all efforts to guarantee the continuity of the Euro. Consequently, most financial institutions were able to issue debt at tighter spreads.

The Fund for Orderly Bank Restructuring, FORB, is a 100 percent state-owned entity created in 2009 on bank restructuring and reinforcement of credit entities' equity. FORB's goal is to manage the restructuring and resolution processes of credit institutions, aimed at ensuring the stability of the financial system, depositor protection and an efficient use of public resources. FORB will grant financial support to merger processes when requested to do so by the entities concerned.

FORB received an initial capital allocation of €9 bn, increased by €6 bn on September 2012. Securities issued by FORB are plain vanilla bonds with an explicit, unconditional and irrevocable guarantee of the Kingdom of Spain. The guarantee is available on up to €13 bn, 0 percent risk-weighted assets and bonds eligible as guarantee assets in ECB monetary policy operations. The bonds will be listed on the Public Debt Entry Book Market with the Bank of Spain acting as payment agents. Finally, they will have an equivalent treatment to Government bonds for tax purposes.

The Spanish Asset Management Company, SAREB, was created in the context of the roadmap established in the MoU signed in July 2012. Its objective was the separation of troubled assets linked to the real estate sector from the balance sheets of aided financial institutions. SAREB is a for-profit vehicle with yield objectives (expected return on equity [ROE] of around 14–15 percent). It is not part of the public sector (majority private owned) and the overall maximum size of SAREB will be €90 000 mn. It will have a maximum life of 15 years and is empowered without limitation to issue securities and borrow from credit institutions, as well as create funds of specific assets.

SAREB started operating on the 1 January 2013 with assets transferred by Group 1 banks (nationalised institutions) in November 2012. The transfer process was completed in February 2013 with assets from Group 2 banks (those who have received public funds but are not nationalised).

sector. These measures included the determination of the capital needs through stress tests; the introduction of recapitalisation, restructuring and/or resolution plans; and the segregation of the troubled assets through the creation of the SAREB (Spanish Asset Management Company), better known as the 'bad bank' (see Box 21.1). All these adjustments have helped to restore confidence in the system, as the better access Spanish banks have had to capital markets since the second half of 2013 seems to indicate. However, mortgage lending was notably restricted during this period as banks were forced to increase their capital base.

Following the difficult adjustment of the mortgage market, some measures were undertaken in order to stimulate rentals. One of these measures was the introduction in 2009 of a new investment instrument: the SOCIMIs (Public Limited Investment companies in real estate market) designed as the Spanish version of Real Estate Investment Trusts (REITs). However, the bigger adjustments occurring within the real estate sector combined with some significant differences between SOCIMIs and international REITs made the investment vehicle largely unattractive for the market. It was not until 2012 – when some aspects of the 2009 regulation of the SOCIMIs were modified to make the vehicle more flexible through a tax harmonisation with the REITs in other countries and to reduce the entry barriers – that SOCIMI became a feasible tool for boosting the rental market (not only residential but also commercial). In addition, another law was passed in 2013 with the aim of normalising the legal regulations of the letting process, aiming to protect the rights of both the lessor and the lessee.

Finally, the rise of non-performing loans as a result of the GFC made clear the need to reform the 2000 Law for the enforcement of civil procedures. This law was intended to liberalise the procedures and protect borrowers while reducing the costs and length of the processes, although this has been difficult to assess due to the lack of foreclosures in the following years. When the number of foreclosures and evictions started to rise in 2009, it became necessary to amend some parts of the 2000 law to address this controversial social issue and to comply with European standards. A new law was passed in 2013 which included measures to protect mortgagees, debt restructuring and social rents. The law amends certain aspects of both the judicial and out-of-court mortgage enforcement proceedings in order to: (i) increase protection of borrowers who have secured their debts with a mortgage on their home residence; (ii) obtain better prices through auction processes; and (iii) allow suspension of the enforcement proceedings when the loan or credit facility secured by the mortgage contains abusive clauses.

The impact of these milestones over the last 25 years

In the last 25 years there have been two booms in the Spanish real estate market. The first took place between mid-1980s and early 1990s, encouraged by increases in foreign investment from those interested in the new member of the economic union. This boom was characterised by a strong increase in housing demand but not in housing offer due to the inelasticity of land supply, which pushed prices up dramatically. House prices doubled during the second half of the 1980s, after having remained stagnant since 1973. The euphoria of the market lasted until 1992. The celebration of the 1992 Olympic Games in Barcelona and the Expo '92 in Seville delayed the effects of the oil crisis of 1991 and the Gulf War in Spain. House prices then adjusted during the recession period, which lasted until 1996.

The second and most intense boom took place between 1997 and 2007, a decade of long expansion during which the economic situation improved dramatically with sharp growth in employment, economic activity and wealth as well as relatively low levels of public deficit and public debt over GDP (one of the lowest of Europe). Household income doubled between 1997 and 2007; unemployment reached its lowest level ever in Spain; and population grew driven by intense immigration. The percentage of immigrants within the Spanish population rose from 1.6 percent in

1998 to 10 percent in 2007. Low income immigrants also had access to the property market, sharing mortgages among several people.

In addition to the exceptional macro conditions, specific factors fueled the property market boom after 1997. The development of the mortgage market and its funding tools enabled Spain to reach one of the highest home-ownership ratios in the EU. In a fully liberalised market with a high level of competition between financial institutions, households benefitted over this period from very favourable terms in mortgage loans and a plentiful supply of credit. Credit liquidity also reached real estate developers as it was a way for financial institutions to achieve new clients through the subrogation mechanism.

Against this background, demand for homes notably increased over this period. Housing transactions peaked in 2006 as a result of population growth (i.e. large scale immigration) and very good performance of the labour market (the number of employed persons in Spain went from 12.5 million in 1997 to 19.4 at the end of 2007). The decreasing trend in long-term interest rates also doubled the debt capacity of Spanish families (Alberdi and San Martin 2004). This facilitated the continuous increase in house prices despite declining affordability. Demand for property was also partly speculative given that the rise in prices and the availability of credit made buying a home an interesting investment as buyers anticipated a speculative gain. Total outstanding residential mortgage lending-to-GDP reached 61 percent at the end of 2007, compared with the European average of 44 percent.

Housing supply followed the same path with housing starts rising from 338 000 in 1997 to a maximum of 865 000 in 2006. Over this 10-year period more than 6 million new houses were constructed. According to the last 2011 Census the total stock of dwellings was 25.2 million, an increase from 21 million in 2001. Credit for construction and real estate activity fed this exponential growth, with banks even funding land acquisition in the last years of the boom. Commercial lending increased by 30 percent on average in annual terms from 1999 to 2007, moving from a €59 bn outstanding volume up to €455 bn at the end of the period. In relative terms it represented 38 percent of total outstanding mortgage lending.

In spite of the plentiful supply of homes and the reduction of input prices in the construction sector, house prices tripled between 1997 and 2007 with an average annual growth of 10 percent. This upward trend was mostly explained by two factors: first, it was driven by increased land values, which could reflect up to 50 percent of the final house price calculated as a residual value; second, the lack of a professional rental market increased demand and drove up prices. As a consequence, housing affordability started to deteriorate (Figure 21.2). The house prices to earnings ratio grew from 4.5 times annual wages needed to buy a house in 1997 to 9.2 in 2007 (Rodriguez-Lopez 2014). As a result some sectors demanding housing (i.e. first-time buyers) started to be driven out of the market and a soft

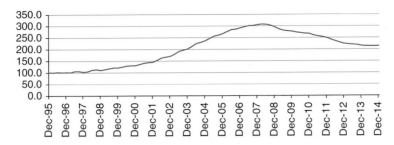

Figure 21.2   Housing price index (1995 = 100).
Source: Ministry of Public Works (2014).

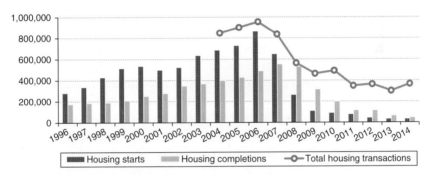

Figure 21.3   Evolution of housing supply and demand.
Source: Ministry of Public Works (2014).

adjustment started to be observed in 2006, which slowed down the growth of both housing transactions and starts.

However, the onset of the GFC in 2008 eliminated the possibility of a soft landing. The financial shock exacerbated the imbalances built up by the Spanish economy during its period of expansion and led to a shrinking of residential real estate activity in terms of both supply and demand (Peña 2011). Housing indicators experienced a large and fast adjustment. In only 1 year, from 2007 to 2008, housing starts reduced by 59 percent down to 265 000, and declined further to just 35 000 in December 2014.

In addition, household confidence and financial wealth notably deteriorated prompting a drop in housing transactions. In 2013 transaction levels were a third of those recorded in 2007. However, in spite of this severe adjustment, demand for housing proved to be more resilient to the crisis and housing transactions have remained above housing completions levels during the entire crisis period (Figure 21.3). This has allowed for a gradual reduction in the excess housing supply generated during the boom, which was estimated to be 650 000 homes at the end of 2008.

House prices also adjusted during the crisis, decreasing by about 40 percent on average terms since the peak of the cycle. This adjustment, linked to the reduction in long-term interest rates, helped to improve affordability levels in the last few years. The number of years of gross disposable income needed to buy a house has decreased, returning to 2003/2004 levels. The main obstacles remaining for housing affordability are unemployment, which reached 27 percent at the end of 2013, and the reduction of net household income.

In terms of lending, restrictions in mortgage lending supply, which began in 2007, were affected by: funding constraints for financial institutions and turmoil in the wholesale funding markets (i.e. Lehman Brothers, sovereign debt crisis); the restructuration and recapitalisation processes of the financial system; and high levels of uncertainty and deterioration in the wider economy. On the other hand, demand for credit also decreased in light of a deteriorating labour market and expectations of further decreases in house prices. As a result, total outstanding mortgage lending of Spanish deposit institutions, which at the end of 2008 amounted to €1.1 trillion (100 percent of GDP), decreased to €721 bn at the end of December 2014 (Figure 21.4). In relative terms, this represented an accumulated drop of 34 percent.

Regarding new loans, gross mortgage lending decreased from a maximum of €284 bn at the end of 2006 to €41 bn at the end of 2013, while the total number of new loans also decreased from 1.6 mn at the end of 2005 to 321 000 at the end of 2013. When considering only residential mortgage lending, the number of new loans granted dropped 85 percent over the same period to 154 000, and residential gross lending reduced by 89 percent to €17 bn. Mortgage lending conditions also changed, with reductions in the average term of the loans and LTV as well as increases in long-term interest rates (i.e. margins) for new loans.

However, for financial institutions, the worst problem was their exposure to the construction and real estate companies, whose outstanding debt amounted to a maximum of €470 bn at the end of 2008. In order to accelerate the coverage of non-performing loans and to provide incentives to banks to

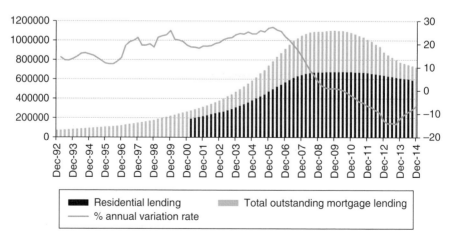

Figure 21.4   Evolution of outstanding mortgage lending.
Source: Spanish Mortgage Association (2014).

take foreclosed assets off the balance sheet in 2010 and later in 2012, the levels of provisioning were tightened. From 2011 to 2012 gross exposure to construction and real estate lending reduced by almost €100000 mn down to €297075 mn (around €90000 mn when considering net provision). It is worth noting that beyond provisions, part of the 2012 correction (around 50 percent) was related to the transfer of certain real estate assets to the newly created asset management company (SAREB) in the months between December 2012 and February 2013.

Regarding the evolution of non-performing loans, doubtful assets for construction and real estate companies have grown much faster than the rest of the portfolio, from below 1 percent in 2007 to over 36 percent at the end of September 2014. This was mainly a result of the bankruptcy of many real estate companies that were heavily in debt with financial institutions, requiring a provision of some 47 percent in 2012 according to the Bank of Spain. Default rates in the retail mortgage portfolio, however, have risen only from 0.7 percent in 2007 to 6.0 percent in September 2014, although much of this rise occurred during the last year (Figure 21.5).

The sound growth of the mortgage market since the end of the 1980s was supported by the development of mortgage funding mechanisms (covered bonds and mortgage backed securities (MBS)). This development took off thanks to Spain's entry into the economic and monetary union in 1999 and high investor appetite for the Spanish debt. Until that moment, the main source of funds for banks and savings banks were deposits, insufficient to meet the demand of mortgage lending. From 2001 to 2006 the issuance of covered bonds and MBS grew at a year-on-year average variation rate of 60 percent and multiplied their outstanding volume 10 times as mortgage credit multiplied by three times in the same period.

At the peak of the period, in 2006, total outstanding of covered bonds and MBS amounted to €307 bn and represented 24 percent and 10 percent of total outstanding mortgage lending, respectively. From 2008 after the bankruptcy

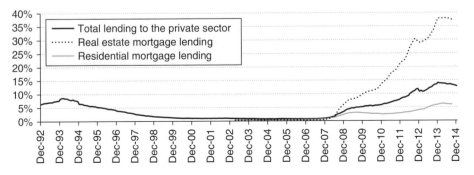

Figure 21.5 Evolution of non-performing loans by credit purpose (percent).
Source: Spanish Mortgage Association (2014).

of Lehman Brothers until 2013, credit institutions faced severe funding constraints related at first to the subprime crisis and, between 2010–2012, with the southern countries' sovereign debt crisis. During this period, the issuance of MBS almost disappeared due to liquidity problems and the generalised credit risk perception of the instrument.

Covered bonds, on the contrary, remained an important funding tool for Spanish financial institutions during the entire period and proved to be a resilient instrument despite the continued downturn in financial markets. In 2012 covered bonds issuances reached a historical maximum level of €104 407 mn. From 2013 on, however, the issuance of covered bonds has notably reduced as a consequence of two factors: fewer needs for funds in light of the deleveraging of the private sector and the maturity scheme of debt. Consequently, the overall volume of outstanding covered bonds reduced over the last year as a result of amortisation and repurchase operations.

Looking to the future: financing into the future

Most indicators in 2014 seem to point to a slight recovery of the housing market in Spain, and some intrinsic features of the Spanish housing and mortgage markets have started to change. The uncertainty during the GFC regarding the evolution of the economy and prices led to an increasing demand for rental housing, forcing sellers to rent their dwellings because of a lack of buyer appetite. Reforms have been implemented in order to improve the rental market; however, it is too soon to see the effects of this. Regarding the second factor, the increase in foreclosures and the acquisition of assets in payment of debt (especially of real estate companies) multiplied the weight of real assets in banks' balance sheets over recent years. In order to manage this situation, financial institutions created big asset management companies, renting part of their stock and becoming the largest property companies in the country. In order to address the social concerns related to increasing household evictions, financial institutions in collaboration with the government have become the largest suppliers of social housing, renting part of their housing stock to troubled households evicted from their main dwellings. However, as the economic situation improves, the nature of the business makes it unsustainable for financial institutions to continue managing real estate assets and providing rented housing. In fact, since the end of 2013 some financial institutions have already started to sell their real estate platforms.

Against this background, the proportion of households living in rented housing has increased in the last few years to 13.5 percent in 2011 (up from 11.4 percent in 2001). To develop a suitable rental market, deeper steps must be taken to correct the structural inefficiencies of the Spanish rental market (i.e. the absence of a public stock of social rental housing, unfavourable taxation, and the lack of a professional rental market). However, the tax changes introduced in 2012 through the SOCIMIS (Spanish REITs) and the changes introduced in 2013, which should foster and increase the flexibility of the rental market, will provide an additional push for the development of this market.

Regarding lending, the prospects for 2014 and the near future include: a gradual recovery of credit to households based on the completion of the process of restructuration and recapitalisation of the banking sector, which will liberate funds; the normalisation of the wholesale funding markets; improved consumer confidence as the growth in unemployment – while still high – slows; and the emergence of positive growth rates in the housing market, already observed in house prices in some areas.

However, the reactivation of lending will be framed in a context of higher prudence and responsibility from both lenders and borrowers. Credit risk analysis will be an essential component in the assessment of granting a loan, which will have an impact on the spread of mortgage interest rates, allowing them to remain competitive although higher than in the pre-crisis period as the risks will be considered in price. In this regard, credit institutions will put greater emphasis on profitability than on increasing the number of customers. Transparency in the relationship with the client and in the information provided will also be very important in the future, as it is increasingly prioritised through European legislation (i.e. the Directive on Credit Agreements for consumers relating to Residential Immovable Property, CARRP).

Finally, as a consequence of the variability shown by EURIBOR (the main reference for variable interest rates in Spain), households are more concerned about the risk of interest rates and have exhibited an increased appetite for halfway formulas as initial fixed period interest rates. Lending to construction and real estate companies is not likely to resume at its pre-crisis levels in the medium term. Financial institutions have become more prudent and a back-to-basics approach has been observed. In this regard, it is likely that over the next few years, the levels of outstanding real estate lending will continue to decrease and new loans will be restricted to profitable operations, with lower LTVs and without land funding.

Will Spain's private finance and housing markets ever recover? This analysis suggests that the reactivation of the housing market over the next few years will be less dependent on private finance. Mortgage lending will be subdued due to the new risk standards, thus limiting the capability of the system to fund housing demand. Alternative mechanisms will likely develop in order to attend unmet demand. The rental market will become increasingly important. If properly stimulated, the rental market could be an efficient tool for young first-time homebuyers, while, at the same time, favouring labour mobility. Additionally, the way in which housing construction has been traditionally funded will need to change. Real estate companies that have survived the GFC are characterised by having sounder capital ratios.

In order to ensure the viability of new residential projects and access to private funding, real estate companies will need to prove that a minimum share of buyers are interested in the project as a common practice. Finally, self-construction projects, REITs and private equity firms will also play an important role in the housing market by helping to curb the dependence on traditional banking finance and diversify housing finance models.

References

Alberdi, B (2014). Social housing in Spain. In: *Social Housing in Europe*, Scanlon, K, Whitehead, C and Fernandez Arrigoitía, M (eds). Wiley-Blackwell, RICS, Oxford.

Alberdi, B and San Martin, I (2004). Policy and market responses to affordability issues in Spain, *Housing Finance International*, June, 18–25.

Alberdi, B and Levenfeld, G (1996). Housing policy in Spain. In: *Housing Policy in Europe*, Balchin, P (ed.). Routledge, London.

Alvarez, P and Gómez, JM (2003). La estructura de los tipos de interés en los préstamos hipotecarios sobre viviendas, *Economic Gazette*, July–August, Bank of Spain.

Galapero, R (1999). Fiscalidad de la vivienda en el Impuesto sobre la Renta de las Personas Físicas. *Revista Impuestos*, Vol II.

INE (2014). *Censo de Viviendas*. [Online] Available: www.ine.es/censos2011_datos/cen11_datos_inicio.htm (accessed 29 July 2015).

Ministry of Public Works (2014). Housing Prices, Housing supply and demand. [Online] Available: www.fomento.gob.es/MFOM/LANG_CASTELLANO/ATENCION_CIUDADANO/INFORMACION_ESTADISTICA/Vivienda/Estadisticas/ (accessed 29 July 2015).

Peña, CI (2011). A review of the Spanish mortgage market, *Mortgage Info September 2011*. European Mortgage Federation. [Online] Available: www.ahe.es/bocms/images/bfilecontent/2008/01/28/2317.pdf?version=3 (accessed 29 July 2015).

Rodriguez-Lopez, J (2014). *Crisis económica y cambios en el sistema financiero*, Editorial Catarata.

Spanish Mortgage Association (2014). Mortgage Lending and non-performing loans. [Online] Available: www.ahe.es/bocms/sites/ahenew/estadisticas/ (accessed 29 July 2015).

22

Milestones in Swedish Housing Finance

Peter Englund
Stockholm School of Economics, Stockholm, Sweden

Background

Institutional framework

Today, housing finance is widely available to Swedish homeowners. Loans are routinely granted up to 85 percent of collateral value, and households can choose between interest-only and amortising loans as well as between variable-interest rate loans and loans with interest fixed for up to 10 years. Banks fund their loans in an active covered-bonds market, today larger in volume than the market for government bonds. Before 1985, in contrast, the total volume of loans was regulated by the Riksbank (the central bank of Sweden) and equity withdrawal was generally not available. There was little choice regarding interest and amortisation. The standard was a 30-year amortising loan with a 5-year fixed interest rate. Funding was by special bonds that were bought by investors subject to placement regulations.

To understand the transformation of Swedish housing finance over the last three decades, it is necessary to start in the early 1980s. Two traits of the Swedish economy at that time stand out. First, financial institutions were limited by tight regulations and lending to various sectors of the economy was largely allocated based on political priorities. While funding of new housing construction was given high priority, the Riksbank put a strict cap on bank lending for low-priority purposes like consumption. In most years, equity withdrawal was more or less ruled out. Second, the tax system was heavily asymmetric with interest payments being deductible at 50–80 percent marginal tax rates. Combined with two-digit inflation rates, this led to sharply negative after-tax real interest rates. As a result, there was a vast amount of

Milestones in European Housing Finance, First Edition.
Edited by Jens Lunde and Christine Whitehead.
© 2016 John Wiley & Sons, Ltd. Published 2016 by John Wiley & Sons, Ltd.

suppressed credit demand. While the rationale for the credit regulations go back to a planning philosophy where monetary policy was conducted by quantitative controls rather than by market operations, the regulations fulfilled an important function in curbing credit demand that was artificially stimulated by an asymmetric tax system in an inflationary environment.

Even though housing finance has been liberalised since the 1980s, housing choices by Swedish households are still today strongly influenced by various regulations and institutional factors. Figure 22.1 shows the distribution of households across the three main tenures. In 1990, 42 percent of all households were owner-occupiers living in single-family homes, 41 percent were renting and the remaining 17 percent lived in units owned by co-operative housing associations (*bostadsrättsföreningar*). Outright ownership of a dwelling in a multi-dwelling building, like a condominium, was not permitted in Sweden until a legal reform in 2009. So far, the number of owned apartments remains minuscule. A significant fraction of the rental housing stock is owned by municipal housing companies operating on a non-profit basis. These companies are owned by local governments and have historically been more or less completely funded by debt at near risk-free rates. Following Sweden's entrance into the EU, this has been regarded as illegal anti-competitive state support and the municipal housing companies now need to have an equity base that should earn a market return. Rents are set in negotiations between organisations representing tenants and landlords. As a result, centrally located rental apartments in the major metropolitan areas are priced way below market-clearing levels and are mainly allocated on a queuing system. On the other hand, shares in co-op associations that give

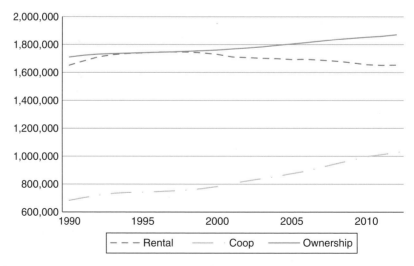

Figure 22.1 Number of dwelling units (one-family houses and apartments) according to tenure mode.
Source: Statistics Sweden.

the right to occupy a dwelling are traded at market prices in a very active market. The market for co-op shares was deregulated in the early 1970s.

Reforms and crisis

It was clear even by 1980 that reforms were badly needed: both credit market deregulation and tax reform were long overdue when they came a few years later. Unfortunately for economic stability, the reforms came in the wrong order, with credit deregulation around 1985 preceding the tax reform that was only implemented in 1992. Financial deregulation occurred in several steps. The key decision was to abolish bank lending ceilings, which took place in 1985. From then on, banks and mortgage institutions were free to make their own lending decisions and compete over market shares. Predictably, this led to a credit boom with bank lending increasing by 136 percent between 1985 and 1990, much of it going into real estate. This fuelled a general macro-economic boom. Between 1985 and 1991, prices of owner-occupied homes doubled in nominal terms and by 36 percent in real terms. New housing construction increased from around 30 000 units per year in the mid-1980s to around 60 000 in 1991 and 1992.

As in so many cases, as documented for example by Reinhart and Rogoff (2009) and Schularick and Taylor (2012), the credit boom was followed by a macro-economic crisis – in fact, three intertwined crises: a currency crisis, a real estate crisis and a banking crisis. High Swedish inflation in the late 1980s led to speculation against the Swedish krona (SEK, which was pegged to a basket of currencies). For some time, the Riksbank managed to counter the currency outflow by increasing the interest rate. This effectively broke the back of the real estate boom and led to falling house prices from 1990 and mounting bank credit losses. With banks at various stages of insolvency and renewed currency speculation, the situation was not tenable for very long. In the fall of 1992, in the context of general European currency turmoil, the krona was left to float. To save the banking system, the government issued a general guarantee for all bank obligations. Two of the six major banks were taken over by the state (see, e.g. Englund 1999, for an account of the crisis).

The crisis left lasting marks on the Swedish economy. It resulted in sizeable output losses. GDP fell by 6 percent from the summer of 1990 to the summer of 1993 and unemployment jumped from 2 to 10 percent. It took a decade for unemployment to get down to 5 percent, still twice the pre-crisis level. The crisis also put a strain on government finances, and government debt reached a high of 77 percent of GDP in 1994.

The crisis also left the banking system much impaired. Total credit losses for Swedish banks between 1990 and 1993 amounted to 17 percent of the 1990 loan stock. Losses were concentrated in the commercial real estate sector. Falling commercial rent levels hit the cash flow of highly leveraged property companies and simultaneously reduced collateral values. Commercial property values fell by half from 1990 to 1993.

In the housing sector, losses were concentrated in multi-family housing, in particular in those located outside the major metropolitan areas where the labour market was weakening. In these regions bankruptcies were widespread among private landlords and some co-op associations had to be reconstructed. Many municipal housing companies ran into financial difficulties and were recapitalised, partly with support from the state. It bears emphasising, however, that bank losses related to household lending, including mortgages, remained small. Only 6 percent of bank losses came from household lending, despite the fact that nominal prices of owner-occupied single-family homes fell by 20 percent from the peak in the first quarter of 1991 to the bottom in the third quarter of 1993. Since Swedish banks have full recourse to borrower income and other assets, default was not an option for households that were under water. In some cases, banks may have given interest concessions to households that were hit by unemployment, but overall this was of minor importance. This experience reinforced the view among Swedish banks and regulators that household mortgage lending is a low-risk activity.

Key milestones

Institutional and regulatory change

The sweeping deregulation of the 1980s included two key elements that directly affected the housing sector. Banks were now free to make their own lending decisions without any quantitative restrictions and with interest rates only limited by competition. Further, insurance companies and pension funds were no longer required to invest in housing bonds. Funding for housing loans was now determined by the market. Combined with tax and subsidy reforms that took place later, this laid the ground for a transformation of the Swedish mortgage markets. The main steps in this process are summarised in the timeline in Table 22.1.

The backbone of the pre-existing system had been one of physical planning based on a quantitative target for new construction. New construction within that target was in principle guaranteed funding. Funding during the construction process was provided by banks and was regarded as high-priority within the total loan ceiling. Funding once the housing unit was completed came in two parts. The primary mortgage – typically 70 percent of approved building costs – was supplied by specialised mortgage institutions, some of which were bank subsidiaries. These mortgage institutions were funded by bonds. Until the deregulation in the mid-1980s, banks and insurance companies were incentivised to buy these bonds through special regulations that required

Table 22.1 Timeline of major reforms and market changes.

1985: Deregulation of bank lending. This led to increased competition and a gradual proliferation of various types of mortgage contracts.

1985: Abolishment of placement requirements for insurance companies and pension funds, requiring investments in housing bonds.

1991: Major tax reform, reducing the tax rate on interest deductions to 30% and introducing a new property tax, proportional to property value.

1993: Gradual abolishment of interest subsidies to new construction (completed in 2007).

2004: Covered bond legislation.

2007: Reduction of the property tax to make it flat for all properties with value above a threshold (roughly half of all properties).

2010: Maximum 85% loan-to-value for new mortgages.

2013: Minimum 15% weight on mortgages in calculating risk-weighted assets for banks.

2014: Minimum amortisation rules for new mortgages.

them to hold a certain proportion of their assets in housing and government bonds. As a result, these bonds could be issued at below general market interest rates. A secondary mortgage – 25 percent of building costs for one-family houses and 28 percent for multi-dwelling units – came directly from a state agency. Both primary and secondary mortgages were subject to government subsidies, taking the form of guaranteed interest rates. To qualify, the dwelling had to fulfil certain quality criteria and not be above a certain maximum size. The intent was to subsidise high-quality housing for ordinary people.

Deregulation removed the link between the physical planning system (which otherwise remained intact) and housing finance. Funding during the construction phase was no longer automatically guaranteed. The system with subsidised interest rates was initially maintained, however, and only abolished gradually during the following decade as described in the section on policy change that follows.

The 1992 crisis triggered several fundamental changes to the institutional framework for macro policy. As a new anchor of monetary policy, the Riksbank announced a 2 percent inflation target from 1993. A few years later new legislation granting the independence of the central bank and explicitly identifying inflation as the central goal of monetary policy was passed by parliament in 1999. Given the nominal and asymmetric character of the Swedish tax system, the reduction in inflation from two-digit levels in the 1980s to around 2 percent had a strong impact on the real cost of housing consumption.

Furthermore, the process for deciding the government budget was reformed. The new process imposed a two-stage structure: first, parliament decides on an overall budget; then any reforms have to be fully funded. So discipline is imposed on both government and parliament. This put a halt to the expansion of public expenditure and the government budget turned from deficit to surplus from 1998. With these new limits imposed on government spending, it became more difficult to encompass generous housing subsidies as detailed in the next section. As a result of these changes,

Sweden came into the recent worldwide financial crisis with among the strongest government finances in Europe and with interest rates down at German levels. Arguably, these low overall interest rates have been more important for housing costs than the removal of interest subsidies.

The financial crisis was the result of a failure not only of macro-economic policy but also of banking regulation and supervision. It led to an increased general awareness among bankers and regulators about the nature of credit risk. The Financial Supervisor (*Finansinspektionen*) was given increased resources. In general, however, the experience from the crisis was that the risks associated with household lending, and mortgage lending in particular, were quite low. Only 6 percent of total credit losses during the crisis came from loans to households. This experience has allowed Swedish banks to operate with relatively little capital. In the standardised version of the Basel rules for bank capital coverage that came into effect in the 1990s, household mortgages carried a relatively high risk weight. But when banks later were allowed to base the capital requirement on internal models, these risk weights were reduced substantially for all Swedish banks. Still today, Swedish banks hold less capital against their mortgage loans than banks in most other countries, even though the regulator has recently imposed a minimum requirement irrespective of what the bank internal models suggests.

Policy change – taxes and subsidies

Traditionally, Sweden had a system of comprehensive income taxation with nominal interest payments fully deductible irrespective of the source of the interest payments; consumption loans and loans invested in housing were treated equally. Owner-occupiers were taxed based on a measure of imputed income calculated in proportion to a tax-assessed value (ideally equal to 75 percent of market value). Combined with a progressive tax scale with rates peaking at 85 percent in the early 1980s, this had dramatic effects on the costs of housing and made user costs effectively negative for large groups of households. A series of tax reforms culminating with a comprehensive reform in 1991 changed the system fundamentally. Now the taxation of capital income was separated from the tax on labour income. Under the new tax system the marginal rate applicable to interest payments was reduced to a uniform 30 percent. Combined with a property tax of 1.5 percent of property value, the tax system was in principle neutral regarding owner-occupied homes. Assuming an interest rate of 5 percent (3 percent real plus 2 percent inflation following the new inflation target), the property tax would be exactly equal to the value of interest deductions for a fully mortgaged house. In practice tax assessed house values, which provide the basis for the property tax, were set at 75 percent of expected market value and remained fixed for several years. The returns to housing were also taxed through a *capital gains tax* and a *tax on net wealth*. From 1993, the capital gains rate was set to

15 percent of the nominal net gain after deduction of repair expenses, brokerage fees and so on. The tax could be rolled forward if the gain was reinvested in more expensive housing. Furthermore, net wealth (above SEK 1.5 mn) was taxed at a rate of 1.5 percent per annum. Overall, neither of these taxes were of major importance to most households, the capital gains tax because it could be postponed – thus reducing the effective tax rate – and the wealth tax because it had many loopholes. Illustrative calculations by Englund *et al.* (1995) suggest that the 1991 reform increased the rental cost of owner-occupied housing by almost 50 percent, from 5.7 percent to 8.2 of house value, based on a 10 percent interest rate, 7 percent inflation and 5 percent operation and maintenance costs.

As mentioned in the previous section, there were also direct subsidies to first mortgages. Nominal interest rates were guaranteed to follow a pre-set path over the course of the loan. The guaranteed interest rates differed between owner-occupied and rental housing to compensate for the asymmetry of the tax system. These loans were amortised over periods of 40–60 years. Berger *et al.* (2000) have calculated the net present discounted value of the interest subsidy to owner-occupied housing in the 1980s as between 13 and 21 percent of building costs depending on the specific assumptions.

The subsidised loans were issued to the first owner of the home. The loans were assumable but any subsequent extra borrowing, in connection with a house sale or as equity withdrawal by the current owner, had to come at regular market terms. Before 1985, access to such funding was restricted by the cap put on low-priority lending. This restriction affected liquidity and mobility in the housing market. Direct loans from seller to buyer were common if bank loans were not available.

Direct interest subsidies remained essentially unchanged during the latter part of the 1980s. It was only in connection with the 1991 tax reform that the system was changed. From 1993 a new system was gradually introduced. The objective was to abolish the interest subsidy to owner-occupied houses altogether and to limit the subsidy to multi-family units, which were taxed as business income, to correspond to 30 percent of a standardised estimate of interest costs. In practice, the new rules meant a reduction in the interest subsidy to rental units of around half in the late 1990s. In the low-interest environment of the 2000s, on the other hand, the new 30 percent subsidy in fact was more generous than the old system of guaranteed interest rates (See Finance Ministry 2005: Tables 9.1 and 9.3). The interest subsidies were finally abolished altogether from 2007.

Under the old system, primary mortgages up to 70 percent of approved building costs were given by private mortgage lenders conditional on the building project being approved by a state agency. Secondary mortgages up to 95–98 percent of costs came directly from a state agency. Reforms in the early 1990s also made it possible for private lenders to grant secondary mortgages. The state agency was transformed into a mortgage bank, SBAB, competing with private lenders on more or less equal terms (arguably not quite, since equity may be cheaper for SBAB than for other lenders). To support secondary mortgages, the state now introduced a system of mortgage insurance. Initially the insurance fee was set below the market rate, thus including a subsidy element. Following reform in 1997 the fees are no longer subsidised.

As house prices started to rise again from the mid-1990s, the property tax – a key element in the reformed tax system – came under increasing attack. It was argued that the tax base was not measured with sufficient precision as values were assessed by the tax authorities that were influenced by observations of neighbouring transactions (natural enough for any property appraiser but seemingly alien to many laymen). Further it was argued that owner-occupied houses did not yield cash income and hence that many households would face liquidity problems in paying their taxes. In attractive areas – for example, the archipelagos outside Stockholm and Gothenburg – long-time residents saw their property values sky-rocketing without feeling any richer and without liquidity to cover the property tax. Gradually this type of critique gained political momentum. As a result tax-assessed values were frozen over extended periods and in 2007 the property tax was abolished, although reintroduced euphemistically as a 'property fee' at the same time. For properties with a tax-assessed value below SEK 800000 the property fee is 1.2 percent of the tax-assessed value, but for the properties with a value above SEK 800000 the fee is capped at SEK 9600. In 2007, 48 percent of all properties were above the cap. With increasing house prices thereafter, the fee is now a lump sum irrespective of the house value for the majority of homeowners.

Partly to compensate for the reduced property tax, capital gains tax was increased from 20 to 22 percent. Further, an interest charge was levied on the tax liability that was rolled over. The cost of homeownership was also affected by the abolition of the gift and estate tax in 2005 and the wealth tax in 2007. Since that year, Sweden has been in the near unique position of having essentially no taxes levied directly on wealth and property. According to calculations by the Ministry of Finance, the net income from the property tax, the wealth tax, the capital gains tax and the mortgage interest deduction has gone from around 2 percent or more of disposable income in the mid-1990s to minus half a percent in the 2010s.

Market changes

In the deregulated environment of the last two decades, the development of housing finance has reflected underlying market forces. Deregulation triggered several structural changes in the market of particular importance for housing finance. Until the 1980s, private housing finance was dominated by financial institutions without equity owners: savings banks and other mutual lenders (in particular the mortgage lender *Stadshypotekskassan*). The boards of these institutions typically involved strong participation by local politicians and business leaders. Lending decisions tended to reflect 'the public interest'. This structure was changed in the 1990s. New legislation enacted in 1991 made it possible to transform savings banks into joint-stock companies. As a result, the majority of savings banks were merged into a commercial bank: the current *Swedbank*, today, is one of the four major Swedish banks. An analogous law change in 1992 allowed the transformation of *Stadshypotekskassan* into a joint stock company, first majority-owned by the state and since 1997 by one of the 'big four' banks, *Handelsbanken*. From this date, if not before, decisions regarding housing loans were no different than any other lending or borrowing decision.

During the same period, the general loan market was also transformed. Deregulation had already unleashed intensified competition in the 1980s. As a result a wave of mergers and acquisitions took place and led to a concentration of the Swedish banking sector. Today, four banks, *Swedbank*, *Handelsbanken*, *Nordea* and *SEB*, account for three-quarters of all bank lending. This transformation was also heavily influenced by the banking crisis in the early 1990s. Prior to the crisis, the state was the majority owner of one of the major banks (out of a total of six in 1991), *Nordbanken*. As a result of the crisis, the government also took over another of the big six, *Gota*. These two banks were subsequently merged forming the starting point for the *Nordea* banking group; today, the only Swedish bank to qualify as of systemic importance within the EU. The majority stake in *Nordea* was sold to private interests in the 1990s. This, like the subsequent sale of *Stadshypotek*, shows the commitment of successive Swedish governments – irrespective of political colour – to the private ownership of financial institutions.

What has this transformation of the Swedish banking industry meant for the structure of housing finance (see Sveriges Riksbank 2014a for an excellent overview of the current Swedish mortgage market)? One major development is an increase in the variety of mortgage contracts. The traditional Swedish mortgage had a very long maturity (40–60 years) typically with linear amortisation and with the interest rate fixed for a period of 5 years, after which the interest rate was reset unilaterally by the lender. In the 1990s banks started to offer a menu of contracts, ranging from flexible interest rates (in practice reset every 3 months) to fixed rates over 10 years and more. Gradually, most households have chosen to benefit from the historical experience that the yield curve is mostly upward sloping. The fraction of borrowers choosing flexible rates has grown from a tenth in 1996 to more than half today. In other respects, however, Swedish mortgage contracts remain quite standardised. There is no prepayment option; in case of prepayment, the lender may charge a fee that corresponds to the interest difference. Nor is there a default option; Swedish lenders have full recourse to borrower income and assets in addition to the collateral.

In a market environment, the availability of mortgage loans depends on the banks' credit risk assessment. The banks learned from the crisis that collateral values can vanish quickly, in particular once the costs of repossession are taken into account. As a consequence, they came to look more closely at the borrowers' income and ability to repay the loan rather than relying on collateral values. In an environment of full recourse loans, income is clearly a more important indicator of credit risk than, say, the loan-to-value ratio (LTV). But the banks had also learned that loans to households rarely give rise to large losses; at worst minor concessions have to be made. Consequently, the availability of mortgage loans has not been a problem for homebuyers, at least not for those with secure employment and an ability to service the loan.

As a result of the integration of the specialised mortgage lenders into the leading commercial banking groups, all Swedish banks have come to rely quite heavily on housing-related lending. As noted, such lending has for long been regarded as virtually riskless. Even during the banking crisis, when prices of single-family homes fell by 20 percent, credit losses related to household mortgages were negligible. As a consequence, mortgages carry low risk weights in Value-at-Risk and other standard risk-assessment models based on statistical inference from historical data. The view of household mortgages as virtually risk-free is controversial however. To understand why, we have to look at the funding side.

Traditionally, when mortgage lending was done through specialised institutions, the loans were funded by regular bonds backed by the entire balance sheet of the institution and not earmarked to any particular set of loans. The maturity structure of these bonds was closely matched to the maturity of the mortgages. The lending institutions did not engage in maturity transformation, and with a low-credit-risk mortgage portfolio they could operate with relatively little equity. The bonds issued by these institutions were transacted in a quite liquid market dominated by domestic Swedish investors like pension funds and insurance companies. Normally, the bonds traded at interest rates 50 or so basis points above those for the corresponding government bonds, to the extent that mortgage lending was done by banks and funded by a mixture of deposits, bonds and equity; they were also seen as low risk, despite the considerable amount of maturity transformation that was involved.

With the increasing integration into international financial markets, the standardisation of financial instruments has assumed more importance. As a sign of this, Sweden adopted new legislation in 2004 allowing banks to issue covered bonds, analogous with similar instruments in Denmark, Germany and other European countries. In case of default, such bonds are secured by a registered pool of high-quality mortgages. In the 2000s, Swedish housing bonds were gradually converted into covered bonds. While this may have made them easier to understand and analyse for international investors, who own around one-third of all outstanding bonds (Sandström *et al.* 2013: diagram 4), it is not clear that the introduction of covered bonds had much of an impact on interest margins over government bonds.

An indicator of the efficiency of the system is the interest margin between government bonds on the one hand and the interest on mortgages on the other. The development of this margin at the shortest end of the yield curve is illustrated in Figure 22.2, which shows how the mortgage interest rate can be decomposed into the overnight repo rate plus three margins: the cost of going from overnight to the 3-month STIBOR (Stockholm inter-bank offered rate) rate; the risk premium between STIBOR and the bank funding rate; and the profit margin between the bank funding rate and the mortgage rate. We can see that the risk premium was essentially absent prior to the crisis, whereas it added 30–50 basis points in 2009–2012 after which it has come down to only a few basis points. The profit margin, on the other hand, has increased substantially and is today around one full percentage point, the highest margin during the period covered by the graph. This seems to indicate a certain lack of competition in the market combined with an attempt by the banks to increase their capital base in the expectation of stricter regulations.

The availability of low-cost bank loans has been particularly important for the market for co-op shares and explains why the fraction of co-ops has

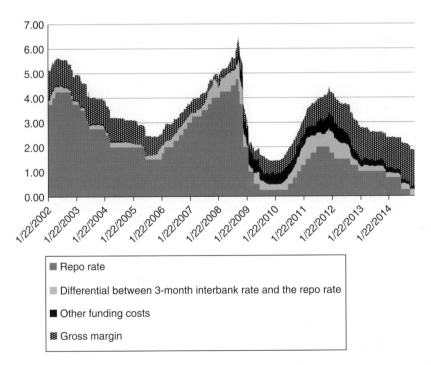

Figure 22.2 Decomposition of the mortgage rate for new mortgages with a 3-month fixed rate.
Source: Sveriges Riksbank (2014b: Chart B2.7) (updated).

increased from 17 percent of the dwelling stock in 1991 to 23 percent in 2012, while the fraction of households living in rental units has fallen from 41 to 36 percent (Figure 22.1). The increased attractiveness of co-ops is explained by two factors. First, rent setting is regulated. As a result access to a rental unit is difficult, in particular in the major metropolitan areas. Second, co-ops are favoured by the tax system just like regular ownership. Rents are set in negotiations between organisations representing tenants and landlords. The underlying principle is that rents should be similar for all dwellings of comparable quality irrespective of owner or age and that the general rent level should be aligned with the cost of producing new dwellings of comparable quality. In practice, negotiated rents have significantly underestimated the importance of location, particularly in the major metropolitan areas. To take Stockholm as an example, the rents in the city centre may be 20 percent above rents in the suburbs, whereas the cost of occupying a co-op apartment (fee to the co-op association plus capital costs) may differ by a factor of two or three. As a consequence, access to rental units in attractive locations is severely limited. In 2013, the average queuing time for a rental apartment in Stockholm was 7 years (Bostadsförmedlingen 2014).

With two levels of housing costs, one for rentals and one for co-ops, an apartment building will also command a different price depending on its tenure. The total market value of all shares of a co-op association is much higher than the net present value of the corresponding negotiated rents. There are, thus, strong incentives to sell apartment buildings to co-op associations. The process of conversion from rental to co-op is not uncomplicated, however. A landlord is only allowed to sell if a two-thirds majority of the tenants agree to form a co-op association and buy the property. By buying, tenants give up the value of occupying their dwellings below market rent, and have to be compensated by a sufficiently low purchase price. Hence, the reservation price will differ among tenants depending on the value the tenant attaches to the right to rent below market price. As a result, the conversion process has been gradual, despite the strong economic incentives. The pace of conversions has also been influenced by political considerations. Communities ruled by social democrats have been less inclined to allow conversion to co-ops than those with liberal-conservative governments.

Impacts

We have followed the evolution of Swedish housing finance from a strictly regulated system with quantitative controls in the early 1980s to today's sophisticated and competitive market. During this period, as shown in Figure 22.3, Sweden has experienced two credit booms. Between 1986 and 1990 the household debt-to-income ratio increased from 100 to 130 percent. As a result of the crisis the ratio came down to 90 percent within a couple

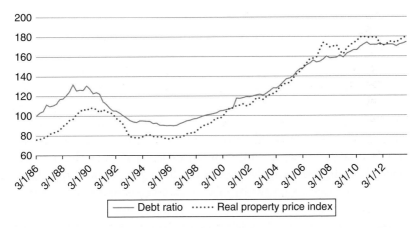

Figure 22.3 The ratio of household debt to disposable income (percent) and an index of the real price of owner-occupied one-family houses.
Source: Sveriges Riksbank, Financial Stability Report (2014b: 2, Diagram 1:6).

of years, but this has been followed by an almost uninterrupted increase to 175 percent today. This extended period of expansion has been a cause of growing policy concern in recent years. In particular, it has been taken as a major reason to maintain a relatively restrictive monetary policy.

As we can see from the figure, the development of the debt ratio has been closely paralleled by the development of housing prices. The question is whether the credit boom has been causing the house price boom or vice versa. In other words: can house prices be explained by fundamental demand and supply factors? On the demand side, user costs have decreased considerably as a result of lower interest rates and eased taxation. Between 1995 and 2014, the nominal interest rate on a 5-year mortgage fell from 11 to 3.5 percent. Arguably, inflationary expectations were relatively constant during this period, so the corresponding fall in the real interest rate is equally large in percentage points (and larger in relative terms). Furthermore, the reduction in the property tax in 2007 may be translated into a price increase of approximately 10 percent. During the same period, real disposable income per capita increased by 55 percent and labour market pressures resulted in continued migration into the main metropolitan areas. It is remarkable and important that this strong demand increase has not so far been met with a corresponding building increase. The number of new units completed has not, by far, kept pace with the population increase. As a consequence, the average number of individuals per dwelling, which had been falling for a long time and continues to fall outside the major metropolitan areas, has now gone up in Stockholm from 2.02 in 1993 to 2.16 in 2012 (Boverket 2012). This lack of additional supply is the more striking given the sharp increase in Tobin's Q during this period: between 1995 and 2014 the factor cost index for one-family homes only increased by 80 percent, whereas house prices increased by 200 percent during the same period, so profitability has increased.

A broad conclusion – backed up by quantitative and econometric studies (e.g. Claussen *et al.* 2011; Englund 2011; Sørensen 2012) – is that the current high prices may reasonably be attributed to fundamentals, conditional on the lack of supply response and the general housing shortage. It does not seem necessary to refer to a 'bubble' driven by optimistic expectations or more generous funding conditions to motivate the price increase. The big question, however, is how permanent is this supply shortage? If a construction boom is around the corner, this ought to feed back into expectations of future price developments. In this sense, today's elevated prices may build on expectations that ultimately will not be sustained. Whether this comes about through a dramatic 'bubble burst' or through a more gradual process, probably depends on the nature of the supply process, not least how it will be influenced by local planning processes.

Compared to many other countries, Sweden's financial system was relatively little affected by the Global Financial Crisis. After a blip in 2008–2009, major trends continued seemingly unperturbed. Household indebtedness as a fraction of GDP continued to grow from 45 percent in the mid-1990s to 75 percent in 2007 to 90 percent today. The increase in lending has become a major policy concern, particularly in the last couple of years. It has even affected monetary policy and caused the Riksbank to maintain a higher interest rate than that proven to be consistent with the inflation target. The Swedish inflation rate has hovered around zero since 2010, short of the 2 percent target, in a situation where unemployment is arguably above its natural rate.

Overall, the cost of mortgage borrowing has remained low, even though the margin between the repo interest rate set by the Riksbank and variable mortgage interest rates has increased somewhat from around 100 basis points before the crisis to around 150 basis points today. This reflects higher funding costs for banks combined with increased bank profit margins. The strong credit growth has also been supported by the banks' switch of focus from collateral values to borrower income and ability to service the loan. In view of this, 85 percent LTV came to be the standard for any household who was deemed creditworthy at all and loans beyond 85 percent LTV were increasingly common. The average LTV across all new housing loans increased from 59 percent in 2002 to 71 percent in 2010 (Finansinspektionen 2014). To put a halt to this development, the *Finansinspektionen* decided in the fall of 2010 to put an 85 percent LTV cap on all new mortgage loans. As a result the average LTV on new loans has fallen slightly to 70 percent in 2013. But as seen in Figure 22.3, this has not prevented house prices from increasing even further. Another source of concern is that an increasing fraction of loans – around 50 percent of new loans granted (Finansinspektionen 2014) – are non-amortising. This has led to an initiative from the supervisor to require that all new loans amortise at a minimum of 2 percent per year down to an LTV of 70 percent and 1 percent per year down to an LTV of 50 percent. This will be implemented in 2015. Yet another issue is that the majority of all mortgages (around two-thirds) have variable rates. This exposes households to considerable interest risk, but also makes monetary policy more powerful. But variable rate loans can also be seen as an insurance against income risk since interest rates typically co-vary positively with the business cycle (i.e. interest rates tend to be high when the average household can best afford paying them).

Mortgage lending to households has traditionally been seen as having low risk to the lender, largely because they come with full recourse to borrower assets and income. Consequently, bank internal models based on historical data yield very low capital coverage according to the Basel rules – on average only 5 percent in 2012. This has been regarded as too low, taking a broader macro-prudential view. Consequently, the supervisor imposed a 15 percent risk-weight floor for mortgage loans from 2013 and there is a suggestion to increase this further to 25 percent. It remains an open, and controversial, issue as to whether this will be enough to maintain financial stability.

Finally, it is striking that most of the policy debate has focused on various restrictions on the supply of credit. Reforms aimed at reducing the demand for loans – such as increasing the property tax or reducing the tax deductibility of interest payments – are still lacking.

Looking to the future

The combination of rent regulation and very high co-op share prices causes major social and economic problems. In particular, young households without very good income prospects and/or wealthy parents (perhaps because the parents are homeowners) are effectively locked out of the housing market in major metropolitan areas. The square metre price of an apartment with a 30-minute commute to the city centre of Stockholm is at least €4000. A well-functioning housing finance system has contributed to this situation. Given the focus on the ability to service a loan, a starting apartment had been within reach for two-earner households with secure employment. With increasing prices, however, the key hurdle has switched from the income of the young household to the income and wealth of their parents. Effectively, it has become even more of an insider market. Just like access to the rental market is limited by connections that allow inheriting a rent-regulated contract, access to the owner market depends on parental support in covering the collateral and/or by guaranteeing the loan. This has obvious negative consequences for labour market mobility. The recent LTV restrictions may well have helped to dampen price increases, but at the expense of limiting outsider access to the expanding metropolitan labour markets even further.

Given this, most observers agree that the housing finance system is not the problem. Instead one can point to three areas where reforms are urgently needed:

1. A tax system that is reasonably neutral between owner-occupied housing, rental housing and other sectors of the economy, while at the same time not preventing mobility. This could be achieved for example by reintroducing a property tax and reducing the capital gains tax.
2. A reform of the rent-setting system. This would have to be done gradually to ensure incumbent tenants security of tenure and could be supplemented by increased housing allowances and a temporary tax on the windfall gains made by landlords.
3. An overhaul of the planning process to increase the flexibility of housing supply.

Since the crisis in the early 1990s, many sectors of the Swedish economy have been deregulated – not just the financial system but also the transportation system, schools, many utilities and social services. Many would argue that this deregulation may have come too fast and has gone too far in some cases. Be that as it may, the housing sector provides a striking contrast. Attempts at reforms in the three areas highlighted previously meet with resistance from insider groups: incumbent tenants who oppose higher rents, incumbent homeowners who oppose higher taxes and resulting capital losses, and incumbent residents who oppose more building in 'their backyard'. On earlier occasions – for example, the 1991 tax reform – the Swedish political system has showed an ability to agree on major reforms across the political spectrum. If the system still has that ability with a more fragmented parliament is an open question.

References

Berger, T, Englund, P, Hendershott, PH and Turner, B (2000). The capitalisation of interest subsidies: evidence from Sweden. *Journal of Money, Credit, and Banking* 32, 199–217.

Bostadsförmedlingen (2014). *Bostadskön i siffror*. [Online], Available: https://bostad.stockholm.se/statistik/ (accessed 29 July 2015).

Boverket (2012). *Bostadsbristen ur ett marknadsperspektiv*, Rapport 2012: 18.

Claussen, CA, Jonsson, M and Lagerwall, B (2011). A macroeconomic analysis of house prices in Sweden. In: *The Riksbank's Inquiry into the Risks in the Swedish Housing Market*. Sveriges Riksbank.

Englund, P (1999). The Swedish Banking Crisis – roots and consequences. *Oxford Review of Economic Policy* 15:3, 80–97.

Englund, P (2011). Swedish house prices in an international perspective. In: *The Riksbank's Inquiry into the Risks in the Swedish Housing Market*. Sveriges Riksbank.

Englund, P, Hendershott, PH and Turner, B. (1995) The tax reform and the housing market. *Swedish Economic Policy Review* 2, 319–356.

Finance Ministry (2005). *Rapport om ny bostadsfinansiering,* Ds 2005:39.

Finansinspektionen (2014). *The Swedish Mortgage Market 2014.*

Reinhart, C and Rogoff, K (2009). *This Time is Different.* Princeton University Press, Princeton.

Sandström, M, Forsman, D, Stenkula von Rosen, J and Fager Wettergren, J (2013). The Swedish covered bond market and links to financial stability. *Sveriges Riksbank Economic Review* 2013: 2.

Schularick, M and Taylor, AM (2012). Credit booms gone bust: monetary policy, leverage cycles, and financial crises, 1870–2008. *American Economic Review* 102, 1029–1061.

Sveriges Riksbank (2014a). From A to Z: the Swedish mortgage market and its role in the financial system, *Riksbank Studies,* April 2014.

Sveriges Riksbank (2014b). *Financial Stability Report.*

Sørensen, PB (2012). The Swedish housing market: trends and risks, report to the Swedish Fiscal Policy Council 2013/5.

Statistics Sweden (various years). Housing Stock. [Online] Available: www.scb.se (accessed 29 July 2015).

23

Housing Finance in Turkey over the Last 25 Years: Good, Bad or Ugly?

Yener Coşkun

Capital Markets Board of Turkey, Izmir University of Economics and the University of Sarajevo, Ankara, Turkey

Introduction

Turkish households traditionally prefer to invest in real estate as opposed to other investments. As a result of experiences during the high inflation, negative real interest rate periods following the 1970s, the majority of Turkish households believe that housing is the strongest available anti-inflationary hedging instrument (Coşkun *et al.* 2014). This economic history may also explain Turkey's high ownership ratio (61 percent) and its patterns of housing demand. Housing finance in the late 1980s was mostly dysfunctional and consequently houses were rarely used as collateral in many parts of the country. Both the Turkish economy and the housing market, however, have benefited from new policies and improved market dynamics since then. This research identifies three important trends which have had great influence on the practices and structure of housing finance in Turkey. These include: (i) the growing impact of central government policies and initiatives on the housing (and real estate) market after the 1980s; (ii) the impressive growth in the housing and primary mortgage markets in last decade; and (iii) the increasing internationalisation of the real estate (and housing) market in Turkey, specifically in last decade. These three key trends reveal that the development of Turkey's housing finance system over the last 25 years has been the result of market dynamics and specific government policies but is also the outcome of a wider socio-political agenda, characterised by the marketisation and liberalisation of the Turkish economy and its housing market.

Milestones in European Housing Finance, First Edition.
Edited by Jens Lunde and Christine Whitehead.
© 2016 John Wiley & Sons, Ltd. Published 2016 by John Wiley & Sons, Ltd.

This study discusses the economic and institutional environment within which the Turkish housing finance system developed over the last 25 years. It does not, however, include a detailed analysis or assessment of market performance, structural problems or the effectiveness of housing (finance) policies. Instead, it seeks to set out a framework for understanding milestones and trends in the development of Turkish housing markets and their impact on housing finance during this period.

The Turkish experience provides an interesting case study for several reasons. First, it is now an example of an almost completely market-based housing finance regime with some limited exceptions, mostly arising from the activities of the Housing Development Agency, hereafter HDA (TOKI). Second, the Turkish experience also suggests that the current housing finance system has not generated positive efficiency benefits for households, the housing finance market and the financial market more broadly because of structural problems and market incompleteness. Third, by documenting the evolution of housing policies after the 1980s and identifying changes in the institutional, regulatory and market structure of Turkish housing finance, we are able to see how the real estate and housing markets have become some of the main policy instruments for Turkey's central government. Essentially, these instruments have been used by the government to manage socio-economic and political pressures over the last decade. We also discuss what we should expect from the Turkish housing finance system in the near future, based on analysis of existing legislative/policy/market structures and emerging trends.

The Turkish housing finance system over the last 25 years from a marketisation perspective

Overview of the Turkish housing market

According to Turkstat data, there are approximately 20 million buildings in Turkey; 40 percent of these buildings are squatter settlements and 67 percent lack a settlement permit. Approximately 14 million of these buildings are residential. Renovation – that is, demolition and rebuilding – is necessary for approximately 6.5 million of these homes within of the next 20 years because of disaster risks (HDA accessed 2013). This picture implies that the housing and land management system in Turkey has important deficiencies, one key reason for an increased governmental role in housing finance.

The supply of housing in Turkey is market based and is dominated by home-ownership. Just less than two in three (61 percent) of the population were owner-occupiers in both 2006 and 2013 (Table 23.1) (for the proportion of households by ownership status of the dwelling, see TurkStat (2013a)). Most of the housing in Turkey is produced by the private sector, but there are two

Table 23.1 Income groups and tenure status in Turkey, 2006–2013.

| | | | Income Groups | | | | | |
| | | | Group I (%) | | Group II (%) | | Group III (%) | |
	2013	2006	2013	2006	2013	2006	2013	2006
NIP* (in thousand)	74 457	67 631	16 706	17 165	28 724	23 229	29 027	27 237
Tenure Status (percent)								
Owner	60.7	60.9	59.3	59.3	56.3	56.6	65.9	65.5
Tenant	21.3	23.5	22.8	25.0	23.3	26.0	18.5	20.5
Lodging**	1.6	1.1	0.4	0.0	1.1	0.9	2.9	2.0
Other***	16.3	14.5	17.4	15.7	19.3	16.5	12.8	12.0

Notes:
*NIP (non-institutional population): Comprises all the population excluding the residents of dormitories of universities, orphanages, rest homes for elderly persons, special hospitals, prisons and military barracks etc. Group I: refers to households who earn below 60% of the median income; Group II includes households who earn between 60% and 120% of the median income; and households in Group III earn above 120% of median income.

**'Lodging' is an ownership status of households who live in a house which belongs to either the government or a workplace or whose rent is paid by the workplace of one of the members of household.

***'Other' includes households that live in housing owned by family members or relatives, etc. and do not make any payment or pay only a a small amount of money (TurkStat 2013c: 173, 379).

Source: TurkStat (2010: 393; 2013c: 374; 2014).

exceptions: first, the HDA currently meets 5–10 percent of the housing need of Turkey (see Box 23.1 later) (HDA accessed 2013) and second, squatter settlements (*gecekondu*), which involve self-build production, are an important part of the existing housing stock. The provision of housing finance by the HDA started in the 1980s but almost stopped in early 2000s; since 2003, however, it has again greatly increased.

Figure 23.1 summarises the key features of the Turkish housing market (see also Coşkun 2011c: 43, 46) and underlines that housing has been a long-standing policy predicament in Turkey. The complexity of addressing housing through policy is the result of political and bureaucratic problems, a lack of sufficient and sustainable government resources (at either the local or central level), rapid urbanisation and rural immigration, income and wealth constraints faced by lower/middle income groups, and the negative impacts of macro-economic instabilities in Turkey.

Marketisation: literature review and periodisation

The Turkish economy has a bank-based financial system. Commercial banks, nearly 40 percent of which are foreign banks, are also main players in capital markets. However, structural problems and financial instabilities have made the Turkish economy fragile and have resulted in less developed financial and mortgage systems. Our primary focus in this section will be on

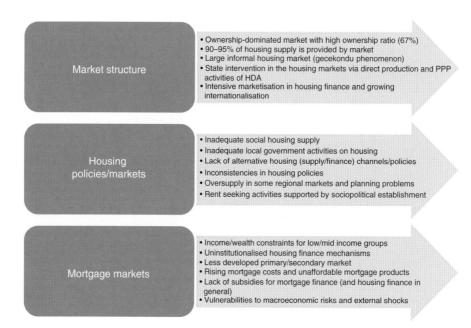

Figure 23.1 Overview of the Turkish housing market.
Source: Author.

the emerging marketisation of the housing market, looking at the critical junctures in Turkish housing policy and the transformation into a market-based housing finance system. We mark the starting point of this periodisation in 1980 as this encompasses key political and economic milestones of the country's development.

Different classification approaches have been used in existing housing literature in Turkey, generally focusing on the features of housing supply or the role of the public sector rather than the evolution of housing finance. For example, Bal (2010: 120–124) categorises housing (production and supply) systems in Turkey into five periods: 1923–1950, 1950–1965, 1965–1980, 1980–1990 and the period after 1990. The author specifically indicates that, although housing was market based from the 1980s, it became more market focused after 2000 when neoliberal policies became even more influential. Özdemir (2011: 1102–1112) analyses the role of the Turkish public sector in housing provision over three periods: 1950–1980, 1980–2000 and 2000 onwards. Concerning mortgage availability, the author says that the market is newly developed and has still only been serving upper income groups since 2000. For different approaches to classification of the Turkish housing (finance) system, see Tekeli (1995), Altaban (1996) (cited in Bal 2010: 120) and Keyder and Öncü (1993).

We suggest that the recent history of the Turkish housing finance system should be classified into three sub-periods. Those periods are: 1980–2000 (the early marketisation period); 2000–2002 (the transitional period) and post-2003 (the full marketisation period) (Figure 23.2).

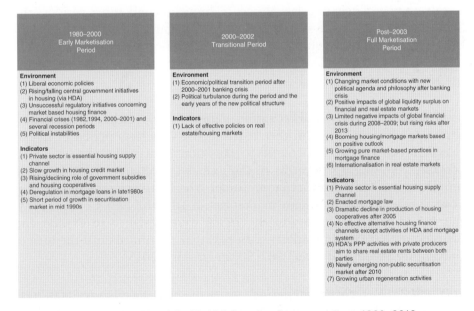

Figure 23.2 Marketisation of the Turkish housing finance system, 1980–2013.
Source: Author.

The three periods

Our attempt at classifying the development of Turkey's housing finance system into three periods is based on observations regarding market dynamics, legislation and policies. Indicators of the evolving marketisation of housing finance and the housing market overall after the 1980s include: the deregulation of the housing credit market in the late 1980s; introduction of secondary mortgage instruments, institutions and rules in capital market regulations from the early 1990s; a short period of growth in the securitisation market in the mid-1990s; a newly emerging non-public securitisation/bond market after 2010 (the first mortgage covered bond was issued in 2015; for an analysis of the Turkish covered bond market, see Coşkun and Gökçeimam 2015); the declining role of housing cooperatives in housing supply after 2005; the increasing importance of market-based mortgage loans after 2003; regulation of new primary/secondary mortgage markets; policy preference to keep subsidies at a minimum level in the housing finance system; the HDA's public-private partnership (PPP) activities with private producers with the goal of sharing real estate rents between both parties and growing internationalisation and urban regeneration activities. Although marketisation has been the overwhelming general trend in the Turkish housing finance system, there have been some exceptions to this privatisation. The provision of selective and limited central government subsidies via the HDA and urban regeneration schemes in the post-2003 period are two important examples of moves in the other direction. Subsidies for housing cooperatives were maintained before 2000 but these have been largely removed over the last decade. Throughout all three periods, the Turkish housing finance system lacked an efficient primary and secondary mortgage system, faced problems of instability concerning government subsidies and the HDA and struggled to develop successful alternative (social) housing finance channels.

1980–2000: The early marketisation period   1980 marked a significant turning point for Turkey in that it paved the way for a period of liberal restructuring. During the country's transition from a closed to a liberal economy, housing was brought to the fore as a profitable area that could provide capital for the new economic order. The 1980s were the transitional years in which housing became market based (Bal 2010: 122). Consequently, the state's housing policies in the 1980s were designed to expand and restructure the housing market – a process that continued until the turn of the century (Aydın and Yarar 2007: 50) and to early 2015.

2000–2002: The transitional period   After the banking crisis of 2000–2001 (see Box 23.3, later), structural reforms were designed to help the banking sector become the engine of economic growth. In order to return to sustainable economic growth, public sector deficits were reduced and the public sector stepped back from financial markets (BRSA 2010: ix, 34). Following the crisis, Turkey was able to enter a period of successful economic restoration as a result of an unusually long period of political and economic stability and the positive impacts of the global liquidity surplus particularly between 2003 and 2007. The banking crisis (2000–2001) and early post-crisis era (2002) can be classified as a transitional period because there were no effective housing finance policies.

Post 2003: The full marketisation period Despite the numerous challenges Turkey faced in addressing the problems after the 2000–2001 banking crisis, the Turkish economy has enjoyed a relatively successful record over the last decade. During this period, the real estate and housing sectors gradually became one of the top policy priorities at both the municipal and national levels. It is important to note that the rapid marketisation in the post-2003 period is based both on the increasing role of the real estate and housing sectors as an economic stabiliser for the general economy and the large increase in available housing credit thanks to the global liquidity surplus and economic stability.

In the full marketisation period, the private sector has continued to provide most of the housing supply in the country. This period represents a further rise in the marketisation of housing as a result of booming housing credit volume, PPP activities of HDA (see Box 23.1), the declining importance of (subsidised) housing cooperatives and more importantly, the lack of government subsidies on mortgage finance. Politically, this period has been characterised by a shift away from subsidies for low and middle income groups alongside the increasing marketisation of mortgage finance.

Box 23.1 The role of the HDA in the post-2003 period

Involvement of the central government in the housing and land markets remained a critical factor in both the early marketisation period (1980–2000) and the full marketisation period (post-2003) in Turkey (see Figure 23.2). Policymakers in Turkey have preferred to employ both market-based housing finance (mortgage) mechanisms (for higher-income groups) and direct housing production through the HDA (for lower-income groups) to address the housing finance problems in the post-2003 period. The beneficiaries of the HDA's social housing projects (constructed on HDA-owned land) make their down payments at the beginning of construction and then continue to pay monthly through a single-index repayment plan (Housing Development Agency 2006). There may also be payment increases, depending on inflation, in the housing finance programmes targeting the poorest citizens. The maturities of the loan repayments of the HDA are set at 10, 15 or 20 years depending on the financial capacities of the target group (HDA accessed 2013).

The following section discusses key institutional, regulatory and policy changes during these three periods and analyses their implications for the Turkish housing finance system, both in the last 25 years and in the future.

Finance milestones: The rise of marketisation and changes in housing finance

Regulation, marketisation and constraints

There were several unsuccessful market-based housing finance initiatives introduced in Turkey after 1980. Affordable mortgage products failed to develop in the market-based housing finance system because of a variety of factors: sub-optimal design of the housing finance instruments and intermediaries, macro-economic instabilities and a lack of efficient subsidy mechanisms. The mortgage law introduced in 2007 – the most important market-based housing finance regulation in Turkey – has seemingly proved unsuccessful in providing effective solutions to the larger structural problems (Coşkun and Yalçıner 2011). It has limited the positive impact on the development of mortgage markets. The economic rationale of the mortgage regulation was to increase housing credit volume within a sound mortgage banking environment. The primary reason for increasing the volume of housing credit in the last decade was mostly related to improving affordability and building upon the unusually successful growth in the Turkish economy after 2003.

While the housing market outlook may appear positive, questions remain about how low and middle-income groups will survive in this highly marketised housing finance environment. As suggested by Coşkun (2015), in the period between January 2005 and September 2011 public policies that sought to expand the money supply and increase the financial income/wealth of households may in fact have had little positive impact on housing credit growth and the development of the mortgage market in Turkey. However market-based housing finance policies do not seem to be the best option for addressing the income and wealth constraints faced by most of the population or for developing a well operating mortgage market. Nevertheless, although these policies appear 'ugly' from a social perspective, it is clear that this type of marketisation of housing finance has become the new norm in the Turkish housing market.

Declining financial support for housing cooperatives

The structure of housing supply in Turkey has a dual character (see Figure 23.1). On the one hand, housing is provided by a formal finance and production sector shaped by laws, private sector initiatives and formal credit mechanisms. On the other hand, there is a large illegal, informal housing finance and production sector, epitomised by the *gecekondu* phenomenon (Coşkun 2011a). Before the 2000s, housing cooperatives (co-ops) represented another core housing supply channel. In the last decade, however, policy changes have reduced financial support for these co-ops, which arguably has had a negative impact on the finance of affordable housing.

The financial support of co-ops by the HDA was one of the important housing supply mechanisms during the 1990s. For moderate income groups, cooperative housing is a tool for securing homeownership via affordable payments. Co-ops pool members' resources and benefit from collectivism during the development process. The HDA supported the production of co-ops through the provision of long-term, cheap housing credits. But mostly because of removed benefits, the share of co-ops in the production of total dwellings has declined from 34.7 percent to 5.6 percent between 2001 and 2011 (Turkstat 2012: 412–413).

The declining role of co-ops in the housing market has had several impacts, and serves as an indicator of the marketisation of Turkey's housing finance system. This change away from supporting co-ops favours market-based finance at the expense of subsidised housing finance. The groups who benefit from the decline of co-ops are probably private sector house suppliers and mortgage banks. In this context, while the housing finance mechanisms that supported co-ops were weakening, mortgage credit volume has been increasing since mid-2003. Instead of providing better governmental (and/or third party) control mechanisms on the HDA's credit subsidies to co-ops, the HDA preferred to be a direct supplier (producer), via contractors, in the social housing sector and almost entirely ceased providing financial incentives to co-ops. The gradual decline in HDA subsidies for co-ops and the shift to direct housing production by the HDA represent a change in philosophy around the state's housing policies after 2003. As a result of these policy changes, some part of housing demand that was originally satisfied by the supply of co-ops may now be met by the free market. Consequently, this policy change represents another step toward marketisation and supports the aims of policy makers who want to increase middle-class housing demand for mortgage markets.

Urban regeneration, marketisation and housing finance markets

Investment in urban regeneration has grown substantially in recent years as an outcome of central government policy. Urban regeneration helps to create economic activity for the construction, banking and state sectors and improves the formal housing finance system. It is expected that the production of regenerated housing units will increase and hence create a new impetus in both the urban area and the macro-economy. From the perspective of Turkish municipal economies and the national economy, the urban regeneration projects are expected to increase government spending on subsidies and infrastructure while also increasing private firm and household spending through construction and housing loans (for the relevant regulations and the outcomes, see Çevre ve Şehircilik Bakanlığı). Additionally, Penpecioğlu (2013: 182) underlines that, in the formation of urban development projects, urban planning as the strategic mechanism in space production has been subordinated to the priorities of economic growth.

As indicated, with the exception of the HDA activities, the housing finance structure of Turkey is almost fully marketised and includes no effective subsidy schemes for specific social groups. Surprisingly, however, recent urban regeneration legislation has included a temporary subsidy framework. According to relevant legislation, the government will pursue selective subsidy policies in urban regeneration projects including rent and interest payment assistance (credit support) for owners whose apartments are to be regenerated. This selective subsidy strategy may help to satisfy general economic expectations from the process. Therefore, it seems that urban regeneration has developed both a new rental sector and housing supply channel while also serving as a new tool of the real estate-based, short-term growth strategy for the country. From a housing (and also construction) finance perspective, the urban regeneration scheme represents a new, profitable face of the marketisation of the Turkish housing finance system, but one that includes a subsidy system for qualified projects.

Impacts of the transformation of the housing finance system

Both the marketisation processes and the introduction of new state initiatives concerning the Turkish housing market gained pace after the 1980s. The Turkish economy faced three economic crises and several recession periods particularly in the 1990s (see Box 23.3). However, in the last decade, the economy has generally showed resilience and both the housing and mortgage markets have experienced spectacular growth. In this respect, 'the good' part of the story includes three positive transformations that resulted from the changing market dynamics of last decade.

According to statistics, housing demand and supply, housing transactions, mortgage rates and house prices have all generally followed positive trends in recent years. Mortgage loan rates declined from 29.3 percent in 2003 to 10.9 percent in 2013. Dramatic declines in interest rates have had positive effects on key housing market variables, including house prices and the volume of loans. Figures 23.3 and 23.4 together show the inverse correlation between mortgage interest rates and house prices/loan volume in Turkey between 2003 and 2013. In this context, lower mortgage rates have positively supported mortgage affordability through to the lower costs of mortgage loans and probably growing refinancing arrangements on better terms.

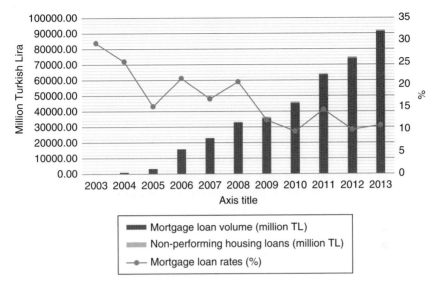

Figure 23.3 Mortgage loan rates/volume and non-performing housing loans in Turkey, 2003–2013.
Source: CBRT (2013); BRSA (2012; 2013).

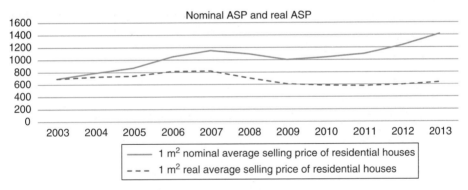

Figure 23.4 Average nominal and real selling price of residential houses per m² in Turkey, 2003–2013.
Source: Reidin (2013) and TurkStat (2013d).
Note: Year-end average house selling price (ASP) data are derived from the arithmetic average of monthly house price data for 2008–2013. Because of the lack of data, the 2007 year-end ASP house price data is the arithmetic average of 7 months (6/2007–12/2007). Longer period house price data starting in 2003 were constructed by combining the actual house price index, provided by Reidin for the term 6/2007–2013, and the construction cost index as a proxy (for the term 2003–2006) (for the methodology, see Coşkun 2015). For a different perspective, researchers may also review Turkish Central Bank house price indexes.

Figure 23.3 shows the boom in mortgage loan volumes between 2003 and 2013. After the 2000–2001 banking crisis, the value of mortgage loans in Turkey increased from $0.04 bn in 2003 to $51.6 bn in 2013 with an insignificant non-performing housing loan portfolio.

Moreover, this positive market environment has fundamentally continued, despite the Global Financial Crisis (GFC: see Box 23.3). The 'good' news is that increasing access to mortgage finance in the last decade has supported formal housing finance at the expense of informal housing finance (see Box 23.2). Yet the ratio of mortgage loans to GDP is roughly 6 percent as of June 2013 and there have been no publicly issued mortgage backed securities since the mid-1990s. This picture suggests that Turkish primary and secondary mortgage market volumes are far below the EU 27 and US averages. Therefore, despite the recent boom in housing loans, the mortgage market in Turkey is comparatively much smaller than markets in more developed countries.

The greater availability of relatively affordable mortgage loans has also helped to increase housing demand and house prices in addition to the volume of mortgage loans. As Figure 23.4 demonstrates, the nominal average selling price of residential houses per m² has almost doubled in last decade, while real house prices by CPI have fallen since 2007.

Box 23.2   Institutional housing finance and housing finance sources in Turkey

Until the establishment of the Mass Housing Fund (MHF) in 1984, there were only two institutionalised finance channels in Turkey: the state-owned Emlak Bank, and the Worker's Social Security Fund. Together, these channels contributed to the financing of less than 10 percent of the housing constructed in the 1970s. Until the inception of the MHF, most housing construction was financed either directly by private savings or by short-term, commercial and supplier credit (Keyder and Öncü 1993: 23–24). Most private housing finance programmes were developed as part of consumer lending initiatives that started in the late 1980s. There were some similarities between the programmes of four private lenders (Pamukbank, Emlak Bank, Yapı Kredi and Is Bank). For example, the loans tended to have maturities of no longer than 5 years, be fully amortising, require monthly payments and have rates that could adjust at least annually. Most were available for finished homes only and loan-to-value ratios (LTVs) tended to be between 50 percent and 80 percent (Fannie Mae 1992: 11–12). Therefore, before the mortgage boom in recent years, formal finance channels were quite restrictive in Turkey with a less developed institutional housing finance framework than existed in other countries (Fannie Mae 2004).

Profiles of Turkish home owners under this finance system can be grouped as follows: self-builders, inheritors, beneficiaries of parental donations and family borrowing, transfers relying on private debts, direct purchasers (with existing assets and savings), purchasers via the HDA, transfers with market debt programmes and those accessing housing through unauthorised channels (*gecekondu*) (Erdoğdu 2010: 110–113). Personal savings remain the most frequent source of capital used to purchase a home, representing a 76 percent share of all housing finance in Turkey. Nearly 62 percent of owner-occupiers who did not use financial markets purchased their property using their own savings (HDA 2006: 62, cited in: Erdoğdu 2010: 110).

On the other hand, it is important to note that the short average mortgage loan maturity in Turkey makes housing less affordable. According to the Turkish Banking Association (2012: 8) the average mortgage loan maturity was only 7.2 years between 2006 and 2010.

Future trends in housing finance markets

The internationalisation of Turkey's housing market

Growing foreign direct investment (FDI) is one of the major recent trends in the Turkish real estate and housing sectors. As discussed previously, policy makers support the real estate sector as a tool for short-term growth purposes. Growing foreign demand in the real estate sector conforms to this policy and also helps to finance current account deficits, one of the most fragile points of the Turkish economy.

The value of the net real estate purchase by foreigners between 2004 and 2012 was $20.9 bn (see Table 23.2). Compared to the net $1 bn of real estate purchases made by foreigners between 1995 and 2003, the 2004–2012 period can be classified as a boom period (Republic of Turkey Ministry of Economy 2012: 9). The Turkish real estate market has thus experienced increasing internationalisation in last decade as a result of foreign demand. According to several local and global industry reports (see DTZ 2013: 1–2; Knight Frank 2013: 29), Istanbul's real estate market is one of the fastest growing markets in the world. However, it is also important to note that this internationalisation may increase the instability and vulnerability of the overall economy and, in turn, the housing market (see Box 23.3).

Gated communities and housing finance

Changing preferences among high-income groups towards gated communities are visible in big Turkish cities. The essential motives for this shift in demand include desire for safety and luxury. The increasing income and wealth of existing and newly emerging social groups and the greater availability of mortgage credit in last decade have also supported this development. New residential units in big cities are of higher quality, have higher prices and are marketed through nationwide campaigns. This commoditisation has socio-economic and political implications for different income groups. In this respect, housing researchers have specifically addressed the following issues: the social impacts of gated communities; social exclusion; new housing supply and new rent economies in regenerated areas through the activities of private firms. From the perspective of housing finance, increasing demand from international buyers and the rise of gated communities have resulted in

Table 23.2 FDI inflows by component, 1995–2011 (USD millions).

	1995–2003*	2004	2005	2006	2007	2008	2009	2010	2011
Cumulative FDI (net)	11 253	2785	10 031	20 185	22 047	19 504	8411	9038	15 904
FDI	10 255	1442	8190	17 263	19 121	16 567	6629	6544	13 891
Capital (Net)	9591	888	8053	16 876	18 100	14 313	5382	5792	13 297
Inflow	10 682	986	8454	17 533	18 843	14 348	5464	5827	15 288
Outflow	–1091	–98	–401	–657	–743	–35	–82	–35	–1991
Reinvested Earnings	132	204	81	106	294	399	788	411	599**
Other Capital***	532	350	56	281	727	1855	459	341	–5
Real Estate Purchases (Net)	998	1343	1841	2922	2926	2937	1782	2494	2013

Notes:
* Cumulative
** Estimate
*** Investment credits received by foreign-owned companies from foreign partner
Source: Republic of Turkey Ministry of Economy (2012: 9).

Box 23.3   Banking crises in Turkey and impacts of the GFC

The Turkish economy has experienced three important financial crises and several periods of financial pressure since 1980. After the 1982 and 1994 banking crises, the third crisis, the 2000–2001 banking crisis, resulted in huge economic losses and a brand new political structure in the country. After the crisis, economic recovery was guided by an International Monetary Fund (IMF) and World Bank-supported financial stability programme, which has been accepted as one of the critical reasons for the recent economic revitalisation (Coşkun 2013: 46). The 5 years between 2003 and 2008 were a period of economic growth for the country and the GFC had little impact on this positive trajectory.

During the GFC, many countries experienced huge financial losses and extraordinarily negative impacts on their housing sectors. Turkey, however, faced limited negative impacts. By analysing the structure of Turkey's primary and secondary mortgage markets, we argue that these limited negative impacts were related to the small and inefficient mortgage economy of the country rather than a positive strategy of successful crisis management or market dynamics. Because securitisation and structured product markets had also been dysfunctional before/during crisis, the Turkish economy was not exposed to significant problems. Therefore, the absence of a secondary mortgage market and the inefficient housing credit market may have, in reality, been beneficial for Turkey during the financial crisis (Coşkun 2011b: 13).

---

higher residential property values and consequently increasing affordability problems in urban areas.

Challenges to housing finance: income and wealth constraints and emerging risks

It is expected that the Turkish mortgage market will pursue further growth into the long-term, but this is not without some short and long-term risks. It may be true that Turkey is a dynamic, emerging economy and that there are several positive factors that resulted from the improved housing and mortgage market performance in recent years. But it is equally true that the housing and mortgage markets will face important challenges. First, income and wealth constraints faced by most households and a lack of effective subsidy policies for middle and low-income groups may create housing affordability problems, and hence limit the development of market based housing finance systems. In this context, Coşkun *et al.* (2014) show empirically that between 2003 and 2013, median priced housing was not affordable for median and average income households in Turkey, despite positive trends in macro-economic variables and even in affordability. Yalçıner and Coşkun (2014) suggest that developments in the Turkish mortgage market are not only directly related to financial stability, affordable mortgage costs, sufficient housing demand and housing market activity level but also to more complex socio-economic and political processes, such as income inequalities.

Second, another potentially 'bad' development may be an increase in risk as the result of housing market growth. In this context, fragilities in the Turkish economy may inevitably create distortions in the housing and mortgage market. Moreover, some have raised questions about whether there are growing risks from rising house prices, growing mortgage and construction loans, unsold new residential units (excess housing supply) and the aggressive marketing campaigns of both the HDA and private firms (Coşkun 2013: 48–50). Volatilities and growing perceptions of risk in international and local financial markets increase these concerns. On the other hand, it has been observed in recent years that the HDA has shown unusually effective performance in social housing production. It seems that hybridity is one of the critical aspects of the HDA's enterprise model and its pragmatic approach called revenue-sharing has worked well. However, as discussed by Coşkun (2011a), concerns also exist about the sustainability and efficiency of the existing policies and the financial structure of the HDA. Therefore, we should note that the lack of transparency about the structure and operation of the HDA may hide potential risks in its current housing finance model. Additionally, the way that real estate and housing markets are working may be one of the most important socio-economic factors in increasing social tensions between different social groups. In this respect, the Gezi Park protests, which occurred in mid-2013 in Istanbul and spread to some other Turkish cities, represent an interesting case study for real estate researchers. This series of events may be also analysed from the perspectives of how the new middle class and urban poor differentially react to income inequalities, rent-seeking activities in real estate and private profit-making in public places (Fukuyama 2013; Gürkaynak 2013; Keyder 2013).

Conclusions

After the collapse of the golden age of economic growth in the early 1970s, developed countries gradually deregulated their economies. This marketisation process slowly but inevitably affected the social sectors, also gradually involving housing. The Turkish economy and housing market were no exception to this almost global phenomenon. Marketisation in the Turkish economy started after 1980, but has rapidly accelerated in the last decade. Moreover, the increasing role of the real estate and housing sectors has acted as an economic stabiliser and a growth channel after the 2000–2001 banking crisis period, which, in turn, has had noteworthy impacts on the marketisation process.

This study aimed to document the economic and institutional environment of the Turkish housing finance system over the last 25 years, in the light of the influence of marketisation in the housing market. It analysed the regulatory, policy and market dynamics related to housing finance and the housing market after 1980. In this context, we have defined three key periods to describe the evolution of the Turkish housing finance system over the last 25 years. These are the early marketisation period (1980–2000), the transitional period (2000–2002) and the full marketisation period (post-2003). Market dynamics in the last decade have resulted in increasing house prices and a growing volume of mortgage loans with falling interest rates. Moreover, it seems that the internationalisation of the market, the growing popularity of gated communities, income and wealth constraints and inequalities as well as some external risks will shape the near future of housing finance and markets in Turkey.

The discussion presented in the study provides a framework for analysing the evolution, problems and future trends of the Turkish housing market. In this context, we can identify three key conclusions. The 'good' thing about the development of the Turkish housing market that has been driven by marketisation over the last 25 years is that it has stimulated economic growth, internationalisation, rapid urbanisation and demographic transformation. These dynamics have helped to increase housing demand and supply into the longer term. The 'bad' thing is that the fragility of the Turkish economy may inevitably create negative pressure on housing and mortgage markets based on the complex relationship between housing and financial markets. The 'ugly' outcome of this evolution is that housing finance in Turkey is now based on households having to finance their own home purchase in pure market conditions with some limited exceptions. In this context, income and wealth constraints and the lack of effective subsidy policies for middle and low-income groups have created housing affordability problems, which are constraining the long term development of the market-based housing finance system. In other words, a fully market-based mortgage market that includes no or ineffectual subsidies for housing finance with a less affordable market structure may not provide a sustainable financial framework for most of the population in Turkey. The direct supply of housing by the HDA is almost the only important exception to the marketisation of housing finance in Turkey. It, too, may be classified as a 'good' outcome of the developments of recent decades, despite remaining concerns about the sustainability and efficiency of the existing policies and the financial structure of the HDA.

Acknowledgements

The first version of this study was submitted to the ENHR Housing Finance Working Group's Brussels Meeting, on 17 September, 2013 in Belgium, and the second version was discussed at the ENHR 2014 Conference, 1–4 July, 2014 in Scotland. The author would like to thank the editors and members of working group for their valuable comments.

References

Altaban, Ö (1996). toplu konut alanlarinda örgütlenme ve işletme. Toplu konut idaresi başkanliği, Ankara.

Aydın, S and Yarar, B (2007). Kentleşme ve Konut Politikaları Açısından Neo-Liberalizmin Eleştirel Bir Değerlendirmesi ve Sosyal Adalet Fikrinin Yeniden İnşaası. *Sosyoloji Araştırmaları Dergisi* 1, 28–56.

Bal, E (2010). Economic restructuring in Turkey: Developments. In: *The Housing Sector Since The 2001 Crisis* (in, *Home Ownership Getting In, Getting From, Getting Out Part III, May.),* Doling, JF, Elsinga, M and Ronald, R (eds), Delft University Press, Delft. pp. 119–135.

Banking Sector Regulatory Agency (BRSA) (2010). *From Crisis to Financial Stability (Turkey Experience).* Working Paper. 3rd Edn. [Online] Available: www.bddk.org.tr/WebSitesi/english/ Reports/Working_Papers/8675from_crisis_to_financial_stability_turkey_experience_3rd_ ed.pdf (accessed 3 August 2015).

Banking Sector Regulatory Agency (BRSA) (2012). *Financial Markets Report. Issue 26, June.* [Online] Available: https://www.bddk.org.tr/WebSitesi/english/Reports/Financial_Markets_ Report/11588financial_markets_report_june_2012.pdf accessed 3 August 2015).

Banking Sector Regulatory Agency (BRSA) (2013). *Turkish Banking Sector Interactive Monthly Bulletin* [Online] Available: http://ebulten.bddk.org.tr/ABMVC/en(accessed 3 August 2015).

Central Bank of Turkey (CBRT) (2013). *Electronic Data Delivery System.* [Online] Available: http://evds.tcmb.gov.tr/ (accessed 29 July 2015).

Çevre ve Şehircilik Bakanlığı Web-Site (n.d.). *Financial Support* [Online] Available: www.csb.gov. tr/gm/altyapi/index.php?Sayfa=sayfaandTur=webmenuandId=13456 (accessed 29 July 2015).

Coşkun, Y (2011a). Does re-design of the policies on housing finance and supply help to solve the housing question of Turkey. *18th Annual ERES Conference.* June 2010. Eindhoven, The Netherlands.

Coşkun, Y (2011b). The Global Financial Crisis and the Turkish housing market: Is there a success story? *Housing Finance International* 25:3, 6–14.

Coşkun, Y (2011c). The Establishment of the Real Estate Regulation and Supervision Agency of Turkey (RERSAT). *Housing Finance International* 25:4, 42–51.

Coşkun, Y (2013). *Housing-Construction Market Risks in Turkey: Over Rated or Under-Estimated? Housing Finance International* 26:4, 47–55.

Coşkun, Y (2015) Housing finance in Turkey: Problems and solution suggestions. Analysis of the institutional housing finance system in Turkey, *The Banks Association of Turkey,* March, Istanbul.

Coşkun, Y and Yalçıner, K (2011). Global financial crisis and market-based housing finance: An assessment for the Turkey. *Finans Politik and Ekonomik Yorumlar Dergisi* 48:558, 81–93.

Coşkun, Y, Watkins, C. and White, M. (2014) Measuring housing affordability in Turkey: Lessons for emerging markets. Working Paper. *2014 ENHR Conference,* July 2014, Scotland.

Coşkun, Y and Gökçeimam, O (2015). Turkish Mortgage Covered Bond Market: Legislation and future prospects. January. *Mortgage Info* 4–5.

DTZ (2013). *Property Times Turkey Q1 2013.* July [Online] Available: http://preview.dtz.com/ portal/site/dtz/menuitem.af9280e60ce624d8ceb3fd10d0a587a0/?vgnextoid=bdf124d7b16ff3 10VgnVCM1000000c02a8c0RCRD&vgnextchannel=771246ff69d1f110VgnVCM1000000d5 a780aRCRD (accessed 3 August 2015).

Erdoğdu, GPS (2010). A comparative analysis of entry to home ownership profiles: Turkey and The Netherlands. *METU JFA* 27:2, 95–124.

Fannie Mae (1992). *Creating a Market Oriented Housing Finance System in Turkiye.* March. Volume I: Final report and appendices A1–A4. March.

Fannie Mae (2004). *Primary and Secondary Mortgage Market Feasibility Study.* July 28. Special Report (for OYAK).

Fukuyama, F (2013). The middle-class revolution. *The Wall Street Journal*, June 28 [Online] Available: http://online.wsj.com/article/SB10001424127887323873904578571472700348086. html (accessed 29 July 2015).

Gürkaynak, RS (2013). *Gezi Olayları ve Türkiye Ekonomisi* [Online] Available: http:// bilimakademisi.org/sites/ default/files/duyuru/Gezi%20Olaylar%C4%B1%20ve%20T%C3% BCrkiye%20Ekonomisi.pdf (accessed 29 July 2015).

Housing Development Agency (2006). Türkiye'de Konut Sektörü ve TOKİ'nin Konut Üretimindeki Yeri. Research Series. No: 2. *Yapı Endüstri Merkezi*, Ankara.

Keyder, Ç (2013). *Keyder: Gezi Olaylarının Seyrini Türkiye'de Yükselmekte Olan Yeni Orta Sınıf Değiştirmiştir*, Interview [Online] Available: http://t24.com.tr/haber/keyder-gezi-olaylarinin-seyrini-turkiyede-yukselmekte-olan-yeni-orta-sinif-degistirmistir/238849 (accessed 29 July 2015).

Keyder, Ç and Öncü, A (1993). Istanbul and the concept of world cities. *Friedrich Ebert Vakfı Yayınları*.

Knight Frank (2013). *The Wealth Report 2013* [Online] Available: www.knightfrank.com/ research (accessed 29 July 2015).

Özdemir, D (2011). The role of the public sector in the provision of housing supply in Turkey, 1950–2009. *International Journal of Urban and Regional Research* 35:6, 1099–1117.

Penpecioğlu, M (2013). Urban development projects and the construction of neo-liberal urban hegemony. The case of Izmir. *METU JFA* 30:1, 165–189.

Reidin (2013). Reidin Turkey Residential Property Price Index (for period of 2007/6–2013).

Republic of Turkey Ministry of Economy (RTME) (2012). *Foreign Direct Investments in Turkey 2011* April. Ministry of Economy.

Tekeli, İ (1995). Yetmiş Yıl İçinde Türkiye'nin Konut Sorununa Nasıl Çözüm Arandı. Konut Araştırmaları Sempozyumu. TC Başbakanlık Toplu Konut İdaresi Başkanlığı Konut Araştırmaları Dizisi 1. *ODTÜ Basım İşliği*, Ankara.

Turkish Banking Association (2012). *Türkiye Mortgage Piyasası İçin Sermaye Piyasası Çözümleri Geliştirilmesi* [Online] Available: www.tbb.org.tr (accessed 29 July 2015).

Turkish Statistical Institute (TurkStat) (2010). *Turkey's Statistical Yearbook 2009*. May.

TurkStat. (2012). Statistical Indicators 1923–2011. Publication No: 3890, December, Turkstat, Ankara, Turkey.

TurkStat (2013a). Population and Housing Census 2011. July.

TurkStat (2013b). House Sales Statistics 2013 Q2. Bulletin No: 13570.

TurkStat (2013c). Turkey's Statistical Yearbook 2012. June.

TurkStat. (2013d). *Building Construction Cost Index* [Online] Available: www.tuik.gov.tr/ UstMenu.do?metod=istgosterge (accessed 29 July 2015).

TurkStat (2014). *Distribution of non-institutional population by equivalised household disposable median income groups and problems with the dwelling and environment, 2006–2013* [Online] Available at: www.turkstat.gov.tr/PreTablo.do%3Falt_id%3D1011 (accessed 3 August 2015).

Yalçıner K and Coşkun Y (2014). Conditions of mortgage market development: A critical empirical review for Turkey. *İktisat İşletme ve Finans* 29:339, 59–94.

24

Milestones in EU Housing and Mortgage Markets

Jennifer Johnson[a], Lorenzo Isgrò[a] and Sylvain Bouyon[b]

[a]*European Mortgage Federation, Brussels, Belgium*
[b]*Centre for European Policy Studies, Brussels, Belgium*

Milestones in EU housing and mortgage markets

At the end of 2013, the volume of outstanding mortgage loans in the EU amounted to €6.7 trillion, which is equal to approximately 51 percent of aggregate EU GDP, making mortgage credit a major driver of the real economy (European Mortgage Federation 2014). Since 1990, EU mortgage markets have grown and evolved at remarkable rates and have also been witness to significant milestones in regulatory terms on the retail, prudential and funding sides of the business (Table 24.1). This article will describe and analyse the development of EU mortgage markets throughout this period, as well as the EU policy milestones and, where possible, their impact on EU mortgage markets.

1990–2000 – Milestones: The Single European Market, deregulation and consolidation and product innovation

The last decade of the twentieth century brought with it a number of changes that had significant and wide-reaching impacts on EU mortgage markets. One of the key catalysts for change during this period was the progress made towards the creation of the *Single European Market* (SEM), which in turn triggered a movement of deregulation and consolidation, product innovation and ultimately a massive expansion of EU mortgage markets.

Milestones in European Housing Finance, First Edition.
Edited by Jens Lunde and Christine Whitehead.
© 2016 John Wiley & Sons, Ltd. Published 2016 by John Wiley & Sons, Ltd.

Table 24.1 Milestones.

	Milestones		
	EU Policy milestones	Market milestones (structural, product)	Market milestones (economic)

1990–2000	Single Market Programme:
	• Preparation and introduction of single currency
	• Progress in creation of single market in banking:
	  ○ 1988 Capital Liberalisation Directive
	  ○ 1989 Second Banking Directive
	  ○ 1989 and 1991 Directives on Own Funds and Solvency Ratio
		Deregulation and consolidation of the financial sector
		Product innovation and allocation of substantial resources to the Internet
			Massive expansion of EU Mortgage Markets, with markets more than doubling over the period

2001–2008	Focus on mortgage credit: • Voluntary European Code of Conduct on Home Loans • Assessment of Integration of EU mortgage markets 2006 Capital Requirements Directive	Focus on covered bonds: • Growing recognition that savings deposits no longer sufficient to meet lenders' funding needs • Establishment of the European Covered Bond Council (ECBC)	Continued steady growth of EU mortgage markets, with 'booms' experienced, e.g. in IE, UK and ES
2008–	Review of the Capital Requirements Directive: CRR/CRD IV Bank Recovery and Resolution Directive Banking Union Mortgage Credit Directive Capital Markets Union	Covered bonds perform very well during crisis and cement their role as a robust long-term financing instrument, even during volatile market conditions European Commission launches plan to encourage high quality securitisation as part of its long-term financing agenda	Differentiated performance of EU mortgage markets as a result of the financial crisis, with some continuing to display robust growth rates, e.g. BE, FR, RO and SE, others slower but nevertheless positive rates, e.g. DK, DE, NL and the UK, and a small number recording y-o-y negative growth rates, e.g. IE, PT and ES

Time period (vertical label, left margin)

The Single European Market

The preparation for and introduction of the single currency in 1999 for 12 EU Member States marked a key turning point for European mortgage markets. Mortgage interest rates had increased during the late 1980s and reached a high in 1990, largely as a result of high interest rates in Germany stemming from the enormous cost of reunification, which in turn pushed interest rates up all over Europe. However, the 1993 Euro convergence criteria, introduced under the 1992 Maastricht Treaty, required Member State governments to ensure that interest rates were not more than 2 percent higher than in the three member states with the lowest inflation in order to qualify for the third stage of the Economic and Monetary Union (EMU). This contributed to the historically low levels of European mortgage interest rates, which steadily converged downwards from their peak at the beginning of the 1990s. This downward trend was reinforced by increased competition across many Member States as a result of the entry of non-specialised mortgage lenders into the market (see next). However, the year 2000 brought with it increases, albeit slight ones, in mortgage interest rates in almost all Member States largely as a result of a tightening of monetary policy by the European Central Bank (ECB) in response to rising energy prices and pressure on wages in some countries. Rates nevertheless remained close to the historically low levels recorded in the previous years.

The introduction of the single currency also had a massive impact on capital markets and this decade saw the establishment of a Euro-denominated bond market, which proved less volatile than the earlier national markets. The subsequent access to lower cost, long-term funding helped to develop wholesale market instruments, such as mortgage bonds and mortgage-backed securities (MBS), as alternatives to the traditional ways of funding mortgage loans, that is, through savings or retail deposits.

In 1988, the EU adopted legislation on *capital liberalisation* in Directive 88/361/EEC (EUR-Lex 1988), which provided for the full liberalisation of capital movements by requiring the abolition of remaining exchange controls, by the mid-1990s. These still remained despite the Treaty of Rome having provided for the free movement of capital in the 1960s (EUR-Lex 1957). Around the same time, the EU took legislative steps to coordinate banking legislation through the *1989 Second Banking Directive*, Directive 89/646/ EEC (EUR-Lex 1989a), which took effect in 1993. This Directive was based on the principles of a single banking license, mutual recognition and home country rule, and subsequently permitted – in principle – free establishment and the provision of banking services on a cross-border basis. Despite its advances, the Second Banking Directive would, however, ultimately fail to create a single market as a result of limitations to the principle of mutual recognition and its 'general good' clause, which Member States used to protect their national markets. It would later be replaced by the Capital Requirements Directive 2006/48/EC (EUR-Lex 2006) (see next) as the main, legislative framework for the banking sector. Nevertheless, this Directive and the Capital Liberalisation Directive were extremely significant for EU mortgage markets: they represented the first concrete steps towards the promotion of the cross-border provision of financial services as part of the Single Market Programme and consequently also led to intensified competition and pressure on markets. In parallel to these legislative developments, the EU Directives on Own Funds and Solvency Ratio – Directives 89/47/EEC and 91/633/EEC (EUR-Lex 1989b,

1991) – which were designed to ensure that all banks in the EU had the same capital standards, also came into effect in 1993. They introduced a preferential risk weighting for residential mortgage loans of 50 percent that translated into a 4 percent own-funds requirement and therefore had a huge impact on lenders' ability to finance mortgage credit

Deregulation and consolidation

The heightened competition and pressure that was generated by progress made in the creation of the single market in banking and the historically low interest rates, which resulted from the preparation for the introduction of the single currency, in turn, contributed to a movement of *deregulation* and *consolidation* in the financial sector. Until the 1980s, housing finance systems were generally strictly regulated at the national level to ensure matching in long-term finance, but also because many governments were keen to encourage access to homeownership at the lowest possible cost. Increasingly, however, the 1990s brought with them a removal of such restrictions and, in the process, a change in the financial institutions offering mortgage credit, with non-specialised lenders, such as commercial banks, entering the market and specialised lenders changing their legal status. As the 1980s and 1990s progressed, consolidation and cross-border mergers and acquisitions also became a feature of the period. These developments occurred despite reluctance on the part of certain governments towards market liberalisation and their determination to support national champions.

Product innovation

In this new environment, lenders were pushed to be dynamic and innovative and to develop new financial products and new methods to market these products to the consumer. *Product innovation* that emerged in several EU Member States during this period included Euro-denominated mortgages as well as foreign exchange (FX) loans that could be sold across borders and flexible mortgages. Flexible mortgages helped households. They provided borrowers with the opportunity to under or over pay and 'take a holiday' from their repayment and therefore to manage less predictable income streams and adapt their mortgages more to their lifestyles. Product innovation would continue into the 2000s with a variety of new products being brought to markets in the EU, including self-certification loans for self–employed borrowers who did not have a sufficiently long run of accounts to satisfy lenders' normal requirements and credit impaired loans for borrowers with poor credit history, who otherwise would have difficulties in accessing credit. After the 2007/2008 financial crisis, deficiencies in the regulation and granting of some of these products became apparent in certain Member States, resulting in the tightening of lending conditions and a more conservative approach generally in terms of products available on these markets. Towards the end of 1990s, mortgage lenders began to allocate substantial resources to the Internet, which became – and remains today – an indispensable source of information and comparison for prospective borrowers.

Market developments

The developments outlined here translated into a *massive expansion of European mortgage markets* between the late 1980s and 1999, with markets more than doubling in nominal terms over the period. At the end of the decade, the volume of outstanding residential mortgage loans amounted to just over €3 trillion, representing more than 35 percent of EU GDP (European Mortgage Federation 2000). As largely remains the case today, mortgage markets retained their strong national characteristics, with markets differing greatly in size and importance, as a result of differences in political and historical environments, and in the legal and regulatory frameworks in which mortgage lenders operated. The largest markets in terms of volume of mortgage loans outstanding were Germany, the UK, France and the Netherlands (the UK would later, in 2004, overtake Germany to become the EU's largest mortgage market, as a result of the boom in the UK market in the preceding years and Germany's slow growth by comparison, while Spain would overtake the Netherlands in 2006 to become the EU's fourth largest mortgage market, as a result of the strength of the Spanish economy and the domestic real estate market). The markets that grew most during the period were Portugal and Ireland, as well as Greece, Spain and the Netherlands (Figure 24.1) (European Mortgage Federation 2001).

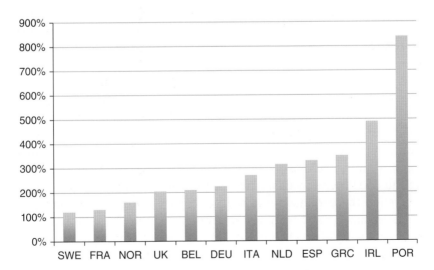

Figure 24.1 Country breakdown for mortgage lending growth, 1990–2000 (as a percentage, based on volume outstanding).
Source: EMF.
Figures provided for 1990 or 2000 refer to the closest available year.

2001–2008 – Milestones: EU focus on mortgage credit, growth of covered bonds and adoption of the Capital Requirements Directive (CRD)

EU focus on mortgage credit

The adoption of the Maastricht Treaty in 1992 (EUR-Lex 1992) and the subsequent introduction of the Euro in 1999 led the European Commission to turn its attention to closing the gap between Europe and its citizens. Consumer policy questions were given a higher priority on the political agenda. In 1996, in the context of a review of the 1987 Consumer Credit Directive (CCD), mortgage credit effectively came on to the EU agenda for the first time, when the European Commission launched an investigation into the possible need for regulation in this area. However, the study team put in place by the Commission concluded that at national level consumer protection standards for mortgage lending were broadly consistent with or exceeded the minimal requirements of the CCD. It therefore suggested that mortgage credit should not be regulated on the basis of the CCD and that harmonisation of mortgage credit through consumer protection rules would not favour cross-border mortgage lending.

As the turn of the century approached, the European Commission therefore opted for a flexible approach to regulation and encouraged a dialogue between mortgage lenders and consumers to work towards the standardisation of pre-contractual information. It was hoped that this would enable prospective borrowers to compare mortgage products both at home and on a cross-border basis, and in this way promote transparency and reinforce consumer confidence. Several years' worth of discussions and negotiations culminated in the signing of the *Voluntary European Code of Conduct on Home Loans* (the Code) in 2001. The Code was later endorsed by the European Commission in 2002 by way of a recommendation inviting EU lenders to adhere to the agreement. Despite the application of the Code by a majority of lenders in a majority of Member States, the Code ultimately floundered. This was largely the result of incompatibilities in some Member States between national legislation and the Code's requirements, the perceived lack of commitment to the Code from the European Commission, as well as the absence of a monitoring and compliance mechanism. The premise of the Code was a good one, however, and the cornerstone of the agreement, the European Standardised Information Sheet (ESIS), would later be taken up in the 2014 Mortgage Credit Directive 2014/17/EU (EUR-Lex 2014b) to become the core of the Directive's pre-contractual information requirements (more on that later).

The Code was the first concrete sign of the European Commission's recognition of the importance of mortgage credit to the EU economy and in 2003 the European Commission once again set its sights on EU mortgage markets. This time, the focus was on how greater *integration of EU mortgage markets* could be achieved, with a view to maximising benefits for lenders, consumers and the economy as a whole. With this in mind, the European Commission launched the Forum Group on Mortgage Credit, which brought together lender and consumer representatives to identify the main obstacles to the functioning of a genuine European mortgage credit market and to formulate policy recommendations on the most appropriate ways to achieve such an integrated market.

Throughout the process, which ultimately culminated in the publication of a Commission White Paper in 2007, the focus steadily converged on the importance of removing legal infrastructural obstacles, such as access to land registers and credit databases, in order to create integrated EU mortgage markets, naturally alongside an emphasis on enhanced consumer protection (EUR-Lex 2007). This movement reflected increasing acknowledgement that further integration would most likely be supply-driven, with lenders crossing borders to offer their products, rather than demand-driven, not least because of the intrinsic link between the mortgage loan and the location of the property. The prospect of EU intervention at some point in the future to open up EU markets to lenders on a truly cross-border basis was short-lived, however; in 2008, the EU was rocked by the financial crisis and the European Commission shifted its policy orientation away from the 'integration' agenda to an emphasis on consumer protection. The result of this, more than 5 years later, was a directive on mortgage credit.

Growth of covered bonds

Lenders were, at the same time, keeping a very close eye on developments on the funding side of the business. In 2004, the European Mortgage Federation (EMF) established the *European Covered Bond Council (ECBC)* as a platform for covered bond market participants (covered bonds are debt instruments secured by a cover pool of mortgage loans or public-sector debt). This initiative was a direct response to the acknowledgement that savings deposits were no longer sufficient to meet lenders' funding requirements and that there was an ever-increasing need for mortgage lenders to tap capital markets. In recent years, the covered bond market has developed at an exceptional rate, which is evidenced by the fact that covered bond legislation now exists in 26 out of 28 EU Member States (Estonia and Malta do not yet have covered bond legislation) and in five other non-EU European countries (Armenian, Azerbaijan, Russia, Turkey and Ukraine).

Adoption of the Capital Requirements Directive (CRD)

The years before the onset of the financial crisis also saw a return to discussions about banks' capital requirements in order to protect against financial and operational risks. 2004 saw the publication of Basel II, a set of recommendations from the Basel Committee on Banking Supervision (BCBS), which established risk-sensitive minimum capital requirements for the banking sector and principles against which banks could assess the adequacy of their capital and supervisors could review these assessments (Basel 2004). The Basel II recommendations were implemented in the EU by way of the *Capital Requirements Directive* in 2006 (EUR-Lex 2006) and marked a major change for the mortgage industry with capital being much more closely aligned to risk. During this process, the EU mortgage industry worked hard to ensure that the low-risk profile of residential mortgage lending was recognised. Significantly, its risk weighting was subsequently reduced from the 50 percent required by Basel I (Basel 1988) to 35 percent (under the foundation and internal ratings based approaches), a weighting that remains in place today. The Industry also secured a preferential treatment for covered bonds on the basis of their intrinsic credit quality, which also continues to apply. The new standards undeniably made significant progress in the management of risk and capital; however, the events of 2007/2008 would later highlight that the standards did not go far enough to safeguard against the consequences of the collapse of a major bank or series of banks.

Market developments

Throughout this period, EU mortgage markets continued to experience steady growth. Between 2001 and 2008, the outstanding residential debt to GDP ratio increased by 50.6 percentage points in Ireland, 29.5 in Spain, 26.6 in the UK, 26.5 in the Netherlands, 23.5 in Denmark, 22.6 in Greece and 21.5 in Sweden. In comparison, the sovereign debt to GDP ratio expanded by 14.6 percentage points in the UK, 9.7 in Ireland, 9.2 in Greece and 7.8 in the Netherlands and contracted by 16.2 in Denmark, 15.9 in Spain and 15.4 in Sweden (European Mortgage Federation 2009).

Prior to the crisis, outstanding residential lending was continuously fed by buoyant gross residential lending. In 2008, flows of residential loans were indeed significantly above their 2001 levels for most EU15 countries: 200.7 percent in Ireland, 123.8 percent in Belgium, 91 percent in Italy, 84.3 percent in France, 59.8 percent in the UK, 57.3 percent in Sweden and 51.6 percent in Spain. There were different factors behind this boom (European Mortgage Federation 2009).

On the supply side, as indicated earlier, the progressive build-up of the Euro area in the second half of the 1990s and the effective introduction of the common currency at the beginning of the 2000s, with the establishment of the ECB, led to a progressive decrease in the funding costs of banks, especially on the wholesale markets of the so-called peripheral markets. As a result, according to the Bank Lending Survey conducted by the ECB, lending standards for housing purchases eased almost continuously between Q3 2004 and Q3 2007 in the Euro area (ECB 2007).

Figure 24.2 Correlation in percent between gross residential lending and different factors (in 2008, 2001 = 100).
Source: EMF.
Note: the sample includes Belgium, Denmark, France, Germany, Ireland, Italy, the Netherlands, Spain, Sweden and the UK.

On the demand side, different variables can explain the substantial growth in residential mortgage loans between 2001 and 2008 (Figure 24.2). First, nominal house prices, which increased markedly in most EU27 markets during these years, can have a direct impact on the average amount of mortgage loans. As a result, the correlation between nominal house prices and gross lending is relatively high (34 percent). As expected, disposable income of households and the population over 18 also play a key role in the demand for housing loans (the correlation is respectively 24 percent and 53 percent). Finally, the number of housing starts, mirroring the activity of the construction market, has a significant positive impact on the volume of gross residential lending (correlation of 50 percent) (European Mortgage Federation, 2009).

2008–2014 – Milestones: Restoring financial stability, consumer protection and unlocking long-term financing

The failure of Lehman Brothers in September 2008 and the subsequent onset of the US subprime crisis triggered a Global Financial Crisis, the effects of which are still being felt today in the EU more than 6 years later, both in terms of mortgage market activity and regulatory responses.

The combination of irresponsible mortgage lending to subprime borrowers in the US, fuelled by abundant liquidity and rising house prices, and the almost exclusive reliance of US banks on securitisation triggered a financial crisis in the US that sent shockwaves through the global economy. The subprime crisis in the US had the knock-on effect of destroying confidence and closing the liquidity 'tap' in the EU, as a result of EU banks having invested in US securitisation portfolios containing toxic, subprime loans. This plunged the Union into crisis. In turn, the financial efforts required by the national governments in some EU Member States to respond to crisis in their banking sectors and support their national economies resulted in a *sovereign debt crisis*, pushing the Union even further into crisis and, in 2009, leading it into the worst recession since the Treaty of Rome established the EEC in 1958.

Restoring financial stability

Both in the Member States and in Brussels, the last 6 years have seen a focus on restoring financial stability. National responses have naturally varied according to respective experiences of the crisis. In Brussels, Frankfurt and London, however, the focus of the European Commission and European Parliament, the ECB and the European Banking Authority respectively has been on measures to improve the resilience of the financial system by implementing the Basel Committee on Banking Supervision's (BCBS) requirements with regard to financial regulatory reform, and, at the same time, on regulating the EU banking sector on the basis of a Single EU Rule Book.

The *CRR/CRD IV Package*, which transposes the Basel III Framework (Basel 2011) into EU legislation, came into force on 1 January 2014 and should be fully applicable by 2018. It consists of both a *Capital Requirements Regulation* (CRR) No 575/2013 (EUR-Lex 2013b), including detailed prudential rules for banks, and a *Capital Requirements Directive* (CRD IV) 2013/36/ EU (EUR-Lex 2013a), covering predominantly supervision. Basel III and CRR/ CRD IV represent a very significant step forward in EU efforts to ensure a resilient banking sector. The challenge now for the EU is to ensure that the global level Basel III Framework is adapted at the EU level to take into account both the specificity of the EU market and the range of different business models and practices that exist in the market. A number of key issues are of specific relevance to the mortgage industry, including the preferential treatment of mortgages in respect of capital requirements, the leverage ratio, the calibration of the liquidity coverage requirement (LCR) and the net stable funding ratio (NSFR), and the recognition of covered bonds. So far, the signs are that the European Commission is taking the need to take account of EU specificities very seriously. This is reflected, for example, in the extensive preferential treatment accorded to covered bonds in the recently published LCR.

As part of the process of reinforcing the resilience of the banking sector and in order to complement the new capital requirements, EU regulators have also been preoccupied with bank recovery and resolution rules. After much deliberation, the final rules were agreed in April 2014 in the form of the *Bank Recovery and Resolution Directive* (BRRD), Directive 2014/59/EU (EUR-Lex 2014a). The BRRD deals with the restructuring and winding-down of failing banks and aims to provide national competent authorities with the necessary tools and powers to ensure that bank failures in the EU are managed in a way that does not threaten financial stability and that minimises costs for taxpayers. The BRRD system took effect in January 2015. The national bank recovery and resolution funds (for non-banking union countries) will be fully capitalised in 2025.

With the two key building blocks well underway, EU policymakers turned their attention back to one of the primary objectives of pre-crisis EU agendas and a key component of resilience, namely deeper and more integrated financial markets that are seen as necessary to restore the efficient functioning of the single market. The idea of developing a *banking union* quickly became a priority on the EU political agenda. In June 2013, the European Commission published its Communication on Completing the Banking Union, in which it set out the Banking Union's constituent elements and their sequencing: *Single Supervisory Mechanism* (SSM) and a *Single Resolution Mechanism* (SRM) (as well as a fiscal backstop in the Euro Area) (European Commission 2012).

Agreement was reached relatively quickly between the EU institutions on the Single Supervisory Mechanism and the Regulation was published in October 2013. In accordance with the agreement, the SSM went live on 4 November 2014, when the ECB took up its role as the single European supervisor for Euro zone financial institutions (as well as financial institutions in those non-Euro Member States that opt for voluntary cooperation). It will be very interesting in the coming months to see what impact the split between SSM and non-SSM banks will have on supervision and therefore on the banking industry more widely, and the mortgage and covered bond industries more specifically.

As a kind of BRRD for banks in those Member States subject to the SSM, the Single Resolution Mechanism is intended to ensure that if an 'SSM bank' faces serious difficulties, its resolution can be managed by way of a common EU-level resolution process, including a Single Resolution Board (SRB) and a Single Resolution Fund (SRF) financed by the EU banking industry, with minimal costs for taxpayers and the real economy. At the end of March 2014, after long and difficult negotiations, agreement was finally reached and the SRM was formally adopted in April. The SRM's provisions on the preparation of resolution planning, the collection of information and cooperation with national resolution authorities took effect on 1 January 2015.

Consumer protection

On the retail side, the EU authorities' initial response to the crisis saw a shift away from the Commission's original objective of further integrating EU mortgage markets, as outlined above, to one focussed very much on consumer protection, in the form of a Proposal for a *Mortgage Credit*

Directive, Directive 2014/17/EU (EUR-Lex 2014b) in 2011. The change in orientation appeared to a large extent to be motivated by the irresponsible mortgage lending that triggered the sub-prime mortgage crisis in the US. This was reflected in a draft proposal for a directive that provided for a significant shift of responsibility from the borrower to the lender across a number of key provisions. After much dialogue with and between the EU Institutions, the final text in February 2014 struck an appropriate balance, at least from a lender point of view, between the respective rights and obligations of lenders and borrowers, whilst ensuring a high level of consumer protection that does not, however, stifle consumer choice and innovation. The Directive, which entered into force in March 2014, includes: provisions on marketing, advertising and consumer information; principle-based rules and standards relating to the execution of lending services (e.g. conduct of business obligations, competence and knowledge requirements for lender staff); requirements on lenders in respect of consumer creditworthiness assessment, provisions on early repayment, foreign currency loans and tying and bundling practices; and some high-level principles covering, for example, financial education, property valuation and arrears and foreclosure.

With the legislative process concluded, attention has now turned to transposition of the Directive into national legislation and implementation by EU lenders, which must be concluded by March 2016. In addition to the usual challenges of transposing European legislation, Member States (and therefore lenders) will have to contend with this requirement in a post-financial – and in some cases, sovereign – crisis context. In some Member States, this will be further complicated by their own recent, or on-going, national efforts to respond to the crisis and, where necessary, reform mortgage legislation, for example in Ireland, Spain and the UK.

In the wake of the crisis, attention at the EU level has also, perhaps inevitably, turned to the issue of *over-indebtedness*. This resulted very much from reports of rising arrears and possessions in certain EU Member States, although, since then, the levels of arrears in the Member States most affected by the crisis have been falling, largely as a result of bank forbearance and improved employment rates on the back of economic recovery in these countries. Concretely, the EU Institutions have launched studies looking at the causes, effects and possible means to address over-indebtedness, including alternatives to foreclosure of the property. At the time of writing, it is still unclear exactly what kind of follow-up there will be to the work already started at EU level.

Unlocking long-term financing

Throughout the crisis, covered bonds continued to demonstrate a strong degree of resilience, which has characterised their performance for more than 200 years as a result of their key safety features: strict legal and supervisory frameworks, asset segregation and a dynamic cover pool maintaining the quality of the collateral. The performance of covered bonds during the crisis cemented the asset class' reputation amongst policymakers as a robust long-term financing instrument contributing to the efficient allocation of capital. As part of its efforts to respond to an increasing focus on transparency in the wake of the crisis, the covered bond industry launched a quality Label in January 2013. The Covered Bond Label is designed to further improve standards, increase transparency in the market and contribute to the enhancement of financial stability.

If the period between 2007/2008 and 2015 has seen covered bonds go from strength to strength and play a crucial role as a crisis management tool, the same cannot be said for securitisation. This market has all but dried up at the onset of the crisis as a result of the market being held largely responsible for the financial crisis, even though losses on instruments originated in the EU were very low compared to the US. Since then, unlike in the US as a result of public guarantees, EU securitisation markets have remained very subdued; this, however, is potentially about to change.

Since the installation of the new European Commission in September and particularly since the beginning of 2015, long-term financing of the EU economy has been at the forefront of the EU's political agenda. In particular, the European Commission is seeking to stimulate new and different ways of unlocking long-term financing and supporting Europe's return to sustainable growth and job creation. The recently announced Capital Markets' Union (CMU) is a key element of the long-term financing agenda. Alongside a focus on a revision to the Prospectus Directive to facilitate the access of smaller firms to markets and investment, on credit information on small-medium enterprises (SMEs) to help bring loans to smaller firms, on private placement regimes and on European Long-Term Investment Funds, a cornerstone of the CMU is a plan to encourage high quality securitisation. At the time of writing, the European Commission is consulting with interested stakeholders on an EU framework for simple, transparent and standardised securitisation with a view to promoting greater integration of EU financial markets, supporting the diversification of funding sources and unlocking capital, to facilitate bank lending to the real economy.

Market developments

Over the last seven years, the financial crisis, which has triggered so much regulatory reform, has also, inevitably, had a direct impact on the performance of EU Mortgage Markets. Depending on the structure of markets, and their lending and funding practices, Member States' experiences of the crisis have differed greatly across the EU (Figure 24.3). Belgium, France, Romania, Poland and Sweden experienced an almost continuous and robust quarter on quarter growth in outstanding mortgage loans between Q1 2007 and Q4 2014

(a)

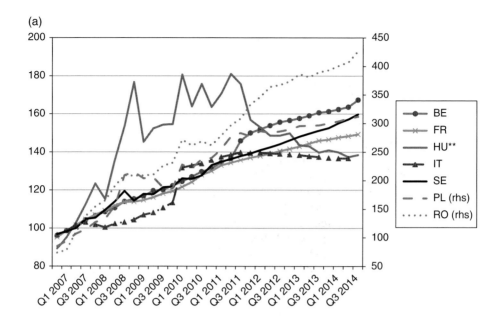

(b)

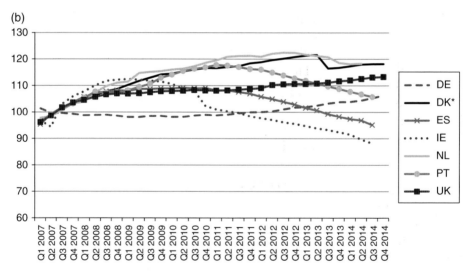

Figure 24.3   Total Outstanding Residential Lending, 2007 = 100. (a) Countries where Total Outstanding Residential Lending rose and is now at least 20 percent above 2007 levels. (b) Countries where Total Outstanding Residential Lending fell, or is now no more than 20 percent above 2007 levels.

Source: EMF.

Note: Please note that figures are calculated on values expressed in local currencies for non-Euro area countries

*Due to the review and implementation of the new MFI statistics in Denmark in the fall of 2013, there is a structural break in Q3 2013 for this time series. The break is due to a revision of the household sector.

**Please note that the positive Hungarian y-o-y change in Q4 2011 is explained by the devaluation of the forint versus the Swiss Franc and the Euro.

(figures are in domestic currency). Some other domestic mortgage markets also registered growth in the same period, albeit at a slower pace (e.g. Denmark, UK and Germany). Finally, within the context of economic recession and household deleveraging, outstanding residential lending had contracted quarter on quarter in Q4 2014 for 22 consecutive quarters in Ireland; 14 in Portugal and 15 in Spain (European Mortgage Federation, 2015).

As regards gross residential lending, the picture has been much gloomier in the years following the economic crisis, though it has already started to show clear signs of recovery (see Figure 24.4). The EU sample countries can be roughly divided into two groups: (a) one with national mortgage markets where gross lending (including new loans and external re-mortgaging: between two banks) has followed a positive or stagnant trend between 2007 and 2014 and (b) the other composed of countries where gross lending has moved along a downward trend in the same period and now stands at least 30 percent below average 2007 levels. The first group notably includes Belgium, Germany and Sweden, among others. The second subclass contains Hungary, Ireland, Italy, Portugal and Spain. In the UK, gross lending remained significantly below 2007 levels in Q1 2014, nonetheless, contrary to other countries of the group, the trend was largely stable between Q1

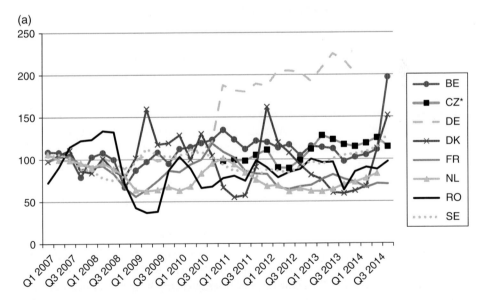

Figure 24.4 Gross residential lending, 2007 = 100 (in domestic currency, seasonally adjusted data). (a) Countries where Gross Residential Lending is now no more than 30 percent below average 2007 levels, or is higher.
Source: EMF.

*2011 = 100

Note: Please note that the time series have been seasonally adjusted by regressing the gross domestic lending of each country on quarter dummies and a constant, and adding the residuals to the sample means. STATA econometric software has been used.

(b)

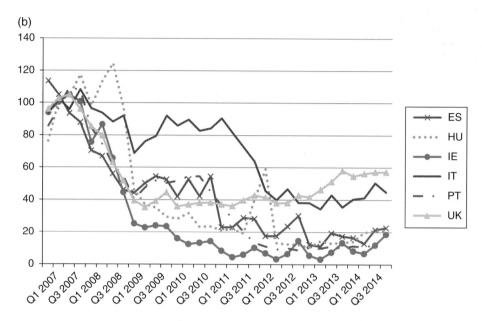

Figure 24.4   (*Continued*) Gross residential lending, 2007 = 100 (in domestic currency, seasonally adjusted data). (b) Countries where Gross Residential Lending rose and is now at least 30 % below average 2007 levels.
Source: EMF.

2009 and Q1 2013, after which it started to rise again. It should be noted that some countries, notably France, Denmark and Romania exhibit very high levels of volatility (despite seasonal adjustments). Broadly speaking, their gross residential lending levels have remained overall quite stagnant since 2007 (maybe slightly risen recently in Denmark). However, this erratic trend makes them more difficult to be clearly classified in one of the two categories presented (European Mortgage Federation 2014).

During the period 2007–2014, different macroeconomic factors contributed to this marked heterogeneity across countries in terms of gross lending dynamics. On one hand, it is likely that variables such as gross domestic product significantly affected the demand dynamics for gross lending. On the other hand, nominal house prices could arguably be an even more important driver of gross lending in the EU27, perhaps because prices affect gross lending via the channels of both lending standards and demand for new loans.

Conclusion

The last 25 years have seen EU mortgage markets grow at incredible rates, with the volume of outstanding mortgage loans almost doubling during the period. To a large extent, this remarkable evolution was driven initially in the 1990s by low interest rates and strong competition, further progress in the Single Market Programme and a subsequent wave of consolidation and deregulation of the sector. Later it was spurred on by economic growth in several EU Member States. The unprecedented events of 2007/2008, however, brought an end to the year-on-year double-digit growth rates that had characterised the years preceding the crisis. Nevertheless, between 2007 and 2012 and despite the differentiated performance of EU markets, with some recording negative growth rates, outstanding mortgage lending in the EU27 continued to grow, albeit at far more moderate rates. At the time of writing, in spring 2015, almost seven years after the onset of the crisis, the markets in many Member States are displaying robust or moderate growth rates, confirming recovery in much of the EU. Other Member States continue to record negative growth rates, however, the expectation is that we will see improvements in these markets and, for some, prospects for new lending in particular are indeed looking brighter.

As mortgage markets have grown and developed, so have secondary markets, and since the early part of this century, we have seen covered bonds in particular go from strength to strength, even during volatile market conditions. The onset of the crisis saw the drying-up of securitisation but the current focus of the European Commission on unlocking long-term financing and stimulating growth and job creation in the EU will see the development of a framework to encourage high quality securitisation, and possibly the kick-starting of this instrument once again.

The last quarter of a century has also seen regulators working hard to keep pace with developments in banking and, for mortgage lenders, new rules and standards at the global and EU level since 1990 have had a huge impact on the way in which they manage risk and capital. The most recent regulatory developments on both the retail and prudential sides of the business, many of which are direct responses to the financial crisis, will continue to influence the way in which mortgage lenders carry out their activities and the shape that mortgage markets take into the future. EU lenders are currently working to absorb the most recent raft of national and EU legislation and are trying to understand the likely effects of the BRRD's bail-in tool and the CRD's leverage ratio among other issues. These could have serious implications for business models, particularly among the EU's specialised mortgage lenders.

Whatever the next quarter of a century brings, one thing is sure: the financial and sovereign debt crises, the effects of which are still being felt today, have changed the European economy irreversibly and the financial services landscape will be marked for many years to come. Hopefully, the EU will move forward into the next 25 years with not only a stronger, stable, more resilient financial system, but also strong and efficient mortgage markets that continue to respond to consumer needs and act as key drivers of growth of the wider economy.

References

Basel Committee on Banking Supervision (1988). *International Convergence of Capital Measurement and Capital Standards (Basel I)* [Online] Available: www.bis.org/publ/bcbs04a.pdf (accessed 30 July 2015).

Basel Committee on Banking Supervision (2004). *International Convergence of Capital Measurement and Capital Standards: A Revised Framework (Basel II)* [Online] Available: www.bis.org/publ/bcbs107.pdf (accessed 30 July 2015).

Basel Committee on Banking Supervision (2011). *International regulatory framework for banks (Basel III)* [Online] Available: www.bis.org/bcbs/basel3.htm (accessed 30 July 2015).

European Central Bank (ECB) (October 2004–October 2007). *Euro Area Banking Lending Survey* [Online] Available: www.ecb.europa.eu/stats/money/surveys/lend/html/index.en.html (accessed 30 July 2015).

European Commission (2012). *Banking Union* [Online] Available: http://ec.europa.eu/internal_market/finances/banking-union/index_en.htm (accessed 30 July 2015).

European Commission (2001). *European Voluntary Code of Conduct on Home Loans* [Online] Available: *http://ec.europa.eu/internal_market/finservices-retail/docs/home-loans/agreement_en.pdf*

European Mortgage Federation (1989–1999, 1990–2000). *Hypostat, Mortgage and Property Markets in the EU and Norway: a 10 year overview.*

European Mortgage Federation (2008, 2014). *Hypostat, A Review of Europe's Housing and Mortgage Markets.*

European Mortgage Federation (2015). *Quarterly Review of European Mortgage Markets, Q4 2014.*

EUR-Lex (1957). *Treaty of Rome* [Online] Available: http://eur-lex.europa.eu/collection/eu-law/treaties.html (accessed 30 July 2015).

EUR-Lex (1988). *Council Directive 88/361/EEC of 24 June 1988 for the implementation of Article 67 of the Treaty (Capital Liberalisation)* [Online] Available: http://eur-lex.europa.eu/LexUriServ/LexUriServ.do?uri=CELEX:31988L0361:EN:HTML (accessed 30 July 2015).

EUR-Lex (1989a). *Second Council Directive 89/646/EEC of 15 December 1989 on the coordination of laws, regulations and administrative provisions relating to the taking up and pursuit of the business of credit institutions* [Online] Available: http://eur-lex.europa.eu/LexUriServ/LexUriServ.do?uri=CELEX:31989L0646:EN:HTML (accessed 30 July 2015).

EUR-Lex (1989b). *Council Directive 89/647/EEC of 18 December 1989 on a solvency ratio for credit institutions* [Online] Available: http://eur-lex.europa.eu/legal-content/en/ALL/?uri=CELEX:31989L0647 (accessed 30 July 2015).

EUR-Lex (1991). *Council Directive 91/633/EEC of 3 December 1991 implementing Directive 89/299/EEC on the own funds of credit institutions* [Online] Available: http://eur-lex.europa.eu/legal-content/EN/TXT/PDF/?uri=CELEX:31991L0633&from=EN (accessed 30 July 2015).

EUR-Lex (1992). *Treaty on European Union – Maastricht Treaty* [Online] Available: http://eur-lex.europa.eu/collection/eu-law/treaties.html (accessed 30 July 2015).

EUR-Lex (2006). *Directive 2006/48/EC of the European Parliament and of the Council of 14 June 2006 relating to the taking up and pursuit of the business of credit institutions (recast)* [Online] Available: http://eur-lex.europa.eu/legal-content/EN/TXT/PDF/?uri=CELEX:32006L0048&from=EN (accessed 30 July 2015).

EUR-Lex (2007). *White Paper on the Integration of EU mortgage credit markets* [Online] Available: http://eur-lex.europa.eu/legal-content/EN/TXT/PDF/?uri=CELEX:52007DC0807&from=EN (accessed 30 July 2015).

EUR-Lex (2013a). *Directive 2013/36/EU of 26 June 2013 on access to the activity of credit institutions and the prudential supervision of credit institutions and investment firms (CRD IV)* [Online] Available: http://eur-lex.europa.eu/legal-content/EN/TXT/PDF/?uri=CELEX:32013L0036&from=EN (accessed 30 July 2015).

EUR-Lex (2013b). *Regulation (EU) No 575/2013 of 26 June 2013 on prudential requirements for credit institutions and investment firms (CRR)* [Online] Available: http://eur-lex.europa.eu/legal-content/EN/TXT/PDF/?uri=CELEX:32013R0575&from=EN (accessed 30 July 2015).

EUR-Lex (2014a). *Directive 2014/59/EU of 15 May 2014 establishing a framework for the recovery and resolution of credit institutions and investment firms (BRRD)* [Online] Available: http://eur-lex.europa.eu/legal-content/EN/TXT/PDF/?uri=CELEX:32014L0059&from=EN (accessed 30 July 2015).

EUR-Lex (2014b). *Directive 2014/17/EU of the European Parliament and of the Council of 4 February 2014 on credit agreements for consumers relating to residential immovable property and amending Directives 2008/48/EC and 2013/36/EU and Regulation (EU) No 1093/2010 Text with EEA relevance* [Online] Available: http://eur-lex.europa.eu/legal-content/EN/ALL/?uri=CELEX:32014L0017 (accessed 30 July 2015).

25

Following On From a Quarter of a Century of Mortgage Debt

Jens Lunde[a] and Christine Whitehead[b]

[a] Department of Finance, Copenhagen Business School, Frederiksberg, Denmark
[b] Department of Economics, London School of Economics, London, UK

Introduction: 1989 and 2014

The last quarter-century has been an extraordinary period for housing finance and particularly for the mortgage market across Europe and indeed most of the industrialised world. During much of the period and in almost all countries included in this text, mortgage debt expanded rapidly: in some countries from a high starting point; in others from almost nothing. Developments in funding mechanisms were just as extraordinary – in some cases evolving from wholly government funding although more usually from special circuits of retail finance to fully liberalised systems using a wide range of wholesale market instruments. The latter part of the period saw the mortgage market blamed as a major cause of the Global Financial Crisis (GFC) followed, in many countries, by the near closure of mortgage markets and increased regulation at both national and international levels. Today, we have very little idea how the 'new normal' with respect to housing finance will play out but at the present time, in most housing markets, supply remains depressed even though house prices have begun to rise again.

The picture around 1989

In Chapter 2 we analysed the results of a questionnaire looking at national mortgage markets in 1989 and again in 2014. The evidence from 1989 suggested that the countries included could perhaps be grouped into three

Milestones in European Housing Finance, First Edition.
Edited by Jens Lunde and Christine Whitehead.
© 2016 John Wiley & Sons, Ltd. Published 2016 by John Wiley & Sons, Ltd.

main categories: countries where much of the liberalisation had already taken place in the 1980s or even the 1970s; others where the process had started but still involved considerable regulation; and finally countries where most funding was government sponsored and entry into owner-occupation was limited to those with their own equity. The implication was that most countries were going in the same direction through the removal of special circuits of housing finance, deregulation of finance markets more generally and a decreasing role for government finance and subsidy. The expectation was that access to cheaper funding would increase, enabling more people to enter owner-occupation as had happened in countries such as the UK and Australia where deregulation had started in the 1970s (Turner and Whitehead 1993).

Even at this stage, however, it was recognised that some countries would not follow the full liberalisation route. Germany in particular would be likely to maintain its more specialist funders using an on-balance sheet funding approach (Tomann 1993). Austria was expected to work on similar lines but with far greater government support (Deutsch *et al.* 1993). Equally it was recognised that the opening up of housing finance markets had tended to increase housing market volatility in some countries that had already experienced significant deregulation – with higher levels of defaults, increasing problems of affordability and some negative impact on housing investment. There was also some evidence of a move away from retail funding to the use of wholesale markets including mortgage backed securities as well as the on-balance-sheet approach already favoured by Denmark, Germany and Austria. Finally, there was considerable discussion of the efficiency of housing finance markets, culminating in a report by Diamond and Lea for Fannie Mae covering five developed countries, four in Europe plus the USA, put in place in part because of concerns about how the European single market would impact on behaviour (Diamond and Lea 1992). The contentious conclusion was that the UK was the most efficient system based on most criteria and on a narrow definition of efficiency – even though it was already showing signs of crisis.

One factor where there was little understanding of the future was with respect to the impact of the fall of the Berlin Wall. Germany had yet to come to terms with the implications of reunification while housing finance was hardly high on the agenda of reform in Russia and Eastern Europe. It was recognised that changes might be seismic but there was as yet no indication of the rapidity of that change. Equally in countries such as Turkey and Portugal where government dominated, the mechanisms by which change might occur were little understood.

Thus at the beginning of the quarter century the questionnaire showed that much of the basic regulatory and market infrastructure was in place in most Western European countries – but no-one imagined the scale of the changes in mortgage markets and had only some nascent understanding of the potential impact on housing markets across Europe.

The picture in 2014

The answers to the 2014 questionnaire with respect to the details of the operation of housing finance systems showed far fewer changes, at least outside Eastern Europe, than perhaps we had expected when specifying the survey. This was for two main reasons: many countries had put in place almost all of the formal legal frameworks for a deregulated system well before our starting date and these were operating fairly effectively by 1989. The second reason was that looking at the end point of 2014 the effects of the GFC and subsequent market and regulatory changes had reversed many of the changes introduced in the early part of the new century.

So was there a clear typology of countries in 2014? Looking at the categorisation suggested for 1989, set out previously, there were still some groupings that have changed relatively little: the first group of already liberalised systems had maintained that position with perhaps the most obvious changes being the further decline in special circuits of housing finance and the consolidation of banking industries in many countries (which had been one of the most important consequences of the GFC). There was more use of wholesale funding but levels of mortgage activity were often very low, again as a result of the unwinding of over-indebtedness following from the GFC and consequent recession. However, some of those who had deregulated the most had run into levels of problems that had totally disrupted their banking systems – Iceland, Ireland and Spain in particular could be regarded as a separate category because their finance systems were still in many ways dysfunctional even in 2014. On the other hand, some of the second group of countries, those that were moving towards greater liberalisation in 1989, had continued to do so and in formal terms looked much more like the better operating countries already liberalised in 1989.

Those countries that in 1989 had been highly dependent on government funding showed the most change. In Eastern Europe in particular, the government had all but fully withdrawn and legal systems had been put in place to enable the growth of private finance markets. Even so these were generally still quite small by Western European standards and households clearly had to rely more on their own resources. There was a similar picture in Turkey and to a lesser extent in Portugal.

The group that had remained least affected was probably the fairly heavily regulated but highly sophisticated countries, such as Germany and Austria (and indeed Switzerland, which is not covered in detail in our text). In these countries there had been big changes on the Treasury management side but relatively few changes in either the role of government or the operation of the mortgage market.

Evaluation

In all the countries covered in this text the objective is basically the same: to build finance markets that enable households to match their payments over their housing careers to their incomes and to widen the choice of housing and tenure wherever possible. In this context, the findings from the questionnaire showed most importantly that housing finance markets now exist in all the countries included in this text and that these have mainly become more efficient, more accessible and cheaper both for lenders and consumers. As a result, in most countries debt finance has grown rapidly and the use of own equity has declined.

Legal systems associated with mortgage markets have become more transparent and have helped to ensure better operating markets. The choice of instruments has increased and the proportions of households able to purchase have become larger. Private funding mechanisms have also expanded, particularly through the use of wholesale and secondary markets. There is much less use of government funding and, with the exception of France, special circuits of housing finance have been much reduced. With deregulation, liberalisation and market competition, risks faced by both lenders and borrowers have undoubtedly increased and, as we discuss below, looking at developments during the period, rising house prices and market volatility have offset at least some of the benefits of greater availability of debt finance.

Finally the questionnaire evidence on the detail of these markets shows considerable convergence in how mortgage markets operate. Yet there remain many differences, reflecting different histories, development paths and cultures as well as different legal and regulatory systems.

Trends in mortgage systems over the quarter century

Looking both at how national housing finance systems have developed and the overall picture, the period 1989–2014 is simply unique in housing and financial market cycles (except to the extent that in a number of countries change started somewhat earlier). House prices and mortgage debt started to move more closely in parallel and both showed unprecedentedly strong growth from the middle of the 1990s onward. Especially after the turn of the century, because the rate of increase in house prices grew so far out of line with incomes the period was perceived as a 'housing bubble' by commentators in many countries.

These prices could not have been realised unless they were funded through easier and cheaper access to (mortgage) credit. Equally, the large-scale growth in outstanding loans could not have occurred unless still larger loans were demanded. Thus was the expansion in housing credit seen to generate an equivalent 'credit bubble'.

This decline in interest rates that started in the early 1990s and was reinforced by government policies after the GFC means that across the continent (and indeed the industrialised world) most countries have ended up with low interest rate regimes. These lower interest rates increased affordability for owner-occupation as debt payments were lowered. But, because of the lack of much supply response, housing markets reacted by capitalising these reduced payments into higher housing prices. Thus falling interest rates became an important driver behind the unprecedented increase in both house prices and in mortgage debt.

Moreover the low interest rates contributed to a low equity/high leverage pattern among homeowners and other property investors. The front loading problem, still an important part of housing markets in the 1980s because of high inflation, disappeared and borrowers were increasingly able to service the debt associated with higher borrowing even in the first year of the mortgage. However, falling inflation also contributed to borrowers facing continuing high leveraging for a larger and larger proportion of their housing careers, as the real value of the debt reduced more slowly over the years.

The use of equity as a source of housing finance for the initial purchase of the dwelling and thereafter over the lifetime of the mortgage has reduced remarkably between 1989 and 2014. Loan terms were lengthened significantly, interest-only mortgages became available in quite a number of countries, homeowners were enabled to make equity withdrawals and even in 2014 downpayment requirements were slightly less common than in 1989. This decline in equity financing was another reason why homeowners became more leveraged over longer proportions of their housing careers. This might be regarded as a common milestone in European housing finance, and as a systemic change resulted in significantly more risk for borrowers and lenders, and thus potentially more volatile and less secure housing markets.

These tendencies were reinforced by regulatory changes, which enabled significant increases in loan terms as well as the introduction and widespread use of interest-only mortgages especially in the early 2000s when worsening affordability made it 'necessary' for institutions competing for business to reduce borrowers' debt servicing (Scanlon *et al.* 2008). In some countries loan terms doubled in length, running for much longer than the mortgagor's working life. A similar reduction in initial payments can be generated by using variable rate or adjustable rate loans instead of (long) fixed interest loans, when the yield curve is increasing. The answers on the questionnaires show that only seven countries used mostly fixed interest rates in 2014, slightly fewer than in 1989, and even in these countries the fixed interest periods seem to have been shortened. Other countries introduced 'taster' discounted short-term fixed interest rates that had to be regularly refinanced if the best deals were to be achieved. This in itself resulted in major problems in refinancing after the near closure of credit markets in 2008.

More fundamentally, the shift to using mortgage loans where the property acts as collateral for the lender and makes it possible to operate with lower interest rates rather than unsecured bank loans has reduced the interest rates paid. Thus the development and expansion of mortgage systems as well as improvements in access to mortgage markets are of themselves perhaps some of the most important innovations (Franklin *et al.* 2014).

Many restrictions on borrowers' access to mortgage funding have been a matter of usual business practise rather than a legal requirement. As with many other constraints, loan-to-value ratios (LTVs) were relaxed in the period of rapid expansion in debt financing in many countries, sometimes to well over 100 percent. In some others there were no generally accepted rules. However, by 2014 all countries used LTV rules, mostly set around 80 percent. This might be seen as a milestone in European mortgage regulation and as a reflection of the harmonisation process within the EU. Possible rules concerning debt-to-income and debt service-to-income ratios were also used but to a much lesser extent.

One exception to this trend has been the growth of loans where the downpayment is kept low by enabling a government guaranteed equity contribution. The borrower then provides a small deposit and the mortgage company makes a traditional loan of less than 80 percent LTV. The UK provides the clearest example of a policy aimed at helping first-time buyers who have little access to capital. But examples are found in other countries, notably the Netherlands.

In some countries borrowers had the capacity to raise mortgage loans in currencies other than their own. Initially this usually occurred in countries such as Austria and Slovenia where large numbers of workers were employed in other countries and their debt was denominated in the currency in which they were paid. However, in the late 1990s and early 2000s opportunities to borrow in other currencies increased, even if there was no income in that currency. This was a temptation that quite a few borrowers could not resist, as they could utilise the difference between their national and the foreign interest rate to reduce their interest payments. Many came to regret this decision as, typically, the exchange rate risk was mispriced, and around the outbreak of the GFC the 'FX model' broke down in these countries and often created large losses for borrowers, lenders and societies.

Access to housing loans forms one side of the housing financing model. The funding method is equally important as it contributes to determining the borrowers' interest rates.

Thus another important, possibly *the* most important, change – milestone – in housing finance has been that in most countries a far more diverse range of funding methods is in use in 2014 than was the case in 1989. Now, only a few countries use retail deposits as their only funding source. Securitised mortgages, that is, the use of mortgage backed security bonds that takes the debts off the balance sheet, were an increasingly important source of funding in the UK, Australia and Ireland in the 1990s and 2000s. However, the crisis in the USA in 2008 closed the market for some time – even though there were few signs of distress in Europe – to the point that without government support very few new issues have been possible. The most important alternative approach has been in the increasing use of covered bonds, which in some form or another can be found in 18 of the 21 countries. Covered bonds are debt instruments secured by a pool of mortgages with properties as collateral that remain on the issuer's balance sheet.

In the questionnaire, the authors of the country chapters were asked how individual mortgage interest rates were determined in their country. Their answers revealed important differences between housing finance systems in Europe. At one extreme, and the most used method in 1989, was the 'banking model', where interest rates were decided for each loan after negotiation between the bank and the borrower. The resultant interest rate then depended on information about of property, earlier savings, downpayment or LTV, loan term (or maturity) and so on. In some countries, borrowers placed in well-defined categories had to be offered the same interest rates. In others it could be more individual. At the other extreme, in the Danish system, the interest rate has always been determined by the sale price of the relevant bond on the stock exchange, so interest rates move constantly, reflecting market conditions. Thus Danish borrowers all pay the same risk premium embedded in the interest rate for a given loan type, which is determined by those who invest in these bonds in the capital market.

By 2014, banks had the power to determine the interest rate on each loan individually in only seven countries. Even in these cases the banks take into account certain 'rules' as well as capital market interest rates that they cannot influence. In addition lenders include a margin to cover fees to the lender that may be determined by competition or may be regulated in many countries. Thus in 2014 mortgage interest rates are generally much more consistent between borrowers of similar type and more likely to be determined by market pressures.

The impact of the GFC

Again it is possible to categorise countries specifically with respect to the GFC – but that categorisation differs from ones in earlier sections. Moreover, the picture can be seen more as a multi-faceted spectrum than being made up of entirely separate categories (an earlier summary of this section was published by the EMF in 2014 – see Lunde and Whitehead 2014).

Experts in seven countries among the 21 represented here suggest that housing finance and housing markets in their countries were *relatively unaffected* by the GFC. These include, in alphabetical order: Austria, Belgium, the Czech Republic, France, Germany, Norway and Sweden. As is obvious from earlier discussion these countries do not come, as many commentators have argued, wholly from particular institutional frameworks. Some of these countries have very open finance markets, for example Norway, Sweden and Belgium; others, such as Germany and Austria, remain quite strongly regulated and France in particular is still fairly dependent on a special circuit of housing finance. Not surprisingly the reasons given for the limited impact also differ greatly – ranging from having quite a small private finance sector in the Czech Republic through to continuing high levels of government involvement as in France and Austria.

It is also important to note that in at least three of these countries there is now considerable concern around current trajectories. In Sweden household debt continues to grow and prices have been rising rapidly in some parts of the country; in Austria there is seen to be major housing shortages resulting in rapid growth in house prices but also political pressures for change and reduced government involvement; in Germany there are similar issues around the rise in house prices although from a low base and only in some cities.

While the mortgage markets in these countries may have hardly been disrupted, some of these countries experienced major problems with respect to the capitalisation and asset holdings of banks. This led in some cases to very significant government intervention to support the banking system and to large scale restructuring as well as consolidation and reduced competition. These funding issues generally had relatively short-term impacts on the flow of funds into mortgage markets but have had longer-term effects on housing supply.

A second, overlapping, group of countries are those that suffered quite badly in the immediate aftermath of the crisis but then, often with the help of specific government intervention to revive and stabilise the housing market and to build stronger regulatory arrangements, were able to come out of the crisis relatively rapidly. Some of those we have identified as relatively unaffected might also be placed in the category of having an *effective government response* – notably the Czech Republic, Norway and Germany. The group also includes Australia, where there was a three pronged approach (stimulation of housing supply, support for financial flows and better targeted regulation); Finland, which had learned a great deal from the early 1990s crisis, and Turkey, where the government moved to rebalance the drivers of housing demand and supply resulting in short-term setbacks but longer-term benefits.

Thus 10 out of our 21 countries either were relatively unaffected in terms of housing finance or the impact was short-term and successfully addressed by government responses. This is not to say that these markets have remained unchanged. Rather it is to say that these finance systems have proved relatively resilient into the medium-term.

The other 11 countries, those much more affected, can be split into three main groups: those that have by 2014 returned to some sort of normality even if there are still underlying longer-term issues; those where there are still continuing problems specifically in the housing finance market but considerable signs of improvement and those where the housing crisis was central to wider economic crises that have yet to be fully resolved.

The first sub-group includes Denmark, Finland and Poland. The initial disruption was undoubtedly very considerable but finance market activity has returned to reasonable levels in the following years. In most cases market demand has anyway fallen so there is no shortage of funding. In Finland, the immediate crisis lasted just a year; in Denmark and Poland the adjustment took a bit longer. But issues of over-indebtedness and consumer risk remain in Denmark and in Finland. The negative effects of the disastrous foreign exchange mortgage lending in Poland that took place prior to the crisis will take years to unravel.

Countries in the second sub group – where the effect of the crisis on housing finance and housing markets was very significant and where, while there has been improvement, financial markets are still seen to be constrained – include the UK, Slovenia, Portugal, the Netherlands and Hungary. In the UK credit constraints have been followed by much tighter regulation and to some extent lack of demand; in Slovenia and Portugal, lending continued to fall for some time after the crisis and signs of recovery are still quite tenuous; in the Netherlands, the nature of the problem has changed as a result of government measures to restrict mortgage tax relief and other housing subsidies so that recovery has been further delayed. Hungary is a special case in part because FX (foreign currency) loans became very popular but more because (unlike in Poland) the mortgage market has been paralysed by the 'unorthodox' mortgage rescue programme and there are as yet no signs of either economic or finance market recovery. In identifying this group it is important to clarify that in all of these finance markets the credit crisis was very significant; there has been major restructuring of both banks and regulatory systems and the levels of activity continues to remain low by historic standards.

The final sub-group made up of three countries – Iceland, Ireland, Spain – and, to a lesser extent, Portugal is distinguished by the fact that the housing market crisis morphed into much broader based financial crises and then into large scale disruption in their real economies. With the exception of Portugal, housing output levels in these countries prior to the GFC had been historically high and in all cases cutbacks in investment in the real economy as well as the near collapse of their financial markets led to international as well as national intervention to support and restructure markets. In all cases there are some limited signs of improvement but the extent of over-indebtedness and the loss of asset values means it will take many more years before well operating finance and housing markets are likely to be observed.

Overview

As soon as the scale of the crisis became obvious the vast majority of countries included in this text took immediate action with respect to housing finance market liquidity. These measures were usually part of a broader approach to keeping finance markets functioning. Many countries, including some where mortgage markets continued to operate quite well, found that parts of their banking system needed restructuring and often recapitalisation. These problems required an immediate response, followed by more structured approaches involving 'bad banks', takeovers and transfers to government ownership and higher capital requirements implemented at both national and EU levels.

Initial interventions are being replaced in many countries by more coherent approaches to evaluating risk and the introduction of more consistent and coherent regulatory requirements addressed at financial institutions in general and mortgage lending in particular. Examples here include Australia, Finland, Ireland, Iceland, Norway, Portugal and the UK. Into the medium and longer-term the majority of countries are working towards compliance with Basel III and the commensurate higher capital requirements. Consistent with these requirements many countries are looking to reduce LTV and loan-to-income ratios – although from very different starting points. In the Netherlands LTV maxima remain above 100 percent although they are planned to reduce to 80 percent over the coming years. In Sweden, Finland and a number of other countries, there are also moves to limit the ratio to 80 percent. Many regulators are also looking to broader based and more detailed affordability assessments that take better account of a household's overall financial commitments.

A particular issue in the run-up to the crisis was the growing use of mortgage instruments (including, depending on the country, variable rate mortgages, interest-only and longer term mortgages and many other variants that improved immediate affordability). These have in the main been withdrawn by the market as much as by governments. There are exceptions, notably Sweden, where interest-only mortgages remain readily accessible, but in the main the evidence is on greater restrictions.

Finally, some countries have chosen to make major policy changes with respect to reducing subsidies to owner-occupation, notably in the Netherlands and Hungary and the regionalisation of support for owner-occupation in Belgium. These and other policy changes impact directly on the operation of housing finance and housing markets in these countries.

This discussion of the varying impact of the GFC has concentrated on financial market changes. Yet in many ways it is the continuing impact of the crisis on housing markets through the subsequent – and probably consequent – recession that followed that has been both more consistent across countries and longer lasting that the financial crisis itself. Credit crunches are usually expected to last little more than 18 months. This one was worldwide and therefore has taken much longer to unravel. But the negative effects on housing markets, particularly in terms of new housing investment but also with respect to market volatility are still very much a current cause for concern.

Conclusions: looking back and looking forward

The past

In many ways the last quarter century can be described by the cliché 'a game of two halves' – expansion and liberalisation before the GFC and adjustment/ additional regulation since. Yet, as in most football games, this is an over-simplification. The period around 1989 saw two major crises where there was little understanding of how these would play out: in the East the fall of the Berlin Wall and consequent political and structural changes in Eastern Europe together with the reunification of Germany, and in the West large scale disruption in property and finance markets as economies went into recession followed by sudden declines in inflation, which limited the capacity readily to readjust over-stimulated markets. Yet in both cases the next few years – although very hard for some countries, notably in Eastern Europe but also in Scandinavia – generated positive results from at least the mid-1990s onward. As a result, from the beginning of our period to around 2007, the general picture, agreed with lots of exceptions, was of expansion in both finance and housing markets with greater consumer choice and less government involvement. Then the crunch came (and looking back it is easy to see that things had been building from the beginning of the century) with housing finance seen as a core source of broader economic crisis and instability. Since then we have, in the main, seen a period of retrenchment and increasing national and international regulation. Housing systems have been disrupted because of continuing worsening affordability even in the face of low interest rates; lower levels of housing investment; declining rates of owner-occupation in many countries; and growing intergenerational inequalities.

Arguably the European finance system has actually survived better than might have been expected in 1989. As Stefan Kofner in his chapter on Germany (Chapter 11) remarked:

> ...four once-in-a-century events changed the financing conditions and the structure of the supply side: German reunification, the introduction of the Euro without a political union, the sub-prime mortgage crisis and the subsequent Euro zone sovereign crisis.

Similar lists of extreme and – to a great degree, exogenous – events could be made for many of the countries included in this text and almost all saw periods of very rapid macro-economic change, both positive and negative. Arguably Europe has survived a roller coaster of a period without major political upheaval, at least until now, and in the main managed to keep in place and even improve housing finance systems. The challenge for the next period is to make the systems far more resilient so that they can effectively support more efficient housing markets into the longer term.

The future

The most important general finding is that none of the country experts see current conditions as equating to longer run equilibrium. In a few, notably countries where mortgage markets are still relatively undeveloped and mortgage finance plays a relatively small part in financing ownership (such as the Czech Republic, Poland, Russia and Turkey), the operation of finance markets is continuing to improve for instance with the development of wholesale markets and greater liquidity. At the other extreme in market oriented systems – especially in highly indebted countries – there is the hope, if not always the expectation, that deleveraging will continue reducing risks to consumers, financial institutions and national economies alike.

In most countries access to funding is expected to remain more difficult into the medium and indeed the longer term, in part because of changing risk attitudes among both consumers and institutions, in part because of government and international finance market intervention. In many countries mortgage markets have anyway become less central to the operation of housing markets as equity makes a comeback. Most fundamentally the recession, which in most countries followed the financial crisis, is still affecting both demand and investment. As a result few expect to see mortgage market activity rates return to past levels even into the medium-term. However, at some point, possibly in the near future but more probably not until the next decade, the cycle will turn upward, generating a period when debt levels and leverage increase again, as was seen in a few more mature mortgage markets in the late 1980s. The big question then is whether systems will have been developed – and maintained – which are more resilient to external shocks. At the moment there is some reason to doubt that this will prove to be the case.

During the 25-year period – and especially after the GFC – housing markets, house prices and not least housing finance became increasingly important in economic and financial stability analysis as well as in theoretical macro-economic analysis, especially with respect to business cycle dynamics and financial stability risks. This was particularly because real estate lending booms were increasingly perceived to be followed by deeper recessions and slower recoveries. It was, and is, also because of the massive levels of political and media attention on housing market and finance conditions, which has grown exponentially as a result of the experience of the past decade. Macro-stabilisation policies have proved to have relatively few tools by which property markets can be managed effectively. Moreover, both popular interest and sudden crises tend to generate herd instincts that can reinforce rather than alleviate problems. Experience over the last few years does not generate much optimism that policy responses to future crises will be more effective than in the past.

One of the greatest concerns is about what will happen when interest rates start to rise again. This adjustment keeps being put off but ultimately macro-economies will be seen to have recovered enough to start to bring interest rates back towards some sort of 'normality'. Then the European Central Bank will increase short-term interest rates, reduce or stop the quantitative easing policy and possibly again sell reserves on the capital market, which will in turn increase longer-term interest rates. Many housing finance systems are still based on variable or adjustable rate mortgages and households will rapidly feel the pinch. No one should disregard the risk that a significant and abrupt interest rate increase might generate major issues of default and consequent falling house prices. Equally countries that have reintroduced government support to address short-term issues may remove that safety net.

The housing crises of the new century and especially the GFC have already resulted in tighter regulation to improve and tighten financial systems, including mortgage lending. Yet much of the liberalisation of the earlier years – which has generally led to more efficient outcomes – in housing financing systems across Europe throughout those 25 years, seems irreversible. Also it seems quite unrealistic that European countries will return to stringent regulatory regimes or even to some sort of 'mortgage corset' as we saw in UK and in many other countries until around 1980.

On the contrary, it may be more likely that after some years the stronger regulation that we are now seeing might be rolled back, being deemed unnecessary. This in the past has been an argument put forward in the USA in the context of the strong regulations introduced after the Great Depression, which was partially reversed or even cancelled over the decades – contributing to the build-up in financial market risks before the GFC. It seems more realistic to imagine that, after some sort of recovery is in place, there will be further financial engineering and financial innovations associated with the housing finance (Franklin *et al.* 2014).

Even so, into the immediate future it is likely that additional regulation will be brought forward. In a number of countries there is considerable discussion about how such regulation might effectively avoid new 'housing and credit bubbles'. This would involve counter-cyclical regulation, which requires new measures such as variable taxation rules, variable LTVs, variable access to some loan types, or similar measures – probably mainly for new buyers and borrowers. But will financial regulation of loan types meet the challenge that most loan types, if forbidden, can be re-done by some clever financial engineering? Moreover, how would the time for action be determined? When will the regulators be able to identify and be convinced that a new bubble is building up? And when will they determine that the market is 'over the peak', when does the tightening have to be eased, and when should possible new rescue operations be brought into operation?

All in all, crises will undoubtedly happen and it is not at all obvious that it will be possible to avoid new housing and credit bubbles by new regulation. As Susan Wachter suggested:

…if banks are unable to go beyond current market prices to determine whether prices are out of line with fundamentals, how will regulators be able to determine this? Beyond these new regulatory stances, are there market-based mechanisms that could be brought to bear in the mispricing episodes? (Wachter 2015: 41)

No matter what changes are introduced, the next 'mortgage market quarter century' will be exciting. Developments in housing markets and in housing finance will be closely followed, not only by national and international governments, market agents, economics and finance specialists, but also by populations across Europe.

References

Deutsch, E, Riessland, B and Shmidigner, J (1993). Recent and future development of private housing finance in Austria. In: *Housing Finance in the 1990s*, Turner, B and Whitehead, C (eds), Research Report SB: 56. The National Swedish Institute for Building Research, Gavle, pp. 173–202.

Diamond, D and Lea, M (1992). Housing finance in developed countries: and international comparison of efficiency. *Journal of Housing Research* 3:1, Washington, Fannie Mae.

Franklin, A, Barth, J and Yago, G (2014). Financial innovations and the stability of the housing market. *National Institute Economic Review* 230, November, R16–R33.

Lunde, J and Whitehead, C (eds.) (2014). Milestones in European housing finance. *Mortgage Info ENHR Special Edition* September 2014, EMF.

Scanlon, K, Lunde, J and Whitehead, C (2008). Mortgage product innovation in advanced economies: more choice, more risk. *European Journal of Housing Policy*, 8:2. 109–131.

Tomann, H (1993). Developments in Germany Housing Finance. In: *Housing Finance in the 1990s*, Turner, B and Whitehead, C (eds), Research Report SB: 56. The National Swedish Institute for Building Research, Gavle, pp. 157–172.

Turner, B and Whitehead, C (eds.) (1993). *Housing Finance in the 1990s*, Research Report SB: 56, The National Swedish Institute for Building Research, Gavle.

Wachter, S (2015). The housing and credit bubbles in the United States and Europe: A comparison. *Journal of Money, Credit and Banking* Supplement to 47:1 (March–April 2015).

Index

References to figures are given in italic type. Reference to tables are given in bold type.

Abbey National (England), 130, 135
ABN (Netherlands), 265, 268
Action Plan for the Risk of Non-compliance
      (PARI) (Portugal), 319
adjustable rate mortgages (ARM) (Denmark),
      109–10, 112, 124
Affordable Housing Guarantee Scheme
      (England), 138
Agency for Housing Mortgage Lending
      (Russia), 331
Allied Irish Banks, 246
ancillary guarantees (France), 174–5
Anglo-Saxon group, 5
Asset Covered Securities Act
      (Ireland), 244
Association of Residential Letting Agents
      (ARLA), 131
Australia, 38–52
   credit boom, 44–5
   deregulation, 34, 38, 39, 41
   economic reform, 38
   economic stability, 46–7
   fiscal policy, 41–2
   Global Financial Crisis, 39, 42, 45
   guarantees, 29, 50
   home-ownership rates, 47–8
   house prices, **11**, 44
   housebuilding, 44
   household debt, 45–7, *46*
   household equity, **19**
   housing debt, 46, *46*
   housing outcomes, 47–8
   housing policy, 42–3, 48–9
   housing supply, 44, 48–9
   income inequality, 39
   inflation, 38
   institutional environment, 37–9
   interest rate periods, **32**
   interest rates, 45
   key milestones, **40**, 43
   loan-to-value ratio, 38, 49–50

   mortgage debt, 38
   regulatory reform, 40–1
   rental housing, 48–9, 50–1
   social housing, 42, 50, 61
   taxation, 38, 41–3
Australian Prudential Regulation Authority
      (APRA), 41, 49–50
Australian Securities and Investment
      Commission (ASIC), 41
Austria, 55–71
   accession to EU, 58
   building boom, 58–63
   covered bonds, 58–61, 62, 66, 68,
      69, 70
   financial stability, 66–71
   foreign exchange mortgages, 63–4
   future prospects, 70–1
   Global Financial Crisis, 57, 66, 68–9
   house prices, 9, **10**, *13*, 69
   household debt, 63, 67
   household equity, **19**
   housing loan composition, 56–7
   institutional environment, 55–7
   interest rate periods, **32**
   interest rates, 58
   key milestones, 57–66, **58–9**
   loan maturities, 63, 66
   loan-to-value ratio, 66, 68
   mortgage debt, 56, 66, 68, 71
   private finance, 64–6
   privatisation, **59**
   rental housing, 56–7, 69–70
   social housing, 69, 70
   special purpose banks, 62
   taxation, 61, 63, 67
authorised deposit-taking
      institutions (ADIs)
      (Australia), 37, 41, 50

Bank of England, 127, 133, 136, 144
Bank of International Settlements, 8

Milestones in European Housing Finance, First Edition.
Edited by Jens Lunde and Christine Whitehead.
© 2016 John Wiley & Sons, Ltd. Published 2016 by John Wiley & Sons, Ltd.

Bank of Portugal, 312, 318
Bank Recovery and Resolution Directive
      (BRRD), 422–3
Bank of Slovenia, 352
Bank of Spain, 365
banking model, 22, 30, 439
bankruptcy systems, 33
Barclays, 134
Basel rules, 380, 419–20
Bausparkasse model, 18, 22
   Austria, 57, 62
   Germany, 183
   see also building societies
Belgian Professional Union for Credit
      (UPC-BVK), 75
Belgium, 75–89
   bank risks and securities, 85–6
   Eurozone membership, 77
   finance system, 76
   first time homeowners, 87
   future prospects, 88–9
   Global Financial Crisis, 77, 82, 88
   guarantees, 29
   house prices, **10**, **11**, 12, *13*, 81–2
   housebuilding, 76, 80, 87
   household debt, 82
   household equity, **19**
   institutional environment, 76–7
   interest rate periods, **32**
   key milestones, 77–86
   lending conditions, 84–5
   loan maturities, 76, 84, 86
   loan-to-value ratio, 76
   mortgage debt, *83*
   regional housing policy, 80–1
   regulatory framework, 78–9
   savings banks, 82
   social housing, 80, 81
   taxation, 79–80, 87, 88–9
BNG (Netherlands), 265
bonds, 22
   Belgium, 86
   Czech Republic, 107
   Denmark, 111, 112, 116
   England, 138
   Germany, 183, 188, 196
   Iceland, 225, 231
   Norway, 276, 277, 282
   Poland, 296, 305
   Russia, 331
   Spain, 365, 366

Sweden, 375, 378, 379, 384
   see also covered bonds
building societies, 22, 136, 227
   England, 129–31
   see also Bausparkassen
Bulgaria, 331
buy-to-let mortgages
   England, 131–2
   France, 170–1
   Ireland, 242–3

Caisse des Dépôts (France), 169
Caisses d'Eparne (France), 168–9, 178
Capital Markets Union, 425
cautions (France), 172–3
Central Bank of Ireland, 246, 249
Central Credit Register (Belgium), 78–9
Compte Epargne Logement (France), 169
Condominium Law (Poland), 293–4
Consortium de Réalisation (CDR)
      (France), 169
construction *see* housebuilding
consumer law, 250–1
consumer protection, 423–4
Contract Savings Banks
   Austria, 55–6, 58, 62, 69
   Hungary, 208
cooperative housing, 94, 99, 327, 385–6
   Czech Republic, 94, 96, 99
   Denmark, 110
   Poland, 295, 297, *302*, 306
   Russia, 327
   Turkey, 401
Covered Bond Label, 425
covered bonds, 22, 23, 24, 419, 425–6
   Austria, 58–61, 62, 66, 68, 69, 70
   Czech Republic, 94, 96, 99
   Finland, 153–4
   France, 169–70
   legislation, 25
   Norway, 279–81, 282
   Poland, 296, 299, 305
   Spain, 360–1, 371–2
Crédit Agricole (France), 169
credit assessment, 16, 25–6, 27
   Denmark, 118
   Norway, 273, 283, 287
Crédit Foncier de France, 168
Crédit Immobilier de France (CIF), 169
Crédit Lyonnais, 169
credit risk, 28–9

CRR/CRD IV Package, 422
Czech Republic, 93–107
  cooperative housing, 94, 96, 99
  covered bonds, 94, 96, 99
  deregulation, 99, 104, 105
  first time homeowners, 98
  future prospects, 106
  Global Financial Crisis, 95, 101, 105
  Gross Domestic Product (GDP), 102, **103**
  guarantees, 102, 105
  house prices, **10**, 94, 95, 105
  housebuilding, 93–4
  housing savings scheme, 103
  inflation, 95, 97, 101–2
  interest rate periods, **32**
  key milestones, 95–102
  legislative framework, 94–5
  loan-to-value ratio, 94, 99–101
  mortgage bonds, 93–4
  mortgage debt, 101, 106
  privatisation, 102
  rental housing, 96, 97, 104, 106
  restitution, 96–7, 104
  savings banks, 93
  taxation, 98, 100

debt service charges, 21
Deferred Interest Mortgage (DIM), 295
Denmark, 109–25, 113, 118, 124
  adjustable rate mortgages (ARM), 109–10,
      112, 124
  banking crisis, 121–2
  cooperative housing, 110
  credit assessment, 25–6
  deregulation, 113
  future prospects, 124–5
  Global Financial Crisis, 117, 121–3
  house prices, **10**, **11**, 117–21
  housebuilding, 121–2
  household debt, 125
  housing debt, *119*
  inflation, 110, 118
  institutional framework, 113–15
  interest rates, 30, 116–17
  loan-to-value ratio, 30, 111, 111–12, 115,
      118–19, 125
  mortgage system, 111–13
  mortgage debt, 115
  net liabilities to income ratio, 119–20
  refinancing, 114, 119, 124
  social housing, 29, 110

  taxation, 109–10, **114**, 115–16, 125
  tenure structure, 109
deposit-financed mortgages, 22
depository systems, 22
deregulation, 2, 3, 5, 6, 9, 13, 17, 18,
      413–15, 434
  Australia, 34, 38, 39, 41
  Czech Republic, 99, 104, 106
  Denmark, 113
  England, 132–3
  European Union, 416
  financial markets, 2
  Finland, 148–51, 159, 166
    rental sector, 150–1
  Germany, 186–7
  Iceland, 229
  Ireland, 240
  Netherlands, 256–8, 266–7
  Norway, 275–6, 283, 288
  Poland, 292
  Portugal, 310, 312
  Slovenia, 354
  Sweden, 377, 378–9, 383
  Turkey, 398
directed credit, 22
downpayments, 18, **19–20**

Economic and Monetary Union (EMU), 415
Eigenheimzulage (Germany), 186–7, 191
endowment mis-selling (England), **128**, 131,
      132–3
England, 127–43
  building societies, 129–31
  buy-to-let mortgages, 131–2
  deregulation, 132–3
  Funding for Lending Scheme, 136
  Global Financial Crisis, 127–8, 131,
      133, 135
  guarantees, 134, 137, 138
  house prices, **10**, **11**, 127, 134, 139–40
  household equity, **19**
  Housing Act, 137
  housing associations, 136–9
  inflation, 127–8
  interest rates, 143
  key milestones, 128–36
  loan-to-value ratio, 134, 135, 140
  mortgage funding, 135–6
  owner-occupation rate, 142–3
  regulatory framework, 132–3
  rental housing, 138

England (*cont'd*)
  social housing, 29, **128**, 136, 137
  taxation, 129
  see also United Kingdom
equity financing, 18–21
equity withdrawal, 28
Estonia, 17
EURIBOR, 32, 170, 349, 373
Euro zone, 77, 160, 187, 196, 197
European Central Bank (ECB), 21, 116, 124–4,
    195, **240**, 243, 247, 365, 366, 415
  Bank Lending Survey, 420–1
European Commission, 418–19, 422-3,
    425, 429
European Economic Area (EEA), 219–20
European Financial Stabilisation
    Mechanism (EFSM), 246
European Financial Stability Facility
    (EFSF), 246
European Mortgage Federation (EMF), 33
European Network of Housing Research
    (ENHR), 3
European Union, 64
  Austria's accession, 58
  deregulation, 416
    Second Banking Directive, 415
  gross lending, 427–8
  key milestones, **414**
  market developments, 417–18
  Mortgage Credit Directive, 423–4
  restoration of financial stability, 422–3
Exchange Rate Mechanism (ERM), 349–50

family equity, 16, 17
  Austria, 57
  Portugal, 310–12
  Turkey, 404
Fannie Mae, 434
Financial Market Authority (Austria), 56
financial markets, 2, 101, 123
  crisis *see* Global Financial Crisis
  deregulation, 6, 147
  interest rates, 99
Financial Supervisory Authority
    (Finland), 154
Finansinspektionen (Sweden), 388
Finland, 6, 147–8
  banking crisis (1994), 150
  covered bonds, 153–4
  deregulation, 148–51, 159, 166
  Eurozone membership, 151

first time homeowners, 151, 154, 159, *159*
future prospects, 161–2
guarantees, 147, 152, 153
house prices, **10**, **11**, 149, 150, 153,
    158–9, 160
housebuilding, 153, 160
household debt, 156–8
household equity, **19**
housing debt, 156–8
housing stock quality, 156–8
inflation, 147, 155
interest rates, **32**, 155–6, *156*
key milestones, 148–54, **149**
loan maturities, 155–6
loan-to-value ratio, 147, 150, 154, 161
property valuation, 26
social housing, 151, 152–3
taxation, **149**, 151, 154
First Home Owners Boost (FHOB)
    (Australia), 42
First Home Owners Grant (FHOG)
    (Australia), 42
first time homeowners, 18
  Belgium, 87
  Czech Republic, 98
  Denmark, 119
  England, 128, 134, 140–1
  Finland, 151, 154, 159
  France, 174
  Netherlands, 263, 270
  Norway, 278
  Russia, 334
fixed rate mortgages
  Czech Republic, 101, 111–13
  England, 142–3
Flanders, 89
Flemish Housing Council, 88–9
flexible mortgages, 99, 416
Fonds de Garantie de l'Accession Sociale
    (France), 172, 173–4
foreclosures, 31–3
foreign exchange (FX) loans, 416
  Austria, 56, 63–5, 68
  Hungary, 210–11
  Iceland, 221–2, 230–1
  Poland, 299
France, 165–80
  ancillary guarantees, 174–5
  buy-to-let mortgages, 170–1
  cautions, 172–3
  covered bonds, 169–70

future prospects, 179
Global Financial Crisis, 173, 177–9
guarantees, 174
housebuilding, 165, 178
house prices, **10**, **11**, 165, 176–7, *177*
household equity, **19**
housing debt, 171, 177
inflation, 166
interest rate periods, **32**
interest rates, *168*
key milestones, 165–71, **167**
loan-to-value ratio, 173, 177
low income guarantee funds, 173–4
mortgage debt, 176–7
property valuation, 26
refinancing, 166, 168, 170, 178
social housing, 169, 176, 178
taxation, 169, 170–1
tenure length, 175–6
universal banks, 171–2
Fund for Orderly Bank Restructuring
    (FORB), 366
Funding for Lending Scheme
    (England), 136
FX loans *see* foreign exchange loans

Germany, 183–98
capital markets, 186–8
deregulation, 186–7
Eigenheimzulage, 186–7, 191
Global Financial Crisis, 184
guarantees, 188, 189, 194, 197
house prices, **11**, 12, *314*
housebuilding, 186, 197
household equity, **19**
housing market, 195–6
housing policy in East Germany, 185
interest rate periods, **32**
labour market, 196
loan-to-value ratio, 189, 194
mortgage funding models, 22–3
mortgage debt, 186, 434
property valuation, 26
refinancing, 189, 194–5, 196–7
rental housing, 190
reunification, 184–6, 434, 443
savings banks, 185, 188
taxation, 178, 186, 190–1
Global Financial Crisis, 1, 21, 25, 28, 34,
    421–9, 439–42, 444–5
Australia, 39, 42, 45, 46, 49

Austria, 57, 66, 68–9
Belgium, 77, 82, 88
Czech Republic, 95, 101, 105
Denmark, 117, 121–3
England, 127–8, 131, 133, 135
France, 173, 177–9
Germany, 184, 188
Hungary, 200, 203, 214–16, **215**
Iceland, 231
Ireland, 246, 248–9, 251
Netherlands, 256, 261–2, 270
Norway, 282
Poland, 291, 298, 299–301
Portugal, 313, 318–19, 320, 321
Russia, 335–7
Slovenia, 3, 52–3, 342, 351
Spain, 360, 364–5, 367, 369
Sweden, 388–9
goods and services tax (GST)
    (Australia), 42
government debt, 4
Belgium, 77
Ireland, 246, 251
Gross Domestic Product (GDP), 11–12
Australia, 38
bank credit ratio, 7, **8**
Czech Republic, 95, 102, **103**
Denmark, 110, 122
Finland, 153
Germany, 196
government debt ratio, 378
household debt ratio, 123
    Iceland, 234
    Portugal, 316
    Slovenia, 349
Hungary, 202, 203, 207, 209
mortgage debt ratio, 8–9, *11*, 17, 67
    Austria, 65, 67
    Denmark, 123
    Finland, 158
    Hungary, *206*
    Russia, *335*, 337–8
    Spain, 360, 368
    Turkey, 404
Poland, 298, 307
Portugal, 319
Slovenia, 351
Spain, 360
Gross National Product (GNP)
Finland, 151
Ireland, 251

guarantees, 9, 28–9
  Czech Republic, 102, 105
  England, 134, 137, 138
  Finland, 147, 152, 153
  France, 174
  Germany, 188, 189, 194, 197
  Netherlands, 29, 259, 260, 261
  Norway, 275
  Portugal, 311, 321
  Russia, 331
Gulf War, 367

habitations à loyers modérés (France), 169
Heerma Memorandum (Netherlands),
    255–6, 266–7
HELIBOR, 148
Help to Buy (England), 134
home-ownership rates, 47–8
Homes and Communities Agency
    (England), 138
House Financing Fund (Iceland), 226
house prices, 2, 6, 9–12, 21
  Australia, **11**, 44
  Austria, 9, **10**, *13*, 69
  Belgium, **10**, **11**, 12, *13*, 81–2
  Czech Republic, **10**, 94, 95, 105
  Denmark, **10**, **11**, 117–21
  England, **10**, **11**, 127, 134, 139–40
  Finland, **10**, **11**, 149, 150, 153, 158–9, 160
  France, **10**, **11**, 165, 176–7, *177*, 179
  Germany, **11**, 12, *314*
  Hungary, *206*, 207, 209
  Iceland, 221, 232–3, *232*
  Ireland, 242, 245–6, 249
  mortgage debt and, **8**, 9–10
  Netherlands, **11**, 257, 260, 261, *267*, *314*
  Norway, **11**, 274, 279, 282, 283–4, 285
  Poland, 298, 300, 303, *304*
  Portugal, 313, *314*, 315, 318
  Russia, 329
  Slovenia, 342, 354
  Spain, 3, **11**, *314*, 360, 364, 368–9, *369*
  Sweden, **11**, 382, 387
  Turkey, 402, 404, 408–9
housebuilding
  Australia, 44
  Austria, 56, 57–8, 66
  Belgium, 76, 80, 87
  Czech Republic, 93–4
  Denmark, 121–2
  Finland, 153, 160

  France, 165, 178
  Germany, 186, 197
  Hungary, *206*, 207, 209, 211, 216
  Ireland, 242, 251
  Netherlands, 261
  Norway, 278, 284
  Poland, 294, 297, 301–2, 303, 305
  Portugal, 312, 315, *316*, 317
  Russia, 327, 330, 337, 342
  Slovenia, 343, 345, 353–4, 356
  Spain, 368
  Sweden, 377, 378, 388
  Turkey, 404
household debt, 7–8, 440
  Australia, 45–6, 46–7, *46*
  Austria, 63, 67
  Belgium, 82
  Finland, 156–8, 160
  Iceland, 233–4
  Portugal, 316–17, 319
housing associations
  Denmark, 110–11
  England, 136, 136–7, 138, 386
  Netherlands, 259
  Sweden, 376
Housing Attitudes 2001 survey (Czech
    Republic), 97
Housing Bank (Norway), 277–9
housing bonds
  Iceland, 225
  Norway, 280
  Sweden, 378, 384
Housing Construction Banks (Austria), 56,
    58, 61–2, 62
Housing Construction Convertible Bonds
    (HCCB) (Austria), 62
housing debt
  Australia, 46
  Denmark, *119*
  Finland, 156–8
  France, 171, 177
housing finance (definition), 3–4
Housing Finance Fund (Iceland), 227–8, 233
Housing Fund of Finland, 153
housing outcomes (Australia), 47–8
housing policy (Australia), 42–3, 48–9
housing supply (Australia), 44, 48–9
HSBC, 134
Hungary, 201–17
  future prospects, 215–16
  Global Financial Crisis, 203, 214–16

house prices, *206*, 207, 209, 211
housebuilding, *206*, 207, 209, 211, 216
household equity, **19**
housing subsidies, 207–9
inflation, 203, 207–8
interest rates, 30, **32**
key milestones, *205*
mortgage market, 209–10
National Asset Management Company
    (NAMC), 213
national savings banks (OTP), 203–4
privatisation, 202, 208
refinancing, 215
rent-to-own scheme, 213, **215**
social housing, 208, 213
state housing system, 203–4
taxation, 203, 209, 215
transition to market-based system, 207–9
Hypo Alpe Adria (Austria), 65
Hypo Real Estate (Germany), 191–2

Iceland, 219–37
    deregulation, 229
    foreclosure, 33
    foreign exchange (FX) loans, 221–2, 230–1
    future prospects, 235–7
    Global Financial Crisis, 231
    House Financing Fund, 227–8, 233
    house prices, 221, 232–3, *232*
    household debt, 233–4
    household equity, **19**
    housing bonds, 225
    indexed mortgages, 224
    institutional environment, 220–1
    interest rate periods, **32**
    key milestones, 221–31, **222–3**, **229**
    loan-to-value ratio, 227
    mortgage debt, 235
    privatisation, 220, 228, 229, 233
    refinancing, 230
    rental housing, 227
    savings banks, 221
    social housing, 221, 225, 226
    taxation, 225
income inequality, 39, 48
indexed mortgages (Iceland), 223, 230,
    232, 235
inflation, 6, 21, 28, 95
    Australia, 38
    Czech Republic, 95, 97, 101–2
    Denmark, 110, 118

England, 127–8
Finland, 147, 155
France, 166
Hungary, 203, 207–8
Iceland, 220–1, 223
Sweden, 387–8
ING (Netherlands), 265
insurance, 29, 81, 85, 132, 173
    life, 64, 79, 99–100, 265
    mortgage, 38, 173, 331
interest rates, 21, 415–16, 437–8
    Australia, 45
    Austria, 58
    Czech Republic, 99–100
    Denmark, 116–17, 125
    determination, 29–31
    England, 143–4
    Finland, 155–6, *156*
    fixed periods, **32**
    France, *168*
    Poland, 297
    Portugal, 318
    reduction, 6
    Slovenia, 349, *350*
    Spain, 363, 373
    Sweden, 381, 385
    see also variable-rate mortgages
International Monetary Fund (IMF), 8, 45,
    203, 228
intramuros (France), 179
Ireland, 239–51
    Asset Covered Securities Act, 244
    buy-to-let mortgages, 242–3
    deregulation, 240
    government debt, 246, 251
    house prices, 242, 245, 245–6, 249
    housebuilding, 242, 251
    household equity, **20**
    interest rate periods, **32**
    key milestones, 239–47, **240**
    loan-to-value ratio, 243, 245, 249
    mortgage debt, 243, 244
    mortgage law, 250–1
    regulatory framework, 248
    social housing, 248, 250
    taxation, 247–8
    unemployment, 241–2
Irish Nationwide Building Society, 246

La Hénin (France), 169
Landesbanken (Germany), 188

Large-Scale Voluntary Transfers
(England), 137
Latvia, 17
Lehman Brothers, 101, 133–4, 421
lending restrictions, 26–7
Limited-Profit Housing Associations
(LPHAs) (Australia), 57, 57–8,
61, 62–3
Ljubljana, 354
Lloyds Bank (England), 134
loan maturities
Austria, 63, 66
Belgium, 76, 84, 86
Czech Republic, 98
Finland, 150, 155–6
Portugal, 310, 320
Slovenia, 347
loan periods, 27–8
loan-to-value (LTV) ratio, 9, 16, 438, 445
Australia, 38, 49–50
Austria, 66, 68
Belgium, 76, 83–4
Czech Republic, 94, 99–101
Denmark, 30, 111, 111–12, 115,
118–19, 125
England, 134
Finland, 147, 150, 154, 161
France, 173, 177
Germany, 189, 194
Iceland, 227, 228, 229, 231, 233, 236
Ireland, 243, 245, 249
Netherlands, 29, 262, 442
Norway, 273, 274, **276**, 279–80,
283, 286
Poland, 300
Portugal, 310, 318, 320
regulation, 18–19
Russia, 336
Slovenia, 351
Spain, 359, 360, 373
Sweden, 388–9
loan-to-value rule, 27, 438

Maastricht Treaty, 187, 258, 415, 418
Mercer Oliver Wyman, 141
MIBOR, 363
Mortgage Arrears Resolution Targets
(MART) (Ireland), 247
mortgage backed securities (MBS), 25, 434
Russia, 334–5
Spain, 271

Mortgage Credit Directive, 423–4
mortgage debt, 2, 7–11
in 1989, 433–4
in 2014, 435
Australia, 38, 45, 46
Austria, 66, 68, 71
Belgium, *83*
Czech Republic, 101, 106
France, 176–7
GDP ratio, **8**, 17
Germany, 186, 434
house prices and, 7–9, **8**, 9–10, 11–13
Iceland, 235
Ireland, 243, 244
Netherlands, 262, 267, *268*
Russia, *335*
Spain, 360
Mortgage Market Review (England),
134–5
mortgage supply, 21–5, **23**, **24**
mortgage systems, 5–7, 16–17
classification, 22
loan currency, 28
loan periods, 27–8
trends, 436–7

National Asset Management Agency
(NAMA) (Ireland), 247
National Asset Management Company
(NAMC) (Hungary), 213
National Bank of Belgium, 75, 79
National Housing Authority (Iceland),
219–20
National Housing Fund (Poland), 295
National Housing Fund (Slovenia),
345–8, 354
National Housing Savings Scheme (NHSS)
(Slovenia), 346–7
National Mortgage Guarantee Fund (NMGF)
(Netherlands), 267
National Rental Assistance Scheme (NRAS)
(Australia), 42–3
negative gearing, 41, 45, 190
net liabilities to income ratio (Denmark),
119–20
Netherlands, 255–71
credit rating, 262
deregulation, 256–8, 266–7
downpayment requirements, 18, 438
equity withdrawals, 28
first time homeowners, 263, 270

Global Financial Crisis, 255
guarantees, 29, 259, 260, 261
house prices, **11**, 257, 260, 261, *267*, *314*
housebuilding, 261
household equity, **20**
housing associations, 259
housing policy, 255–6
key milestones, 256–265, **265**
interest rate periods, **32**
loan-to-value ratio, 29, 262, 442
mortgage debt, 262, 267, *268*, 270
mortgage interest deduction, 263–4
mortgage market, 257
regulatory framework, 261–2, 267
rental housing, 264
social housing, 259, 260, 260–1, 264, 269
taxation, 257–8, 260
New Housing Act (Slovenia), 343
Nordea Bank, 147, 383
Norges Bank, 274, 275, 281, 284, 286
Northern Rock (England), 133–4, 135
Norway, 273–88
covered bonds, 279–81, 282
credit assessment, 273, 283, 287
deregulation, 275–6, 283, 288
Global Financial Crisis, 281–2
guarantees, 275
house prices, **11**, 274, 279, 282, 283–4
housebuilding, 278, 284
household equity, **20**
Housing Bank, 277–9
institutional framework, 275–6
interest rate periods, **32**
key milestones, 275–81
loan-to-value ratio, 273, 274, **276**, 279–80
macro-economic development, 273–4
market changes, 382–3
oil fund, 273
subsidies, 381–2
taxation, 279, 287, 382

Olympic Games (1992), 367
Organisation for Economic Co-operation
    and Development (OECD), 7–8, 262
Australia, 38
Austria, 67–9
Belgium, 80
Denmark, 118, 124–5
Netherlands, 262
OTP (Hungary), 203–4
Own House programme (Russia), 328

PAP loans (France), 166, 168–9
Pfandbriefe, 22, **24**
Austria, 56
Germany, 187, 188–9
PKO BP (Poland), 296
Plan Epargne Logement (France), 169
Pohjola Group (Finland), 147
Poland, 291–308
cooperative housing, 295, 297, *302*, 306
deregulation, 292
future prospects, 307–8
Global Financial Crisis, 291, 299–301
Gross Domestic Product (GDP), 307
house prices, 298, 300, 303, *304*
housebuilding, 294, 297, 301–2, 303, 305
household equity, **20**
housing boom, 298, 303–4
housing sector reform, 294
interest rate periods, **32**
interest rates, 30
key milestones, **293**
loan-to-value ratio, 300
mortgage banking models, 305–6
mortgage funding, 24
privatisation, 293–4, 294–5, 301
refinancing, 296
regulatory framework, 298–9
rental housing, 295
social housing, 295, 301, 306, 307
taxation, 294, 297–8
Polish-American Mortgage Bank (PAM), 296
Portugal, 309–22
1974 revolution, 311
construction rates, 309–10
deregulation, 310, 312
equity withdrawal, 28
family equity, 310–12
guarantees, 311, 321
house prices, 313, *314*, 315, 318
housebuilding, 312, 315, *316*, 317
household debt, 316–17, 319
household equity, **20**
key milestones, 313–19
loan-to-value ratio, 310, 318, 320
rental housing, 315, 322
social housing, 312
Strategic Housing Plan, 318
taxation, 313–14
Prague Interbank Offered Rate (PRIBOR), 99
Prague Spring, 203
principal dwelling houses (PDH), 249

privatisation, 2
  Australia, 40
  Austria, **59**
  Czech Republic, 94, 96–7, 102
  Hungary, 202, 208
  Iceland, 220, 228, 229, 233
  Netherlands, 256–7, 266
  Poland, 293–4, 294–5, 301
  Portugal, 310, 313, 315
  Russia, **327**
  Slovenia, 343, 344, 353–4
  Turkey, 398
product innovation, 416–17
property valuation, 26

Rabobank (Netherlands), 265
Real Estate Investment Funds (Spain), 362
refinancing, 31, 69, 437
  Austria, 58, 61, 66, 69
  Belgium, 89
  Denmark, 114, 119, 124
  France, 166, 168, 170, 178
  Germany, 189, 194–5, 196–7
  Hungary, 215
  Iceland, 230
  Poland, 296
  Russia, 331–2, 336, 338
  Turkey, 402
Regional Mortgage Banks (Austria),
    58–9, 62
regulatory frameworks, 445
remortgaging, 4
rental housing
  Australia, 48–9, 50–1
  Austria, 56–7, 69–70
  Czech Republic, 96, 97, 104, 106
  England, 138
  Finland, 150–1
  Germany, 190
  Hungary, 213
  Iceland, 227
  Netherlands, 264
  Poland, 295
  Portugal, 315, 322
  Spain, 361–2
residential mortgage backed securities *see*
    mortgage backed securities
restitution, 344–5
  Czech Republic, 96–7, 104
  Russia, 344–5
Riester pension (Germany), 191

right-to-buy (RTB), 63
  Czech Republic, 95
  England, 136–7
Riksbank (Sweden), 377, 379
Rodzina na Swoim (RnS) (Poland), 297–8
Romania, 425–7
Royal Bank of Scotland, 134
Russia, 325–39
  cooperative housing, 327
  downpayment requirements, 18
  first time homeowners, 334
  foreclosure, 33
  future prospects, 337–9
  Global Financial Crisis, 335–7
  guarantees, 331
  housebuilding, 327, 330, 337, 342
  household equity, **20**
  housing stock, 331
  interest rate periods, **32**
  law on mortgages, 329
  loan-to-value ratio, 336
  mortgage debt, *335*, 337
  privatisation, **327**, 328, 329, 330
  refinancing, 331–2, 336, 338
  restitution, 344–5
  social housing, 329
  Soviet era housing, 326–7
  transition to market economy, 328

Santander (Spain), 362
savings banks
  Belgium, 82
  Czech Republic, 93, 97
  Germany, 185, 188
  Iceland, 221
Scandinavian group, 5
securitised mortgages, 22
self-building (Austria), 57
self-managed superannuation funds (SMSF)
    (Australia), 41–2
Single European Market (SEM), 413–17,
    414–16, **414**
Single Resolution Mechanism, 423–4
Single Supervisory Mechanism, 423
Slovakia, 17
Slovenia, 341–59
  deregulation, 354
  future prospects, 356–7
  Global Financial Crisis, 52–3, 342
  house prices, 342, 354
  housebuilding, 343, 345, 353–4, 356

housing policy, 342–3, 354–5
interest rate periods, **32**
interest rates, 349, *350*
key milestones, **344**
loan-to-value ratio, 351
National Housing Fund, 345–8
National Housing Savings Scheme
    (NHSS), 346–7
pre-market economy, 342–3
privatisation, 343, 344, 353–4
social housing, 342, 344
taxation, 349
SNS (Netherlands), 265
social housing, 9
    Australia, 42
    Austria, 69, 70
    Belgium, 80
    Czech Republic, 106
    Denmark, 29, 110
    England, 29
    Finland, 151, 152–3
    France, 169, 176, 178
    Hungary, 208, 213
    Iceland, 221, 225, 226
    Ireland, 248, 250
    Netherlands, 259, 260
    Poland, 295, 301, 306, 307
    Portugal, 312–13
    Russia, 329
    Slovenia, 342, 344
    Spain, 372
    Turkey, 399, 401
social mortgage credit (Belgium), 80–1
sociétés de crédit foncier (France), 170
sociétés de financement (France), 170
SOCIMI (Spain), 366–7
Spain, 28, 359–74
    covered bonds, 360–1, 371–2
    equity withdrawal, 28
    future prospects, 372–3
    Global Financial Crisis, 360, 364–5, 367, 369
    housebuilding, 368
    house prices, 3, **11**, *314*, 360
    interest rate periods, **32**
    interest rates, 363, 373
    key milestones, **361**
    legislative framework, 360–4
    lending supply, 370
    loan-to-value ratio, 359
    mortgage backed securities (MBS), 271
    mortgage debt, 360

Real Estate Investment Funds, 362
rental housing, 361–2
social housing, 372
taxation, 364, 367, 373, 375
Spanish Asset Management Company
    (SAREB), 366
STIBOR, 385
structured finance (Austria), 67
subrogation (Spain), 362
Superannuation Guarantee Scheme
    (Australia), **40**, 42
Sweden, 375–90
    deregulation, 377, 378–9, 383
    future prospects, 389–90
    Global Financial Crisis, 388–9
    house prices, **11**, 382, 387
    housebuilding, 377, 378, 388
    household debt, 387
    household equity, **20**
    housing bonds, 378, 384
    housing reform, 377–8
    institutional framework, 378–9
    interest rates, 385
    key milestones, 378–9
    loan-to-value ratio, 388
    taxation, 375–6, 380–1
Switzerland, 435

taxation
    Australia, 38, 41–3
    Austria, 61, 63, 67
    Belgium, 79–80, 87, 88–9
    Czech Republic, 98, 100
    Denmark, 109–10, **114**, 115–16
    England, 129
    Finland, **149**, 151, 154
    France, 169, 170–1
    Germany, 178, 186, 190, 190–1
    Hungary, 203, 209, 215
    Iceland, 225
    Ireland, 247–8
    Netherlands, 257–8, 260
    Norway, 279, 287, 382
    Poland, 294, 297–8
    Portugal, 313–14
    Slovenia, 349
    Spain, 364, 367, 373, 375
    Sweden, 375–6, 380–1, 382, 387
tilt problem, 21
    Czech Republic, 97
tracker mortgages (Ireland), 242–4

Turkey, 393–409
  cooperative housing, 401
  deregulation, 398
  future prospects, 405
  gated communities, 405–8
  Global Financial Crisis, 407
  house prices, 402, 404
  housebuilding, 404
  household equity, **20**
  Housing Development Agency, 394, 396,
      398, 399–400, 407–8
  housing market overview, 394–6, 396
  key milestones, 400–402
  marketisation, *397*
    early (1980–2000), 398
    full (2003–), 399
    impacts, 402–5
    transitional (2000–2002), 398–9
  privatisation, 398
  refinancing, 402
  regulatory framework, 400
  social housing, 399, 401
  tenure status, **395**
  urban regeneration, 400–1

unemployment benefits, 196
United Kingdom, 438
  house prices, **11**

  interest rate periods, **32**
  see also England
United States, 1, 282, 445

Value Added Tax (VAT)
  Belgium, 79
  France, 171
  Poland, **293**, 299
variable-rate mortgages
  Australia, 37–8
  England, 127
  Finland, 155
  Hungary, 209
  Ireland, 243–4
  Sweden, 389
Vienna, 57, 63, 68–9
Voluntary European Code of Conduct on
      Home Loans, 418
Vorarlberg (Austria), 64

Waarborgfonds Eigen Woningen
      (Netherlands), 258–9
Waterschapsbank (Netherlands), 265
WIBOR, 297
woonbonus (Belgium), 79–80, 88–9
World Bank, 208, 294, 296, 407

zero interest loans (France), 167, 168, 169